11·10

P9-ARB-591

YANKEE LIFE

CHARACTERISTICS OF NEW ENGLAND

YANKEE LIFE

BY THOSE WHO LIVED IT

Edited by BARROWS MUSSEY

1947

NEW YORK : ALFRED A. KNOPF

THE LIBRARY
COLBY JUNIOR COLLEGE
NEW LONDON, N. H.

F
3
M87

THIS IS A BORZOI BOOK,
PUBLISHED BY ALFRED A. KNOPF, INC.

Copyright 1937, 1947 by Barrows Mussey. All rights reserved. No part of
this book may be reproduced in any form without permission in writing
from the publisher, except by a reviewer who may quote brief passages or
reproduce not more than three illustrations in a review to be printed in a
magazine or newspaper. Manufactured in the United States of America.

First published as *We Were New England* in 1937 by Stackpole Sons.
This edition has been revised, expanded, and reset.

FIRST BORZOI EDITION

28312

Foreword

NEW ENGLAND *holds our hearts in a mother's grip. We read now of snow-chilled dawn on a New Hampshire farm, now of Mather's horrid joylessness, now of Chinese opulence at Salem. Some dim ancestral memory makes each picture familiar.*

But after reading histories and novels of New England for a time, one begins to wonder: was it really like this? Is this New England, or only a writer's knack? And which was the real New England? That of Mather? That of Emerson? Or that of the men whom John Neal called "the true Yankees, dealers in cuckoo clocks, horn gunflints, and wooden-nutmegs"?

I wondered about it until I felt an urge to do something. This book is the result.

The final authority on a life is the man who lived it, and in the following pages New Englanders of three centuries speak for themselves. By sea and land, in pulpit, camp and shop we see these men build New England. They are real: they tell us their own lives, their own thoughts, in their own language. If we still cannot choose which is the real essence among Cotton Mather hounding witches, George Hewes throwing tea into the harbor, and John Neal watering rum, the fault belongs to New England — a hard land, but rich in many men.

The method of the book is simple. I have taken from the autobiographies of New Englanders those passages which show what it felt like to live in the cradle of the nation. For this reason I have had to pass by some thrilling moments and some great writing; but at any rate the books are there to read, and I shall be glad if somebody after tasting my appetizers goes on to make a full meal of John Neal's Wandering Recollections, *Chester Harding's* My Egotistography, *or Thomas Low Nichols'* Forty Years of American Life. *The necessity for leaving out so much was the only unhappy part of my task. Beyond a connective or inserting a date or place, I have made no changes in the words of the autobiographers; their spelling and punctuation are their own — sometimes very much their own.*

The book stops at the Civil War; since then a different New England has started to grow up, which in its turn deserves another book.

1937   BARROWS MUSSEY

THE *lapse of a decade has left me better satisfied with the original choice of material than I had dared to hope. There is nothing I re-*

[v]

gret having put in, and astonishingly little that I have since learned to regret having left out.

Wilson Follett and the other wise heads on the Knopf editorial staff, however, did offer a number of excellent suggestions beyond my own afterthoughts; if the present edition is better rounded than its predecessor, the merit is largely theirs.

Almost no book of this kind is ever finished without the editor's owing his gratitude to the New York Public Library; in this case I have particularly to thank Gerald McDonald.

Valuable suggestions and material came from three learned booksellers: Charles P. Everitt of New York, A. J. Huston of Portland, Maine, and Robert Kolvoord of Walpole, New Hampshire.

The contributions of Edwin Valentine Mitchell have been going on steadily for so many years that I very nearly forgot to mention his name.

The illustrations are from the collections of the Museum Society, of Brattleboro, Vermont.

1947   B. M.

Contents

YANKEE LIFE

How Dear to My Heart . . . (Early Childhood)   3

My Book and Heart (School Days)   51

College   76

IN THE SWEAT OF THY FACE

Life Ashore   107

Life Afloat   167

Wooden Nutmegs (Commerce)   197

Down by the Old Mill Stream (Manufacturing)   224

Timber !   236

Mightier Than the Sword (The Printed Word)   251

Painters and Other Vagabonds   271

Stop Thief !   280

And Now, Fellow Citizens (Politics and Law)   309

The Practice of Physic   325

The Meeting-House (Spiritual Life)   333

CONTENTS

STIRRING TIMES

FURIOUS TAWNIES (Indian Captivity)   387

SPIRIT OF 'SEVENTY-SIX   411

SECOND WAR WITH GREAT BRITAIN   444

YANKEES   459

TRAVELS IN NEW ENGLAND   487

❖❖❖❖❖❖❖❖❖❖❖❖

YANKEE LIVES   535

INDEX   *follows page* 543

YANKEE LIFE

HOW DEAR TO MY HEART

❖◇❖◇❖◇❖◇❖◇❖◇❖◇❖

[Anna Green Winslow, Boston]

30th Nov., 1771. I wore Miss Griswold's Bonnet on my journey to Portsmouth, & my cousin Sallys Hatt ever since I came home, & now I am to leave off my black ribbins tomorrow, & am to put on my red cloak & black hatt — I hope aunt wont let me wear the black hatt with the red Dominie — for the people will ask me what I have got to sell as I go along street if I do, or, how the folk at New guinie do ? Dear mamma, you dont know the fation here — I beg to look like other folk. You dont know what a stir would be made in sudbury street, were I to make my appearance there in my red Dominie & black Hatt.

Jany. 4th, 1772. I was dress'd in my yellow coat, my black bib & apron, my pompedore shoes, the cap my aunt Storer sometime since presented me with (blue ribbins on it) & a very handsome loket in the shape of a hart she gave me — the last pin my Hond. Papa presented me with in my cap, My new cloak & bonnet on, my pompedore gloves, &c, &c. And I would tell you, that *for the first time, they all lik'd my dress very much.* My cloak & bonnett are really very handsome, & so they had need be. For they cost an amasing sight of money, not quite £45 tho' Aunt Suky said, that she sup-

[3]

pos'd Aunt Deming would be frighted out of her Wits at the money it cost. I have got *one* covering, by the cost, that is genteel, & I like it much myself.

Jany. 11th, 1772. There was a large company assembled in a handsome, large, upper room in the new end of the house. We had two fiddles, & I had the honor to open the diversion of the evening in a minuet with miss Soley . . . There was a little Miss Russell & the little ones of the family present who could not dance . . . — our treat was nuts, rasing, Cakes, Wine, punch, hot & cold, all in great plenty. We had a very agreeable evening from 5 to 10 o'clock. For variety we woo'd a widow, hunted the whistle, threaded the needle, & while the company was collecting, we diverted ourselves with playing of pawns, no rudeness Mamma I assure you. Aunt Deming desires you would *perticularly observe,* that the elderly part of the company were *spectators only,* they mix'd not in either of the above describ'd scenes.

I was dress'd in my yellow coat, black bib & apron, black feathers on my head, my past comb, & all my past garnet marquesett & jet pins, together with my silver plume — my loket, rings, black collar round my neck, black mitts & 2 or 3 yards of blue ribbin, (black & blue is high tast) striped tucker and ruffels (not my best) & silk shoes compleated my dress.

May 25. I had my HEDDUS roll on, aunt Storer said it ought to be made less, Aunt Deming said it ought not to be made at all. It makes my head itch, & ach, & burn like anything Mamma. This famous roll is not made *wholly* of a red *Cow Tail,* but is a mixture of that, & horsehair (very course) & a little human hair of yellow hue, that I suppose was taken out of the back part of an old wig. But D—— made it (our head) all carded together and twisted up. When it first came home, aunt put it on, & my new cap on it, she then took up her apron & mesur'd me, & from the roots of my hair on my forehead to the top of my notions, I mesur'd above an inch longer than I did downwards from the roots of my hair to the end of my chin. Nothing renders a young person more amiable than virtue & modesty without the help of false hair, red *Cow Tail,* or D—— (the barber).

❖❖❖❖❖❖❖❖❖❖❖❖

[*Lyman Beecher, D.D., North Guilford, Conn.*]

1775. As the nurse's milk did not agree with me, she was dismissed, almost heart-broken at having to give me up, and I was given in charge to a girl named Annis, to be brought up by hand.

Annis was a noble girl, and had a great influence over my character. She was nurse, mother, sister, and all. She and Aunt Benton fill up the memory of my early days.

She was pious, and though little was said to children then, talked with me about my soul. I remember one night, when the northern lights were very bright, a blood-red arch from horizon to zenith, and light enough to read out of doors. Every body was out looking at it, and Uncle Stephen Benton said, " Ah ! we don't know at what time the day of judgment will come — at midnight or at cock-crowing."

The thought flashed through my mind, "It has come now," and I felt all the dismay of the reality. I began to cry. Annis quieted me, and, after I went to bed (I always slept with her), she talked with me about my soul.

Uncle Lot Benton was a substantial farmer, an upright, tall, bright, dark-eyed man of pleasant countenance. He had strong feelings, hid under a don't-care look, yet spilling over at the corner of the eye.

If a neighbor came to borrow a hoe, Uncle Lot would say, "Why don't ye have hoes o' your own ? What d'ye hang on to your neighbors for ?" Then, when the borrower was going away, "Here, come back; *take* the hoe, can't ye ? You'll break it, I s'pose."

Uncle Lot was a saving, contriving, scheming man, who farmed on the principle of making his ground yield the most with the least outlay.

He made and mended his own tools, harness, and plow. His farm was on a ridge of good, quick, strong land, sloping to the east and west — a beautiful situation. He had forty head of cattle, two horses, and forty sheep.

There was a rotation of crops, corn following grass, and oats corn, and then grass again. We made as stout oats as could stand.

Raised an acre or two of flax, though it was impossible to keep Aunt Benton and niece in spinning for the winter.

We raised our own breadstuffs, and fodder for stock, and cut salt hay on the marsh.

Flax-pulling was hard enough to break your back the first day, the second lighter, the third easy enough. We had about three days' pulling for Uncle Benton and me, boy and man. Then we rotted it, beat it, and bleached it. I knew my business about flax.

In the fall and winter there was wood to be cut and hauled from the wood-lot. We kept no spirits in the house. Uncle Lot always bought a gallon of rum, which answered for haying and harvest. One pint bottle served for seven or eight hands. In June we filled our gallon bottle with cider and water, and went down to Quinnepaug Outlet to wash and shear the sheep. We built an enclosure of rails and drove the sheep in. The old ram we boys used to drag in and souse under. He would come out and stand dripping.

Then, after a day or two, we sheared them. The only difficulty with me was, I used to cut in and take out a little piece of the skin now and then.

Then the fleece was washed, salted, carded, and spun. Aunt Benton spun it all in the house. Flax in winter, wool in summer; woman's work is never done.

They made all sorts of linen work, table-cloths, shirting, sheets, and cloths. If it hadn't been for this household manufactory we never should have succeeded in the Revolution.

I remember in those days how the selectmen visited the farmhouses, and took an inventory and gave receipts. We paid in beef. The kitchen was full, and they came with carts and carried it to the army.

Harriet Beecher Stowe: "Was there no complaining?"

No complaint; not a word.

H.B.S. "We were independent already, and only determined we would remain so."

Yes. If we had been slaveholders we should have gone to the dogs.

H.B.S. "Were there not some that held slaves then?"

Yes, a few. Darb, the fiddler, was a slave; belonged to old Mr. Ben Rossiter. Darb came in one evening and played dancing tunes after I was abed. There were about a dozen slaves in North Guilford, but the slavery was very lenient. Old Priest Fowler's Moses was quite the man of business; sent Johnny Fowler to college, and paid the bills, managed the farm, rung the church bell, and was factotum. He lived a slave because he was a king.

"How did they live in those days? Tell us something about Aunt Benton's kitchen."

I can see her now as plain as I can see you. She and Annis got breakfast very early. We had wooden trenchers first, then pewter, and finally earthenware. Our living was very good. Rye bread, fresh butter, buckwheat cakes, and pie for breakfast. After the dishes were washed, Annis and I helped aunt milk. Then they made cheese and spun till dinner. We dined on salt pork, vegetables, and pies; corned beef also; and always, on Sunday, a boiled Indian pudding. We made a stock of pies at Thanksgiving, froze them for winter's use, and they lasted till March.

After dinner aunt put things "to rights." Annis spun, and I worked at flax and foddering.

In the evening we visited, chatted, ate apples, drank cider, and told stories. On Sunday nights the boys went a courting.

I used to have the heartburn after eating puddings and pies, and Aunt Benton had a notion I was weakly. "Lyman," she would say, "won't you go into the milk-room and get a piece of cake? You don't look *well*."

H.B.S. "Well, father, you had to work hard; but what did you do for amusement?"

Hunting and fishing were my amusements, except that I used to play checkers with Sam Bartlett, and go to singing-school with Annis, and sing from Law's Collection.

The first time I went a fishing Uncle Benton took me down to Beaver Head, tied a brown thread on a stick, put a crooked pin on it and a worm, and said, "There Lyman, throw it in." I threw it in, and out came a shiner! The first time I caught a perch was at Quinnepaug Outlet. He got off my hook and fell in the shallows, and began to flapper off, and away I went after him down the shallows on all fours, quicker than a flash.

Another time I found a school of perch in a hole under the roots of a tree, and took them all out with my hand.

I always liked "training-day," because then I could go a fishing. Fished all day till dark, and felt sorry when night came. That was my passion. Couldn't leave off till the bullheads had done biting. Once, at the saw-mill, I hooked a pickerel without bait; how I whopped him out!

Used to follow the trout-brook round to the mill-dam. Once, below the dam, in a deep hole, I saw six salmon-trout. Dropped my hook with a grasshopper; none of 'em bit. Tried a worm, squirmed lively; one of 'em struck it; took him out. Cut a stick, strung him; baited my hook, threw in; another of 'em struck it; pulled him out, strung him; another, and another, till I had the whole six.

H.B.S. "Did you hunt any ?"

Yes, down between home and the western road — squirrels, quail, partridges, and what not. Used to catch muskrats and minks; deer were scarce. The wolves used to howl in the woods; never heard them but once since, and that was in the black swamp in Indiana.

H.B.S. "Did you care anything about flowers then ?"

Well, Aunt Benton had a beautiful garden in front of the house. All the common sorts of flowers grew there — peonies, pinks, feath-erfew, balsams, roses, and the like.

H.B.S. "Was that a healthy country ?"

Healthy ? In eighteen years of early life I never went to the fu-neral of a young person of our circles. Never knew but one case of fever and ague. The ground sloped away to the marsh so far that there was no miasm. The drainage was swift, and the trout-brook did not dry up the year round. Every storm threw floods down the mountainside and swept every thing clean. Sometimes a cloud broke on the mountains, filled the channel, carried away bridges, and went past like a wave of the sea.

When I used to be out hoeing corn, and saw two thunder-clouds rising, my nerves braced up, as it grew darker, the excitement in-creased, till, finally, when the thunder burst, it was like the effect of a strong glass of wine.

H.B.S. "Were you afraid ?"

Not I. I wished it would thunder all day. I never heard such thunder since, except once in the hills round Marietta, Ohio.

H.B.S. "And were you never sick ?"

I had the mumps, measles, hooping-cough and all that sort of thing. One or two narrow escapes too; I stumbled over the dye-pot, and sat down in a kettle of scalding water. That threw me into con-vulsions. Came near being crushed by a falling tree; should have been if it had not *lodged:* that saved me.

[*J. T. Buckingham, Windham, Conn.*]

The death of my father in 1783 was, of course, but the prelude to further domestic calamity. My mother was naturally of a delicate constitution, and had been broken down by frequent and severe attacks of rheumatic fever. She continued, however, to keep the tavern for some months — perhaps a year. At length, the establishment was abandoned, and the family necessarily dispersed. The second son went to sea; the next was apprenticed to a saddler; the third to a shoemaker; and for the next two, places were provided, at which they were supplied with food and clothing for such services as they were able to perform, till they should be of an age suitable to go out as apprentices. The furniture of the tavern was sold to pay off debts; and my mother, with a few articles, indispensable in housekeeping, and with two young children, me and a sister two years older, hired a couple of rooms in the house which her husband had built in the days of his prosperity, and which she had once expected to call her own for life. Here amidst occasional sickness, and constant destitution and sorrow, she supported her two remaining children, by the labor of her hands, chiefly needle-work.

But the depth of her destitution and distress she had not yet reached. There were still some demands against her late husband's estate pressing for payment. How long she continued with us in this house, I cannot tell, but I think I could not have been more than four years and a half old, when another portion of her scanty stock of furniture was taken from her by an officer of the law. With one bed, a case of drawers, two or three chairs, and a few cooking utensils, she left the rooms she had occupied and took refuge in the adjoining building, which my father had erected some twenty years before for a workshop. She held me and my sister by the hand, while a constable sold, at the door, the only andirons, shovel and tongs, chairs, beds, table, &c. which she had reserved when she left the tavern; — leaving her one bed, one table, three chairs, the old case of drawers, a frying-pan and tea-kettle, and probably the articles absolutely necessary to enable a woman and two children to eat their food with decency; — but of this I am not positive. I went to a wheelwright's shop on the opposite side of the street, and gathered some chips to build a fire in our new habitation. The place of andirons was supplied with stones, taken from the street, and the service of shovel and tongs was performed by a spoke from a broken wheel, — the gift of our neighbor the wheelwright.

At this time we had no dependence for subsistence but the labor of my mother. She was often sick and unable to work. When in a condition to labor, she was employed in sewing for a neighbor who was a tailor, or in *"binding* and *closing"* women's shoes, which were then made principally of cloth, for another neighbor. This was a business in which she was expert, having done much of it when her husband carried on the manufacture. I was sometimes employed in sticking card-teeth, for a manufacturer of cards. But, with all these poor resources, we must have suffered with cold and hunger but for the charity of a few friends.

I have no recollection of any time when I could not read. Probably I had attended a school in the summer after my father's death, but of this I have no remembrance. While we were living in this state of abject poverty, some one gave me a few coppers on a training day, with which I bought a New-England Primer, and no speculator who makes his thousands by a dash of the pen ever felt richer than I did with my purchase. To my mother I was indebted for constant daily instruction, and I may say, without boasting, that her pupil repaid her attention, and at this moment feels an emotion of gratitude, which time has not destroyed or enfeebled. My elder brothers, when they came home to see us, (Heavens, what a home !) sometimes brought me a picture-book, and I was the owner of Robinson Crusoe, Goody Two-Shoes, Tom Thumb, and perhaps half-a-dozen other books of a similar character. I have a confused idea of going to a woman's school in the summer after I was four years old; but, as the district schools were then kept but two months in the winter and two in the summer, two months was the longest term that I could have attended, and probably I was not there half of the time.

In December, 1784, the month in which I was five years old, I went to a master's school, and, on being asked if I could read, I said I could read in the Bible. The master placed me on his chair and presented a Bible opened at the fifth chapter of Acts. I read the story of Ananias and Sapphira falling down dead for telling a lie. He patted me on the head and commended my reading. It was that winter, I believe, that Noah Webster's Spelling Book was first introduced into the schools. I could not read with the class, to which I properly belonged, because they read from that book; *mine* was an old Dilworth, and my mother had not the means to buy a Webster.

Of what are called "perquisites," I had none before I was fourteen years old. *Then* I was allowed the privilege of selling to a brush-maker the bristles that came from the swine as they were slaughtered. For a small bunch of these I received ninepence, (the eighth of a dollar,) and this was the first bit of silver that I could call mine. It was kept for years as a *pocket-piece,* and, when parted with, it was to pay the postage of a letter to my mother. At the same time, the privilege was granted to me of selling a certain quantity of walnuts, of which the woods and pastures afforded a plentiful supply. A bushel or two, in the autumn of 1794, produced a sum sufficient to enable me to buy a slate and pencil, Dilworth's Arithmetic, and the Second and Third Parts of Noah Webster's "American Institute," — the Grammar and the Selection of Reading Lessons. Grammar was not then a study in the district schools; but I had conceived an idea that the knowledge of it was a desirable accomplishment. I therefore undertook to study it, *by myself.* But my ambition soon received a check. After a number of evenings spent in committing twenty or thirty pages to memory, and confusing my head with numbers and cases, modes and tenses, declensions and conjugations, I discovered that my attempt to learn, without an instructor, was vain and useless, and my Grammar was thrown aside as a seven-sealed book.

◇◇◇◇◇◇◇◇◇◇◇◇◇

[*S. G. Goodrich, Ridgefield, Conn.*]

To the New House we removed in 1797, when I was four years old. On that great occasion, every thing available for draft or burden was put in requisition; and I was permitted, or required, I forget which, to carry the *peel,* as it was then called, but which would now bear the title of shovel. Birmingham had not then been heard of in those parts, or at least was a great way off; so this particular utensil had been forged expressly for my father by David Olmstead, the blacksmith, as was the custom in those days. I recollect it well, and can state that it was a sturdy piece of iron, the handle being four feet long, with a hemispherical knob at the end. As I carried it along, I doubtless felt a touch of that consciousness of power, which must have filled the breast of Samson as he bore off the gates of Gaza. I recollect perfectly well to have perspired under the operation, for the distance of our migration was half a mile, and the season was summer.

One thing more I remember: I was barefoot; and as we went up the lane which diverged from the main road to the house, we passed over a patch of earth, blackened by cinders, where my feet were hurt by pieces of melted glass and metal. I inquired what this meant, and was told that here a house was burned down * by the

* Lossing says, in his Field Book, p. 409, vol. i.: "Having repulsed the Americans, Tryon's army encamped upon *high ground,* about a mile south of the Congregational church in Ridgefield, until daylight the next morning, when they resumed their march toward Norwalk and Compo, through Wilton. Four dwellings were burned in Ridgefield, and other private property was destroyed, when the marauders struck their tents."

The "high ground" here spoken of was High Ridge, the precise spot where the house I have described, stood. Doubtless the vestiges here mentioned were those of one of the four houses alluded to.

[11]

British troops already mentioned — and then in full retreat — as a signal to the ships that awaited them on the Sound where they had landed, and where they intended to embark.

It was the custom in those days for boys to go barefoot in the mild season. I recollect few things in life more delightful than, in the spring, to cast away my shoes and stockings, and have a glorious scamper over the fields. Many a time, contrary to the express injunctions of my mother, have I stolen this bliss, and many a time have I been punished by a severe cold for my imprudence, if not my disobedience. Yet the bliss then seemed a compensation for the retribution. In these exercises I felt as if stepping on air — as if leaping aloft on wings. I was so impressed with the exultant emotions thus experienced, that I repeated them a thousand times in happy dreams, especially in my younger days. Even now, these visions sometimes come to me in sleep, though with a lurking consciousness that they are but a mockery of the past — sad monitors of the change which time has wrought upon me.

As to the black patch in the lane, that too had its meaning. The story of a house burned down by a foreign army, seized upon my imagination. Every time I passed the place, I ruminated upon it, and put a hundred questions as to how and when it happened. I was soon master of the whole story, and of other similar events which had occurred all over the country.

I was of course subjected to the usual crosses incident to my age — those painful and mysterious visitations sent upon children — the measles, mumps, whooping-cough, and the like; but they have almost passed from my memory, as if overflowed and borne away by the general drift of happiness which filled my bosom. Among these calamities, one monument alone remains — the small-pox. It was in the year 1798, as I well remember, that my father's house was converted into a hospital, or, as it was then called, a "pest-house," where, with some dozen other children, I was inoculated for this disease, then the scourge and terror of the world.

It will be remembered that Jenner published his first memoir upon vaccination about this period, but his discoveries were generally repudiated as mere charlatanism, for some time after. There were regular small-pox hospitals in different parts of New England, usually in isolated situations, so as not to risk dissemination of the dreaded infection. One of these, and quite the most celebrated of its time, had been established by my maternal grandfather upon Duck Island, lying off the present town of West Brook — then called Pochaug — in Long Island Sound; but it had been destroyed by the British during the Revolution, and was never revived. There was one upon the northern shore of Long Island, and doubtless many others; but as it was often inconvenient to send children to these places, several families would unite and convert one house, favorably situated, into a temporary hospital, for the inoculation of such as needed it. It was in pursuance of this custom that our habitation was selected, on the present occasion, as the scene of this somewhat awful process.

There were many circumstances which contributed to impress this event upon my mind. In the first place, there was a sort of popular horror of the "pest-house," not merely because of the virulent nature of small-pox, but because of a common superstitious feeling in the community — though chiefly confined to the ignorant classes — that voluntarily to create the disease, was contrary to nature, and a plain tempting of Providence. In their view, if death ensued, it was esteemed little better than murder. Thus, as our house was being put in order for the coming scene, and as the subjects of the fearful experiment were gathering in, a gloom pervaded all countenances, and its shadow naturally fell upon me.

The lane in which our house was situated was fenced up, north and south, so as to cut off all intercourse with the world around. A flag was raised, and upon it were inscribed the ominous words "SMALLPOX." My uncle and aunt, from New Haven, arrived with their three children. Half a dozen others of the neighborhood were gathered together, making, with our own children, somewhat over a dozen subjects for the experiment. When all was ready, like Noah and his family we were shut in. Provisions were deposited in a basket at a point agreed upon, down the lane. Thus, we were cut off from the world, excepting only that Dr. Perry, the physician, ventured to visit us in our fell dominion.

As to myself, the disease passed lightly over, leaving, however, its indisputable autographs upon various parts of my body. Were it not for these testimonials, I should almost suspect that I had escaped the disease, for I only remember, among my symptoms and my sufferings, a little headache, and the privation of salt and butter upon my hasty-pudding. My restoration to these privileges I distinctly recollect: doubtless these gave me more pleasure than the clean bill of health which they implied. Several of the patients suffered severely, and among them my brother and one of my cousins. The latter, in a recent conversation upon the subject, claimed the honor of two thousand pustules, and was not a little humbled when, by documentary evidence, they were reduced to two hundred.

❖❖❖❖❖❖❖❖❖❖❖❖❖

[13]

[*Julia Cowles, Farmington, Conn.*]

Thursday, September 28, 1799. At home in the morning. **P. M.**, rode out in the stage upon the plain with 17 in the stage; staid a few hours and became quite tired of Fielday. I was shocked to see the indelicacy with which some of my sex appeared in. One, perhaps a woman of 40, went far enough to use very vulgar expressions and even to strike a gentleman who sat upon his horse, with whom she

was an entire stranger. It wounded my delicacy to see girls of 17 encircled in the arms of lads; what a pity that their reason could not have taught them better ! Why could reason dictate thus ? Could not sweet Charity lend them assistance ? How ridiculous must such appear in the eyes of persons of sense; would quite degrade the whole sex in their opinion. Girls who perhaps would have made (with a little education) fine women, good mothers, and happy wives, will now make neither, entirely destitute of the common rules of decency. Why should the rich spend a fortune upon dress and other outward equipage; why not share with the poor (whom Nature has given equally the same) and give us all a common education and wherewith to get a living by ? should we not be much happier ? Happiness would take a seat in every breast and hush every rising murmur, where Hope would lend his aid; and Despair, the most unhappy passion, would not reign among us. From the field I repaired to the ball. I was agreeably surprised at seeing Mr. Ely, I returned home about 12 with Mr. E.

Monday, April 25, 1802. Rode uptown. Found the little girl breathless. Staid some time. Went to Mary's. Called to see Sally Gleason, who had a blister applied last night; had not rise(n). How many have changed this life for another and put on immortality since I have been unwell; some in old age, some in the bloom of life, some in childhood. This child was a week since a picture of health; that is no security, it withstands not the arrests of death. Why have all these been taken, and I am still left? I many times think when I see a corse, perhaps mine will be next; we know not what a day may bring forth. What reason have this family for thankfulness, what great cause for praise! How much mercy and favor have they received a year past! First my sickness last summer, when I was supposed to be dangerous. From that, I was mercifully raised to an apparent state of health. In the last winter I was attacked with complaints, different but in their nature far more dangerous. I was reduced almost to a state of consumption, from which Providence has graciously raised me to tolerable health. What great reason have I to admire and adore the goodness of God! Next to this my little sister was violently ill, considered dangerous; she is now healthy. This spring I am again to appearance losing my health. A few days since, my Father was in imminent danger. His life was miraculously preserved and lent longer to a needy family by the kind interposition of Providence; in a week he was much better and able to walk out. These favors, unmerited as they are, we have received, and which, I am sorry to say, are too much disregarded. I have sewed today, and evening spent in writing, among which I wrote a line to Mary. Retired early.

Tuesday, 26th. The morning was very blustering and cool. After breakfast, took Emily and Betsey, as I had before engaged them, in the chaise; carried them to see the little corpse. Staid there some time. Went on to Mary's. Took her and went to Dr. Tod's. He directed me to continue the medicine. Then called on Lucy T—ll and took a ride in the meadows. Returning, met John going to his day's labour. I called to see Sally Gleason, who is much emaciated and altered since I last saw her. Methought, "I am approaching her situation." Returned home. Fixed Mama's bonnet and prepared for the funeral. Mr. Pitkin spoke a few words. Mr. Washburn made an excellent address to the mourners, to all. Closed with a fervent, engaged prayer in which all were concerned. What consolation would it be to these afflicted parents, had they the comforts of religion, could they look up and say, "not my will *but thine be done!*"

After funeral I carried Mary home and took another short ride.

[15]

Lucy and I drank tea there. Returned about dusk. Spent part of the eve in writing and part in reading extracts from "Sacred Biography" with T—ll.

Sabbath Day. After breakfast, rode in the meadows. Admired nature in her beauty. The morning very pleasant. My thoughts turned upon my state of health and the sensations of myself and friends, should I be necessitated to bid them an eternal adieu. The time is perhaps at hand. We know not what a day may bring forth; no time but the present moment is ours. "Our best happiness is short, precarious, and uncertain; man cometh up and is cut down like a flower."

Prepared and attended meeting. The death of my cousin, with that of a negro girl, was mentioned. The prayer was excellent. The text in Corinthians 2.20. The aforementioned series of discourses are continued. Today it was shown the necessity of divine revelation to depraved, fallen man, and that what was discoverable from the light of nature would not teach us to worship alone an eternal, self-existent, uncreated God, neither in what way we should display our gratitude. Afternoon text the same. Truman Cowles' child was baptized. How solemn the ordinance of baptism! Evening, T—ll and Horace were here.

June 1st. Another month of our allotted time is gone, is past and can never be recalled. We should have no cause to complain or repine at the rapidity of time, provided we spent it in the way an impartial Judge would commend and in the most probable way to lead to a happy hereafter when never-ending time dissolves into eternity.

Since Election, have continued the medicine untill about a week since, when their operation proved so violent as to weaken me very considerably and induce my physician to omit them and try that. My fever was apparently reduced. Riding, with temperate living, was prescribed. I found myself better and have taken no more since. A syrup I have taken which has appeared to be serviceable. No efforts or exertions have been wanting; my parents, friends, and self, each in our turns, have used our endeavors to conquer this stubborn fever, and we have reason to think our wishes will still be gratified.

I have been to East Hartford with Maj. Hooker, Dolly, Lucy, and F. Norton. The girls are going to Hebron to school. I was considerably fatigued riding and much affected parting with the girls. Perhaps, I thought, the time of my dissolution draws nigh, and this may be seeing them for the last time. Tho' I am much better now, yet soon it may be said of me:

The feeble pulse, the panting breath,
Bespeak the near approach of death;
Exhausted nature now gives way,
In ruin falls the tottering clay,
The moment's come, she sinks, she dies,
Breathless and cold, alas ! she lies !

I spent the P. M. very agreeably with Mr. and Mrs. Olcott. Am much pleased with both. Their situation is very pleasant, and a pretty family of children, four in number. Retired fatigued. Slept 'til late the next morning. Mrs. Olcott came home with Maj. H. and myself in the waggon, also one of her little daughters. Called on Horace, who refreshed us with port wine, and saw Mary, whom I rejoiced to see. Evening, Betsey, Horace, and T—ll were here.

October 18th, 1802. One year more is past and gone, never to be recalled. Seventeen years have past over this guilty head. Where I shall be at the end of 17 more, is not for human beings to determine. The command is, "Redeem the time, because the days are evil," but instead of redeeming the precious time I have wasted it in idleness and folly. It becomes me at this anniversary day to look back and enquire where and in what situation I stood one year ago. Then I had good health; now my health is poor. I have advanced one year more in life and in sin. I have to render an account for one year more of wasted time. I have seen, and still see, that the delusive joys of this world are insufficient to satisfy the desires of an immortal soul. But the world and its fascinating allurements have and still do find it in their power to draw this foolish weak heart to taste and partake of their pleasure. But they are frail and unsatisfying. Their joys are the joys of a day or an hour.

[Julia Cowles died May 21, 1803]

❖❖❖❖❖❖❖❖❖❖❖❖❖

[*John Neal, Maine*]

Among my earliest recollections is that of being obliged to stand upon a table, and say over, "Pity the sorrows of a poor old man, whose trembling limbs have borne him to your door," at the special instance and request of my dear old grandfather, and a few of what were called with singular *propriety* his particular friends; for they overlooked nothing, and were always in the way of prodigies and portents. How I quitted myself, I do not remember, nor am I quite sure that I remember of myself what I have already mentioned; for I was not over two and a half, or three years of age at the time, (about 1795 or 6) , as I found out by letters which were in my possession before the [Portland] fire; but I do remember, and without help or misgiving, incidents yet earlier.

The very first was the following. It was a second birth to me, and all before was a dead blank, and continues to be so, up to this hour. But how old was I? My vouchers being all destroyed, I can judge only by circumstances. On my way from Falmouth, now Portland, to Kittery, now Elliot, where my grandfather lived, I remember, as if it were but yesterday, going through water so deep that it flowed over the bottom of our carriage. I remember, too, the strange appearance of the trees growing out of the water, with no sign of road or pathway, and nothing to guide us. There had been a great freshet; and the whole country up to Doughty's Falls, they say, was flooded. We stayed with my grandfather a year and a half; and I was not put into jacket-and-trousers, till after our return to Portland, so that I could not have been much older than I have said.

But while I remember many other little incidents with distinctness, I remember nothing at all — absolutely nothing — of a somewhat serious accident, which occurred to me while we were at my grandfather's. It seems he was furnishing shiptimber for Portsmouth; that one of his workmen stood up a broad axe by the handle, with the blade resting against the fence, while away to dinner; that I went after some chips, barefooted; and, while gathering them, the old sow began rooting about in my neighborhood, and at last overthrew the axe, which, in falling, struck me, and cut off my great toe, so that it only hung by a bit of skin. How strange that, while a score of other incidents, absolutely trivial in comparison, are crowding upon my recollection with the vividness and clearness of recent experience, I remember nothing of the fright or pain which I must have suffered, and was obliged to rely upon others for the fact, while carrying the scar with me to the grave!

Among these are the following. I give them in the order they occur to me. I took it into my head one day to clamber into an empty hogshead; and let some of my playfellows roll me about, until I received a serious gash over the left temple, from a peg or a nail, which had been overlooked. They say that I was taken up and carried into the house, and laid upon a table, where the wound was sewed up; and that when it was all over, and I was asked how I felt, I said to Uncle James, who had given me a fig to encourage me under the operation, that I should be willing to go through the whole of it again, for another fig.

About this time, they put me into jacket-and-trousers; whereupon, they say that I gathered up my petticoats and flung them to my sister, saying, "Sis may have these: they're too good for me." Here was a touch of human nature. Being twins, we had always been dressed alike, till then; but, from that time forward, I was the man-child and she — poor thing! only "Sissy," and obliged to wear petticoats.

I remember also, and this without help — for when I mentioned it to my mother, not long before her death, she had wholly forgotten the circumstance — that, having been provided with a new hat, I amused myself one sabbath-morning — and the neighbors also, I dare say — with kicking the old one, of which I had long been heartily ashamed, up and down the street, on my way to meeting.

And this reminds me of a narrow escape I had — to say nothing of the poor boy I aimed at, one day, with a cross-bow, as he was leaning over and drinking from the nose of a pump, standing by what used to be known as the Fosdick House, on the corner of Federal and Church Streets. I stood upon the steps of the Friends' meeting-house, lately occupied by Thompson, the marble-cutter, when I snapped the string and let fly, with no more idea of hitting the poor fellow than of hitting a swallow on the wing; but my little crooked arrow, whittled out of a shingle, struck him just between the eyes, as he lifted his head after drinking. Half an inch, one way or the other would have cost him an eye, myself undying remorse, and my mother a pretty penny, I dare say; for we Down-Easters are a litigious people, and lawyers are always to be had.

And yet another. Having been furnished with a pine-sled by my uncle Simeon Hall, which, owing to a little oversight when it was put together was always running against the grain, I was obliged to do my sliding on the steepest hills I could find, or run the risk of stopping half way, and tumbling off into the snow. I went with two or three companions, one beautiful moonlight evening, to try my luck on Titcomb's Wharf, near Clay-cove, just below our new custom-house. Not being well acquainted with the neighborhood, I followed in the wake of the other boys; but instead of turning off, as they did, at a particular bend of the highway, which they were acquainted with, and of course had prepared for, I kept on and on, till I found myself in the dock fifteen or twenty feet below, with a sheet of ice under me, and great blocks of salt-water ice piled up in every direction about me. I had been going a "belly-plumper;" and, for a minute or two, I thought I should never breathe again, so completely was the wind knocked out of me. The boys were not to blame, however. They did not know that I was there for the first time, and never thought of warning me, 'til it was too late, and they saw me going head-first over the wharf, and into the sea. Luckily for us all, the tide was out.

With that unhappy sled, there is another sorrowful recollection associated. Not being able to make much headway on the common street-slopes, I had taken a fancy to neighbor McLellan's front-steps, when they were heaped with snow. They were not more than three feet high, or, at the most, four; though I had an impression, till I saw them after my return from abroad, that they were high enough to be dangerous, and therefore to justify the course of my good Uncle James with me.

Finding me, one day, just on the point of launching my sled from the top of this elevation, he pulled me up short, and assured me in a way peculiar to himself, that if he caught me sliding on anybody's steps again, he would take my sled away, and split it up, and burn it. Hardly had he turned the corner, before I was up, and at it once more. Happening to look around, he caught me in the act, and, being a man of his word — he had also been a school-master, and a great disciplinarian — my poor sled was taken away, split in pieces, and burned before my face — the monster ! — and I never had another. I am afraid I have never quite forgiven him to this day, though he has been dead thirty years, and meant to make me his heir; but dying in a hurry, as old bachelors often do, he failed to carry out his avowed intentions, and I lost a handsome estate — a loss, by the way, which I never felt a twentieth part as much as I did the loss of my little rough-and-tumble pine-sled.

Long after this, when I reached the age of ten or eleven, I had another experience of a similar nature. Next my mother's in Fish-Street, now called Exchange-Street, lived a Widow Deering. The back addition to her house had a low, sloping roof, which I took a prodigious fancy to, for a variety of reasons. One was, that I could mount a large cane at the end of the ridge-pole and slid down, at a tremendous pace, to the very edge of the roof; and from thence leap to the platform, without much risk. To be sure, the noise I made was terrific; you would have thought a hurricane had got among the old shingles, and was ripping them off, by the wheel-barrow-load.

The Widow Deering was a kind-hearted, patient woman; but she could not bear everything, even from a neighbor's boy — about as mischievous a little wretch as ever breathed, I dare say, though not absolutely vicious nor heartless; and so she gave my good uncle a hint, I suppose. He had a private insurance-office just over the way, where the wealthiest men of the time used to congregate, as under-writers and gossips, and where I was then going through a "course of Sprouts" with my uncle.

Calling me up, he questioned me about my horsemanship on the widow's roof, and about the cane; and taking it from me, with a cuff or two, which set my head ringing like a brass kettle, he put it away behind some old painted canvas hangings, which had been there from time immemorial; certainly from the time of the old Indian wars, if we might believe the stories that were told about the talks held there, when it was the council-chamber of Massachusetts-Bay. They were the first I ever saw, and the last; and I can recall the trees and blue waters, and the birds, and the squirrels, and the bright, clear sky, as if I had but seen them the other day. Perhaps my uncommon relish for painting, and especially for landscape, originated there. But to return: before the sound of my good uncle's footsteps died away, I had got possession of the cane, and was careering down that roof, with more vehemence than ever, al-most ripping off the shingles as I went; and fully persuaded that I was not only revenging myself, on my uncle and the widow, for the cuff-ing I had been favored with, but that I was showing off my horse-manship, and my pluck, in a way not to be misunderstood. N. B. I think so now; but I cannot understand how I ever had the courage to disobey such a man, knowing him as I did, without a moment's hesitation, and without regard to consequences. That these were in-dications of a character headstrong, adventurous, and rash, I must acknowledge.

One evening — and this I regard as my first *pitched* battle, for I had to do with a young sailor in *tarred* clothes (not so bad) — one evening, I was called out by some boys, who announced that the Lower-Enders were coming up in a body to thrash the Middle-End-ers, as we were called. They wanted a champion. I was now behind a counter, well dressed, and tall for my age, with quite a reputation among the schoolboys and counter-jumpers for courage and pluck; having only a few days before accepted a challenge from Bill Gibbs, the greatest bully among us, when he dared me to come on board a vessel, one sabbath-day, which he had undertaken to hold against all comers. Whereupon, I jumped aboard at once, and waited the issue; having a crowd of spectators on the wharf to see fair play. But he failed to redeem his pledge; and when the boys began crowing over him, I verily thought he would jump overboard, to conceal his mortification. He was the eldest of a large family, all given to fisticuffs; and his father kept the county-jail, for amusement.

Though far from desiring such a distinction, and by no means qualified for the championship, I did not refuse; but went with them to the head of Exchange-Street, then called Fish-Street, where we found the rival faction, headed by a sailor-boy named Wiley, at least two years my elder; according to my present recollection; somewhat heavier, and accustomed all his life to being knocked about, both at sea and ashore.

After a brief, though clamorous parley it was agreed that the two parties, instead of going into the battle head-first, every boy for himself, should fight by proxy; we to do the hammering, and they the hurrahing. Of course, having gone so far, I could not say no. My reputation was at stake — my self-respect indeed. Fools that we are ! I had never seen Wiley before, though I had been told of his doings. Nor am I sure that he knew me, otherwise than by the reputation I had among the boys. We were both natural fighters, game-cocks without feathers; but wholly ignorant of boxing, or, as it is called now, "the manly art of self-defense," under color of which the well-trained pugilist sets a fellow spinning, with a slap in the mouth;, or drops him, with a blow under the ear, as dead as a herring.

Not a moment was lost. There was no palavering, no backing and filling. We did not even off coats, and roll up our sleeves; nobody thought of *peeling* in that day; and I had on, I well remember, that London-made coat of blue broadcloth, with gilt buttons, which had been made for a young merchant for whom I had been writing, and who gave it to me because it did not fit him, though it fitted me to a charm, after a few alterations.

And so to work we went, hammer and tongs; and, before five minutes were over, I had a lift under the right ear, which I did not get entirely over for two months, while he, poor fellow, was bleeding like a pig, and actually crying with vexation and shame. At last, he called for a pole; he wouldn't fight, as we had begun, rough and tumble, though neither of us had gone down, and there was no pulling hair, no kicking shins; but a pole he must and would have, or he should leave it for somebody else to polish me off. This delighted me, of course; for it was an acknowledgment, before all the belligerent youth of Portland, that I was too much for him. I forget whether a pole was brought; although I have some recollection of seeing two boys of my own age, who were either bottle-holders or pole-bearers, jumping about, like two young bears learning to dance on hot bricks, barefooted. The battle was soon over, and I came off with flying colors; though, in consequence of being remonstrated with by the late John Fox, who happened along, just as we had got through, and I was buttoning up, I began to feel most heartily ashamed of myself; and am to this hour, whenever I recall the circumstances. For what business had I, a young gentleman in comparison with all the rest, and a Quaker, to be battling the watch with a set of graceless vagabonds, at the head of a great thoroughfare, and within sight of my poor mother's windows? But, after all, it did me good; for it cured me of championship. And, though I have never seen Wiley from that hour to this, I have always felt a desire to thank him for that rap under the ear. It made me cautious, though "sudden and quick in quarrel" as ever, until I knew how to guard against similar visitations.

◆◇◆◇◆◇◆◇◆◇◆◇◆

[*Harriot Kezia Hunt, M.D.* (*born 1805*) , *Boston*]

Our fingers were kept busy out of school and play hours, aiding the shirt-maker — helping her in the fine stitching, ruffled bosoms, and button-holes. In the making of the latter, even now, I am considered an adept. But with all this work, (which would be accounted a terrible hardship in 1855 !) there was always blended a merriment and joy, for our mother managed to make us feel that younger eyes were aiding older ones. The books we read were carefully examined, as our eager curiosities seized these intellectual treasures; healthful imagination was encouraged; pains were taken that beautiful pictures of Truth should impress our minds with its power. With scrupulous care, our apparel was ever alike; but with thoughtful wisdom, our individualisms were respected.

Taught at home while young by our mother, we received the impress of her mind. The remembrance of sitting on my father's knee at twilight, learning the multiplication table, by the bright light of a wood fire in a Franklin stove flashing softly on the shadows of the cheerful room, comes to me now like an interior illumination.

I think again of our little garden, fragrant with the early rose and fleur-de-lis. There, on spring mornings, our mother was seen, as many may remember, training and weeding her choice plants and flowers. The early lettuce and peppergrass on our table spoke of her thrift.

Whoever can look back to childhood, and recall, with gratitude, a good and kind teacher, remembers — no matter what that teacher's name — Mrs. Carter of Friend street. I am sure all who were her pupils, reading this work, will agree with me in her unfailing suavity, kindness, and tenderness to children. Her husband was a dancing-master. His hall adjoined our school-house; and many an hour she permitted me to enjoy the music and dancing as a spectator. When the time came for me to be a scholar in this school, my joy seemed complete. Mrs. Carter's was a private school: — we never attended the public schools; they were not then the carefully modelled institutions they now are, and did not bear their present relation to the public. I have my first school bill to Mrs. Carter, dated 1810. Our bills were always carefully preserved by our mother, that we might realize in maturer years the expense of our education. Friend street was at some distance from our house; this distance being objectionable in the winter season, we went, while yet quite young, to a school in an old house (now removed) at the junction of Garden court and Fleet street, kept by Misses Hannah and Elizabeth Brown. My early school mates will remember vividly the Misses Brown, and their peculiar tact in *leading* the minds of their pupils to knowledge.

The simplicity of our lives, the nearness of our spirits, and our limitation to home delights, placed us where we were little understood by our neighbors. When we were mere children we read the newspaper to our parents. (How long the President's messages seemed to us then !) While other children were walking out in the evening, we were quietly in bed — too often awake ! — and talking over when *we* should be old enough to be up in the evenings !

I can aid memory in these glances at my life by reference to my journal, which was commenced in 1815, and has to this day been kept up in the family. I find the first entry: — "Business very dull; father being now a juryman, fifty-three days at the supreme judicial court gladdens us, because his *mind* will be employed." I find reference to my desire to write my first letter to a cousin, and to my mother's refusal, on the ground of incompetency. This was just the thing for my sanguine nature, because now I would prepare myself. Here is an entry, dated January 13, 1815, referring to the close of the war of 1812–14. "The joyful news of peace is announced. Mother says the greatest emotion of our hearts must be gratitude to God." The next morning, I remember, we were awakened by the ringing of the bells, whose merry peals lasted, at intervals, all day; for it was the day of the ratification of the treaty. The morning following, we were again awakened by the ringing of bells and the firing of guns; for that was the day of celebration. Mother aroused and shared our joy; and that evening when the town was illuminated, was our first evening out, away from her. In 1855, at the Fourth of July Celebration in Dorchester, her grandchildren were out for the first evening, to see fireworks !

My journal, under the date of May, 1818, speaks of our grass being mown. The entry refers to the plot in front of our house; and in this connection I remember the old man who regularly came from year to year, for some medicinal plant which grew there, mixed with the grass. Quietly he helped himself, left his thanks quietly, and quietly departed. What a magic mirror is memory ! It now shows me our sweet little garden in the rear of the dwelling, filled with flowers, and fragrant with the cinnamon-rose trees trellised on bars, from which we were wont to cut wreaths to grace the rooms of our friends. Among the flowers, the Iris was my mother's favorite. Its broad green, decided leaf, appearing when the frost was gone from the earth, with the snow of the early spring resting upon it, had a charm for her. At that time, as I have before observed, the North End abounded in beautiful gardens, and very fine fruit was then abundant, — not doled out in scanty quart boxes, as now. My father always wished to avoid the doctor and his bills; he, therefore expended liberally for choice, ripe fruit. While our school mates were suffering from summer complaints, we were exempt.

◇◇◇◇◇◇◇◇◇◇◇◇◇

[Harriet Beecher Stowe (born 1812), Litchfield, Conn.]

My father was fond of excursions with his boys into the forests about for fishing and hunting. At first I remember these only as something pertaining to father and the older boys, they being the rewards given for good conduct,. I remember the regretful interest with which I watched their joyful preparation for departure. They were going to the Great Pond — to Pine Island — to the wonderful blue pine forest which I could just see on the horizon, and who knew what adventures they might meet ? Then the house all day was so still; no tramping of laughing, wrestling boys — no singing and shouting; and perhaps only a long seam on a sheet to be over-sewed as the sole means of beguiling the hours of absence. And then dark night would come down, and stars look out from the curtains, and innuendoes would be thrown out of children being sent to bed, and my heart would be rent with anguish at the idea of being sent off before the eventful expedition had reported itself. And then what joy to hear at a distance the tramp of feet, the shouts and laughs of older brothers; and what glad triumph when the successful party burst into the kitchen with long strings of perch, roach, pickerel, and bullheads, with waving blades of sweet-flag, and high heads of cattail, and pockets full of young wintergreen, of which a generous portion was bestowed always upon me. These were the trophies, to my eyes, brought from the land of enchantment. And then what cheerful hurrying and scurrying to and fro, and waving of lights, and what cleaning of fish in the back shed, and what calling for frying-pan and gridiron, over which father solemnly presided; for to his latest day he held the opinion that no feminine hand could broil or fry fish with that perfection of skill which belonged to himself alone, as king of woodcraft and woodland cookery.

I was always safe against being sent to bed for a happy hour or two, and patronized with many a morsel of the supper which followed, as father and brothers were generally too flushed with victory to regard very strictly dull household rules.

Somewhat later, I remember, were the expeditions for chestnuts and walnuts in the autumn, to which all we youngsters were taken. I remember the indiscriminate levy which on such occasions was made on every basket the house contained, which, in the anticipated certainty of a great harvest to bring home, were thought to be only too few. I recollect the dismay with which our second mother, the most ladylike and orderly of housekeepers, once contemplated the results of these proceedings in her well-arranged linen-room, where the contents of stocking-baskets, patch-baskets, linen-baskets, yarn-baskets, and thread-baskets were all pitched into a promiscuous heap by that omnipotent marauder, Mr. Beecher, who had accomplished all this confusion with the simple promise to bring the baskets home full of chestnuts.

What fun it was, in those golden October days, when father dared William and Edward to climb higher than he could and shake down the glossy chestnuts. To the very last of his life, he was fond of narrating an exploit of his climbing a chestnut-tree that grew up fifty feet without branches slantwise over a precipice, and then whirling himself over the abyss to beat down the chestnuts for the children below. "That was a thing," he said, "that I wouldn't let any of the boys do." And those chestnuts were had in everlasting remembrance. I verily believe that he valued himself more on some of those exploits than even his best sermons.

My father was famous for his power of exciting family enthusiasm. Whenever he had a point to carry or work to be done, he would work the whole family up to a pitch of fervent zeal, in which the strength of each one seemed quadrupled. For instance: the wood of the family used to be brought in winter on sleds, and piled up in the yard, exactly over the spot where father wished in early spring to fix his cucumber and melon frames; for he always made it a point to have cucumbers as soon as Dr. Taylor, who lived in New Haven, and had much warmer and drier land; and he did it by dint of contrivance and cucumber frames, as aforesaid. Of course, as all this wood was to be cut, split, and carried into the wood-house before an early garden could be started, it required a miracle of generalship to get it done, considering the immense quantity required in that climate to keep an old windy castle of a house comfortable. How the axes rung, and the chips flew, and the jokes and stories flew faster; and when all was cut and split, then came the great work of wheeling in and piling; and then I, sole little girl among so many boys, was sucked into the vortex of enthusiasm by father's well pointed declaration that he "wished Harriet was a boy, she would do more than any of them."

I remember putting on a little black coat which I thought looked more like the boys, casting needle and thread to the wind, and working almost like one possessed for a day and a half, till in the afternoon the wood was all in and piled, and the chips swept up. Then father tackled the horse into the cart and proclaimed a grand fishing party down to Little Pond. And how we all floated among the lilly-pads in our boat, christened "The Yellow Perch," and every one of us caught a string of fish, which we displayed in triumph on our return.

There were several occasions in course of the yearly housekeeping requiring every hand in the house, which would have lagged sadly had it not been for father's inspiring talent. One of these was the apple-cutting season, in the autumn, when a barrel of cider-apple-sauce had to be made, which was to stand frozen in the milk-room, and cut out from time to time in red glaciers, which, when duly thawed, supplied the table. The work was done in the kitchen, an immense brass kettle hanging over the deep fireplace, a bright fire blazing and snapping, and all hands, children and servants, employed on the full baskets of apples and quinces that stood around. I have the image of my father still as he sat working the apple-peeler. "Come, George," he said, "I'll tell you what we'll do to make the evening go off. You and I'll take turns, and see who'll tell the most out of Scott's novels;" for those were the days when the Tales of my Landlord and Ivanhoe had just appeared. And so they took them, novel by novel, reciting scenes and incidents, which kept the eyes of all the children wide open, and made the work go on without flagging.

Occasionally he would raise a point of theology on some incident narrated, and asked the opinion of one of his boys, and run a sort of tilt with him, taking up the wrong side of the question for the sake of seeing how the youngster could practice his logic. If the party on the other side did not make a fair hit at him, however, he would stop and explain to him what he ought to have said. "The argument lies so, my son; do that, and you'll trip me up."

In regard to Scott's novels, it will be remembered that, at the time they came out, novel writing stood at so low an ebb that most serious-minded people regarded novel reading as an evil. Such a thing as a novel was not to be found in our house. And I well recollect the despairing and hungry glances with which I used to search through father's library, meeting only the same grim sentinels — Bell's Sermons, Bogue's Essays, Bonnet's Inquiry, Toplady on Predestination, Horsley's Tracts. There, to be sure, was Harmer on Solomon's Song, which I read, and nearly got by heart, because it told about the same sort of things I had once read of in the Arabian Nights. And there was The State of the Clergy during the French Revolution, which had horrible stories in it stranger than fiction. Then there was a side-closet full of documents, a weltering ocean of pamphlets, in which I dug and toiled for hours to be repaid by disinterring a delicious morsel of a Don Quixote that had once been a book, but was now lying in forty or fifty *dissecta membra,* amid Calls, Appeals, Sermons, Essays, Reviews, Replies, and Rejoinders. The turning up of such a fragment seemed like the rising of an enchanted island out of an ocean of mud.

Great was the light and joy, therefore, when father spoke *ex cathedra,* "George, you may read Scott's novels. I have always disapproved of novels as trash, but in these is real genius and real culture, and you may read them." And we did read them; for in one summer we went through Ivanhoe seven times, and were both of us able to recite many of its scenes, from beginning to end, verbatim.

One of father's favorite resorts was Aunt Esther's room, about half a minute's walk from our house. How well I remember that room ! A low-studded parlor, looking out on one side into a front yard shaded with great elm-trees; on the other, down a green hillside, under the branches of a thick apple-orchard. The floor was covered with a neat red and green carpet; the fireplace resplendent with the brightest of brass andirons; small hanging book-shelves over an old-fashioned mahogany bureau; a cushioned rocking-chair; a neat cherry tea-table; and an old-fashioned looking-glass, with a few chairs, completed the inventory. I must not forget to say that a bed was turned up against the wall, and concealed in the day time by a decorous fall of chintz drapery.

This room, always so quiet, so spotlessly neat, was a favorite retreat, not only of father, but of all us children, who were allowed, as a reward of good behavior, to go and pass an hour or two with Aunt Esther. She rented the apartment of a motherly old body, of a class whom every body in a Yankee village calls aunt. And Aunt Bull was a great favorite with all children, being always provided with a kind word and a piece of gingerbread for each and every one. Aunt Esther, too, had a deep, shady mysterious closet in her room, most stimulating to our childish imaginations, from whence, when we went to take tea with her, came forth delicate India china, quaint old-fashioned glass, and various dainties, for the making of which she was celebrated, and some of which bear her name to this day in the family.

But Aunt Esther herself, with her sparkling hazel eyes, her keen, ready wit, and never-failing flow of ancedotes and information, interested us even more than the best things she could produce from her closet. She had read on all subjects — chemistry, philosophy, physiology, but especially on natural history, where her anecdotes were inexhaustible. If any child was confined to the house by sickness, her recounting powers were a wonderful solace. I once heard a little patient say, "Only think: Aunt Esther has told me *nineteen rat stories* all in a string." In fact, we thought there was no question we could ask that she could not answer.

I remember once we said to her, "Aunt Esther, how came you to know so much about every sort of thing ?" "Oh," said she, "you know the Bible says the works of the Lord are great, sought out of them that have pleasure therein. Now I happen to have pleasure therein, and so I sought them out."

◇◇◇◇◇◇◇◇◇◇◇◇◇

[*Edward Everett Hale (born 1822) , Boston*]

Drawing was the most popular of evening occupations, and took the most of our time and thought. The provisions for it were very simple, and there was only the faintest pretence at instruction. There was one particular brand of lead pencils, sold by one particular grocer in West Street at twelve cents a dozen. These were bought by us at this wholesale rate, and kept in the drawer. One piece of India rubber was also kept there for the crowd. As we gathered at the table, a quarter-sheet of foolscap was given to each child and to each guest, and one pencil.

The reader must imagine the steady flow of voices. "Who's got the India rubber ?" "Here it is under the Transcript." "This horse looks as if he were walking on foot-balls." "Oh, you mustn't draw his shoes; you never see his shoes!" "I wish I knew how to draw a chaise." "I don't see how they make pictures of battles. My smoke covers up all the soldiers." Battle pieces, indeed, were, as usual with children, the favorite compositions. We were not so far from the last war with England as the children of to-day are from the Civil War.

Perhaps two of us put together our paper, folded it and pinned it in the fold, and then made a magazine. Of magazines there were two — *The New England Herald,* composed and edited by the two elders of the group, and *The Public Informer,* by my sister Lucretia and me. I am afraid that the name "Public Informer" was suggested wickedly to us little ones, when we did not know that those words carry a disagreeable meaning. But when we learned this, afterwards, we did not care. I think some of the Everetts, my uncles, had had a boy newspaper with the same name. When things ran with perfect regularity *The New England Herald* was read at the breakfast-table one Monday morning, and *The Public Informer* the next Monday morning. But this was just as it might happen. They were published when the editors pleased, as all journals should be, and months might go by without a number. And there was but one copy of each issue. It would be better if this could be said of some other journals.

I must not give the idea, however, by speaking of these evenings thus that our lives were specially artistic or literary. There were devoted to play, pure and simple, with no object but having a good time. The principal part of the attics — or, as we called them, garrets — in every house we lived in was surrendered to us boys. In Tremont Place we had the valuable addition of a dark cockloft over the garret chambers. It had no windows, but was all the better place to sit and tell stories in. Then we controlled the stairs to the roof, and we spent a good deal of time, in the summer days, on the ridge-pole. There were not twenty houses in Boston on higher land, so that from this point we commanded a good view of the harbor.

We were close by the Common. The Common was still recognized as

| 1. A pasture for cows. | 3. A place for beating carpets. |
| 2. A play-ground for children. | 4. A training ground for the militia. |

It had served these purposes, or some of them, for two hundred years, since Blackstone had first turned in his cows among its savins and blackberries and rocks to pick up a scanty living. In modern days it had not been fenced until 1815. The rails of this fence were hexagonal — two or three inches in diameter, perhaps. If a flat side were on top, as was generally the case, it made a good seat for boys, as they sat on the top rail with their feet on the second. If the corner came uppermost it was not so good. The fence was double — inside the mall and outside. When a muster took place, or Artillery Election, or when the Sacs and Foxes danced on the Common,

space within the inner fence was cleared. Then boys and girls sat on it to witness the sports within, and those taller stood in rows behind.

There cannot be a square yard of the Common on which I have not stood or stepped, and the same could be said of most boys of that time. As for the cows, we saw but little of them. I cannot think that in our time there were ever fifty at once there. They retired to the parts near Charles Street, with which we had less, though much, to do. So did the people who beat carpets. Practically the Common was ours to work our own sweet will upon.

This may be my last chance to put on paper a note of Lord Percy's encampment. His brigade, in the winter of 1775–76, and perhaps of the previous year, was encamped in tents, in a line stretching south-west from the head of West Street. As the weather grew cold the tents were doubled, and the space between the two canvas roofs was filled with straw. The circles made by such tents and the life in them showed themselves in a different color of the grass for a hundred years after Percy's time. The line is now almost all taken up by what I may call the highway from the Providence station down town.

As the snow melted, and the elms blossomed, and the grass came, the Common opened itself to every sort of game. We played marbles in holes in the malls. We flew kites everywhere, not troubled, as boys would be now, by trees on the crosspaths, for there were no such trees.

Of all the entertainments of the Common, however, nothing, to our mind, compared with the facilities which the malls gave for driving hoop and for post-offices. The connection of the two may not be understood at first, and I will describe it. When the season for driving hoops came round, we examined last year's hoops, and, if they had come to grief, Fullum negotiated some arrangements by which we had large hoops from sea-going casks. I see none such now. My hoop was named Whitefoot. With these hoops it was our business to carry a daily mail.

The daily mail was made chiefly from small newspapers, which were cut from the leading columns of larger ones. In an editor's house we had plenty. The Quebec *Gazette* was specially chosen, because its column head was a small copy of its larger head, and squares cut from that column made very good little papers. With a supply of these folded, we started at the head of Park Street, two or three of us, secret as the grave, to leave the day's mail.

No, I will not, even after sixty years, tell where those post-offices were. I have no doubt that the ashes of the Quebec *Gazette* are now fertilizing some of these elms. But one was near Joy Street, one was in a heart which some landscape gardener had cut in the turf near Spruce Street, one was halfway along Charles Street. They were holes in the ground, or *caches* between the roots of trees. At each was a box — or, in one case, two tight-fitting oyster shells — which received the mail. From it the yesterday's mail was taken to the next office.

When the mail-riders with their hoops arrived at one of these postoffices they threw themselves negligently upon the ground, as if tired; but one dug with care for the box buried below. Of course he found it, unless some fatal landscape gardener, of whom the Common knew but few, had interfered. When found, the paper or letter from the last office was left here, the sods of stones or sand were replaced, and the cautious mail-riders galloped on. At the end of a winter the chances were worse for finding a mail, or after a long rain or vacation.

There were four holidays in the year — 'Lection proper, Artillery Election (generally called 'Tillery 'Lection), the Fourth of July (called Independence Day, I think, more than it is now), and, in October, Muster, or the Fall Training.

What was truly important was the festivity, principally on the Common, of Election Day. Early in the morning, perhaps even Tuesday evening, hucksters of every kind began to put up their tables, tents, and stalls on each side of the Tremont Street mall, and, to a less extent, on the other malls. On the Common itself a mysterious man — in a mysterious octagonal house painted green and red, as I remember — displayed camera views of the scene. Of these I speak from hearsay, for I never had money enough to pay for admission to this secret chamber.

To prepare for these festivities every child in Boston expected "'Lection money." 'Lection money was money given specifically to be spent on the Common on Election Day. The day before Election my mother sent Fullum to the office for three or four dollars' worth of silver; for she knew that all her train of vassals, so far as they could pretend to be children, would expect "'Lection money" from her. First, she had her own children, to whom she gave twelve and a half cents each. There was a considerable number of nephews and nieces who might or might not look in; but if they did, each of them was also sure to have a "ninepence," which was the name given to the Spanish piece which was a half a "quarter dollar." American silver coinage was still very rare.

Other retainers expected election money. There were families of black children, who never appeared at any other time, who would come in with smiling faces and make a little call. Mother would give each one his or her ninepence. On the other hand, if in the street I happened to meet an uncle, he would ask me if I did not want some Election money, and produce his ninepence. I never heard of "tipping" in any other connection, except when a boy held water for a horse as you rode any where; then you always gave him a bit of silver or a few cents.

Thus provided with the sinews of war, we went up on the Common with such company as might have happened along — girls with girls, and boys with boys. The buying and selling were confined almost wholly to things to eat and drink.

It happened oddly enough that tamarinds, in the curious "original packages," were always for sale, and dates, of which we did not see much on other occasions. At home we never had oysters, I believe because my father did not like them; but on the Common we could buy two oysters for a cent, and we ate them with rapture. Candy of all kinds then known was for sale, but the kinds were limited. There was one manufactured form which, I am sorry to say, has died out. One or two dealers sold large medals of checkerberry stamped with a head. Whom this originally represented I do not know, but very early we all said it was John Endicott, because he was the first Governor of Massachusetts Bay, and we called them "John Endicotts." You would see sailor-looking men eating lobsters, but those we were quite sure of at home. Ginger beer and spruce beer were sold from funny little wheelbarrows, which had attractive pictures of the bottles throwing out the corks by their own impro-

[33]

THE LIBRARY
COLBY JUNIOR COLLEGE
NEW LONDON, N. H.

28312

vised action. You might have a glass of spruce beer for two cents, and, to boys as impecunious as most of us were, the dealers would sell half a glass for one cent.

The military system of the State in those days required two annual parades, in which every militiaman should appear with his gun and other equipments. It is by a comparatively modern arrangement that the State or the United States furnishes the arms for the militia. Under the simpler arrangements of the colony, and of the State at the beginning, every man who considered himself a man was obliged to have a gun, a cartridge-box, a belt, a "primer," * and the other necessaries for an infantry soldier.

The interest among young men which now goes largely to the keeping up of military companies was then expended in great measure on the volunteer fire department. Still, when the fall training came, the interest of the boys was naturally in the companies which were in uniform; and when the parade was formed on the Common these companies always held the right of the line, either by courtesy or because they were entitled to it by law. According as the major-general commanding had more or less enthusiasm there would or would not be a sham fight. The whole Common was cleared for these exercises. Of course a considerable detail of melancholy sentinels was required to keep the boys from running in, and the principal fights, sham or real, on these occasions, were their contests with these sentinels. But as the army to be reviewed really amounted to nearly one-third of the men of Boston, even after this large detail of sentries, there would be a considerable force in the field. It seems to me that the line always extended, with its back to the Tremont Street mall, for the whole length of that mall.

We boys, sitting on the fence, criticised the manoeuvres of this Waterloo, with such information on tactics as we had got from reading Botta's "History of the American Revolution" or Caesar's "Commentaries on the War with Gaul"! I recollect a sham fight in which the hill — still fortified — was defended against an attack. It appears to me, however, that the attacks were generally made by the whole force against an unseen enemy. This mode of fighting has its advantages. Practically, however, after the Rangers had been thrown out as skirmishers, and the different companies had moved backward and forward across the Common, at about five in the afternoon the whole line was formed again, and a discharge of blank cartridges began, which lasted till all the cartridges of all the soldiers were burned up. I say all the cartridges, but we would solicit Fullum to

* Pronounce i as in "pine."

slip one or more cartridges into his pocket instead of firing them off, and on rare occasions he succeeded in doing this.

The actual presence of war, as it showed itself in this discharge of powder, was of course very attractive, and "Muster" had a certain value which belonged to none of the other holidays of the year.

When, in 1833, the Worcester Railroad was opened, our walking trips gave way, for a family as largely interested in that railroad as we were, to excursions out of town to the point where the walk was to begin. The line to West Newton was opened to the public on the 7th of April, 1833, but from the day when the *Meteor,* which was the first locomotive engine in New England, ran on her trial trip, we two boys were generally present at the railroad, on every half-holiday, to take our chances for a ride out upon one of the experimental trips. We knew the engine-drivers and the men who were not yet called conductors, and they knew us. My father was the president of the road, and we thought we did pretty much as we chose. The engine-drivers would let us ride with them on the engine, and I, for one, got my first lessons in the business of driving an engine on those excursions. But so soon as the road was open to passengers, these rides on the engine dropped off, perhaps were prohibited. Still we went to Newton as often as we could in the train, and afterwards to Needham. There were varied cars in those days, some of them open, like our open trolley-cars of to-day, and all of them entered from the side, as in England up to the present time.

We "went to meeting" Sunday morning and afternoon always, and so, I am apt to think, did all respectable people; certainly in the earlier part of those years. I know that I never observed any distinction between the size of the congregation in the afternoon and that of the morning. Frequently, Mr. Palfrey, the minister, would say, at the end of the morning's sermon, "I shall continue this subject in the afternoon." He did so with the perfect understanding that he would have the same hearers.

In the interior of the State, as at my grandfather's, for example, the observance of "the Sabbath" stopped at sunset. For instance, we watched at his house for the sun to go down on Sunday afternoon, and then brought out our little cannons and fired a *feu de joie* in honor of its departure. We then played blindman's-bluff all Sunday evening, and this in the parsonage of a stiff Calvinistic minister. No such excesses as this would have been permitted in Boston.

Perhaps the great central day which gave distinction and hope to the duty of going to meeting was the proclamation of Thanksgiving. Let me describe a scene in Brattle Street Meeting-House.

The time is the middle of November, on a Sunday morning. A boy of four years old, who has the fortunate privilege of sitting on the cross-seat of the pew, is the person who describes, after sixty-six years, what he remembers. The little boy, whose self and successor is now trying to reproduce him, could sleep, if he chose, extended on the cross-seat with his head in his mother's lap, while she listened to the minister. I will not say that on this particular day, he, or I, had been asleep. What is important to the present business is that she whispers to him that he had better listen now, for the minister is going to read the proclamation. The boy stands up on his seat, and with that delight with which even conservative childhood sees any custom defied watches with rapture Mr. Palfrey unfolding the large paper sheet, which might have been a large newspaper, and sees the sheet cover even the pulpit Bible.

Mr. Palfrey is a young man of thirty or thereabouts, who is afterwards to be the distinguished Dr. Palfrey, a leader of the Anti-Slavery opinion of Massachusetts. He reads the Governor's proclamation with sense and feeling, so that even a child follows along, about the taking care of the poor, the happiness of home, but specially about the success of the fisheries. But home, poor people, fisheries, and all sink into their own insignificance when with resonant voice the minister ends — with the grand words:

Given in the Council Chamber at Boston, in the year of our Lord, 1826, and of the Independence of the United States the fiftieth.

Levi Lincoln, Governor.

This fine relationship between "Thanksgiving Day" and "Independence Day," of which the glories, six months ago, are a certain hazy dream, is not lost upon the child. And then follow the words, most grand in all rituals:

By his Excellency the Governor, with the advice and consent of the Council.

Edward D. Bangs, Secretary.

GOD SAVE THE COMMONWEALTH OF MASSACHUSETTS!

That words so inspiring, pronounced with such a clarion voice, should be uttered in a church on Sunday — this was indeed something to fill high the cup of wild, intoxicating joy. That Edward D. Bangs, the secretary, should be sitting himself, watching, as it were, his own petard, on the other side of the aisle, with his finger resting on his right ear, in a peculiar manner such as was unknown to

others — he clad in a brown coat with a velvet collar — that he should see and hear all this unmoved — this added to the grandeur and solemnity and high dignity of the whole. A certain emphasis on the D added to the effect. The minister said that, in accordance with the instructions of the Executive, the church would be open on Thanksgiving Day, and that, before that day — namely, on the next Sunday — a contribution would be taken for the poor. The boy asked his mother if he might bring some money — and was told that he should have a fo'pence for the occasion. "Fo'pence" in the language of the time meant fourpence-halfpenny of the currency of New England. But New England, though she coined threepences with her own pine-tree, never coined fourpence-ha'penny pieces. She used instead the half-real of the Spanish coinage. The boy was to put in the box, and did put in for many years at Thanksgiving, one of these coins, small to kings, but almost the largest known in familiar use to children.

Had we children been asked what we expected on Thanksgiving Day we should have clapped our hands and said that we expected a good dinner. As we had a good dinner every day of our lives this answer shows simply that children respect symbols and types. And indeed there were certain peculiarities in the Thanksgiving dinner which there were not on common days. For instance, there was always a great deal of talk about the Marlborough pies or the Marlborough pudding. To this hour, in any old and well-regulated family in New England, you will find there is a traditional method of making the Marlborough pie, which is a sort of lemon pie, and each good housekeeper thinks that her grandmother left a better receipt for Marlborough pie than anybody else did. We had Marlborough pies at other times, but we were sure to have them on Thanksgiving Day; and it ought to be said that there was no other day on which we had four kinds of pies on the table and plum pudding beside, not to say chicken pie. In those early days ice creams or sherbets or any other kickshaws of that variety would have been spurned from a Thanksgiving dinner.

Every human being went to "meeting" on the morning of Thanksgiving Day, the boy of four years including. At that age he did not know that the sermon was, or might be, political. Still an attentive ear might catch words from the pulpit which would not have been heard on Sunday. It was when all parties came home from "meeting" that the real festival began. Not but what frequent visits to the kitchen the day before had familiarized even Young Boston with the gigantic scale on which things were conducted. For it was the business of the kitchen, not simply to supply the feast in that house but the other feasts in the houses of feudal dependents of different colors, who would render themselves for their pies and their chickens.

The hours absolutely without parallel in the year were the two hours between twelve and two. We were in our best clothes and it was Thanksgiving Day. We therefore did not do what we should have done on other days, and we were the least bit bored by the change. On other days we should have gone and coasted had the snow fallen; or we should have gone into the "garret" and fought an imaginary battle of Salamis on the floats. But this was Thanksgiving Day, and we therefore went into the best parlor, not very often opened, and entertained ourselves, or entertained each other, by looking at picture-books which we could not always see. The Hogarths were out, the illustrated books of travel, the handsome annuals which were rather too fine for our hands at other periods. We were in the position of the boy and girl invited to a party where they know nobody, standing in a corner and pretending to be interested by photographs. But before a great while the cousins would begin to arrive, and then all would be well. The cousins also were in their best clothes, to which we were not accustomed. But if we could show them the Hogarths, or they could tell us some experience of theirs in private theatricals, then the joys of society began.

And at two the party, larger than we ever saw it at any other time, went into the back parlor, where the large table was set. Observe that this large table never appeared, unless the "club" met with my father, except on Thanksgiving Day. Christmas Day, as a holiday of this sort, was absolutely unknown in this Puritan family.

There would be a side-table for the children at which the oldest cousin in a manner presided, with his very funny stories, with his very exciting lore about the new life on which he was entering, either in the first class at the Latin School or possibly after he had left the Latin School. Occasionally the revelry at the side-table became so loud that it had to be suppressed by a word from the elders. At the elders' table great talk about genealogy: whether Gib Atkins did or did not leave a particular bit of land to certain successors who now own it; whether the Picos and the Robbs were on good terms after the marriage of one of them to an Everett. I will say, in passing, that, as we grew older, we children had the wit to introduce these subjects for the purpose of seeing the mad rage with which different aged cousins advanced to the attack, as a bull might to a red flag.

It may readily be imagined that, with twenty or thirty guests and the innumerable courses, the company, who were indeed in no haste, sat a good while at the table. This was one of the marvels to us children, that it was possible to be at dinner two hours. There was no desire to slip down from the chair and go off to play. There was no soup dreamed of, and I think, to this day, that there never should be any at a Thanksgiving dinner. Neither did any fish follow where no soup led the way. You began with your chicken pie and your roast turkey. You ate as much as you could, and you then ate what you could of mince pie, squash pie, Marlborough pie, cranberry tart, and plum pudding. Then you went to work on the fruits as you could. The use of dried fruits at the table was much more frequent in those days than in these. Dates, prunes, raisins, figs, and nuts held a much more prominent place in a handsome dessert than they do now. Recollect that oranges were all brought from the West Indies or from the Mediterranean in sailing vessels, and were by no means served in the profusion with which they are served now.

And when at last the last philopoena had been given between two of the children, or the last "roast turkey" had been broken out of an English walnut and saved as a curiosity, all parties slid from their chairs, or rose up from them, as the length of their legs might be, and adjourned to the large parlor again.

At the bottom of my heart I think that here came a period in which the elders quailed. I think it was rather hard for them to

[39]

maintain the conversation about genealogy and lost inheritances. But we children never quailed. We either returned to the picture-books or we sat in the corner and told stories, or possibly the expert cousins, who were skilled in the fine arts, drew pictures for us. I have not the slightest recollection, either at that first Thanksgiving or any subsequent Thanksgiving of childhood, of any moment of tediousness or gloom, such as I have since found to hang over even the bravest in the midst of a high festivity. Before long we would be in the corner playing commerce, or old maid, or possibly "slap everlasting"; or the Game of Human Life would be produced, with the teetotum, and one would find himself in the stocks, or in a gambling-room, or in prison perhaps, or happily, at the age of sixty-three years, in glory.

❖❖❖❖❖❖❖❖❖❖❖

[*Lucy Larcom*]

I first saw the light in 1824, in the very middle of Beverly, in full view of the town clock and the Old South steeple. (I believe there is an "Old South" in nearly all these first-settled cities and villages of Eastern Massachusetts.) The town wore a half-rustic air of antiquity then, with its old-fashioned people and weather-worn houses; for I was born while my mother-century was still in her youth, just rounding the first quarter of her hundred years.

Primitive ways of doing things had not wholly ceased during my childhood; they were kept up in these old towns longer than elsewhere. We used tallow candles and oil lamps, and sat by open fireplaces. There was always a tinder-box in some safe corner or other, and fire was kindled by striking flint and steel upon the tinder. What magic it seemed to me, when I was first allowed to strike that wonderful spark, and light the kitchen fire !

The fireplace was deep, and there was a "settle" in the chimney corner, where three of us youngest girls could sit together and toast our toes on the andirons (two Continental soldiers in full uniform, marching one after the other), while we looked up the chimney into a square of blue sky, and sometimes caught a snow-flake on our foreheads; or sometimes smirched our clean aprons (high-necked and long-sleeved ones, known as "tiers") against the swinging crane with its sooty pot-hooks and trammels.

The coffee-pot was set for breakfast over hot coals, on a three-legged bit of iron called a "trivet." Potatoes were roasted in the ashes, and the Thanksgiving turkey in a "tin-kitchen," the business of turning the spit being usually delegated to some of us small folk, who were only too willing to burn our faces in honor of the annual festival.

There were brick ovens in the chimney corner, where the great bakings were done; but there was also an iron article called a "Dutch oven," in which delicious bread could be baked over the coals at short notice. And there never was anything that tasted better than my mother's "fire-cake," — a short-cake spread on a smooth

piece of board, and set up with a flat-iron before the blaze, browned on one side, and then turned over to be browned on the other. (It required some sleight of hand to do that.) If I could only be allowed to blow the bellows — the very old people called them "belluses" — when the fire began to get low, I was a happy girl.

In those early days, towns used to give each other nicknames, like school-boys. Ours was called "Bean-town"; not because it was especially devoted to the cultivation of this leguminous edible, but probably because it adhered a long time to the Puritanic custom of saving Sunday-work by baking beans on Saturday evening, leaving them in the oven over night. After a while, as families left off heating their ovens, the bean-pots were taken by the village baker on Saturday afternoon, who returned them to each house early on Sunday morning, with the pan of brown bread that went with them. The jingling of the baker's bell made the matter a public one.

The Sabbath mornings in those old times had a peculiar charm. They seemed so much cleaner than other mornings ! The roads and the grassy footpaths seemed fresher, and the air itself purer and more wholesome than on week-days. Saturday afternoon and evening were regarded as part of the Sabbath (we were taught that it was heathenish to call the day Sunday) ; work and playthings were laid aside, and everybody, as well as every thing, was subjected to a rigid renovation. Sabbath morning would not have seemed like itself without a clean house, a clean skin, and tidy and spotless clothing.

The Saturday's baking was a great event, the brick oven being heated to receive the flour bread, the flour-and-Indian, and the rye-and-Indian bread, the traditional pot of beans, the Indian pudding, and the pies; for no further cooking was to be done until Monday. We smaller girls thought it a great privilege to be allowed to watch the oven till the roof of it should be "white-hot," so that the coals could be shoveled out.

Then it was so still, both out of doors and within ! We were not allowed to walk anywhere except in the yard or garden. I remember wondering whether it was never Sabbath-day over the fence, in the next field; whether the field was not a kind of heathen field, since we could only go into it on week-days. The wild flowers over there were perhaps Gentile blossoms. Only the flowers in the garden were well-behaved Christians. It was Sabbath in the house, and possibly even on the doorstep; but not much farther. The town itself was so quiet that it scarcely seemed to breathe. The sound of wheels was seldom heard in the streets on that day; if we heard it, we expected some unusual explanation.

I liked to go to meeting — not wholly oblivious to the fact that going there sometimes implied wearing a new bonnet and my best white dress and muslin "vandyke," of which adornments, if *very* new, I vainly supposed the whole congregation to be as admiringly aware as I was myself.

But my Sabbath-day enjoyment was not wholly without draw-backs. It was so hard, sometimes, to stand up through the "long prayer," and to sit still through the "ninthlies," and "tenthlies," and "finallys" of the sermon ! It was impressed upon me that good children were never restless in meeting, and never laughed or smiled, however their big brothers tempted them with winks or grimaces. And I did want to be good.

When I first opened my eyes upon my native town, it was already nearly two hundred years old, counting from the time when it was part of the original Salem settlement — old enough to have gained a character, an individuality of its own, as it certainly had. We children felt at once that we belonged to the town, as we did to our father or mother.

The sea was its nearest neighbor, and penetrated to every fireside, claiming close intimacy with every home and heart. The farmers up and down the shore were as much fishermen as farmers; they were as familiar with the Grand Banks of Newfoundland as they were with their own potato-fields. Every third man you met in the street, you might safely hail as "Shipmate," or "Skipper," or "Captain." My father's early seafaring experience gave him the latter title to the end of his life.

It was hard to keep the boys from going off to sea before they were grown. No inland occupation attracted them. "Land-lubber" was one of the most contemptuous epithets heard from boyish lips. The spirit of adventure developed in them a rough, breezy type of manliness, now almost extinct.

Men talked about a voyage to Calcutta, or Hong-Kong, or "up the Straits," — meaning Gibraltar and the Mediterranean, — as if it were not much more than going to the next village. It seemed as if our nearest neighbors lived over there across the water; we breathed the air of foreign countries, curiously interblended with our own.

The women of well-to-do families had Canton crape shawls and Smyrna silks and Turk satins, for Sabbath-day wear, which somebody had brought home for them. Mantel-pieces were adorned with nautilus and conch-shells, and with branches and fans of coral; and children had foreign curiosities and treasures of the sea for playthings. There was one imported shell that we did not value much, it was so abundant — the freckled univalve they called a "prop." Yet it had a mysterious interest for us little ones. We held it to our ears, and listened for the sound of the waves, which we were told that it still kept, and always would keep. I remember the time when I thought that the ocean was really imprisoned somewhere within that narrow aperture.

We were accustomed to seeing barrels full of cocoa-nuts rolled about; and there were jars of preserved tropical fruits, tamarinds, ginger-root, and other spicy appetizers, almost as common as barberries and cranberries, in the cupboards of most housekeepers.

I wonder what has become of those many, many little red "guinea-peas" we had to play with ! It never seemed as if they really belonged to the vegetable world, notwithstanding their name.

We had foreign coins mixed in with our large copper cents, — all kinds, from the Russian "kopeck" to the "half-penny token" of Great Britain. Those were the days when we had half cents in circulation to make change with. For part of our currency was the old-fashioned "ninepence," — twelve and a half cents, and the "four pence ha'penny," — six cents and a quarter. There was a good deal of Old England about us still.

And we had also many living reminders of strange lands across the sea. Green parrots went scolding and laughing down the thimbleberry hedges that bordered the cornfields, as much at home out of doors as within. Java sparrows and canaries and other tropical song-birds poured their music out of sunny windows into the street, delighting the ears of passing school children long before the robins came. Now and then somebody's pet monkey would escape along the stone walls and shed-roofs, and try to hide from his boy persecutors by dodging behind a chimney, or by slipping through an open scuttle, to the terror and delight of juveniles whose premises he invaded.

And there were wanderers from foreign countries domesticated in many families, whose swarthy complexions and un-Caucasian features became familiar in our streets, — Mongolians, Africans, and waifs from the Pacific islands, who always were known to us by distinguished names, — Hector and Scipio, and Julius Caesar and Christopher Columbus. Families of black people were scattered about the place, relics of a time when even New England had not freed her slaves. Some of them had belonged in my great-grandfather's family, and they hung about the old homestead at "The Farms" long after they were at liberty to go anywhere they pleased. There was a "Rose" and a "Phillis" among them, who came often to our house to bring luscious high blackberries from the Farms woods, or to do the household washing. They seemed pathetically out of place, although they lived among us on equal terms, respectable and respected.

The pathos of the sea haunted the town, made audible to every ear when a coming northeaster brought the rote of the waves in from the islands across the harbor-bar, with a moaning like that we heard when we listened for it in the shell. Almost every house had its sea-tragedy. Somebody belonging to it had been shipwrecked, or had sailed away one day, and never returned.

Our own part of the bay was so sheltered by its islands that there were seldom any disasters heard of near home, although the names of the two nearest — Great and Little Misery — are said to have originated with a shipwreck so far back in the history of the region that it was never recorded.

But one such calamity happened in my infancy, spoken of always by those who knew its victims in subdued tones; — the wreck of the "Persia." The vessel was returning from the Mediterranean, and in a blinding snowstorm on a wild March night her captain probably mistook one of the Cape Ann light-houses for that on Baker's Island, and steered straight upon the rocks in a lonely cove just outside the cape. In the morning the bodies of her dead crew were found tossing about with her cargo of paper-manufacturers' rags, among the breakers. Her captain and mate were Beverly men, and their funeral from the meeting-house the next Sabbath was an event which long left its solemnity hanging over the town.

"Old Election," "'Lection Day" we called it, a lost holiday now, was a general training day, and it came at our most delightful season, the last of May. Lilacs and tulips were in bloom, then; and it was a picturesque fashion of the time for little girls whose parents had no flower-gardens to go around begging a bunch of lilacs, or a tulip or two. My mother always made "'Lection cake" for us on that day. It was nothing but a kind of sweetened bread with a shine of egg-and-molasses on top; but we thought it delicious.

Among other domestic traditions of the old times was the saying that every girl must have a pillow-case full of stockings of her own knitting before she was married. Here was another mountain before me, for I took it for granted that marrying was inevitable — one of the things that everybody must do, like learning to read, or going to meeting.

I began to knit my own stockings when I was six or seven years old, and kept on, until home-made stockings went out of fashion. The pillow-case full, however, was never attempted, any more than the patch-work quilt. I heard somebody say one day that there must always be one "old maid" in every family of girls, and I accepted the prophecy of some of my elders, that I was to be that one. I was rather glad to know that freedom of choice in the matter was possible.

It did not take long to turn over the new leaf of our home experience. One sunny day three of us children, my youngest sister, my brother John, and I, took with my mother the first stage-coach journey of our lives, across Lynnfield plains and over Andover hills to the banks of the Merrimack. We were set down before an empty house in a yet unfinished brick block, where we watched for the big wagon that was to bring our household goods from Beverly to Lowell.

It came at last; and the novelty of seeing our old furniture settled in new rooms kept us from being homesick. One after another they appeared, — bedsteads, chairs, tables, and, to me most welcome of all, the old mahogany secretary with brass-handled drawers, that had always stood in the "front room" at home. With it came the barrel full of books that had filled its shelves, and they took their places as naturally as if they had always lived in this strange town.

There they all stood again side by side on the shelves, the dear, dull, good old volumes that all my life I had tried in vain to take a sincere Sabbathday interest in, — Scott's Commentaries on the Bible, Hervey's "Meditations," Young's "Night Thoughts," "Edwards on the Affections," and the Writings of Baxter and Doddridge. Besides these, there were bound volumes of the "Repository Tracts," which I had read and re-read; and the delightfully miscellaneous "Evangelicana," containing an account of Gilbert Tennent's wonderful trance; also the "History of the Spanish Inquisition," with some painfully realistic illustrations; a German Dictionary, whose outlandish letters and words I liked to puzzle myself over; and a descriptive History of Hamburg, full of fine steel engravings — which last two or three volumes my father had brought with him from the countries to which he had sailed in his sea-faring days. A complete set of the "Missionary Herald," unbound, filled the upper shelves.

Other familiar articles journeyed with us: the brass-headed shovel and tongs, that it had been my especial task to keep bright; the two card-tables (which were as unacquainted as ourselves with ace, face, and trump) ; the two china mugs, with their eighteenth-century lady and gentleman figures, curiosities brought from over the sea, and reverently laid away by my mother with her choicest relics in the secretary-desk; my father's miniature, painted in Antwerp, a treasure only shown occasionally to us children as a holiday treat; and my mother's easy-chair — I should have felt as if I had lost *her,* had that been left behind. The earliest ambition of my infancy had been to grow up and wear a cap, and sit in an easy-chair knitting, and look comfortable, just as my mother did.

◇◇◇◇◇◇◇◇◇◇◇◇◇

[*Charles T. Congdon, New Bedford, Mass.*]

I sometimes divert myself by making an inventory of things which we have now [1880] which we did not have when I was a boy. There are many who remember all about the clumsy, old-fashioned tinderbox, and who have scraped their knuckles piteously while imitating Prometheus, and striking the flint against the steel, until at last the tinder caught the divine spark. A better way was to bank up the wood fire at night, for we had wood fires then, and live coals enough for kindling would be found in the morning. The wonted fire (see Gray) lived in the ashes. The first inventions for obtaining the desired flame were clumsy. There was the French fire-box, as it was called; the matches in them it was necessary to dip in a little bottle of acid; sometimes they were inflamed by the process, but oftener, as I remember it, they were not. The friction match was at

A NEW ENGLAND FIRESIDE

first very clumsy. The lucifers it was necessary to pull briskly through folded sand-paper. At last came the match as we have it now, handy, certain, and convenient. The improvement in pens was similarly slow. The good gray goose-quill was all we had at first. When our stern old pedagogue tried to teach us the art of making a pen, we blundered and cut our fingers, and some of us, myself among the number, never mastered the mystery after all. The first metallic pens, which were of silver, were the very worst instruments of the kind which I ever saw. The first steel pens were not much better. There was a certain horrible "oblique pen," as it was called, which did nothing but spatter and blot and catch in the paper, and do everything which a pen should not do. Metallic pens were then sold in little cases containing half a dozen, and cost ten or fifteen cents apiece.

In housekeeping, also, there have been innumerable changes. Alas! we had firesides then, around which we cosily gathered to watch dreamily the consumption of the well-seasoned oak-wood, and to indulge in social converse. Possibly people may enjoy themselves now quite as well huddled about a register; I have no doubt of the fact that their backs are warmer, for our backs, I am sorry to say, were often cold while our faces were aflame: but to sit there and chat and dream while the firelight flickered upon the ceiling and in the mirror, and made the great brass andirons two separate and distinct glories; to read by that light, with our young eyes, some fairy tale, or to con the lesson of the next day; to see in the glowing log castles and caverns, giants and fairies, and even excellent maps of the United States; to repeat verses which maternal taste and tenderness took care should be good ones, — how charming it all seems to me now! How we dreaded the stroke of nine, which sent us off to our cold beds! But we needed a plenty of sleep, and we got it, though during the winter months breakfast was eaten by candle-light. Dinner was at noon, and even that was two hours later than Queen Elizabeth ate hers. Tea at five concluded the eating for the day, unless there were nuts and apples in the course of the evening. It was all a simple, but it was a happy life, — much happier than any which I anticipate in the days which remain to me.

◇◇◇◇◇◇◇◇◇◇◇◇◇◇

[J. M. Bailey, (The Danbury News)]

The boys on Liberty Street are rather down on Willie Cliver. They were playing mumblety peg, all of them together, Saturday afternoon. Mumblety peg is a very exciting game if you are a spectator.

It got on to a little boy named Mose, first. He got down on his knees and rooted around in the earth to get a hold of that peg, with the wisdom and decorum of a man forty years old. When he came up with the peg in his teeth, his mouth and nose looked like a vacant asparagus bed. Willie enjoyed it hugely, and was fairly insane with delight when three other boys got caught and wore the newness off their noses and the enamel from their teeth in the mighty endeavors to encompass the obstinate peg. Then it got on to Willie, and the boys whose faces were smarting acutely under the pressure of preceding defeats, drove that peg with a velocity that would have depressed any other boy but Willie; but he had been educated by religious parents, and when the peg was fairly settled, he went into the house to get his Sunday-School lesson — and while he was in there looking pure, and good, and attentive, Mose and the three other little boys put up their shamefully-abused noses and lips and howled and roared around like mad.

Rafting is the prevailing popular amusement with juveniles this month. The boy whose parents own the pond, is generally chosen captain of the craft. The raft quite frequently consists of a couple of boards the captain's father has laid away to season. The captain stands at the bow and hollers, and the other officers, whose claim to the berth principally rests on the fact that they have dry pants at home, stand at the stern, and spatter water on outsiders who are on the shore with their hands in their breeches' pockets and guile in their hearts. They thus navigate for hours at a time, and then fight over the distance they have made, and finally go home to see their parents about it, and are dried with a bed cord, and put to bed, where they can feel of their injuries without molestation.

Calling a boy up in the morning can hardly be classed under the head of "pastimes," especially if the boy is fond of exercise the day before. And it is a little singular that the next hardest thing to getting a boy out of bed is getting him into it. There is rarely a mother who is a success at rousing a boy. All mothers know this; so do their boys. And yet the mother seems to go at it in the right way. She opens the stair door and insinuatingly observes: "Johnny." There is no response. "John-ny." Still no response. Then there is a short, sharp "John," followed a moment later by a prolonged and emphatic "John Henry." A grunt from the upper regions signifies that an impression has been made, and the mother is encouraged to add, "You'd better be getting down here to your breakfast, young man, before I come up there an' give you something you'll feel." This so startles the young man that he immediately goes to sleep again. And the operation has to be repeated several times. A father knows nothing about this trouble. He merely opens his mouth as a soda bottle ejects its cork, and the "John Henry" that cleaves the air of that stairway, goes into that boy like electricity, and pierces the deepest recesses of his very nature. And he pops out of that bed and into his clothes, and down the stairs, with a promptness that is commendable. It is rarely a boy allows himself to disregard the paternal summons. About once a year is believed to be as often as is consistent with the rules of health. He saves his father a great many steps by his thoughtfulness.

MY BOOK AND HEART

❖❖❖❖❖❖❖❖❖❖❖❖

[*Lyman Beecher*]

I WENT to school first in North Guilford, in a great barn of a
school-house, with desks around, and a long desk through the center.
The best writers sat at the end next to the fire. The fireplace took in
wood cart length, and it was hot enough at that end to roast an ox,
and that was all the heat there was. I was about the fourth or fifth
from the fire, and the ink always froze in my pen. So it was, "Master,
may I go to the fire?" all day long.

They had a parish meeting once to see about moving the old
thing, but quarreled and broke up in a row. It never would have
been set straight if it hadn't been for our old neighbor, Tim
Baldwin.

Next morning he said he wasn't going to have any quarreling
about that school-house; so he yoked his oxen, and Tim Rossiter's,
and went down, hitched on — "Whoa, haw, Bright — gee up !" and
dragged the school-house along where he wanted it. Then he un-
hitched and left it there, and there it stood. And, when people
found it was done, they stopped quarreling.

Bishop was our first teacher — a poor creature who didn't know
what else to do, so he kept school. I worked all summer, and went
to school in winter, and learned my letters out of Dilworth.

Dan Bartlett came next, and taught me Daboll's Arithmetic. Jones was next — pretty good in common things. I came late that quarter, and stood at the foot in reading. After we had done reading, he said to me, "Come up here next the head."

Afterward, I remember, we chose sides; two pretty girls drew lots for first pick. After we had done, "Very well," said he. "Lyman Beecher is the best reader in school." Oh, how proud I felt!

Then came Augustus Baldwin. He really took hold and gave us a start. We thought him the most wonderful man in the world. He was "college-learned," and a little vain. After lecturing us on manners, he would wind up by saying, "Be as I am!" and strutted about. We swallowed it all, admiring. I went in arithmetic through the Rule of Three; but nobody ever explained any thing. We only did sums. The only books we had at Uncle Benton's were the great Bible and Psalm-book. Father came over once and made me a present of Robinson Crusoe and Goody Two-shoes. They thought me a genius because I took Robinson Crusoe out to the barn to read and beat flax. But I was not much of a reader.

Catharine Beecher: "Well, father, what sort of religious training did you have?"

We always had family prayers, and I heard the Bible read every morning. Aunt Benton became pious when I was about ten. I remember Parson Bray's coming to see her, and talking about "inability." I never heard Parson Bray preach a sermon I understood.

They say every body knows about God naturally. A lie. All such ideas are by teaching. One Sunday evening I was out playing. They kept Saturday evening, and children might play on Sunday evening as soon as they could see three stars. But I was so impatient I did not wait for that. Bill H. saw me, and said,

"That's wicked; there ain't three stars."

"Don't care."

"God says you mustn't."

"Don't care."

"He'll punish you."

"Well, if he does, I'll tell Aunt Benton."

"Well, he's bigger than Aunt Benton, and he'll put you in the fire and burn you forever and ever."

That took hold. I understood what fire was, and what forever was. What emotion I had thinking. No end! no end! It has been a sort of mainspring ever since.

I had a good orthodox education; was serious-minded, conscientious, and had a settled fear of God and terror of the day of judgment. Conscience, however, only troubled me about particular sins.

[52]

I knew nothing about my heart. For instance: I got to pulling hair with Alex. Collins one training-day, and Granny Rossiter told Aunt Benton, "I'm afeared Lyman's been a fighting." I felt so ashamed, as if I had lost my character. It laid heavy on my heart long after. Again: one Sunday, Spring (my first dog) and I staid at home in the forenoon. Spring and Spot (Uncle Tim's dog) would visit on Sundays, and off they went to the woods to hunt squirrels. This time they found a rabbit. I had great workings. I knew it would be wrong. But nobody was there. After holding back as long as I could, I let go, and went down to the branch.* The rabbit had run to his burrow, and the dogs could not reach him. I staid a while, but conscience tormented me so that I went back. Then I had nothing to do; so I took the big Bible, and read Susanna, Bel and the Dragon, and the Revelations till I was tired. Then I fell to whittling, and made elder pin-boxes. But, when they were made, I was so conscience-smitten that I gathered them up and threw them into the fire.

At sixteen I went to school in New Haven, taught by Colonel Mansfield, father of Mansfield of Cincinnati. Harry Baldwin, my college chum, was there too. I began to study my Accidence there, but did not stay long. My mother's sister, Aunt Williston, of West Haven, took me to board, in exchange for their son at college, who boarded with father.

Uncle Williston was a very pious man; but, like most ministers of that day, fond of his pipe. He used a ton or more of tobacco in his life-time. Had a little shelf by the side of his writing-table — a piece of plank — on which he cut tobacco; it was nearly cut through. Never saw him without a pipe in his mouth. Aunt Williston was kind, and kept good watch over us young folks. Her niece, Lucy, about my age, was a pretty girl, and I liked to sit up nights cosily chatting with her. But no, Aunt Williston came in and ordered me off to bed.

Harriet Beecher Stowe: "Was she *very* pretty?"

Why — (hesitation). She was really a sensible girl, of fair form and presence, which, I dare say, would have waxed into beauty.

H.B.S. "Was Uncle Williston a good preacher?"

Well, he always read his morning sermon to us Saturday evening, and the other at noon, and catechised us on them in the evening. Lucy and I were bored alike. He was not weak — every body loved him — but he was not keen. I remember one sermon on "My son, eat thou honey, because it is good." He repeated it over and over, and turned it this way and that, and scratched it as a hen does an

* A little brook.

[53]

ear of corn, and wound up — "And what other reason shall I give why virtue should be chosen ? My son, eat thou honey, for it is good."

I studied Latin grammar. The grammar was written in Latin. I studied, parsed, recited every thing in Latin. A deadly trial; but the best fortune I ever had. Really, a thorough-going thing. I got it by heart, every word of it. In that thing none of my class surpassed me.

I staid all winter at Uncle Williston's, and then went to Parson Bray's at North Guilford, who fitted boys for college. He gave us sums to do in arithmetic, but never explained. I suffered in that department through his neglect. He was a farmer; had two slaves to till his farm, and abundance of cattle and hogs. He preached twice on the Sabbath, and attended funerals, and that was all except the quarterly sacramental lecture. That was the average of ministerial work in those days.

H.B.S. "That is one reason why they lived longer, and staid longer in the same place."

True. Nowadays they wear a man out in a few years. They make him a slave, worse than on the plantation. The old way was healthier.

I remember the Association met there, and dined at Uncle Benton's. As soon as Aunt Benton saw them coming, she threw the irons in the fire, and ran down cellar to draw a pail of beer. Then the hot irons were thrust in hissing and foaming, it was sweetened, and the flip was ready. Then came pipes, and in less than fifteen minutes you could not see across the room.

Parson Bray took a newspaper, the first one I ever read. Those were French Revolutionary days, and the paper was full of battles between the French and Austrians. I have read the papers regularly ever since, and kept up with the times.

◇◇◇◇◇◇◇◇◇◇◇◇◇◇

[David L. Dodge, Brooklyn, Conn.]

The summer I was six years of age (1780) I attended the school of a venerable Irish maiden lady, Mary Moxley, I suppose then about sixty years of age, who had taught schools in the country about forty years. Of her I learnt my A B C, went wholly through the spelling and reading lessons in Fanning's Spelling Book. I was, however, taken from the school before the term closed, as I was feeble and raised blood. This excellent lady, though strict in discipline, imparted much religious instruction adapted to our ages. Most of the scholars learned a majority of Watt's Divine Songs, several of which I have never forgotten, also texts of scripture, and answers in the shorter catechism. I received my first serious impressions under the instruction of this pious lady, whom I was permitted to visit several years afterward, when she would receive me with the kindness of a parent, give me sweetmeats and cakes, then put her hand upon my head, warn me against evil example, and urge me to seek the favor of Christ as all important. She had acquired considerable property, and quite a library, from which she often loaned me books suitable to my age. She resided with a nephew, about a mile and a half from my father's, and diffused a savor of piety all around her. She lived to a quite old age, and died in peace.

◇◇◇◇◇◇◇◇◇◇◇◇◇◇

[*Timothy Dwight, S.T.D., LL.D., New Haven*]

A stranger traveling through New-England, marks with not a little surprise the multitude of school-houses, appearing every where at little distances. Familiarized as I am to the sight, they have excited no small interest in my mind; particularly as I was travelling through the settlements recently begun. Here, while the inhabitants were still living in log-huts, they had not only erected school-houses for their children, but had built them in a neat style; so as to throw an additional appearance of deformity over their own clumsy habitations. This attachment to education in New-England, is universal; and the situation of that hamlet must be bad indeed, which, if it contain a sufficient number of children for a school, does not provide the necessary accommodations. In 1803, I found neat school-houses in Colebrook, and Stewart, bordering on the Canadian line.

◇◇◇◇◇◇◇◇◇◇◇◇◇◇

[*Samuel Griswold Goodrich, Ridgefield, Conn.*]

1799. The site of the school-house was a triangular piece of land, measuring perhaps a rood in extent, and lying, according to the custom of those days, at the meeting of four roads. The ground hereabouts — as everywhere else in Ridgefield — was exceedingly stony, and in making the pathway the stones had been thrown out right and left, and there remained in heaps on either side, from generation to generation. All around was bleak and desolate. Loose, squat stone walls, with innumerable breaches, inclosed the adjacent fields. A few tufts of elder, with here and there a patch of briers and pokeweed, flourished in the gravelly soil. Not a tree, however, remained, save an aged chestnut, at the western angle of the space. This, certainly, had not been spared for shade or ornament, but probably because it would have cost too much labor to cut it down, for it was of ample girth. At all events it was the oasis in our desert during summer; and in autumn, as the burrs disclosed its fruit, it resembled a besieged city. The boys, like so many catapults, hurled at it stones and sticks, until every nut had capitulated.

Two houses only were at hand: one, surrounded by an ample barn, a teeming orchard, and an enormous wood-pile, belonged to Granther Baldwin; the other was the property of "Old Chich-es-ter," an uncouth, unsocial being, whom everybody for some reason or other seemed to despise and shun. His house was of stone and of one story. He had a cow, which every year had a calf. He had a wife — filthy, uncombed, and vaguely reported to have been brought from the old country. This is about the whole history of the man, so far as it is written in the authentic traditions of the parish. His premises, an acre in extent, consisted of a tongue of land between two of the converging roads. No boy, that I ever heard of, ventured to cast a stone, or to make an incursion into this territory, though it lay close to the school-house. I have often, in passing, peeped timidly over the walls, and caught glimpses of a stout man with a drab coat, drab breeches, and drab gaiters, glazed with ancient grease and long abrasion, prowling about the house; but never did I discover him outside of his own dominion. I know it was darkly intimated that he had been a tory, and was tarred and feathered in the revolutionary war, but as to the rest he was a perfect myth.

The school-house itself consisted of rough, unpainted clapboards, upon a wooden frame. It was plastered within, and contained two apartments — a little entry, taken out of a corner for a wardrobe, and the schoolroom proper. The chimney was of stone, and pointed with mortar, which, by the way, had been dug into a honeycomb by uneasy and enterprising penknives. The fireplace was six feet wide and four feet deep. The flue was so ample and so perpendicular, that the rain, sleet, and snow fell direct to the hearth. In winter, the battle for life with green fizzling fuel, which was brought in sled lengths and cut up by the scholars, was a stern one. Not unfrequently, the wood, gushing with sap as it was, chanced to be out, and as there was no living without fire, the thermometer being ten or twenty degrees below zero, the school was dismissed, whereat all the scholars rejoiced aloud, not having the fear of the schoolmaster before their eyes.

It was the custom at this place, to have a woman's school in the summer months, and this was attended only by young children. It was, in fact, what we now call a primary or infant school. In winter, a man was employed as teacher, and then the girls and boys of the neighborhood, up to the age of eighteen, or even twenty, were among the pupils. It was not uncommon, at this season, to have forty scholars crowded into this little building.

I was about six years old when I first went to school [1799]. My teacher was Aunt Delight, that is, Delight Benedict, a maiden lady of fifty, short and bent, of sallow complexion and solemn aspect. I remember the first day with perfect distinctness. I went alone — for I was familiar with the road, it being that which passed by our old house. I carried a little basket, with bread and butter within, for my dinner, the same being covered over with a white cloth. When I had proceeded about half way, I lifted the cover, and debated whether I would not eat my dinner, then. I believe it was a sense of duty only that prevented my doing so, for in those happy days, I always had a keen appetite. Bread and butter were then infinitely superior to *pâté de foie gras* now; but still, thanks to my training, I had also a conscience. As my mother had given me the food for dinner, I did not think it right to convert it into lunch, even though I was strongly tempted.

I think we had seventeen scholars — boys and girls — mostly of my own age. Among them were some of my after companions. I have since met several of them — one at Savannah, and two at Mobile, respectably established, and with families around them. Some remain, and are now among the grey old men of the town; the names of others I have seen inscribed on the tombstones of their native village. And the rest — where are they ?

The school being organized, we were all seated upon benches, made of what were called *slabs* — that is, boards having the exterior or rounded part of the log on one side: as they were useless for other purposes, these were converted into school-benches, the rounded part down. They had each four supports, consisting of straddling wooden legs, set into augur-holes. Our own legs swayed in the air, for they were too short to touch the floor. Oh, what an awe fell over me, when we were all seated and silence reigned around !

The children were called up, one by one, to Aunt Delight, who sat on a low chair, and required each, as a preliminary, to make his manners, consisting of a small sudden nod or jerk of the head. She then placed the spelling-book — which was Dilworth's — before the pupil, and with a buck-handled penknife pointed, one by one, to the letters of the alphabet, saying, "What's that?" If the child knew his letters, the "what's that ?" very soon ran on thus:

"What's that ?"

"A."

" 'Sth-a-t ?"

"B."

"Sna-a-a-t ?"

"C."

"Sna-a-a-t ?"

"D."

"Sna-a-a-t ?"

"E," &c.

I looked upon these operations with intense curiosity and no small respect, until my own turn came. I went up to the school-mistress with some emotion, and when she said, rather spitefully, as I thought, "Make your obeisance!" my little intellects all fled away, and I did nothing. Having waited a second, gazing at me with indignation, she laid her hand on the top of my head, and gave it a jerk which made my teeth clash. I believe I bit my tongue a little; at all events, my sense of dignity was offended, and when she pointed to A, and asked what it was, it swam before me dim and hazy, and as big as a full moon. She repeated the question, but I was doggedly silent. Again, a third time, she said, "What's that ?" I replied: "Why don't you tell me what it is ? I didn't come here to learn you your letters !" I have not the slightest remembrance of this, for my brains were all a-woolgathering; but as Aunt Delight affirmed it to be a fact, and it passed into a tradition, I put it in.

I believe I achieved the alphabet that summer, but my after progress, for a long time, I do not remember. Two years later [1801] I went to the winter-school at the same place, kept by Lewis Olmstead — a man who had a call for plowing, mowing, carting manure, &c., in summer, and for teaching school in the winter, with a talent for music at all seasons, wherefore he became chorister upon occasion, when, peradventure, Deacon Hawley could not officiate. He was a celebrity in ciphering, and 'Squire Seymour declared that he was the greatest "arithmeticker" in Fairfield county. All I remember of his person is his hand, which seemed to me as big as Goliath's judging by the claps of thunder it made in my ears on one or two occasions.

The next step of my progress which is marked in my memory, is the spelling of words of two syllables. I did not go very regularly to school, but by the time I was ten years old I had learned to write, and had made a little progress of arithmetic. There was not a grammar, a geography, or a history of any kind in the school. Reading, writing, and arithmetic were the only things taught, and these very indifferently — not wholly from the stupidity of the teacher, but because he had forty scholars, and the standards of the age required no more than he performed.

Ridgefield, being a village, had a right to follow its own whim, and therefore West Lane, instead of being the aristocratic end of the place, was really rather the low end. It constituted in fact what was called *Down-town*, in distinction from the more eastern and northern section, called *Up-town*. In this latter portion, and about the middle of the main street, was the Up-town school, the leading seminary of the village, for at this period it had not arrived at the honors of an academy. At the age of ten years I was sent here, the institution being then, and many years after, under the charge of Master Stebbins. He was a man with a conciliating stoop in the shoulders, a long body,

short legs, and a swaying walk. He was, at this period, some fifty years old, his hair being thin and silvery, and always falling in well-combed rolls, over his coat-collar. His eye was blue, and his dress invariably of the same color. Breeches and knee-buckles, blue-mixed stockings, and shoes with bright buckles, seemed as much a part of the man as his head and shoulders. On the whole, his appearance was that of the middle-class gentleman of the olden time, and he was in fact what he seemed.

This seminary of learning for the rising aristocracy of Ridgefield was a wooden edifice, thirty by twenty feet, covered with brown clapboards, and except an entry, consisted of a single room. Around, and against the walls ran a continuous line of seats, fronted by a continuous writing-desk. Beneath, were depositories for books and writing materials. The center was occupied by slab seats, similar to those of West Lane. The larger scholars were ranged on the outer sides, at the desks; the smaller fry of a-b-c-darians were seated in the center. The master was enshrined on the east side of the room, contrary, be it remembered, to the law of the French savans, which places dominion invariably in the west. Regular as the sun, Master Stebbins was in his seat at nine o'clock, and the performances of the school began.

According to the Catechism — which, by the way, we learned and recited on Saturday — the chief end of man was to glorify God and keep his commandments: according to the routine of this school, one would have thought it to be reading, writing, and arithmetic, to which we may add spelling. From morning to night, in all weathers, through every season of the year, these exercises were carried on with the energy, patience, and perseverance of a manufactory.

Master Stebbins respected his calling: his heart was in his work; and so, what he pretended to teach, he taught well. When I entered the school, I found that a huge stride had been achieved in the march of mind since I had left West Lane. Webster's Spelling-book had taken the place of Dilworth, which was a great improvement. The drill in spelling was very thorough, and applied every day to the whole school. I imagine that the exercises might have been amusing to a stranger, especially as one scholar would sometimes go off in a voice as grum as that of a bullfrog, while another would follow in tones as fine and piping as a peet-weet. The blunders, too, were often ineffably ludicrous; even we children would sometimes have tittered, had not such an enormity been certain to have brought out the birch. As to rewards and punishments, the system was this: whoever missed went down; so that perfection mounted to the top. Here was the beginning of the up and down of life.

Reading was performed in classes, which generally plodded on

[60]

without a hint from the master. Nevertheless, when Zeek Sanford — who was said to have a streak of lightning in him — in his haste to be smart, read the 37th verse of the 2d chapter of the Acts — "Now when they heard this, they were *pickled* in their heart" — the birch stick on Master Stebbins's table seemed to quiver and peel at the little end, as if to give warning of the wrath to come. When Orry Keeler — Orry was a girl, you know, and not a boy — drawled out in spelling: k-o-n, *kon* s-h-u-n-t-s, *shunts*, konshunts — the bristles in the master's eyebrows fidgeted like Aunt Delight's knitting-needles. Occasionally, when the reading was insupportably bad, he took a book and read himself, as an example.

We were taught arithmetic in Daboll, then a new book, and which, being adapted to our measures of length, weight, and currency, was a prodigious leap over the head of poor old Dilworth, whose rules and examples were modeled upon English customs. In consequence of the general use of Dilworth in our schools, for perhaps a century — pounds, shillings, and pence were classical, and dollars and cents vulgar, for several succeeding generations. "I would not give a penny for it," was genteel; "I would not give a cent for it," was plebeian. We have not yet got over this: we sometimes say *red cent* in familiar parlance, but it can hardly be put in print without offense.

Master Stebbins was a great man with a slate and even beyond the Rule of Three, and making forays into the mysterious region of Vulgar Fractions. Several daring geniuses actually entered and took possession.

But after all, penmanship was Master Stebbins's great accomplishment. He had no magniloquent system; no pompous lessons upon single lines and bifid lines, and the like. The revelations of inspired copy-book makers had not then been vouchsafed to man. He could not cut an American eagle with a single flourish of a goose-quill. He was guided by good taste and native instinct, and wrote a smooth round hand, like copper-plate. His lessons from A to &, all written by himself, consisted of pithy proverbs and useful moral lessons. On every page of our writing-books he wrote the first line himself. The effect was what might have been expected — with such models, patiently enforced, nearly all became good writers.

Beyond these simple elements, the Up-town school made few pretensions. When I was there, two Webster's Grammars and one or two Dwight's Geographies were in use. The latter was without maps or illustrations, and was in fact little more than an expanded table of contents, taken from Morse's Universal Geography — the mammoth monument of American learning and genius of that age and generation. The grammar was a clever book; but I have an idea that neither Master Stebbins nor his pupils ever fathomed its depth. They floundered about in it, as if in a quagmire, and after some time came out pretty nearly where they went in, though perhaps a little obfuscated by the dim and dusky atmosphere of these labyrinths.

The fact undoubtedly is, that the art of teaching as now understood, beyond the simplest elements, was neither known nor deemed necessary in our country schools in their day of small things. Repetition, drilling, line upon line, and precept upon precept, with here and there a little of the birch — constituted the entire system.

◇◇◇◇◇◇◇◇◇◇◇◇◇◇

[*Edward Everett Hale, Boston, 1824*]

At my own imprudent request, not to say urgency, I was sent to school with two sisters and a brother, older than I, when I was reckoned as about two years old. The school was in an old-fashioned wooden house which fronted on a little yard entered from Summer Street.

I supposed the room to be a large hall, though I knew it was not nearly so large as our own parlors at home. It may have been eighteen feet square. The floor was sanded with clean sand every Thursday and Saturady afternoon. This was a matter of practical importance to us, because with the sand, using our feet as tools, we made sand pies. You gather the sand with the inside edge of either shoe from a greater or less distance, as the size of the pie requires. As you gain skill, the heap which you make is more and more round. When it is well rounded you flatten it by a careful pressure of one foot from above. Hence it will be seen that full success depends on your keeping the sole of the shoe exactly parallel with the plane of the floor. If you find you have succeeded when you withdraw the shoe, you prick the pie with a pin or a broom splint provided for the purpose, pricking it in whatever pattern you like. The skill of a good pie-maker is measured largely by these patterns. It will readily be seen that the pie is better if the sand is a little moist. But beggars cannot be choosers, and while we preferred the sand on Mondays and Fridays, when it was fresh, we took it as it came.

I cannot tell how we were taught to read, for I cannot remember the time when I coud not read as well as I can now.

In an old desk, of which the cover had been torn off, in the closet at the left of the fireplace, were a number of bows made of yellow, pink, and blue ribbon. When Saturday came, every child "who had been good" during the week was permitted to select one of these bows, choosing his own color, and to have it pinned on his clothes under his chin to wear home. If, on the other hand, he had been very bad, he had a black bow affixed, willy nilly.

In winter Fullum, the factotum, put my two sisters, my brother, and myself into a little green sleigh which he had had made, in which he dragged us over the snow to school. I believe that if any Fullum of to-day should start from the upper door of the Parker House, and drag four little children down School Street, through Washington Street, to Summer Street, and stop at a door opposite Hovey's, he would attract a fair share of attention. But there was room enough for all of them. The "main street " was what the chief street of a good country town would be now, and this equipage seemed strange to nobody.

At the Latin School in 1831 we had not much room for playing, but we might take a turn at tag or some other out-door game before the school-bell rang. But at last, at eight o'clock in summer and at nine in winter, the bell began to ring. It rang for five minutes, and before the end of the five minutes every boy must be in his place. The masters, four or five of them, had been standing in the meanwhile on the sidewalk in front of the school door; as the bell rang they bowed to each other and repaired one by one to their rooms.

By the time the bell struck its last stroke every boy would be in his seat. The boys of the present generation have little idea what such seats were. At first they were simply long benches with what we call long "forms" in front. About midway of my school career, there were substituted for these benches separate desks, somewhat like what boys have now, but with the very hardest and smallest seat which was ever contrived for an unfortunate boy to wriggle upon. Still we could open the desks and support them with our heads while we pretended to be arranging our books. No school-boy who has ever had the felicity of such a desk, needs to be told what various orgies we could carry on under such shelter of protection.

To this school we repaired at eight o'clock in the morning for the months between April and October, and at nine o'clock from the 1st of October to the 1st of April. School lasted till twelve o'clock, excepting for the little boys, who, in the latter part of my time, were "let out" at eleven o'clock. School began again at three, and lasted, in winter, as long as there was light, and in summer till six o'clock.

The other fellows would urge us to go down on the wharves, as they did. The fathers of most of them were in mercantile life, for Boston was still largely a shipping town. I can remember asking one of them what we should do on the wharves, with a horrified feeling which I have to this day about any vague future entertainment of which the lines are not indicated. He said, "Oh, we can go about the vessels, we can talk with the men." Perhaps they would be landing molasses, and we could dip straws in the bung-holes; or once a cask had broken open, and the fellows had gathered up brown sugar in their hands. To this day, when I hear of persons going abroad or anywhere else

BACON ACADEMY, COLCHESTER, CONNECTICUT

in search of an undefined amusement, I imagine them dipping straws into casks of West India molasses, and then drawing those straws through their mouths.

◇◇◇◇◇◇◇◇◇◇◇◇◇

[*Timothy Dwight*]

By an *Academy,* as the term is used in New-England, and generally throughout the United States, is intended a school, between a parochial school, and a College, and approximating indefinitely towards either. In such a school are usually taught the English, Latin, Greek, and sometimes the French, languages; reading, with propriety, writing, speaking, composition, various branches of Mathematical science, and sometimes Logic, and Natural Philosophy. No system has, however, been formed, hitherto, for the regulation of Academies. A large proportion of those, who are destined to a liberal education, are here prepared for their admission into Colleges. At the same time, multitudes, who never receive such an education, are furnished with the knowledge, which qualifies them to enter upon various kinds of useful business.

Of these schools there are more than twenty in the state of Connecticut. The exact number I do not know. About ten or twelve of them may be incorporated. Seven or eight are sustained by funds. Some have sprung from the combined exertions of numbers; and some, from the efforts of individuals. Of those, which have funds, the principal are Bacon Academy, at Colchester, amply endowed by a Mr. Bacon, one of its inhabitants; the Episcopal Academy at Cheshire; the Hopkins Grammar School at Hartford; and the Staples Academy at Weston.

In Massachusetts there are forty eight of these schools; all incorporated, and most, if not all of them, endowed to some extent by the State. The principal of these is Phillips' Academy at Andover. Two of those in Connecticut, and three in Massachusetts, are exclusively female seminaries. Some others admit children of both sexes.

Of the Academies in Massachusetts the District of Maine has its full proportional share.

In New-Hampshire, the number of schools, which may with propriety be placed on this list, is thirteen. The principal of these is Phillips' Academy at Exeter.

The number of these schools in Vermont is twelve, all of which are incorporated.

❖❖❖❖❖❖❖❖❖❖❖❖

[*John Neal*]

I had been to a Quaker boarding-school at Windham, Maine, where they starved and froze me for two long winters, and where I learned, to the best of my knowledge and belief, just nothing at all; to a Quaker private school, to the town school, kept by Master Gregg and Master Patten; to the Portland Academy, when the late Dr. Payson was preceptor; and finally, to Master Moody's in Union Street. In both of these two last-mentioned establishments, the "Columbian Orator" was a text book; and elocution was taught in a way I never shall forget — never !

We had a yearly exhibition at the Academy, and the favorites of the preceptor were allowed to speak a piece; and a pretty time they had of it. Somehow, I was never a favorite with any of my teachers, after the first two or three days; and, as I went barefooted, I dare say it was thought unseemly, or perhaps cruel, to expose me upon the platform. And then, as I had no particular aptitude for public speaking, and no relish for what was called oratory, it was never my luck to be called up. Among my schoolmates, however, was one, a very amiable, shy boy, to whom — partly on account of his good clothes,

I dare say, and partly on account of his father, one of our wealthiest merchants — was assigned, at the last exhibition I attended, that passage in Pope's Homer, beginning with, *"Aurora, now fair daughter of the dawn."* This the poor boy gave with so much emphasis and discretion, that, to me, it sounded like "O roarer !" and I was wicked enough, out of sheer envy, I dare say, to call him "O roarer !" — a nickname which clung to him for a long while, though no human being ever deserved it less; for, in speech and action both, he was quiet, reserved, and sensitive, as everybody who knew Edward Cobb will acknowledge.

My next experience in elocution was still more disheartening, so that I never had a chance of showing what I was capable of in that way, till I set up for myself. Master Moody was thought to have uncommon qualifications for teaching oratory. He was a large, handsome, heavy man, over six feet high; and having understood that the first, second, and third pre-requisite in oratory was *action,* the boys he put in training were encouraged to most vehement and obstreperous manifestations. Let me give an example, and one that weighed heavily on my conscience for many years after the poor man passed away.

Among his pupils were two boys, brothers, named Simpson, who were thought highly gifted in elocution. The master, who was evidently of that opinion, had a habit of parading them on all occasions before visitors and strangers; though one had lost his upper front teeth and lisped badly, and the other had the voice of a penny-trumpet. Week after week these two boys went through the quarrel of Brutus and Cassius, for the benefit of myself and others, to see if their example would not provoke us to a generous competition for all the honors.

On coming to the passage, "Be ready, gods, with all your thunderbolts — dash him in pieces !" the elder of the two gave it after the following fashion: "Be ready, godths, with all your thunderbolths — dath him in pietheth !" — bringing his right fist down into his left palm with all his strength, and his lifted foot upon the platform, which was built like a sounding-board, so that the master himself, who had suggested the action, and obliged the poor boy to rehearse it, over and over again, appeared to be utterly carried away by the magnificent demonstration; while to me — so deficient was I in rhetorical taste — it sounded like the crash of broken crockery, intermingled with chicken-peeps.

◇◇◇◇◇◇◇◇◇◇◇◇◇

[Josiah Quincy, Boston]

We had come to Andover to get religion, and the pursuit of this object was seldom interfered with. During the first years of my stay, starting in 1811, we were taken to worship in the church of the town, which was supported by a tax laid upon all citizens. What the winter services were in that old meeting-house no description can reproduce. The building was in decay, and the windows rattled with every blast.

There was no pretence of stove or furnace, and the waters of life, which were dispensed from the pulpit, froze to solid ice before they reached us. There were, to be sure, a few pans of ignited charcoal, which the sexton carried to certain old ladies of great respectability, and which were supposed to impart some warmth to their venerable feet. But this luxury was never provided for the voting sex; and boys, as a matter of course, received their ghostly instruction with a chill on. We muffled ourselves up in comforters, as if to go on a sleigh ride, and shivered through the long services, warmed only by such flickering flames of devotion as they were calculated to kindle. The vivid descriptions of those sultry regions to which the vast majority of the human race were hastening lost something of the terror they were meant to excite. If we could only approach the quarters of the condemned near enough to get thoroughly warmed through, the broad road that led to them might gain an additional attraction. The boys were required to remember the text, as well as the heads of the discourse, and were duly examined thereupon the next day. My own memory was good, — so good, indeed, that some of those sermons stick there yet. And they were not difficult to remember either; for, give the preacher his premises, and let him start his machine of formal logic, and the conclusions ground themselves out with unerring certainty. An exception to this rule was found in the doctrine of election as not inconsistent with individual freedom. This was a craggy theme with which the Andover divines were accustomed to grapple with great spirit. They certainly showed, or appeared to show, that we were perfectly free to choose a destiny which, nevertheless, had been absolutely decreed beforehand; but the reasoning which dissolved this formidable paradox was altogether too subtle for the youthful brain to follow.

A report of an occasional sermon may give some idea of the gallant style in which the Andover ministers faced sin — or what seemed to them sin — under difficulties. It happened that a proposition to teach dancing in the town had been made by some rash professor of that accomplishment. Under this visitation there was clearly but one subject for the next Sunday's discourse. The good minister rose in the pulpit fully armed for the encounter; but he was not the man to take unfair advantages. The adversary should be allowed every point which seemed to make in his favor. In pursuance of this generous design, a text was given out which certainly did seem a little awkward in view of the deductions which must be drawn from it. It was taken from the Book of Ecclesiastes, and was announced with unflinching emphasis, "There is a time to dance." The preacher began by boldly facing the performance of King David,

> When before the Ark
> His grand *pas seul* excited some remark !

But, notwithstanding the record, we were assured that David did not dance. A reference to the original Hebrew made it plain that "he took no steps." All he did was to jump up and down in a very innocent manner, and it was evident that this required no professional instruction. And now, having disposed of the example of the father, the way was clear to take up the assertion of Solomon that there was a time to dance. Were this the case, it were pertinent to consider what that time might be. Could a man find time to dance before he was converted ? To ask such a question as that was to answer it. The terrible risks to which the unregenerate were exposed, and the necessity that was upon them to take summary measures for their avoidance, clearly left no time for dancing. And how was it with a man while he was being converted? Overwhelmed with the sense of sin, and diligently seeking the remedy, it was simply preposterous to imagine that *he* could find time for dancing. And how was it with the saints who had been converted ? Surely such time as they had must be spent in religious exercises for the conversion of others; obviously *they* had no time to dance. And so the whole of human life had been covered, and the conclusion was driven home with resistless force. What time for dancing Solomon might have had in mind it was unnecessary to inquire, for it was simply demonstrable that he could not have referred to any moment of the time allotted to man on this earth. After this discourse it is needless to say that no dancing-master showed his face in Andover during my acquaintance with the town.

But if it shall happen that I speak freely of forms which have no longer the spiritual meaning that once filled them, I must also emphasize the fact that a stern pressure towards morality was characteristic of the school. Emulation was abandoned because it appealed to lower motives than Christians should entertain, and the phrase "unhallowed ambition" was applied to the pursuit of excellence for any selfish end. A society for the cultivation of the moral virtues, composed of candidates for the Divinity Department and some of the smaller boys, existed in the school, and a pledge to abstain from intoxicating liquors was exacted from its members.

During the six years I spent in Andover there were several revivals of religion. The master believed in their utility and did everything in his power to encourage them. We had prayer meetings before school, after school, and in recess, and a strong influence was exerted to make us attend them. I am tempted to give a little circumstance in this connection because it shows the absolute sincerity with which our teachers held their religious views. One summer's day, after a session of four hours, the master dismissed the school in the usual form. No sooner had he done so than he added, "There will now be a prayer meeting: those who wish to lie down in ever-lasting burning may go; the rest will stay." It is probable that a good many boys wanted to get out of doors. Two of them only had the audacity to rise and leave the room. One of these youngsters has since been known as an eminent Doctor of Divinity; the other was he who now relates the incident. But no sooner was the prayer meeting over than Mr. Adams sought me out, asked pardon for the dreadful alternative he had presented, and burst into a flood of tears. He said with deep emotion that he feared that I had committed the unpardonable sin and that he had been the cause. His sincerity and faith were most touching; and his manliness in confessing his error and asking pardon from his pupil makes the record of the occurrence an honor to his memory.

It was provided that every pupil of the Academy should be taught to sing, and a special master was kept to train us in an accomplishment which was held to be of the first importance in the next world, if not in this. English literature was presented in the sober guise of "Vincent's Explanations of the Westminster Catechism," and "Mason on Self-Knowledge," and from each of these books we were required to recite once a week. The sole work of imagination tolerated by the authorities was the "Pilgrim's Progress." There was, nevertheless, an awful rumor, only to be mentioned under one's breath, that Doctor Porter, professor of rhetoric in the divinity school, had upon his shelves the writings of a person called William Shakespeare, a play-actor, whose literary productions were far from edifying. I mention this scandal, not as asserting its truth; it may be one more specimen of those reckless stories boys will get up about their betters.

❖❖❖❖❖❖❖❖❖❖❖

[*Lucy Larcom, Beverly, Mass. (born 1824)*]

The school was kept by a neighbor whom everybody called "Aunt Hannah." It took in all the little ones about us, no matter how young they were, provided they could walk and talk, and were considered capable of learning their letters.

A ladder-like flight of stairs on the outside of the house led up to the schoolroom, and another flight, also outside, took us down into a bit of a garden, where grew tansy and spearmint and southernwood and wormwood, and, among other old-fashioned flowers, an abundance of many-tinted four o'clocks, whose regular afternoon-opening just at the close of school, was a daily wonder to us babies. From the schoolroom window we could watch the slow hands of the town clock, and get a peep at what was going on in the street, although there was seldom anybody in sight except the Colonel's gardener or coachman, going into or out of the driveway directly opposite. It was a very still street; the front windows of the houses were generally closed, and a few military-looking Lombardy poplars stood like sentinels on guard before them.

Another shop — a very small one — joined my father's, where three shoemakers, all of the same name — the name our lane went by — sat at their benches and plied their "waxed ends." One of them, an elderly man, tall and erect, used to come out regularly every day, and stand for a long time at the corner, motionless as a post, with his nose and chin pointing skyward, usually to the north-east. I watched his face with wonder, for it was said that "Uncle John" was "weather-wise," and knew all the secrets of the heavens.

Aunt Hannah's schoolroom and "our shop" are a blended memory to me. As I was only a baby when I began to go to school, I was often sent downstairs for a half hour's recreation not permitted to the older ones. I think I looked upon both school and shop entirely as places of entertainment for little children.

Aunt Hannah used her kitchen or her sitting room for a school-room, as best suited her convenience. We were delighted observers of her culinary operations and other employments. If a baby's head nodded, a little bed was made for it on a soft "comforter" in the cor-ner, where it had its nap out undisturbed. But this did not often happen; there were so many interesting things going on that we sel-dom became sleepy.

Aunt Hannah was very kind and motherly, but she kept us in fear of her ferule, which indicated to us a possibility of smarting palms. This ferule was shaped much like the stick with which she stirred her hasty pudding for dinner, — I thought it was the same, — and I found myself caught in a whirlwind of family laughter by reporting at home that "Aunt Hannah punished her scholars with the pudding-stick."

There was one colored boy in school, who did not sit on a bench, like the rest, but on a block of wood that looked like a backlog turned endwise. Aunt Hannah often called him a "blockhead," and I sup-posed it was because he sat on that block. Sometimes, in his absence, a boy was made to sit in his place for punishment, for being a "block-head" too, as I imagined. I hoped I should never be put there. Stupid little girls received a different treatment, — an occasional rap on the head with the teacher's thimble; accompanied with a half-whispered, impatient, ejaculation, which sounded very much like "Numskull!" I think this was a rare occurrence, however, for she was a good-natured, much-enduring woman.

One of our greatest school pleasures was to watch Aunt Hannah spinning on her flax-wheel, wetting her thumb and forefinger at her lips to twist the thread, keeping time, meanwhile, to some quaint old tune with her foot upon the treadle.

A verse of one of her hymns, which I never heard anybody else sing, resounds in the farthest corner of my memory yet: —

> Whither goest thou, pilgrim stranger,
> Wandering through this lowly vale?
> Knowest thou not 'tis full of danger?
> And will not thy courage fail?

Then a little pause, and the refrain of the answer broke in with a change, quick and jubilant, the treadle moving rapidly, also: —

> No, I'm bound for the kingdom!
> Will you go to glory with me?
> Hallelujah! Praise the Lord!

I began to go to school when I was about two years old, as other children about us did. The mothers of those large families had to resort to some means of keeping their little ones out of mischief, while they attended to their domestic duties. Not much more than that sort of temporary guardianship was expected of the good dame who had us in charge.

But I learned my letters in a few days, standing at Aunt Hannah's knee while she pointed them out in the spelling-book with a pin, skipping over the "a b abs" into words of one and two syllables, thence taking a flying leap into the New Testament, in which there is concurrent family testimony that I was reading at the age of two years and a half. Certain it is that a few passages in the Bible, whenever I read them now, do not fail to bring before me a vision of Aunt Hannah's somewhat sternly smiling lips, with her spectacles just above them, far down on her nose, encouraging me to pronounce the hard words. I think she tried to choose for me the least difficult verses, or perhaps those of which she was herself especially fond. Those which I distinctly recall are the Beatitudes, the Twenty-third Psalm, parts of the first and fourteenth chapters of the Gospel of St. John, and the thirteenth chapter of the First Epistle to the Corinthians.

◇◇◇◇◇◇◇◇◇◇◇◇◇

[*Thomas Low Nichols, Orford, N. H. (born 1851)*]

Every year, at town-meeting, the paupers of the town were sold at auction to those who would keep them cheapest, taking into account the work they were capable of doing. The pauper was a slave, sold for a year at a time, but sold yearly as long as he lived. The schoolmaster was treated in the same inglorious fashion. The cheaper he could be boarded, the longer the money would last, and the longer the school-term continued. A well-to-do farmer, with an abundance of food, and children who might have some extra assistance in their lessons, would be glad to board the master for a very trifling consideration. I have known one to be sumptuously entertained for less than seventy-five cents a-week.

But even this amount was often saved to the district by the master or mistress boarding round — taking turns of a week or two at the houses of his or her pupils. This gave a pleasing variety to the life of the teacher, and enabled the people of the district to vie with each other in their hospitalities. I think that this was the most popular system. It gave all the young misses a fair chance at a possible admirer, and though the teacher might have long walks when boarding at the extremities of the district, he was treated everywhere with the attentions due to a transient and honored guest. The best room in the house and the best fare that could be provided were ready for the schoolmaster.

◇◇◇◇◇◇◇◇◇◇◇◇◇

[Stephen Burroughs, Hanover, N. H. (born 1765)]

I took a school in a town called Orford,* eighteen miles below Haverhill, and twelve miles from Hanover. Fortunately for me, I had kept this school long enough to get established, before Mr. Ripley [of Dartmouth] knew where I was, and of course, his efforts for my overthrow were ineffectual. I continued this school until the expiration of the time agreed for, to the universal satisfaction of all concerned. I began this school in November, and ended with the month of February. The usual time for schooling, in all the towns throught the eastern states, is only in the winter, some few populous towns excepted.

Whilst I taught this school, I became acquainted with a woman, who was supposed to be a widow, possessing those amiable qualifications calculated to attract the attention of every admirer of the fair part of creation. I paid strict attention to gain her affections, and flattered myself I had in a measure succeeded. After the school was ended, I returned to my father's. I had not been long with my father, before I had a visit from Joseph Huntington, who was a member of Dartmouth College. He came in a sleigh, and brought a classmate, who was of that peculiar turn of mind, as to be a butt for the ridicule of all the wits in College; and it was certain, he would be led into all the scrapes then in vogue. Huntington proposed to me to take a ride that evening in his sleigh, telling me at the same time, he had brought A—— with him to steal a beehive. For the diversion of drawing A—— into a ludicrous situation, I immediately consented to be one of the party. We accordingly all got into the sleigh, and drove away about two miles, when, coming near where bees were kept, we sent A—— after them, who was ever prompt to do what he was set about by any one. He soon returned with a hive to the sleigh, when we drove off with great speed to the College, where I found a number assembled, ready to partake of the repast which the honey afforded. All were regaled with this delicious morsel but myself, having an insuperable antipathy to honey, which wholly incapacitates me from ever making use of it.

* Compare the description, elsewhere in these pages, by Thomas Low Nichols. — B. M.

[73]

I am now, sir, at a place in my narrative which has caused me pain in relating, because I view my conduct entirely wrong, and my mode of reasoning upon such subjects, at that age, quite ridiculous. For some unaccountable reason or other, youth are carried away with false notions of right and wrong. I know, for instance, that Huntington possessed those principles of integrity, that no consideration would have induced him to deprive another, by stealth, of any species of property, except fruits, bees, pigs, and poultry. And why it is considered by youth generally, that depriving another of those articles is less criminal, than stealing any other kind of property, I cannot tell; but it is a fact, that almost all do esteem this so; and robbing others of those articles is thought to be only the playful wantonness of thoughtless inexperience. I will ask you, sir, whether our treatment of those things does not give too much reason to convince youth, that we view them in that light ourselves.

We parted at 11 o'clock that evening, and I returned home. The man who lost the bees, suspected the scholars as the authors of this depredation, and accordingly, went to the governors to enter his complaint. Search was made, and by the inattention of A——, a discovery was effected. It was found, likewise, in the discovery, that I was of the party. This was a fine bone for my friend Ripley to pick. He did not fail to fulfil the office of a clergyman, by setting his face against iniquity. He was determined I should be made a public example. After Huntington and A—— had settled with the owner of the bees, Ripley represented to him the necessity of not making any settlement with me, but prosecute in the law, and there have it terminate. Coffin was ready to back this representation with all his oratory. They succeeded; I was informed into the circumstances; and as another circumstance had now taken place, which co-operated with this, it is necessary I should go back a little in my narrative, and bring forward this event to the present time. The lady, of whom mention has been made, and who was supposed to be a widow, I still addressed on the terms of courtship: matters between us had proceeded to considerable length. I went to visit her one day, after I had left Orford, and coming to a neighbor of hers about six rods distant, I saw a man standing in the door of her house, a stranger whom I never before saw; and upon inquiring who he was, received information that her husband was alive, and had come home. This intelligence was like heaven's artillery, charged with tenfold vim. The wheels of nature ran backward ! The blood curdled in my veins, and I fell almost senseless into a chair ! I was aroused from this stupor, by female shrieks ! Howlings of bitter lamentation as-

[74]

sailed my ears . . . God of nature ! what greater scenes of distress are reserved in store? What sharper arrows yet remain in thy quiver ?

[*Henry Adams, Boston*]

The atmosphere of education in which he lived was colonial, revolutionary, almost Cromwellian, as though he were steeped, from his greatest grandmother's birth, in the odor of political crime. Resistance to something was the law of New England nature; the boy looked out on the world with the instinct of resistance; for numberless generations his predecessors had viewed the world chiefly as a thing to be reformed, filled with evil forces to be abolished, and they saw no reason to suppose that they had wholly succeeded in the abolition; the duty was unchanged. That duty implied not only resistance to evil, but hatred of it. Boys naturally look on all force as an enemy, and generally find it so, but the New Englander, whether boy or man, in his long struggle with a stingy or hostile universe, had learned also to love the pleasure of hating; his joys were few.

Politics, as a practice, whatever its professions, had always been the systematic organizations of hatreds, and Massachusetts politics had been as harsh as the climate. The chief charm of New England was harshness of contrasts and extremes of sensibility — a cold that froze the blood, and a heat that boiled it — so that the pleasure of hating — one's self if no better victim offered — was not its rarest amusement; but the charm was a true and natural child of the soil, not a cultivated weed of the ancients. The violence of the contrast was real and made the strongest motive of education. The double exterior nature gave life its relative values. Winter and summer, cold and heat, town and country, force and freedom, marked two modes of life and thought, balanced like lobes of the brain. Town was winter confinement, school, rule, discipline; straight, gloomy streets, piled with six feet of snow in the middle; frosts that made the snow sing under wheels or runners; thaws when the streets became dangerous to cross; society of uncles, aunts, and cousins who expected children to behave themselves, and who were not always gratified; above all else, winter represented the desire to escape and go free. Town was restraint, law, unity. Country, only seven miles away, was liberty, diversity, outlawry, the endless delight of mere sense impressions given by nature for nothing, and breathed by boys without knowing it.

YALE COLLEGE

COLLEGE

❖❖❖❖❖❖❖❖❖❖❖

[*Timothy Dwight*]

In Massachusetts, all instructors of the university, colleges, academies and schools, and all private instructors, are required to take diligent care and exert their best endeavors to impress on the minds of children and youth committed to their care, the principles of piety, justice, and a sacred regard to truth, love to their country, humanity, and universal benevolence, sobriety, industry, and frugality, chastity, moderation, and temperance, and all other virtues; and to show them the tendency of these virtues, to secure the blessings of liberty, and the tendency of the opposite vices to slavery and ruin. School-masters of grammar schools must have received an education at some college or university; must produce a certificate from a learned minister well skilled in the Greek and Latin languages, or from two such ministers in the vicinity, that they have reason to believe him well qualified to discharge the duties of his office, and a certificate from the minister of the place where he belongs, or from the select-men of the town, or from the committee of the parish, that to the best of his, or their knowledge he sustains a good moral character. This certificate is unnecessary to a person who is to keep school in his native place; but the select-men or committee are in this case required specially to attend to his morals.

❖❖❖❖❖❖❖❖❖❖❖❖❖

[*Samuel Sewall, Harvard*]

Monday, June 15, 1674. Mr. Thatcher, Fellow. The Corporation met and chose Sir Thatcher Fellow, Mr. Johnson, Printer. N. B. There were this day two boyes killed at Watertown with the tumbling of a load of brush on them, on which they road: the one was about the age of 12 years, and the other 9.

Thomas Sargeant was examined by the Corporation: finally, the advice of Mr. Danforth, Mr. Stoughton, Mr. Thatcher, Mr. Mather (then present) was taken. This was his sentence.

That being convicted of speaking blasphemous words concerning the H. G. [Holy Ghost] he should be therefore publickly whipped before all the Scholars. 2. That he should be suspended as to taking his degree of Bachelour (this sentence read before him twice at the Pr^{ts} before the committee, and in the library 1 up before execution.) 3. Sit alone by himself in the Hall uncovered at meals, during the pleasure of the President and Fellows, and be in all things obedient, doing what exercise was appointed him by the President, or else be finally expelled the Colledge. The first was presently put in execution in the Library (Mr. Danforth, Jr. being present) before the Scholars. He kneeled down and the instrument Goodman Hely attended the President's word as to the performance of his part in the work. Prayer was had before and after by the President. July 1, 1674. Sir Thacher Commonplaced, Justification was his head. He had a solid good piece: stood above an hour, and yet brake of before he came to any use. By reason that there was no warning given, none (after the undergraduates) were present, save Mr. Dan Gookin, Sr. the President and myself. July 3, 1674. N. B. Mr. Gookin, Jr. was gone a fishing with his brothers.

Had my hair cut by Goodman Barret, July 6.

July the 8th being Cambridge lecture day, Mr. Wallie set sail, with whom went Mr. Chauncy and Mr. Epps.

July 10. I Commonplaced. Nobody save the 6 plm. [placemen ?] was present.

July 17. Sir Weld commonplaced. His subject was Man as created in God's Image.

July 21. Sir Bowles * Commonplaced. His subject was the Creation of the Soul.

August 7, 1674. New Colledge raised. John Francis helping about raising of the new Colledge had his right legg (both bones) broke

* John Bowles — sometimes written Bowels — and Thomas Weld were Sewall's classmates. The title *Sir* designated graduates before they took the Master's degree.

a little above his anckle, and his left thigh about 4 inches below the joint, by a peece that fell on him, and had like to have killed several others and yet hurt none.

Friday, August 14. I with my two Brothers went home to Newbury.

[*Timothy Dwight (President of Yale)*]

Cambridge was the fourth township colonized in the County of Middlesex: Charlestown being the first, Watertown the second, and Medford the third. The settlement of Cambridge was begun under the immediate direction of the government in the year 1631. The town was laid out in squares; one of which was left open for a market, and is now known by the name of Market-place. Four of the streets run from North to South, and three others from East to West. The houses exhibit every gradation of building, found in this country, except the log-hut. Several handsome villas, and other handsome houses are seen here, a considerable number of decent ones, and a number not small, of such as are ordinary and ill-repaired. To my eye this last appeared as if inhabited by men, accustomed to rely on the University for their subsistence: men, whose wives are the chief support of their families by boarding, washing, mending and other offices of the like nature. The husband, in the mean time, is a kind of gentleman at large; exercising an authoritative controul over every thing within the purlieus of the house; reading newspapers, and political pamphlets; deciding on the characters, and measures, of an Administration; and dictating the policy of his country. In almost all families of this class, the mother and her daughters lead a life of meritorious diligence, and economy: while the husband is merely a bond of union, and a legal protector of the household. Accordingly he is paid, and supported, not for his services, but for his presence. In every other respect he is merely "nugae canorae;" just such another talking trifle as a parrot; having about as much understanding and living just about as useful a life; a being, creeping along the limits of animated and unanimated existence; and serving, like an oyster, as a middle link between plants and animals. If such men are not found here, Harvard-College may boast of exclusive privileges.

I ought to have mentioned, that the greatest disadvantage, under which this Seminary labours, is the proximity of Boston. The allurements of this Metropolis have often become too powerfully seductive to be resisted by the gay, and sometimes even by the grave, youths, who assemble here for their education. Since the erection of West Boston bridge, the distance between these towns is reduced from five to little more than three miles. This fact, as I have been informed by the Governours of the University, has rendered the evil, alluded to, still greater. The bustle and splendour of a large commercial town are necessarily hostile to study. Theatres, particularly, can scarcely fail of fascinating the mind at so early a period of life.

◇◇◇◇◇◇◇◇◇◇◇◇◇◇

[*Josiah Quincy, Harvard 1821*]

One day early in November, 1818, I find a dry twig pasted upon the leaf of my journal and underneath this inscription: "Resistance to tyrants is obedience to God. This twig was my badge; all the class tore them from the Rebellion Tree, and agreed to wear them in their bosoms." The rough and unmannerly proceedings which characterized this memorable outbreak have long since ceased to be possible in first-class colleges. Boarding in Commons was at that time compulsory, and the freshmen and sophomores were fed in two large halls which were separated by folding doors. These portals were generally kept carefully locked and bolted; but, one Sunday evening, they had unhappily been left open. Taking advantage of this circumstance, some sophomore threw a plate into the quarters of the freshmen. It was promptly returned; every one started up from the tables; and a hot and furious battle commenced. Cups, saucers, and dishes were used as missiles, and the total destruction of the crockery belonging to the college was the result. Of course it was necessary for the government to take notice of such an outrage as this; and it was soon anounced that five of my classmates were suspended and must leave town. Two of these victims were from New York, two from South Carolina, and one from Massachusetts. The students selected happened to be very popular, and it seemed to us unjust that they alone should be punished for an offence of which so many others were equally guilty. Accordingly we followed them out of Cambridge with shouts and cheers, and, on returning, assembled about the Rebellion Tree and awaited results. After a little time the president's freshman came upon the scene, and summoned Adams, Otis, and myself to appear at once in his study. Doctor Kirkland * told us that he was a good friend of our fathers, and wished

* John Thornton Kirkland, President of Harvard, 1810–1828. The Harvard professors mentioned in the ensuing pages can be identified and dated no less easily.

to get us out of mischief; he must accordingly advise us to leave town for the present, and should command us at our peril not to return to the tree. Under the excitement which ruled the hour, we promptly went back to the rendezvous; and Adams, who was appointed our spokesman, addressed the assembly in a vigorous speech.

I happen to remember the climax of his remarks: "Gentlemen, we have been commanded, at our peril, not to return to the Rebellion Tree: *at our peril we do return!*" This morsel of defiance seemed to us to have as fine a ring as the famous, "Sink or swim, live or die, survive or perish," which Daniel Webster subsequently attributed to the grandfather of the speaker. The applause was immense, and we voted to remain in session all day, and to absent ourselves from all college exercises. Even the rain which soon began to descend was powerless to disperse us; for we adjourned in force to the great porch which then stood in front of University Hall. The end of it was that there was a new crop of rustications and suspensions; and this burlesque of patriots struggling with tyrants gradually played itself out and came to an end. But the events of that fervid time impressed themselves so deeply upon us, that, when "the great rebellion" is spoken of, my first thought is that the allusion must be, not to Charles I and the Puritans, nor yet to the American colonists and England, but to that mangnificent protest against oppression that was made at Harvard College sixty-three years ago.

Harvard College, at the time of which I am writing, was very different from the noble university which at present bears the old name. Some students entered at twelve years of age, though fifteen was nearly the average among those whose parents were well off. We were treated as boys, and not without reason. The law declared that we must not go to Boston without permission, or pass a night away from Cambridge without a special license from the authorities. Moreover, in the early part of 1819, the president, in behalf of the corporation, promulgated a statute to the effect that a fine of ten dollars would be exacted from every student who was caught at the theatre, while five dollars must be paid by any one who attended a party in Boston. But it is probable that the corporation made no attempt to carry out the system of espionage which their savage edict seemed to necessitate. We certainly used to go to the theatre and to parties with some freedom, and seldom got into difficulty from doing so.

But there were natural impediments to leaving Cambridge, which would have astonished the pampered young gentlemen who are now complaining that a horse car every three minutes does not furnish suitable communication with the metropolis, and demand an elevated railroad to give them their full rights in this particular. We knew but a morning and evening stage. At nine and at two o'clock, Morse, the stage driver, drew up in the college yard, and performed upon a tin horn to notify us of his arrival. He was a great hero among the students, for coachmen have some mysterious charm about them which wins the regard of young gentlemen in their teens. Those who went to Boston in the evening were generally forced to walk. It was possible, to be sure, to hire a chaise of Jemmy Reed (who held the same place that Hobson did in the Cambridge of Milton) , yet his horses were expensive animals, and he was very particular in satisfying himself of the undoubted credit of those to whom he let them. And it was probably well for us that we were so often compelled to resort to the primitive means of locomotion; for the necessity of regular exercise for students was unrecognized at the time, and such as we obtained was taken very irregularly and with some end in view. There was a favorite summer walk to Sweet Auburn, which was then as Nature made it; and when the skies were perfectly favorable we consented to avail ourselves of its attractions. This beautiful piece of country was afterwards christened Mount Auburn, and became the first garden cemetery in the country.

There were some half a dozen houses on the avenue leading from the colleges to Sweet Auburn; they had been built before the Revolution, and were abandoned by their Tory proprietors. The largest and most conspicuous was the fine mansion which had been the headquarters of Washington, and which has since gained additional interest as the residence of the poet Longfellow. It was then occupied by Mrs. Craigie, the widow of a gentleman very notable in his day.

[81]

He had made a large fortune by buying up government promises, and by other speculations during the Revolution. He kept a princely bachelor's establishment at the old house, and was in the habit of exercising a generous hospitality.

I have said that the decrees of the corporation did not prevent us from going to the theatre; but if I am to tell the whole truth, I fear

THE CRAIGIE HOUSE

it must be acknowledged that they actually added a zest to that forbidden enjoyment. For there is a good deal of human nature in the familiar story of the gentleman who, being very fond of pork, protested that fate had been cruel to him in not so arranging matters as to have caused him to be born a Jew, — "for then," said he, "I should have had the pleasure of eating pork and of sinning at the same time." The latter delight, whatever it may have amounted to, the authorities of Andover and of Harvard College had taken good care that we should have in connection with all scenic representations. There was but one theatre in Boston, and performances were held three days in the week. The box office was opened only on the day of the play, and a battle often occurred in the efforts of the crowd to reach the window from which tickets were dispensed. Morse, the stage driver, was our champion upon these occasions, and we waited his return with eagerness to know how the fight had gone, and what spoils he had brought us from the box office.

I make the following extract from my journal of July 7, 1820:

After breakfast the College Company went to town accompanied by the full band. We marched through a great number of the dustiest and dirtiest streets. At last we arrived at Chestnut Street, where we partook of a most splendid collation at the house of General

Sumner. We were received in a room in which there were all kinds
of refreshments, and ladies among other things. This gave it a very
genteel effect, though none were remarkably handsome except Misses
S --- and B ---. After parading before the house, we went to the
Common, and then to Mr. Gray's, where we got good drink. From
there we went to State Street, and after performing a variety of evolutions, we dined at the Washington Garden, where toast, songs,
etc., abounded. This being finished, we returned to Cambridge,
where, wonderful to relate, the President gave us a treat, and we
were dismissed. The day was exceptionally hot, and we all perspired
in glory. I drank an enormous quantity, to say nothing of what I
ate, and finished my exploits with hasty pudding and molasses at the
club.

After this the next day's entry is not surprising: "Stayed at home
to recruit after our labors."

The Harvard Washington Corps, one of whose excursions is
chronicled above, was composed of students of the two higher classes,
but was officered exclusively by seniors. It was very popular among
the under-graduates, though by no means approved by the older
friends of the college. To hold a command in the company was considered a great distinction, and there was much rivalry among candidates. There was one condition necessary to promotion: the aspir-
ant must have a good leg; for the uniform required the officers to
appear in tights, and any crural deficiency was an obstacle which
could not be surmounted. And so it came to pass that the first question asked concerning any candidate was this, "How is the man off
for a leg ?"

Now it happened that there was exhibited daily before the students what may be called an ideal leg, by which all others might be
measured and their shortcomings noted. This shapely limb was the
property of Doctor Popkin, the Greek professor; and the owner
seemed fully conscious of the beauty of its proportions, for he was in
the habit of nursing and smoothing it, while hearing recitations, to
the great delight of his classes. And so, when inquiries were made
touching the calves of any would-be officer, there was but one answer that was really satisfactory, "Why, sir, his leg is as good as Doctor Pop's !"

The Greek professor, I may say in passing, possessed an individuality that, if somewhat odd, was clearly cut and impressive. He was
once asked by a lady who admired a system of theology then much
discussed, whether ne was a Hopkinsian. "Not a bit of it, madam;
I am always a Popkinsian," was the prompt reply. And it was even
so, for never was man more vigorously himself. His antique simplic-

[83]

ity, dry humor, and hatred of all shams were just the qualities to win the regard of young men; and it was more affection than offensive familiarity which led to the universal abbreviation of his name. It is said he once turned suddenly upon a stranger whom he had overheard designating him by the familiar college title with, "What right have you to call me Doctor Pop, sir? you were never one of my boys at Harvard?"

Years after this, I happened to meet the Doctor wearing the baggy pantaloon which reduced all legs to that democratic equality which Jefferson's manifesto declares to be the birthright of the people who go about on them. I could not help remarking that he, of all men, had reason to lament the departure of breeches and the accompanying stocking. The old gentleman seemed much gratified with the allusion, and declared that the fashion was detestable which caused Apollo and a Satyr to be equally presentable.

I have said that there were grave doubts in the minds of conservative citizens respecting the propriety of the College Company; but it is safe to say that there was no doubt whatever concerning the College Fire Department. From an outside point of view it was an unmitigated nuisance, — a circumstance which did not render it less dear to the hearts of the students. Like most vested interests, the college engine struck its roots into the good old times of our ancestors, and was very difficult to abolish. The corporation had long owned a little tub of a machine, which would be thought scarcely fit to water a flower bed at the present day, and the under-graduates had always enjoyed the privilege of tearing off with this instrument whenever there was an alarm of fire. The captain of the engine was appointed by the president of the college, but as all the minor offices were filled by the suffrages of the students, the organization was democratic enough to be interesting. No sooner did the fire bell ring than we got into all sorts of horrible and grotesque garments. Hats in the last stages of dilapidation and strange ancestral coats were carefully kept for these occasions. Feeling that we were pretty well disguised, there seemed nothing to hinder that lawless abandonment to a frolic which is so delightful to unregenerate man when youthful blood bubbles in his veins. I cannot remember that we ever rendered the slightest assistance in extinguishing a fire; indeed, there were so many good reasons for stopping on the way that we commonly arrived after it was out. And then, if we were tired, we had an impudent way of leaving the tub upon the ground, well knowing that the government would send for their property the next day.

Among the memorable fires that were attended by the college engine, the burning of the Exchange Coffee-House was the most impressive. This building was said to be the finest in the Union, and was certainly the pride and boast of Boston. It had noble halls, and over two hundred lesser apartments. It was quite a little town in itself, giving shelter to brokers, insurance companies, foreign consuls, and masonic lodges. It had cost about $600,000, which was then thought to be an immense sum to be put in bricks and mortar. The light was so great as to be seen over a large area of country, and far out to sea; and when, at nine o'clock in the evening, the dome came crashing down, a shudder ran through thousands of excited spectators. Strange to say, no life was lost through all the tumult and confusion of the night. It was not until the next day that an accident occurred which called to mind the end of Clarence in his butt of Malmsey. An immense caldron of beer lay open among the ruins, and into this a poor boy managed to fall with consequences quite as fatal as the wine brought to the royal duke.

On our return from this fire, exhausted with excitement and fatigue, we repaired to the engine-house, as was our custom, and were there regaled upon "black strap," a composition of which the secret, as I fervently hope, now reposes with the lost arts. Its principal ingredients were rum and molasses, though it is probable there were other simples combined with these conspicuous factors. Of all the detestable American drinks, upon which the inventive genius of our countrymen has exercised itself, this "black strap" was surely the most outrageous. It finally broke up the engine company, and this was perhaps the only good thing which ever came of it. For matters at last reached a crisis; the government came to their senses, sold the engine, and broke up the association. But to take the edge off the cruelty of this necessary act, it was decided that the company should be allowed a final meeting. And so we celebrated the obsequies of the old machine with an oration and a poem, following up these exercises with other proceedings of which a detailed account is unnecessary.

Few realize that college life sixty years ago was just a year longer than it is now. Cambridge was not deserted during the vacation; while at present from July to October everybody is off and all the rooms are vacant. The students' apartments of my day were not so attractive that one would wish to linger in them. I cannot remember a single room which had carpet, curtain, or any pretence of ornament. In a few of them were hung some very poor prints, representing the four seasons, emblematical representations of the countries of Europe, and imaginative devices of a similar nature. Our light came from dipped candles, with very broad bases and gradually narrowing to the top. These required the constant use of snuffers, — a circumstance which hindered application to an extent that in these days of kerosene and gas can scarcely be appreciated. Indeed, the dual brain with which men are furnished seemed to us to show intelligent design, not less than the famous illustrations presented by Paley. One brain was clearly required to do the studying, while it was the business of the other to watch the candles and look after the snuffers.

Our fuel was wood, which was furnished by the college; it being cut from some lands in Maine which were among its possessions, and brought to the wharf in the college sloop, the *Harvard*. This arrangement was supposed to cause a great saving, and the authorities naturally prided themselves upon the sagacity which made this Eastern property so productive. It was not until Doctor Bowditch, the great mathematician, was given a place in the government that this arrangement was quietly abandoned. This eminent gentleman — perhaps from his natural aptitude for figures — succeeded in demonstrating to his associates that it would be much cheaper for the college to buy wood from the dearest dealer than to cut it on its own land and transport it in its own sloop. It is strange how long-established methods of obtaining the necessaries of life will continue, when a little thought will show that better ones may be substituted.

When speaking just now of the decoration (or absence of decoration) of college rooms, I ought to have noticed one significant exception. My class-mate, Otis, had ornamented his mantelpiece with two curious black stones, which excited great interest in his visitors. He had made a journey to Washington, to see his father, who was a Senator; and had brought these rarities home, as precious memorials of his travels. He had a strange tale to tell concerning them. It seemed that the people in Baltimore actually burned just such stones as these; and, wonderful to relate, there was no smoke in the chimneys. I believe that these singular minerals have become so popular in Harvard College that they are now brought there in considerable quantities. The only change is that they are no longer displayed on the mantel-piece, but just below it — in the grate. They will be recognized under the name of anthracite coal.

There were two college clubs, to which admission depended on scholarship. These were the Hasty Pudding and the Phi Beta Kappa. In the former there were nominally an essay and a discussion at every meeting. In reality there was nothing of the sort. There were pudding and molasses, and nothing more. The latter, with the exception of its annual dinner, had no meetings, whatever, except those necessary to receive new members; but it possessed the attraction of being a secret society, and we were solemnly sworn never to reveal the mighty mysteries that were confided to us at the ceremony of initiation. During the great anti-Masonic excitement John Quincy Adams brought it to pass that all pledges of secrecy were removed, by a formal vote of the society; so that I am perfectly free to expose all its mysteries, could I only remember what they were. The secret of the brilliant annual dinners of the Phi Beta, under the presidencies of Edward Everett, Judge Story, Judge Warren, and others, lies near the surface. It was very difficult for outsiders to gain admission, so that the company was one in which distinguished men were willing to unbend. Add to this — as the secret within the secret — that we were absolutely secured against reporters.

COMMENCEMENT DAY IN 1821

Sixty years ago Commencement Day was a State holiday. The banks were closed, business was pretty generally suspended, and numbers of sight-seers repaired to Cambridge, as their ancestors had been accustomed to do a hundred years before. The college exercises were held, as they had been for a century, in the old Congregational meeting-house; and the building was by no means ill-adapted to this purpose. The galleries, which sloped at an angle of about forty-five degrees, displayed to great advantage the beautiful and fashionably dressed ladies with which they were crowded. At the end of each of the four aisles a wooden desk was erected, and from these forensics had formerly been read. The speakers, of course, delivered their parts from the platform. The students belonging to Boston families of wealth gave elaborate parties in honor of the occasion. These were frequented by all the strangers who happened to be in town, and advertised the college in a way that was thought useful. Indeed, the government were accused of giving parts to inferior scholars, whose sumptuous entertainments would be likely to lend dignity to the day.

The account of the conclusion of my college life shall be copied just as it stands written in my diary. I need not apologize for any crudities or egotism which may be found in the wholly private records of a youth who was legally a minor.

July 16, 1821. Attended a dissertation of [Ralph Waldo] Emerson's in the morning on the subject of Ethical Philosophy. I found it long and dry. In the afternoon we went to our last lecture on exhilarating gas. Gorham fought, Dinsmore danced, Curtis laughed, and Bunker swore, according as the ruling passion swayed their breasts. In the evening I paid my last visit to the Miss Hills. In the afternoon, went to the President and got my dissertation, which he had mislaid. He was quite facetious, for I had painted my coat against the wall. This is the last evening we spent in college. May I never look back upon it with regret ! It strikes eleven, and I must go to bed.

July 17th. At nine in the morning I read my dissertation, and it had the good fortune to please our college critics. At half past ten we assembled at Keating's room, and marched from there to the President's, and escorted him, with the rest of the government, to the chapel, where Barnwell and Emerson performed our valedictory exercises before all the scholars and a number of ladies. They were rather poor and did but little honor to the class. We returned with the President to his house immediately after the exercises. At one o'clock all those who were fortunate enough to obtain *deturs* went to the President to receive them. There were but eighteen who got them. I had Westall's edition of "Young's Night Thoughts," one of the best books that was given out. At two we marched down to Porter's, where we had a fine dinner. After the cloth was removed, Mr. Cushing (afterward well known as Honorable Caleb Cushing) came in, and gave for a toast: "The bands of friendship, which always tighten when they are wet." After he had gone, Wood delivered an oration, which was very witty and appropriate; and then Alden rehearsed the woes and pleasures of college life in his usual style. There were a number of original songs sung: Alden sung one much to the amusement of us all. When we had all drunk our skins full, we marched round to all the professors' houses, danced round the Rebellion and Liberty Trees, and then returned to the hall. A great many of the class were half-seas-over, and I had the pleasure of supporting one of them. This was as hard work as I ever desire to do. Many ladies came to witness our dancing, and were much scandalized by the elevation of spirit which some exhibited. We parted with more grief than any class I ever saw, every one of us being drowned in tears. Had I been told that I should have felt so much, I should have laughed at the idea. When it came to the point, however, I cried like the rest of them. In the evening Frank Lowell and I went over to Mr. John Lowell's, where we had a very pleasant time. Miss Eliza S --- looked prettier and talked better than I ever knew her to before.

August 29, 1821, Commencement Day. In the morning I went to prayers, to hear Mr. Cushing pray; for it is always customary for the particular tutor of the graduating class to perform that duty on Commencement morning. He read us an account of the fall of Babylon and of the emancipation of the oppressed Jews. This seemed very applicable to our escape from the government, though I do not believe he ever thought of it. His prayer was short and not impressive. About eight o'clock the ladies came over; and I got them into the meeting-house by opening the door while the sexton was away, for which I had a good scolding on his return. That, however, was but a small matter. I then went to Mr. Higginson's, and returned to wait on the ladies. The house was full of very beautiful women, and every one who spoke paid them some compliment or other; but most of them were rather lame ones. Hill Second, Sampson Reed in the master's oration, Burton, and Leverett were very pathetic toward them. A Miss - - - -, from Salem, attracted much attention on account of the beauty of her neck; and she, to oblige admirers, wore no ruffles. All the Amorys, Sullivans, Crowninshields, with long *et ceteras*, filled the house. After the exercises, which were very short, I went over to Porter's, where all the relations of our family were assembled. They appeared gratified with my performance. We had a very handsome dinner; and after it was over the Governor, Council, and all the great and learned men, both friends and strangers, came in and took wine with us. They all complimented me on my success, — in part payment, I suppose, for the wine which they drank. Among my relations was Mrs. Storer, who is eighty-six years old, and who attended the Commencements of my father and grandfather. She seemed to enjoy the day as highly as anybody. We visited Mrs. Farrar, after our company had gone, and found there many young ladies, in addition to all the gentlemen who had visited us. In the evening my sisters and myself went to Mr. Otis's great ball (given in honor of the graduation of his son) , and there we enjoyed ourselves highly. It was nearly twelve o'clock before we returned. Thus ends my college life. I must now begin the world.

◈◇◈◇◈◇◈◇◈◇◈◇◈

[*Edward Everett Hale, Harvard 1839*]

Class day seems to have originated as early as the beginning of the century. The class itself chose a favorite speaker as orator, and someone who could write a poem, and had its own exercises of farewell. There grew up side by side with those farewell exercises the custom by which the class treated the rest of the college, and eventually treated every loafer in Cambridge. As I remember the first class days which I ever saw, they were the occasions of the worst drunkenness I have ever known. The night before class day some of the seniors — I do not know but what all — went out to the lower part of the yard, where there was still a grove of trees, and "consecrated the grove," as the phrase was, which meant drank all the rum and other spirits that they liked. Then, on the afternoon of class day, around the old elm tree, sometimes called Rebellion Tree and sometimes Liberty Tree, which stood and stands behind Hollis, all the college assembled, and every other male loafer who chose to come where there was a free treat. Pails of punch, made from every spirit known to the Cambridge innkeepers, were there for everybody to drink. It was a horrid orgy from end to end, varied perhaps, by dancing round the tree.

With such memories of class day President Quincy, in 1838, sent for my brother and one or two others of the class of that year in whom he had confidence, to ask what could be done to break up such orgies. He knew he could rely on the class for an improvement in the customs. They told him that if he would give them for the day the use of the Brigade Band, which was then the best band we had in Boston, and which they had engaged for the morning, they felt sure that they could change the *fête*. The conditions, observed, were a lovely July day, the presence in the morning at the chapel, to hear the addresses, of the nicest and prettiest girls of Boston and neighborhood with their mammas, and the chances of keeping them there through the afternoon. Mr. Quincy gladly promised the band, and when the day came, it became the birthday of the modern "class day," the most charming of *fêtes*. Word was given to the girls that they must come to spend the day. In the chapel Coolidge delivered a farewell oration. Lowell, alas ! was at Concord, not permitted to come to Cambridge to recite his poem; it had to be printed instead. When the ode had been sung the assembly moved up to that shaded corner between Stoughton and Holworthy. The band people stationed themselves in the entry of Stoughton, between 21 and 24, with the window open, and the "dancing on the green," of which there are still traditions, began. The wind instrument men said afterward that they never played for dancing before, and that their throats were bone dry; and I suppose there was no girl there who had ever before danced to the music of a trombone. When our class came along, in 1839, we had the honor of introducing fiddles. I shall send this paper to the charming lady — the belle of her time — with whom I danced in the silk gown in which I had been clad when I delivered the class poem of my year. Does she remember it as well as I do ?

◇◇◇◇◇◇◇◇◇◇◇◇◇◇

[*Lyman Beecher, Yale*]

After spending about two years in fitting for college, I went home to father's in New Haven, and spent a month before Commencement. I was eighteen [1793]. Farmer's life and farmer's fare had made me strong and hearty beyond any thing I should have reached if I had grown up in father's family, though that was far more intellectual. I built up the physical first, the intellectual afterward.

Father was now living with his fifth wife, and Esther, her daughter, was about thirteen, and forever reading. Then there were Polly, Lydia, and David, so that there was a pretty good fam-

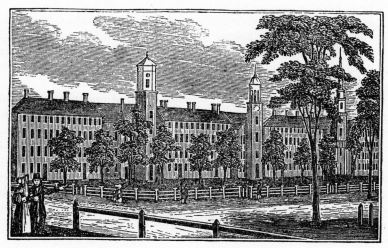

ily of us. Besides, there were several boarders, and, at Commencement, the house was always filled to overflowing with company.

That was the first house that President Day ever stopped at in New Haven. His father used to put up there at Commencement.

We young folks thought it a fine thing to sleep on the straw in the barn, and high times we had up in the old hay-loft.

Yale College then was very different from what it is now [1863].

The main building was Connecticut Hall, three stories high, now South Middle College.

What is now the Athenaeum was then the chapel, with a tall spire, and the present Laboratory was then the dining-hall.

The present South College, then Union Hall, was commenced the year I entered, 1793, and finished the next.

The stairs in the main building were worn nearly through, the rooms defaced and dirty.

As to apparatus, we had a great orrery [clockwork planetary system], almost as big as the wheel of an ocean steamer, made in college by Joseph Badger, afterward missionary to the Sandwich Islands. It was made to revolve, but was all rusty; nobody ever started it.

There was a four-foot telescope, all rusty; nobody ever looked through it, and, if they did, not to edification. There was an air-pump, so out of order that a mouse under the receiver would live as Methusaleh.

There was a prism, and an elastic hoop to illustrate centrifugal force.

We were taken up to see those dingy, dirty things, and that was all the apparatus the college had.

James Gould was our first tutor, and then Roger Minot Sherman, a great man, one of the first at the bar afterward. He loved us, and we him. He was our tutor till the spring of our Junior year. After Gould left us, the president heard us recite for a season, till Sherman took us.

President [Ezra] Stiles was well made, trim, of medium height, of strong prejudices, not profound, but very learned, one of the politest, most urbane gentlemen I ever knew — that is, out of college; for, as a man, he was one thing, but as president quite another. I remember that, in my first vacation, Ben Baldwin got me to keep school for him while he went a journey. This kept me out three weeks of the next term. When I went up to President Stiles's study to get excused, I told him the whole story. "Notetur," said he (you must be fined) ; and that was all he said. In those days the students were fined for any misdemeanors.

One of our class once snapped a copper on the floor at recitation. The old gentleman paused; looked up severe and stern, and, when all was hushed, went on again.

One evening he brought a foreign ambassador or other dignitary with him to prayers, but being rather late, the students were in a row, stamping, etc., all over the chapel. This mortified him exceedingly. He reached the stage; tried to speak to quell the tumult; couldn't be heard; then up with his cane and struck on the stage, shivering it to splinters, and broke out in a rage. He was of the old regime — the last of that age — had it in his heart and in his soul. He liked the old college laws derived from the English universities; and when the Freshmen complained of the oppression of the Sophomores, he sent them back. Those laws were intensely aristocratic, and it was in my day that the reaction came, and the modern democratic customs were introduced.

I had some hand in that myself. The first part of the year I lived in George Street, and escaped the tyranny of the Sophomores; but, on taking a room in college (it was the northwest corner, lower story) , I soon experienced its effects. I was sent for to a room so full of tobacco-smoke you could not see across it. There I was asked all

[92]

manner of questions, in English and Latin, and received all manner of solemn advice. Then Forbes, a big fellow, took me as his fag, and sent me on errands. Every day he contrived to send me on some business or other, worrying me down to indignation.

One moonlight evening, as a few of our class was standing together as the nine o'clock bell rang, some one said, "Come, let's go down and break Forbes's windows."

"No, no," said I, "the streets are full of people."

"Coward !"

"You've missed your man this time. I'm not a coward, but I'm not a fool. If any man will go at twelve o'clock tonight, I will."

"I'll go !" said Parker. And so, when twelve o'clock came, we went down, each armed with a couple of bricks. We marched past, and let drive one after another. One struck the wall just above his head.

Next day father said to me, "Lyman, Mr. Hubbard has been talking with me; he thinks it likely you were concerned in breaking Forbes's windows."

"Well," said I, "he can't prove it, and you can't prove it; and God only can publish it if it's true."

"Well, well," said he, "I'll tell you what you had better do. Just stop your class and contribute enough to mend the windows, and say nothing."

So said, so done. The windows were mended, and the thing passed over; but they never sent me errands any more after that.

The old system was abolished soon after.

The spring vacation came, and I went home to North Guilford to recruit by making maple-sugar. We had about a hundred trees. Oh, I wish you could see them now, with their great spreading roots ! I used to delight in that work, tapping the trees, boiling down the sap, and carrying it home.

In my Sophomore year (September, 1794–5) I did comparatively little. My early instructors had never explained the principles of arithmetic, so that for this part of the course I had small qualification. Mathematics I lost totally.

In May of this year Dr. Stiles died, and Dr. Dwight * became president at the next Commencement. He had the greatest agency in developing my mind.

Before he came college was in a most ungodly state. The college church was almost extinct. Most of the students were skeptical, and rowdies were plenty. Wine and liquors were kept in many rooms;

* Timothy Dwight, quoted at great length in this volume. — B. M.

[93]

intemperance, profanity, gambling, and licentiousness were common. I hardly know how I escaped. Was invited to play, once, in a classmate's room. I did so, and won. Next day I won again, then lost, and ended in debt. I saw immediately whereunto that would grow; obtained leave of absence, went home for a week, till cured of that mania and never touched a card afterward.

That was the day of the infidelity of the Tom Paine school. Boys that dressed flax in the barn, as I used to, read Tom Paine and believed him; I read, and fought him all the way. Never had any propensity to infidelity. But most of the class before me were infidels, and called each other Voltaire, Rousseau, D'Alembert, etc., etc.

They thought the Faculty were afraid of free discussion. But when they handed Dr. Dwight a list of subjects for class disputation, to their surprise he selected this: "Is the Bible the word of God ?" and told them to do their best.

He heard all they had to say, answered them, and there was an end. He preached incessantly for six months on the subject, and all infidelity skulked and hid its head.

He elaborated his theological system in a series of forenoon sermons in the chapel; the afternoon discourses were practical. The original design of Yale College was to found a divinity school. To a mind appreciative like mine, his preaching was a continual course of education and a continual feast. He was copious and polished in style, though disciplined and logical.

There was a pith and power of doctrine there that has not been since surpassed, if equalled. I took notes of all his discourses, condensing and forming skeletons. He was of noble form, with a noble head and body, and had one of the sweetest smiles that ever you saw. He always met me with a smile. Oh, how I loved him ! I loved him as my own soul, and he loved me as a son. And once at Litchfield I told him that all I had I owed to him. "Then," said he, "I have done a great and soul-satisfying work. I consider myself amply rewarded."

Intellectually, the Senior year was the best to me. We all looked forward to Dr. Dwight's instructions with interest. We began with Blair's Rhetoric, half an hour's recitation, and an hour or hour and a half of extempore lecture. He was full of anecdote and illustration, and delighted to talk as much as we did to listen, and often he was very eloquent in these class lectures. It was not all ornament, however, but he showed a thorough-going mastery of the subject. Then we took up logic and metaphysics — Duncan and Locke were our authors. In ethics we studied Paley, our recitations all conducted as before. This took up three days of each week. On two other days we had written or extempore debates before Dr. Dwight, he summing up at the close. On Saturday we had the Catechism, Vincent's Exposition, followed by a theological lecture. You see it was more than a college — it was partly a divinity school. That was the idea of its original founders.

I spent my vacations at Uncle Lot Benton's. He had moved to Old Guilford. Uncle Lot was proud of me. He had *mind*. I used to carry over my compositions and read them to him. He would cock up his eye and say, "Ef I'd had a college edication, don't ye think I could have written as well as that ?" Oh, he was very proud. It was a great delight to him afterward to hear my sermons. It was a great reward.

Harriet Beecher Stowe: "Did he ever argue the point with you ?"

Argue ? Yes, indeed, he did argue, but was always committed so as never to yield. He never did yield. He wouldn't yield even to me. *Couldn't* give up.

H.B.S. "Did Uncle Lot pay your bills through college ?"

In great part, and what he did not pay father paid himself. Father used to have the "hypo" dreadfully about supporting me. Esther heard him telling her mother he could not stand it; he should certainly have to take me out of college, or they should all go to ruin. She answered, nobly (she was my step-mother), that she couldn't have it so; and said that her property might go to pay my bills. There was some property of hers, and he had the use of it.

H.B.S. "Did you know how he felt ?"

Yes; I knew he was bankrupt, as he supposed. I recollect saying, "Father, you needn't be concerned; you have enough to live on at present; and when I get through and have a home, I'll take care of you."

"Pooh ! poor fellow !" said he, "you'll scratch a poor man's head all your life-time."

I did help myself a little, though. Staples, the butler, left college six weeks before the end of the year, and I took the buttery and bought out his stock for about $300, which I borrowed. I went into it hot and heavy. One day I bought a lot of watermelons and canta-loupes and trundled them across the green on a wheelbarrow, in the face of the whole college. I sent to New York by an English parson (a judge of the article) and bought a hogshead of porter. It's odd; but I can remember selling things to Moses Stuart, [the great theo-logian] — two classes below me.

That buttery was a regular thing in those days; it has wholly disappeared since, and is almost forgotten. The old Latin laws are a curiosity.*

H.W. "Did it pay well ?"

Well, I paid my note, and, besides $100 in bad debts, cleared my Commencement expenses, bought a suit of clothes, and had $100 in cash. I worked hard. If I had gone into business then I should have made money.

❖❖❖❖❖❖❖❖❖❖❖❖

[*Stephen Burroughs, Dartmouth 1785*]

My father placed me at school under the tuition of the late Joseph Huntington, D.D., whose fame for an instructor was very noted throughout all the New England States; where I continued one year, and was then removed to Dartmouth College, of which I became a member.

Whilst I was with Doctor Huntington, many of those boyish pranks which students are apt to practice, in order to give themselves the tone of wits, were performed by me to the no small diversion of myself and the other students, and to the great hindrance of my pursuits in literary acquirements. This was the hour of folly. From the effect of this age flowed a continued stream of crude, undigested whims, which kept the school and myself in a constant uproar. I became an inmate in the family of my preceptor, which consisted of the Doctor, Mrs. Huntington, two sons by a former wife, nearly my own age, and a number of small children, how many I do not recollect. The Doctor himself was a character whose parallel is not commonly found. A man of very considerable oratorical abilities, which consisted more in smooth figures, and ingenious declamation, than in close metaphysical reasoning. A mind by no means tied down to establish modes and forms, but internally despising them; possessing an unbounded ambition; fond of flattery. A temper, when undisturbed, philanthropic, but disappointment and chagrin changed it into the boisterous rage of a northwest whirlwind. Mrs. Huntington, a character truly amiable. Joseph, second son to the Doctor, after his own name, about one year younger than

* The following is an extract:

"Promo licentia in promptuario vendendi vinum pomaceum, hydromelem, crevisiam fortem (non plus quam cados duodecim, annuatim), saccharum rigidum, tubulos, tabacum, et talia scholaribus necessaria, non a dispensatore in culina venalis."

"The butler may sell in the buttery cider, metheglin, strong beer (not more than twelve barrels a year), loaf-sugar, pipes, tobacco, and other necessaries of students not furnished by the steward in the commons."

myself. This youth was truly the son of his father, the fire of his ambition was great; his resolution was equal to his ambition; and his eccentricity was equal to both; with a strong mind, equal to his father, he despised the shackles of education, broke through all the

little obstacles of vulgar prejudice, and pursued those paths to which the fire of genius, and the want of judgment at that time directed him. The rest of the family had nothing uncommon in their characters which distinguished them from mankind in general.

But being full of vivacity, Joseph and I were almost perpetually prosecuting some scene of amusement and diversion. Some of those pastimes were graduated upon a scale of innocence, and some, I am sorry to say, embraced for their object the vexation and detriment of the neighbors. Our chief force was aimed at a neighbor, commonly known by the name of Tiger, on account of his morose misanthropic disposition. One night we repaired to his house and took logs from his woodpile, about two feet in length, and piled them up against his door, until they reached the top, laying them in such a manner as to incline into the house. After arranging matters in this order, we made a noise as if attempting to get into the old man's garden, sufficiently loud for him to hear; immediately upon this the old man crept softly to the door, and opening it suddenly, down came the logs so rapidly as to knock him to the floor, and cover him over. The noise which this made alarmed the family universally, with an idea that they felt the shock of an earthquake, and that the last judgment had arrived, which set some a-screaming and some a-praying, and for a long time these ideas so wholly occupied the minds of the family, that the old man could not get any assistance from the load of timber, under which he was buried. Immediately upon his being freed from his confinement, he put on some clothes and repaired to Doctor Huntington's, in order to enter a complaint against Joseph and myself, whom he suspected of being the agents in this disagreeable scene; and the reason of his suspicion was founded in this, viz. but a few days before, Joseph and I were caught by him, picking some early apples off a tree in his garden; a complaint of which was made, and we obliged to pay three shillings. But as we were seen to go to bed that night and found in bed when he came with this last complaint, and no evidence that we had left our bed, it was concluded that his suspicions wanted proof, and there this matter ended.

Soon after this, we contrived another plan to disturb the old man's quiet. Joseph went to him, and with a woeful countenance professed his sorrow for his having given him trouble, and in order to evince his sorrow, told him he had to inform of an intention of some of the scholars to rob his apple trees that night, and advised him to watch, that he might detect them; and if he should, they would have to pay him a considerable sum of money. This bait the old man eagerly swallowed, and took his stand accordingly for watching.

The other part of this contrivance I was to act myself, as being the best fitted for it, on account of my superior agility. Accordingly, about ten at night, I crept along close to the garden fence till I came, as though by accident, near to the old man, at which I turned and ran, and he after me. Being able abundantly to outrun him, I kept but a very small distance before him, pretending to run with all my might, in order to raise his expectations of being able to overtake me; when coming to the edge of a ditch, which contained about three feet depth of mud and filth, I clapped down on my hands and knees before the old man, and he stumbled over me plump into the ditch; but catching hold of the skirt of my coat, tore it off and carried it into the ditch with him. This was a clue which served the next day to unravel the plot in part, as it related to me; and when complaint was made to our Preceptor, he acquitted us entirely, as not having done anything unlawful, nor having attempted it according to the proof.

This was a scene of great diversion to the Doctor. The woeful countenance which Tiger made about falling into the ditch, together with my strutting about without a skirt to my coat, altogether made so ludicrous an appearance, that notwithstanding all the exertion of the Doctor, he could not suppress the rising inclination to laugh, but would, once in a while, burst forth in spite of himself.

At commencement, 1781, I was presented, examined, and admitted a member of Dartmouth College. Here I had a new situation before me, and another part to act; not possessing all the advantages to act it with éclat. The reports of my many wild eccentricities had come before me, magnified in a tenfold degree, and I found all were waiting with open mouths to see an explosion. Those, who were fond of such scenes, of diversion, were disappointed at my neglect in exhibiting some specimens of fun, which I had determined to lay by entirely. Others, who were of a different cast, lowered upon me with a threatening brow, indicative of their intention to check my wildness in its first appearance.

Here, I found my situation very different and disagreeable; on the one hand, I was excited, invited and flattered to gratify those who were fond of amusement; on the other, I was watched, with the scrutinizing eye of jealousy, for misconduct, and a readiness to censure in me what would be thought innocent in others, to humble and check that growing propensity to disorder, as was alleged. My father was careful to have me take a room with one Jacob Wood, A. M., who, of all others, was best calculated to humble and mortify any, whom he entertained a suspicion against, as differing from his own principle or practice. A man of small stature, and yet greater mental abilities; rigid and enthusiastic in his notions of religion, which consisted in a sour, morose, misanthropic line of conduct towards all who were not of his party. To be an inmate with such a character, you will readily conceive, no way comported with a disposition like mine; and consequently, we never enjoyed that union and harmony of feelings in our intercourse as roommates, which was necessary for the perfect enjoyment of social life. Possessing a mind very unstable, he was often out of humor, at his want of success, in making me submissive and humble to his caprice; and being desirous of my sharing a part of his chagrin, he assailed my ears with a perpetual stream of petulant criminations. He sought opportunities to mortify me before company, by representing me as a person inattentive to matters of religion, and consequently, wanting every virtue. This mode of procedure, I could not tamely dispense with; my invention was the only means of resort for retaliation.

One night, while he was paying his devoirs to a young lady, word was brought him, that in a fit of the epilepsy, I was about expiring, and wished for him to perform the last kind office of a friend, to pray with, and for me. This was a business he always attended with great promptitude; his Dulcinea being equally possessed with the laudable ambition of proselyting, agreed to accompany him to the room. But when they came there, they found it empty of every living thing, and not even the appearance of any person's being there that night! for the truth was, I had, the day preceding, obtained leave of absence, and was gone to my father's. This was readily understood as a pun upon his sacerdotal character, than which, nothing could have wounded him more. His character, in that respect, he wished to have considered as sacred; and to trifle with that, that was striking at the very root of all his sanctimonious self-importance. He suspected me to be the author of this mortifying scene, and was unwearied in his endeavors to gain some evidence of the fact; but all his exertions were ineffectual. Notwithstanding all these singularities and eccentricities, I believe him to be a man of an honest heart, led to practice those ridiculous plans by a misguided zeal for religion.

About this time, the Indians had made inroads upon some of the frontier settlements, and destroyed them. It was feared they would make a descent upon Hanover, and burn Dartmouth College, with the buildings in its vicinity; and consequently, the minds of the people were full of fear, and easily aroused by an alarm of any kind. One evening, being in company with a number of others, we proposed and agreed, to make a visit to a yard of watermelons, belonging to a man in the vicinity, who kept them for sale, and help ourselves to some of them. We accordingly put our plan in execution; and went as far as the river, half a mile out of town, in order to eat them more securely. After we had finished our repast, every one took his own way, in order to get to his room unperceived. I came directly into town, by the most obvious route, in company with one Paine. When we had gotten to the green, around which the buildings stand, we discovered some person walking before my door, suspecting, as I supposed, my absence from my room; which being against the laws of College, at that time of night, would give him an opportunity, if he made the desired discovery, to involve me in difficulty.

All these circumstances were very apparent to me, and therefore, I wished to avoid being known to him, as well as to avoid the discovery of the watermelons. We therefore turned off another course, than directly to the College, and rolled our gowns close together, and tucked them up on our backs, so as to make the appearance of men with packs on their backs. This man, Higgins by name, seeing us by this time, came on towards us; we quickened our pace — he pursued us with equal speed — we ran — he ran after us, and halloed with all his might. I was now sensible, that an alarm would be made among the inhabitants, and of course, some immediate and decisive measures must be taken to prevent discovery, or a suspicion of the watermelon business falling on me; I therefore, turned a short corner, where my pursuer lost sight of me, and ran directly back to the College, and got into my room undiscovered.

Fortunately, my roommate was not at his lodgings this night. I heard an enquiry in the rooms adjoining respecting the noise; I went into one of them, and found they were about starting after Higgins, to learn the difficulty. We accordingly all started together, and after running about one hundred rods, came up to him, who was still hallooing for help. On enquiry, he told us that he had discovered two men, carrying packs on their backs, lurking about the town, whom he supposed to be spies from the Indians, and that they had fled on discovering him. The town was alarmed, the militia turned out; the boats up and down the river were stopped; the woods were scoured, but nothing found, nothing discovered; all night, the fruitless search was continued.

About the dawn of day, the people returned, weary and fatigued, into town, and assembled for mutual consultation. Some thought one thing, some another. Some thought the whole difficulty began in nothing, and ended in the same. Some thought it a trick of the scholars to make themselves diversion. At the suggestion of this idea, one Capt. Storrs observed, that he saw Burroughs and Paine pass by his house, about six minutes before he heard the outcry. The name of Burroughs cast a suspicious appearance upon the business; they all turned their eyes on me, as the author of this alarm and uproar. I cited those who ran from the College with me, on the first of the outcry, to vouch for my innocence; they readily did it. All were satisfied, on my account, except my good friend Mr. Wood. He rolled the eye of jealousy over the business — he was dissatisfied. He took Paine to a private room in the College, and there, by a reiterated course of flattery, threatening, terrors, and soothings, he obtained the mighty secret, as it related to me. I was immediately informed of the business, by a person whom I had placed in a room adjoining, to overhear whatever should be the result of this conference.

It was now about sunrise. I immediately went to the owner of the watermelons, and told him, that passing his yard last evening, after he was in bed, I had taken twelve of his watermelons, knowing he kept them for sale, and came to let him know it, and pay for them. After counting his watermelons, and finding twelve taken, according to my account, he took the pay, and gave me his receipt. I now

returned to my room, ready to meet the heavy blow I saw was preparing against me.

By this time it had taken air, that I was the author of last night's
alarm. Every countenance was turned upon me in an oblique direction. They had all heard that theft was combined in the business;
they had all determined I must fall under this blow; therefore, they
were waiting for the awful moment of my being summoned before
the authority of College. Ten o'clock, the all tremendous hour, arrived ! I appeared; a number had gathered, which crowded the room.
After the charge was made against me, Mr. Ripley, one of the
Tutors, addressed me in a speech of half an hour's length, stating
the enormous crime I had been guilty of, the course of iniquity I
must have led through life, to be detected in such an atrocious high-
handed breach of law, at the age of sixteen; the disgrace I had
brought on my family connections, and the seminary of which I
was a member; that my expulsion, which would undoubtedly succeed, would be but only a prelude to my punishment by the civil
law: that ruin and disgrace were the only effects, which would fall
on my devoted head.

This rant I heard with the coolness of a stoic. After he had talked
himself out of breath, I had liberty to answer. I mentioned the hard-
ness of my case, in being accused, condemned and executed without any proof, or even being heard in my own defence. That I
did not know what evidence they could produce of my being guilty
of the crime laid to my charge, but whatever it was, I hoped to be
sufficiently able to overturn its validity, and clearly establish my innocence. At least, the humane language of candor taught us to hold
every man innocent till he was proved guilty. True it was, I had
taken watermelons from Mr. Smith the night preceding, but had
early that morning informed him of the fact, and paid for them.
This information was like a thunder-clap to some of the spectators.
All their hopes of seeing ruin fall heavy on my head were now
quashed in the twinkling of an eye. Mr. Smith, the owner of the
watermelons, having been sent for, testified to all the facts which I
had stated; and of course, here the business ended.

When a youth has spent four years at a University, and has gone
the common round of establishing a character for ability, by stealing watermelons, robbing henroosts, geese-houses, etc., and playing
tricks upon the inhabitants' cows and horses, and can speak a number of sentences which others do not understand, his fond mother
looks at him with a pleasing significance, and tells her inquisitive
neighbors, that her son has got to be a man of science, and in order
to establish her doctrine recounts all the manoeuvres he has prac-

ticed at College, in order to get a hen out of the roost. The father thinks these are marks of greatness of mind and depth of knowledge, and from these evidences, forms the most pleasing expectations of his son's future greatness. These anecdotes are recounted by the neighbors to their families, through a long course of succeeding winter evenings' amusements. They drink deeply at this fountain of entertainment. When they hear of the foolish pranks of scholars, they are exhilarated at the recital; they dwell upon them with pleasure, and behold the performers with admiration. Whereas, let it be said, that such or such persons have out-stripped their fellows in depth of thought, or perspicuity of reasoning and invention, the tale becomes lifeless, and is soon forgotten.

◇◇◇◇◇◇◇◇◇◇◇◇◇

[*Timothy Dwight*]

The students at Dartmouth are usually about one hundred and fifty in number; and as in the other New-England Colleges, are divided into four classes. The freshmen study the learned Languages, the rudiments of speaking and writing, and the elements of Mathematics. The sophomores beside the Languages, and Mathematics, study also Geography, and Logic. The junior sophisters, beside the Languages, are employed in Natural and Moral Philosophy, and Composition. The senior sophisters compose in English and Latin, and study Metaphysics, together with the elements of Natural and Political Law. There is in this Institution a Professor of Divinity, a Professor of Mathematics and Natural philosophy, and a Professor, who teaches Medical science and Chemistry. The President is also Professor of History. The number of Tutors is small, and variable. Frequently there has been but one. The annual Commencement is held on the fourth Wednesday of August: and is attended by a numerous assembly of gentlemen and ladies, from the surrounding country. The annual revenue of this college, arising from tuition, was in the year 1793 about $2,000; and the rent of its land near $500 more. By contracts made that year, it was to amount, in 1797, to $1,500, and, in 1805, to $2,166⅔.

There are two Vacations in this Institution: one, immediately succeeding the Commencement, and continuing six weeks and two days; and the other, beginning on the fourth Monday in February, and continuing five weeks and five days.

The first Collegiate building erected here, stood almost twenty years; and was then consumed by fire. Another has been since erected, (in 1786), one hundred and fifty feet long, and fifty feet

[103]

wide; of three stories. It is built of wood. The figure is the same, as that at Providence, formerly described, and both are copies of that of Princeton. The public rooms, containing the library, philosophical apparatus, and a number of natural and artificial curiosities, are in a projection at the centre. This building has a decent appearance. At a small distance from the College Southward stands a Chapel; the arched ceiling of which, ascending from the four sides, produces the same effect, as the whispering gallery in the dome of St. Paul's. A whisper, uttered in one of the angles, with so low a sound as not to be audible six feet from the speaker, is very distinctly heard in the opposite angle. These buildings stand on the Eastern side of a square, surrounded by decent houses, and covered with a lively verdure.

IN THE SWEAT OF THY FACE

LIFE ASHORE

◈◈◈◈◈◈◈◈◈◈◈◈◈

[Samuel Maverick, Massachusetts]

1660. On the Coast within Cape Sable, as in Nova Scotia, Port Royall, and those other fforts now in possession of Collonel Temple is mutch Beaver & other Peltry gotten, and more might be if fully Stocked.

And for the Southern part of New-England, It is incredible what hath been done there.

In the yeare 1626 or thereabouts there was not a Neat Beast Horse or sheepe in the Countrey and a very few Goats or hoggs, and now it is a wonder to see the great herds of Catle belonging to every Towne I have mentioned, The braue Flocks of sheepe, The great number of Horses besides those many sent to Barbados and the other Carribe Islands, And withall to consider how many thousand Neate Beasts and Hoggs are yearly killed, and soe have been for many yeares past for Provision in the Countrey and sent abroad to supply Newfoundland, Barbados, Jamaica, @ other places, As also to victuall in whole or in part most shipes which comes there.

Betweene the years 1626 and 1633, Indian Corne was usually sold at 10ˢ or 12ˢ the Bushell, now not esteemed worth 2ˢ. Beefe and Porke then Brought from England and Irland sold at excessive rates.

At that time all the Houses there, except three or fower at New Plymouth, and those which I had could not be valued worth 200ˡᵇ, and now to behold the handsome Houses & Churches in so many Townes as I have named is a wonder, And the place in which Boston (the Metropolis) is seated, I knew then for some yeares to be a Swamp and Pound, now a great Towne, two Churches, a Gallant Statehouse & more to make it compleate, then can be expected in a place so late a wilderness.

And wheras about the time before mentioned wee could not make in all three Hundred men in the whole Countrey, those scattered a hundred and ffiftie Miles assunder, Now almost every Towne which I have named is able to bring into the feild a full Company of Foote and some Horse, some Townes two or three Companyes compleate with Horse proportionable and Boston more

And the great abundance of English Fruite, as Apples, Pears, Apricocks, Plumbs, Cherries, Musk-Mellons, Water-Mellons &c. is not to be beleeved but by those that have seene it

And about those times also there were not within the now Great Government of the Massachusetts above three Shallops and a few Cannoes, Now it is wonderfull to see the many Vessels belonging to the Country of all sorts and seizes, from Shipps of some reasonable burthen to Skiffes and Cannoes, many other great Shipps of Burthen from 350 Tunns to 150 have been built there, and many more in time may be, And I am confident there hath not in any place out of so small a number of People been raised so many able Seamen and Commanders as there hath been.

❖❖❖❖❖❖❖❖❖❖❖

[*Samuel Sewall*]

Monday, Octr 6. 1701. Very pleasant fair Wether; Artillery trains in the Afternoon [Sewall in command]. March with the Company to the Elms; Go to prayer, March down and Shoot at a Mark. Mr. Cushing I think was the first that hit it, Mr. Gerrish twice, Mr. Fitch, Chauncy, and the Ensign of the Officers. By far the most missed, as I did for the first. Were much contented with the exercise. Led them to the Trees agen, perform'd some facings and Doublings. Drew them together; propounded the question about the Colours; twas voted very freely and fully. I inform'd the Company I was told the Company's Halberds &c. were borrowed; I understood the Leading staff was so, and therefore ask'd their Acceptance of a Half-Pike, which they very kindly did; I deliver'd it to Mr. Gibbs for their Use.

They would needs give me a Volley, in token of their Respect on this occasion. The Pike will, I suppose, stand me in fourty shillings, being headed and shod with Silver: Has this Motto fairly engraven:

Agmen Massachusettense
est in tutelam Sponsæ
AGNI Uxoris.
1701.

The Lord help us to answer the Profession. Were treated by the Ensign in a fair chamber. Gave a very handsome Volley at Lodging the Colours. The Training in Septr. was a very fair day, so was this.

7^r. 30. 1720. Mr. Coleman's Lecture: Daughter Sewall acquaints Madam Winthrop that if she pleas'd to be within at 3. p. m. I would wait on her. She answer'd she would be at home.

8ʳ. 1. Satterday, I dine at Mr. Stoddard's: from thence I went to Madam Winthrop's * just at 3. Spake to her, saying, my loving wife died so soon and suddenly, 'twas hardly convenient for me to think of Marrying again; however I came to this Resolution, that I would not make my Court to any person without first Consulting with her. Had a pleasant discourse about 7 [seven] Single persons sitting in

Samuel Sewall.

the Fore-seat 7ʳ. 29ᵗʰ, viz. Madᵐ Rebekah Dudley, Catharine Winthrop, Bridget Usher, Deliverance Legg, Rebekah Loyd, Lydia Colman, Elizabeth Bellingham. She propounded one and other for me; but none would do, said Mrs. Loyd was about her Age.

Octobʳ. 3. 2. Waited on Madam Winthrop again; 'twas a little while before she came in. Her daughter Noyes being there alone with me, I said, I hoped my Waiting on her Mother would not be disagreeable to her. She answer'd she should not be against that that

* Madam Winthrop was Katherine, daughter of Thomas Brattle, born Sept. 26, 1664. She married, first, John Eyre, and had twelve children, who all died young except Katherine, wife of David Jeffries and Oliver Noyes; Bethiah, wife of John Walley; and John Eyre, born in 1700. She married, secondly, Wait Still Winthrop, as his second wife, and became a widow again Nov. 7, 1717. She was fifty-six years old at this time. She did not marry again, and died at Boston, Aug. 5, 1725. Sewall was now in his sixty-ninth year.

might be for her Comfort. I Saluted her, and told her I perceiv'd I must shortly wish her a good Time; (her mother had told me, she was with Child, and within a Moneth or two of her Time). By and by in came Mr. Airs, Chaplain of the Castle, and hang'd up his Hat, which I was a little startled at, it seeming as if he was to lodge there. At last Madam Winthrop came too. After a considerable time, I went up to her and said, if it might not be inconvenient I desired to speak to her. She assented, and spake of going into another Room; but Mr. Airs and Mrs. Noyes presently rose up, and went out, leaving us there alone. Then I usher'd in Discourse from the names in the Fore-seat; at last I pray'd that Katharine [Mrs. Winthrop] might be the person assign'd for me. She instantly took it up in the way of Denyal, as if she had catch'd at an Opportunity to do it, saying she could not do it before she was asked. Said that was her mind unless she should Change it, which she believed she should not; could not leave her Children. I express'd my Sorrow that she should do it so Speedily, pray'd her Consideration, and ask'd her when I should wait on her agen. She setting no time, I mention'd that day Sennight. Gave her Mr. Willard's Fountain open'd with the little print and verses; saying, I hop'd if we did well read that book, we should meet together hereafter, if we did not now. She took the Book, and put it in her Pocket. Took Leave.

8ʳ. 5. Midweek, I din'd with the Court; from thence went and visited Cousin Jonathan's wife, Lying in with her little Betty. Gave the Nurse 2ˢ. Although I had apointed to wait upon her, Mᵐ. Winthrop, next Monday, yet I went from my Cousin Sewall's thither about 3. p. m. The Nurse told me Madam dined abroad at her daughter Noyes's, they were to go out together. I ask'd for the Maid, who was not within. Gave Katee a peny and a Kiss, and came away. Accompanyed my Son and dâter Cooper in their Remove to their New House. Went to tell Joseph, and Mr. Belcher saw me by the South Meetinghouse though 'twas duskish, and said I had been at House-warming, (he had been at our house). Invited me to drink a Glass of Wine at his house at 7. and eat part of the Pasty provided for the Commissioners voyage to Casco-Bay. His Excellency, Madam Belcher, S. S. Col. Fitch, Mr. D. Oliver, Mr. Anthony Stoddard, Mr. Welsteed, Mr. White, Mr. Belcher sat down. At coming home gave us of the Cake and Ginger-Bread to carry away. 'Twas about Ten before we got home; Mr. Oliver and I waited on the Governour to his Gate; and then Mr. Oliver would wait on me home.

8ʳ. 6ᵗʰ. A little after 6. p. m. I went to Madam Winthrop's. She was not within. I gave Sarah Chickering the Maid 2ˢ, Juno, who brought in wood, 1ˢ. Afterward the Nurse came in, I gave her 18ᵈ, having no other small Bill. After awhile Dr. Noyes came in with his Mother; and quickly after his wife came in: They sat talking, I think, till eight a-clock. I said I fear'd I might be some Interruption to their Business: Dr. Noyes reply'd pleasantly: He fear'd they might be an Interruption to me, and went away. Madam seem'd to harp upon the same string. Must take care of her Children; could not leave that House and Neighbourhood where she had dwelt so long. I told her she might doe her children as much or more good by bestowing what she laid out in Hous-keeping, upon them. Said her Son would be of Age the 7ᵗʰ of August. I said it might be inconvenient for her to dwell with her Daughter-in-law, who must be Mistress of the House. I gave her a piece of Mr. Belcher's Cake and Ginger-Bread wrapped up in a clean sheet of Paper; told her of her Father's kindness to me when Treasurer, and I Constable. My daughter Judith was gon from me and I was more lonesom — might help to forward one another in our Journey to Canaan. — Mr. Eyre came within the door; I saluted him, ask'd how Mr. Clark did, and he went away. I took leave about 9 aclock. I told [her] I came now to refresh her Memory as to Monday-night; said she had not forgot it. In discourse with her, I ask'd leave to speak with her Sister; I meant to gain Madᵐ Mico's favour to persuade her Sister. She seem'd surprised and displeas'd, and said she was in the same condition !

In the Evening I visited Madam Winthrop, who treated me with a great deal of Curtesy; Wine, Marmalade. I gave her a News-Letter about the Thanksgiving; Proposals, for sake of the verses for David Jeffries. She tells me Dr. Increase Mather visited her this day, in Mr. Hutchinson's Coach.

It seems Dr. Cotton Mather's chimney fell a-fire yesterday, so as to interrupt the Assembly a. m. Mr. Cutler ceased preaching ¼ of an hour.

8ʳ. 11ᵗʰ. I writ a few Lines to Madam Winthrop to this purpose: "Madam, These wait on you with Mr. Mayhew's Sermon, and Account of the state of the Indians on Martha's Vineyard. I thank you for your Unmerited Favours of yesterday; and hope to have the Hapiness of Waiting on you to-morrow before Eight aclock after Noon. I pray GOD to keep you, and give you a joyful entrance upon the Two Hundred and twenty ninth year of Christopher Columbus his Discovery; and take Leave, who am, Madam, your humble Servᵗ.

S. S.

Sent this by Deacon Green, who deliver'd it to Sarah Chickering, her Mistress not being at home.

8ʳ. 12. Go to the Meeting at the Wido Emon's: Mr. Manly pray'd,

I read half Mr. Henry's 12ᵗʰ Chapter of the L. Supper. Sung 1., 2, 3, 4, 5, 10, and 12ᵗʰ Verses of the 30ᵗʰ Psalm. Broʳ Franklin concluded with Prayer. At Madᵐ Winthrop's Steps I took leave of Capt Hill, &c.

Mrs. Anne Cotton came to door (twas before 8.) said Madam Winthrop was within, directed me into the little Room, where she was full of work behind a Stand; Mrs. Cotton came in and stood. Madam Winthrop pointed to her to set me a Chair. Madam Winthrop's Countenance was much changed from what 'twas on Monday, look'd dark and lowering. At last, the work, (black stuff or Silk) was taken away, I got my Chair in place, had some Converse, but very Cold and indifferent to what 'twas before. Ask'd her to acquit me of Rudeness if I drew off her Glove. Enquiring the reason, I told her twas great odds between handling a dead Goat, and a living Lady. Got it off. I told her I had one Petition to ask her, that was, that she would take off the Negative she laid on me the third of October; She readily answer'd she could not, and enlarg'd upon it; She told me of it so soon as she could; could not leave her house, children, neighbours, business. I told her she might do som Good to help and support me. Mentioning Mrs. Gookin, Nath, the widow Weld was spoken of; said I had visited Mrs. Denison. I told her Yes! Afterward I said, If after a first and second Vagary she would Accept of me returning, Her Victorious Kindness and Good Will would be very Obliging. She thank'd me for my Book, (Mr. Mayhew's Sermon), But said not a word of the Letter. When she insisted on the Negative, I pray'd there might be no more Thunder and Lightening, I should not sleep all night. I gave her Dr. Preston, The Church's Marriage and the Church's Carriage, which cost me 6ˢ at the Sale. The door standing open, Mr. Airs came in, hung up his Hat, and sat down. After awhile, Madam Winthrop moving, he went out. Jnᵒ Eyre look'd in, I said How do ye, or, your servant Mr. Eyre: but heard no word from him. Sarah fill'd a Glass of Wine, she drank to me, I to her, She sent Juno home with me with a good Lantern, I gave her 6ᵈ. and bid her thank her Mistress. In some of our Discourse, I told her I had rather go to the Stone-House adjoining to her, than to come to her against her mind. Told her the reason why I came every other night was lest I should drink too deep draughts of Pleasure. She had talk'd of Canary, her Kisses were to me better than the best Canary. Explain'd the expression Concerning Columbus.

8ʳ. 13. I tell my Son and daughter Sewall, that the Weather was not so fair as I aprehended.

8ʳ. 15. I dine on Fish and Oyle at Mr. Stoddard's. Capt. Hill

wish'd me Joy of my proceedings i. e. with M-. Winthrop; Sister
Cooper applauded it, spake of Visiting her: I said her Complaisance
of her Visit would be obliging to me.

8ʳ. 16. L. Day, I upbraided my self that could be so solicitous
about Earthly things; and so cold and indifferent as to the Love of
Christ, who is altogether Lovely. Mr. Prince administered. Din'd
at my Son's with Mr. Cutler, and Mr. Shurtleff. Mr. Cutler preaches
in the Afternoon from Ezek. 16. 30. How weak is thy heart. Son
reads the Order for the Thanksgiving.

8ʳ. 17. Monday, In the Evening I visited Madam Winthrop, who
Treated me Courteously, but not in Clean Linen as sometimes. She
said, she did not know whether I would come again, or no. I ask'd
her how she could so impute inconstancy to me. (I had not visited
her since Wednesday night being unable to get over the Indisposi-
tion received by the Treatment received that night, and *I must* in it
seem'd to sound like a made piece of Formality.) Gave her this
day's Gazett. Heard David Jeffries say the Lord's Prayer, and some
other portions of the Scriptures. He came to the door, and ask'd me
to go into Chamber, where his Grandmother was tending Little
Katee, to whom she had given Physick; but I chose to sit below. Dr.
Noyes and his wife came in, and sat a Considerable time; had been
visiting Son and dâter Cooper. Juno came home with me.

8ʳ. 18. Visited Madam Mico, who came to me in a splendid Dress.
I said, It may be you have heard of my Visiting Madam Winthrop,
her Sister. She answered, Her Sister had told her of it. I ask'd her
good Will in the Affair. She answer'd, If her Sister were for it, she
should not hinder it. I gave her Mr. Holmes's Sermon. She gave me
a Glass of Canary, entertain'd me with good Discourse, and a Respectful Remembrance of my first Wife. I took Leave.

8ʳ. 19. Midweek, Visited Madam Winthrop; Sarah told me she
was at Mr. Walley's, would not come home till late. I gave her
Hannah 3 oranges with her Duty, not knowing whether I should
find her or no. Was ready to go home: but said if I knew she was
there, I would go thither. Sarah seem'd to speak with pretty good
Courage, She would be there. I went and found her there, with Mr.
Walley and his wife in the little Room below. At 7 a-clock I mentioned going home; at 8. I put on my Coat, and quickly waited on
her home. She found occasion to speak loud to the servant, as if she
had a mind to be known. Was Courteous to me; but took occasion
to speak pretty earnestly about my keeping a Coach: I said 'twould
cost £100. per anum: she said twould cost but £40. Spake much
against John Winthrop, his false-heartedness. Mr. Eyre came in and
sat awhile; I offer'd him Dr. Incr. Mather's Sermons, whereof Mr.

Apleton's Ordination Sermon was one; said he had them already. I said I would give him another. Exit. Came away somewhat late.

8ʳ. 20. At Council, Col. Townsend spake to me of my Hood: Should get a Wigg. I said twas my chief ornament: I wore it for sake of the Day. Broʳ. Odlin, and Sam, Mary, and Jane Hirst dine with us. Promis'd to wait on the Govʳ about 7. Madam Winthrop not being at Lecture, I went thither first; found her very Serene with her dâter Noyes, Mrs. Dering, and the widow Shipreev sitting at a little Table, she in her arm'd Chair. She drank to me, and I to Mrs. Noyes. After awhile pray'd the favour to speak with her. She took one of the Candles, and went into the best Room, clos'd the shutters, sat down upon the Couch. She told me Madam Usher had been there, and said the Coach must be set on Wheels, and not by Rusting. She spake something of my needing a Wigg. Ask'd me what her Sister said to me. I told her, She said, If her Sister were for it, She would not hinder it. But I told her, she did not say she would be glad to have me for her Brother. Said, I shall keep you in the Cold, and asked her if she would be within to morrow night, for we had had but a running Feat. She said she could not tell whether she should, or no. I took Leave. As were drinking at the Governour's, he said: In England the Ladies minded little more than that they might have Money, and Coaches to ride in. I said, And New-England brooks its Name. At which Mr. Dudley smiled. Govʳ said they were not quite so bad here.

8ʳ. 21. Friday, My Son, the Minister, came to me p. m. by apointment and we pray one for another in the Old Chamber; more especially respecting my Courtship. About 6. a-clock I go to Madam Winthrop's; Sarah told me her Mistress was gon out, but did not tell me whither she went. She presently order'd me a Fire; so I went in, having Dr. Sibb's Bowels * with me to read. I read the two first Sermons, still no body came in: at last about 9. a-clock Mr. Jnᵒ Eyre came in; I took the opportunity to say to him as I had done to Mrs. Noyes before, that I hoped my Visiting his Mother would not be disagreeable to him; He answered me with much Respect. When twas after 9 a-clock He of himself said he would go and call her, she was but at one of his Brothers: A while after I heard Madam Winthrop's voice, enquiring somthing about John. After a good while and Clapping the Garden door twice, or thrice, she came in. I mention'd somthing of the lateness; she banter'd me, and said I was later. She receiv'd me Courteously. I ask'd when our proceedings should be made publick: She said They were like to be no more

* "Bowels opened; or, a Discovery of the Union betwixt Christ and the Church."

[114]

publick than they were already. Offer'd me no Wine that I remember. I rose up at 11 a'clock to come away, saying I would put on my Coat, She offer'd not to help me. I pray'd her that Juno might light me home, she open'd the Shutter, and said twas pretty light abroad; Juno was weary and gon to bed. So I came hôm by Star-light as well as I could. At my first coming in, I gave Sarah five Shillings. I writ Mr. Eyre his Name in his book with the date Octob^r. 21. 1720. It cost me 8^s. Jehovah jireh ! Madam told me she had visited M. Mico, Wendell, and Wm Clark.

Octob^r. 22. Dâter Cooper visited me before my going out of Town, staid till about Sun set. I brought her going near as far as the Orange Tree. Coming back, near Leg's Corner, Little David Jeffries saw me, and looking upon me very lovingly, ask'd me if I was going to see his Grandmother ? I said, Not to-night. Gave him a peny, and bid him present my Service to his Grandmother.

Octob^r. 24. I went in the Hackny Coach through the Comon, stop'd at Madam Winthrop's (had told her I would take my departure from thence) . Sarah came to the door with Katee in her Arms: but I did not think to take notice of the Child. Call'd her Mistress. I told her, being encourag'd by David Jeffries loving eyes, and sweet Words, I was come to enquire whether she could find in her heart to leave that House and Neighbourhood, and go and dwell with me at the South-end; I think she said softly, Not yet. I told her It did not ly in my Lands to keep a Coach. If I should, I should be in danger to be brought to keep company with her Neighbour Brooker, (he was a little before sent to prison for Debt) . Told her I had an Antipathy against those who would pretend to give themselves; but nothing of their Estate. I would a proportion of my Estate with my self. And I suppos'd she would do so. As to a Perriwig, My best and greatest Friend, I could not possibly have a greater, began to find me with Hair before I was born, and had continued to do so ever since; and I could not find in my heart to go to another. She comended the book I gave her, Dr. Preston, the Church Marriage; quoted him saying 'twas inconvenient keeping out of a Fashion commonly used. I said the Time and Tide did circumscribe my Visit. She gave me a Dram of Black-Cherry Brandy, and gave me a lump of the Sugar that was in it. She wished me a good Journy. I pray'd God to keep her, and came away. Had a very pleasant Journy to Salem.

8^r. 25. Sent a Letter of it to my Son by Wakefield, who delivered it not till Wednesday; so he visited her not till Friday p. m. and then presented my Service to her.

31. 2. At night I visited Madam Winthrop about 6 p. m. They told me she was gon to Madam Mico's. I went thither and found she

was gon; so return'd to her house, read the Epistles to the Galatians, Ephesians in Mr. Eyre's Latin Bible. After the Clock struck 8. I began to read the 103. Psalm. Mr. Wendell came in from his Warehouse. Ask'd me if I were alone? Spake very kindly to me, offer'd me to call Madam Winthrop. I told him, She would be angry, had been at Mrs. Mico's; he help'd me on with my Coat and I came home: left the Gazett in the Bible, which told Sarah of, bid her present my Service to Mrs. Winthrop, and tell her I had been to wait on her if she had been at home.

Novr. 1. I was so taken up that I could not go if I would.

Novr. 2. Midweek, went again, and found Mrs. Alden there, who quickly went out. Gave her about ½ pound of Sugar Almonds, cost 3^s per £. Carried them on Monday. She seem'd pleas'd with them, ask'd what they cost. Spake of giving her a Hundred pounds per annum if I dy'd before her. Ask'd her what sum she would give me, if she should dy first? Said I would give her time to Consider of it. She said she heard as if I had given all to my Children by Deeds of Gift. I told her 'twas a mistake, Point-Judith was mine &c. That in England, I own'd my Father's desire was that it should go to my eldest Son; 'twas 20£ per annum; she thought 'twas forty. I think when I seem'd to excuse pressing this, she sem'd to think 'twas best to speak of it; a long winter was coming on. Gave me a Glass or two of Canary.

Novr. 4th. Friday, Went again about 7 a-clock; found there Mr. John Walley and his wife: sat discoursing pleasantly. I shew'd them Isaac Moses's [an Indian] Writing. Madam W. serv'd Comfeits to us. After a-while a Table was spread, and Supper was set. I urg'd Mr. Walley to Crave a Blessing; but he put it upon me. About 9. they went away. I ask'd Madam what fashioned Neck-lace I should present her with, She said, None at all. I ask'd her Whereabout we left off last time; mention'd what I had offer'd to give her; Ask'd her what she would give me; She said she could not Change her Condition: She had said so from the beginning; could not be so far from her Children, the Lecture. Quoted the Apostle Paul affirming that a single Life was better than a Married. I answer'd That was for the present Distress. Said she had not pleasure in things of that nature as formerly: I said, you are the fitter to make me a Wife. If she held in that mind, I must go home and bewail my Rashness in making more haste than good Speed. However, considering the Supper, I desired her to be within next Monday night, if we liv'd so long. Assented. She charg'd me with saying, that she must put away Juno, if she came to me: I utterly deny'd it, it never came in my heart; yet she insisted upon it; saying it came in upon discourse about the

Indian woman that obtained her Freedom this Court. About 10. I
said I would not disturb the good orders of her House, and came
away. She not seeming pleas'd with my Coming away. Spake to her
about David Jeffries, had not seen him.

Monday, Novr. 7th. My Son pray'd in the Old Chamber. Our time
had been taken up by Son and Daughter Cooper's Visit; so that I
only read the 130th. and 143. Psalm. Twas on the Account of my
Courtship. I went to Mad. Winthrop; found her rocking her little
Katee in the Cradle. I excus'd my Coming so late (near Eight). She
set me an arm'd Chair and Cusheon; and so the Cradle was between
her arm'd Chair and mine. Gave her the remnant of my Almonds;
She did not eat of them as before; but laid them away; I said I came
to enquire whether she had alter'd her mind since Friday, or remained of the same mind still. She said, Thereabouts. I told her I
loved her, and was so fond as to think that she loved me: She said
had a great respect for me. I told her, I had made her an offer, without asking any advice; she had so many to advise with, that twas a
hindrance. The Fire was come to one short Brand besides the Block,
which Brand was set up in end; at last it fell to pieces, and no Recruit was made: She gave me a Glass of Wine. I think I repeated
again that I would go home and bewail my Rashness in making
more haste than good Speed. I would endeavour to contain myself,
and not go on to sollicit her to do that which she could not Consent
to. Took leave of her. As came down the steps she bid me have a
Care. Treated me Courteously. Told her she had enter'd the 4th year
of her Widowhood. I had given her the News-Letter before: I did
not bid her draw off her Glove as sometime I had done. Her Dress
was not so clean as somtime it had been. Jehovah Jireh!

March, 29th, 1722. Samuel Sewall, and Mrs. Mary Gibbs were
joined together in Marriage by the Rev^d. Mr. William Cooper.

Lord's day, April, 1. Sat with my wife in her Pue.

April, 2. Brought her home to my House.

April, 8. introduc'd her into my Pue, and sat with her there.

April, 15. Conducted my wife to the Fore-Seat; having been invited by David Jeffries esqr. Danl Oliver esqr, and Mr. Ezekiel
Lewis, March, 31. as overseers.

Harriet Beecher Stowe: "Well, father, how did it happen that you did not become a farmer ?"

[*Lyman Beecher*]

I should, [have become a farmer] if Uncle Benton had not cleared a fifteen-acre lot, and I driven plow over the whole three times. He always meant I should be his heir, and have the homestead, and be a farmer as he was. I wish you could see his old plow. It was a curious thing of his own making — clumsy, heavy, and patched with old hoes and pieces of iron to keep it from wearing out. That plow is the most horrible memorial of that time.

If that plow could tell the story of my feelings it would be a development. Uncle Lot, however, thought a great deal of it. One day I drove the ox-team so as to graze it with the wheel.

"There, there, Lyman, you've run over that plow and broke it all to pieces."

"Why, Uncle Lot, I haven't touched the plow."

"Well, I'd a great deal rather you had than to have gone so plaguy nigh it."

Now I am naturally quick, and that old plow was so slow — one furrow a little way, and then another — and the whole fifteen acres three times over, some of it steep as the roof of a house. I became inexpressibly sick of it. What should I do, then, but build castles in the air. First I knew I would be a rod ahead, and the plow out, and Uncle Lot would say "Whoa," and come and give me a shake.

Not long after the job was finished Uncle Benton and I were walking together over to Toket Hill, and I had got so used to driving that I fell into a brown study, and kept saying "Whoa !" "Haw !" "Gee !" as if the oxen were along.

"Why, Lyman," said Uncle Lot, "did you think you were driving the oxen ?" It was then, I believe, he gave up. Next day we were out behind the barn picking up apples.

"Lyman," said he, "should you like to go to college ?"

"I don't know, sir," said I. But the next day we were out picking apples again, and, without his saying a word, I said, "Yes, sir, I should." So he drove over to New Haven, and talked with father, and they settled it between them. Uncle Lot was to clothe me — Aunt Benton could make nearly every thing — and father was to do the rest. Uncle took his nephew, Lot Benton, for his heir, and gave him the homestead, and moved to Old Guilford. When he died he left me his Guilford house, and land worth about $2000 besides.

[*Timothy Dwight*]

Vermont has been settled entirely from the other States of New England. The inhabitants have, of course, the New-England character, with no other difference beside what is accidental. In the formation of Colonies, those, who are first inclined to emigrate, are usually such, as have met with difficulties at home. These are commonly joined by persons, who, having large families, and small farms, are induced, for the sake of settling their children comfortably, to seek for new and cheaper lands. To both are always added the discontented, the enterprizing, the ambitious, and the covetous. Many, of the first, and some, of all these classes, are found in every new American country, within ten years after its settlement has commenced. From this period, kindred, friendship, and former neighbourhood, prompt others to follow them. Others, still, are allured by the prospect of gain, presented in every new country to the sagacious, from the purchase and sale of lands: while not a small number are influenced by the brilliant stories, which every where are told concerning most tracts during the early progress of their settlement. A considerable part of all those, who *begin* the cultivation of the wilderness, may be denominated *foresters,* or *Pioneers.* The business of these persons is no other than to cut down trees, build log-houses, lay open forested grounds to cultivation, and prepare the way for those who come after them. These men cannot live in regular society. They are too idle; too talkative; too passionate; too prodigal; and too shiftless; to acquire either property or character. They are impatient of the restraints of law, religion, and morality; grumble about the taxes, by which Rulers, Ministers, and School-masters, are supported; and complain incessantly, as well as bitterly, of the extortions of mechanics, farmers, merchants, and physicians; to whom they are always indebted. At the same time, they are usually possessed, in their own view, of uncommon wisdom; understand medical science, politics, and religion, better than those, who have studied them through life; and, although they manage their own concerns worse than any other men, feel perfectly satisfied, that they could manage those of the nation far better than the agents, to whom they are committed by the public. After displaying their own talents, and worth; after censuring the weakness, and wickedness, of their superiors; after exposing the injustice of the community in neglecting to invest persons of such merit with public offices; in many an eloquent harangue, uttered by many a kitchen fire, in every blacksmith's shop, and in every corner of the streets; and finding all their efforts vain; they become at length discouraged:

[119]

and under the pressure of poverty, the fear of a gaol, and consciousness of public contempt, leave their native places, and betake themselves to the wilderness.

Here they are obliged either to work, or starve. They accordingly
cut down some trees, and girdle others; they furnish themselves with
an ill-built log-house, and a worse barn; and reduce a part of the
forest into fields, half-enclosed, and half-cultivated. The forests fur-

nish browse; and their fields yield a stinted herbage. On this scanty
provision they feed a few cattle; and with these, and the penurious
products of their labour, eked out by hunting and fishing, they
keep their families alive.

A farm, thus far cleared, promises immediate subsistence to a better husbandman. A log-house, thus built, presents, when repaired
with moderate exertions, a shelter for his family. Such a husbandman is therefore induced by these little advantages, where the soil
and situation please him, to purchase such a farm; when he would
not plant himself in an absolute wilderness. The proprietor is always ready to sell: for he loves this irregular, adventurous, half-
working, and half-lounging life; and hates the sober industry, and
prudent economy, by which his bush pasture might be changed into
a farm, and himself raised to thrift and independence. The bargain
is soon made. The forester, receiving more money for his improvements than he ever before possessed, and a price for the soil, somewhat enhanced by surrounding settlements, willingly quits his
house, to build another like it, and his farm, to girdle trees, hunt,

and saunter, in another place. His wife accompanies him only from a sense of duty, or necessity; and secretly pines for the quiet, orderly, friendly society, to which she originally bade a reluctant farewell. Her husband, in the mean time, becomes less and less a civilized man: and almost every thing in the family, which is amiable and meritorious, is usually the result of her principles, care, and influence.

The second proprietor is commonly a *farmer;* and with an industry and spirit, deserving no small commendation, changes the desert into a fruitful field.

The institutions, and the habits, of New-England, more I suspect than those of any other country, have prevented, or kept down, this noxious disposition; but they cannot entirely prevent either its existence, or its effects. In mercy, therefore, to the sober, industrious, and well-disposed inhabitants, Providence has opened in the vast Western wilderness a retreat, sufficiently alluring to draw them away from the land of their nativity. We have many troubles even now: but we should have many more, if this body of foresters had remained at home.

It is however to be observed, that a considerable number even of these people become sober, industrious citizens, merely by the acquisition of property. The love of property to a certain degree seems indispensable to the existence of sound morals. I have never had a servant, in whom I could confide, except such as were desirous to earn, and preserve, money.

In forming new settlements, it will be easily believed, the planters are necessitated to struggle with many difficulties. To clear a farm covered with a thick growth of large trees, such as generally abound in this country, is a work of no small magnitude. Especially is this true, when, as is usually the fact, it is to be done by a single man; and still more especially, when that man is poor, and obliged to struggle with many other discouragements. Yet this is the real situation of multitudes, who undertake enterprises of this nature.

When a planter commences this undertaking, he sets out for his farm with his axe, gun, blanket, provision, and ammunition. With these he enters the forest; and builds himself a shed, by setting up poles at four angles, crossing them with other poles, and covering the whole with bark, leaves, and twigs of trees, except the South side, purposely left open to the sun and a fire. Under this shelter he dresses his food; and makes his bed of straw, on which he sleeps soundly beneath his blanket. Here he usually continues through the season: and sometimes without the sight of any other human being. After he has completed this shelter, he begins to clear a spot of ground: i. e. to remove the forest, by which it is covered. This is done in two ways; *girdling,* and *felling,* the *trees.* The former of these I have already described. The latter has now become almost the universal practice: and wherever it can be adopted, is undoubtedly to be preferred. The trees are cut down, either in the autumn, or as early as it can be done in the spring; that they may become so dry as to be easily burnt up in the ensuing summer. After they have lain a sufficient length of time, he sets fire to them, lying as they fell. If he is successful, the greater part of them are consumed in the conflagration. The remainder he cuts with his axe into pieces of a convenient length; rolls them into piles; and sets fire to them again. In this manner they are all consumed; and the soil is left light, dry, and covered with ashes. These, so far as he can, he collects, and conveys to a manufactory of potashes if there be any in the neighbourhood; if not, he leaves them to enrich the soil. In many instances the ashes, thus gathered, will defray the expense of clearing the land.

After the field is burned over, his next business is to break it up. The instrument, employed for this purpose, is a large and strong harrow; here called *a drag,* with very stout iron teeth; resembling in its form the capital letter A. It is drawn over the surface, a sufficient number of times to make it mellow, and afterwards to cover the seed. A plough would here be of no use; as it would soon be broken to pieces by the roots of the trees. In the same manner the planter proceeds to another field, and to another; until his farm is sufficiently cleared to satisfy his wishes.

The first house which he builds, is formed of logs and commonly contains two rooms, with a stone chimney in the middle. His next labour is to procure a barn; generally large, well framed, covered, and roofed. Compared with his house, it is a palace. But for this a saw-mill is necessary, and is therefore built as early as possible.

Among the enjoyments of these people, health, and hardihood, ought never to be forgotten. The toils, which they undergo; the difficulties, which they surmount; and the hazards which they escape; all increase their spirits, and their firmness. A New-England forest, formed of hills and vallies, down which the waters, always pure and sweet, flow with unceasing rapidity; or of plains, dry, and destitute of marshes, is healthy almost of course. The minds of these settlers, therefore possess the energy, which results from health, as well as that, which results from activity: and few persons taste the pleasures, which fall to their lot, with a keener relish. The common troubles of life, often deeply felt by persons in easy circumstances, scarcely awaken in them the slightest emotion. Cold and heat, snow and rain, labour and fatigue, are regarded by them as trifles, deserving no attention. The coarsest food is pleasant to them; and the hardest bed refreshing. Over roads, encumbered with rocks, mire, and the stumps and roots of trees, they ride upon a full trot; and are apprehensive of no danger. Even their horses gain, by habit, the same resolution; and pass rapidly, and safely, over the worst roads, where both horses and men, accustomed to smoother ways, merely tremble, and creep. Even the women of these settlements, and those of every age share largely in this spirit. The longest journies, in very difficult roads, they undertake with cheerfulness, and perform without anxiety. I have often met them on horseback; and been surprised to see them pass fearlessly over those dangers of the way, which my companions and myself watched with caution and solicitude. Frequently I have seen them performing these journies alone.

Another prime enjoyment of these settlers is found in the kindness, which reigns among them universally. A general spirit of good neighbourhood is prevalent throughout New-England; but here it prevails in a peculiar degree. Among these people, a man rarely tells the story of his distresses to deaf ears; or asks any reasonable assistance in vain. The relief given is a matter, not of kindness merely, but of course. To do kind offices is the custom; a part of the established manners. This is seen every where; and is regularly experienced by the traveller; whom they receive as a friend rather than as a stranger; as an object of good will, and not as a source of gain.

❖❖❖❖❖❖❖❖❖❖❖❖

[Henry David Thoreau]

The deeper you penetrate into the [Maine] woods, the more intelligent, and, in one sense, less countrified do you find the inhabitants; for always the pioneer has been a traveler, and, to some extent, a man of the world; and, as the distances with which he is familiar are greater, so is his information more general and far reaching than the villagers. If I were to look for a narrow, uninformed, and countrified mind, as opposed to the intelligence and refinement which are thought to emanate from cities, it would be among the rusty inhabitants of an old-settled country, on farms all run out and gone to seed with life-everlasting, in the towns about Boston, even on the high-road in Concord, and not in the backwoods of Maine.

❖❖❖❖❖❖❖❖❖❖❖❖❖

[*Seth Hubbell*]

In the latter part of February, 1789, I set out from the town of Norwalk, in Connecticut, on my journey for Wolcott, Vermont, to commence a settlement and make that my residence; family consisting of my wife and five children, they all being girls, the eldest nine or ten years old. My team was a yoke of oxen and a horse. After I had proceeded on my journey to within about one hundred miles of Wolcott, one of my oxen failed, but I however kept him yoked with the other till about noon each day; then turned him before, and took his end of the yoke myself, and proceeded on in that manner with my load to about fourteen miles of my journey's end, when I could get the sick ox no further, and was forced to leave him with Thomas W. Connel, in Johnson; but he had neither hay nor grain for him. I then proceeded on with some help to Esq. McDaniel's in Hydepark: this brought me to about eight miles of Wolcott, and to the end of the road. It was now about the 20th of March; the snow not far from four feet deep; no hay to be had for my team, and no way for them to subsist but by browse. As my sick ox at Connel's could not be kept on browse, I interceded with a man in Cambridge for a little hay to keep him alive, which I backed, a bundle at a time, five miles, for about ten days, when the ox died. On the 6th of April I set out from Esq. McDaniel's, his being the last house, for my intended residence in Wolcott, with my wife and two eldest children. We had eight miles to travel on snow-shoes, by marked trees — no road being cut: my wife had to try this new mode of travelling, and she performed the journey remarkably well. The path had been so trodden by snow-shoes as to bear up the children. Esq. Taylor, with his wife and two small children, who moved on with me, had gone on the day before. We were the first families in Wolcott: in Hydepark there had two families wintered the year before. To the east of us it was eighteen miles to inhabitants, and no road but marked trees: to the south, about twenty, where there was infant settlements, but no communication with us; and to the north, it was almost indefinite, or to the regions of Canada.

I had now got to the end of my journey, and I may say almost to the end of my property, for I had not a mouthful of meat or kernel of grain for my family, nor had I a cent of money left to buy with, or property that I could apply to that purpose. I however had the good luck to catch a saple. The skin I carried fifty miles, and exchanged for half a bushel of wheat, and backed it home. We had now lived three weeks without bread; though in the time I had bought a moose of an Indian, and backed the meat five miles, which answered to subsist upon. I would here remark that it was my fate to move on my family at that memorable time called the "scarce season," which was generally felt through the state, especially in the northern parts in the infant settlements: no grain or provision of any kind, of consequence, was to be had on the river Lamoille. I had to go into New Hampshire, sixty miles, for the little I had for my family, till harvest, and this was so scanty a pittance that we were under the painful necessity of allowancing the children till we had a supply. The three remaining children that I left in Hydepark, I brought one at a time on my back on snow-shoes, as also the whole of my goods.

I moved from Connecticut with the expectation of having fifty acres of land given me when I came on, but this I was disappointed of, and was under the necessity soon after I came on of selling a yoke of oxen and a horse to buy the land I now live on, which reduced my stock to but one cow; and this I had the misfortune to loose the next winter. That left me wholly destitute of a single hough of a creature: of course the second summer I had to support my family without a cow. I would here notice that I spent the summer before I moved, in Wolcott, in making preparation for a settlement, which, however, was of no avail to me, and I lost the summer; and to forward my intended preparation, I brought on a yoke of oxen, and left them, when I returned in the fall, with a man in Johnson, to keep through the winter, on certain conditions; but when I came on in the spring, one of them was dead, and this yoke of oxen that I put off for my land was made of the two surviving ones. But to proceed, in the fall I had the good fortune to purchase another cow; but my misfortunes still continued, for in the June following she was killed by a singular accident. Again I was left without a cow, and here I was again frustrated in my calculations: this last cow left a fine heifer calf that in the next fall I lost by being choaked. Soon after I arrived, I took two cows to double in four years. I had one of my own besides, which died in calving. In June following, one of those taken to double, was killed while fighting: the other was found dead in the yard; both of which I had to replace. In the same spring, one of my neighbor's oxen hooked a bull of two years old, which caused his death soon after. Here I was left destitute — no money to buy, or article to traffic for one: but there was a door opened. I was informed that a merchant in Haverhill was buying snakeroot and sicily. This was a new kind of traffic that I had no great faith in; but I thought to improve every means or semblance of means in my power. Accordingly, with the help of my two oldest girls, I dug and dried a horse-load, and carried this new commodity to the merchant; but this was like most hearsay reports of fine markets, always a little way ahead, for he knew nothing about this strange article, and would not even venture to make an offer; but after a long conference I importuned with the good merchant to give me a three year old heifer for my roots, on certain conditions too tedious to mention. I drove her home, and with joy she was welcomed to my habitation, and it has been my good fortune to have a cow ever since. Though my faith was weak; yet being vigilant and persevering, I obtained the object, and the wilderness produced me a cow.

When I came into Wolcott, my farming tools consisted of one axe and an old hoe. The first year I cleared about two acres, wholly without any team, and being short of provision was obliged to work the chief of the time till harvest with scarce a sufficiency to support nature. My work was chiefly by the river. When too faint to labor, for want of food, I used to take a fish from the river, broil it on the coals, and eat it without bread or salt, and then to my work again. This was my common practice the first year till harvest. I could not get a single potato to plant the first season, so scarce was this article. I then thought if I could but get enough of this valuable production to eat I would never complain. I rarely see this article cooked, but the thought strikes my mind; in fact to this day I have a great veneration for this precious root. I planted that which I cleared in season with corn; and an early frost ruined the crop, so that I raised nothing the first year: had again to buy my provision. My seed corn, about eight quarts, cost me two and a half yards of whitened linen, yard wide, and this I had to go twenty miles after. Though this may be called extortion, it was a solitary instance of the kind; all were friendly and ready to assist me in my known distress, as far as they had ability. An uncommon degree of sympathy pervaded all the new settlers, and I believe this man heartily repented the act, for he was by no means indigent, and was many times reminded of it by way of reproof.

My scanty supply of bread-corn made it necessary to improve the first fruits of harvest at Lake Champlain, to alleviate our distress, it being earlier than with us. Accordingly, on the last days of July or first of August, I took my sickle, and set out for the Lake, a distance of better than forty miles. When I had got there, I found their grain was not ripe enough to begin upon; but was informed that on the Grand Isle they had began their harvest. I was determined to go on, but had nothing to pay my passage. I finally hired a man to carry me over from Georgia for the small compensation of a case and two lances that I happened to have with me; but when I had got on to the Island, I found I was still too early. There was no grain ripe here, but I found the most forward I could, plead my necessity, and stayed by the owner till I got one and a half bushel of wheat, and worked for him to pay for it: it was quite green; I dried it and sat out for home; but my haste to get back prevented my drying it sufficiently. I found a boat bound for Mansfield's mills, on the river Lamoille, and got my grain on board, and had it brought there free from expense. I got it ground, or rather mashed, for it was too damp to make meal. I here hired my meal carried on to Cambridge borough for my sickle, and there got it ground the second time, but it was still far from good meal. From the Borough I was so fortunate as to get it home on a horse. I was a fortnight on this tour. My wife was fearful some accident had happened, and sent a man in pursuit of me, who met me on my way home. I left my family without bread or meal, and was welcomed home with tears: my wife baked a cake, and my children again tasted bread.

I had the good fortune to buy on trust, the winter after I lost my corn, of a man in Cambridge, twenty four miles from home, twelve bushels of corn, and one of wheat. This, by the assistance of some kind friends, I got to Esq. McDaniel's. I also procured by digging on shares in Hydepark, twelve or thirteen bushels of potatoes. This grain and potatoes I carried eight miles on my back. My common practice was one half bushel of meal, and one half bushel of potatoes at a load.

The singular incidents that took place in getting this grain on, though tedious to mention, may be worthy of notice. Soon after I set out from home, sometime in the month of March, it began to rain, and was a very rainy day and night. The Lamoille was raised — the ice became rotten and dangerous crossing — many of the small streams were broken up. The man of whom I purchased the grain was so good as to take his team and carry it to the mill. The owner of the mill asked me how I expected to get my meal home. I answered him as the case really was, that I knew not. The feeling man then offered me his oxen and sled to carry it to the Park, and I thankfully accepted his kind offer. He then turned to the miller, and directed him to grind my grist toll free. While at the mill a man requested me to bring a half hogshead tub on my sled up to Johnson. By permission of the owner of the oxen, he put the tub on the sled, and it was a Providential circumstance; for when I came to Brewster's branch, a wild stream, I found it broken up, run rapid and deep. At first I was perplexed what to do. To go across with my bags on the sled would ruin my meal; I soon thought of the tub; this held about half of my bags; the other half I left on the shore, and proceeded into the branch and crossed with safety. Though I was wet nearly to my middle, I unloaded the tub and returned into the branch, holding the tub on the sled, but the stream was so rapid, the tub being empty, that in spite of all my exertions I was washed off the sled and carried down the stream, holding on to the tub, for this I knew was my only alternative to get across my load. At length I succeeded in getting the tub to the shore, though I was washed down the stream more than twenty rods, sometimes up to my armpits in the water, and how I kept the tub from filling in this hasty struggle, I know not, but so it was. The oxen, though turned towards home, happily for me, when they had got across the stream, stopt in the path, till I came up with the tub. I then put in the other half of my load, and succeeded in getting the whole across the branch, and traveled on about three miles and put up for the night. Wet as I was, and at that season of the year, it is easy to conceive my uncomfortable situation, for the thaw was over, and it was chilly and cold. In the morning I proceeded for home — came to the river; not being sensible how weak the ice was, I attempted to cross, but here a scene ensued that I can never forget. When about half across the river, I perceived the ice settling under my oxen. I jumped on to the tongue of my sled, and hastened to the oxen's heads and pulled out the pin that held the yoke. By this time the oxen were sunk to their knees in water. I then sprang to the sled, and drew it back to the shore, without the least difficulty, notwithstanding the load, and returned to my oxen. By this time they had broken a considerable path in the ice, and were struggling to get out. I could do nothing but stand and see them swim round — sometimes they would be nearly out of sight, nothing scarcely but their horns to be seen — they would then rise and struggle to extricate themselves from their perilous situation. I called for help in vain; and to fly for assistance would have been imprudent and fatal. Notwithstanding my unhappy situation, and the manner by which I came by the oxen, &c. I was not terrified in the least — I felt calm and composed; — at length the oxen swam up to where I stood and laid their heads on the ice at my feet. I immediately took the yoke from off their necks; they lay still till the act was performed, and then returned to swimming as before. By this time they had made an opening in the ice as much as two rods across. One of them finally swam to the down stream side, and in an instant, as if lifted out of the water, he was on his side on the ice, and got up and walked off; the other swam to the same place and was out in the same way. I stood on the opposite side of the opening, and saw with astonishment every movement. I then thought, and the impression is still on my mind, that they were helped out by supernatural means; most certainly no natural cause could produce an effect like this: that a heavy ox six and a half feet in girth, can of his own natural strength heave himself out of the water on his side on the ice, is too extraordinary to reconcile to a natural cause: — that in the course of Divine Providence events do take place out of the common course of nature, that our strongest reasoning cannot comprehend, is impious to deny; though we acknowledge the many chimeras of superstition, ignorance and barbarism in the world; and when we are eye witnesses to such events, it is not for us to doubt, but to believe and tremble. Others have a right to doubt my testimony: but in this instance, for me to doubt would be perjury to my own conscience, and I may add ingratitude to my Divine Benefactor. In fact a signal Providence seemed to direct the path for me to pursue to procure this grain. Though I was doomed to encounter perils, to suffer fatigue and toil, there was a way provided for me to obtain the object in view. In the first onset I accidentally fell in with the man of whom I purchased at the Park. I found he had grain to sell. I requested of him this small supply on trust: we were strangers to each other — a peculiar friend of mine, happening to be by, volunteered his word for the pay. I knew not where nor how to get the money, but necessity drove me to make the purchase, and in the course of the winter I was so fortunate as to catch saple enough to pay the debt by the time it was due. Though I hazarded my word, it was in a good cause — it was for the relief of my family, and so it terminated. But to return.

I had now gone to the extent of my abilities for bread corn, but was destitute of meat; and beef and pork were scarcer in those times. Accordingly I had to have recourse to wild meat for a substitute, and had the good luck to purchase a moose of a hunter; and the meat of two more I brought in on shares — had the one for bringing in the other. These two were uncommonly large — were judged to weigh seven hundred weight each. The meat of these three moose I brought in on my back, together with the large bones and heads. I backed them five or six miles over rough land, cut up by sharp ridges and deep hollows, and interspersed with underbrush and windfalls, which made it impracticable to pass with a hand sled, which, could I have used, would much eased my labour. A more laborious task was this than that of bringing my meal, &c. from the Park.

My practice was to carry my loads in a bag, to tie the ends of the bag so nigh that I could but comfortably get my head through, so that the weight of my load would rest on my shoulders. I often had to encounter this hardship in the time of a thaw, which made the task more severe, especially in the latter part of winter and fore part of the spring, when the snow became coarse and harsh, and will not so readily support the snow-shoe. My hold would often fail without any previous notice to guard against — perhaps slide under a log or catch in a bush and pitch me into the snow with my load about my neck. I have repeatedly had to struggle in this situation for some time to extricate myself from my load, it being impossible to get up with my load on. Those who are acquainted with this kind of burden may form an idea of what I had to encounter — the great difficulty of carrying a load on snow-shoes in the time of a thaw, is one of those kinds of fatigue that it is hard to describe, nor can be conceived but by experience. It is wearisome at such times to travel without a load; but with one, especially at this late season, it is intolerable: but thaw or freeze, my necessities obliged me to be at my task, and still to keep up my burthen. I had to draw my fire-wood through the winter on a hand sled: in fact, my snowshoes were constantly hung to my feet.

Being destitute of team for four or five years, and without farming tools, I had to labor under great embarrassments: my grain I hoed in the three first years. After I raised a sufficiency for my family, I had to carry it twelve miles to mill on my back, for the three first years: this I had constantly to do once a week. My common load was one bushel, and generally carried it eight miles before I stopped to rest. My family necessities once obliged me to carry a moose hide thirty miles on my back, and sell it for a bushel of corn, and bring that home in the same way.

For a specimen of the hardships those have often to encounter who move into the wilderness, I will give the following, that took place the winter after I came on: We had a remarkable snow, the first, of consequence, that fell; it was full two feet deep. Our communication was with the inhabitants of Hydepark, and it was necessary for us to keep the road, or rather path, so that we could travel; we were apprehensive of danger, if we did not immediately tread a path through this snow. I was about out of meal, and had previously left a bushel at a deserted house about five miles on the way. I agreed with Esq. Taylor, he being the only inhabitant with me, to start the next day on the proposed tour. We accordingly started before sunrise; the snow was light, and we sunk deep into it. By the middle of the day it give some, which made it still worse; our snow-shoes loaded at every step: we had to use nearly our whole strength to extricate the loaded shoe from its hold. It seemed that our hip joints would be drawn from their sockets. We were soon worried —

could go but a few steps without stopping; our fatigue and toil became almost insupportable — were obliged often to sit down and rest, and were several times on the point of giving up the pursuit, and stop for the night, but this must have been fatal, as we had no axe to cut wood for a fire; our blood was heated, and we must have chilled. We finally, at about dusk, reached the deserted house, but was in effect exhausted. It seemed we could not have reached this house had it been twenty rods further: so terrible is the toil to travel through deep snow, that no one can have a sense of it till taught by experience. This day's journey is often on my mind; in my many hard struggles it was one of the severest. We struck up a fire and gathered some fuel that lay about the house, and after we had recovered strength, I baked a cake of my meal. We then lay down on some hewn planks, and slept sound till morning. It froze at night; the track we had made rendered it quite feasible travelling. The next day I returned home with my bushel of meal.

Another perilous tour I will mention, that occurred this winter. It was time to bring on another load of meal from Esq. McDaniel's. I proposed in my mind to go early the next morning. There had been a thaw, and in the time of the thaw a man had driven a yoke of oxen from Cabot, and went down on my path, and trod it up. The night was clear — the moon shone bright, and it was remarkably cold. I woke, supposing it nearly day, and sat out, not being sensible of the cold, and being thinly clad I soon found I was in danger of freezing, and began to run, jump, and thrash my hands, &c. The path being full of holes, and a light snow had just fallen that filled them up, I often fell, and was in danger of breaking my limbs, &c. The cold seemed to increase, and I was forced to exert my utmost strength to keep from freezing: my limbs became numb before I got through, though I ran about every step of the eight miles, and when I got to McDaniel's the cocks crowed for day. I was surprised upon coming to the fire to find that the bottoms of my mockasins and stockings were cut and worn through, the bottoms of my feet being entirely bare, having cut them by the holes in the path, but notwithstanding the severity of the frost, I was preserved, not being frozen in any part. Had I broken a limb, or but slightly spraint a joint, which I was in imminent danger of doing, I must have perished on the way, as a few minutes of respite must have been fatal.

In the early part of my residence in Wolcott, by some means I obtained knowledge of their being beaver on a small stream in Hardwick; and desirous to improve every means in my power for the support of my family, and to retrieve my circumstances, I determined on a tour to try my fortune at beaver hunting. Accordingly, late in the fall, I set out in company with my neighbor Taylor on the intended enterprise. We took what was called the Coos road, which was nothing more than marked trees: in about seven miles we reached the stream, and proceeded up it about three miles farther, and searched for beaver, but were soon convinced that they had left the ground. We, however, set a few traps. Soon after we started it began to rain, and before night the rain turned to a moist snow that melted on us as fast as it fell. Before we reached the hunting ground, we were wet to our skins; night soon came on — we found it necessary to camp (as the hunters use the term) ; with difficulty we struck up a fire; but our fuel was poor, chiefly green timber — the storm increased — the snow continued moist; our bad accommodations grew worse and worse; our fire was not sufficient to warm us and much less to dry us; we dared not attempt to lay down, but continued on our feet through the night, feeding our fire and endeavoring to warm our shivering limbs. This is a memorable night to me — the most distressing I ever experienced; we anxiously looked for day. At length the dawn appeared, but it was a dismal and a dreary scene. The moist snow had adhered to every thing in its way; the trees and underwood were remarkably loaded, were completely hid from sight — nothing to be seen but snow, and nothing to be heard but the cracking of the bended boughs under the enormous weight, we could scarcely see a rod at noon day. When light enough to travel, we sat out for home, and finding it not safe to leave the stream for fear of getting bewildered and lost, we followed it back; it was lined the chief of the way with beaver meadow, covered with a thick growth of alders; we had no way to get through them but for one to go forward and beat off the snow with a heavy stick. We thus proceeded, though very slowly, down the stream to the Coos road, and worried through the ten miles home at the dusk of the evening, nearly exhausted by fatigue, wet and cold, for it began to freeze in the morning; our clothes were frozen stiff on our backs; when I pulled off my great coat it was so stiff as to stand up on the floor. In order to save our traps we had to make another trip, and one solitary muskrat made up our compensation for this hunting tour.

A painful circumstance respecting my family I must here mention: In the year 1806 we were visited with sickness that was uncommonly distressing, five being taken down at the same time, and several dangerously ill. In this sickness I lost my wife, the partner of my darkest days, who bore her share of our misfortunes with becoming fortitude. I also lost a daughter at the same time, and another was bedrid about six months, and unable to perform the least labour for more than a year. This grievous calamity involved me in debts that terminated in the loss of my farm, my little all; but by the indulgence of feeling relatives I am still permitted to stay on it. Though I have been doomed to hard fortune I have been blest with a numerous offspring; have had by my two wives seventeen children, thirteen of them daughters; have had forty-seven grand-children, and six great grand-children, making my posterity seventy souls.

I have here given but a sketch of my most important sufferings. The experienced farmer will readily discover, that under the many embarrassments I had to encounter, I must make but slow progress in clearing land; no soul to help me, no funds to go to: raw and inexperienced in this kind of labor, though future wants pressed the necessity of constant application to this business, a great portion of my time was unavoidably taken up in pursuit of sustenance for my family; however reluctant to leave my labor, the support of nature must be attended to, the calls of hunger cannot be dispensed with. I have now to remark, that at this present time, my almost three score years and ten, I feel the want of those forced exertions of bodily strength that were spent in those perils and fatigues, and have worn down my constitution, to support my decaying nature.

When I reflect on those past events, the fatigue and toil I had to encounter, the dark scenes I had to pass through, I am struck with wonder and astonishment at the fortitude and presence of mind that I then had to bear me up under them. Not once was I discouraged or disheartened: I exercised all my powers of body and mind to do the best I could, and left the effect for future events to decide, without embarrassing my mind with imaginary evils. I could lay down at night, forgetting my troubles, and sleep composed and calm as a child; I did in reality experience the just proverb of the wise man, that "the sleep of the laboring man is sweet, whether he eat little or much." Nor can I close my tale of sufferings without rendering my feeble tribute of thanks and praise to my benign Benefactor, who supplies the wants of the needy, and relieves the distressed, that in his wise Providence has assisted my natural strength both of body and of mind to endure those scenes of distress and toil.

County of Orleans, Nov'r. 1824.

The undersigned, having read in manuscript the foregoing Narrative, and having lived in habits of intimacy with, and in the neighborhood of Mr. Hubbell at the time of his sufferings, we are free to inform the public, that we have no doubt but his statements are, in substance, correct. Many

[133]

of the circumstances therein narrated we were at the time personally knowing to, and are sensible more might be added without exaggeration, in many
instances wherein he suffered.

> Thomas Taylor, *Justice of Peace.*
> Darius Fitch, *J. of Peace.*
> John McDaniel, *J. P.*
> Jesse Whitney, *J. P.*

[*Timothy Dwight*]

1797. In New Concord [N. H.] township we began to find the
bridges, and causeys, made of round sticks, and logs. These are built
in the following manner. Two large logs are laid from one bank to
the other: and these are covered by other small logs, laid in contact,
transversely. The surface, which they present, is slippery, cylindrical,
and of course unpleasant. They are also liable to speedy, and unperceived, decay; and when they appear still to be sound, sometimes
yield suddenly to the foot, and hazard the lives both of the horse
and his rider. When these bridges are once broken, they are frequently left a long time without repair. The inhabitants in the most
recent settlements, you will remember, are few, thinly scattered, and
poor; and are also engrossed by their domestic difficulties. At the
same time they are so used to these and other inconveniences, that
they feel them very little. Hence the necessary repairs are often neglected for a long time. It ought, however, to be by no means forgotten, that these settlers, amidst all their embarrassment, labour,
and contribute, for the improvement of roads and bridges, more in
proportion to their means, than any other people.

A *log-house* is built in the same manner, as the weekwams, which
have been constructed in later times by the Indians, having been
derived from their intercourse with the Colonists. The logs, intended for this purpose, are chosen of one size, and hewn on two
opposite sides. They are then cut down to half the thickness at each
end, on one of the hewn sides. After this, they are laid upon each
other at right angles, and fastened together with wooden pins so as
to form the external walls of the building. In this manner they are
carried up to a sufficient height; and covered with a roof, usually
of shingles. The crevices are then stopped with mortar; and the interiour is finished according to the fancy, and circumstances, of the
proprietor; always, however, in a plain, and usually a coarse and
indifferent, manner. It will be sufficient to observe here, that, although they are often absolutely necessary to the planter, when he

first adventures into the forest, yet they are certainly no ornaments to the landscape. By the New-England planters they are intended only to shelter their families, until they can erect better habitations.

As to the opinion, that the Climate has already become milder, and is gradually advancing towards the mildness of the European Climates in the same latitudes, I can only say, that I doubt the fact. Indeed, the observation of this subject has been so loose, and the records are so few and imperfect, as to leave our real knowledge of it very limited. Within my own remembrance no such change has taken place. It is unquestionably true, that very severe seasons existed in the early periods of New-England; and it is equally certain that they exist now. The winters of 1780, 1784, 1788, and 1805, were probably as severe, as those of 1641 and 1696; and the snow, which fell in 1717, was, I am persuaded, not so great, as that which began to fall on the 20th of February, 1802. In 1641, and 1696, sleighs and sleds crossed the Harbour of Boston; and some of them went down on the ice to Nantasket, nine miles. In 1780 the British Dragoons passed from New-York to Staten Island: a distance of ten miles. In 1784 the sound was frozen entirely across at Fairfield; where it is eighteen miles wide. The effects of the cold on the apple-trees, and peach trees, were in 1788 greater in the County of Fairfield, than are recorded of any other period. The Western sides of the Apple trees were, in many instances, killed to a considerable extent: a fact, unprecedented within the knowledge of any living inhabitant: and the peach trees were destroyed in very great multitudes: a fact, which rarely, if ever, from the same cause, takes place in a single instance. The Sound was, indeed, not frozen: but the reason was obvious. The wind blew violently, with hardly any intermission, either by night or by day. The water was, of course, too much agitated to admit of its being frozen. In streams, and ponds, thicker ice was, I believe, never known in this country. In 1792 the Sound was frozen at Fairfield about five weeks. The snow in 1717 fell six feet deep. It fell to an equal depth, in Northampton, in 1740. From February 21, 1802, it fell during the principal part of a week. It ought rather to be called hail; for it was a mixture of hail with snow, in which the former predominated, and was so dense, that it contained more than double the quantity of water usually found in the same depth of snow. Had it been snow only: it would, at least, have been eight feet deep.

The husbandry of New-England is far inferior to that of Great-Britain. It is, however, superiour to that of any other class of people in the United States; unless the Germans, settled in the counties of

Lancaster and York in Pennsylvania, and in the valley of the Shenandoah in Virginia, are to be excepted. I speak, here, of a body of people, not of individuals; nor of a little collection of persons on a small tract. With this cultivation the average produce of wheat in Connecticut is by information, on which I rely, fifteen bushels an acre; and that of maize twenty five bushels. The greatest crop of wheat, which I have known in Connecticut was forty bushels an acre; the greatest crop of maize one hundred and eighteen. The quantity of wheat, usually sown is one bushel and a half peck, to the acre.

Wheat is sown with the broad cast. Maize is planted in hills, from three to four feet apart, in a manner resembling a quincunx. The number of stalks in a hill should be not more than four nor less than three. The ground is afterwards broken, sometimes with a harrow, made in the form of a triangle, and sometimes with a plough; each drawn by a single horse. In stony grounds a larger plough is used; and is drawn by a yoke of oxen. The ground is then cleaned with the hoe. The process is repeated at least three times, and not unfrequently four: at the last of which the earth is raised to the height of from four to six inches, around the corn, and is denominated a hill; whence every planting is called a *hill of corn*. The hill is made, to give a better opportunity for the roots, which, when the stalk is grown to a considerable height, shoot from it several inches above the surface, to insert themselves in the ground with more ease, and less hazard of failure. These roots are called braces; because they appear to be formed for the sole purpose of supporting the stalk.

The principal defects in our husbandry, so far as I am able to judge, are a deficiency in the quantity of labour, necessary to prepare the ground for seed; insufficient manuring; the want of a good rotation of crops; and slovenliness in cleaning the ground. The soil is not sufficiently pulverized; nor sufficiently manured. We are generally ignorant of what crops will best succeed each other; and our fields are covered with a rank growth of weeds. Those, indeed, which are planted with maize, and potatoes, are kept, during the vegetation of these plants, tolerably clean; but whenever the hoe ceases from its task, become again very weedy. I have often thought, when passing by a field, from which a crop of wheat or rye had been taken, that the crop of weeds, which grew the same year, would weigh more than either. These evils are understood, and felt; but the price of labour, not unfrequently twelve dollars a month, prevents them from being removed. Superiour skill would, however, remove them in part.

[136]

But, defective as our Agriculture is, it has been considerably improved within the last thirty years; and is now fast improving.

We have in New-England no such class of men, as on the Eastern side of the Atlantic are denominated *peasantry*. The number of those, who are mere labourers, is almost nothing, except in a few of the populous towns; and almost all these are collected from the shiftless, the idle, and the vicious. A great part of them are foreigners. Here every apprentice originally intends to establish, and with scarcely an exception, actually establishes himself in business. Every seaman designs to become, and a great proportion of them really become, mates, and masters, of vessels; and every young man, hired to work upon a farm, aims steadily to acquire a farm for himself; and hardly one fails of the acquisition. We have few of those amphibious beings, of whom you have such a host; who pass through life under the name of *journeymen*. All men, here, are masters of themselves: and such is the combined effect of education, and society, that he who fails of success in one kind of business, may almost of course betake himself with advantage to another.

The means of comfortable living, are in New-England so abundant, and so easily obtained, as to be within the reach of every man who has health, industry, common honesty, and common sense. Labour commands such a price, that every labourer of this character may earn from one hundred and twenty-five to two hundred and fifty dollars a year. Hence every one may within a moderate period purchase himself a farm of considerable extent in the recent settlements, and a small one in those which are older. Even those, who are somewhat below the common level in these attributes, may, and do, acquire small houses, and gardens, where they usually live comfortably.

The food of the inhabitants at large, even of the poor, is principally flesh, and fish; one or other of which is eaten by a greater part of the inhabitants twice and three times a day. A breakfast, in the large towns, is chiefly bread and butter; the bread in the cool season generally toasted. In the country almost universally this is accompanied with smoke-dried beef, cheese, or some species of fish or flesh broiled, or otherwise fitted to the taste of the family. So universal is this custom, that a breakfast without such an addition is considered as scarcely worth eating. At dinner, the vegetables, which I formerly mentioned, continually succeed each other in their varieties. Fruits also, which you will remember are here very numerous and various, as well as very rich and luscious, are brought upon the dinner-table, or are eaten in other parts of the day, throughout most of the year. Supper, in most parts of the country, is like the breakfast; except that it is made up partially of preserved fruits, different kinds of cake, pies, tarts, &c. The meats, used at breakfast and supper, are generally intended to be dainties.

Puddings, formed of rice, flour, maize, and sometimes of buckwheat, very frequently constitute a part of the dinner.

Pork, except the hams, shoulders, and cheeks, is never converted into bacon. I do not know, that I ever saw a flitch of bacon, cured

in New-England, in my life. The sides of the hog are here always pickled; and by the New England people are esteemed much superiour to bacon. The pork of New-England is fatted upon maize; a sweeter and richer food for cattle of all kinds, than any other; is more skilfully cured; and is, therefore, better than that of any other country. It is also a favourite food with most of the inhabitants.

Tea and coffee constitute a part of the breakfast, and supper, of every class; and of almost every individual. The principal drink of the inhabitants is cider. Wine, which is here very cheap, is extensively used: so in the mild season is punch. Porter, also, is drunk by fashionable people; and in small quantities, ale. In the large towns, particularly in Boston, dinners are given without number; but much more unfrequently in the smaller ones. The favourite entertainment in them is the supper. For this there are two potent reasons. One is, every body is here employed in business through the day. The evening, being the only season of leisure, furnishes the best opportunity for that agreeable intercourse, which is the primary object of all entertainments. The other is, the want of a sufficient number of servants to take the burden of superintending the preparation of dinners from the mistress of the family. I have been present at a very great multitude of entertainments of both kinds; and am compelled to say, that those of evening are much the most pleasant, and rational. There is less excess, and more leisure; the mind is more cheerful; and the conversation almost of course more sprightly, interesting, and useful.

The hours of breakfast vary in the country from six to eight in the summer, and from seven to nine in the winter: those of dinner from twelve to two: those of supper from five to eight. In the large towns all these hours vary still more. The most fashionable people breakfast late; and dine from three to four. The food of such people is principally taken at a single meal. In the summer many of the labouring people make their principal meal at supper.

The proportion of animal food, eaten in this country, is, I think, excessive.

At entertainments, the dining-table is loaded with a much greater

variety of dishes than good sense will justify. A fashion, which it is difficult to resist, prevails, in this respect, over every rational consideration.

The quantity of ardent spirits, consumed chiefly by the middle and lower classes of people, is scandalous to its character, although much less in its amount than that drunk by the same number of people in Great-Britain.

The dress of the inhabitants is chiefly formed of the manufactures, and made up in the fashions, of Europe; particularly of Great-Britain.

The principal amusements of the inhabitants are visiting, dancing, music, conversation, walking, riding, sailing, shooting at a mark, draughts, chess, and unhappily in some of the larger towns, cards, and dramatic exhibitions. A considerable amusement is also furnished in many places by the examination, and exhibitions, of the superiour schools; and a more considerable one, by the public exhibitions of Colleges.

Our countrymen also fish, and hunt.

Journeys, taken for pleasure, are very numerous; and are a very favourite object.

Boys, and young men, play at foot-ball, cricket, quoits, and at many other sports of an athletic cast; and in the winter are peculiarly fond of skating. Riding in a sleigh, or sledge, is also a favourite diversion in New-England.

People of wealth, and many in moderate circumstances, have their children taught music; particularly on the piano-forte; and many of the young men play on the German flute; violin, clarionet, &c. Serenading is not unfrequent.

Visiting, on the plan of sociality and friendship, is here among all classes of people, especially among those who are intelligent, and refined, a very agreeable, and very rational, source of enjoyment; and is usually free from the crowds and confusion, the ceremony and frivolity, which so often render scenes of this nature wearisome in great cities, and force the hours, devote to them, to drag heavily: while

> The heart, distrusting, asks if this be joy.

Visits are here formed for the purposes of interchanging thought, affection, hospitality, and pleasure. With far less parade, less inconvenience to the family visited, and less trouble to the visitors, they are fraught with more cordiality, more good sense, more sprightliness, and incomparably more pleasure. The themes of conversation are of a superior class; the affections, and sentiments, are set upon a higher key; and the company part, not with eagerness, but with regret.

Reading also is a favourite employment with persons in almost all conditions of life. A considerable collection of books throughout a great part of this country, is furnished to the inhabitants by the social libraries, heretofore mentioned. Private libraries are undoubtedly much more limited than in Great-Britain. Many of them are, however, sufficient collections to extend much useful information, and to supply not a small fund of pleasure to their proprietors and others. By these means a great number of persons are enabled to read as extensively as their other avocations will permit; and all, who love reading, will find, or make, opportunities for pursuing it, which in the aggregate, will constitute a considerable, as well as valuable and delightful, part of their lives. Accordingly this employment is pursued by men, and women, in almost every sphere of life.*

* The reading of Newspapers in this country is undoubtedly excessive; as is also the number of such papers annually published. Yet it cannot be denied that newspapers, conducted with moderation, integrity, and skill, are capable of being useful to a community; or that the reading of them to some extent is a pleasant, rational, and profitable employment. Several newspapers in this country are conducted by men of education and talents.

There is not, there never was, a more quiet, or more orderly state of society than that, which has existed in Connecticut from the beginning, and in all the old settlements of New-England, with too few exceptions to deserve notice. Against this proof from experience, the conjectures of the most learned men on the other side of the Atlantic, will to a New-Englander, be urged in vain. The Magistrate in the mean time will here see his official duty stripped of half its incumbrances; and peace established around him by the good sense, and good principles, of those whom he governs. The Minister will behold his church and congregation, ordinarily settled upon firmer foundations, and yielding less to every wind of doctrine, than in most other countries. The neighbourhood, also will be rendered social, and pleasant; and life pass on with more peace, and comfort, than were ever yielded by ignorance.

To the individuals, who are thus enlightened; enlightened, I mean, when compared with those of other countries in the same circumstances; the advantages are often incalculable. A New-Englander imbibes from this education an universal habit of combining the objects of thought, and comparing them in such a manner, as to generalize his views with no small degree of that readiness, and skill, which in many countries are considered as peculiar to a scientifical education. Hence he often discerns means of business, and profit, which elsewhere are chiefly concealed from men of the same class. Hence, when prevented from pursuing one kind of business, or unfortunate in it, he easily, and in very many instances successfully, commences another. Hence he avails himself of occurrences which are unregarded by most other men.

From this source have been derived many original machines for abridging human labour, and improving its results; not a small number of which have been invented by persons, who had received no education, except that, which has excited these observations. A house-joiner in Massachusetts, if I have been correctly informed, has invented a stocking loom, which weaves six stockings a day. Universally, our people are by this degree of education fitted to make the best of their circumstances, both at home and abroad; to find subsistence where others would fail of it; to advance in their property, and their influence, where others would stand still; and to extricate themselves from difficulties, where others would despond. Universally also, they teach their children more, and better things, than persons of less information teach theirs; and are regularly induced to give them, if possible, a better education than themselves have received.

In a war on the land, and on the water, the New-Englanders, with the same discipline, and experience, will be found more expert, both as soldiers and seamen, than the inhabitants of most other countries.

[*Samuel Griswold Goodrich*]

At the date of my earliest recollection, in the 1790's, the society of Ridgefield was exclusively English, and the manners and customs such as might have been expected, under the modifying influence of existing circumstances. I remember but one Irishman, one negro, and one Indian in the town. The first had begged and blarneyed his way from Long Island, where he had been wrecked; the second was a liberated slave; and the last was the vestige of a tribe, which dwelt of yore in a swampy tract, the name of which I have forgotten. We had a professed beggar, called Jagger, who had served in the armies of more than one of the Georges, and insisted upon crying "God save the king!" even on the 4th of July, and when openly threatened by the boys with a gratuitous ride on a rail. We had one settled pauper, Mrs. Yabacomb, who, for the first dozen years of my life, was my standard type for the witch of Endor.

Nearly all the inhabitants of Ridgefield were farmers, with the few mechanics that were necessary to carry on society in a somewhat primeval state. Even the persons not professionally devoted to agriculture, had each his farm or at least his garden and home lot, with his pigs, poultry, and cattle. The population might have been 1200, comprising two hundred families. All could read and write, but in point of fact, beyond the Almanac and Watts' Psalms and Hymns, their literary acquirements had litle scope. There were, I think, four newspapers, all weekly, published in the State: one at Hartford, one at New London, one at New Haven, and one at Litchfield. There were, however, not more than three subscribers to all these in our village. We had, however, a public library of some two hundred volumes, and what was of equal consequence — the town was on the road which was then the great thoroughfare, connecting Boston with New York, and thence it had means of intelligence from travelers constantly passing through the place, which kept it up with the march of events.

If Ridgefield was thus rather above the average of Connecticut villages in its range of civilization, I suppose the circumstances and modes of life in my father's family, were somewhat above those of most people around us. We had a farm of forty acres, with four cows, two horses, and some two dozen sheep, to which may be added a stock of poultry, including a flock of geese. My father carried on the farm, besides preaching two sermons a week, and attending to other parochial duties — visiting the sick, attending funerals, solemnizing marriages, &c. He personally laid out the beds and planted the garden, he pruned the fruit-trees, and worked with the men in the meadow in the press of haying-time. He generally cut the corn-stalks himself, and always shelled the ears; the latter being done by drawing them across the handle of the frying-pan, fastened over a wash-tub. I was sometimes permitted, as an indulgence, to spell my father in this, which was a favorite employment. With these and a few other exceptions, our agricultural operations were carried on by hired help.

The household, as well as political, economy of these days lay in this, that every family lived as much as possible within itself. Money was scarce, wages being about fifty cents a day, though these were generally paid in meat, vegetables, and other articles of use — seldom in money. There was not a factory of any kind in the place.* There was a butcher, but he only went from house to house to slaughter the cattle and swine of his neighbors. There was a tanner, but he only dressed other people's skins: there was a clothier, but he generally fulled and dressed other people's cloth. All this is typical of the mechanical operations of the place. Even dyeing blue a portion of the wool, so as to make linsey-woolsey for short-gowns, aprons, and blue-mixed stockings — vital necessities in those days — was a domestic operation. During the autumn, a dye-tub in the chimney corner — thus placed so as to be cherished by the genial heat — was as familiar in all thrifty houses, as the Bible or the back-log. It was covered with a board, and formed a cosy seat in the wide-mouthed fireplace, especially of a chill evening. When the night had waned, and the family had retired, it frequently became the anxious seat of the lover, who was permitted to carry on his courtship, the object of his addresses sitting demurely in the opposite corner. Some of the first families in Connecticut, I suspect, could their full annals be written, would find their foundations to have been laid in these chimney-corner courtships.

Being thus exposed, this institution of the dye-tub was the frequent subjects of distressing and exciting accidents. Among the early, indelible incidents in my memory, happening to all vigorous

---

* I recollect, as an after-thought, one exception. There was a hatter who supplied the town; but he generally made hats to order, and usually in exchange for the skins of foxes, rabbits, muskrats, and other chance peltry. I frequently purchased my powder and shot from the proceeds of skins which I sold him.

characters, turning this over is one of the most prominent. Nothing so roused the indignation of thrifty housewives, for besides the ignominious avalanche of blue upon the floor, there was an infernal appeal made to another sense than of sight. Every youth of parts was laden with experience in this way. I have a vague impression that Philip N . . ., while courting H . . . M . . ., was suspended

for six weeks, for one of these mischances. If it was not he, it was some other spark of that generation.

To this general system of domestic economy our family was not an exception. Every autumn, it was a matter of course that we had a fat ox or a fat cow, ready for slaughter. One full barrel was salted down; the hams were cut out, slightly salted, and hung up in the chimney for a few days, and thus became "dried" and "hung beef," then as essential as the staff of life. Pork was managed in a similar way, though even on a larger scale, for two barrels were indispensable. A few pieces, as the spare-ribs, &c., were distributed to the neighbors, who paid in kind when they killed their swine.

Mutton and poultry came in their turn, all from our own stock, save that on Thanksgiving-day some of the magnates gave the parson a turkey. This, let me observe, in those good old times, was a bird of mark; no timid, crouching biped, with downcast head and pallid countenance, but stalking like a lord and having wattles red as a "banner bathed in slaughter." His beard, or in modern parlance, his *goat,* without the aid of gum and black-ball, was so long, shining, and wiry, that it might have provoked the envy of his modern human rival in foppery. There was, in fact, something of the genius of the native bird still in him, for though the race was nearly extinct, a few wild flocks lingered in the remote woods. Occasionally in the depths of winter, and along to the early spring, these stole to the barnyard, and held communion with their civilized compatriots. Severe battle ensued among the leaders for the favors of the fair, and as the wild cocks always conquered, the vigor of the race was kept up.

Our bread was of rye, tinged with Indian meal. Wheat bread was reserved for the sacrament and company; a proof not of its superiority, but of its scarcity and consequent estimation. All the vegetables came from our garden and farm. The fuel was supplied by our own woods — sweet-scented hickory, snapping chestnut, odoriferous oak, and reeking, fizzling ash — the hot juice of the latter, by the way, being a sovereign antidote for the ear-ache. These were laid in huge piles, all alive with sap, on the tall, gaunt andirons. You might have thought you heard John Rogers and his family at the stake, by their plaintive simmerings. The building of a fire was a real architectural achievement, favored by the wide yawning fireplace, and was always begun by daybreak. There was first a back-log, from fifteen to four and twenty inches in diameter and five feet long, imbedded in the ashes; then came a top log; then a fore stick; then a middle stick, and then a heap of kindlings, reaching from the bowels down to the bottom. A-top of all was a pyramid of smaller fragments, artfully adjusted, with spaces for the blaze.

Friction matches had not then been sent from the regions of brimstone, to enable every boy or beggar to carry a conflagration in his pocket. If there were no coals left from the last night's fire, and none to be borrowed from the neighbors, resort was had to flint, steel, and tinder-box. Often, when the flint was dull, and the steel soft, and the tinder damp, the striking of fire was a task requiring both energy and patience. If the edifice on the andirons was skilfully constructed, the spark being applied, there was soon a furious stinging smoke, which Silliman told the world some years after, consisted mainly of pyroligneous acid. Nevertheless, in utter ignorance of this philosophical fact, the forked flame soon began to lick the sweating sticks above, and by the time the family had arisen, and assembled in the "keeping room," there was a roaring blaze, which defied even the bitter blast of winter — which, by the way, found abundant admittance through the crannies of the doors and windows. To feed the family fire in those days, during the severe season, was fully one man's work.

But to go on with our household history. Sugar was partially supplied by our maple-trees. These were tapped in March, the sap be-

MAKING MAPLE SUGAR

ing collected, and boiled down in the woods. This was wholly a domestic operation, and one in which all the children rejoiced, each taking his privilege of an occasional sip or dip, from the period of the limpid sap, to the granulated condiment. Nevertheless, the chief supply of sugar was from the West Indies.

Rum was largely consumed, but our distilleries had scarcely begun. A half-pint of it was given as a matter of course to every day laborer, more particularly in the summer season. In all families, rich or poor, it was offered to male visitors as an essential point of hospitality, or even good manners. Women — I beg pardon — ladies, took their schnapps, then named "Hopkins' Elixir," which was the most delicious and seductive means of getting tipsy that has been invented. Crying babies were silenced with hot toddy, then esteemed an infallible remedy for wind on the stomach. Every man imbibed his morning dram, and this was esteemed temperance. There is a story of a preacher about those days, who thus lectured his parish: "I say nothing, my beloved brethren, against taking a little bitters before breakfast, and after breakfast, especially if you are used to it. What I contend against is this dramming, dramming, dramming, at all hours of the day. There are some men who take a glass at eleven o'clock in the forenoon, and at four in the afternoon. I do not purpose to contend against old established customs, my brethren, rendered respectable by time and authority; but this dramming, dramming, is a crying sin in the land."

However absurd this may seem now, it was not then very wide of the public sentiment. Huxham's tincture was largely prescribed by the physicians. Tansey bitters were esteemed a sort of panacea, moral as well as physical, for even the morning prayer went up heavily without it. The place of Stoughton — for this mixture was not then invented — was supplied by a tuft of tansey which Providence seemed to place somewhere in every man's garden or home lot.

As to brandy, I scarcely heard of it, so far as I can recollect, till I was sixteen years old, and as apprentice in a country store, was called upon to sell it. Cider was the universal table beverage. Cider brandy and whisky were soon after evoked from the infernal caldron of evil spirits. I remember, in my boyhood, to have seen a strange, zigzag tin tube, denominated a "still," belonging to one of our neighbors, converting, drop by drop, certain innocent liquids into the infernal fire-water. But, in the days I speak of, French brandy was rather confined to the houses of the rich, and to the drug shop.

Wine in our country towns was then almost exclusively used for the sacrament. I remember to have heard a story of these days, which is suggestive. The Rev. Dr. G . . . of J . . . had a brother who had lived some years in France, and was familiar with the wines of that country. On a certain occasion, he dined with his clerical brother, who after dinner gave him a glass of this beverage. The visitor having tasted it, shrugged his shoulders, and made wry faces.

"Where did you get this liquor, brother?" said he.

"Why it is some that was left over from the sacrament, and my deacons sent it to me."

"I don't wonder, brother," was the reply, "that your church is so small, now that I know what wine you give them."

There was, of course, no baker in Ridgefield; each family not only made its own bread, cakes, and pies, but their own soap, candles, butter, cheese, and the like. The fabrication of cloth, linen, and woolen was no less a domestic operation. Cotton — that is, raw cotton — was then wholly unknown among us at the North, except as a mere curiosity, produced somewhere in the tropics; but whether it grew on a plant, or an animal, was not clearly settled in the public mind.

We raised our own flax, rotted it, hackled it, dressed it, and spun it. The little wheel, turned by the foot, had its place, and was as familiar as if it had been a member of the family. How often have I seen my mother, and my grandmother too, sit down to it — though this, as I remember, was for the purpose of spinning some finer kind of thread — the burden of the spinning being done by a neighbor of ours, Sally St. John. By the way, she was a good-hearted, cheerful old maid, who petted me beyond my deserts. I grieve to say, that I repaid her partiality by many mischievous pranks, for which I should have been roundly punished, had not the good creature, like charity, covered a multitude of sins. I did indeed get filliped for catching her foot one day in a steel-trap, but I declare that I was innocent of malice prepense, inasmuch as I had set that trap for a rat instead of the said Sally. Nevertheless, the verdict was against me, not wholly because of my misdemeanor in this particular instance, but partly upon the general theory that if I did not deserve punishment for that, I had deserved it, and should deserve it for something else, and so it was safe to administer it.

The wool was also spun in the family, partly by my sisters, and partly by Molly Gregory, daughter of our neighbor, the town carpenter. I remember her well as she sang and spun aloft in the attic. In those days, church singing was one of the fine arts — the only one, indeed, which flourished in Ridgefield, except the music of the drum and fife. The choir was divided into four parts, ranging on three sides of the meeting-house gallery. The tenor, led by Deacon Hawley, was in front of the pulpit, the base to the left, and the treble and counter to the right * — the whole being set in motion by a pitch-pipe, made by the deacon himself, who was a cabinet maker. Molly took upon herself the entire counter, for she had excellent lungs. The fuging tunes, which had then run a little mad, were her delight, and of all these, Montgomery was the general favorite. In her solitary operations aloft, I have often heard her send forth from the attic windows, the droning hum of her wheel, with fitful snatches of a hymn, in which the base began, the tenor followed, then the treble, and finally, the counter — winding up with irresistible pathos. Molly singing to herself, and all unconscious of eavesdroppers, carried on all the parts, thus:

Base. Long for a cooling —
Tenor. Long for a cooling —
Treble. Long for a cooling —
Counter. Long for a cooling stream at hand,
And they must drink or die !

The knitting of stockings was performed by the female part of the family in the evening, and especially at tea parties. According to the theory of society in that golden age, this was a moral as well as an economical employment, inasmuch as Satan was held to find

Some mischief still   For idle hands to do.

Satan, however, dodged the question, for if the hands were occupied, the tongue was loose; and it was said that in some families, he kept them well occupied with idle gossip. At all events, pianos, chess-boards, graces, battledoors, and shuttlecocks with other safety-valves of the kind, were only known by the hearing of the ear, as belonging to some such Vanity Fair as New York or Boston.

The weaving of cloth — linen, as well as woolen — was performed

* This separation of a choir is seldom practiced now in our churches, but was in general use at this period.

[149]

by an itinerant workman, who came to the house, put up his loom, and threw his shuttle, till the season's work was done. The linen was bleached, and made up by the family; the woolen cloth was sent to the fuller to be dyed and dressed. Twice a year, that is, in the spring and autumn, the tailor came to the house and fabricated the semi-annual stock of clothes for the male members — this being called "whipping the cat."

Mantuamakers and milliners came in their turn, to fit out the female members of the family. There was a similar process as to boots and shoes. We sent the hides of the cattle — cows and calves we had killed — to the tanner, and these came back in assorted leather. Occasionally a little morocco, then wholly a foreign manufacture, was bought at the store, and made up for the ladies' best shoes. Amby Benedict, the circulating shoemaker, upon due notice, came with his bench, lapstone, and awls, and converted some little room into a shop, till the household was duly shod. He was a merry fellow, and threw in lots of singing gratis. He played all the popular airs upon the lapstone — as hurdygurdies and hand-organs do now.

Carpets were then only known in a few families, and were confined to the keeping-room and parlor. They were all home-made: the warp consisting of woolen yarn, and the woof of lists and old woolen cloth, cut into strips, and sewed together at the ends. Coverlids generally consisted of quilts, made of pieces of waste calico, elaborately sewed together in octagons, and quilted in rectangles, giving the whole a gay and rich appearance. This process of quilting generally brought together the women of the neighborhood, married and single, and a great time they had of it — what with tea, talk, and stitching. In the evening, the beaux were admitted, so that a quilting was a real festival, not unfrequently getting young people into entanglements which matrimony alone could unravel.

I am here reminded of a sort of communism or socialism which prevailed in our rural districts long before Owen or Fourier was born. If some old Arcadian of the golden age had written his life, as I now write mine, I have no doubt that it would have appeared that this system existed then and there, and that these pretended inventors were mere imitators. At all events, at Ridgefield we used to have "stone bees," when all the men of a village or hamlet came together with their draft cattle, and united to clear some patch of earth which had been stigmatized by nature with an undue visitation of stones and rocks. All this labor was gratuitously rendered, save only that the proprietor of the land furnished the grog. Such a meeting was always of course a very social and sociable affair.

When the work was done, gymnastic exercises — such as hopping, wrestling, and foot-racing — took place among the athletic young men. My father generally attended these celebrations as a looker-on. It was indeed the custom for the clergy of the olden time, to mingle with the people, even in their labors and their pastimes. For some reason or other, it seemed that things went better when the parson gave them his countenance. I followed my father's example, and attended these cheerful and beneficial gatherings. Most of the boys of the town did the same. I may add that, if I may trust the traditions of Ridgefield, the cellar of our new house was dug by a *bee* in a single day, and that was Christmas.

House-raising and barn-raising, the framework being always of wood, were done in the same way by neighborly gatherings of the people. I remember an anecdote of a church-raising, which I may as well relate here. In the eastern part of the State, I think at Lyme, or Pautipaug, a meeting-house was destroyed by lightning. After a year or two, the society mustered its energies, and raised the frame of another on the site of the old one. It stood about six months, and was then blown over.

In due time, another frame was prepared, and the neighborhood gathered together to raise it. It was now proposed by Deacon Hart that they should commence the performance by a prayer and hymn, it having been suggested that perhaps the want of these pious preliminaries on former occasions, had something to do with the calamitous results which attended them. When all was ready, therefore, a prayer was made, and the chorister of the place deaconed * the first two lines of the hymn thus:

> If God to build the house deny,
> The builders work in vain.

This being sung, the chorister completed the verse thus, adapting the lines to the occasion:

> Unless the Lord doth shingle it,
> It will blow down agin!

I must not fail to give you a portrait of one of our village homes — of the middle class — at this era. I take as an example that of our

* Deaconing a hymn or psalm, was adopted on occasions when there was but a single book, or perhaps but one or two books, at hand — a circumstance more common fifty years ago, when singing-books were scarce, than at present, when books of all kinds render food for the mind as cheap and abundant as that for the body. In such cases, the leader of the choir, or the deacon, or some other person, read a verse, or perhaps two lines of a hymn, which being sung, other stanzas were read, and then sung in the same way.

neighbor, J . . . B . . ., who had been a tailor, but having thriven in his affairs, and now advanced to the age of some fifty years, had become a farmer — such a career, by the way, being common at the time; for the prudent mechanic, adding to his house and his lands, as his necessities and his thrift dictated, usually ended as the proprietor of an ample house, fifty to a hundred acres of land, and an ample barn, stocked with half a dozen cows, one or two horses, a flock of sheep, and a general assortment of poultry.

The home of this, our neighbor B . . ., was situated on the road leading to Salem [N. Y.], there being a wide space in front occupied by the wood-pile, which in these days was not only a matter of great importance, but of formidable bulk. The size of the wood-pile was indeed in some sort an index to the rank and condition of the proprietor. The house itself was a low edifice, forty feet long, and of two stories in front; the rear being what was called a *breakback*, that is sloping down to a height of ten feet; this low part furnishing a shelter for garden tools, and various household instruments. The whole was constructed of wood; the outside being of the dun complexion assumed by unpainted wood, exposed to the weather for twenty or thirty years, save only that the roof was tinged of a reddish-brown by a fine moss that found sustenance in the chestnut shingles.

To the left was the garden, which in the productive season was a wilderness of onions, squashes, cucumbers, beets, parsnips, and currants, with the never-failing tansey for bitters, horseradish for seasoning, and fennel for keeping old women awake in church time. A sprig of fennel was in fact the theological smelling-bottle of the tender sex, and not unfrequently of the men, who, from long sitting in the sanctuary — after a week of labor in the field — found themselves too strongly tempted to visit the forbidden land of Nod — would sometimes borrow a sprig of fennel, and exorcise the fiend that threatened their spiritual welfare.

The interior of the house presented a parlor with plain, whitewashed walls, a home-made carpet upon the floor, calico curtains at the window, and a mirror three feet by two against the side, with a mahogany frame: to these must be added eight chairs and a cherry table, of the manufacture of Deacon Hawley. The keeping or sitting room had also a carpet, a dozen rush-bottom chairs, a table, &c. The kitchen was large — fully twenty feet square, with a fireplace six feet wide and four feet deep. On one side, it looked out upon the garden, the squashes and cucumbers climbing up and forming festoons over the door; on the other a view was presented of the orchard, embracing first a circle of peaches, pears, and plums, and beyond, a wide-spread clover field, embowered with apple-trees. Just by, was the well, with its tall sweep, the old oaken bucket dangling from the pole. The kitchen was in fact the most comfortable room in the house; cool in summer, and perfumed with the breath of the garden and the orchard: in winter, with its roaring blaze of hickory, it was a cosy resort, defying the bitterest blast of the season. Here the whole family assembled at meals, save only when the presence of company made it proper to serve tea in the parlor.

The chambers were all without carpets, and the furniture was generally of a simple character. The beds, however, were of ample size, and well filled with geese feathers, these being deemed essential for comfortable people. I must say, by the way, that every decent family had its flock of geese, of course, which was picked thrice a year, despite the noisy remonstrances of both goose and gander. The sheets of the bed, though of home-made linen, were as white as the driven snow. Indeed, the beds of this era showed that sleep was a luxury, well understood and duly cherished by all classes. The cellar, extending under the whole house, was a vast receptacle, and by no means the least important part of the establishment. In the autumn, it was supplied with three barrels of beef and as many of pork, twenty barrels of cider, with numerous bins of potatoes, turnips, beets, carrots, and cabbages. The garret, which was of huge dimensions, at the same time displayed a labyrinth of dried pumpkins, peaches, and apples — hung in festoons upon the rafters, amid bunches of summer savory, boneset, fennel, and other herbs — the floor being occupied by heaps of wool, flax, tow, and the like.

The barn corresponded to the house. It was a low brown structure, having abundance of sheds built on to it, without the least regard to symmetry. I need not say it was well stocked with hay, oats, rye, and buckwheat. Six cows, one or two horses, three dozen sheep, and an ample supply of poultry, including two or three broods of turkeys, constituted its living tenants.

The farm I need not describe in detail, but the orchard must not be overlooked. This consisted of three acres, covered, as I have said, with apple-trees, yielding abundantly — as well for the cider-mill as for the table, including the indispensable winter applesauce — according to their kinds. In the spring, an apple orchard is one of the most beautiful objects in the world.

In most families, the first exercise of the morning was reading the Bible, followed by a prayer, at which all were assembled, including the servants and helpers of the kitchen and the farm. Then came the breakfast, which was a substantial meal, always including hot viands, with vegetables, apple-sauce, pickles, mustard, horseradish, and various other condiments. Cider was the common drink for laboring people; even children drank it at will. Tea was common, but not so general as now. Coffee was almost unknown. Dinner was a still more hearty and varied repast — characterized by abundance of garden vegetables; tea was a light supper.

The day began early; breakfast was had at six in summer and seven in winter; dinner at noon — the work people in the fields being called to their meals by a conch-shell, usually winded by some kitchen Triton. The echoing of this noon-tide horn, from farm to farm, and over hill and dale, was a species of music which even rivaled the popular melody of drum and fife. Tea — the evening meal, usually took place about sundown. In families where all were laborers, all sat at table, servants as well as masters — the food being served before sitting down. In families where the masters and mistresses did not share the labors of the household or the farm, the meals of the domestics were had separate. There was, however, in those days a perfectly good understanding and good feeling between the masters and servants. The latter were not Irish; they had not as yet imbibed the plebeian envy of those above them, which has since so generally embittered and embarrassed American domestic life. The terms democrat and aristocrat had not got into use: these distinctions, and the feelings now implied by them, had indeed no existence in the hearts of the people. Our servants, during all my early life, were of the neighborhood, generally the daughters of respectable farmers and mechanics, and respecting others, were themselves respected and cherished. They were devoted to the interests of the family, and were always relied upon and treated as friends. In health, they had the same food; in sickness, the same care as the masters and mistresses or their children. This servitude implied no degradation, because it did not degrade the heart or manners of those subjected to it. It was never thought of as a reproach to a man or woman — in the stations they afterwards filled — that he or she had been out to service.

At the period of my earliest recollections, men of all classes were dressed in long, broad-tailed coats, with huge pockets, long waistcoats, and breeches. Hats had low crowns, with broad brims — some so wide as to be supported at the sides with cords. The stockings of the parson, and a few others, were of silk in summer and worsted in winter; those of the people were generally of wool, and blue and gray mixed. Women dressed in wide bonnets — sometimes of straw and sometimes of silk: the gowns were of silk, muslin, gingham, &c. — generally close and short-waisted, the breast and shoulders being covered by a full muslin kerchief. Girls ornamented themselves with a large white Vandyke. On the whole, the dress of both men and women has greatly changed. As to the former, short, snug, close-fitting garments have succeeded to the loose latitudinarian coats of former times: stove-pipe hats have followed broad brims, and pantaloons have taken the place of breeches. With the other sex — little French bonnets, set round with glowing flowers, flourish in the place of the plain, yawning hats of yore; then it was as much an effort to make the waists short, as it is now to make them long. As to the hips, which now make so formidable a display — it seems to me that in the days I allude to, ladies had none to speak of.

The amusements were then much the same as at present — though some striking differences may be noted. Books and newspapers — which are now diffused even among the country towns, so as to be in the hands of all, young and old — were then scarce, and were read respectfully, and as if they were grave matters, demanding thought and attention. They were not toys and pastimes, taken up every day, and by everybody, in the short intervals of labor, and then hastily dismissed, like waste paper. The aged sat down when they read, and drew forth their spectacles, and put them deliberately and reverently upon the nose. These instruments were not as now, little tortoise-shell hooks, attached to a ribbon, and put off and on with a jerk; but they were of silver or steel, substantially made, and calculated to hold on with a firm and steady grasp, showing the gravity of the uses to which they were devoted. Even the young approached a book with reverence, and a newspaper with awe.

The two great festivals were Thanksgiving and "training-day" — the latter deriving, from the still lingering spirit of the revolutionary war, a decidedly martial character. The marching of the troops, and the discharge of gunpowder, which invariably closed the exercises, were glorious and inspiring mementoes of heroic achievements, upon many a bloody field. The music of the drum and fife resounded on every side. A match between two rival drummers always drew an admiring crowd, and was in fact one of the chief excitements of the great day.

Tavern haunting — especially in winter, when there was little to do — for manufactures had not then sprung up to give profitable occupation, during this inclement season — was common, even with respectable farmers. Marriages were celebrated in the evening, at the house of the bride, with a general gathering of the neighborhood, and usually wound off by dancing. Everybody went, as to a public exhibition, without invitation. Funerals generally drew large processions which proceeded to the grave. Here the minister always made an address, suited to the occasion. If there was any thing remarkable in the history of the deceased, it was turned to religious account in the next Sunday's sermon. Singing meetings, to practice church music, were a great resource for the young, in winter. Dances at private houses were common, and drew no reproaches from the sober people present. Balls at the taverns were frequented by the young; the children of deacons and ministers attended, though the parents did not. The winter brought sleighing, skating, and the usual round of indoor sports. In general, the intercourse of all classes was kindly and considerate — no one arrogating superiority, and yet no one refusing to acknowledge it, where it existed. You would hardly have noticed that there was a higher and a lower class. Such there were certainly, for there must always and everywhere be the strong and the weak, the wise and the foolish — those of superior and those of inferior intellect, taste, manners, appearance, and character. But in our society, these existed without being felt as a privilege to one which must give offence to another. The feuds between Up and Down, which have since disturbed the whole fabric of society, had not then begun.

The mechanical operations especially of the weaver and carpenter stimulated my curiosity, and excited my emulation. Thus I soon became familiar with the tools of the latter, and made such windmills, kites, and perpetual motions, as to extort the admiration of my playmates, and excite the respect of my parents, so that they seriously meditated putting me apprentice to a carpenter. Up to the age of fourteen, I think this was regarded as my manifest destiny. I certainly took great delight in mechanical devices, and became a celebrity on pine shingles with a penknife.

In this age of excitement, perpetual motion was the great hobby of aspiring mechanics, as it has been indeed ever since. I pondered and whittled intensely on this subject before I was ten years old. Despairing of reaching my object by mechanical means, I attempted to arrive at it by magnetism, my father having bought me a pair of horse-shoe magnets in one of his journeys to New Haven. I should have succeeded, had it not been a principle in the nature of this curious element, that no substance will instantly intercept the stream of attraction. I tried to change the poles, and turn the north against the south; but there too nature had headed me, and of course I failed.

A word, by the way, on the matter of whittling. This is generally represented as a sort of idle, fidgety, frivolous use of the penknife, and is set down by amiable foreigners and sketchers of American manners as a peculiar characteristic of our people. No portrait of an American is deemed complete, whether in the saloon or the senate-chamber, at home or on the highway, unless with penknife and shingle in hand. I feel not the slightest disposition to resent even this, among the thousand caricatures that pass for traits of American life. For my own part, I can testify, that, during my youthful days, I found the penknife a source of great amusement and even of instruction. Many a long winter evening, many a dull, drizzly day, in spring and summer and autumn — sometimes at the kitchen fireside, sometimes in the attic, amid festoons of dried apples, peaches, and pumpkins; sometimes in a cosy nook of the barn; sometimes in the shelter of a neighboring stone-wall, thatched over with wild grape-vines — have I spent in great ecstasy, making candle-rods, or some other simple article, of household goods, for my mother, or in perfecting toys for myself and my young friends, or perhaps in attempts at more ambitious achievements.

In these early days, I was a Nimrod, a mighty hunter — first with a bow and arrow, and afterward with the old hereditary firelock, which snapped six times and went off once. The smaller kinds of game were abundant. The thickets teemed with quails; * partridges drummed in every wood; the gray-squirrel — the most picturesque animal of our forests — enlivened every hickory copse with his mocking laugh, his lively gambols, and his long bannered tail. The pigeons in spring and autumn migrated in countless flocks, and many lingered in our woods for the season.

Everybody was then a hunter, not of course a sportsman, for the chase was followed more for profit than for pastime. Game was, in point of fact, a substantial portion of the supply of food at certain seasons of the year. All were then good shots, and my father could not be an exception: he was even beyond his generation in netting pigeons. This was not deemed a reproach at that time in a clergyman, nor was he the only parson that indulged in these occupations. One day, as I was with him on West Mountain, baiting pigeons, we had seduced a flock of three or four dozen down into the bed where they were feeding — my father and myself lying concealed in our bush-hut, close by. Suddenly, whang went a gun into the middle of the flock! Out we ran in great indignation, for at least a dozen of the birds were bleeding and fluttering before us.

* The American quail is a species of partridge, in size between the European quail and partridge. The *partridge* of New England is the *pheasant* of the South, and the *ruffed grouse* of the naturalists.

Scarcely had we reached the spot, when we met Parson M . . . of Lower Salem, who had thus unwittingly poached upon us. The two clergymen had first a flurry and then a good laugh, after which they divided the plunder and parted.

The stories told by Wilson and Audubon as to the amazing quantity of pigeons in the West, were realized by us in Connecticut half a century ago. I have seen a stream of these noble birds, pouring at brief intervals through the skies, from the rising to the setting sun, and this in the county of Fairfield.

I can recollect no sports of my youth which equaled in excitement our pigeon hunts, generally taking place in September and October. We usually started on horseback before daylight, and made a rapid progress to some stubble-field on West Mountain. The ride in the keen, fresh air, especially as the dawn began to break, was delightful. My memory is still full of the sights and sounds of those glorious mornings: the silvery whistle of the wings of migrating flocks of plover — invisible in the gray mists of dawn; the faint murmur of the distant mountain torrents; the sonorous gong of the long-trailing flocks of wild geese, seeming to come from the unseen depths of the skies — these were among the suggestive sounds that stole through the dim twilight. As morning advanced, the scene was inconceivably beautiful — the mountain sides, clothed in autumnal green and purple and gold, rendered more glowing by the sunrise — with the valleys covered with mists and spreading out like lakes of silver; while on every side the ear was saluted by the mocking screams of the red-headed woodpecker, the cawing of congresses of crows, clamorous as if talking to Buncombe; and finally the rushing sound of the pigeons, pouring like a tide over the tops of the trees.

By this time of course nets were ready, and our flyers and stool-birds on the alert. What moments of ecstasy were these, and especially when the head of the flock — some red-breasted old father or grandfather — caught the sight of our pigeons, and turning at the call, drew the whole train down into our net-bed. I have often seen a hundred, or two hundred of these splendid birds, come upon us, with a noise absolutely deafening, and sweeping the air with a sudden gust, like the breath of a thundercloud. Sometimes our bush-hut, where we lay concealed, was covered all over with pigeons, and we dared not move a finger, as their red, piercing eyes were upon us. When at last, with a sudden pull of the rope, the net was sprung, and we went out to secure our booty — often fifty, and sometimes even a hundred birds — I felt a fullness of triumph, which words are wholly inadequate to express !

[158]

I trust I have all due respect for my little fat, paternal grand-mother. She was quite lame, having broken her leg some years before, and appeared to me shorter than ever; nevertheless, she was active, energetic, and alive to every thing that was passing. She welcomed me heartily, and took the best care of me in the world — lavishing upon me, without stint, all the treasures of her abundant larder. As to her Indian puddings — alas, I shall never see their like again ! When she saw me eating with a good appetite, her benignant grandmotherly face beamed like a lantern.

She was a model housekeeper, and as such had great administrative talents. Every thing went right in the household, the garden, the home lot, the pasture, and the little farm. The hens laid lots of large fresh eggs, the cows gave abundance of milk, the pigs were fat as butter; the woodpile was always full. There was never any agony about the house: all was methodical, as if regulated by some law of nature. The tall old clock in the entry, although an octogenarian, was still staunch, and ticked and struck with an emphasis that enforced obedience. When it told seven in the morning, the breakfast came without daring to delay even for a minute. The stroke of twelve brought the sun to the noon-mark, and dinner to the table. The tea came at six. At sunset on Saturday evening, the week's work was done, and according to the Puritan usage, the Sabbath was begun. All suddenly became quiet and holy. Even the knitting-work was laid aside. Meditation was on every brow; the cat in the corner sat with her eyes half shut, as if she too were considering her ways.

On the morning of the Holy Day, all around was silent. The knife and fork were handled quietly, at the table. The toilet, though sedulously performed, was made in secret. People walked as if they had gloves on their shoes. Inanimate nature seemed to know that God rested on that day, and hallowed it. The birds put on a Sunday air; the cows did not low from hill to hill as on other days. The obstreperous hen deposited her egg, and cackled not. At nine o'clock, the solemn church bell rang, and in the universal stillness, its tones swelled over the village like a voice from above. At ten, the second bell rang, and the congregation gathered in. There, in the place she had held for forty years, was my good grandmother, in rain and shine, in summer and in winter. Though now well stricken in years, and the mother of staunch men — their names honored in the pulpit, the senate, and at the bar — she still faltered not in the strait and narrow path of duty.

◇◇◇◇◇◇◇◇◇◇◇◇◇

[Thomas Low Nichols, M.D., Orford, N.H. (born 1815)]

All men love the land of their birth — it may be that all men think the scenes they first looked upon beautiful. It is forty years since I have seen the Upper Connecticut valley, and the more mountainous regions of the Old Granite State.

Forty years ! but my native State glows in my memory, — a land of craggy mountains, whose summits glisten in the sun, or fade in the blue distance; of silvery lakes cradled in the forests and among the hills; of crystal springs, singing brooks, roaring waterfalls, and clear arrowy rivers, swollen in the spring-time to magnificent torrents; of the loveliest of green valleys, walled by the grandest of precipitous mountain ranges, with villages of white cottages and mansions with green blinds, shaded by broad-spreading elms and shining sugar-maples. The forests are pine, hemlock, spruce, odorous balsam-fir, the great white birch (of whose bark the Indians made canoes, and which I rolled into torches for night-fishing), beech, maple, oak, and more trees than I can remember. The ground was fragrant with pine-leaves, mosses, and the winter-green, with its bright red berries, alive with playful squirrels and musical with singing birds. The ponds are full of fish; the mountains and pasture lands are covered with berries. A glowing landscape in summer; in winter a robe of glittering snow.

My birthplace is about the same latitude as Lyons, in France, yet the snows fall three or four feet deep, and lie on the ground three months at a time. The ice froze twenty inches in thickness; the thermometer went down at times to twenty, thirty, and in some mountain regions forty degrees below the absurd zero of Fahrenheit. Then the trees would burst with the frost with a sound like a cannon, and the ground, frozen a yard deep, would crack open with a noise like thunder, shaking the house like an earthquake. These cracks go across the fields in straight lines for a long distance, and are as deep as the frost extends, and nearly an inch wide; still, such weather is not as bad as it may seem. After reaching a certain point of cold, ten or twenty degrees make little difference with the feelings. Protect the hands and feet, and prevent the ears and nose from freezing, and the cold stimulates the system to resist it, and is less uncomfortable than a drizzly chill above the freezing point. Steady intense cold makes the blood circulate briskly, and the system put forth its energies. The cold, condensed air is rich in oxygen, and the frost exhilarating. Then the sleigh-rides ! The snow is four feet deep, but trodden in the roadway hard as rock. All the landscape is glistening white in the dazzling sunshine. The trees are cased all in diamonds with glittering prismatic light. You glide along swiftly to the music of the jingling bells, just feeling the motion, and wrapped in buffalo robes, bearskins, or softer furs. Fancy a line of twenty sleighs, loaded with as many loving couples, gliding through the frozen landscape by moonlight, with the silvery ringing of a thousand bells and shouts of merry laughter, the gay frolic ending with a supper and a dance, and then home again before the day breaks.

Skating, too. It is hardly worth buying skates, or learning the beautiful exercise, for the chance one has of enjoying it in England; but in the Northern States of America you can calculate on two or three months of skating when the snow is not too deep upon the ice. Sometimes the snow falls before the large ponds and rivers freeze over; sometimes it is blown from the ice. I used to skate miles up and down the Connecticut River, and when thirsty would creep carefully to the edges of the airholes, or "glades," in the ice, and drink. The water, clear as crystal, ten or twelve feet deep, ran in a strong current under me. It seems very absurd now that I should have run such a risk for a drink of water; but every boy runs many such, and shudders at the danger in after years.

The township in which I was born had about 1000 inhabitants. There was a pretty village, with a Congregational meeting-house, post-office, tavern, two or three shops called stores, each with its assortment of draperies, ironmongery, groceries, wines, liquors, tobacco, crockery, glass — almost everything, in fact. There were also two or three lawyers, and a blacksmith, hatter, shoemaker, wheelwright, cabinet-maker, tailor. A small village, two or three miles back among the hills, supplied its own neighbourhood. Grist-mills which ground our corn, and saw-mills which supplied our timber, were upon a mill brook which brawled down from the hills and wound through the loveliest of meadows into the Connecticut.

There were no landlords in this country. Almost every man owned the land he cultivated. And they believed in the motto of Poor Richard: —

> He that by the plough would thrive,
> Must either hold himself, or drive.

The proprietor of hundreds of acres worked harder than any man he could hire. And whom could he hire? That was the great difficulty. There were very few men to go out at "day's works." The sons of small farmers, wishing to raise a little money for themselves, would sometimes hire out at about fifteen dollars a month and found. They lived with their employer, fared as he did, ate at the same table, worked by his side; and when the young man put on his Sunday suit, he offered his arm to the prettiest of the farmer's daughters and escorted her gallantly to meeting. The term servant, and the idea of service, were unknown. He was a "hand," or a "hired man." And the young lady who in rare cases assisted a neighbour in doing the housework associated on terms of perfect equality with her employer's family, and considered that she was conferring an obligation, as indeed she was, and was entitled to gratitude and very respectful treatment, as well as what were then considered good wages.

The two or three richest men in our parts were wildly reputed to be worth forty or fifty thousand dollars. But the possessor of property worth ten thousand dollars was called rich. No one ever spoke of incomes; they were not much reckoned. The farmer who made both ends meet, with a little increase of his stock, thought himself doing well enough.

Let me give an idea of such a farmer's home, as I remember it, forty years ago. The farm was about a hundred acres of land, running back from the river in a series of three level terraces, and then up a steep, rocky hill. These alluvial terraces or levels appeared to me to have been at some period the successive bottoms either of a much broader river, or, more probably, of a great lake, bounded by the chain of precipitous mountains that girt our valley, excepting where they were broken through at the north and south. This farm was fenced with the stumps of the great pine-trees that had once covered the meadows, which had been cut down at an earlier period and sawn into boards, or made into shingles, or rafted down the river to become

Fit masts for some tall admiral.

The fences were made by placing these stumps — extracted from the ground with great labour and the aid of machinery — on their sides, with their gnarled roots stretching into the air, and forming a *chevaux de frise* which few animals would venture to jump over, but which, with an occasional tear of trousers, I managed to climb with great facility. There were no hedges. In the rocky uplands there were stone walls, elsewhere board fences and palings.

The stage road passed along the second terrace, and here were the farm buildings — a storey-and-a-half wooden house, with a steep shingled roof, having ten rooms, and close by a wash-house, dairy, wood-house, where the year's firewood was stored, and hog-house. At a little distance was the barn-yard, with two large barns for hay, unthreshed grain, and stables for horses and cattle, and a corn-barn for storing Indian corn and the threshed and winnowed grain.

Back of the buildings was an orchard of ten or fifteen acres; and back of this, by a rich bank of blue clay, a brick-yard.

Our neighbour was an industrious man. He raised large crops of wheat, rye, maize, potatoes, and flax. He kept horses, cattle, sheep, and swine. The women carded, spun, and wove the wool and flax, making the blankets, full cloth, woollen stuffs, stockings, and mittens, and linen of the family. They also made plenty of butter and cheese. The farmer and his stout boys chopped their wood, shaved pine-shingles, converted the apples into cider, made bricks, washed and sheared the sheep, prepared the flax, and had plenty of work for every week in the year. They raised their food, made their clothing, and a large surplus of everything to exchange for what they could not manufacture or produce — tea, coffee, tobacco, and all the goods furnished by the stores. In those days the buzz of the spinning-wheel and the clang of the loom were heard, and the odour of the dye-pot smelt, in every farmer's dwelling. Now, these instruments of domestic manufacture are stowed away in the garret, and the young ladies, dressed in the produce of the looms of Manchester, Lyons, or Lowell, "spin street yarn," exercise at the pianoforte, and are learned in the mysteries of crochet. They are educated at Female Seminaries, they graduate at female or mixed colleges, but I doubt if they are the better for all these modern improvements.

When the crops are gathered there is another job to do, best done in company. At least, it is an excuse for an evening gathering, and the settler is able by this time to give a little treat to those who help him. So all the neighbours, and especially the young men and girls, are invited to a "husking." The Indian corn has been gathered into one end of the house, if there is no barn. It is still upon the stalk, and the long yellow ears, or white they may be, with sometimes a red one, are still enclosed in their tough, fibrous husks.

The husking takes place in the evening, by the light of a good fire of pine-knots, or candles, where civilisation has advanced so far. Both sexes join in the pleasant labour, with songs, stories, chaffing,

and the pleasant excitement arising from the rule that the fellow who husks a red ear of maize has the privilege of kissing the girl next him. The baskets are filled, the pile diminishes, the stalks and husks are cleared away. Then comes a supper of pork and beans, pumpkin-pie, dough-nuts, apples and cider, if the orchards have grown, or other and perhaps stronger beverages. Then, if the Puritanism is not too strong, a fiddle and a dance; if it is, games of romps and forfeits, supposed to be less objectionable, and a walk home of happy couples in the moonlight.

When the orchards have grown, then come the "apple-paring bees." They did come, at least, before ingenious Yankees invented paring machines. The apples were pared with sharp knives and rapid hands, quartered, cored, strung on twine, and hung up to dry in festoons over the kitchen ceiling. The paring bee was a milder kind of evening party than the husking, and ended with the same festivities.

The quilting is mostly a feminine arrangement. Its ostensible object is the manufacture of a bed-quilt. This involves a social gathering — talk, tea, probably a little gossip and scandal, and in the evening the accession of masculinity, with more or less of fun and frolic. The upper surface of the quilt is that marvelous result of feminine industy — patchwork; the lower stratum is more modest calico; the interior cotton or wool; and the whole is united by quilt-ings in elaborate figures, composed of a vast number of stitches, made by as many old and young ladies as can sit around the frame, beginning on the borders, and, as the frame is rolled up, gradually working towards the centre. The reasons for making this a social undertaking are obvious. When the quilt is in the frame it occupies a large space. It would take a long time for one or two persons to do it, and would be a long time in the way. Finally, it is an excuse for a social gathering.

The men have shooting-matches all to themselves. These come off in the autumn, when turkeys are fat and thanksgiving is coming. Turkeys are put up to be shot at so many rods' distance, at so much a shot, and the poor shots pay for the turkeys which the good ones carry home. In my memory good shots were very common. Every man and every boy could shoot. Guns and rifles were in every house; and when I was eight or nine years old, a light fowling-piece, with which I shot at birds or squirrels, or at a mark, was my favourite plaything. I shot with a rifle resting over a rail in the fence, or across the stump of a tree, long before I could hold one out at arm's length. Crack shots did what were considered very handsome feats in those days, before arms of precision and long ranges were invented. These riflemen, who killed their game with-out injuring their skins, barked squirrels off the trees, and shot wild turkeys in the head, would hold candles in the night for each other to snuff with a bullet without extinguishing the light, drive a nail into a tree without bending it, or split a bullet into equal halves on a knifeblade.

◇◇◇◇◇◇◇◇◇◇◇◇◇◇

[Uriel Crocker, Boston]

Somewhere about the year 1820, I was a member of a fire company called the "Conservative Society." Each of us had two leather buckets to take with us when we ran to the fire, and we always kept the buckets ready for use with a bed-key and two large canvas bags in them. I still have those buckets and bags. The bed-key was for the purpose of taking apart the bedsteads that we might find in the houses that were on fire or liable to take fire, and the canvas bags were to be used to put small articles in that might be saved from the fire. The "rules and regulations" of this "Conservative Society," printed in 1811, provided in Article 4 that "Every member shall constantly keep together, in the most suitable place in his house, two leather buckets, two canvas bags, and one bed-key; the buckets and bags to be uniformly painted, agreeably to the directions of the society." Article 5 further provided that "If a building, occupied by any member of the society, be in danger from fire, every other member shall immediately repair to such building, with his buckets, bags, and bed-key, and use his best endeavors to preserve the building, and to remove and secure the goods and effects."

◇◇◇◇◇◇◇◇◇◇◇◇◇

[*J. M. Bailey,* The Danbury News]

DRIVING A HEN

When a woman has a hen to drive into the coop, she takes hold of her hoops with both hands, and shakes them quietly toward the delinquent, and says, "Shew, there !" The hen takes one look at the object, to convince herself that it's a woman, and then stalks majestically into the coop, in perfect disgust of the sex. A man don't do that way. He goes out of doors and says, "It is singular nobody in this house can drive a hen but myself." And, picking up a stick of wood, hurls it at the offending biped, and observes, "Get in there, you thief." The hen immediately loses her reason, and dashes to the opposite end of the yard. The man straightway dashes after her. She comes back again with her head down, her wings out, and followed by an assortment of stove-wood, fruit-cans, and coal-clinkers, with a much-puffing and very mad man in the rear. Then she skims up on the stoop, and under the barn, and over a fence or two, and around the house, and back again to the coop, all the while talking as only an excited hen can talk, and all the while followed by things convenient for handling, and by a man whose coat is on the sawbuck, and whose hat is on the ground, and whose perspiration and profanity appear to have no limit. By this time the other hens have come out to take a hand in the debate, and help dodge the missiles — and then the man says every hen on the place shall be sold in the morning, and puts on his things and goes down the street, and the woman dons her hoops, and has every one of those hens housed and contented in two minutes, and the only sound heard on the premises is the hammering by the eldest boy as he mends the broken pickets.

LIFE AFLOAT

❖❖❖❖❖❖❖❖❖❖❖❖❖

[Stephen Burroughs, Hanover, N. H.]

I left my father's house, about the 20th of November, 1782, at the age of seventeen, and directed my course for Newburyport, a small seaport town in the state of Massachusetts, where they fitted out many small vessels for privateering.

Intending to sell my horse, saddle and bridle, and with the avails to prepare myself for sea, I found the market for horses so low, that a sale for him would not be easily obtained, without great loss; I therefore concluded to send my horse back to my father. I arrived at Newburyport and delivered my letter of introduction to Capt. McHurd, to whom it was addressed. This man kept a house for boarders and lodgers; I accordingly put up with him. Not finding any privateers going to sea soon, I concluded to go in a packet, which had a letter of marque, to France. Having no doctor engaged, I undertook to act in that capacity; and after obtaining the assistance, advice and direction of an old practitioner in physic, together with marks set on each parcel of medicine, I thought myself tolerably well qualified to perform the office of a physician on board the ship. We did not sail till the first day of January, 1783. When I lost sight of America, I cannot say but what my feelings were more disagreeably affected than I expected. Those attachments which we form in childhood, to places, to persons and things, are pretty strong, I believe, in the minds of all.

Soon after we had lost sight of land, I began to grow intolerably seasick, which continued without intermission for four days. This is a species of sickness, though not dangerous, yet as disagreeable to bear as the most violent disorder to which the human constitution is subject. This served, in a great measure, to cool my ardor for spending my days on the salt water. On the fifth day I began to feel more at ease; the motion of the vessel was not so irksome; my appetite began to recover, which before was quite gone. We made the island of Sable, lying in 45° north latitude, where we went on shore. This island is a dreary barren place, about thirty miles in length. Some wild horses and hogs were placed on this spot, for the support of seamen who might be cast away. Accidents of this kind being very common here, on account of the shoals extending from its shores at a great distance into the sea. Here was likewise a small hut, a porridge pot, and fire-wood, flint and tinder box. Here, the sailors recounted many circumstances of the marvellous, representing this as the abode of spirits, hobgoblins, etc. They affirmed with much positive assurance, that many families had attempted living here, induced by great rewards from government, but all their attempts were in vain, owing to sights and noises, which had disturbed them. It was said that this island, in times of an easterly storm, would shake with great violence, which I was rather induced to believe, because a natural reason can be assigned for this phenomenon. Leaving this place, we proceeded on our voyage, till the eighth day of our departure, when, about 10 o'clock in the morning, the man at the masthead cried out, a sail ! a sail was discovered ahead; we hove to, in order to see which way she was going. We soon found her making from us with all her force. We put about and made sail after her, till about sunset. We found her a merchant's brig from New York, bound to London, with pearl-ash, commanded by one Pratt. After we had manned our prize, we pursued our route, without any material occurrence, till the twenty-third.

About 11 o'clock in the morning, we espied a sail astern, which we soon saw was in pursuit of us; we made all the sail we could, to run from her and found she carried to it (a sea term for not taking in sail) through some pretty severe squalls. We lost sight of her about sunset: we made an island on the coast of France, pronounced in the French language, Graw — how they spell it, I do not recollect. We came to under this island, and fired for a pilot. One soon came off to us: about 1 o'clock at night, we got under way again.

About 10 o'clock the next morning, we made Bellisle, and soon after saw a sail standing for us, right ahead. We thought her the same that pursued us the day preceding; she proved to be the same. She was a Lugger, carrying 12 six pounders, and was chasing a brig mounting 6 guns. We soon passed the brig, and speaking with her, found her from Boston, bound to Nantz. We entreated her to put about with us, and look at the Lugger, which by this time, was hove to, waiting for us. All our entreaties were in vain; she ran in under the fort of Bellisle. We carried 18 guns, but unfortunately, ten of them were wood so that little advantage could be expected from them. We hauled up our courses, put up our boarding netting, cleared our decks, lit our matches, and made all ready for action. We had on board twenty-one men besides the prisoners. The thirteen stripes of the United States were flying; but the Lugger, as yet, showed no colors. We came so near as to hail — she answered in French — and after understanding we came from America and were bound to Nantz, she offered us a pilot, and when we told them we had a pilot already on board, she affected not to understand, but made towards us with a pretended design of accommodating us with a pilot. Not more than ten men were to be seen on her deck. By this time, she was sufficiently near to discover those on board by their countenances. Mr. Severe, our first mate, knew the commander of the Lugger to be a man from the Isle of Jersey, having been taken by him the preceding year. The mate vociferated like a stentor, "give them a gun! give them a gun!" We fired, but so strongly prepossessed were the gunners, that the Lugger was a Frenchman, that they pointed over her, and did her no damage. She ported her helm, and fell astern as much as half a mile, expecting that we fought with 18 guns. We kept on our course — seeing this, she made all the sail possible after us, hung out the English colors, and her deck became instantly filled with men. She first came up on our windward board, but now altered her intention, and came round on our lee-side. We began to fire stern chases at them, and they returned our salute with bow chases. While Mr. Severe was elevating the gun at our bow he received a swivel ball, which carried away his right cheek, went through and broke his right arm, and two of his ribs. We caught him up, and carried him into the cockpit, where I dressed his wounds, and at the desire of one,

Bootman, a passenger, left Mr. Severe in his care, and returned on deck. Our ship was thinly manned, and the help of every hand was felt. A chest of loaded small arms stood on the quarter deck, where I took my station. The Lugger, by this time, was grappled to our ship, and attempted sword in hand to cut away our boarding nettings. Every man was ordered to his boarding pike, and for ten minutes, the conflict was truly sharp, but the issue was in our favor. They retreated on board their own vessel, the guns were their next resort. With cannon and small arms they poured in upon us a shower of balls, and we endeavored to pay them in like kind, to the full amount of our receipt, so that a balance should be left in our favor, and not against us. The captain and myself had fired nearly all the small arms which were loaded. The commander of the Lugger kept bellowing from his quarter deck, that if we did not strike, he would give us no quarter. I took a blunderbuss, which remained loaded, and taking aim very leisurely, at the mouth of his trumpet, let fly. I believe this did his business; at least, I heard no more of this bravado. Twice more did they attempt to cut away our boarding nettings, but, to as little effect as at first. We by this time, had disabled their fore-top-mast, and carried away their gib-boom. They cut from us, and made all the sail possible towards the Penmarks, which were hidden and dangerous rocks, lying under water, where they expected we should not follow them. In this conjecture they were right. We arrived the same day in the river Loire, and came to an anchor at a town called Penbeef, thirty miles below the city of Nantz.

◇◇◇◇◇◇◇◇◇◇◇◇◇

[*Richard Henry Dana, Cambridge, Mass.*]

The change from the tight dress coat, silk cap and kid gloves of an undergraduate at Cambridge, to the loose duck trowsers, checked shirt and tarpaulin hat of a sailor, though somewhat of a transformation, was soon made, and I supposed that I should pass very well for a jack tar. But it is impossible to deceive the practised eye in these matters; and while I supposed myself to be looking as salt as Neptune himself, I was, no doubt, known for a landsman by every one on board as soon as I hove in sight. A sailor has a peculiar cut to his clothes, and a way of wearing them which a green hand can never get. The trowsers, tight round the hips, and thence hanging long and loose round the feet, a superabundance of checked shirt, a low-crowned, well varnished black hat, worn on the back of the head, with half a fathom of black ribbon hanging over the left eye, and a peculiar tie to the black silk neckerchief, with sundry other minutiae, are signs, the want of which betray the beginner, at once. Besides the points in my dress which were out of the way, doubtless my complexion and hands were enough to distinguish me from the regular *salt*, who, with a sunburnt cheek, wide step, and rolling gait, swings his bronzed and toughened hands athwartships, half open, as though just ready to grasp a rope.

"With all my imperfections on my head," I joined the crew, and we hauled out into the stream, and came to anchor for the night. The next day we were employed in preparations for sea, reeving studding-sail gear, crossing royal yards, putting on chafing gear, and taking on board our powder. On the following night, I stood my first watch. I remained awake nearly all the first part of the night from fear that I might not hear when I was called; and when I went on deck, so great were my ideas of the importance of my trust, that I walked regularly fore and aft the whole length of the vessel, looking out over the bows and taffrail at each turn, and was not a little surprised at the coolness of the old salt whom I called to take my place, in stowing himself snugly away under the long boat, for a nap. That was a sufficient look-out, he thought, for a fine night, at anchor in a safe harbor.

There can be no better place to describe the duties, regulations, and customs of an American merchantman, of which ours was a fair specimen.

The captain, in the first place, is lord paramount. He stands no watch, comes and goes when he pleases, and is accountable to no one, and must be obeyed in everything, without a question, even from his chief officer. He has the power to turn his officers off duty, and even to break them and make them do duty as sailors in the forecastle. Where there are no passengers and no supercargo, as in our vessel, he has no companion but his own dignity, and no pleasures, unless he differs from most of his kind, but the conscious-ness of possessing supreme power, and, occasionally, the exercise of it.

The prime minister, the official organ, and the active and super-intending officer, is the chief mate. He is first lieutenant, boat-swain, sailing-master, and quarter-master. The captain tells him what he wishes to have done, and leaves to him the care of over-seeing, of allotting the work, and also the responsibility of its being well done. *The* mate (as he is always called, *par excellence*) also keeps the log-book, for which he is responsible to the owners and insurers, and has the charge of the stowage, safe keeping, and de-livery of the cargo. He is also, ex-officio, the wit of the crew; for the captain does not condescend to joke with the men, and the second mate no one cares for; so that when "the mate" thinks fit to enter-tain "the people" with a coarse joke or a little practical wit, every one feels bound to laugh.

The second mate's is proverbially a dog's berth. He is neither officer nor man. The men do not respect him as an officer, and he is obliged to go aloft to reef and furl the topsails, and to put his hands into the tar and slush, with the rest. The crew call him the "sailors' waiter," as he has to furnish them with spun-yarn, marline, and all other stuffs that they need in their work, and has charge of the boatswain's locker, which includes serving-boards, marline-spikes, etc., etc. He is expected by the captain to maintain his dignity and to enforce obedience, and still is kept at a great distance from the mate, and obliged to work with the crew. He is one to whom little is given and of whom much is required. His wages are usually double those of a common sailor, and he eats and sleeps in the cabin; but he is obliged to be on deck nearly all his time, and eats at the second table, that is, makes a meal out of what the captain and chief mate leave.

The steward is the captain's servant, and has charge of the pantry, from which every one, even the mate himself, is excluded. These distinctions usually find him an enemy in the mate, who does not like to have any one on board who is not entirely under his control; the crew do not consider him as one of their number, so he is left to the mercy of the captain.

The cook is the patron of the crew, and those who are in his favor can get their wet mittens and stockings dried, or light their pipes at the galley on the night watch. These two worthies, together with the carpenter and sailmaker, if there be one, stand no watch, but, being employed all day, are allowed to "sleep in" at night, unless all hands are called.

The crew are divided into two divisions, as equally as may be, called the watches. Of these the chief mate commands the larboard, and the second mate the starboard. They divide the time between them, being on and off duty, or, as it is called, on deck and below, every other four hours. If, for instance, the chief mate with the larboard watch have the first night-watch from eight to twelve; at the end of the four hours, the starboard watch is called, and the second mate takes the deck, while the larboard watch and the first mate go below until four in the morning, when they come on deck again and remain until eight; having what is called the morning watch. As they will have been on deck eight hours out of twelve, while those who had the middle watch — from twelve to four, will only have been up four hours, they have what is called a "forenoon watch below," that is, from eight, a.m., till twelve, m. In a man-of-war, and in some merchantmen, this alternation of watches is kept up throughout the twenty-four hours; but our ship, like most merchantmen, had "all hands" from twelve o'clock till dark, except in bad weather, when we had "watch and watch."

An explanation of the "dog watches" may, perhaps, be of use to one who has never been to sea. They are to shift the watches each night, so that the same watch need not be on deck at the same hours. In order to effect this, the watch from *four* to *eight,* p.m., is divided into two half, or dog watches, one from four to six, and the other from six to eight. By this means they divide the twenty-four hours into *seven* watches instead of *six,* and thus shift the hours every night. As the dog watches come during twilight, after the day's work is done, and before the night watch is set, they are the watches in which everybody is on deck. The captain is up, walking on the weather side of the quarter-deck, the chief mate on the leeside, and the second mate about the weather gangway. The steward has finished his work in the cabin, and has come up to smoke his pipe with the cook in the galley. The crew are sitting on the windlass or lying on the forecastle, smoking, singing, or telling long yarns. At eight o'clock, eight bells are struck, the log is hove, the watch set, the wheel relieved, the galley shut up, and the other watch goes below.

The morning commences with the watch on deck's "turning-to" at day-break and washing down, scrubbing and swabbing the decks. This, together with filling the "scuttle-butt" with fresh water, and coiling up the rigging, usually occupies the time until seven bells, (half after seven,) when all hands get breakfast. At eight, the day's work begins, and lasts until sundown, with the exception of an hour for dinner.

Before I end my explanations, it may be well to define a *day's work*, and to correct a mistake prevalent among landsmen about a sailor's life. Nothing is more common than to hear people say — "Are not sailors very idle at sea ? — what can they find to do ?" This is a very natural mistake, and being very frequently made, it is one which every sailor feels interested in having corrected. In the first place, then, the discipline of the ship requires every man to be at work upon *something* when he is on deck, except at night and on Sundays. Except at these times, you will never see a man, on board a well-ordered vessel, standing idle on deck, sitting down or leaning over the side. It is the officers' duty to keep every one at work, even if there is nothing to be done but to scrape the rust from the chain cables. In no state prison are the convicts more regularly set to work, and more closely watched. No conversation is allowed among the crew at their duty, and though they frequently do talk when aloft, or when near one another, yet they always stop when an officer is nigh.

With regard to the work upon which the men are put, it is a matter which probably would not be understood by one who has not been at sea. When I first left port, and found that we were kept regularly employed for a week or two, I supposed that we were getting the vessel into sea trim, and that it would soon be over, and we should have nothing to do but to sail the ship, but I found that it continued so for two years, and at the end of the two years there was as much to be done as ever. As has often been said, a ship is like a lady's watch, always out of repair. When first leaving port, studding-sail gear is to be rove, all the running rigging to be examined, that which is unfit for use to be got down, and new rigging rove in its place: then the standing rigging is to be overhauled, replaced, and repaired, in a thousand different ways; and wherever any of the numberless ropes or the yards are chafing or wearing upon it, there "chafing gear," as it is called, must be put on. This chafing gear consists of worming, parcelling, rounding, battens, and service of all kinds — both rope-yarns, spun-yarn, marline and seizing-stuffs. Taking off, putting on, and mending the chafing gear alone, upon a vessel, would find constant employment for two or three men, during working hours, for a whole voyage.

The next point to be considered is, that all the "small stuffs" which are used on board a ship — such as spun-yarn, marline, seiz-ing-stuff, etc., etc. — are made on board. The owners of a vessel buy up incredible quantities of "old junk," which the sailors unlay, after drawing out the yarns, knot them together, and roll them up in balls. These "rope-yarns" are constantly used for various pur-poses, but the greater part is manufactured into spun-yarn. For this purpose every vessel is furnished with a "spun-yarn winch;" which is very simple, consisting of a wheel and spindle. This may be heard constantly going on deck in pleasant weather; and we had employ-ment, during a great part of the time, for three hands in drawing and knotting yarns, and making spun-yarn.

Another method of employing the crew is, "setting up" rigging. Whenever any of the standing rigging becomes slack, (which is continually happening,) the seizings and coverings must be taken off, tackles got up, and after the rigging is bowsed well taut, the seizings and coverings replaced; which is a very nice piece of work. There is also such a connection between different parts of a vessel, that one rope can seldom be touched without altering another. You cannot stay a mast aft by the back stays, without slacking up the head stays, etc., etc. If we add to this all the tarring, greasing, oiling, varnishing, painting, scraping, and scrubbing which is re-quired in the course of a long voyage, and also remember this is all to be done in *addition* to watching at night, steering, reefing, furl-ing, bracing, making and setting sail, and pulling, hauling and climbing in every direction, one will hardly ask, "What can a sailor find to do at sea ?"

If, after all this labor — after exposing their lives and limbs in storms, wet and cold,

> Wherein the cub-drawn bear would couch;
> The lion and the belly-pinched wolf
> Keep their furs dry: —

the merchants and captains think that they have not earned their twelve dollars a month, (out of which they clothe themselves,) and their salt beef and hard bread, they keep them picking oakum — *ad infinitum*. This is the usual resource upon a rainy day, for then it will not do to work upon rigging; and when it is pouring down in floods, instead of letting the sailors stand about in sheltered places, and talk, and keep themselves comfortable, they are separated to different parts of the ship and kept at work picking oakum. I have seen oakum stuff placed about in different parts of the ship, so that the sailors might not be idle in the *snatches* between the frequent squalls upon crossing the equator. Some officers have been so driven to find work for the crew in a ship ready for sea, that they have set them to pounding the anchors (often done) and scraping the chain cables. The "Philadelphia Catechism" is,

> Six days shalt thou labor and do all thou art able,
> And on the seventh — holystone the decks and scrape the cable.

This kind of work, of course, is not kept up off Cape Horn, Cape of Good Hope, and in extreme north and south latitudes; but I have seen the decks washed down and scrubbed, when the water would have frozen if it had been fresh; and all hands kept at work upon the rigging, when we had on our pea-jackets, and our hands so numb that we could hardly hold our marline-spikes.

We met with nothing remarkable until we were in the latitude of the river La Plata. Here there are violent gales from the south-west, called Pamperos, which are very destructive to the shipping in the river, and are felt for many leagues at sea. They are usually preceded by lightning. The captain told the mates to keep a bright look-out, and if they saw lightning at the south-west, to take in sail at once. We got the first touch of one during my watch on deck. I was walking in the lee gangway, and thought that I saw lightning on the lee bow. I told the second mate, who came over and looked out for some time. It was very black in the south-west, and in about ten minutes we saw a distinct flash. The wind, which had been south-east, had now left us, and it was dead calm. We sprang aloft immediately and furled the royals and top-gallant-sails, and took in the flying jib, hauled up the mainsail and trysail, squared the after yards, and awaited the attack. A huge mist capped with black clouds came driving toward us, extending over that quarter of the horizon, and covering the stars, which shone brightly in the other part of the heavens. It came upon us at once with a blast, and a shower of hail and rain, which almost took our breath from us. The hardiest was obliged to turn his back. We let the halyards run, and fortunately were not taken aback. The little vessel "paid off" from the wind, and ran for some time directly before it, tearing through the water with everything flying. Having called all hands, we close-reefed the topsails, and trysail, furled the courses and jib, set the fore-topmost staysail, and brought here up nearly to her course, with the weather braces hauled in a little, to ease her.

This was the first blow, that I had seen, which could really be called a gale. We had reefed our topsails in the Gulf Stream, and I thought it something serious, but an older sailor would have thought nothing of it. As I had now become used to the vessel and to my duty, I was of some service on a yard, and could knot my reef-point as well as anybody. I obeyed the order to lay * aloft with the rest, and found the reefing a very exciting scene; for one watch reefed the fore-topsail, and the other the main, and every one did his utmost to get his topsail hoisted first. We had a great advantage over the larboard watch, because the chief mate never goes aloft, while our new second mate used to jump into the rigging as soon as we began to haul out the reef-tackle, and have the weather ear-ing passed before there was a man upon the yard. In this way we were almost always able to raise the cry of "Haul out to leeward" before them, and having knotted our points, would slide down the shrouds and back-stays, and sing out at the topsail halyards to let it be known that we were ahead of them. Reefing is the most exciting part of a sailor's duty. All hands are engaged upon it, and after the halyards are let go, there is no time to be lost — no "soger-ing," or hanging back, then. If one is not quick enough, another runs over him. The first on the yard goes to the weather earing, the second to the lee, and the next two to the "dog's ears;" while the others lay along into the bunt, just giving each other elbow-room. In reefing, the yard-arms (the extremes of the yards) are the posts of honor; but in furling, the strongest and most experienced stand in the slings, (or, middle of the yard,) to make up the bunt. If the second mate is a smart fellow, he will never let any one take either of these posts from him; but if he is wanting either in seamanship, strength, or activity, some better man will get the bunt and earings from him; which immediately brings him into disrepute.

After all hands were called, at daybreak, three minutes and a half were allowed for every man to dress and come on deck, and if any were longer than that, they were sure to be overhauled by the mate, who was always on deck, and making himself heard all over the ship. The head-pump was then rigged, and the decks washed down by the second and third mates; the chief mate walking the quarter-deck and keeping a general supervision, but not deigning to touch a bucket or a brush. Inside and out, fore and aft, upper deck

* This word "lay," which is in such general use on board ship, being used in giving orders instead of "go"; as, "*Lay* forward !" "*Lay* aft !" "*Lay* aloft !" etc., I do not understand to be the neuter verb *lie*, mispronounced, but to be the ac-tive verb *lay*, with the objective case understood; as, "Lay *yourselves* forward !" "Lay *yourselves* aft!" etc.

and between decks, steerage and forecastle, rail, bulwarks, and
water-ways, were washed, scrubbed and scraped with brooms and
canvas, and the decks were wet and sanded all over, and then holy-
stoned. The holystone is a large, soft stone, smooth on the bottom,
with long ropes attached to each end, by which the crew keep it
sliding fore and aft, over the wet, sanded decks. Smaller hand-
stones, which the sailors call "prayer-books," are used to scrub in
among the crevices and narrow places, where the large holystone
will not go. An hour or two, we were kept at this work, when the
head-pump was manned, and all the sand washed off the decks and
sides. Then came swabs and squilgees; and after the decks were dry,
each one went to his particular morning job. There were five boats
belonging to the ship, — launch, pinnace, jolly-boat, larboard quar-
ter-boat, and gig, — each of which had a coxswain, who had charge
of it, and was answerable for the order and cleanness of it. The rest
of the cleaning was divided among the crew; one having the brass
and composition work about the capstan; another the bell, which
was of brass, and kept as bright as a gilt button; a third, the har-
ness-cask; another, the man-rope stanchions; others, the steps of
the forecastle and hatchways, which were hauled up and holy-
stoned. Each of these jobs must be finished before breakfast; and,
in the meantime, the rest of the crew filled the scuttle-butt, and the
cook scraped his kids (wooden tubs out of which the sailors eat)
and polished the hoops, and placed them before the galley, to await
inspection. When the decks were dry, the lord paramount made his
appearance on the quarter-deck, and took a few turns, when eight
bells were struck, and all hands went to breakfast. Half an hour
was allowed for breakfast, when all hands were called again; the
kids, pots, bread-bags, etc., stowed away; and, this morning, preparations were made for getting under weigh. We paid out on the
chain by which we swung; hove in on the other; catted the anchor;
and hove short on the first. This work was done in shorter time
than was usual on board the brig; for though everything was more
than twice as large and heavy, the cat-block being as much as a man
could lift, and the chain as large as three of the Pilgrim's, yet there
was a plenty of room to move about in, more discipline and system,
more men, and more good will. Every one seemed ambitious to do
his best: officers and men knew their duty, and all went well. As
soon as she was hove short, the mate, on the forecastle, gave the
order to loose the sails, and, in an instant, every one sprung into
the rigging, up the shrouds, and out on the yards, scrambling by
one another, — the first up the best fellow, — cast off the yard-arm
gaskets and bunt gaskets, and one man remained on each yard,

holding the bunt jigger with a turn round the tye, all ready to let go, while the rest laid down to man the sheets and halyards. The mate then hailed the yards — "All ready forward ?" — "All ready the cross-jack yards ?" etc., etc., and "Aye, aye, sir !" being returned from each, the word was given to let go; and in the twinkling of an eye, the ship, which had shown nothing but her bare yards, was covered with her loose canvas, from the royal-mast-heads to the decks. Every one then laid down, except one man in each top, to overhaul the rigging, and the topsails were hoisted and sheeted home; all three yards going to the mast-head at once, the larboard watch hoisting the fore, the starboard watch the main, and five light hands, (of whom I was one,) picked from the two watches, the mizen. The yards were then trimmed, the anchor weighed, the cat-block hooked on, the fall stretched out, manned by "all hands and the cook," and the anchor brought to the head with "cheerily men !" in full chorus. The ship being now under weigh, the light sails were set, one after another, and she was under full sail, before she had passed the sandy point. The fore royal, which fell to my lot, (being in the mate's watch,) was more than twice as large as that of the Pilgrim, and, though I could handle the brig's easily, I found my hands full, with this, especially as there were no jacks to the ship; everything being for neatness, and nothing left for Jack to hold on by, but his eyelids.

The sailmaker was the head man of the watch, and was generally considered the most experienced seaman on board. He was a thoroughbred old man-of-war's-man, had been to sea twenty-two years, in all kinds of vessels — men-of-war, privateers, slavers, and merchantmen; — everything except whalers, which a thorough sailor despises, and will always steer clear of, if he can. He had, of course, been in all parts of the world, and was remarkable for drawing a long bow. His yarns frequently stretched through a watch, and kept all hands awake. They were always amusing from their improbability, and, indeed, he never expected to be believed, but spun them merely for amusement; and as he had some humor and a good supply of man-of-war slang and sailor's salt phrases, he always made fun.

◇◇◇◇◇◇◇◇◇◇◇◇◇◇

[Reuben Delano, Fair Haven, Mass.]

In the spring of 1824 I went to live with a ship owner in the town of Fair Haven.

He had a ship at sea, which my older brother was aboard of. She was called the Stanton and in July she returned from a whaling voyage.

It was a pleasing thing to me, to meet my brother on his return, after an absence of three years, and when I visited the ship with him, strong ideas of entering on a seafaring life entered my mind, though he strove hard to dissuade me from it. I made my intentions known to my employer, he offered to raise my wages if I would re-

main, and sought by every means to dissuade me from the undertaking. My mother also used all her efforts to the same effect, but in vain. My brother on learning that I was determined to sail in the same ship with him and on her next voyage, painted the dangers of the sea in all their most appalling colors, but yet I would suffer nothing to turn me from my resolution. Short sighted boy! here was my first step to sorrow, trodden unheeded.

Having resolved to go to sea, I now commenced getting a proper fit out for the undertaking; a more anxious soul never slept, every hour seemed a day. Never shall I forget the first encasement of my boyish limbs in a red flannel shirt. Lord Nelson at the moment of his victory on the Nile, never felt half the importance that I did, my new glazed tarpaulin was more to my boyish vision than a kingly crown. I felt that I was a man then, and, though not fifteen, as big as the largest.

It is the usual practice before the sailing of a ship, to haul her into the stream and hire hands to take care of her until all is ready. Our ship was hauled out of dock on the 8th of August and on the 9th all was ready and the crew on board. The first officer asked me if I did not wish to go and see my mother. I replied, no; so fascinated was I with the idea of a sea voyage that I forgot mother, friends and every thing besides.

On the 10th we weighed anchor to beat out of the harbor, and made good progress in working ship, considering that two thirds of our crew were green hands; at 6 o'clock, p.m. the pilot left us off Nomans land.

As we cleared the land and entered upon the great ocean, I found I was governed by some new notions, and was not long in changing my opinion of a sea-faring life. At 9 p.m., the breeze freshened, we clewed down and single reefed our top sails. There seemed to be considerable swell, which while it kept the ship in active motion set me to casting up my accounts, and caused my mind to look back towards home.

Our ships company consisted of twenty-one souls and a singular assemblage they were, these were of almost all nations and various opinions and manners, in short I found myself in a new school and in my sickness almost wished myself back under the tutorage of my old mistress.

Our owners in this expedition were as short sighted as some of their crew, for it is a true proverb that " a man who skins a flint to save a cent will spoil a knife worth a shilling."

The first night out, the officers chose their watches and boats' crews, according to custom. I was placed in the larboard watch commanded by the first officer. Our main object now was to keep a good lookout for whales, and make the best of our way to the Western Islands.

The Sabbath after our departure, we found ourselves in the Gulf Stream, of which I had heard much as being remarkable for its continuous squalls of thunder, lightning and much rain. I found all that I had heard of it to be true, as on the following morning all hands were employed in getting down top gallant-yards, and I wished myself more at home than ever. In the Gulf Stream the weather is always very changeable. A ship one hour will be under a close-reefed main topsail, and the next, her top gallant sails will be set and with a fair wind, she will speed on her course. A sailor's life, is called an up and down life, and no one would ever doubt it who had sailed in the Gulf Stream. The winds, however, favored us and we were soon clear of it, much to the satisfaction of all on board.

The whole conversation was now upon things connected with our voyage, and every mind was full of bright anticipations for our future success. Some of the green ones were now so far recovered from their sea-sickness as to overhaul their chests and examine their outfit and the bills from the fitters out. They found, to use Jack's expression, that "the insides were like a southerly wind in a bread bag," which is seldom otherwise when sailors become intoxicated on shore and fall into the hands of the land sharks.

The next object of note, was a school of black fish which we fell in with about ten days out. Boats were lowered and we pulled an hour or so for them, but without success. So we kept on our course, with fine breezes and pleasant weather, with a bright look out at the mast heads, every one eager to discover the spoutings of a sperm whale, as the captain had offered a bounty of eighteen dollars to the discoverer of the first one which should be captured this side the land.

At 9, a.m., on the 20th day out, "breakers" were cried from the mast head, by one of our green hands; but the boat steerer at the main mast cried out that it was a large school of sperm whales, which Paddy had mistaken for breakers. Pat fancied himself already in possession of the bounty, but he learned that there is many a slip between the cup and the lip.

Our boats were cleared away, and our first officer was soon "on and fast" to a good sized whale, with a *one flud* iron which did not hold him in tow fifteen minutes before it drew, and Pat's fairy dream vanished.

On the 25th day from our departure we were up with the island of Florez one of the Western Islands. This island is inhabited by the Portuguese. We backed our main topsail and sent a boat on shore for provisions, which the island yields in great abundance and variety.

We spent that day and part of the next in taking in our supplies, and then took our departure for Cape Horn, a bright look out aloft as usual.

Nothing of note occurred until crossing the line when our main topsail was again laid to the mast, for the purpose of receiving old Neptune on board with the proper ceremonies. The old fellow's visit seemed to afford a deal of amusement to the officers and old hands, but was much to the chagrin of us green ones.

These ceremonies being over, we again stood on our course for Cape Horn, and in 56 days from our last departure, we made the Falkland Islands. By this time the weather began to grow cold and squally, and we made all snug for doubling Cape Horn. To avoid as much as possible the heavy squalls that blow from the land, we gave it a good birth and doubled it in the latitude of 58 deg. south.

After passing the Cape, the weather soon began to soften and we manned our mast heads again for a bright look out along the coast of Chili, but with no success, and then made our way for what is called the "off shore ground." As all three of the mast heads were to be manned, boys were stationed at the mizzen top gallant mast head. There was still a bounty to the one who should first discover a whale, but it was much reduced, as it consisted of but a bottle of rum, and a pair of duck trousers. I had not been long in the cross trees one foggy morning when it was my station aloft, before to my great joy I discovered something which very much resembled Pat's breakers. I quickly gave the alarm lest I should be anticipated by the look-out at the fore and main. It proved to be a school of cows and calves. (whales.) The boats were cleared away, and our chief mate went in and fastened to a small cow whale which ran him from the ship hull down; but he finally succeeded in turning her up, while the rest of the school made good their escape. I was much astonished after this whale was tried out and stowed away, that the oil could be put in so small a compass as she made us but ten barrels, and I began to feel disheartened and cried out to my brother that if whales were so scarce and no bigger I should never get home in the world.

After this, whales seemed to be more plenty and we took in 350 barrels in the next three months. We might have taken double that quantity, had it not been for a quarrel among the officers, who, regardless of the reputation of the voyage, refused to assist each other where they individually, could not have the honor of killing the whale. Therefore many escaped after they were struck.

Having taken on board a good supply of provisions and water we will bid farewell to the Sandwich Islands which have entertained us so well for the space of three weeks.

Our anchor is at the bow, and Jack is once more in his element, bound for the Japan coast, a cruising ground for sperm-whales which extends from latitude 30 deg. to 45 deg. North. The season there is something like our own, in the three summer months which is the best season for whaling.

Nine days from the Sandwich Islands, we raised a school of large bull whales, it was a fine pleasant day and in our proceedings the *honor* of our officers shone bright. The proverb of the flint and jacknife was illustrated in full; our owners had purchased a lot of damaged hemp because it was *cheap* and had their whale lines manufactured from it, their harpoons were purchased with the same end in view, to save expense, and were poor in quality. We were fast to three different whales during the day, but the dignity and honor of our officers, which would not suffer one to assist the other, our miserable harpoons and rotten lines, caused us to come on board at night as well off as we were when we started in the morning and not oil enough to grease our fingers. This days work caused much hard feeling and a great deal of high flown conversation among the crew, and it was plainly perceived in the conduct of our officers who walked the decks as if strangers to each other.

But in a few days this coldness wore off and every thing went on as usual. It was the custom in those days for every ship to carry rum. But our ship was stocked quite moderately in comparison to some, as she had but three barrels on board for a three years cruise, but this in my estimation was just three too many.

The captain and his officers were temperate men for those times, and always drank in moderation. It was served out in small quantities, in "boiling out," and "heaving in," and in wet and disagreeable weather.

Being a mere boy some old tar would often demand my share, which I readily complied with, and I have often wished that some one else had drank my share during all the future years of my life. We had now been nine months at sea, but as good luck would have it we fell in with a large school of whales.

We lowered this day with better success, than common, and fastened to five, and out of the five brought three along side of our ship.

It is remarkable to witness the motherly affection displayed by a cow whale: in time of danger, when the calf is small, she frequently takes it under her fin for protection and loses her own life to save it. In going into a school of whales to strike, a young one will generally cause the whole school, to bring to, in a "gallied" and confounded state, and at such times selfish officers can display their *honor* to advantage as it gives a fine opportunity for each to do as he likes with his own, and more to the satisfaction of a ships company than it would be along side of a large lone whale where all three boats are commonly wanted to assist each other.

It is my opinion that a whale can see as far in his element, as we can in ours, and my reason for this is I have often seen a lone whale raised when as far as the eye could extend no other was in sight and we would not be fast more than ten minutes before we could see hundreds around us.

I had now become a tolerable seaman and could hand, reef and steer, knot and splice quite well.

But here I will digress from my narrative a little to give the reader a plain account of the manner of killing, cutting in and boiling out a whale.

Whales being raised from the mast head, the hands are at once employed in getting the lines into the boats and "bending on the craft," which consists of two harpoons one to a short warp and one to the line. They are then placed in the harpooner crotch, which is situated on the starboard bow of the boat being within a convenient distance for our operations, the main yard is hauled aback, the boats are hoisted and cranes swung, the boat steerer and boat header jumps in, the order is given to "lower away" and she is followed down the ships side by the respective crews.

All hands are now seated at the oars; the boat steerer taking the

harpooneer oar, and the word now is "pull my boys for the whale" whilst those left in charge of the ship are hauling up the davit tackles, bracing, forward the main yard, with one hand aloft, looking out for the boats and whales.

As the boat approaches near the whale, the boat steerer stands up, and, when within striking distance, throws his line iron, and then the short warp, and the cry is now, "stern all." This being accomplished, he changes places with the boat-header, who takes the lance, and the boat steerer, the steering oar, and with the assistance of the crew he manages the boat, and wets the line, the bight of which is in the after part of the boat with a round turn round the "logger head."

The crew is now occupied in hauling the boat on to the whale, while the boat steerer is coiling away the line. When the boat is brought again within a convenient distance the heads-man throws his lance, and if he be expert kills the whale sometimes at a single dart.

[185]

The cry is now "there she spouts blood." On such an occasion the shark of the Pacific is nearly as attentive as the land sharks of our cities and seaports are to poor Jack, on his first arrival, with this difference, that while one is contented with destroying the body, the other destroys both body and soul.

The whale being dead, if the ship is to windward signals are made for her to run down, meanwhile, a hole is cut in her head and one in the fluke and lines made fast for the purpose of hauling along side.

The captain's boat now comes along side the ship and is hoisted up and preparations commence, for taking the whale alongside which is done by hauling aback the head yards, jib hauled down, main and mizen top-sails braced forward, and the spanker set. The boat which has the whale in tow, now takes her line to the ship, and all come on board and commence hauling in the whale. When along side, she is fluke roped and made fast to the bowsprit bits, and the boats are all hoisted up to their proper stations. By this time Jack begins to feel the want of a fresh nip, and the welcome sound comes from aft to "splice the main brace," which causes Jack's eyes to glisten and makes his heart rejoice. This operation being performed some are employed in reeving the "cutting falls" and others the "guys" for heaving in the blubber. The falls being to the windlass, and the guys hauled out, and the hooks lashed on, the stages are over the side and the respective officers for cutting out, are at their places. The first mate in the after staging, and the second in the forward which is slung between the gang-way and main chesstree. Then comes the boat steerer, who goes over the side on to the whale to put in the hook and raise the piece. The hole is now cut and the "monkey rope" on the hook being entered, the word is given to "heave away" and the boat-steerer comes on board and takes his place in the blubber room for the purpose of stowing away the blubber. While the other two, with two edged knives, with blades three feet in length made for the purpose stand by to "board the piece," which, being hove a proper distance above the plankshear, a hole is cut close down, a block, with strap of sufficient length is put in the hole and togled on the outside; they surge on one fall, and heave on the other, till our last fall has sufficient strain. We then lower a bit on the first piece, cut it off and lower it down into the blubber room. Now commences the process of cutting off the head, which generally takes from an hour to an hour and a half by an expert workman with a sharp blade. We now heave away on the body, which in the operation of heaving and cutting, rolls over until the blubber is all peeled off to the tail;

which being unjointed, the carcase is let go, and numerous are the ravenous birds and sharks, the dread of the sailor, that attend it. We now lash on our hooks, for the purpose of hooking to the head, this being hauled along-side for that purpose. And now the main brace must be spliced again, which agreeable ceremony being performed, we heave away and separate the "junk" from the "case." This being on board, we now hook to the case, which is hove up high enough to bail it without intermixture with the salt water. The hole is now cut in the head of the size of a barrel, a "tail

CUTTING IN

block" made fast to the cutting falls above with a line and bucket attached to it. We now commence bailing out the case which in a large whale, often contains from 15 to 20 barrels of "head matter" which is made into spermaceti candles. The whale being now on board, all hands are at their stations; some are cutting, some are mincing, while the boat steerers are lighting the fires for the purpose of boiling out.

The head matter is boiled out first, and we generally calculate that a sixty barrel whale will yield us 20 barrels of head oil, which is the best. In a sperm whale voyage we calculate one third of our cargo to be head oil; but I once knew a Nantucket Captain on his arrival from the Pacific ocean, who turned out a cargo to his owner which was marked to be one half head. One of the broad brimed owners being a little more foxy than some of the rest of his brethren, finding his "capstan somewhat palled" at this, determined not to swallow it whole, or chew it too long but at a convenient season spit it out. But when the ship was ready for sea again, he bid the captain adieu, requesting him at the same time to cut off no more whales heads abaft the fins. Leaving him to take or not the advice of Broadbrim, I will now resume my narrative. In this season we were fast to 19 large whales and our *honorables* succeeded in cap-

BOILING OUT

turing but two of them; we were more successful among the small ones, for during the season we obtained 700 barrels.

We are now 15 months out with 1050 barrels; our small stores meantime had grown short. We had neither tea or coffee on board and had but 4 ounces of meat per day for each man.

The season here was about to close and the weather grew rugged and boisterous, our spars were poor and our rigging often falling down about our heads, the crew in many respects debilitated being attacked by that formidable disease called the scurvy, the consequence of being too long at sea and the want of vegetables. Our officers now concluded to make the best of our way to Owyhee one of the Sandwich islands; accordingly made our course, running for the islands in the day time and lying too at night, as it is considered good whaling ground the whole distance.

On whaling ground it is customary for the Captain, first and second officers, to lie in all night while the night is divided into three "watches" each headed by a boatsteerer which is called "quarter watches." On board of a whale ship when no whale are in sight, the sailor has a great deal of leisure time which properly spent would be a benefit to him; but, too often this time is wasted by the pernicious habit of gambling, and I am sorry to say that our crew was greatly addicted to it; as it was a source of a good deal of ill

feeling among us, causing serious difficulties among the officers and crew.

On the seventh day from our departure from the Japan coast, at 2 p.m. a whale was seen from the mast head, and the cheering cry of "there she blows" resounded through the ship. Our Captain the day before had put a new boat upon his cranes, of which, my brother was steersman. At the time of raising the whale the wind blew fresh and caused a heavy sea. The whale being to leeward at no great distance we hauled back our main yard, lowered away our boats, and made the best of our way for the whale. The monster lay fore and aft in the trough of the sea. The Captain's boat was ahead and going with great speed before the wind and sea. As the boat approached, the boat steerer put himself in the attitude to strike; the Captain fearing danger cried to him to "hold his hand;" but he disregarded the Captain's orders and threw both irons, plunging them to the socket, in the monster's side. For this rashness they were all made bitterly to repent. At one instant the motion of his gigantic fluke cut our boat completely in two which left us completely in the suds; here was a pretty kettle of fish. The first officer's boat being nearest, quickly came to our assistance, and found us clinging to the pieces, and extricated us from this perilous situation. Our formidable foe had in the meantime a course downward, and came up again and lay motionless on the water, a splendid sight to behold. Our second mate acted in this emergency like a motherless colt struck with the Spanish mildew, for though but two boats lengths from him he made no effort for his capture. Our crew was now put on board the ship and our first officer started to capture the whale and pick up the broken boat. The fish now began to see his danger, and started off again with great speed; so we soon gave up the chase and with the fragments of the boat, and the empty line tub, all came on board. This adventure put a damper upon many of the crew; night had arrived and sail was taken in, but as some recompense for our disappointment, grog was served all around which caused us to forget our troubles and made our tongues run lively.

Night passed off as usual and with the morning light we were again on our course. Nothing remarkable took place and in ninety-eight days we made the island of Owyhee. Our first officer with his boats crew was sent to sound the passage into Caricakore Bay, and in his absence a school of whales made their appearance between the ship and the land. The ship at this time lay becalmed, and our captain and second officer lowered away: our second officer pulled directly on to the whale's eye and frightened him, but as good luck would have it, he run in favor of the Captain's boat; and we soon had two irons into him.

The whale being turned up and brought along side, the Captain reprimanded the second mate, for his disobedient conduct, and received from him nothing but abusive language. For this he was turned off duty. At 6 p. m. our boat which had been on a voyage of discovery came along side. Our first and second officer had been opposed to the Captain all the voyage, and it was manifested to a high degree in this case. Our first officer seemed to be quite indignant at the Captain's success, but he was taken sick during the night. In the morning the Captain and the boatsteerer commenced the work of cutting in the whale which we accomplished by two o'clock.

In the month of November I returned from my southern cruise, and having experienced much rough weather in a miserable little Sloop, I was content to remain at home during the months of winter.

I was not fond of society, but preferred above all things to be alone. This trait of character has ruined many a young man. By mingling with the world only, can our faults be brought out; we do not know ourselves except by intercourse with others.

I was naturally industrious and an early riser, but not always to take the worm belonging to the early bird, for in most cases I was gnawed by it, as my first landfall was the decanter.

My mother remonstrated with me on the danger of my conduct, with tears in her eyes, but in vain. The baleful influence of intemperance was spread around me, and I was already a slave to the intoxicating bowl. She would often repeat to me the words of holy writ. "Wo unto him who riseth early in the morning to follow strong drink during the day !" but I heeded not the voice of maternal tenderness, or of divine warning. Sometimes she resorted to prayer in my behalf, and petitioned heaven to turn me from the paths of evil, with all the eloquence of a mother's love for her erring boy.

The sound of her voice in prayer struck on my ear like the sentence of a convicted criminal, and sometimes I would resolve to mend my course, but as often as any thing would turn up to cause the least unpleasant feelings in my mind, I resorted to my cups to drown my sorrows.

I spent the three winter months at school, and made good progress, much to the satisfaction of my teacher and myself.

On the following spring, a Boston gentleman removed to Fairhaven for the purpose of engaging in the whaling business. I applied to him for a birth on board his ship, and procured one at once, much to the dissatisfaction of my mother, who begged of me to remain at home, as I was the only one to comfort her in her old age. My heart sometimes misgave me for deserting her, and fearing lest I should be induced by her to remain, I plunged deeper than ever into the abyss of drunkenness, and scarcely drew a sober breath, until I was on board ship and out at sea.

Strange that men will never profit by the experience of others, or of themselves — that they will pursue the evil rather than the good, and seek the transitory pleasures which destroy, rather than the lasting ones that never fail as a constant joy to the possessor. When fairly out to sea, my conscience smote me, as I considered my past conduct; but I had taken six gallons of my enemy with me, and to drown my serious reflections, I resorted to my keg. We were bound to the Brazil coast, on a right whale voyage, and our ship was fitted for a year.

The fifth day out we encountered a gale, during which we carried away some of our spars and rigging, and sprung a leak; but we soon made the necessary repairs and were on our course again.

The owners of the ship had purchased her, supposing she was staunch and sound. She was bored into by the carpenter and pronounced so on our leaving; but she already leaked from five to seven hundred strokes an hour in carrying heavy sail. Some of us were for going aft and requesting the Captain to put back, and in case of refusal, to refuse to do duty; but the most of our crew were boys, and we finally concluded to leave it with the officers, knowing that they shared with us the risk and danger.

On our passage out, we put into the Western Islands, and obtained a good supply of vegetables, and then made for the False Banks, a cruising ground for right whales.

This season we encountered an abundance of squally heavy weather.

The day on which we took the first whale alongside, it began to blow heavy, and we accordingly paid out on our fluke-chain to let him ride easy. All night the gale continued, and the leak increased, much to the alarm of the Captain, who broached the expediency of casting the whale adrift, as every time the vessel pitched, her transom timbers were so rotten, and her stern frame so open, that the water would dash into the cabin.

The next morning the wind abated, and we commenced cutting in.

The weather being rugged, and whales scarce, we took but 300 barrels during the season, and then shaped our course for the Main Banks, the Sally Ann of New Bedford in company.

Both ships carrying a heavy press of canvass, we found that night that our leak increased to such a rate that 1,500 strokes an hour did not free her. All hands were called, sail taken in, and the ship hove to under a close reefed main top sail, with a lantern at the mizen peak as a signal for the other ship to do the same.

Early next morning, all hands were employed in getting things from forward, and rolling them aft, in order to stop one of the leaks in the bow. Meantime the New Bedford ship came down, and the Captain came on board.

He recommended our proceedings, and after wishing us much success, manned his boat and went on board.

In examining the ship, we found her very open at the hood ends. It was a wet, difficult job; but we succeeded in driving in some pine wedges, and with a coat of tarred parcelling and sheet lead nailed over it, we came on board, replaced our cargo, and putting the ship under short sail, stood on our way. This decreased our leak a trifle. In a few days we had moderate weather, and performed the same operation on the stern leaks that we had on the bows.

Many of the crew now began to complain of sore breasts and weak stomachs from standing so long at the pump breaks, and it became necessary to resort to some machinery for working the pumps, differing from a hand brake. For this purpose a roller was got out, two feet in length and nine inches in diameter, the ends of which were hooped and gudgeoned. A cleet was then nailed to the main-mast six feet above the circle rail, in which was a hole one inch in diameter, boxed with iron, a stanchion was raised abaft the circle rail, of the same height and bushed in the same manner; holes were morticed into the roller opposite each, and pump brakes nine feet in length were shipped into them, standing upwards. This being done holes were morticed in the brakes six inches from the roller, and our upper boxes were attached to the brakes with wooden spears instead of iron. Our apparatus was then hung to the main-mast and stanchion before mentioned, ropes were then attached to the ends of the brakes, which were nearly twelve feet from the deck. By a see-saw motion with the ropes both pumps played admirably, and we could work faster and with twice the ease of the hand brakes, and relieved us greatly.

In a short time the pumps became chamber worn, and we took the boxes out and bagged them, and were now enabled to keep the ship free.

We fell in with a number of ships on this cruise, and oftentimes sailed in company with some of our townsmen.

On lowering upon one occasion, the weather being rugged, we succeeded in fastening to a whale. He soon sounded taking overboard with him the 2d mate and boatsteerer, entangled in the line. Fortunately the line parted between the whale and boatsteerer, and they both rose to the surface and were helped into the boat much exhausted, and the steersman badly mangled.

We here experienced much heavy weather, sometimes compelled to lie to for fifteen or twenty days in succession.

During the season we took but 250 barrels of oil. Some of our crew were sick with the scurvy, and the rest were worn down by short allowance and hard work at the pumps, for she still leaked badly.

We had been nine months at sea, when the Captain gave orders to get the standing-sail booms aloft. We rove our gear, and with a smart south wind, gave her the rag for home, the pumps being strictly attended to every half hour.

When we got into the tropics, we painted ship as usual, touched at Pernambuco, and obtained a boat load of oranges.

Our crew by this time become much debilitated with disease, and had we not spoken the U. S. frigate Hudson, before our arrival here, and obtained from her Commander, Com. Crayten, lime juice and oranges, some of us would have been piped down to Davy Jones' Locker.

In my voyage to the Southern States, I had seen something of slavery in the U. S. But the treatment of the slaves in Pernambuco, by the Portuguese, is horrible beyond description. They were used worse than any brute beasts of the field, and it was heart-rending to witness the lacerated bodies of these unfortunate beings, doomed to a life of misery, and servitude for their passionate and cruel task-masters.

Not unfrequently, they are punished by death at the stake, for the most trifling offences. We stopped but one day at Pernambuco, and with a fair wind, stood on our course. The heavy weather in the Gulf, made the ship leak badly, and our first landfall was Block Island.

It was quite foggy and we were becalmed near the shore, so we let go our anchor.

At ten in the evening it cleared away, and a light breeze sprung up from the Southward, manned our windlass, hove up our anchor and made sail; and at 9 a.m. the next day, took a pilot on-board, and at 3 o'clock in the afternoon our ship was along side of Fair Haven wharf, after an absence of twelve months and twenty-five days, with 550 barrels of oil; and I again shook hands with my mother.

With slate and pencil, the next day I sat down to cipher up my accounts with the world; and finding myself $40 minus on this voyage, I throwed by the slate, and was out of the house in an instant, forgetting every thing over the intoxicating cup.

After I became sober, finding myself so much in arrears, I determined to go to the sea once more, and that as soon as possible, and accordingly, shipped that day in a privateer built ship bound for the Indian Ocean. When I informed my mother of this transaction, she said to me, there is plenty of business on shore, you are capable of doing well, if you will only cease drinking, leave off old habits, and resolve to live a sober and temperate life. You will be beloved and respected, if you take my advice; if not, utter ruin awaits you.

At night we were visited by a severe gale, and at nine in the evening were obliged to put out our fires. At eleven it blew a perfect gale; our decks were covered with oil, which rendered it very difficult to keep on our feet. The sea ran so high, that it became necessary to take our boats from the cranes, and get them in on deck. This was performed after much toil and difficulty.

Our ship had been built at Salem for a privateer during the last war, and was the most uneasy craft in a gale that I ever saw; but

she was of a beautiful model, and a very fast sailer, being very heavy sparred according to her hull.

On trying the pumps we found that she made water quite fast. Every sea that struck her, made her complain fore and aft. On going forward we found that our outer bobstay was gone, and we were obliged to get a preventer tackle on as soon as possible. With much difficulty we succeeded in hooking it, and this purchase served to save the spars. We now lay aloft and sent down top gallant yards. The gale continuing to increase, we goose-winged our main topsail, and set the mizzen stay sail. During the whole of the next day it continued to blow with unabated fury. At four in the afternoon, the Island Inaccessible appeared on the lee beam, at only a league distant.

By this time her upper timbers worked like an old hand basket; her spar-shores that supported the cross timbers, upon which the boats were placed over head, displayed so much weakness that we were obliged to hook on our tackle purchase, and set them up amid ships.

We were now in the greatest extremity of danger. Before us was a high and rocky coast, and every moment shortened the distance between our ship and the shore. There was no alternative, but to carry sail and claw off if possible, even at the risk of carrying away every mast and spar in her.

We now close reefed our fore and mizzen topsails, reefed down our courses, sheeted home our topsails, hoisted them up, set our braces, boarded our tacks, hauled aft our sheets, set the fore top-mast stay sail and hauled out our mizzen. With so much sail on her, the old ship increased her leak, and her timbers creaked and groaned at every surge. Our lives now depended on the strength of our canvass, and our efforts at the pump. Old Davy threatened us now pretty hard; but at seven in the evening we succeeded in clearing the point of the island; shortened sail and hove the ship to. Our danger was soon forgotten, lamps were lighted, and the watch below were soon as sound asleep as if there was no such thing as danger in the world.

WORTHINGTON, CONNECTICUT

WOODEN NUTMEGS

◇◆◇◆◇◆◇◆◇◆◇◆◇◆◇

[*Timothy Dwight*]

THE inhabitants of Worthington, Conn., make great quantities of
tin ware; or utensils, formed of tinned plates. As this species of
manufacture, on the Western side of the Atlantic, probably commenced here; I will give you an account of the manner, in which
it was introduced.

About the year 1740, William Pattison, a native of Ireland, came
to this country, and settled in this town. His trade was that of a
tinner; and soon after his arrival, he commenced manufacturing
tin ware, and continued in that business until the Revolutionary
war. He was then under the necessity of suspending it, as the raw
material could not be obtained. After the war, this manufacture
was carried on at Berlin, by those young men who had learned the
art from Mr. Pattison; and these persons have since extended the
business over a number of the neighbouring towns.

For many years, after tinned plates were manufactured in this
place into culinary vessels, the only method used by the pedlars for

conveying them to distant towns, for sale, was by means of a horse and two baskets, balanced on his back. After the war, carts and waggons, were used for this purpose, and have, from that time to the present, been the only means of conveyance which have been adopted.

The manner, in which this ware is disposed of, puts to flight all calculation. A young man is furnished by the proprietor with a horse, and a cart covered with a box, containing as many tin vessels, as the horse can conveniently draw. This vehicle within a few years has, indeed, been frequently exchanged for a waggon; and then the load is doubled. Thus prepared, he sets out on an expedition for the winter. A multitude of these young men direct themselves to the Southern States; and in their excursions travel wherever they can find settlements. Each of them walks, and rides, alternately, through this vast distance, till he reaches Richmond, Newbern, Charleston, or Savannah; and usually carries with him to the place of his destination no small part of the gain, which he has acquired upon the road. Here he finds one or more workmen, who have been sent forward to co-operate with him, furnished with a sufficient quantity of tinned plates to supply him with all the ware, which he can sell during the season. With this he wanders into the interiour country; calls at every door on his way; and with an address, and pertinacity, not easily resisted, compels no small number of the inhabitants to buy. At the commencement of summer they return to New-York; and thence to New-Haven, by water; after selling their vehicles, and their horses. The original load of a single horse, as I am told, is rarely worth more than three hundred dollars; or of a waggon, more than six hundred. Yet this business is said to yield both the owner and his agent valuable returns; and the profit to be greater than that, which is made by the sale of any other merchandise of equal value. Even those, who carry out a single load, and dispose of it in the neighbouring country, find their employment profitable. In this manner considerable wealth has been accumulated in Worthington, and in several towns in its vicinity.

Every inhabited part of the United States is visited by these men. I have seen them on the peninsula of Cape Cod, and in the neighbourhood of Lake Erie; distant from each other more than six hundred miles. They make their way to Detroit, four hundred miles farther; to Canada; to Kentucky; and, if I mistake not, to New-Orleans and St. Louis.

All the evils, which are attendant upon the bartering of small wares, are incident to this, and every other mode of traffic of the same general nature. Many of the young men, employed in this business, part, at an early period with both modesty, and principle. Their sobriety is exchanged for cunning; their honesty for imposition; and their decent behaviour for coarse impudence. Mere wanderers, accustomed to no order, control, or worship; and directed solely to the acquisition of petty gains; they soon fasten upon this object; and forget every other, of a superiour nature. The only source of their pleasure, or their reputation, is gain; and that, however small, or however acquired, secures both. No course of life tends more rapidly, or more effectually to eradicate every moral feeling.

Berlin has, I suspect, suffered not a little from this source. Were their manufactures sold, like other merchandize; the profits would undoubtedly be lessened: but the corruption of a considerable number of human beings would be prevented.*

◇◇◇◇◇◇◇◇◇◇◇◇◇

["Lord" Timothy Dexter, Newburyport]

How did Dexter make his money ye says bying whale bone for staing for ships in grossing three houndred & 40 tons — bort all in boston salum and all in Noue york under Cover oppenly told them for my ships they all laffed so I had at my oan pris I had four

* The business of selling tin ware, has within a few years undergone a considerable change. Formerly the pedlar's load was composed exclusively of this manufacture: now he has an assortment of merchandise to offer to his customers. He carries pins, needles, scissars, combs, coat and vest buttons, with many other trifling articles of hardware; and children's books, and cotton stuffs made in New-England. A number set out with large waggons loaded with dry goods, hats and shoes; together with tin ware, and the smaller articles already mentioned. These loads will frequently cost the proprietor from one to two thousand dollars; and are intended exclusively for the Southern and Western States.

It is frequently the fact, that from twenty to thirty persons are employed by a single house, in the manufacturing and selling of tin ware and other articles. The workmen, furnished with a sufficient quantity of the raw materials to employ them for six months, are sent on by water, in the autumn, to Virginia, North and South Carolina, or Georgia. They station themselves at some town in the interiour, where the employer, or his agent, has a store, well furnished with such articles as the pedlars require. As the stock of each pedlar is exhausted, he repairs to the store for a supply. In this way, a large amount of goods are vended during the six or eight months they are absent.

Some idea may be formed of the extent to which this business is sometimes carried, from the fact, that immediately after the late war with Great Britain, which terminated in 1815, ten thousand boxes of tinned plates were manufactured into culinary vessels in the town of Berlin, in one year. Since that time, however, the quantity demanded for the market, has greatly diminished. — *Pub.*
(1821)

Counning men for Rounners thay found the horne as I told them to act the fool I was full of Cash I had nine tun of silver on hand at that time — all that time the Creaters more or less laffing it spread very fast here is the Rub — in fifty days thay smelt a Rat —

found where it was gone to Nouebry Port — spekkelaters swarming like hell houns — to be short with it I made seventey five per sent — one tun and halfe of silver on hand and over — one more spect — Drole a Nuf — I dreamed of worming pans three nites that thay would doue in the west inges I got no more than fortey two thousand — put them in nine vessels for difrent ports that tuck good hold I cleared sevinty nine per sent the pans thay made yous of them for Coucking — very good masser for Coukey — blessed good in Deade missey got nise handel Now burn my fase the best thing I Ever see in borne days I found I was very luckky in spekkelation. I Dreamed that the good book was Run Down in this Countrey nine years gone so low as halfe prise and Dull at that — the bibel I means I had the Ready Cash by holl sale I bort twelve per sent under halfe pris thay Cost fortey one sents Each bibbel — twentey one thousand — I put them into twenty one vessels for the west inges and sent a text that all of them must have one bibel in every familey or if not thay would goue to hell — and if thay had Dun wiked flie to the bibel and on thare Neas and kiss the bible three times and look up to heaven annest for forgivnes My Captteins all had Compleat orders — here Coms the good luck I made one hundred per sent & littel over then I found I had made money anuf I hant speckalated sense old time by government secourities I made or cleared forty seven thousand Dolors — that is the old afare Now I toald the all the sekrett Now be still let me A lone Dont wonder Noe more houe I got my money boaz

DEXTER'S MANSION

(Note to Dexter's Second Edition.)

fouder mister printer the Nowing ones complane of my book the fust edition had no stops I put in A Nuf here and thay may peper and solt it as they plese

,,,
,,,
....
,,,
....
....
.................................!!!!!!!!!!!!!!!!!!..................................
.................................!!!!!!!!!!!!!!......................................
.................................!!!!!!!..
.................................!...
,,,
.... ??????????????????????????????? ....

❖❖❖❖❖❖❖❖❖❖❖❖❖

[*David L. Dodge, Connecticut*]

I began to think of giving up teaching, and preparing myself for trade, as a more active business, calculated to restore to me vigorous health.

A young gentleman who had the principal charge of his father's store, one of the most respectable in the city, kindly invited me to examine their whole stock at my leisure, giving me their private marks. The general practice at that day was to make goods in New York currency at cost, and sell them at the same prices in New England currency, which was an advance of 33 1-3 per cent., deducting expenses.

NORWICH, CONNECTICUT

In the spring of 1799, I had an offer to take charge of a store as a clerk for one year, though the salary was not half equal to my tuition bills; yet as I lacked experience, I accepted it, to commence at the close of my quarter, and notified accordingly the proprietors of the school house, who expressed their regret to me.

I entered upon my new business as the chief clerk, the owner residing in New London, with considerable anxiety for want of experience, and soon found, from the complication and extent of the business, that I had hurried myself into a serious responsibility. It required all my efforts of body and mind; and, to keep up the books, I often had to take them to the house, and write till near midnight, and I now seriously found the need of a regular mercantile education. The store was established in Norwich on account of the great mortality, 1798, by yellow fever, in New London, and was considered as a temporary establishment.

Near the close of my year, I inquired of the owner if he intended to continue the store, and, if he did, whether he wanted my services; he answered he had not decided, and if he should continue the business he might employ me another year, but could not very much advance my wages. I gave him distinctly to understand I should not again engage without at least fifty per cent. advance on my salary.

Shortly after, Joshua Raymond, Esq., considered a wealthy man, who resided in Montville, a deacon in the church, called upon me and asked me how I should like to enter a copartnership with him to establish a store of a general assortment of goods for retail, and keep salt, crockery, rum, sugar, and molasses, at wholesale; stating that he had one ship in the Liverpool trade, and two schooners in the West India business. I told him I would take the subject into consideration, and would be pleased to see him again in a few days hence. One of the most judicious and respectable merchants in the place was very friendly to me, with whom I confidentially advised on the subject. He said he had known Mr. Raymond many years, considered him a correct, honorable man, who was generally estimated to be worth about fifty thousand dollars; but he was of opinion that he had unwisely entered into navigation, without much experience, in very hazardous times. He, however, thought I might join him safely in a retail store, if I kept out of navigation. Soon after, Squire Raymond, as he was generally called, came in, and asked if I had considered the subject he had suggested. I answered that I had, and must wholly decline entering without experience into navigation, but should be willing to unite with him in a retail store. After some interviews, we formed an agreement. By close industry and economy I had saved some property, and we were each to put into joint stock specific amounts, and not to reduce them during our copartnership, which was to continue only during the satisfaction of the parties.

I purchased a small assortment of dry goods, hardware, crockery, and groceries, to begin with, until I had gained more experience. My partner purchased more vessels, and repaired and loaded them at the wharf, and drew orders freely on the store until he had drawn out more than he had put in. I reminded him of the necessity of replacing his capital, which he was always going to do on the arrival of some vessel. Before the close of the year he was largely indebted to the store. I then pressed for a dissolution; he then turned in some groceries, still leaving a considerable balance against him for the extent of our business. Being determined to dissolve the connection, it was effected at the close of the year, I being solely authorized to settle the concern. Within two years Mr. Raymond was declared bankrupt, and I received from the commissioners about forty cents on a dollar upon the balance due me. I went immediately to closing our late concern, and in the meantime I was appointed the only auctioneer in the county, under the law of the United States. I was called upon to sell bankrupt estates, goods for merchants, closing their concerns, and received some consignments from New York.

In the fall of 1801, I made a trip to Boston and Salem, to gain a better knowledge of the market, where my wife's brothers resided, who invited me to spend the winter with them, and attend the auc-

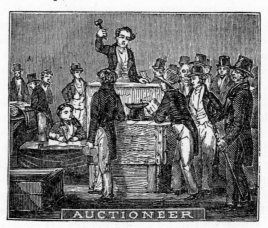

tions to gain a better general knowledge of dry goods. I purchased at auction an extra-fine piece of broadcloth, brought it home in the stages, and sold it to a merchant tailor beyond the expenses of my journey. I collected what funds I could command, put all my notes and accounts into the hands of an attorney for collection, under restrictions, and made preparations for leaving my family for the winter, and proceeded to Boston and Salem. Through the introduction of two of my brothers-in-law, who were gentlemen of high respectability, I gained, in Salem, a knowledge of the names, the cost, the expenses of importation, and qualities of most kinds of East India goods; and in Boston, by auction sales, and at S. & H. Higginson's store, who were cousins of my wife, where another brother of hers was a clerk, they having given me the kind invitation to examine their importations of European goods, which were general and extensive, by which I not only learned the names and costs, but was the better able to judge when most kinds of goods sold at a sacrifice by auction.

In February, 1802, goods generally were greatly depressed, failures occurred, and staple dry goods often sold by auction from twenty-five to fifty per cent. loss, for cash. I determined to commence purchasing. My wife's brothers offered me a loan for a year of two thousand dollars, and guaranteed a supercargo's adventure from India at ninety days. I purchased trunks and neatly packed my goods; hired two wagoners to carry them to Plainfield in Connecticut, where I effected the sale of about four thousand dollars, for cash. The balance I transported to Norwich, where I closed the sale for cash, and in about two weeks I returned to Salem with the proceeds in my pocket, having a net gain on an average of my sales beyond my expectations. I immediately invested my funds again in piece goods, mainly by auction, and purchased on time an entire invoice of India silk handkerchiefs. I again hired wagons to convey my goods to Connecticut, spending about a week in Connecticut in making sales to advantage. In March, I shipped my handkerchiefs on board a Norwich packet for New York, and embarked myself. We had a severe gale in the sound, and just escaped shipwreck. On arriving I soon disposed of most of my handkerchiefs, and closed the balance by auction, making a fair average profit for cash. I returned to Norwich, remitted what I owed in Salem, spent a while with my family, and determined to give up an irregular business, and open a regular dry goods cash store, as I had acquired confidence in my own judgment in most kinds of staple goods, and some knowledge of fancy articles.

I visited Hartford, I think in May, to look for a good location. I was an entire stranger to every one, except to Mr. Asa Corning, a respectable, pious man. After leisurely surveying the place, noticing the course of business, and inquiring the prices of some leading articles, I observed that most of the retailers had large amounts of old goods on hand, and that there was an opening for fresh goods, at reduced prices, and at fair profit. I therefore determined to locate myself there if practicable. I fortunately obtained one of two brick stores, nearly finished, at a reasonable rent, for one or more years, in the center of business, and engaged a house for my family in the fall. I then returned to Norwich, made preparations to move to Hartford, and then proceeded to Boston and Salem to select my stock of goods, and there spent some weeks, before they were purchased, packed, and shipped for Hartford. I returned to Norwich, packed and shipped our furniture, and proceeded with my wife and two babes by land, and arrived in Hartford about the 1st of August, 1802, and took lodgings until September, when our house was to be in readiness for our family. My goods soon arrived, and were marked and displayed on the shelves. I exhibited an outside sign, "D. L. Dodge," "Cash Store." I had engaged an experienced clerk but was obliged to get a lad in addition. Before August closed,

I found it necessary to go to Boston and Salem for a new supply of goods. I did not advertise, as my neighbors did that for me, by advertising "as cheap as the cheap store." One day Mr. A. Corning came into the store, and I inquired of him who kept the cheap store. He replied, I should think you had found out before now. He then informed me that it was currently reported that I had obtained goods on credit, and was selling them less than cost; and as the chance for cheap goods was expected to be short, I had a prodigious run, not only from the city but also from the neighbouring towns. I found myself well repaid for the time and expense I had bestowed to gain a knowledge of goods generally, and the state of foreign and domestic markets.

I followed the course of frequently replenishing my stock with goods in immediate demand, and gradually increased my variety, until the winter, I think, of 1804, when we had but little good sleighing in Hartford, which greatly diminished the winter sales. In March, I understood that there was good sleighing in Litchfield county. I immediately selected goods of such as were an overstock for the season, obtained the services of Mr. Stephen Dodge, who had been unfortunate in business, an excellent, pious man, not related to me by blood. We loaded a sleigh and proceeded to Litchfield, found a good store unoccupied, hired it at a cheap rate, while I might need it, and erected a sign — "Cash Store, for a short time." I remained with him one week and received more than two thousand dollars. Thus encouraged, I returned and replenished; and finally, the prospects were so flattering, I engaged Mr. Dodge permanently with the aid of a clerk, and it became a branch of my Hartford store.

I will here remark, and I trust with gratitude to God, that all the clerks whom I have employed in my mercantile life, who were non-professors, and who remained six months or longer, with one exception, became professors of religion, and I trust most were truly pious; I may add such was the case with several laboring men also. I generally boarded all my clerks in our own family, though often inconvenient; and I wish to say to my descendants who are engaged in business, to take their clerks and even laborers, as far as practicable, into their own families, if you wish them trusty and efficient, where they may be under the restraint by means of family devotion and instruction, where their consciences will be kept alive by a tone of moral influence, where they will habitually attend church and come under the influence of the proclamation of the gospel of peace.

[*John Neal, Portland, Maine*]

My next adventure, in the way of business, I must acknowledge, had a flavor of what would now be called rather sharp practice. I began to manufacture lollipop — at first, in small quantities, but soon after by the dollar's worth; retailing it myself by the stick, or wholesaling it by the ninepenny-worth, and thereby saving the profits both of a jobber and middleman; using my mother's molasses, when there was enough on hand, which was not often, as her purchases were always made with a half-gallon jug; and licking the boys, who, after being trusted, failed to pay at the time fixed between us, thereby saving lots of shoe-leather, interest on capital, and all the costs of attorney-ship. Sharp's the word ! This occurred, I should say, around 1803, when I was about ten.

But after I took to the counter, instead of the highway, as, on the whole, somewhat safer, if not always the more respectable, my business tendencies took a new "start." My masters, with a view to my encouragement, I suppose, or perhaps to quicken my appetite for trade, as hawks are trained with offal and garbage to begin with, allowed me the privilege of selling horn combs, which were manufactured at Woodford's Corner, and went by the name of mock-turtle. They were in great demand: the sale was steady; and the profits, though small, were sure; and though what I did was in the retail way, where any sort of wholesale business might have interfered with my masters, I managed to lay up enough spending-money for the holidays, without touching my capital, which amounted at one time to no less than fourteen or fifteen hundred — cents.

In addition to this privilege, I was allowed to share in the boxes and wrappers and cordage, that came round the bales, with a young man from Boston, who "understood the *ropes;*" and, between us, we managed to earn — we called it earning — I dare not say how much, in the course of a year, but certainly not less than twenty-five dollars apiece. Nor should this be wondered at, when we were allowed to charge just what we pleased for boxing and baling to our country customers; and had constantly before us the example of our friends over sea, whose charges were so extravagant as to astonish us, until we found in them the very justification we needed for ourselves.

And here, two or three little incidents of my shop-keeping life occur to me, which may be worth mentioning, by way of illustration.

One day, a fat Frenchman wanted to look at some pantaloon-stuff. Velvets and velveteens were the go just then; and, while I was trying to persuade him that a drab corduroy was the thing, his eyes fell on a piece of dark purple tabby-velvet, which he fastened upon with such eagerness, I had not the heart to tell him it was not intended for pantaloons. That, and that only, would he have; and so, having measured off three yards, I attempted to tear it across, instead of cutting with the scissors. In tearing, there happened to be a coarse thread in the way; and off it went, with a rip that startled my master at the desk, lengthwise of the roll, for about three-quarters of a yard, but, luckily for my customer, not into his portion of the velvet. Seeing him look up, I huddled the whole together, and threw the piece behind me, lest he might be disheartened if he saw the rent; and giving him his bundle, with the "trimmings," which we used to lump, after a very profitable fashion, so that twists, buttons, and lining yielded nearly as much profit as the cloth itself, took his money, and got rid of him about the quickest. Some few days afterwards, he called with a bundle under his arm, which turned out to be all that remained of his purple velvet pantaloons: he had blown them all to pieces, I know not how — perhaps by trying to sit down in a hurry. The poor fellow was ready to burst with rage and vexation; and, when I reminded him that I had recommended quite a different article, which we would warrant, he grew furious. I then threw the blame on the tailor, who ought to have told him before it was too late; for how should I know that tabby-velvet pantaloons wouldn't bear to be "sneezed at" — or in? This appeared to strike him favorably, and, according to my present recollection, he set off in search of the tailor, before Messrs. Munroe and Tuttle, my masters, had time to interfere, and that was the last we saw of him.

At another time — and these were the transactions that made me so necessary to my good masters, and served to distinguish me for shop-keeping smartness, at the very outset of my career — at another time, the elder of my two principals, Tilly Merrick Munroe, was trying to sell a black Barcelona handkerchief to a backwoodsman, with a beard like a carding machine. He was afraid his *"baird,"* as he called it, passing his hand over his chin, as if it hurt him, would be too much for the Barcelona, if he didn't shave at least every day. "All a mistake," said I, interfering, as I had no business to do, " all a mistake, sir. If you buy that handkerchief, you'll never want shaving again." This was a little too much for my masters. They tried to keep their countenances, and smother a laugh; but in vain. And when they had recovered their self-command, it was too late. I had seen the effect, and the countryman had vanished; so that we lost the sale of the Barcelona, which he had begun to believe beard-proof, double twilled, with "two knocks in the weaving."

Another achievement just occurs to me, which I shouldn't like to forget. I had an uncle David, who was reckoned among the sharpest and shrewdest of our customers. He used to laugh at me, when I was setting a trap for others; and the roguish twinkle of his eyes, I never shall forget, the first time I ever tried "my 'prentice hand on him"; but I succeeded at last, and had the pleasure of see-ing him bait a trap with his own fingers.

There had slowly accumulated in our back shop a large box of remnants, which we wanted to be rid of. There were bits of calico, and copper-plate, or furniture-patch, with the fag-ends of cassimere, calamanco (calimink), and corduroy, and fearnought, and gro-gram, and faded waistcoating; all sorts of worthless rubbage indeed. Occasionally, he had seen me overhauling the pile, and favoring customers with a prodigious bargain; and at last he began teasing and bantering me, till I could bear it no longer. So I tumbled the whole out on the floor, and stumped him to make me an offer. But no: there was nothing there he wanted; and he had no idea of buy-ing a pig in a poke. Yet, as I seemed so much in earnest, he would consent to indulge me so far as to set his own value upon the trash, measuring all the remnants, article by article, and then make me an offer for the whole. Agreed. So to work we went, he appraising every fragment as he lugged it forth, and I measuring it honestly — for his eye was upon me, and I was obliged to "give thumbs" — and then setting it down *as* honestly, and for the same reason, till I had chalked down a column of figures, on the partition, a foot or two long. Then he undertook to add up for himself. I did not inter-fere, but kept aloof until he had finished, when I saw at a glance, though standing a good way off, that he had make a mistake of ten dollars against himself. Then came the offer, with a chuckle; which I accepted, with another; taking care to rub out the figures, while we were finishing up the business, with a laugh, lest he might be tempted to review them. I think he had some suspicion of my pur-pose, though he never would own it; for I well remember the startled expression of his countenance, as I wiped off the figures with a single sweep of my arm, so far at least as to derange the col-umn and put a stop to any proposed verification. Many years after this, I told my good uncle the truth: he was a Quaker, and, on the whole, seemed rather pleased with my smartness, though I do not remember that he laughed outright; for his children were about him, and he had just been bragging about his own cleverness. No

[209]

wonder the temptation was too much for me; and that I lost no time in showing that the smart uncle had a smarter nephew.

We had other tricks of the trade, which now begin to crowd upon my recollection. We used to sell India-cottons by the piece, for example: and when they fell short a yard or two, we comforted the purchaser, by assuring him, that although they came for twelve yards, it was an advantage for him to have them actually measure but ten and a half, or eleven yards, because they all weighed alike.

All our prints, or calicoes, as they were then called, were marked up, when sold by the piece, either half a yard or three-quarters. In England they were always reckoned twenty-eight yards, but would overrun from one fourth to three-fourths of a yard, and sometimes a whole yard. With broadcloths and cassimeres and woollens generally, when sold by the piece, it was the same. The leads were always marked up from one-fourth of a yard to a yard, sometimes by altering the fraction, and sometimes by adding, as the case might require. Pins went up from number two, to two and a half, from number three, to three and a half, and from number four, to four and a half.

It was an established principle with us, no matter what was wanted, always to show the poorest first, thereby enhancing the best by comparison; to keep the windows and doorway so dark, partly by hanging shawls and other showy goods both inside and out, and partly by painting the back windows, that people were often astonished at their bargains, after they got back to their own houses; not only the quality, but the very color of their purchases, undergoing a change for the worse.

Another charming trick we had — or rather some of us had; for the boys were not allowed to understand these delicacies of trade. To show the fineness of a linen or of a linen cambric, we used to draw it over our finger, and wet it with our tongues. This, tending to show how much finer it would be after the stiffening was out, seldom failed to satisfy even pretty good house-keepers. And an-

other, and the worst of all I now remember, was this. The whole
country was deluged with counterfeit money, ten percent, I should
say, of all that was in circulation was absolutely worthless; being
either counterfeit, or the floating issue of broken banks, like the
Farmers'-Exchange Bank, of Massachusetts. Of course, with shop-
boys and inexperienced clerks, it was no easy matter for a business-
man to escape; and the consequence was, that, after a little time, it
became a sort of settled maxim, that, if you buy the devil, the
sooner you sell him, the better. In *our* establishment, all such
moneys, whether counterfeit, or only questionable, were always put
back into the till; and, though nothing was ever said to me on the
subject, it was understood that I had charge of the circulation, or
re-issue; I being the youngest, and by far the most innocent-looking,
with my blue eyes, golden hair, and Quaker bobcoat. And so little
sense of shame had I, that, for a long while, it was my pride and
boast, that I never failed in putting off a bad bill, once committed
to my charge; often passing it to another person, while some one
who had just returned it, was in the shop. And, what is very
strange, I do not believe that we ever lost a customer by such a procedure; it being my practice, at least, whatever others might do,
always to take the bad bill back, without hesitation or delay, and
give a good one for it, upon the positive assurance of the party,
that she could not be mistaken, and that she was sure she had it of
me — I say *she*, because we found it easier and safer to cheat women
than men — and often sending her away with tears of thankfulness
in her eyes, and securing a customer for life.

I longed for something to do — something, I cared little what, so
that I could be earning my bread, and not living on my poor
mother — she got me a place at forty dollars a year, with board and
washing — nothing was said about *mending*, to my knowledge — in
the store of Mr. Benjamin Willis, father of William Willis, the an-
nalist of Portland. There I remained one whole year, working early
and late, in season and out of season, and learning many new tricks
of the trade; Mr. Willis dealing in West-India goods and groceries,
and country produce, as well as in dry-goods from all parts of the
world: for example, how to convert a hogshead of old Jamaica or
Santa Cruz into a hogshead and a half, or thereabouts, by rolling
it back and forth between the store and a town-pump that stood
just in front of the old city-hall; and how to give Spanish brandy
the flavor of cognac, by charging it with burnt sugar. On the whole,
however, the year I spent in Mr. Willis' store was of great advantage to me. In the first place, it kept me busy, and out of mischief;

and in the next, as goods were high, and growing higher every day, it obliged me to economize, and manage in every possible way to make both ends meet, which I did, nevertheless, and should have done, had my wages been less, and goods higher. For mark you, I had stipulated for myself, without consulting my good mother, who had never kept shop, that I was to have what goods I wanted for myself, at cost. Now, Mr. Willis used to buy all his goods at auction for cash, and was the first of our Portland traders who ever went beyond Boston for supplies. Most of his purchases were made in New York; and he would often buy a lot of merchandise of many different qualities at one price, "all round." Of course, therefore, if I happened to take a fancy to any of these, the cost was always the average as marked on the tally. In this way, I got my clothing for half-price at the most and often for less. Then, again, I always bargained with my bootmaker and tailor to take their pay out of the shop. Whatever they had, therefore, I charged to myself at cost; and if they happened to make a little more than just enough to pay their bills, I charged myself with the goods, and the balance of cash went into my pocket, of course, which I accounted for *at cost*. In this way, my forty dollars a year I found to be quite sufficient for my clothing, though I dressed handsomely, and came off with flying colors at the end of the year; having one good suit for special occasions, and another quite passable for every day, with nothing showy or superfluous.

But this could not last. Business grew worse and worse, and so did I; and, at the end of my first year, I was cut adrift, and, for a while, went back to my studies, taking care to fall into no bad habits, and to keep clear of bad company.

Happening to find myself in Hallowell, my attention was attracted by an advertisement, in a Boston paper, for a clerk in a wholesale and retail drygoods establishment; "inquire of the printer." Here was a direct, personal invitation, which I durst not overlook. I lost no time in sending off a letter to Messrs. Young and Minns, in answer to the advertisement. In due time, I received a few lines from a Mr. M., saying, "Come on at once; and, if we cannot agree, your board shall cost you nothing, till you find a place to suit you." Of course, I jumped at the offer. On my way through Portland, where I had long been reported lost, or missing, I called upon some of the old standards, who best knew me as business-men, and, at their suggestion, wrote a "recommend" for myself, which they all signed, and which I have now before me, dated May, 1811. Being brief and to the purpose, I will give it here. "We the subscribers merchants of Portland have known the bearer John Neal for a number of years and believe him to be *honest capable* and *active* and well-qualified for the wholesale or retail English goods bussiness," no stops from beginning to end, and "bussiness" spelled with double *s;* and hurried off by the very next conveyance to Boston, where I arrived late of a Saturday evening, and put up at the stage-tavern kept by Earle, in Ann Street.

At last then, I found myself in Boston, — a stranger among strangers; for I knew but one or two persons at most, and was afraid of meeting either of them, before I had secured a resting-place for the sole of my foot. I rose early, long before the rest of the world, on the first sabbath-morning that followed, and took my way of course, toward Marlboro'-Street, wishing to see how the land lay, before I stopped long enough anywhere to take root. With some difficulty, I found the number — it was nearly opposite the Marlboro'-Hotel — and there saw the name of my correspondent. There were two large bay-windows in the store, and all overhead was occupied by the family. For a wholesale and retail dry-goods establishment, in a large city, as Boston was then regarded, though not larger than Portland is now, (1867) this did not seem to me very magnificent, I must acknowledge; for, up to this time, all the stores I had ever been employed in, were at least three stories high, with no part occupied for dwellings. It is very true that the upper stories were almost always empty, with one single exception, that of Mr. Willis in Haymarket Row; but still they were stores, or warehouses, and not finished chambers, for dwellings or offices.

I found the "store" open Monday at a very early hour, and Mr. M. arranging for the business of the day. On entering, I was not a little amused — astonished, I might say — at the general aspect of the establishment. On one side, there were show-cases with cheap jewellery, silver tea-spoons, and all sorts of Brummagem knick-knackery, a chest of tea, and a long array of japanned waiters, with landscapes and figures and blazonry of the choicest patterns; on the other, and in front, a large assortment of what seemed to be the refuse of many a retail-shop, and many a small auction of haberdashery. And this was the wholesale and retail dry-goods establishment, to which I was invited.

Mr. M. I found to be a tall, thin man, with black hair, just beginning to change, and cut very close. Nothing could be more precise, nothing more serious, than his bearing and equipment. His hat you could see your face in; and his pepper-and-salt clothes looked as if they had never been tumbled, since they came out of the hands of the tailor. With small sharp eyes — very black, in appearance — a rather strange cadaverous complexion, and a solemnity of manner which seemed wholly out of place behind the counter, the first impression that I received, was far from favorable. But, upon introducing myself, and entering into conversation with him, his countenance lighted up; and, at the end of ten or fifteen minutes, we had entered into an arrangement, and I found my prejudices giving way.

I was to have either eighty or a hundred dollars a year, I forget which, with board and washing in the family; to have the whole charge of the business — to open shop, sweep, and dust, and be always on hand, from a very early hour, until we shut up in the evening.

To all this, I made no objection, for I longed to be at work once more; and the smell of the goods, though most of them were musty and shop-worn, was grateful to me.

I had no acquaintances, and never passed an evening out of the house, I believe; and though I used to be called out of bed at a most unreasonable hour, and didn't half like Mr. Murphy's way of doing business, nor his long prayers before we parted for the night, still we managed to get along pretty well together, for nearly a twelvemonth. His wife, a very pleasant, amiable woman, treated me like a younger brother; and I was glad to pass what spare time I had at my own disposal, in her society. I used to go to bed soon after nine o'clock, at all seasons; and though I took a stroll on the sabbath, and sometimes wandered away off into the country, yet I always went to meeting at least once a day, and, if I am not greatly mistaken, twice. The Old South, in which Mr. Huntington then preached, was reckoned among the fashionably orthodox; and Mr. M. was a leading professor.

And, when I mention a few of his peculiarities, it will not be wondered at, that I was troubled with certain misgivings, *not* of a religious character, but of a nature to make me suspicious of all sanctimonious pretension.

The first thing I saw that disturbed my faith in the man, was seeing him smooth his hat with the most elaborate carefulness, wiping it with a fine towel after it had been brushed with a very soft brush over and over again, while the bells were ringing for church, and his wife was waiting for him in the passage-way; and this, after one of his longest prayers for grace to keep the sabbath holy.

But certain of his business habits, after I had got acquainted with them, had a still more disastrous effect upon me. They were too much of a piece with what I had been accustomed to among the heterodox, the world's people, who cared for none of these things. For example: —

[214]

He had acquired a reputation for selling the best teas in the market; and, although he charged a high price, there were certain wealthy families who depended altogether upon him for their supplies, without regard to cost. And yet I never knew him to have more than two or three chests on hand at any time; and that always of the same kind, "Old Hyson," if I recollect rightly. On receiving a new chest into the store, the tea-drinking *cognoscenti* were confidentially notified; a large part was weighed out, and put up into pound bundles, ready for applicants, who always took it for a favor; and so long as that particular brand was on tap, Mr. Murphy went no further into the speculation. One would have supposed the article had come, over land, by the way of Russia, or that it had been smuggled, so much whispering was there between him and his tea-drinking customers, after a fresh arrival, and so mysterious were some of the proceedings. But with his advanced price, and settled reputation for selling the best, and only the best, he managed to make of it a very pretty business.

Another way he had of turning an honest penny was, under pretense of keeping a goldsmith's shop, to *take in* all sorts of trinkets — with their proprietors — for repair. These he would sometimes mend in his own way with shellac or sealing-wax, or send off to a working-jeweller, and then charge three times the price he paid for the work. But people never complained, or never but once, to my knowledge, when a pair of large golden hoops parted, before the owner had fairly reached her home; they had been stuck together by Mr. M. at a cost which seemed rather unreasonable, even if they had been faithfully mended. The matter was finally settled — I know not how — perhaps with a plausible explanation, and another dip into the glue-pot, or a touch of the blowpipe.

One other incident, and I have done with my illustrations of character *here*. The late Deacon Samuel May's family were among his best customers, and always had their tea of him, I believe. One day, it happened that they wanted mourning for the family; and it was not to be had, in a hurry. But Mr. M. had a quantity of cotton cambric remnants on hand, which had been lately dyed, and were warranted not to smut. They were shop-worn, to be sure, and of different qualities and colors and widths; but, then, they would do for mourning. And the whole family were provided for, as a great favor; the war having made new goods impossible, and shopworn, old-fashioned, worthless rubbish, of unspeakable value, especially in the case of sudden death.

After the funeral was over, two of the family called to remonstrate with me, and to show me their dresses: they were absolutely ragged, full of holes, and so different in color that some of the breadths appeared changeable, and not unlike what was then called chambray.

What the worthy man said, I do not now remember; but, preserving his gracious perpendicularity, and seriousness of look, and answering all they could say, as if wondering at their unreasonable pertinacity, he got rid of them at last — and they were among his best customers — upon the ground that he had to buy what he could, where he could, for the supply of his friends, and, of course, would not buy anything unmerchantable, if he knew it. And this was all the satisfaction they ever got.

◇◇◇◇◇◇◇◇◇◇◇◇

[*Amos A. Lawrence, Boston*]

When I first came to this city, in 1807, I took lodgings in the family of a widow who had commenced keeping boarders for a living. I was one of her first, and perhaps had been in the city two months when I went to this place; and she, of course, while I remained, was inclined to adopt any rules for the boarders that I prescribed. The only one I ever made was, that, after supper, all the boarders who remained in the public room should remain quiet at least for one hour, to give those who chose to study or read an opportunity of doing so without disturbance. The consequence was, that we had the most quiet and improving set of young men in the town. The few who did not wish to comply with the regulation went abroad after tea, sometimes to the theater, sometimes to other places, but, to a man, became bankrupt in after life, not only in fortune, but in reputation; while a majority of the other class sustained good characters, and some are now living who are ornaments to society, and fill important stations. The influence of this small measure will perhaps be felt throughout generations. It was not less favorable on myself than on others.

I will state that I practised upon the maxim, '*Business before friends,*' from the commencement of my course. During the first seven years of my business in this city, I never allowed a bill against me to stand unsettled over the Sabbath. If the purchase of goods was made at auction on Saturday, and delivered to me, I always examined and settled the bill by note or by crediting it, and having it clear, so that, in case I was not on duty on Monday, there would be no trouble for my boys; thus keeping the business *before* me, instead of allowing it to *drive* me.

I adopted the plan of keeping an accurate account of merchandise bought and sold each day, with the profit as far as practicable. This plan was pursued for a number of years; and I never found my merchandise fall short in taking an account of stock, which I did as often at least as once in each year. I was thus enabled to form an opinion of my actual state as a business man. I adopted also the rule always to have property, after my second year's business, to represent forty per cent. at least more than I owed; that is, never to be in debt more than two and a half times my capital. This caution saved me from ever getting embarrassed. If it were more generally adopted, we should see fewer failures in business. Excessive credit is the rock on which so many business men are broken.

When I commenced, the embargo had just been laid, and with such restrictions on trade that many were induced to leave it. But I felt great confidence, that, by industry, economy, and integrity, I could get a living; and the experiment showed that I was right. Most of the young men who commenced at that period failed by spending too much money, and using credit too freely.

I made about fifteen hundred dollars the first year, and more than four thousand the second. Probably, had I made four thousand the first year, I should have failed the second or third year. I practised a system of rigid economy, and never allowed myself to spend a fourpence for unnecessary objects until I had acquired it.

[It is known to many of Mr. Lawrence's friends that his father mortgaged his farm, and loaned the proceeds to his son; thereby enabling him, as some suppose, to do what he could not have done by his own unaided efforts. To show how far this supposition is correct, the following extract is given. It is copied from the back of the original mortgage deed, bearing date of September 1, 1807. The extract is dated March, 1847.]

The review of this transaction always calls up the deep feelings of my heart. My honored father brought to me the one thousand dollars, and asked me to give him my note for it. I told him he did wrong to place himself in a situation to be made unhappy, if I lost the money. He told me he *guessed I wouldn't lose it,* and I gave him my note. The first thing I did was to take four per cent. premium on my Boston bills (the difference then between passable and Boston money), and send a thousand dollars in bills of the Hillsborough Bank to Amherst, New Hampshire, by my father, to my brother L. to carry to the bank and get specie, as he was going there to attend court that week. My brother succeeded in getting specie, principally in silver change, for the bills, and returned it to me in a few days. In the mean time, or shortly after, the bank had been sued, the bills discredited, and, in the end, proved nearly worthless. I determined not to use the money, except in the safest way; and therefore loaned it to Messrs. Parkman, in whom I had entire confidence. After I had been in business, and had made more than a thousand dollars, I felt that I could repay the money, come what would of it; being insured against fire, and trusting nobody for goods. I used it in my business, but took care to pay off the mortgage as soon as it would be received. The whole transaction is deeply interesting, and calls forth humble and devout thanksgiving to that merciful Father who has been to us better than our most sanguine hopes.

This incident shows how dangerous it is to the independence and comfort of families, for parents to take pecuniary responsibilities for their sons in trade, beyond their power of meeting them without embarrassment. Had my Hillsborough Bank notes not been paid as they were, nearly the whole amount would have been lost, and myself and family might probably have been ruined. The incident was so striking, that I have uniformly discouraged young men who have applied to me for credit, offering their fathers as bondsmen; and, by doing so, I have, I believe, saved some respectable families from ruin. My advice, however, has been sometimes rejected with anger. A young man who cannot get along without such aid will not be likely to get along with it. On the first day of January, 1808, I had been but a few days in business; and the profits on all my sales to that day were one hundred and seventy-five dollars and eighteen cents. The expenses were to come out, and the balance was my capital. In 1842, the sum had increased to such an amount as I thought would be good for my descendants; and, from that time, I have been my own executor. How shall I show my sense of responsibility ? Surely by active deeds more than by unmeaning words. God grant me to be true and faithful in his work !

◇◇◇◇◇◇◇◇◇◇◇◇◇◇

[*Phineas Taylor Barnum, Danbury, Conn.*]

My father was a tailor, a farmer, and sometimes a tavern-keeper, and my advantages and disadvantages were such as fall to the general run of farmers' boys. I drove cows to and from the pasture, shelled corn, weeded the garden; as I grew larger, I rode horse for ploughing, turned and raked hay; in due time I handled the shovel and the hoe, and when I could do so I went to school.

I was six years old when I began to go to school, and the first date I remember inscribing upon my writing-book was 1818. The ferule, in those days, was the assistant school-master; but in spite of it, I was a willing, and, I think, a pretty apt scholar; at least, I was so considered by my teachers and schoolmates, and as the years went on there were never more than two or three in the school who were deemed my superiors. In arithmetic I was unusually ready and accurate, and I remember, at the age of twelve years, being called out of bed one night by my teacher who had wagered with a neighbor that I could calculate the correct number of feet in a load of wood in five minutes. The dimensions given, I figured out the result in less than two minutes, to the great delight of my teacher and to the equal astonishment of his neighbor.

My organ of "acquisitiveness" was manifest at an early age. Before I was five years of age, I began to accumulate pennies and "four-pences," and when I was six years old my capital amounted to a sum sufficient to exchange for a silver dollar, the possession of which made me feel far richer and more independent than I have ever since felt in the world.

Nor did my dollar long remain alone. As I grew older I earned ten cents a day for riding the horse which led the ox team in ploughing, and on holidays and "training days," instead of spending money, I earned it. I was a small peddler of molasses candy (of home make), ginger-bread, cookies and cherry rum, and I generally found myself a dollar or two richer at the end of a holiday than I was at the beginning. I was always ready for a trade, and by the time I was twelve years old, besides other property, I was the owner of a sheep and a calf, and should soon, no doubt, have become a small Croesus, had not my father kindly permitted me to purchase my own clothing, which somewhat reduced my little store.

As I grew older, my settled aversion to manual labor, farm or other kind, was manifest in various ways, which were set down to the general score of laziness. In despair of doing better with me, my father concluded to make a merchant of me. He erected a building in Bethel, and with Mr. Hiram Weed as a partner, purchased a stock of dry goods, hardware, groceries, and general notions and installed me as clerk in this country store.

Of course I "felt my oats." It was condescension on my part to talk with boys who did out-door work. I stood behind the counter with a pen over my ear, was polite to the ladies, and was wonderfully active in waiting upon customers. We kept a cash, credit and barter store, and I drove some sharp bargains with women who brought butter, eggs, beeswax and feathers to exchange for dry goods, and with men who wanted to trade oats, corn, buckwheat, axe-helves, hats, and other commodities for tenpenny nails, molasses, or New England rum. But it was a drawback upon my dignity that

I was obliged to take down the shutters, sweep the store, and make the fire. I received a small salary for my services and the perquisite of what profit I could derive from purchasing candies on my own account to sell to our younger customers, and, as usual, my father stipulated that I should clothe myself.

There is a great deal to be learned in a country store, and principally this — that sharp trades, tricks, dishonesty, and deception are by no means confined to the city. More than once, in cutting open bundles of rags, brought to be exchanged for goods, and warranted to be all linen and cotton, I have discovered in the interior worthless woolen trash and sometimes stones, gravel or ashes. Sometimes, too, when measuring loads of oats, corn or rye, declared to contain a specified number of bushels, say sixty, I have found them four or five bushels short. In such cases, some one else was always to blame, but these happenings were frequent enough to make us watchful of our customers. In the evenings and on the wet days trade was always dull, and at such times the story-telling and joke-playing wits and wags of the village used to assemble in our store, and from them I derived considerable amusement, if not profit. After the store was closed at night, I frequently joined some of the village boys at the houses of their parents, where, with story-telling and play, a couple of hours would soon pass by, and then as late, perhaps as eleven o'clock, I went home and slyly crept up stairs so as not to awaken my brother with whom I slept, and who would be sure to report my late hours. He made every attempt, and laid all sorts of plans to catch me on my return, but as sleep always overtook him, I managed easily to elude his efforts.

I did my best to please my employers and soon gained their confidence and esteem and was regarded by them as an active clerk and a 'cute trader. They afforded me many facilities for making money on my own account and I soon entered upon sundry speculations and succeeded in getting a small sum of money ahead.

I made a very remarkable trade at one time for my employers by purchasing, in their absence, a whole wagon load of green glass bottles of various sizes, for which I paid in unsalable goods at very profitable prices. How to dispose of the bottles was then the problem, and as it was also desirable to get rid of a large quantity of tin ware which had been in the shop for years and was considerably "shop-worn," I conceived the idea of a lottery in which the highest prize should be twenty-five dollars, payable in any goods the winner desired, while there were to be fifty prizes of five dollars each, payable in goods, to be designated in the scheme. Then there were one hundred prizes of one dollar each, one hundred prizes of fifty cents each, and three hundred prizes of twenty-five cents each. It is unnecessary to state that the minor prizes consisted mainly of glass and tin ware; the tickets sold like wildfire, and the worn tin and glass bottles were speedily turned into cash.

In February, 1828, I returned to Bethel and opened a retail fruit and confectionery store in a part of my grandfather's carriage-house,

which was situated on the main street, and which was offered to me rent free if I would return to my native village and establish some sort of business. This beginning of business on my own account was an eventful era in my life. My total capital was one hundred and twenty dollars, fifty of which I had expended in fitting up the store, and the remaining seventy dollars purchased my stock in trade. I had arranged with fruit dealers whom I knew in New York, to receive my orders, and I decided to open my establishment on the first Monday in May — our "general training" day.

It was a "red letter" day for me. The village was crowded with people from the surrounding region and the novelty of my little shop attracted attention. Long before noon I was obliged to call in one of my old schoolmates to assist in waiting upon my numerous customers and when I closed at night I had the satisfaction of reckoning up sixty-three dollars as my day's receipts. Nor, although I had received the entire cost of my goods, less seven dollars, did the stock seem seriously diminished; showing that my profits had been large. I need not say how much gratified I was with the result of this first day's experiment. The store was a fixed fact. I went to New

York and expended all my money in a stock of fancy goods, such as pocket-books, combs, beads, rings, pocket-knives, and a few toys. These, with fruits, nuts, etc., made the business good through the summer, and in the fall I added stewed oysters to the inducements.

My grandfather, who was much interested in my success, advised me to take an agency for the sale of lottery tickets, on commission. In those days, the lottery was not deemed objectionable on the score of morality. Very worthy people invested in such schemes without a thought of evil, and then, as now, churches even got up lotteries, with this difference — that then they were called lotteries, and now they go under some other name. While I am very glad that an improved public sentiment denounces the lottery in general as an illegitimate means of getting money, and while I do not see how any one, especially in or near a New England State, can engage in a lottery without feeing a reproach with no pecuniary return can compensate; yet I cannot now accuse myself for having been lured into a business which was then sanctioned by good Christian people, who now join with me in reprobating enterprises they once encouraged. But as public sentiment was forty years ago, I obtained an agency to sell lottery tickets on a commission of ten per cent, and this business, in connection with my little store, made my profits satisfactory.

❖❖❖❖❖❖❖❖❖❖❖❖❖

[Asa G. Sheldon, Wilmington, Mass.]

Capt. Joseph Bond had just given his business of baking into the hands of his sons Joseph and William. To increase their manufactures, they were at a loss how to procure faggots, which were then used exclusively for oven heating.

I told them there would be no trouble if they would pay enough for them. "It is such mean business, nobody will make them," they said.

"It will not be a mean business if you will pay a fair price for them."

"Who will make them, if we will pay well for it ?"

"I will," said I.

"I should laugh to see you making faggots."

"I should laugh to see you paying me the money for it," said I.

The bargain was concluded between us, that I should make all I could in five days, anywhere in Wilmington where they could go with a team, and they would draw them and pay 1½ cents per bundle. At work I went, and in five days made 1000 bundles, for which they paid me $15. In less than a fortnight after, many respectable citizens, together with the minister, his two sons and the deacon, employed themselves in making faggots for the Bonds. And from that day to this it has never been considered mean business. Many a laboring man has earned a few dollars, who could not get it in any other way. Besides the benefit arising from the faggots themselves, it has been the cause of clearing many acres of swamp or low land, which proves the best land for cultivation we have in Wilmington.

WATERBURY, CONNECTICUT

DOWN BY THE OLD MILL STREAM

◇◇◇◇◇◇◇◇◇◇◇◇◇

[*Timothy Dwight, 1798*]

THE morals of Waterbury are not on a high scale. Beside the usual evils of political division, litigation has, for a long time, spread a malignant influence over the people of Waterbury. Its well known effects have been extensively suffered here; and will in all probability be unhappily realized to an indefinitely future period.

Several manufactures have been carried on in this town with spirit and success; particularly that of clocks, principally formed of a particular species of wood. These are considered as keeping time with nearly as much regularity, as those which are made of the customary materials. They also last long: and being sold at a very moderate price, are spread over a prodigious extent of country, to the great convenience of a vast number of people who would otherwise have no means of regulating correctly their various business. Gilt buttons also have been made here in considerable quantities; not inferiour in strength and beauty to those which are imported.

◇◇◇◇◇◇◇◇◇◇◇◇◇

[*Thomas Low Nichols*]

The rivers of New England cannot fall ten feet at any point in their progress to the sea without being made to propel some kind of machinery. Cities cluster round the falls of every large river, with great manufactories, as those of Lowell, Lawrence, Manchester, Holyoke, &c. Many years ago I visited the village of Waterbury, in Connecticut, and spent a day among its curious factories. Water and Steam power were at work, but comparatively few human operatives. In one large room, full of machinery in rapid motion, there was but one man, whose business was to watch the machines and supply them with material. Each machine had a great coil of brass wire on a reel beside it. The end of the wire was placed in the machine, and from it flowed hooks or eyes into a basket as fast as one could count. These machines required only to be fed with coils of wire as they were used. In another room, automatic machines were eating up coils of iron-wire and discharging hair pins. Brass-wire went into other machines and came out common pins, with heads and points all perfect, and only requiring to be tinned and papered. The papering was done by a machine which picked out the pins, laid them in rows, and then pushed each row into a paper. One pin factory made three hundred thousand dozens of pins a-day. Another machine took wire from a coil and bits of brass from a hopper, and turned out buttons with the eyes made, set, and riveted.

◇◇◇◇◇◇◇◇◇◇◇◇◇◇

[*Samuel G. Goodrich*]

I have said that in the year 1800 there was but a single chaise in Ridgefield [Conn.], and this was brought, I believe, from New Haven. There was not, I imagine, a coach, or any kind of pleasure vehicle — that crazy old chaise excepted — in the county of Fairfield, out of the two half-shire towns. Such things, indeed, were known at New York, Boston, and Philadelphia — for already the government had laid a tax upon pleasure conveyances; but they were comparatively few in number, and were mostly imported. In 1798, there was but one public hack in New Haven, and but one coach; the latter belonging to Pierpoint Edwards, being a large four-wheeled vehicle, for two persons, called a chariot.

About that time, there came to our village a man by the name of Jesse J. Skellinger, an Englishman, and chaisemaker by trade. My father engaged him to build him a chaise. A bench was set up in our barn, and certain trees of oak and ash were cut in our neighboring

[225]

woods. These were sawed and seasoned, and shaped into wheels and shafts. Thomas Hawley, half blacksmith and half wheelwright, was duly initiated, and he cunningly wrought the iron necessary for the work. In five months the chaise was finished, with a standing top — greatly to the admiration of our family. What a gaze was there, my countrymen, as this vehicle went through Ridgefield-street upon its first expedition !

This was the beginning of the chaise manufactory in Ridgefield, which has since been a source of large revenue to the town. Skellinger was engaged by Elijah Hawley, who had formerly done something as a wagon-builder, and thus in due time an establishment was founded, which for many years was noted for the beauty and excellence of its pleasure vehicles.

At the time I speak of, in 1809, Eli Whitney's Gun-factory, two miles north of New Haven, was the great curiosity of the neighborhood. Indeed, people traveled fifty miles to see it. I think it employed about a hundred men. It was symmetrically built in a wild romantic spot, near the foot of East Rock, and had a cheerful, tasteful appearance — like a small tidy village. We visited it of course, and my admiration was excited to the utmost. What a bound did my ideas make in mechanics, from the operations of the penknife, to this miracle of machinery ! It was, at the time, wholly engaged in manufacturing muskets for the government. Mr. Whitney was present, and showed us over the place, explaining the various processes. Every part of the weapons was made by machinery, and so systematized that any lock or stock would fit any barrel. All this, which may seem no wonder now, was remarkable at the time, there being no similar establishment in the country. Among other things, we here saw the original model of the Cottongin, upon which Mr. Whitney's patent was founded.

◇◇◇◇◇◇◇◇◇◇◇◇◇

[David L. Dodge]

I often met with some of my old Christian friends; on one occasion, five of us were together, and as regular business was interrupted, the subject of manufacturing was discussed, which resulted in appointing me an agent to visit manufactories and gain information on the subject. A young gentleman who had formerly been in my employ as a clerk, was then an agent of a large cotton manufacturing establishment. I made him a visit of two days, and he kindly gave me all the information in his power. I then proceeded to visit most of the important manufactories in Connecticut, Rhode Island and Massachusetts, and communicated to my friends the result of my inquiries and observations. A meeting was appointed for consideration of the subject, and after deliberation we unanimously agreed to undertake a cotton establishment on a moderate scale. As we were all professors of religion, it was suggested whether it was not our duty to look to God for His guidance and blessing on our undertaking; after which, we individually signed a kind of covenant, binding ourselves, by divine assistance, to maintain as a primary object as far as practicable, a moral and religious establishment. We therefore felt a moral obligation to regard religious principles in all our movements, giving a preference, as far as practical, to religious artizans and operatives. We united in selecting and purchasing a site in the north-west corner of the town of Bozrah, in the valley of the Yantic, a tributary to the Thames, six miles from Norwich town. We obtained a liberal charter from the State of Connecticut by the name of the "Bozrah Manufacturing Company"; our first directors were appointed, the company organized, and I was chosen the general agent, with the help of a permanent assistant agent. The plan of our buildings and machinery was approved and put in rapid progress.

In the winter of 1819 it became necessary for me to visit Bozrahville, and examine the state of the manufactory, as there was a great reversion of business, mainly from the great influx of foreign goods which followed the return of peace. Many failures, both of merchants and manufacturers occurred. After spending nearly two months, it was found that the establishment was considerably in debt, and it was difficult to ascertain its real situation. Our agent had great care on his hands, in very difficult times, and aimed to do the best he could. Three of our original stockholders had failed in business, (one assigned his shares to me, for borrowed money, before I knew of his failure), and their stocks passed into other hands. We had now only two of the original directors in the board. On presenting my report, I was earnestly pressed to move to the manufactory, and again to take the general superintendence, which I acceded to, yielding up a promising commission business.

We moved from New York to Bozrahville early in May, 1819. I found my situation embarrassing, but by a vigorous effort, and the aid of an extra book-keeper, the accounts were adjusted and the books balanced. A thorough repair of every machine was effected also, by which means, in the course of a year or two, we were able to turn out weekly twenty-five to thirty per cent. more and better work, without additional expense in operation.

By 1823, our debts were much reduced, but domestic goods were greatly depressed by importations and improvements in machinery. The domestic competition was such, that none but new factories with modern improvements in machinery could sustain themselves. Early in 1824, I reported to our stockholders that we must replace a large proportion of our machinery for the most improved kinds, at an expense of about twenty-five thousand dollars, to stand on equal ground with new establishments, or we must sell the whole concern for what it might command in the depressed state of things. After much debate there was a small majority in favor of closing the concern, which I was authorized to do.

I will now look back to the moral state of things in Bozrahville and the vicinity during our residence there. I would first mention our schools. By our own request, we were set off as a separate district, where we built a large, convenient house and sustained for ten months yearly what the visiting committee complimented as the best school in town. Our rules required, ordinarily, one third of the children to attend school summer and winter, in rotation; and all under a certain age to attend sabbath school steadily.

It was unanimously desired by the professors, consisting of Methodist, Baptist, Presbyterians, Congregationalists, Episcopalians, and one Moravian, to sustain a union meeting at the village, and that when we had no regular authorized minister present, myself and my excellent, pious associate, Erastus Hyde, Esq., (Justice of the Peace), should alternately take the lead of all our social religious meetings. Our meetings at the village soon became solemn, and the inhabitants gave good attention. When I led the meeting, I often read portions of some of the most pungent evangelical sermons with which I was acquainted, interspersing remarks, and Mr. Hyde would generally add an exhortation in unison. Early in 1820, I was impressed with the duty of obtaining a private interview with every adult in the village. When I had nearly completed my object, I found, by conversation with individuals, that Mr. Hyde was pursuing the same course. On conversing with him, I found he had been impressed with the same feelings and that we had privately been pursuing the same course, without any concert.

◆◇◆◇◆◇◆◇◆◇◆◇◆

[Lucy Larcom]

Our house at Lowell was quickly filled with a large feminine family. As a child, the gulf between little girlhood and young womanhood had always looked to me very wide. I supposed we should get

[228]

across it by some sudden jump, by and by. But among these new companions of all ages, from fifteen to thirty years, we slipped into womanhood without knowing when or how.

Most of my mother's boarders were from New Hampshire and Vermont, and there was a fresh, breezy sociability about them which made them seem almost like a different race of beings from any we children had hitherto known.

We helped a little about the housework, before and after school, making beds, trimming lamps, and washing dishes. The heaviest work was done by a strong Irish girl, my mother always attending to the cooking herself. She was, however, a better caterer than the circumstances required or permitted. She liked to make nice things for the table, and, having been accustomed to an abundant supply, could never learn to economize. At a dollar and a quarter a week for board, (the price allowed for mill-girls by the corporations) great care in expenditure was necessary. It was not in my mother's nature closely to calculate costs, and in this way there came to be a continually increasing leak in the family purse. The older members of the family did everything they could, but it was not enough. I heard it said one day, in a distressed tone, "The children will have to leave school and go into the mill."

I went to my first day's work in the mill with a light heart. The novelty of it made it seem easy, and it really was not hard, just to change the bobbins on the spinning-frames every three quarters of an hour or so, with half a dozen other little girls who were doing the same thing. When I came back at night, the family began to pity me for my long, tiresome day's work, but I laughed and said, —

"Why, it is nothing but fun. It is just like play."

And for a little while it was only a new amusement; I liked it better than going to school and "making believe" I was learning when I was not. And there was a great deal of play mixed with it. We were not occupied more than half the time. The intervals were spent frolicking around among the spinning-frames, teasing and talking to the older girls, or entertaining ourselves with games and stories in a corner, or exploring, with the overseer's permission, the mysteries of the carding-room, the dressing-room, and the weaving-room.

I never cared much for machinery. The buzzing and hissing and whizzing of pulleys and rollers and spindles and flyers around me often grew tiresome. I could not see into their complications, or feel interested in them. But in a room below us we were sometimes allowed to peer in through a sort of blind door at the great water-wheel that carried the works of the whole mill. It was so huge that we could only watch a few of its spokes at a time, and part of its dripping rim, moving with a slow, measured strength through the darkness that shut it in. It impressed me with something of the awe which comes to us in thinking of the great Power which keeps the mechanism of the universe in motion. Even now, the remembrance

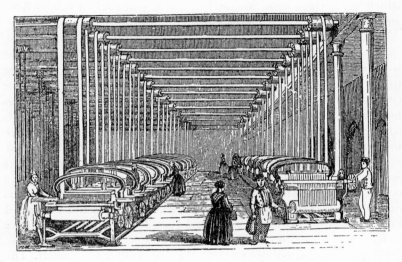

of its large, mysterious movement, in which every little motion of every noisy little wheel was involved, brings back to me a verse from one of my favorite hymns: —

> Our lives through various scenes are drawn,
> And vexed by trifling cares,
> While Thine eternal thought moves on
> Thy undisturbed affairs.

There was but one summer holiday for us who worked in the mills — the Fourth of July. We made a point of spending it out of doors, making excursions down the river to watch the meeting of the slow Concord and the swift Merrimack; or around by the old canal-path, to explore the mysteries of the Guard Locks; or across the bridge, clambering up Dracut Heights, to look away to the dim blue mountains.

On that morning it was our custom to wake one another at four o'clock, and start off on a tramp together over some retired road whose chief charm was its unfamiliarity, returning to a very late breakfast, with draggled gowns and aprons full of dewy wild roses. No matter if we must get up at five the next morning and go back to our hum-drum toil, we should have the roses to take with us for company, and the sweet air of the woodland which lingered about them would scent our thoughts all day, and make us forget the oily smell of the machinery.

The printed regulations forbade us to bring books into the mill, so I made my window-seat into a small library of poetry, pasting its side all over with newspaper clippings. In those days we had only weekly papers, and they had always a "poet's corner," where standard writers were well represented, with anonymous ones, also. I was not, of course, much of a critic. I chose my verses for their sentiment, and because I wanted to commit them to memory; sometimes it was a long poem, sometimes a hymn, sometimes only a stray verse.

Some of the girls could not believe that the Bible was meant to be counted among forbidden books. We all thought that the Scriptures had a right to go wherever we went, and that if we needed them anywhere, it was at our work. I evaded the law by carrying some leaves from a torn Testament in my pocket.

The overseer, caring more for law than gospel, confiscated all he found. He had his desk full of Bibles. It sounded oddly to hear him say to the most religious girl in the room, when he took hers away, "I did think you had more conscience than to bring that book here." But we had some close ethical questions to settle in those days. It was a rigid code of morality under which we lived. Nobody complained of it, however, and we were doubtless better off for its strictness, in the end.

The last window in the row behind me was filled with flourishing house-plants — fragrant-leaved geraniums, the overseer's pets. They gave that corner a bowery look; and perfume and freshness tempted me there often. Standing before that window, I could look across the room and see girls moving backwards and forwards among the spinning-frames, sometimes stooping, sometimes reaching up their arms, as their work required, with easy and not ungraceful movements. On the whole, it was far from being a disagreeable place to stay in. The girls were bright-looking and neat, and everything was kept clean and shining. The effect of the whole was rather attractive to strangers.

The pleasure we found in making new acquaintances among our work-mates arose partly from their having come from great distances, regions unknown to us, as the northern districts of Maine and New Hampshire and Vermont were, in those days of stage-coach traveling, when railroads had as yet only connected the larger cities with one another.

It seemed wonderful to me to be talking with anybody who had

really seen mountains and lived among them. One of the younger
girls, who worked beside me during my very first days in the mill,
had come from far up near the sources of the Merrimack, and she
told me a great deal about her home, and about farm-life among
the hills. I listened almost with awe when she said that she lived
in a valley where the sun set at four o'clock, and where the great
snow-storms drifted in so that sometimes they did not see a neighbor
for weeks.

To have mountain-summits looking down upon one out of the
clouds, summer and winter, by day and by night, seemed to me
something both delightful and terrible. And yet here was this girl
to whom it all appeared like the merest commonplace. What she
felt about it was that it was "awful cold, sometimes; the days were
so short ! and it grew dark so early !" Then she told me about the
spinning, and the husking, and the sugar-making, while we sat in a
corner together, waiting to replace the full spools by empty ones,
— the work usually given to the little girls.

I had a great admiration for this girl, because she had come from
those wilderness-regions. The scent of pine-woods and checkerberry-
leaves seemed to hang about her. I believe I liked her all the better
because she said "daown" and "haow." It was part of the mountain-
flavor.

I tried, on my part, to impress her with stories of the sea; but I
did not succeed very well. Her principal comment was, "They don't
think much of sailors up *aour* way."

◇◇◇◇◇◇◇◇◇◇◇◇◇◇

[*Thomas Low Nichols*]

At the time of my residence in Lowell, in 1835, the population did
not exceed ten thousand. Two-thirds of the whole were operatives,
and a large proportion of these were young women, not residents,
but daughters of the country farmers a hundred miles around, who
had come to the factories to work a few months or years, and lay
up money for their marriage-portions. Great covered waggons —
such as are called vans in England — went about the country collecting the rosy maidens from villages and rural districts, and conveying them to the factories.

Among these girls were many of exceeding beauty — that delicate
beauty nowhere else found in greater perfection. Many were well
educated. Some of them were contributors to a monthly magazine,
called the *Lowell Offering*. Some of these young ladies cultivated
music in their leisure hours, and had pianofortes in their private

parlours, and tended their looms none the worse for it. It is certain that while the greater part came to earn money for their own setting-out in life, many came to relieve a father from debt, to help a widowed mother and younger orphan children; and there were instances of brave girls who earned in the cotton-mill the money which supported a brother in college — the brother who afterwards became a senator, perhaps.

The Lowell of that day was a curious place. The girls all boarded in blocks of regularly built boarding-houses, owned by the manufacturing corporations, and managed by persons in their employ, under very strict rules of their making. No girl was allowed to be out after a certain hour. Up to that time the brilliantly lighted shopping streets would be full of girls; then the bells rang, they hasted home, the shops closed, and the streets were desolate. The boarding-house regulations were as strict as those of a fashionable boarding-school.

It was well worth going to some of the churches on Sunday. There were a thousand girls from fifteen to twenty-five — rarely one older — all dressed with neatness and even a degree of elegance, and, scattered about, a hundred men perhaps, who seemed quite lost and unprotected — as forlorn as one man with eleven women in an omnibus. In the dog-days, 90° in the shade, what a whirr it was, with the flutter of a thousand fans ! And how the Methodist hymns rang out with a thousand soprano and contralto voices with the almost inaudible undertones of bass and tenor !

In congregational churches the girls, being in such an overwhelming majority, exercised their right to vote; and as the few men were of no account against them, they deposed disagreeable ministers, and invited those they liked better, at their own sweet wills; and as they paid their salaries, why not ? They paid their money, and they took their choice; and if they preferred a young, handsome, and agreeable preacher, to an old, ugly, and sour one, who shall blame them ? The Methodist girls were obliged to take those who were sent them; but bishops and presiding elders had enough of the wisdom of serpents not to appoint those who would empty the seats, and drive these lambs of the flock to other and more gentle shepherds.

Not in the churches only did these self-reliant Yankee girls act for themselves. It was at their peril that the factory corporations added half an hour to their time of work, or took sixpence from their weekly wages. The girls would turn out in processions, hold public meetings, make speeches and pass resolutions, and held the whole manufacturing interest at their mercy. Every mill was

[233]

stopped; there were no other hands to be had; there was not a girl in New England would come to take their places. The managers had nothing to do but quietly knock under. The men took no part in these *émeutes*, except as sympathising spectators. And what could

STATE STREET

be done? I should like to see the magistrate who would read the Riot Act to four or five thousand Yankee girls, the police that would arrest, or the military that would charge upon them. So they had their own way in these matters, while they submitted without a murmur to the social regulations which were made for their benefit and protection.

❖❖❖❖❖❖❖❖❖❖❖❖

[*Henry Adams*]

The effect of the Quincy [memorial] service was deepened by the
official ceremony which afterwards took place in Faneuil Hall,
when the boy was taken to hear his uncle, Edward Everett, deliver
a Eulogy. Like all Mr. Everett's orations, it was an admirable piece
of oratory, such as only an admirable orator and scholar could create; too good for a ten-year-old boy to appreciate at its value; but
already the boy knew that the dead President could not be in it,
and had even learned why he would have been out of place there;
for knowledge was beginning to come fast. The shadow of the War
of 1812 still hung over State Street; the shadow of the Civil War to
come had already begun to darken Faneuil Hall. No rhetoric could
have reconciled Mr. Everett's audience to his subject. How could
he say there, to an assemblage of Bostonians in the heart of mercantile Boston, that the only distinctive mark of all the Adamses, since
old Sam Adams's father a hundred and fifty years before, had been
their inherited quarrel with State Street, which had again and
again broken out into riot, bloodshed, personal feuds, foreign and
civil war, wholesale banishments and confiscations, until the history of Florence was hardly more turbulent than that of Boston ?
How could he whisper the word Hartford Convention before the
men who had made it ? What would have been said had he suggested
the chance of Secession and Civil War ?

TIMBER!

[John S. Springer, Maine]

WHILE the Pines, growing in clusters, seem to constitute the aristocracy — families of nobility — the rest of the forest seems to make up the populace; and I may add, that backwoodsmen are accustomed to pay them the same deferential regard above other gentlemen foresters which is awarded to superiors in human society. Indeed, the Pine has claims upon our regard, not only on account of its unequaled dimensions, but "from the importance of its products in naval, and especially in civil and domestic architecture, in many of the arts, and in some instances in medicine."

"As it affords timber and boards of a greater size than any other soft-wooded tree, and is lighter and more free from knots, it is used in preference for the masts of ships, for the large beams, posts, and covering of wooden buildings, and for the frame-work of houses and bridges, as well as for clap-boards and shingles. The clearness, softness, and beauty of this wood recommend it for the panels and frames of doors, for wainscotings, for the frames of windows, for cornices and moldings, and for all the uses of the joiner. As it receives paint perfectly, it is employed for floors which are to be painted. Varnished without paint, it gradually takes a yellowish or light reddish color, and has considerable beauty. It is excellent for the carver in wood, and is used for the figure-heads of vessels; and as it takes gilding well, it is preferred for the frames of looking-glasses and pictures."

Its importance may be estimated, also, from the vast amount of employment it furnishes and the revenue it produces. Its history is full of interest from the hour it leaves the stump in the forest, through the various processes it passes until taken from the hold of the ship and piled away upon our market piers. The amount of employment it furnishes to lumbermen, mill-men, rafters, coasters, truckmen, merchants, and mechanics, exceeds that furnished by any other single product in Maine or the province of New Brunswick. On the Penobscot alone there are said to be ten thousand men engaged in lumbering.

◇◇◇◇◇◇◇◇◇◇◇◇◇

[*Henry David Thoreau, Concord, Massachusetts, 1853*]

Within a dozen miles of Bangor we passed through the villages of Stillwater and Oldtown, built at the falls of the Penobscot, which furnish the principal power by which the Maine woods are converted into lumber. The mills are built directly over and across the river. Here is a close jam, a hard rub, at all seasons; and then the once green tree, long since white, I need not say as the driven snow, but as a driven log, becomes lumber merely. Here your inch, your two and your three inch stuff begin to be, and Mr. Sawyer marks off those spaces which decide the destiny of so many prostrate forests. Through this steel riddle, more or less coarse, is the arrowy Maine forest, from Ktaadn and Chesuncook, and the head-waters of the St. John, relentlessly sifted, till it comes out boards, clapboards, laths, and shingles such as the wind can take, still, perchance, to be slit and slit again, till men get a size that will suit. Think how stood the white-pine tree on the shore of Chesuncook, its branches soughing with the four winds, and every individual needle trembling in the sunlight, — think how it stands with it now, — sold, perchance, to the New England Friction-Match Company ! There were in 1837, as I read, two hundred and fifty saw-mills on the Penobscot and its tributaries above Bangor, the greater part of them in this immediate neighborhood, and they sawed two hundred millions of feet of boards annually. To this is to be added the lumber of the Kennebec, Androscoggin, Saco, Passamaquoddy, and other streams. No wonder that we hear so often of vessels which are becalmed off our coast, being surrounded a week at a time by floating lumber from the Maine woods. The mission of men there seems to be, like so many busy demons, to drive the forest all out of the country, from every solitary beaver-swamp and mountain-side, as soon as possible.

I talked with one of them, telling him that I had come all this distance partly to see where the white-pine, the Eastern stuff of which our houses are built, grew, but that on this and a previous excursion into another part of Maine I had found it a scarce tree; and I asked him where I must look for it. With a smile, he answered, that he could hardly tell me. However, he said that he had found enough to employ two teams the next winter in a place where there was thought to be none left. What was considered a "tip-top" tree now was not looked at twenty years ago, when he first went into the business; but they succeeded very well now with what was considered quite inferior timber then. The explorer used to cut into a tree higher and higher up, to see if it was false-hearted, and if there was a rotten heart as big as his arm, he let it alone; but now they cut such a tree, and sawed it all around the rot, and it made the very best of boards, for in such a case they were never shaky.

One connected with lumbering operations at Bangor told me that the largest pine belonging to his firm, cut the previous winter, "scaled" in the woods four thousand five hundred feet, and was worth ninety dollars in the log at the Bangor boom in Oldtown. They cut a road three and a half miles long for this tree alone. He thought that the principal locality for the white-pine that came down the Penobscot now was at the head of the East Branch and the Allegash, about Webster Stream and Eagle and Chamberlain lakes. Much timber has been stolen from the public lands. (Pray, what kind of forest-warden is the Public itself?) I heard of one man who, having discovered some particularly fine trees just within the boundaries of the public lands, and not daring to employ an accomplice, cut them down, and by means of block and tackle, without cattle, tumbled them into a stream, and so succeeded in getting off with them without the least assistance. Surely, stealing pine-trees in this way is not so mean as robbing hen-roosts.

◇◇◇◇◇◇◇◇◇◇◇◇◇

[*John S. Springer*]

A distinguishing characteristic of this kind of business is the unceasing encounter by our lumbermen with the blood-thirsty millions of flies who swarm and triumph over these sanguinary fields. In the use of fire-arms these unvanquishable hosts are not skilled, to be sure, but in a charge they are invincible. No amount of slaughter will intimidate them. Though the sweeping hand of destruction annihilates them by thousands, still, with full ranks, the contest is carried on with unabated vigor, a respite only being afforded in rainy weather, or when high winds prevail; then they retire from the field.

At night the musquito lancers take up the action — the Indian tribes of the insect species — and all night they keep up their ceaseless war-whoop, as they repeat their sallies upon the weary, disturbed sleeper. No coat of mail is proof against the attacks of one species of fly commonly called the midget, which is so small as to be almost imperceptible to the naked eye. The black fly and the musquito can only reach the exposed parts of the body, but to the midget every portion is accessible. He insinuates himself under the collar, the wristband, and through the texture of the garments, and the whole region between the shirt and the skin is a field for his operations.

No little pains are bestowed upon the conveniences designed for the team. With the exception of sporting horses, never have I witnessed more untiring devotion to any creature than is bestowed upon the ox when under the care of a good teamster. The last thing before "turning in," he lights his lantern and repairs to the ox hovel. In the morning, by the peep of day, and often before, his faithful visits are repeated to hay, and provender, and card, and yoke up. No man's berth is so hard, among all the hands, as the teamster's. Every shoe and nail, every hoof and claw, and neck, yokes, chains, and sled, claim constant attention. While the rest of the hands are sitting or lounging around the liberal fire, shifting for their comfort, after exposure to the winter frosts through the day, he must repeatedly go out to look after the comfort of the sturdy, faithful ox. And then, for an hour or two in the morning again, while all, save the cook, are closing up the sweet and unbroken slumbers of the night, so welcome and necessary to the laborer, he is out amid the early frost with, I had almost said, the care of a mother, to see if "old Turk" is not loose, whether "Bright" favors the near fore-foot (which felt a little hot the day before), as he stands upon the hard floor, and then to inspect "Swan's" provender-trough, to see if he has eaten his meal, for it was carefully noted that at the "watering-place" last night he drank but little; while at the further end of the "tie-up" he thinks he hears a little clattering noise, and presently "little Star" is having his shins gently rapped, as a token of his master's wish to raise his foot to see if

[239]

some nail has not given way in the loosened shoe; and this not for once, but every day, with numberless other cares connected with his charge.

A competent hand in this profession generally calculates to do a good winter's hauling, and bring his team out in the spring in quite as good flesh as when they commenced in the early part of the season. But as in all other matters, so in this, there are exceptions to the general rule. Some teamsters spoil their cattle, and bring them out in the spring miserably poor, and nearly strained to death. Such a practice, however, can not be regarded as either merciful or economical. So far as true policy is concerned, it is much better to keep a team well. What may be gained by hard pushing during the former part of the season will be more than made up during the latter, when the teams are moderately urged and well kept, and then you have a good team still for future labor.

There are some recreations to relieve the monotony of a Sabbath in the wilderness. Sometimes a short excursion in search of spruce gum; for many a young urchin at home has had the promise of a good supply of this article, to be furnished on the return of the campers. Others go in pursuit of timber for ax-helves. As neither the White Oak nor Walnut grow in the latitude of Pine forests in the eastern section of Maine, the White Ash, Rock Maple, Beech and Elm, and sometimes the Hornbeam, are in general use. Others spend, it may be, a portion of the day in short timber-hunting excursions. Where the contiguity of encampments allow it, visits are exchanged among the denizens of the camps.

◇◇◇◇◇◇◇◇◇◇◇◇◇◇

[*H. D. Thoreau*]

About noon we reached the Mattawamkeag, fifty-six miles from Bangor by the way we had come, and put up at a frequented house still on the Houlton road, where the Houlton stage stops. Here was a substantial covered bridge over the Mattawamkeag, built, I think they said, some seventeen years before. We had dinner, — where, by the way, and even at breakfast, as well as supper, at the public-houses on this road, the front rank is composed of various kinds of "sweet cakes," in a continuous line from one end of the table to the other. I think I may safely say that there was a row of ten or a dozen plates of this kind set before us two here. To account for which, they say that, when the lumberers come out of the woods, they have a craving for cakes and pies, and such sweet things, which there are almost unknown, and this is the *supply* to satisfy that *demand*. The supply is always equal to the demand, and these hungry men think a good deal of getting their money's worth. No doubt the balance of victuals is restored by the time they reach Bangor — Mattawamkeag takes off the raw edge. Well, over this front rank, I say, you, coming from the "sweet cake" side, with a cheap philosophic indifference though it may be, have to assault what there is behind, which I do not by any means mean to insinuate is insufficient in quantity or quality to supply that other demand, of men, not from the woods, but from the towns, for venison and strong country fare.

[*J. S. Springer*]

It would be difficult to give an exaggerated sketch of the drunken practices among loggers twenty-five years ago. I recollect that matters were carried so far at Milltown, that the loggers would arrest passers-by, take them by force, bring them into the toll-house grog-shop, and baptize them by pouring a quart of rum over their heads.

But a change has come over, not the spirit of their dreams, but their practices and estimate of such excesses. I doubt whether any portion of society, or class of men whose intemperate habits were so excessive, and whose excuses, at least for a moderate use of liquor, were so reasonable, can be found where the principles of total abstinence have wrought so thorough and complete a change. Not that the evil is wholly eradicated, for many still continue its use. But it has now been fully demonstrated that men can endure the chilling hardships of river-driving quite as well, and, indeed, far better, without the stimulus of ardent spirits, and perform more and better-directed labor.

It would be a match for "Dame Nature" to locate a handsome Pine-tree beyond the grasp of the logmen. Where the Eastern hunter pursues the mountain goat, the logger would pursue the stately Pine. We have seen them in the deep ravine, on the abrupt hill-top, and far up the rugged mountain side, or peering down from some lofty cliff upon the insignificant animal at its base who is contemplating its sacrifice; a few minutes, and the crash of its giddy plunge is heard, "and swells along the echoing crag," causing the earth to tremble under the stroke of its massive trunk; and if it does not break in pieces, as is sometimes the case, in falling, it will in time find its way to the slip of the sawmill. The resolution, daring, skill, and physical force of the men engaged in this business can find no rival, to say the least, in any body or class of men whatever.

In many cases logs are hauled on to the ice of the lakes, streams, and rivers, instead of being left upon the banks or landing-places. When hauled on to the lakes, they are laid together as compactly as possible, and inclosed in a "boom," which is made by fastening the ends of the trunks of long trees, so as to prevent them from scattering over the lake on the breaking up of the ice. A strong bulk-head or raft is constructed of the logs, with a capstan or windlass for the purpose of warping the whole forward in a calm, or when the wind is ahead. In this operation, two or three men take an anchor into the boat, to which, of course, the warp is attached, when they row out to the extent of the rope, let go the anchor, and haul up by working the windlass. Sometimes a tempest breaks up the boom, and the logs are scattered, which gives much trouble, and not unfrequently causes a delay of one year before they reach the mills.

From lakes and tributary streams, the various parcels of logs cut and drove by different companies issue forth, and form one grand drive on the main river, where the separate crews unite, and make common cause in the driving operation. In other instances one drive may precede another, making the river for miles one general scene of logs and river-drivers. Sometimes the foremost logs of one drive, unobstructed, pass on and mingle with what is called the "tail end" of the preceding drive. Under such circumstances, if there be any grudge to gratify by the foremost crew, or a substantial joke to be put, such truant logs are run aground, into creeks, in meadow land, among the bushes, and on the shore. A crew of thirty or forty men will take a log belonging to another crew and run it up high and dry on to the land, stand it on end, prop it up, and leave it in that position. The rear crew, on coming up, stimulated by the prank, knock away the props, and throw it down; a score of pikes pierce its sides, when they shove it upon the run perhaps twenty rods to the river again, amid the most vociferous hurrahs and whooping, enough to give one quite an idea of the Indian war-whoop. Some, perhaps, who may trace these lines may be curious to know how the logs of one party can be distinguished from those of another. The answer is, precisely as one farmer distinguishes his sheep from those of his neighbor by the particular mark they bear, each differing in some particular from every other. A representation of these marks, which are cut in the side of the log, would remind one of the letters or characters of the Chinese.

On the falls, and the more difficult portions of the river, sometimes immense jams form. In the commencement, some unlucky log
swings across the narrow chasm, striking some protruding portions
of the ledge, and stops fast; others come on, and, meeting this obstruction, stick fast also, until thousands upon thousands form one
dense breastwork, against and through which a boiling, leaping
river rushes with terrible force. Who that is unaccustomed to such

scenes, on viewing that pile of massive logs, now densely packed,
cross-piled, and interwoven in every conceivable position in a deep
chasm with overhanging cliffs, with a mighty column of rushing
water, which, like the heavy pressure upon an arch, confines the
whole more closely, would decide otherwise than that the mass
must lay in its present position, either to decay or be moved by
some extraordinary convulsion. Tens of thousands of dollars' worth
lay in this wild and unpromising position. The property involved,
together with the exploits of daring and feats of skill to be performed in breaking that "jam," invest the whole with a degree of
interest not common to the ordinary pursuits of life, and but little
realized by many who are even familiar with the terms *lumber* and
river-driving. In some cases many obstructing logs are to be removed singly. Days and weeks sometimes are thus expended before
the channel is cleared. In other cases a single point only is to be
touched, and the whole jam is in motion. To hit upon the most
vulnerable point is the first object; the best means of effecting it
next claims attention; then the consummation brings into requisition all the physical force, activity, and courage of the men, more
especially those engaged at the dangerous points.

From the neighboring precipice, overhanging the scene of operation, a man is suspended by a rope round his body, and lowered

near to the spot where a breach is to be made, which is always selected at the lower edge of the jam. The point may be treacherous,
and yield to a feeble touch, or it may require much strength to
move it. In the latter case, the operator fastens a long rope to a log,
the end of which is taken down stream by a portion of the crew,
who are to give a long pull and strong pull when all is ready. He
then commences prying while they are pulling. If the jam starts, or
any part of it, or if there be even an indication of its starting, he
is drawn suddenly up by those stationed above; and, in their excitement and apprehensions for his safety, this is frequently done
with such haste as to subject him to bruises and scratches upon the
sharp-pointed ledges or bushes in the way. It may be thought best
to cut off the key-log, or that which appears to be the principal barrier. Accordingly, he is let down on to the jam, and as the place to
be operated upon may in some cases be a little removed from the
shore, he either walks to the place with the rope attached to his
body, or, untying it, leaves it where he can readily grasp it in time
to be drawn from his perilous position. Often, where the pressure
is direct, a few blows only are given with the ax, when the log snaps
in an instant with a loud report, followed suddenly by the violent
motion of the "jam"; and, ere our bold river-driver is jerked half
way to the top of the cliff, scores of logs, in wildest confusion, rush
beneath his feet, while he yet dangles in air, above the rushing,
tumbling mass. If that rope, on which life and hope hang thus suspended, should part, worn by the sharp point of some jutting rock,
death, certain and quick, would be inevitable.

The deafening noise when such a jam breaks, produced by the
concussion of moving logs whirled about like mere straws, the crash
and breaking of some of the largest, which part apparently as easily
as a reed is severed, together with the roar of waters, may be heard
for miles; and nothing can exceed the enthusiasm of the river-
drivers on such occasions, jumping, hurraing, and yelling with joy-
ous excitement.

◇◇◇◇◇◇◇◇◇◇◇◇◇

[*H. D. Thoreau*]

Our course here crossed the Penobscot, and followed the southern
bank. One of the party, who entered the house in search of some
one to set us over, reported a very neat dwelling, with plenty of
books, and a new wife, just imported from Boston, wholly new to
the woods. We found the East Branch a large and rapid stream at
its mouth, and much deeper than it appeared. Having with some

difficulty discovered the trail again, we kept up the south side of
the West Branch, or main river, passing by some rapids called Rock-
Ebeeme, the roar of which we heard through the woods, and,
shortly after, in the thickest of the wood, some empty loggers'
camps, still new, which were occupied the previous winter. Though
we saw a few more afterwards, I will make one account serve for
all. These were such houses as the lumberers of Maine spend the
winter in, in the wilderness. There were the camps and the hovels

for the cattle, hardly distinguishable, except that the latter had no
chimney. These camps were about twenty feet long by fifteen wide,
built of logs, — hemlock, cedar, spruce or yellow birch, — one kind
alone, or all together, with the bark on; two or three large ones
first, one directly above another, and notched together at the ends,
to the height of three or four feet, then of smaller logs resting upon
transverse ones at the ends, each of the last successively shorter than
the other, to form the roof. The chimney was an oblong square
hole in the middle, three or four feet in diameter, with a fence of
logs as high as the ridge. The interstices were filled with moss, and
the roof was shingled with long and handsome splints of cedar, or
spruce, or pine, rifted with a sledge and cleaver. The fire-place, the
most important place of all, was in shape and size like the chimney,
and directly under it, defined by a log fence or fender on the
ground, and a heap of ashes, a foot or two deep within, with solid
benches of split logs running round it. Here the fire usually melts
the snow, and dries the rain before it can descend to quench it.

The faded beds of arbor-vitae leaves extended under the eaves on either hand. There was the place for the water-pail, pork-barrel, and wash-basin, and generally a dingy pack of cards left on a log. Usually a good deal of whittling was expended on the latch, which was made of wood, in the form of an iron one. These houses are made comfortable by the huge fires, which can be afforded night and day. Usually the scenery about them is drear and savage enough; and the loggers' camp is as completely in the woods as a fungus at the foot of a pine in a swamp; no outlook but to the sky overhead; no more clearing than is made by cutting down the trees of which it is built, and those which are necessary for fuel. If only it be well sheltered and convenient to his work, and near a spring, he wastes no thought on the prospect. They are very proper forest houses, the stems of the trees collected together and piled up around a man to keep out wind and rain, — made of living green logs, hanging with moss and lichen, and with the curls and fringes of the yellow-birch bark, and dripping with resin, fresh and moist, and redolent of swampy odors, with that sort of vigor and perennialness even about them that toadstools suggest. The logger's fare consisted of tea, molasses, flour, pork (sometimes beef), and beans. A great proportion of the beans raised in Massachusetts find their market here. On expeditions it is only hard bread and pork, often raw, slice upon slice, with tea or water, as the case may be.

The lumberers rarely trouble themselves to put out their fires, such is the dampness of the primitive forest; and this is one cause, no doubt, of the frequent fires in Maine, of which we hear so much on smoky days in Massachusetts. The forests are held cheap after the white-pine has been culled out; and the explorers and hunters pray for rain only to clear the atmosphere of smoke.

◈◈◈◈◈◈◈◈◈◈◈◈◈

[J. S. Springer]

The boom, which constitutes the general receptacle of all logs, is worthy a few lines of observation.

On the Penobscot it stretches up the side of the river in the vicinity of numerous islands, whose location is peculiarly favorable; the boom-sticks run from one island to another, and, where the distance is too great, a pier is sunk — a square frame of stout timber filled with stones. These piers sometimes span the whole river, united by the boom-sticks. This is true of the main boom on the St. Croix. On the Penobscot it stretches up the river about two

WOODS ON FIRE

miles; at the upper end there being a shear boom, which swings out to intercept and turn the logs floating down the river into its ample embrace.

The Boom Corporation, on the Penobscot, is regulated by legislative enactments, and all logs running into it, or within the limits of its charter, are subject to its laws and regulations. Its bounds embrace a section of the river six miles in length, and to the care of all logs coming within its limits the agent is obligated to give his attention, and the company responsible. It is the duty of the boom-master, with the men under him, to raft the logs of each individual in parcels by themselves previous to their delivery for the mills, guided in his selection by the particular marks cut on the logs, for which service and safe-keeping the owner or owners of the boom receive thirty-three cents per *M.* feet, board measure, which makes the property of the boom very valuable. In addition to this, every log found in the boom without a mark is a "prize log."

Among other duties devolving on the boom agent is to inspect, personally, every raft of logs, setting down the number and mark in a memorandum kept for the purpose. This course of management protects each log-owner's property from plunder, as, in case any and all persons were indiscriminately allowed to raft out logs, the temptation might prove too strong, in some cases, to regard with due honesty logs bearing marks of a different character. Besides these main booms, there are many lesser ones, up and down the river, subject to no special legislation or law except the will of the owner.

At East Machias village there are seventeen saws in operation, and eleven lath machines; the latter, for the most part, are situated in the base of the saw-mills, and manufacture laths from the slabs made in the mill. At this place the saws cut, on an average, about six hundred thousand feet, board measure, to a saw, one half of this lumber being sawed from Pine, and the other from Spruce logs. The same quality of lumber brings fifty cents more per thousand here than on the St. Croix. In answer to the question, *Why is this so?* the reply was, "We saw nearly all our lumber *to order,* and of prescribed dimensions."

Annexed is a table showing at a glance the state of the lumber trade per annum on each river:

EAST MACHIAS.

		Average price per M.	*Total.*
No. of Saw-mills	17.		
" Lath Machines	11.		
Amount of Long Lumber	10,200,000.	$8 00.	$81,600.

		Average price per M.	Total.
No. of Laths	13,200,000.	1 00.	13,200.
			$94,800.
" Men employed	450.		
" Oxen and Horses, do. ...	380.		

WEST MACHIAS.

		Average price per M.	Total.
No. of Saw-mills	20.		
" Lath Machines	14.		
Amount of Long Lumber	18,000,000.	$8 00.	$144,000.
No. of Laths	16,800,000.	1 00.	16,800.
			$160,800.
" Men employed	475.		
" Oxen and horses, do. ...	400.		

The following table, showing the condition of the lumber manu-facture and trade on the Penobscot, has been obtained from the most reliable sources of information, and is presented for the inspection of those interested in such matters.

Number of saw-mills on the Penobscot and tributaries, 240.
" " clap-board machines, 20.
" " lath machines, 200.

Amount of long lumber sawed annually,* 200,000,000 feet, at $10.00 per M.

Amount of laths sawed annually, 400,000,000 pieces, at $1.00 per M.

Amount of clap-boards sawed annually, 5,500,000 pieces, at $18.00 per M.

Amount of shingles † sawed and split annually, 110,000,000 pieces, at $2.50 per M.

Amount of pickets ‡ sawed annually, 10,000,000 pieces, at $6.50 per M.

The number of men, oxen, and horses employed directly and indirectly on this river alone, would not vary, probably, much from twenty thousand.§

* The amount varies from year to year, sometimes exceeding, and then again falling short of the amount above stated.
† Sawed on the river and from the country.
‡ There are various other flinds of short lumber, such as staves, sash and window-blind stuff, not enumerated.
§ The author, in preparing the above statement, has availed himself of the most reliable sources of information, and would particularly mention the following gentlemen, to whose intelligence and kindness he is particularly obligated: Mr. S. Harris, of the surveyor general's office; Rufus Dwinel, Esq., and Mr. Taylor, of Bangor; also A. W. Babcock, Esq., and several other gentlemen of Orono.

The reader may inquire with some curiosity, "Where does all this lumber find a market ?" We may remind such that Maine has furnished, in times past, the principal part of the lumber consumed in the United States and the West India Islands, though other states in the Union possess immense tracts of fine timber land, which, as the lumbering interests of Maine diminish, will be cut and brought into market.

[H. D. Thoreau]

We visited Veazie's mills, just below the island, where were sixteen sets of saws, — some gang saws, sixteen in a gang, not to mention circular saws. On one side, they were hauling the logs up an inclined plane by water-power; on the other, passing out the boards, planks, and sawed timber, and forming them into rafts. The trees were literally drawn and quartered there. In forming the rafts, they use the lower three feet of hard-wood saplings, which have a crooked and knobbed butt-end, for bolts, passing them up through holes bored in the corners and sides of the rafts, and keying them. In another apartment they were making fence-slats, such as stand all over New England, out of odds and ends, — and it may be that I saw where the picket-fence behind which I dwell at home came from. I was surprised to find a boy collecting the long edgings of boards as fast as cut off, and thrusting them down a hopper, where they were *ground up* beneath the mill, that they might be out of the way; otherwise they accumulate in vast piles by the side of the building, increasing the danger from fire, or, floating off, they obstruct the river. This was not only a saw-mill, but a grist-mill, then. The inhabitants of Oldtown, Stillwater, and Bangor cannot suffer for want of kindling stuff, surely. Some get their living exclusively by picking up the drift-wood and selling it by the cord in the winter. In one place I saw where an Irishman, who keeps a team and a man for the purpose, had covered the shore for a long distance with regular piles, and I was told that he had sold twelve hundred dollars' worth in a year. Another, who lived by the shore, told me that he got all the material of his out-buildings and fences from the river; and in that neighborhood I perceived that this refuse wood was frequently used instead of sand to fill hollows with, being apparently cheaper than dirt.

MIGHTIER THAN THE SWORD

◇◇◇◇◇◇◇◇◇◇◇◇◇

[Timothy Dwight]

THERE are three Printing-Offices in Worcester. Isaiah Thomas, Esq. the proprietor of one of them, has probably done as much printing business as any other man in New-England, within the same period of time. He has printed a folio, a quarto, and an octavo, edition of the Bible; and, I believe, was the first person in this country, who purchased a complete font of standing types for printing the Bible in the duodecimo form. He has, also, published a considerable number of large and expensive works, together with a great multitude of small ones; and has for many years had a well furnished book-store in this Town. At the same time he is at the head of an extensive establishment of the same kind in Boston.

◇◇◇◇◇◇◇◇◇◇◇◇◇

[Isaiah Thomas, Worcester, Mass.]

October, 1806. 6. Finished work on the new Street. The Selectmen came and surveyed it & laid it out in form. The Light Infantry Company, under arms, commanded by Capt. Flagg, marched thro it, halted on the bridge, and discharged three vollies. The Gentlemen of the Street prepared a large tub and two pails full of excellent punch, and the Selectmen, at the request of those present and in conformity to their own proposal, named the street Thomas street. The Infantry Company were refreshed with as much punch as they chose to drink and all present. Three Cheers were given, and the Company marched off.

April, 1808. 1. Miss Weld left us in dudgeon. Pleasant for the season. Miss C. returned, and went again to Gov. Lincoln. Began writing a Sketch of the Origin and progress of Printing. A child fell in a kettle of boiling Soap, and died. Its Grandmother going in haste from a neighboring house to administer relief taken with Asthma, died instantly. Her name was Harrington.

4. Hard struggle for Governor, &c. President at Fire Club.

May, 1809. 15. Agreed with Elijah Burbank to make for (me) 100 Reams — Medium printing to Weigh 22 lb. per ream, of the same quality and size as the sample shown him of paper on which Mr. Harris' Sermon, preached at Plymouth on the Anniversary of our forefathers is printed on.

October, 1809. 10. Note at the bank 1600 dols. for my son.

11. Bargained with Cheever Felch for all my Stock in trade at Walpole [N. H. —one of Thomas's branches] & printing materials, to take payment in 20,000 Watts' Psalms & Hymns at 17 Cents each in Sheets; and 5000 Bibles in 8vo. With Apocrypha, in sheets, at 110 cents each — 3 years' credit on interest.

1810. Last year I held more offices in Society than I could attend to — Grand Master of Freemasons in Massachusetts; this office I resigned 27th. of Decr: Grand H.P. of the royal arch Chapters in Massachusetts, having served in this office as long as the Constitution of this order permitted; I was released from it in September: One of the Directors of Worcester Bank, an office I have held since the bank was instituted: One of the Directors of Worcester Turnpike Corporation: Magistrate of the County of Worcester; this office not troublesome, as I but seldom officiate in it, never but from necessity, and always without fees; Member of the Massachusetts Charitable Fire Society, at Boston: Member of the Massachusetts Charitable Mechanic Association, at Boston: Member of the Massachusetts Humane Society: Member of the Massachusetts Agricultural Society: Member of the Christian Monitor Society: Member of Foresters Association: Member and Proprietor Boston Athenaeum Society: Member and Librarian and a Director of the Worcester Library Company: Member of Evangelical Missionary Society of Massachusetts. I cannot boast of being a useful member of many of the above-mentioned Institutions.

January, 1810.

1. Visited by all my son's children.

2. Went to the Bank.

4. Put History of Printing to Press

5. First proof sheets. Lucretia Maccarty died at Charlestown, New Hampshire.

August 1820. 12. Went to South Boston early this morning.

Settled with my partner Eben^r. T. Andrews, and dissolved our Copartnership [Thomas & Andrews, a leading Boston publishing house] which has continued 31 years. I sold out to Mr. Andrews, in order to bring our concerns to a close. *My part* of the Stock, which part had been estimated at 70,000 dollars, (whole of the Co'y's property at 140,000 in 1819) for 13000 Cash payable in one and two years, without interest, and a part of the Stock nominal value 18000 dollars, but will not sell for Cash for 6000 dols. Thus have I lost — not having for 70,000 dols. more than 19,000 — and 6000 of this poor property — on no other terms could I close this long concern with my partner, who served his time with me, and who I sat up in Business — he then had no property — but now is rich, and by his management is worth 4 times as much as myself — so things go ! — At this time I find that my property is at least 90,000 less than what it was estimated at ten years ago; but I hope I shall be able to get through with the concerns of business, and leave something for my heirs, and for publick benefit — "We bring nothing with us into this world, and we can carry nothing away with us."

June 31, 1825. My Grandson Isaiah Thomas received his degree of B.A. at the Commencement of Harvard University this day. I have paid for his College Education, and his private expences whilst at College $1643.60 besides which he is in debt for his expences on 4 or 5 weeks Tour for pleasure, and extra clothing, and for Books towards a private library $191.76.

Let Daniel Golding half the house on the Common at 4 dollars per month till 1st of April next.

November 1825. 8. Value of my bound and Sheet Stock, as taken by Mr. Harris during the last and the present month, according to former prices, about 7 years since, amount to $28,185. several articles not included — which at this time deducting two thirds would amount to $9395 — There are 5800 Bibles 800 with Apocrypha, in the Sheet Stock, for which I gave $1.50 for each copy, but which are now charged only $1.50 and deducting two thirds from this price allows but 41 2-3 cents for each copy, which is not the amount of the paper.

[*Joseph Tinker Buckingham, Windham, Conn.*]

In December, 1795, my term of service with Mr. Welsh expired. I had formed a resolution to learn the trade of a printer. Through the agency of my brother, whom I looked upon as a sort of guardian, a place for me was provided in the office of David Carlisle [another partner of Isaiah Thomas], at Walpole, N. H., and there I was initiated in the mystery of type-setting. My apprenticeship began on the 5th of March, 1796, and owing to a difficulty in accommodating myself, with the "steady habits" in which I had been educated in Connecticut, to the less economical propensities of some of the other and older apprentices, my service there was closed about the beginning of September following. During these six months, I never spent a happy day. Two hours had not elapsed after my entrance into the office, before I was called upon "to treat." I resisted the call for several days, but was at length overcome by the daily and almost hourly annoyance, and more than half of the small amount of money I possessed was expended for brandy, wine, sugar, eggs, crackers, cheese, &c. &c. Till then my lips had never been in contact with either of those liquors. Now, I was literally *compelled* to swallow them, distasteful and nauseous though they were. I say *compelled,* for what boy of sixteen could stand up against the sneers and ribaldry of eight or ten older ones, who laughed at his scruples and reproached him for his lack of honor and manhood in having never been drunk ? After having "treated," as I was the youngest apprentice, I was not called upon for change to buy the wine and eggs, which were taken by my seniors three or four mornings in a week; but it was my lot to go to the store for these articles, and to be on the watch to see if they were not likely to be disturbed by the appearance of Carlisle.

A few days after leaving Walpole, I found myself in the office of Thomas Dickman, publisher of the *Greenfield Gazette,* at Greenfield, Mass. The terms, on which I here commenced anew my apprenticeship, were such as would have contented me, if the business had been more extensive. It was agreed that I should be paid five dollars a year, to supply me with shoes, (!) and that I should be paid a certain fixed price for all the work done over the prescribed daily task. The difficulty was, that when the stint was done there was no more work to do. Of course I could earn nothing for myself, and before the first winter expired, my wardrobe was in a most degenerate condition. The apprentices (there were two beside me) had the privilege of printing such small jobs as they might obtain, without interfering with the regular business of the office — and, as we clubbed our labors, we not unfrequently gathered a few shilling by printing ballads and small pamphlets for peddlers, who, at that time, were tolerably good customers to country printers.

Being the youngest apprentice, it was a part of my duty, on publication days, to distribute the *Gazette* to the subscribers living in the village, the number of which amounted to no more than thirty or thirty-five. According to time-indefinite customs, I had a New-Year's Address, with which to salute my customers. It was written by an acquaintance, about my own age, and a clerk in a store at Guilford, Vt. It consisted of five stanzas of six lines each; but, though short, it was rich in patriotic sentiment, and expressions of regard for the patrons of the *Gazette*. O Croesus ! how mean and insignificant was thy grandeur, how poor and unenvied thy treasures, when I compared (or might have compared) thy lot with mine! when, on the evening of the first day of January, 1797, I counted my wealth, — SIX DOLLARS AND SEVENTY-FIVE CENTS, — all in quarters and eighths of a dollar, — and locked it in my chest ! Never before had I been the owner of so much money, — never before so rich. Yet I was sadly puzzled to decide how I should employ my cash; for my wants were so numerous that the amount, *large as it was,* was altogether inadequate to supply them. The first appropriation was for a new hat. The purchase of a pocket-handkerchief, a cravat, and a pair of stockings soon followed, and occasioned, in my treasury, a deficit of a shilling or two, for which the shopkeeper civilly gave me a short credit. This was the first debt I had contracted. How supremely happy might I have been had it been the last !

In the course of the first year of my apprenticeship at Greenfield, my attempt to form an acquaintance with English grammar was renewed. I foresaw that it would be useful to me, as a printer, but indispensable as an editor, — a profession, to which I looked forward as the consummation of my ambition. I still had my Webster, and chance threw in my way a small treatise by Caleb Alexander. Curiosity induced me to read a page or two of one and then a page or two of the other, to see if they differed, and if so, wherein the difference consisted. While thus engaged, a gleam of light broke through the dark cloud that had hitherto enveloped this intricate science. For some months, most of my leisure hours were spent in study; but, as I had no instructor, my progress was not very rapid: It was my usual practice, after I had obtained some general notion of what grammar was, to compare the copy I had to put in type with the rules, and to correct it, if it was wrong. Shortly after I adopted this exercise, it became pleasant and even fascinating. No romance was ever more interesting than this practice of comparing Noah Webster and Caleb Alexander, — noting their differences, — and forming a system of my own, which I had the vanity to think was better than either! To this day, no species of literary composition has interested me more than works of philology and criticism.

In August, 1798 Dickman sold his entire printing establishment, to Francis Barker, a young man, who had served an apprenticeship in the office of Messrs. Thomas & Andrews, Boston. Not being an indented apprentice, I was at liberty to seek my fortune where I would, but was content to remain with Barker on the liberal terms which he offered. Barker became dissatisfied with his position, and, in June, 1799, he resold the establishment to Dickman. Following his advice, I resolved to seek a place in Boston, where I could obtain a more thorough knowledge of the business of book-printing, and to avail myself of advantages not attainable in a small country office. I left Greenfield on the fourth of July, 1799, with my wardrobe tied up in a handkerchief, and with about forty cents in my pocket, and walked to Northampton. I sought and obtained employment for a few months in the printing-office of Andrew Wright, and afterwards, for a few months more, in the office of William Butler. Having obtained the means of supplying some necessary wants, I started for Boston, and pursuing my way, partly on foot, and sometimes in sleighs, when invited by wayfarers to ride, I completed my journey in three days and a half. On the fourth day, which was Saturday, the eighth of February, 1800, I arrived in Boston, and immediately sought employment. It was obtained, before one o'clock, in the office of Manning & Loring, who were then the principal book-printers in the town.* They were men of strong religious tendencies, and conscientious observers of all religious times and services. They were at this time much pressed with work, — orations, sermons, and other tracts, occasioned by the death of General Washington, and all hands worked, as requested, till twelve o'clock, but were not permitted to hold a *composing-stick* in their hands after the clock struck that hour.

The reminiscences of a journeyman printer will not be esteemed as very valuable contributions to the literature of the present day. If written out in full, mine would be a volume composed chiefly of notices of hard-laboring contemporaries, — of privations and sufferings that the world knew nothing of, — of physical and mental toil by day and by night, which brought neither wealth nor reputation to the laborer, though it transformed many a production

* Thomas & Andrews were among their principal customers. B. M.

into a shape fit for the public eye, which would otherwise have been cast aside as discreditable to its author.

Let us now take the reader into Congress-street, and give him an interior view of an editor's closet. In doing this, we shall observe with religious scrupulousness the maxim of the immortal bard, —

> Nothing extenuate,
> Nor set down aught in malice.

If the reader, after viewing this exhibition, should wonder how *we* manage to publish a daily and a weekly paper, keeping the two entirely distinct, and preserving their *individuality,* he may be assured that he is not *solus* in his admiration; for it is a fact that has frequently confounded *us;* we only know what the reader knows, too, that it *is done,* but how it is done, we can tell him nothing about it, except that it is *not done* without some hours of hard labor, and at hours when he probably is frolicking or asleep.

Our room, (or rather *one* of our rooms,) is about five feet square, one side of which is occupied by a narrow table and desk, over which are some shelves for papers, pamphlets, &c.; and in one corner is a small bookcase, containing our library, consisting chiefly of Fourth-of-July orations, election and ordination sermons, two old dictionaries, Fessenden's Law of Patents, Holt's Law of Libel, Degrand's Tariff of Duties, an odd volume of Stewart on the Mind, Hutchinson's History of Massachusetts, Joseph Bartlett's Aphorisms on Men and Manners, Paul Allen's American Revolution, an odd volume of Morse's Gazetteer, Dictionary of Quotations, Laws and Resolves of Massachusetts for the year 1820, two copies of Billings's Music, a few odd volumes of plays, all the numbers of the New Monthly Magazine which the *punctuality* and *honesty* of borrowing friends have returned, a piece of Chambaud's French Grammar, Maffitt's Tears of Contrition, and a few, a very few others, equally valuable standard works, but still too numerous to be here particularized. Surrounded by this superb collection of the literature of *past* ages, with about seventy or eighty newspapers received by the morning's mail, we seated ourself at the aforesaid table, on which were scissors, paste-dish, pen and ink, the indispensable implements of our profession, to commence our ordinary labor. And first, to prepare the subject-matter of the next day's *daily* journal. Having cast our eye over the New-York Gazette, and the Daily Advertiser, (our invariable standards for news from that city,) and clipped out a few paragraphs, the Washington papers were next put in requisition. An article in the National Journal, or the National Intelligencer, we undertook to *remanufacture*, (giving the Journal, or the Intelligencer, credit for *raw material*,) and having written two lines and a half, a gentleman in the outer apartment inquired if the editor was within, and having stated to the attendant at the clerk's desk, that his business was *very* particular, he was shown into the closet. He wished to know what was the price of the Galaxy. 'Three dollars a year, sir.' 'I thought it was only two and a half.' 'How many times a week is it printed?' 'Once a week, sir,' 'You have raised the price.' 'No, sir.' 'I thought the weekly papers were only two dollars and a half. Two or three of my neighbors thought they should like to take it, — we will subscribe for it for one quarter, if you will put it at two dollars and a half.' 'The price is the same it ever was; if you subscribe by the quarter, it is one dollar for the quarter.' 'That is too high; but I suppose you make a deduction if I pay in advance.' 'No, sir, the condition is payable in advance.' 'I suppose you pay the postage?' 'No, sir.' 'I don't like to pay in advance. I paid in advance once for a paper, and it stopped in two or three weeks.' (Here we took up our pen, finished the third line of our paragraph, and began upon the fourth.) 'Do you think the paper won't stop in three or four weeks?' 'I hope not, sir.' 'Suppose you should die before the quarter is up, what will become of the paper? We can get nothing paid back.' 'That is a subject, sir, which must be left to time and chance.' 'And so, we may lose half our subscription money. I don't like the plan of paying in advance; it's a good paymaster that pays when the work is done. Shall we get the papers regularly?' 'They shall be mailed according to your directions: if they are not received, the fault will not be in this office.' 'Well, I've a great mind to take it one quarter, and try it, but I suppose it will stop before the quarter is up.' 'I hope not; the young man at the desk will take your directions, sir.' 'Shall you continue to send it after the quarter is up, if I pay you a quarter in advance?' 'That shall be as you direct. The paper is never discontinued when a subscriber has complied with the conditions, without his order.' 'Well, I will take it a quarter, and you may direct it to the Postmaster. He lives close by us, and it will save the postage. I suppose he will get the first reading of it.'

The gentleman was again referred to the clerk at the desk to transact his *very particular* business, and as he left the room very reluctantly, another stranger passed by him, and wished to know if we would be kind enough to let him look at the Worcester Spy of week before last 'We haven't it here, sir.' 'Don't you take it?' 'Yes, sir, but it would be impossible to find it now. We doubtless had it, but it is put away with other papers that came at the time.' 'I should think it might be among *them;* may I look among them and seek for it ?' 'It is not there, — those are the papers of this morning.' 'My gracious ! do you take all them papers in one day ? I should like to look at them a few minutes, if it won't interrupt you, (seating himself in a vacant chair, and seizing hold of the paper which contained the article I had been endeavoring to make use of.) I should think it would cost you a good deal for postage.' 'Printers are allowed to exchange papers free of postage.' 'Oh, oh ! How many papers do you take in this way ?' 'Perhaps a hundred.' 'A hundred ! I didn't think there were so many printed in America. I don't see how you get time to read 'em all. Which do you consider the best paper you take ?' 'That is a difficult question to answer.' 'I wish to gracious you could find the Salem Register of last Thursday. What do you do with them all ?' 'They are the perquisite of one of the boys, who sells them, after I have done with them.' 'How much does he get for them ?' 'A trifle, sir.' 'How many papers do you print ?.' 'Two thousand.' 'Gracious father ! where do they all go to ? I suppose you send 'em all over the country. How many of 'em are taken in Boston ?' 'Probably half of them.' ('Is there any copy ready ?' said a workman at the door; and we gave him the few paragraphs cut from the papers before mentioned.) 'How many hands do you keep employed ?' Before we had time to reply, a military company passed, and the gentleman, eager to gratify his curiosity, rushed down stairs, and left us once more to ourself; but carried with him the paper he had so *ceremoniously* pulled from our table. Our paragraph, being unfinished, of course, was useless, and we resumed the examination of our mail papers.

After spending three minutes and five eighths in lonely solitude, during which time we had selected a few straggling articles, and seized the pen with an intention of writing a paragraph or two for 'the daily,' another gentleman called for the editor. He was told the editor was engaged, but that would not do, see him he must, and in he bolted. It was a gentleman who had been arraigned at the Police Court, on Saturday, for an assault and battery, and came to request that his name might not be mentioned in the paper. He was told we had no report of his case, and expected none, but if one was offered, we should adopt the usual course. He said he was a peaceable man, that he got a little groggy, and in one of his *turns,* he committed the offence for which he had been fined in the court. He thought it hard that a *gentleman* should have his name published, and was going on to give a history of his birth, parentage, education, temper, and various good qualities, but was interrupted by a call for 'more copy.' Proceeding with his tale, another man came in and wished to look at the Eastern Argus; but, as we had it not, he took the liberty of casting his eye on the paper we were writing upon, and seeing a line beginning with 'PRESIDENTIAL ELECTORS,' asked if we were going to support the general ticket, or the Crawford ticket. Not receiving a very direct reply, he entered upon a discussion of the expediency of Congress providing by law for a uniform mode of choosing electors in all the states. Just as he was letting off a most terrific explosion to blow up Crawford, hang Jackson, and annihilate Clay, two or three customers called for papers, and, as was very natural, stopped to listen to his eloquence, and one of them stepped into our closet. Recollect, reader, this editorial *retreat* is but five feet square, and now contained, beside the furniture beforementioned, *ourself,* the assault-and-battery gentleman, who had not finished the history of his life, the Adams-man, and the spectator, whom his eloquence had attracted. Four of us in a *five foot* room ! Seeing the boy approach for 'more copy,' we thought it a good opportunity, — under pretence of handing to him, what it was impossible for him to get near enough in our present situation to take, — to endeavor to make our escape, which with some difficulty we effected, leaving our whole *cargo* of mail papers to the mercy of those who had possession of our room. The company filed off, one after another, and left the Adams-man in quiet possession, who stopped about two hours to amuse himself at our expense.

Driven from our own appropriate domains, we retired to another apartment, and took refuge among the workmen. Here, in our elbow-chair, we again went to work, and the door being closed, in the course of half an hour, wonders were accomplished, and the immediate demands for 'more copy' were satisfied, and we commenced writing a most *glorious* description of 'National Feeling;'* when, the door being accidentally opened, a friend coming up stairs, espied us in our retreat, came up and very deliberately looked upon our manuscript, and asked what we were writing about, — wondered how we could ever write enough to fill up the paper, interrupted as we must be, and expressed his astonishment that people could be so uncivil as to call upon an editor, and intrude into his private apartment. Having read that part of our manuscript which was before him, he expressed his approbation; asked what we thought of the parade in honor of La Fayette, if we had shaken hands with him, &c. &c. and after an hour's chat upon things in general, very politely took his leave.

* An article describing the public reception of General La Fayette.

We had scarcely resumed the pen, when a message came that a gentleman wished for an interview. He wanted to know whether job-printing was done there, and what it cost to print a hundred hand-bills. We referred him to the clerk and continued scribbling. In about five minutes, another called to ask it as a favor that a certain article in the Statesman might be inserted next day; and another to say, that there was an error in the price-current of that morning in the article of *Fish,* and that a price current, if it was not correct, was good for nothing. He was told that the gentleman who corrected the price-current was responsible for its correctness, and did not send it into the world anonymously. He animadverted with great earnestness on the utility of a good price-current, the advantage it would be to the public, and the benefit it would be to the proprietor, and the great detriment it was to all parties to have goods quoted at a higher or lower price than they could be bought for; to all of which we assented and kept writing. After he had gone, information was received that there was a note in the bank to be provided for. This was a damper to the imagination, and 'National Feeling' was thrust into the desk, till the rites of Mammon were performed. It was now dinner-time.

On our return at three o'clock, 'National Feeling' was again spread upon the table, another paragraph nearly finished, when a stranger inquired for the editor. It was a celebrated 'DRAMATIC VENTRILOQUIST.' He produced a card, containing a specification of what he was going to perform at the Pantheon, and desired to know the charge for advertising. For this information he was referred to the clerk, and having settled that matter to his apparent satisfaction, he took from his pocket-book three or four pieces cut from Canadian and Portland papers, containing some choice puffs upon his performances in various places, which he wished us first to read, and then to publish, or to write something similar to them. Our reply was, 'It is contrary to our practice to publish such articles in advance.' 'Will you write an editorial paragraph, pointing the attention of the public to the advertisement?' 'I cannot, sir; were I to adopt such a practice, there would be no end to similar applications.' 'The advertisement will be of no use without such a paragraph; no one will read it, unless you direct their attention to it. Three lines under the editorial head will be of more service than a whole column of advertisements.' 'I am aware of that, sir; but is it fair to beat down the price of advertising to its lowest possible terms, and then make a demand upon the editor for a puff?' 'It was never refused to me before; and I expected you would do it without hesitation, for one of your own countrymen. I understand you are a countryman of mine.' 'What country is yours, sir ?' 'England; I have understood you are an Englishman.' 'Indeed, you have been misinformed; I am an American, sir, a Yankee; was never out of New-England but once in my life.' 'What do you ask for writing a paragraph of three or four lines, just referring to the advertisement ?' 'Nothing, sir; I cannot consent to do it.' 'Will you not publish it as a communication ?' 'No, sir.' 'The first people of Quebec and Portland have spoken highly of the performance, and' — 'I dare say the performance will be very good; if I see it, and think it deserves a paragraph, I shall perhaps be disposed to give it one.'

It is not necessary to tire the reader with a continuation of this *small talk*. Suffice it to say, that the gentleman's importunities for an editorial puff were unsuccessful; and after exhausting his persuasive eloquence to no purpose, he left us. It may be proper to add in this place, that his advertisements were published for several successive days according to his orders, and that he left town shortly after, *forgetting to pay his trifling bill*. We thought it possible that he might have forgotten us, because we refused to write and insert the puff preliminary; but we have since ascertained that two or three of our neighbors who did give him the *editorial paragraph*, are equally the objects of his *inattention*. Advertisements in the Worcester and Hartford papers, accompanied by the puff editorial, indicate that the 'dramatic ventriloquist' is wending his way to the south, where we hope he will find pliant editors, generous audiences, and lots of the *shinery*.

◇◇◇◇◇◇◇◇◇◇◇◇

[*Uriel Crocker*]

My father heard of a place in the printing-office of Mr. Samuel Turell Armstrong, and on Saturday, Sept. 14, 1811, the day after I was fifteen years old, my father took me up to Boston to place me as an apprentice with Mr. Armstrong. I had to spend a good part of my birthday cleaning up the old chaise and getting the horse ready, and in the morning my father got me up at four o'clock and we drove to Boston. In the afternoon my father drove home and left me. I did not know a soul in the city. On the next morning (Sunday) I got up and looked out of the front door of my boarding-house, which was a few doors north of Mr. Armstrong's store. I looked around, but was afraid to go far for fear of getting lost. Afterwards, hearing the bell of the Brattle Square Church ring, I went there and heard Dr. Buckminster preach.

At first I was "printer's devil" in the printing-office, and had to do all the errands. I had to put the wool on the balls, and had to go on foot to Cambridge to Mr. Dowse (who gave his library to the Massachusetts Historical Society) to buy sheepskins to make the balls out of. Sometimes I bought two or three skins at a time so that I should not have to go again soon. When not doing errands, I used to learn to set type. I learned this so fast that by Thanksgiving I could set up more type in an hour than any one else in the print-ing-office. For the first four years I got my board (which cost Mr. Armstrong two dollars and a half a week) and thirty dollars a year for clothes, and if I set up more than four thousand types in a day, I got twenty-five cents a thousand for all above that number. I could set up six thousand, and sometimes seven thousand in a day. This money I had for myself, and my father gave me a dollar now and then, but other than that I never got anything from my father or from my grandfather after I was fifteen.*

I remained "printer's devil" for a little more than two months, or until the coming of Osmyn Brewster, who afterwards became my partner. After he came, he was "printer's devil," and I was a "com-positor." He came from Worthington, Mass., and was a chubby, fair-complexioned boy dressed in a blue corduroy suit, when I first knew him.

In January, 1817, when I was nineteen years old, Mr. Ezra Lin-coln, the foreman of our printing-office, purchased a printing-office on Congress Street and left Mr. Armstrong's employ. Mr. Arm-strong requested me to take Mr. Lincoln's position, and I did so, though with some reluctance, as there were upwards of twenty com-positors and pressmen and seven apprentices in the office, and of the apprentices four were older than I was, — namely, William A. Parker, Amasa Porter, Edward Tufts, and Thomas W. Shepard. I had always been, however, the one who had been called on to do the difficult things that the other men could not manage, and I was able to earn two or three dollars a week over my stint, and after my stint was done I could go out when I had a mind to. Mr. Arm-strong told me if I would take the place of foreman I should go out as much as I wished. Well, I took the place, and I never had any trouble. I never assumed anything, but went right along and at-

* From an original account-book kept by Mr. Crocker it appears that during the first four years of his apprenticeship he received, in addition to the $120.00 allowed for clothes, the further sum of $180.02, on account of extra type-setting, making in all the sum of $300.02. It further appears that of this sum $95.15 re-mained at the end of this time uncollected in the hands of his employer, thereby showing that Mr. Crocker's total expenses during the four years, exclusive of his board, which was furnished by Mr. Armstrong, amounted to $204.87, or less than $1.00 a week.

tended to my duty. I never had an unpleasant or unkind word from any of my fellow-apprentices. From this time until I was free Mr. Armstrong allowed me two dollars a week for my services as foreman. He told me to manage the office just the same as if it was my own, and if any of the men did not do what I told them to, I was to order them to go downstairs and get their money. The office then ran seven presses. Mr. Brewster left the printing-office about this time and went downstairs into the book store. Mr. Armstrong had at first wished me to go into the store, but I told him I did not wish to do so, as I wanted to learn the printing business so that I should have a trade by which I could earn a living.

We printed a good deal at that time for Jeremiah Evarts. He used to write thousands of pages of manuscript in a round, plain hand, hardly altering so much as a word, and it never required more than a few minutes to make all the corrections when the proof was returned. Jeremiah Evarts was an extraordinary man. He could recollect the dates of about everything that had happened since the beginning of the world. He was the father of the Hon. William M. Evarts. Others for whom we printed, Rev. Ethan Smith. Rev. Lyman Beecher, Elijah Parish, of Byfield, Rev. Heman Humphrey, and Rev. Dr. Morse * of Charlestown, were more or less careless in their manuscripts, and hours were spent by us in deciphering their words. Frequently, if we could not succeed in making out the words, we would put in words of about the same length that made nonsense, or would leave a vacant space or turn the type upside down.

When I was free, the journeymen claimed that I must give them a treat. I told them I would do so, but that it must be postponed until Saturday. We fixed up some tables in the attic of the printing-office, and I sent out and got some ham, corned beef, etc., etc. I also had lemonade, punch, and Jamaica rum. I bought a dozen bottles of Madeira wine and paid a dollar a bottle for it. The men, however, did not take kindly to the Madeira, but preferred the lemonade and the rum. I kept a bottle of that Madeira for many years, and finally opened it when my grandson, George Uriel Crocker, came of age in 1884. The men came in from the other printing-offices, and I think there was hardly an office in Boston that was not represented. I guess that treat cost me a pretty round sum, one hundred dollars or more, but I had promised to do it.

At this time we used to begin work at six o'clock in the morning. We had an hour (from seven to eight) for breakfast and an hour for dinner. In summer we worked till dark, but after September

* Jedidiah Morse, "father of American geography" and of Samuel F. B. Morse, the painter and inventor. B. M.

20th, we had to go back after tea and work till eight p. m. by candle-light (candles ten to the pound). After eight o'clock we went home and "played saw wood" till ten o'clock, and then went to bed.

◇◇◇◇◇◇◇◇◇◇◇◇◇◇

[John Neal]

I was now fairly under way. A young book-seller — which, of course, may account for the rash adventure — James Adams, Jr., had applied to me, at the suggestion of others, to establish a paper. I refused; though willing enough to be an editor, nothing would induce me to became a proprietor. After a brief negotiation, he undertook to publish, what I was to *edit*, for five hundred dollars a year, payable out of the store; that is, in law-books and stationery.

Subscription-papers were issued, a very satisfactory list of subscribers obtained, and on the first of January, 1828, "The Yankee" burst like a northern meteor upon our people. It was continued with triumphant success; entirely original; most of it — seven-eighths perhaps — written by myself; and altogether literary, without a single advertisement, for a year and a half, when, having swallowed Mrs. Sarah J. Hale's * Monthly — the "Ladies' Magazine," perhaps — the "Bachelor's Journal," and the "Boston Literary Gazette," editor and all, it appeared in Boston, conducted by myself and James W. Miller, the poet, and a true poet he was, though he has been allowed to die out by his contemporaries; and then, as if the publishers and proprietors were beside themselves, they changed it from a weekly folio of eight pages, to a monthly magazine, which, as I foretold, gave up the ghost within the next following six months, although under the guardianship of Lilly and Wait, successors to Wells and Lilly.

While burning its way into public favor, I had for contributors, from all parts of the country, such men as Chief-Justice Appleton, whose first published writings appeared in the "Yankee," on Balance of Trade, Usury, Evidence, and Lotteries; John G. Whittier, who began his career with me, I believe; B. B. Thatcher, author of "Indian Biography;" Albert Pike, then of Newburyport, now of Little Rock; the Rev. Mr. Greenwood; James O. Rockwell, whose lines "To an Iceberg" ought never to be forgotten; Edgar A. Poe; Grenville Mellen, Dr. Isaac Ray, and half a hundred, more or less, of writers who have since become distinguished. Poe sent his first poems to the "Yankee," and proposed to dedicate a volume to me;

* Later famous as the editor of *Godey's Lady's Book*. B. M.

but I discouraged him, saying, that, in the existing state of public opinion, it would be a hindrance, instead of a help, and he forebore. And as for Whittier, I have just fished up a letter of his, which I had entirely forgotten, dated "10th Mo., 1828," and showing on what terms we were, forty years ago. A part of it ran thus: —

"My dear Neal, — I have just written something for your consideration. You dislike — I believe you do, at least — the blank verse of our modern poets and poetesses. Nevertheless, I send you a long string of it. If you don't like it, say so privately; *and I will quit poetry, and everything else of a literary nature,* for I am sick at heart of the business . . . Insult has maddened me. The friendless boy has been mocked at; and, years ago, he vowed to triumph over the scorners of his boyish endeavors. With the unescapable sense of wrong burning like a volcano in the recesses of his spirit, he has striven to accomplish this vow, until his heart has grown weary of the struggle." Of course, I wrote a most encouraging letter in reply; for he persisted, as we see, like Mr. Neal Dow, and William Garrison, after they had both threatened to be distinguished in some way, until he has become one of the glories in our upper-sky; but just think of the Quaker poet, and a poet, so much of a Quaker (he is a distant relation of mine, by the way) making a *vow,* and going about with a *volcano* in his heart, like Sumner Lincoln Fairfield, "full of the *unescapable sense of wrong.*"

About the same time, N. P. Willis, whom I had been watching over a long while, wrote me as follows, while engaging me to write for the "Token," of which he was the editor: "Three of the verses you have *quoted* in the 'Review' of the 'Token,' as specimens of the excellence of pieces, *were inserted by the editor, in the place of expunged stanzas.*" I had always thought highly, and spoken highly, of the poor fellow's poetry, long before I knew the name of the author, and while he was writing occasional verses for a Boston paper, without a signature; but the fact he mentions here, must have been very gratifying. That I should select three verses, to speak highly of, and that all three should turn out to be his, must have satisfied him that I recognized, as by elective affinity, the true spirit in him, and the golden ore of true poetry.

Soon after I had opened fire, and lay with my ground tier double-shotted, and matches lighted, I came to the knowledge of what had always been a provoking mystery to me. I did not mind being abused: I rather throve on it, indeed; but then, I did want to know what it was for. I knew that I had been cruelly slandered, not only misrepresented, but lied about, year after year, while abroad, by at least twelve hundred newspapers of the land; but I never quite understood *why*. At last, it came to me like a revelation from — I will not say where.

In the year 1818, Mr. Pierpont had made me acquainted with Mr. Joseph Tinker, alias Joseph Tinker Buckingham, a parishioner of his, editor and proprietor of the "New-England Galaxy," wretchedly poor, desperate, and living from hand to mouth. I liked the man, I liked his energy and boldness; and after taking upon my hands a personal quarrel, which he had with a fourth-rate English actor, who had come into his office to thrash him — and would have done so, but for me — I advised him to go on, and lay about him, right and left, as with a flail, until his power should be felt and acknowledged, and the abuses he complained of, should be put a stop to; offering, at the same time, to send him occasional communications, without pay. And this I did for two or three years, until, having disposed of Joseph Lancaster,* whom he greatly wronged, by the way, and some others, he began to assail me. Instead of being vexed with him, however, I laughed heartily at the freak, which was intended to prove his independence, even of friendship, and bade him "God speed !"

While abroad, he consigned his son Joseph to my special care, at London. I did my best to promote his views, without well understanding what they were, beyond this, that having interchanged a "sentiment" with Edward Everett, at some public meeting, he felt himself qualified for any thing, and therefore had established, or was about establishing, a new daily paper, the "Boston Courier," I believe. After introducing him to most of my friends, I helped him off to Paris. Meanwhile, the press-gang, the whole paperhood of America, were baiting and badgering me, at every turn, without my knowledge at the time, because, forsooth, in dealing with our American authors, and painters, and poets, from recollection, I had told the truth of them. Buckingham knew this, and knew, also, that the growing prejudice against me had no just foundation; that hundreds of lies were bandied about, which a word from him — "fiery darts," though most of them were — would have quenched for ever. Yet that word he never wrote, and, of course, never spoke. I did not know this at the time, or I should have helped him to something he would have been sorry to sup, even with a long-handled spoon. He was so unscrupulous, not to say unprincipled, that everybody was afraid of him, I found. This rather amused me; for I had flung down my gauntlet in our first issue of the "Yankee," and said to my calumniators, "There's my hand ! open or shut; take your choice."

* Much talked about at the time for his "Lancastrian system" of elementary education. B. M.

[267]

After a while, he ventured on a fling or two, which I did not quite understand nor relish; but I kept my temper. And then, having hinted that something he had allowed himself to say about a Methodist preacher — Huntington, I believe — who had prayed himself into a new pair of breeches — was not calculated to make friends of the religious community, Methodists or not, he had the insolence and folly to threaten me, that, if I gave him any more advice, he would let the people of Portland know who I was. Whereupon, I replied, that I understood him, and that if he did not tell the story — it was about a woman I had sent to Boston, to the care of Cooper, the tragedian — and in the very next paper, I would tell it. By that day's mail, I received a frightened warning letter, from my old friend Pierpont, who knew to what I referred, and all the circumstances, asking if I was mad, and saying that the "giant" — meaning my adversary, *Mr. Joseph Tinker Buckingham* — "was beginning to stir." To this I had nothing to say, just then. The result was, that Buckingham did not tell the story, and I did; and in the very next issue of the "Yankee." From that moment, having declared war, by proclamation, according to established usage, sending a herald into the enemy's camp, we had it broadside after broadside, hot and heavy, till he struck his colors, and said, with a piteous wail, that if it were any satisfaction for me to know that I had almost ruined the "Galaxy," I was welcome to the knowledge. And there the war ended between us, and for ever; and within a few months, he sold out the "Galaxy" to Mr. Moses Kimball, of the Museum, who engaged me as editor, with H. Hastings Weld, now an Episcopal clergyman, some where in New Jersey, for an associate; and then, Mr. Henry F. Harrington. My duties, I find, began on the 1st of January, 1835, and continued for one year — a long while, for any thing I had to do with. I wrote voluminously, but with so faint a recollection of what I did, that not long since, on being asked, by Mr. Edmund Quincy, about my editorship of the "Galaxy" I had entirely forgotten it, though I well remember writing for the paper.

◇◇◇◇◇◇◇◇◇◇◇◇◇◇

[*Phineas Taylor Barnum, Danbury, Conn.*]

In a period of strong political excitement, I wrote several communications for the Danbury weekly, setting forth what I conceived to be the dangers of a sectarian interference which was then apparent in political affairs. The publication of these communications was refused and I accordingly purchased a press and types, and

[268]

October 19, 1831, I issued the first number of my own paper, *The Herald of Freedom.*

I entered upon the editorship of this journal with all the vigor and vehemence of youth. The boldness with which the paper was conducted soon excited widespread attention and commanded a circulation which extended beyond the immediate locality into nearly every State in the Union. But lacking that experience which induces caution, and without the dread of consequences, I frequently laid myself open to the charge of libel and three times in three years I was prosecuted. A Danbury butcher, a zealous politician, brought a civil suit against me for accusing him of being a spy in a Democratic caucus. On the first trial the jury did not agree, but after a second trial I was fined several hundred dollars. Another libel suit against me was withdrawn and need not be mentioned further. The third was sufficiently important to warrant the following detail:

A criminal prosecution was brought against me for stating in my paper that a man in Bethel, prominent in the church, had "been guilty of taking *usury* of an orphan boy," and for severely commenting on the fact in my editorial columns. When the case came to trial the truth of my statement was substantially proved by several witnesses and even by the prosecuting party. But "the greater the truth, the greater the libel," and then I had used the term "usury," instead of extortion, or note-shaving, or some other expression which might have softened the verdict. The result was that I was sentenced to pay a fine of one hundred dollars and to be imprisoned in the common jail for sixty days.

The most comfortable provision was made for me in Danbury jail. My room was papered and carpeted; I lived well; I was overwhelmed with the constant visits of my friends; I edited my paper as usual and received large accessions to my subscription list; and at the end of my sixty days' term the event was celebrated by a large concourse of people from the surrounding country. The court room in which I was convicted was the scene of the celebration. An ode, written for the occasion, was sung; an eloquent oration on the freedom of the press was delivered; and several hundred gentlemen afterwards partook of a sumptuous dinner followed by appropriate toasts and speeches. Then came the triumphant part of the ceremonial, which was reported in my paper of December 12, 1832, as follows:

"P. T. Barnum and the band of music took their seats in a coach drawn by six horses, which had been prepared for the occasion. The coach was preceded by forty horsemen, and a marshal, bearing the national standard. Immediately in the rear of the coach was the carriage of the Orator and the President of the day, followed by the Committee of Arrangements and sixty carriages of citizens, which joined in escorting the editor to his home in Bethel.

When the procession commenced its march amidst the roar of cannon, three cheers were given by several hundred citizens who did not join in the procession. The band of music continued to play a variety of national airs until their arrival in Bethel, (a distance of three miles,) when they struck up the beautiful and appropriate tune of 'Home, Sweet Home!' After giving three hearty cheers, the procession turned to Danbury. The utmost harmony and unanimity of feeling prevailed throughout the day, and we are happy to add that no accident occurred to mar the festivities of the occasion."

PAINTERS AND OTHER VAGABONDS

◇◇◇◇◇◇◇◇◇◇◇◇◇◇

[John Trumbull, Lebanon, Conn.]

My taste for drawing began to dawn early. It is common to talk of natural genius; but I am disposed to doubt the existence of such a principle in the human mind; at least, in my own case, I can clearly trace it to mere imitation. My two sisters, Faith and Mary, had completed their education at an excellent school in Boston, where they both had been taught embroidery; and the eldest, Faith, had acquired some knowledge of drawing, and had even painted in oil, two heads and a landscape. These wonders were hung in my mother's parlor, and were among the first objects that caught my infant eye. I endeavored to imitate them, and for several years the nicely sanded floors, (for carpets were then unknown in Lebanon,) were constantly scrawled with my rude attempts at drawing.

The tranquillity of the arts seemed better suited to me than the more bustling scenes of life, and I ventured to remonstrate with my father, stating to him that the expense of a college education would be inconvenient to him, and after it was finished I should still have to study some profession by which to procure a living; whereas, if he would place me under the instruction of Mr. (John Singleton) Copley, (then living in Boston, and whose reputation as an artist was deservedly high,) the expense would probably not exceed that of a college education, and that at the end of my time I should possess a profession, and the means of supporting myself — perhaps of assisting the family, at least my sisters. This argument seemed to

TRUMBULL HOUSE, LEBANON, CONNECTICUT

me not bad; but my father had not the same veneration for the fine arts that I had, and hoped to see me a distinguished member of one of the learned professions, divinity in preference. I was overruled, and in January, 1772, was sent to Cambridge, under the care of my brother, who in passing through Boston indulged me by taking me to see the works of Mr. Copley. His house was on the Common, where Mr. Sears's elegant granite *palazzo* now stands. A mutual friend of Mr. Copley and my brother, Mr. James Lovell, went with us to introduce us. We found Mr. Copley dressed to receive a party of friends at dinner. I remember his dress and appearance — an elegant looking man, dressed in a fine maroon cloth, with gilt buttons — this was dazzling to my unpracticed eye ! — but his paintings, the first I had ever seen deserving the name, riveted, absorbed my attention, and renewed all my desire to enter upon such a pursuit. But my destiny was fixed, and the next day I went to Cambridge, passed my examination in form, and was readily admitted to the Junior class, who were then in the middle of the third year, so that I had only to remain one year and a half in college.

[He passed through a turbulent military career before actually becoming a patriarch of early American painting.]

◇◇◇◇◇◇◇◇◇◇◇◇◇

[*Chester Harding*]

The summer of 1822 I spent in Pittsfield and Northampton. Mr. Mills, United States Senator from Massachusetts, resided in the latter town. He had seen my pictures in Washington, and had spoken favorably of them and of me; and I found that I had already a high reputation. I at once got orders, and soon my room was tolerably well filled with pictures.

While I was there, the annual cattle-show came off. I allowed my pictures to be exhibited among the mechanical arts. They elicited great admiration, and formed one of the chief attractions. I went into the room one day when there was a great crowd, and was soon pointed out as the artist. Conversation ceased, and all eyes were turned upon me. This was altogether too much for my modesty, and I withdrew as quickly as possible.

I one day received an invitation to a large party, to be given by Mrs. Ashmun (the stepmother of George Ashmun), which I accepted; but, as the evening drew near, began to regret that I had done so. I finally went into my room, and sat down on the bed, before beginning to dress, and took the matter into serious consideration. Should I go ? or should I not ? It was a fearful ordeal to go through. I had never been to a fashionable lady's party, and should not know how to behave. My heart grew faint at the thought of my ignorance and awkwardness. But then, I reflected, there must be a first time; and, with a mighty effort, resolved that this should be it ! So I went, and passed through the trial better than I anticipated; but I was glad when it was over.

While in Northampton, I painted the portrait of two gentlemen from Boston. They encouraged me to establish myself in that city. I did so, and for six months rode triumphantly on the top wave of fortune. I took a large room, arranged my pictures, and fixed upon one o'clock as my hour for exhibition. As soon as the clock struck, my bell would begin to ring; and people would flock in, sometimes to the number of fifty. New orders were constantly given me for pictures. I was compelled to resort to a book for registering the names of the numerous applicants. As a vacancy occurred, I had only to notify the next on the list, and it was filled. I do not think any artist in this country ever enjoyed more popularity than I did; but popularity is often easily won, and as easily lost. Mr. [Gilbert] Stuart, the greatest portrait painter this country ever produced, was at that time in his manhood's strength as a painter; yet he was idle half the winter. He would ask of his friends, "How rages the Harding fever ?"

[1827]. As to financial matters, my dear friend, I can say that I am doing tolerably well. Since I commenced I have painted to the amount of $1,400, and I have little doubt that my business will increase rather than diminish. I find my pictures give satisfaction, and if I am not gaining popularity to the degree that I did when I was here before, I feel that I am gaining fame, which is a thousand times preferable. It is rather against me that I created such an excitement then, — an interest that could not by any human interest be kept alive. I am identified with my former pictures, and as they are not worthy the high encomiums that were passed upon them, the natural consequence is a reaction, which I have to contend with; but perseverance will do wonders.

I began my career again in Boston in 1829; not as I did on my first appearance in that city, for then I was entirely self-taught, and little could be expected from one from the back-woods: but now I came fresh from the schools of Europe, and with some reputation. I felt keenly how much more would be required of me, to fill the expectations of the connoisseurs and patrons of art.

My first picture was of Emily Marshall, then the reigning beauty of Boston. No artist's skill could be put to a severer test; for her beauty depended much upon the expression of her animated face, which, when lighted up in conversation, was bewitchingly lovely. I did not succeed to my own satisfaction, though others seemed well pleased.

Much interest was shown in my paintings, and I soon had enough to do; though of the eighty applicants on my list when I left Boston, not one came to renew his engagement. Many whom I had painted previously wanted their pictures altered, either because the dress was out of fashion, or the expression did not please them, etc.; but I found it would never do to begin to alter the old pictures. So I adopted for a rule, that I would paint a new picture in place of the old one, and deduct the price of the latter. I now charged $100 for a head: my former price was $50.

Among the sitters I had at this time was Timothy Pickering of Salem. He was far advanced in years, but as bright in intellect as a man of thirty. His conversation was extremely interesting, though it mostly pertained to the early days of our government. One day, I felt a strong desire to know how a man would feel who knew that his allotted time was nearly spent, and thought I might venture to put the question to him; so I said, "You have lived beyond the average of human life; how do you feel upon the subject of the final departure to the other world?" His reply was, "It was only the other day that I was asking old Dr. Holyoke the same question.' The doctor was some ten years his senior.

✧✧✧✧✧✧✧✧✧✧✧✧✧

[*Phineas Taylor Barnum*]

In April, 1836, I connected myself with Aaron Turner's travelling circus company as ticket-seller, secretary and treasurer, at thirty dollars a month and one-fifth of the entire profits, while Vivalla was to receive a salary of fifty dollars. As I was already paying him eighty dollars a month, our joint salaries reimbursed me and left me the chance of twenty per cent of the net receipts. We started from Danbury for West Springfield, Massachusetts, April 26th, and on the first day, instead of halting to dine, as I expected, Mr. Turner regaled the whole company with three loaves of rye bread and a pound of butter, bought at a farm house at a cost of fifty cents, and, after watering the horses, we went on our way.

We began our performances at West Springfield, April 28th, and as our expected band of music had not arrived from Providence, I made a prefatory speech announcing our disappointment, and our intention to please our patrons, nevertheless. The two Turner boys, sons of the proprietor, rode finely. Joe Pentland, one of the wittiest, best, and most original of clowns, with Vivalla's tricks and other performances in the ring, more than made up for the lack of music. In a day or two our band arrived and our "houses" improved.

While we were at Cabotville, Massachusetts, on going to bed one night one of my room-mates threw a lighted stump of a cigar into a spit-box filled with sawdust and the result was that about one o'clock T. V. Turner, who slept in the room, awoke in the midst of a dense smoke and barely managed to crawl to the window to open it, and to awaken us in time to save us from suffocation.

At Lenox, Massachusetts, one Sunday I attended church as usual, and the preacher denounced our circus and all connected with it as immoral, and was very abusive; whereupon when he had read the closing hymn I walked up the pulpit stairs and handed him a written request, signed "P. T. Barnum, connected with the circus, June 5, 1836," to be permitted to reply to him. He declined to notice it, and after the benediction I lectured him for not giving me an opportunity to vindicate myself and those with whom I was connected. The affair created considerable excitement and some of the members of the church apologized to me for their clergyman's ill-behavior.

✧✧✧✧✧✧✧✧✧✧✧✧

[*J. M. Bailey,* The Danbury News]

CIRCUS DAY IN DANBURY

A pretty fair index of Mr. Barnum's control over the credulity of an American public, was given on Saturday. The day was unpleasant, to use the mildest type of expression, but the streets were thronged with a mass of people — some of them coming twenty miles over the very bad roads. It was an enthusiasm no rain could dampen — no possible combination of circumstances flatten.

There were three tents — two small and one very large one. The former enclosed the menagerie and museum — the latter the arena. I attended the afternoon performance out of curiosity, and the evening entertainment out of revenge. I was a little disappointed in the menagerie, because I had depended on that and the museum for the bulk of my happiness on this occasion. The most noted specimens of the forest and jungle were those which appeared on the bills but not in the cages. Here was a discrepancy I could not reconcile with the proprietor's well-known honesty and enterprise. I cast a few reproachful glances upon the specimens that good living and virtuous percepts had preserved to such a good old age, and passed to the museum. There was a visible improvement in this place. The mind was illuminated by the lady who wrote the autograph with her toes, and the heart made glad by various other articles I cannot recall to mind.

When I got inside the large tent I was surprised. A sea of faces spread out before and around me. The tier seats are crowded, the ring seats are crowded, the gang-ways are crowded. It is a mass of suffocation, fun, and sweat. I don't think I ever saw so large an attendance at a prayer meeting, and I have never been to many of them.

I really enjoyed the sight. Here was one of the grandest views to be seen. Myriads of people of every clime — every temper, disposition, mind, and heart. Here, embraced in an area of a few hundred yards, might be observed —

"Why don't that bald-headed reptile set down?" cried a coarse voice behind me. I looked around. A red-faced, illiterate man was glowing down upon me from a tier seat. Passion disturbed his features; the man was really mad. I cast a sorrowful glance upon him and sat down. There were fifty or sixty people between me and the ring. I had not made any calculation for this when I came, and so I didn't appreciate it. Occasionally somebody hollered, "Down in front." Whenever I heard the cry I singled out the author and bestowed a grateful glance upon him. It was the finest oration I ever heard, and my appreciation of it was sharpened, I think, by the remarkably uncomfortable position I had got into. I had an excellent view of the tent, and, once in a while, of the ridge pole of the giant who stood nearly opposite. I knew there was something going on in the ring, but if I had been prostrated on my dying couch I could not have told what it was. But I knew whenever a different act commenced, because the folks in front of me stood up on the seats, and the folks behind me put their children on my head, and their umbrellas down my back, and remarked audibly to each other, —

"Was there ever anything like it ?"

And I, staring idiotically into the back of the man in front of me, fervently hoped there was not.

But all things have an end, and the dreary afternoon performance was not an exception. The last act was performed; the clown finally convulsed the audience; the children in the rear were pulled out of my hair, and I was permitted to fall over, roll around, and eventually get on my feet. With the crowd gone I stole back to the tent and took one fond, piercing glance at what I had not yet seen, — the ring.

The oldest inhabitant will never forget the severity of the storm in the evening. The rain descended in torrents, the air was chilly and raw, and the night was one in which all the sores in your heart are made bare to the sight. I knew there would be no attendance upon the show, but I thought I would go over. When I got there I found about one thousand people present, mostly ladies and umbrellas. They flocked into the tent, by wax figures, and up to the arena — the umbrellas shining in the light of the lamps, and a thousand irresponsible rivulets falling swiftly. The huge crowd looked like a party of immigrants on their way to colonize the Atlantic Ocean. The short people labored under a striking disadvantage. The prongs of the surrounding alpaca caught in their bonnet strings, and tried to disengage themselves by washing off those articles. Men who had acquired the filthy habit of profanity held the highest position in the party, and were much sought after. Everybody sincerely regretted he had come, and at the same time renewed his exertions to get close to the ring. Occasionally some one fell down, and his neighbors stepped on him and walked over him, and facetiously enquired, "How was that for high ?" Little girls with dazzling patches of fashionable glory on their heads were jammed, jarred, and impartially stirred up. The man who held on to his wife with one hand, five fractious children in the other, and balanced a ten-shilling umbrella on his chin, attracted general attention. The enthusiasm was really sublime during the entire show. What it

would have been if the bulk of the audience could have occasionally seen what was going on in the ring, the human mind fails to
calculate. But the rain came through the canvas in torrents, although several men were sent on the roof with patches, and the
ghastly dreariness of the spectacle became more and more condensed. The giant loomed up through the fog and misery like a
wart on a popular man's nose. The clown retired to the recesses of
the dressing room and wrung himself out, while the great basso
player emptied his instrument over the profane drummer, and the
crowd of disgusted and dilapidated people clawed and pushed their
way out doors.

❖❖❖❖❖❖❖❖❖❖❖❖❖

[*Edward Everett Hale, Boston*]

One of the societies would arrange a course of lectures. The whole
course might be on chemistry. I remember such a course from Professor Webster. It was conducted with all his brilliant power of experiment, and listened to with enthusiasm by four or five hundred
people. I remember another course by John Farrar on the steam-
engine. I heard in the Useful Knowledge course several of Mr.
Waldo Emerson's biographical lectures. The Useful Knowledge
course would be perhaps on Tuesday evening, the Mercantile Library on Wednesday, the Mechanics' on Thursday. Eventually halls
were built specially for such lectures. There was one favorite hall
in the Masonic Temple, which I suppose would hold five hundred
people. The seats rose rapidly, as in the lecture-room of a medical
college, so that people could see all the experiments or pictures on
the platform.

To such an entertainment you went, and if you were old enough
you took a friend of the other sex. You arrived there half an hour
before the lecture began, and walked from seat to seat, talking with
the people whom you found there. After the lecture had gone on
half an hour or more there was a recess, and again you walked
about from seat to seat, perhaps chose another seat, if the first had
not been satisfactory. At the end of a lecture of maybe an hour and
a half in length you went home with anybody who chose to invite
you. At the house you went to there was the invariable dish of oysters, or crackers and cheese, or whatever was the evening meal of
that particular evening.

The function of tea-parties was quite different from that of dinner
parties. You would invite two or three boys and girls who were

friends of your children to come and take tea, where now you would hardly invite children of the same age to come and dine. Now if this function happened to be exercised in the house of old-fashioned people it had some rather queer attendants — or what would seem queer to the boy of the present day. For instance, one of the relics of Revolutionary times was the general impression that no boy could ever serve his country, unless he were trained as a public speaker. I think this is true now, and it was known to be true then. Consequently when you were at such a party as I have described, the evening's entertainment of playing old maid, teetotum games, jack-straws, or whatever might occupy the young people, would be interrupted, from time to time, by an appeal to the boys of the party to "speak a piece" for the benefit of the elders. There was a certain compliment implied in being asked to "speak a piece," but it was not a great compliment, for every boy was asked, not to say compelled, to do so. It would have been bad form to decline to speak quite as much as it would be to sit at a dinner-table and decline to eat anything before you, as if it were of a quality poorer than that to which you were accustomed.

Accordingly you had one or two "pieces" in mind which you were prepared to "speak." When you were called upon — when the old ladies, at their side of the room, had made up their minds that it was time for this exercise to go forward — you were told, "Master Edward" (or Master Oliver, or Master Alexander), "the company would like to have you speak a piece." You demurred as little as you could, you went into a corner, you made a bow, and you spoke a piece. You then went back to your cards or other entertainment. I do not remember that the girls sang songs, as it seems to me they should have done, under the circumstances.

At such a little party invariably the tray was brought in as the evening went by, and you ate the nuts and raisins or figs, which were generally something you did not have at home. Perhaps this is always one of the charms of social life.

STOP THIEF!

◇◇◇◇◇◇◇◇◇◇◇◇◇◇

[Henry Tufts, New Hampshire]

I LAID a scheme, in concert with two other young fellows of my own standing to steal some bread and cheese, and at the same time, to rob a cucumber yard, owned by one Stevens, a steady old farmer. My two accomplices, not being versant in exploits of this kind, were both extremely timid and doubtful, as to the issue of the enterprise, and, when the case came really in hand, one of them declined entering the yard at all, by reason it was contiguous to the mansion of the proprietor. To induce our dispensing with his farther attendance, he offered to procure the bread and cheese, as he said he could take those articles from his own father's house. On condition of his so doing, we agreed to excuse him, and he set out for home accordingly. In the meantime the other youngster and myself (it being now late in the evening) ventured into the yard and stripped the vines of as many cucumbers as we could well carry away. We all three met again, the same evening at a preconcerted place of rendezvous, when, to our transport, it appeared that our pusillanimous companion had made shift to acquire half a loaf of bread, and a large cheese weighing fourteen pounds. We all sat down in order to commence a pleasing repast; but the thought struck my fancy, that I should much rather have the whole plunder to myself, than to share it in partnerships with my associates. No sooner did the idea enter my imagination, than slyly I took up a small pebble, threw it at one of my messmates, and with it hit him on the back. He was much startled at the stroke, as not knowing from what quarter it proceeded; while I also pretending to be panic-struck,

[280]

jumped up, exclaiming with affected surprise, "they are coming in pursuit of us." We all instantly took to our heels, myself in a different route from the other two, but they sped only a small distance; wherefore least they should find out the mistake, and return, I counterfeited a variety of strange voices; at the hearing of which the young novices were so sadly frighted, that they scampered away home as fast as their legs would carry them, adventuring no more back for the night. In a few minutes I returned to the cheese and cucumbers, and conveyed the whole away to a place of better security. The next day, meeting with the two young chaps, I told them, that, in trying to escape the night before, I had been unluckily overtaken by old Stevens, who found also and took possession of our booty, and besides threatened me so harshly that I was obliged to promise him three days work to compromise the affair. The young lads readily swallowed this fictitious account, and were very well pleased that I had escaped so easily. Soon after they paid me a day's work apiece, as their due share of the common penalty.

Now that the revolving wheel of time had rolled away twenty-one years of my existence, I began to think it high time to think of providing for myself. To this end I made application to my father desiring him to bestow on me some part of his property, as an encouragement to industry, and towards my obtaining a comfortable subsistence in the world, in proportion as he had done by my elder brother.

After my father had been sufficiently teased (as perhaps he thought) with my importunities, he finally rejected my suit, declaring it his intention, that his eldest son should possess the whole of his estate, which, might be worth (as I supposed) one thousand dollars.

Thus being disappointed in my hopes, and cut off from that, which had long been the ground of my only dependence, I grew angry and discontented, not well knowing what steps to pursue. The reflection that I had pretty diligently served my father during minority, (the whole term of which had been applied to the business of husbandry) and that my labor had contributed in a great measure to the support of the family, was constantly present to my indignant view. Whereupon I determined at all events to seek redress, and that too in some clandestine manner, if unable to persuade him to do me justice.

It is written (as 'tis said) in the Hebrew annals, that the man, who gave his son, neither property, education nor trade, brought him up to be a thief. The truth of this was verified in me, for after ruminating a while in order to concert the most eligible method, in which to be even with my sire, I at last concluded (as the outset and beginning of what I had further in view) to take his horse; that being the most convenient article of his domestic inventory, and best suited to the dispatch, that seemed needful in my novel undertaking. Accordingly, at a convenient season, under pretense of riding but a few miles, I made my flight with the horse to Chester, in Hampshire, where I sold him for about thirty dollars, in ready money.

Never till now had I been in possession of so considerable a sum. It appeared, in my enraptured view, as a plentiful fund, and sure earnest of future riches and prosperity.

Leaving Chester, I strolled from place to place, defraying itinerary expenses, in part by occasional labor, though principally with the contents of my purse. This mode of life continued for nearly two months. Meantime the money, which, at first, I had contemplated with so much delight, continuing to dwindle, till scarce a moiety of its original sum remained; my dreams of happiness became wholly dispelled, and I resolved (however fearfully) to return home, like the prodigal son, and apologize for my misconduct in the best manner I could, hoping to pacify my parent, by paying him what money I had left, and which I thought might pretty well compensate for the loss of his horse.

With these views I set off on foot for Lee, and arrived thither in the course of a few days. When I approached the much dreaded presence of my father he appeared sorely displeased, and reprimanded me sharply for eloping with his horse, desiring to know where I had bestowed him. I replied, that I had sold him in Chester, and taking out the money I had left, presented it most respectfully, expressing, at the same time, great sorrow and contrition for all past offenses. He took the money, but complained that his horse was worth much more, and rebuked me sharply for my past bad conduct, which he predicted would bring me to the gallows in the end, if I persisted in such pernicious practices. But my father's displeasure subsided by degrees, and I continued to reside with him as formerly.

Awhile after our reconciliation, I repaired to Nottingham, a neighboring town, with intention to reside there for a season. In this place I contracted some acquaintance with a young woman, named Sally Hall. As lasciviousness I have every reason to suppose was an original ingredient in my composition, I made love to this damsel, and continued the courtship, with ardor, for a time; but at last her pregnancy was the result of our frequent intimacy. She gave me to understand her situation, and hinted expectations of my healing the transgression by marriage. This however I had no intention of doing. At present I was averse from all thoughts of matrimonial alliance, especially so with the young woman in question, of whose virtue and accomplishments I had not the most exalted opinion. Nevertheless I gave her flattering encouragement, that, I would in due season comply with her wishes, only our connection must be kept secret, 'till things should be arranged to our liking. In this she fully acquiesced — my discourse as the sugar plum was pleasing to the credulous miss, and inasmuch, as her reliance was strong on my assurances, she remained confidently easy for several months. But after that, as I neglected the accustomed visits, she became fully convinced of my duplicity and intention to deceive her, and, being at this crisis, urged on by her friends, she went and entered a complaint before Esq. Butler, a neighboring magistrate, whose warrant for my arrestation was committed to one Dearborn, a constable, with directions to see me forthcoming with all speed.

This man dealt so craftily in the business, that, one day, he caught me by surprise, as I was walking in a bye crossway, without suspicion of his or any other person's being near. I was carried before Esquire Butler, and requested to find sureties for my personal appearance at the next Court of General Sessions of the peace, which then took cognizance of such matters. To be handled in this compulsatory manner was to me, at that early period of life, an entire novelty, for which reason I was greatly intimidated, not knowing in what way the affair would terminate. But as my propitious stars ordained, I was at this juncture, pretty well furnished with cash, and, by a judicious distribution of seven dollars to one man, three to another, and so on, made a number of fast and able friends, who promised to stick by and see the matter through. They fulfilled articles to a tittle, for, through their management, the girl was brought to settle for ten dollars, receiving which, she signed the back of the warrant satisfied, giving me a receipt too in full of all further demands.

Myself and fellow laborer Dennis soon contracted a very familiar acquaintance, nature had endowed him with convertible powers, and for me he had imbibed no small predilection.

Hearing me complain of inability to support self and family in the manner I desired, he started as from a reverie, and said, if I would be led by his counsels, he would put me in a way to acquire some considerable property. I requested an explanation, so he went on to say, that he knew of a store in Saco, (Mr. Pickard's of Ipswich) with every avenue to which he was perfectly acquainted, and out of which we might take goods to any amount whatever. The goods might be carried, without danger of discovery, into the country and be disposed of for ready money. This he observed would be a more expeditious method to acquire the *desiderata*, than was the dull employment to which we then submitted. In short, the scheme he had laid down far surpassed anything of the kind, which had ever entered my imagination. Being no adept in the art of appropriating to myself, in a genteel manner, the property of others, I was suspicious of ill consequences, and therefore made objections, not only as to the feasibility of his plan, but to the danger of detection in its execution. But my demurs were all overruled by his engaging to be accountable for our success ultimately, in case of my submission to his particular management. As I had no contemptible opinion of the man's capacity, I consented without more ado, and thereon, collecting my arrear of wages, accompanied him forthwith to Saco, the compact part of which lay only seven miles distant. Dennis was very confident of success, and strove to encourage his drooping companion, but, to confess the truth, the fear of detection was a prevailing ingredient with me, pending the whole voyage.

We reached the village of Saco a little before nightfall, and entered a shop to procure the means of exhilarating our spirits, and of fitting us for the arduous enterprise. As the moments seemed precious we resolved on effecting our business that very evening. Wherefore, after tippling till near bedtime, we sallied forth, and drew near the store in question, concealing ourselves by the wayside, so as to observe all that passed. In this posture we waited till all was still, and the people in bed and asleep, as we presumed. Then we set forward, and coming up to the store, carefully reconnoitered every avenue. We were at some loss about matters, so withdrew to a small distance to hold consultation in what shape to commence the attack. My Irish friend began by observing that one end of the shop had been fitted up for a wash house, and he rather supposed this the most vulnerable quarter. In short, we agreed to make a first essay on the wash house door. To this end Dennis led the van, while I, staggered at the magnitude of the attempt, followed with trepidation.

On examination we found the door less strongly fastened, than we had imagined, for means were readily devised to force it open without disturbance. Instantly we entered the wash room, and waited a few minutes, in a listening attitude, to catch the smallest echo, that might float through the air; but no sounds vibrated on the ear; a profound silence prevailed, as the general pulse of life stood still.

It being tolerably dark we ventured, at length, to light a candle, which, by groping about, we found near the fireplace. The only obstruction that now remained, was the door communicating with the store room. This entrance we found to be fast locked, but Dennis drew out his knife and cut the hinges. This was not difficult, seeing they were made only of leather. Every impediment being thus removed, Dennis directed me to leave the house, and watch by the side of the outer door, while he should explore the premises; and since he knew me to be unversed, at that time, in the flash tongue, he desired me to preserve silence, and knock only against the door in case of alarm. I took post accordingly; meanwhile my file leader went into the store and proceeded with prosperity and dispatch. He found, however, but little money, for which reason it was needful to take the greater hold of other articles. Finally, he packed together two large bundles, consisting of English goods, and a few other commodities, to the value of about two hundred dollars, and brought them forth to the outer door. This whole business was completed in about thirty minutes, by which time we were ready for departure. But here I would just give a small piece of cautionary advice to shopkeepers in general: it is, to leave but little cash in such stores, as are remote from their dwelling houses, since the loss of goods may possibly be sustained with less inconveniency, than that of ready money.

With the booty we made our way through the compact part of the town, and then (veering) traveled westwardly six or eight miles, highly elated indeed with our fortunate acquisition. But now we arrived at the house of one Richard Dutton, an old acquaintance of Dennis's, where we proposed to make a stand, and deposit our booty for the present. We acquainted Dutton and wife with the manner in which we had acquired the articles, they engaging to secrete them effectually, and befriend us. After devoting ourselves to rest and refreshment, during the residue of the night and greater part of the next day, and regaling upon good cheer and agreeable drink till we became merry as so many Greeks, Dennis and Dutton, a little before the close of day, went out with a few trinkets to dispose of them for cash and such necessaries as our present inclination demanded. In transacting this business they took it into their heads, that, as the goods had been obtained at a cheap store, they might afford to sell cheap too, especially for cash in hand. In this, however, they overshot themselves, for their customers, supposing they sold at too low a rate to come by the things honestly, seized and detained both them and their lading. A magistrate and other officers being called in, the culprits were so hardly handled, and besieged withal to acknowledge how they came by the articles, that Dutton (the privilege of admission as King's evidence being promised him) at last confessed all, informing, more particularly, of the commodities secreted at his own house. Dennis, too, was so closely pressed that he confessed every fact, and betrayed what he knew respecting his young proficient, Henry Tufts.

When those ministers of justice (or rather vengeance) had gathered the necessary information, they speedily set out for Dutton's abode, in quest of me and the other articles. Their arrival was excessively early in the morning, so that I, who happened to be quietly in bed with my friend Dutton's wife, dreaming, I protest, of no harm, till I heard them thundering at the door, had scarce time to retreat from the arms of my playmate, ere they entered the room and made me prisoner. Seeing but one bed in the cottage, they demanded where I had lodged the night preceding. I replied "on the floor." They charged me with fallacy, intimating, that from appearances, I must have bundled with Dutton's wife, but it being no part of my creed to criminate myself, where the facts could not be fairly proved, I positively denied their assertions. Dutton seemed to trouble his pate but little about the business, but being requested to produce the residue of the goods, he did it alertly, to the satisfaction of the whole company. This over, they bade Dennis and me prepare for jail, and presently after hurried us to Saco, where having undergone another examination, we were escorted under a strong guard to Falmouth [now Portland] jail, and there confined in irons.

It was late in autumn (1770) when it was our mishap to become inmates of this horrid mansion, wherefore, being destitute of fire and bedding, we suffered miserably during imprisonment. We continued in the most comfortless situation for fifteen days together, without making a single effort for effecting our escape. At length, growing uneasy, we thought it high time to devise some stratagem for that purpose. We concerted several, but on trial, the means proved inadequate to the undertaking. We had instruments of no sort to force a breach through the prison walls, so that in our desponding view, the obstacles to deliverance appeared insuperable.

This was the first time I had ever been immured within the walls of a prison, consequently I sustained my sufferings with less patience and fortitude than did Dennis. My handcuffs I thought intolerable, and bitterly regretted the part I had taken (thus unwarily) in breaking Pickard's store. We remained awhile longer in

the same gloomy situation, when Dennis, who was remarkably
fertile in expedients, suggested, that if we could prevail with Mr.
Modley, the prison keeper, to allow us a little fire, he did not
scruple but we might burn a passage through the side of the jail,
and so make our escape. Had we been provided with implements of
any kind, fire, undoubtedly had been our *dernier resort,* but destitute, as we were, of every requisite, we knew of nought else, of
which to avail ourselves, so resolved, at all hazards, to try the event
of that, if so lucky as to obtain the article.

Accordingly, the next day, we represented to the jailor how much
we had suffered already from the severity of the cold and from
nakedness, beseeching him, withal, to allow us a little fuel, to warm
our benumbed limbs in this inclement season. The keeper was a
benevolent man and truly pitied, I believe, our sufferings, wherefore, he granted our request, but had the precaution, to extinguish
the fire with a bucket of water, every evening, lest we might compass some mischief. Yet we soon found a remedy for this evil, for
having a large piece of a broken earthen milk pan, we contrived to
place it crosswise in the funnel of the chimney, as far above the
mantle piece, as we could well reach. In this vessel, one certain evening, we deposited a small brand of fire, a few minutes previous to
the customary return of the jailor. Presently, coming, he quenched
the embers as usual, but, to our satisfaction had no suspicion of our
plan.

On his leaving us, we reclaimed the hidden fire, and were careful
not to lose it for lack of feeding. With some anxiety we watched the
passing hours, till about eleven o'clock at night, when thinking it
high time for all to be sound asleep, we set fire to the broadside of
the jail, a few feet above the flooring, intending to burn a hole
through sufficiently large for our exit. The timbers, which composed the sides of the prison, were fourteen inches in thickness, being placed hard by one another, and sheathed on the inside with
two inch oak plank, the outside was boarded and clapboarded. We
attended the fire unremittingly by the space of two hours, an
burned away the wood with an expedition that scarce seemed tedious to our eager wishes. By this time we had made an opening
quite through the wall, as large in circumference, as the head of
our gallon keg. "Courage, (said Dennis, whose eyes, I perceived,
were nearly closed with smoke), courage, my good lad, the game
goes well; if we manage the fire rightly, there'll be no kind of danger." I thought so too, and, upon the whole, we both grew pretty
confident of success, but presently a provoking accident occurred,
which disconcerted the whole scheme; overturned our fond hopes,

[287]

and rendered escape, in this way impracticable. The new disaster was this. The fire had been creeping, though very gradually, through the interstices of the timber, from the time of kindling it, yet we had made shift to control it by the help of a pail of water. But by this time we had burned through as above, our water was all expended, the fire then increased with surprising rapidity, and began blazing, inside and out, with much briskness. So that our room was immersed in such thick volumes of smoke, as to admit the fetching of scarce a single breath. One pailful of water more would have done the thing completely, as, by means of that, the flames had been checked long enough for all purposes. But the room being thus filled with smoke and fire; water all spent; the flames spreading and our design impracticable further, we were constrained, at last, to shout for help. Our loud vociferations aroused, anon, the whole family, which drawing near, found us, poor devils, on the very point of suffocation. The whole posse were collected in a few minutes, who united their efforts to conquer the unruly element, which raged by this time, with ungovernable fury. Full three hours were expended in this disagreeable service, though water (not to mention crow bars and axes) was used in abundance. At last, however, they succeeded in arresting the progress of the fire, but the jail was nearly ruined, for the breach in the wall was sufficient for the admission of a team of oxen. I gazed on the fruits of our labor with some admiration, and wished my hands at liberty, that I might have escaped; but my sighs were in vain.

All this while we had been treated with civility by the bystanders, except that I received one stroke of the hand from the prison keeper at his first entrance.

The jail was now adjudged unsuitable for the retention of prisoners, so it was thought advisable to send us packing to Old York jail; but Thanksgiving being near, we were kept under guard, in Mr. Modley's family, till that solemnity should be over.

After a circuitous ramble I ventured to revisit Lee, where my first wife yet held possession of the cattle. She had heard of my extraordinary marriage, during my late elopement, and therefore gave me an uncouth welcome; however I cohabited with the dame, as formerly.

Soon after this I hired out, as a day laborer, with one deacon Tash, of Newmarket. On a certain day, while mowing grass in his meadow, I accidentally came across a huge wasp's nest. Having a mind for a little sport with the honest deacon, who was indeed quite a worthy and zealous man, I slyly cut the twig, from which the nest was suspended, and, in a gentle manner, conveyed it to a cock of hay, where I concealed it for the present. All this I did without the smallest disturbance to the meddlesome race. In the afternoon the Deacon and I went out with the team to haul hay. He mounted the wheels, as usual, to make the load, leaving me behind to manage the team. At length I drove in course to the bunch containing the waspy tribe, when pushing my fork through the nest, so as to break it pretty well to pieces, I pitched it up, hay and all, to the unsuspecting deacon, who was stripped entirely to the shirt. An armed host of those mischievous insects now seized him conjunctly, and stung him so intolerably, that not being able to keep his post he pitched head foremost to the ground. Being still surrounded with his troublesome assailants, he scrabbled up with what agility he could muster, in order to retreat to a more respectful distance, but scampering away with more speed than forecast, he again lost his center of gravity and had the fresh misfortune to plunge precipitately into the main ditch. This had lately been thrown up to drain the meadow, and was, moreover, full of water, so that the old gentleman lay floundering in both water and mud, 'till I seeing the catastrophe, and fearing he might be suffocated, ran up to his assistance. We had a fearful time of it, to be sure, for in trying to clear him, I was prodigiously stung by the wasps myself. The deacon was in a sweet pickle, but no sooner did he recover breath for articulation, then he accused me of doing him this piece of roguery intentionally, and desired I would instantly quit his service. I asserted my innocence with much gravity, protesting I was extremely sorry for his misfortune; so that on further reflection, the good-natured man imputed the whole to mere accident, and expressed his thankfulness at escaping with no greater injury.

About this period I met with one James Smith, a Dutchman, whose disposition, I perceived, was analogous to my own. As kindred souls naturally agree, we became intimately associated. I took some pains to cultivate an acquaintance with this convenient blade, and to acquire his confidence; in both of which I succeeded to my wishes. At length we entered into partnership, and agreed to stick close by each other, for the present; but, being both in want of the means of support, we were compelled to have recurrence to furtive pursuits, my usual resort on pressing occasions. Hens, turkeys, sheep and the like, became the victims of our rapacious industry, and supplied our wretched larder with just sufficient to enable us to continue the unlawful pursuit. Farmers had to regret the loss of their fleecy tribes, and wives of the poultry, which were immolated daily on the altars of our hungry deities. But the solicitude of the sufferers was unavailing, for Smith and I concealed our plunder so artificially, as to baffle all attempts at detection, though we had frequent visits from such as suspected us to be the demons, who had thus *spirited* away their substance.

My partner and I not having accumulated property by such spoliations, but in lieu thereof becoming destitute of apparel and other conveniences, we saw the necessity of striking some more important blow than any we had hitherto attempted. And the way to affect this readily presented; for Smith was familiar with a man belonging to the *Newfields* (in Newmarket) who had hinted that a certain store, the property of Smith Gilman and Levi Chapman, might be opened without difficulty. Moreover (Smith my informant) was well assured, that the same man would lend some assistance, though he bore at the time, the character of a gentleman. In expectation of this, we set out for the Newfields, and repaired to the house of Smith's friend and confident. We communicated the secret of our embassy and requested his advice. The project we found was far from displeasing our entertainer, for with much volubility, he went on to digest the proper mode of procedure, advising us to enter the store through a particular casement, which he represented as slightly fastened. We followed punctually his prescriptions, and our efforts were crowned with brilliant success; we forced a passage through the window, as directed, and took out of the store, clothes to the value of about one hundred dollars, two guineas in money, sundry pieces of silver, with a large quantity of other articles.

The goods we carried directly to the gentleman's house, and presented him with a pail of sugar, several rolls of ribband, and a piece of gauze, as a recompense for his trouble, then took our leave. As we intended to steer southwestwardly with the booty, we took, under cover of darkness, the highway leading through Stratham. I was mounted on a horse I had picked up a day or two before, but Smith being destitute of such conveniency, we contrived to supply the defect, by stealing a horse from one Barker, as we passed through the town last mentioned. Being now whole footed, we pushed on, full tilt, till we gained Haverhill ferry. It was about dawn of day, when we arrived at this place; so that, nobody being stirring, we took a boat, and crossed over without observation; and then drove on, with our half-famished steeds, to Pepperell, in Massachusetts; ourselves and horses, by the time we had recovered this station, being sufficiently fatigued with a forced march of forty-five miles.

Here we made a final halt for the day, and exposed our goods to sale, the same afternoon. On the edge of the evening, Gilman and Chapman entered Pepperell in pursuit of the thieves, and, if possible, to recover their property. Their coming was so abrupt that they surprised us effectually, before we had opportunity to secrete the goods, or make the smallest arrangement for a personal escape. Thus were we suddenly arrested, and taken into custody; when to our no small surprise, we found that the man who had contrived so conveniently, the method of breaking the store, and who had received also his quota of the stolen commodities, had turned informant against us, and had revealed the probable route we had taken. Deceitful and treacherous as this person proved, I am unwilling to reveal his name to the public, especially as he has since removed to a distance from Newmarket, and now supports the character of a better man.

The next day Smith and I were conveyed back as far as Exeter. He was shut up in the common prison; but my doom was close confinement in the dungeon.

As they expected that I should try hard to give them the slip, every precaution was taken for its prevention. My feet were shackled together with a large iron bolt, of two feet in length, which, at either end, was fastened with rivets to the irons surrounding my ankles; a strong chain, of two feet only, proceeded from the bolt to the floor, and was there secured with a huge iron staple. These iron appendages kept my feet at just such a distance asunder, and rendered my stepping one foot before the other upon the floor, altogether impossible. It was with extreme difficulty I could reach the place of office, or stretch my limbs on a miserable couch of straw. In such deplorable condition I continued, ninety days and nights, or rather one continued night of so long duration.

The dampness of the dungeon, the offensive effluvia of the prison vault, my want of necessary food and clothing, and the troublesome vermin, which are generally the undisturbed inhabitants of a jail, altogether, so much dispirited and afflicted me, that I could obtain none, or very little rest, night or day. The consequence was that my health visibly declined, and my strength daily decayed. At length, after a lapse of ninety tedious days, which seemed an entire age, the superior court sat at Exeter, and I, with my accomplice, Smith, were brought fourth for trial. The proof of the felony being full against us, we were adjudged *guilty*. Our sentence was to receive thirty-five lashes on the naked back, of which twenty were assigned to my peculiar share. The whole were to be inflicted on the Monday then next ensuing; receiving which, we were to be imprisoned thirty-one days longer, and to pay, moreover, a certain sum in damages with costs; but in default of payment to be sold to make good the same.

After hearing sentence, Smith was recommitted to the common prison, but I was immured in the dungeon and loaded with chains as before. On the Monday succeeding we were carried out to receive the destined punishment. The stripes were laid on by one of the prisoners of the yard, Jacob Hardy; who, thinking to gratify the spectators, labored hard in fulfilling his odd vocation, administering the strange medicine, with so lavish a hand, that one had been led to imagine he intended this potion should be our last. But had he known the minds of the people, he would have abated (I presume) somewhat of his exertions; for being afterwards blamed by several of the bystanders for exceeding the bounds of his duty, and his conscience (I suppose) smiting him severely, for punishing so greedily two of his unfortunate fellow prisoners, and that without offense received at their hands, he offered to treat us with a dollar's worth of punch; and doubtless would have done us that favor, had he not been discouraged by the keeper of the prison.

In a few days my friends supplied me with instruments, by which, with much toil, I drilled a hole through the wall, sufficiently capacious when stripped to the skin for my corporal exit. The process of cutting I had concealed so effectually, by filling up the cavities with bread, whenever I ceased to work, that none mistrusted my undertaking; and before the thirty-one days were fully elapsed, I was prepared to evacuate that most odious of tenements, the jail at Exeter. During all this while, no chapman (I intend no pun) appeared for the purchase of either Smith or me, though exposed to sale every day. But being thus ready to leave my detested abode, I determined to improve the first convenient season for that purpose. This occurred the ensuing evening. Yet, previous to departure, I had a fancy for a small matter of merriment with my fellow prisoner, Smith, who was in the cell overhead.

With a view to this, I acquainted him with my intention of quitting the premises that very night. He was importunate to learn by what means. I replied, "By the help of the devil, who is now at my beck and call, whenever I need his assistance." Smith had heard it reported that I was a wizard, and, being always the dupe of his own credulity, had now the simplicity to credit my ridiculous tale. Anxious of deliverance from his tedious confinement, he begged me to extricate him in a similar way. "Yes," said I, "provided you will follow, with exactitude, my directions." He assented: so waiting till I presumed the people of the house were sound asleep, I called again to Smith, in a low key, and told him it was time to be doing, and that the first thing necessary was to strip off all our clothes, turn them inside out, and fling them out at the window. This injunction Smith executed with alertness, and so did I (bating the inversion of apparel) from more substantial motives. Being both stripped to the buff, I told him I should break bulk first, ten minutes after which he might follow, by repeating the following distich, to wit:

> Come in old man, with that black ram,
> And carry me out, as fast as you can.

After giving my fellow sufferer this lesson, I crept out at the partition fracture, and flipping on my clothes, stepped into the yard just under Smith's window, who was listening at the grates, with no small solicitude, to learn the issue of my experiment. I informed him of my success, bade him repeat his creed as instructed, which would certainly procure his enlargement also. He promised a punctilious performance, while I, without more colloquy, gathered up Smith's apparel, which I expected in all likelihood to need, and with it, sped away precipitately, leaving the poor wight to mumble over his ceremony at leisure.

The science of deception, as my readers must suppose, had been ever my favorite study, and, among other acquirements, I had learned to disguise a horse so artificially, by various methods, most frequently by the help of different paints, that the owner, to have known his property again, must have had uncommon sagacity. A trick of this kind I put in practice on the present occasion; for happening to meet, one evening, with a valuable horse belonging to one Johnson, I did not lose the propitious moment, but seized the prize, and rode him to a secluded place, where I so altered him, by painting his face white, spotting his feet and legs, and clipping his mane and tail, that he had altogether another appearance.

The next day I was overtaken on the road by Johnson himself, who, on missing the horse, had set out in quest of him and the thieves. He surveyed the nag repeatedly, but never recognized his property. We traveled in company several miles, and then parted without his entertaining the smallest suspicion of the deceit. The horse I kept but a day or two longer, for not daring to appear with him at Lee, I sold him for the money, and with it repaired thither.

Having passed through Number four [now Charlestown, N. H.], I wheeled to the right about; came, in a short time to Nottingham, and soon arrived at Hampton-Falls. Here I wheedled away a large dog, and sold him near Newbury, for ten shillings; but had crossed the Ferry, scarce twenty minutes, when the dog returned to me by swimming. I ventured into a house in Newburyport, and sold him a second time for six shillings, good money; then taking the road to Bradford, I went on about two miles, when my faithful dog again overtook me. At Bradford I parted with him a third and last time, for about one dollar more; so that, on the whole, my trusty dog turned to a pretty good account. I halted at Bradford just long enough to replenish with food, when my journey was renewed with increased ardor, adopting a sort of disguise, and altering my name, frequently, with a view to baffle pursuit.

About this period was completed a collection of necessaries, that had cost me no small time and trouble in preparing. It consisted of a number of augers, with a compass and other saws of various descriptions, calculated to facilitate the breaking through strongholds; to which were added a variety of false and spring keys, so constructed, as to open almost any sort of lock. Those instruments I deposited in several places, in order to have them in readiness upon special occasions. My inducements in providing this resource, resulted not only from past experience of their utility; but from the probability, that yet existed, of my needing such implements in future; unless eventually I should cultivate some emendation of morals, and forsake the illicit game of thieving, of which, at present, I did not see the most remote prospect. I imagine my keys must have been viewed, as a curiosity, by such as were unused to the sight of such rarities; the construction of them, however, is so simple, as to easily be imitated or made by any smith of common ingenuity; and when judiciously fashioned, are of such extensive application, that one key will fit a great variety of locks. I am positive, that, with this assortment of keys, I could have opened, without violence, almost any lock I ever saw; this I am assured by experience, which is indeed the touchstone of truth.

While noticing these particulars, I would observe likewise, that I now kept on hand, or in suitable places of deposit, a variety of paints of different colors; by means of which, I could so alter the looks of any horse, that the owner must be puzzled to know him again while the disguise lasted, which was usually a week or more, unless the paint were sooner displaced by hard riding or rainy weather.

I also kept on hand, several setts of cork shoes, covered with sole leather; these I used frequently, to fasten round my horses feet, to prevent the sound of his footsteps being heard; I have often surprised people, for favorite purposes, by this contrivance.

I also furnished myself with vitriol, aqua fortis, and other corrosive ingredients, to soften or eat away iron. Those liquids I some-times carried in a phial, tied up in the club of my hair; while the blades of my compass-saws were frequently concealed, between the soles of my shoes. A number of the articles, above enumerated, I confided to the keeping of confidential friends, of whom I had now a connected string, reaching from New York, to the District of Maine; and from thence through Vermont to Canada line.

One day, we went to a pasture, three miles distant, for the purpose of docking a number of Steers; having made the purposed amputa-tion, and feeling fatigued with the exercise, we called into a house, hard by, to rest ourselves. Here taking in hand, one of the tails, I transformed it so as to resemble an elegant false tail; then in fash-ion. On our way homeward we called into one Hilton's, who was absent; but to his son, a young man, who was at home, I proffered the false tail, for about a dollar. Want of money was his only ob-jection to the purchase; I therefore offered to take corn, which, in-deed, was at that time a scarce article. Accordingly the young fel-low coveting the curiosity, measured me up a bushel and a half of this staff of life, which, throwing upon Doe's horse, and resigning the dear-bought bubble, I scoured off with all imaginable industry.

◇◇◇◇◇◇◇◇◇◇◇◇◇◇◇

[Stephen Burroughs, Hanover, N. H.]

We arrived at Boston about 11 o'clock; stopped and dined at the sign of the Lamb. I found many of my former acquaintances now shunned me, as though I carried some pestilential disorder about me. One in a particular manner, who was a classmate of mine in Dartmouth college, coming in sight of the sleigh, in which the pris-oners were conveyed, and discerning me in the sleigh, stopped short; ran into a shop contiguous and viewed me through the window with great attention.

After dinner, we were taken to the commissary's store, who pro-vided for the Castle, and all the prisoners, excepting myself, re-ceived their clothes, which consisted of a parti-colored suit; I was entirely willing to be excused from receiving this bounty from the state.

After the clothing had been delivered, we were taken to Long Wharf, put on board a small sailboat, and left the mainland for the island, on which the Castle stood. As we put off from the wharf, the people standing on this, and the neighboring wharves, gave three cheers, declarative of their satisfaction in our leaving them for a state of confinement. We returned three cheers immediately after; endeavoring to retort their insult, by letting them understand that we were also glad to leave them, even for a state of confinement.

We soon arrived on the island, were conveyed into the Castle, our irons taken off, and we left to view the situation in which we were confined.

The island is situated three miles below the town of Boston, its figure being nearly circular, containing eighteen or twenty acres of land. The main channel of the river runs on the east side of this island, very near the shore, and not wider than would be sufficient for two vessels to sail up a-breast; of course, the east side of the island is much the stronger fortified. A platform extends the greater part of the east side, on which are mounted cannon, twenty-four and thirty-two pounders. This platform is nearly the height of the island. Nearly on a level with the water, at full tide, is a place where another tier of cannon were placed, during the time in which the British had possession of it; but destroyed by them and never since rebuilt. The remaining part of the island is but very indifferently guarded by fortifications.

The buildings, when I came to this island, were the governor's house, standing upon the most elevated spot on the island, under which was what was called the bombproof, in which we were confined; a stone magazine, barracks for the officers and soldiers, and a blacksmith's shop.

On this island I found a company of fifty soldiers, commanded immediately by three officers, viz. In the first place, Lieutenant Perkins, formerly holding the title of Major in the continental army. Secondly, Lieut. Treat; and thirdly, Burbeck, holding an Ensign's commission, if I mistake not, and doing the duty of gunner. The lieutenant-governor of the state was Captain of the company.

When I first came on to this island, there were in all only sixteen prisoners. The principal part of them were kept at work in the blacksmith's shop. The remainder did little or nothing. Our provision was one pound of bread and three-fourths of a pound of meat per day.

Immediately after my confinement on this island, I began to look about, to see whether a possibility for escaping remained. I viewed the building in which I was confined. It was made of brick, the walls of which were five feet thick, laid in cement, which was much harder than the brick themselves. I searched every corner for a spot upon which I could work without detection, our room being searched every day, to see whether the prisoners had made any attempt to break away. I at length hit upon a place. There was a chimney at one end of the room, grated in a very strong manner, about twelve feet above its funnel, which was sufficiently large for a man to go up. About three feet above the mantlepiece of this fire-place, I concluded to begin my operation. Here I could work, and not have my labors discovered, unless very critical search was made up the chimney. I had not been at work long before I had made a beginning of a hole sufficiently large to crawl through; I then took a board, and blacking it like the chimney-back made it of the proper size, and put it into the hole, so that the strictest search could produce no discovery. The prisoners in the room with me were seven in number. These prisoners were all turned out to work about sunrise, when the doors of the prison were again shut, and not opened until 12 o'clock, when the prisoners came from work, and continued half an hour; they were then taken back again to work, and there remained until sunset. Therefore, I had as much as sixteen hours in the twenty-four in which I could work upon the brick wall, which work I continued with the most unremitting attention.

The labor was incredible ! I could, in the first place, work only with a large nail, rubbing away the brick gradually, not daring to make the least noise, lest the sentries, who stood round the prison, should overhear me at work, and thereby become discovered. One night I rubbed the bricks so hard, as to be overheard by the sentry, standing on the other side of the wall. The alarm was immediately given, and the guard and officers rushed into the room to detect us in our operations. Fortunately, I overheard the sentry tell the ser-geant of the guards, that Burroughs was playing the devil in the jail. The sergeant ran to inform the officers, and I had but just time to put my board in its place, and set down to greasing my shoes, when the officers entered, and with a great degree of sternness, inquired where I had been at work ? I told them that I had been rubbing some hard soot off the chimney and grinding it fine to mix with the grease, and put on to my shoes. They laughed at my nicety about my shoes, that I should wish for sleek shining shoes in this situa-tion. Major Perkins knowing my inattentiveness to dress, could not so readily believe that blacking my shoes was the only object in view; he therefore made a very strict search for some other matter, which should account for the noise the sentry had heard: but after a fruitless pursuit, they gave over their search, concluding that one among the thousand strange whims which marked my character, had prompted me to set about blacking my shoes, at that time.

After they were gone, I felt as strong a disposition to laugh at them for the deception under which they were laboring, as they did whilst present to laugh at me, for the whim of greasing and black-ing my shoes. This temporary check was of the utmost importance in my further prosecution of this business. It made me more care-ful for the future, not to pursue my labors with too much impatient impetuosity, a failing I ever was subject to.

The prisoners in the room were merry on the occasion of my turning the suspicion of the officers so entirely from the real object to another very foreign from it. They thought it a manifestation of ability. In fine, I had gained such an ascendency over the prisoners, that they implicitly gave up to my opinion in all but little matters: and more particularly, when any contention arose among them, I generally succeeded in amicably terminating the difficulty without their proceeding to blows.

I determined to be more careful in prosecuting my labor on the wall for the future, and check that impatience which often hurried me on beyond the dictates of prudence. I now wrought with the greatest caution, and made slow but sure advances. After I had been employed in this business about a week, I found I could work to greater advantage if I had a small iron crow; therefore, I ordered one of the prisoners, who wrought in the shop, to make me one about a foot long, and sharp at one end. This he found an oppor-tunity to do, undiscovered by the overseer, and brought it to me. I found that with this crow I could pry off half a brick at a time without the least noise, after I had worn a hole with my nail, suffi-ciently large to thrust in my crow. The rubbish which I took out of the wall I put every night into a tub, standing in our room for necessary occasions, and this was emptied by one of the prisoners every morning into the water.

After I had labored with unceasing assiduity for two months, I found one night, after I had pried away a brick, that I could run my arm out of the prison into the open air. This circumstance made my heart leap with joy. After such a length of labor, to find my toils crowned with apparent success, gave me a tone of pleasure of which you can have no idea.

Upon examination, I found the breach through the wall was just below a covered way, so that it would remain unseen in the day-time, unless discovered by some accident. I had measured the height of the covered way by a geometrical operation, not being permitted to come near it: and this was done with an instrument made by my penknife; that penknife which had done me such excellent service in Northampton jail.

When the prisoners saw my measurement was exact, their idea of my profound knowledge was greatly raised; and they appeared to

[298]

entertain the most sanguine assurance, that their liberty was certain when their operations were directed under my auspices.

After I had found the hole through the wall was entirely secreted by the covered way, I proceeded to make it sufficiently large to pass through.

After all this was accomplished, one difficulty still remained. The sentry standing on the covered way would undoubtedly hear us in going out at this hole; and moreover, if we should be so fortunate as to get, unheard, into the covered way, yet we must come out of that within five feet of the place where he stood, and therefore could not prevent a discovery.

Under these circumstances, we found it necessary to lie quiet until some rainy night should remove the sentry from his stand on the covered way, to some place of shelter. This was generally the case when the weather was foul or uncomfortable, unless some special cause should detain him to this particular spot. I recollect, that soon after the officers had found me blackening my shoes with soot, the sentinels kept their post, invariably, on the covered way, in every kind of weather; but they had, by this time, become more at ease in their feelings, and consequently would, at such time, retire into an alley leading through the bombproof.

We did not wait many days for the happy moment, before we heard the sentry leave his station on the covered way, and enter the alley, for shelter from the rain.

About 11 o'clock at night, I made the necessary arrangements for the expedition. The island being in a circular form, I ordered seven men to go round it to the south, whilst I went around to the north. The reason why I did this was of the following nature, viz. There was a wharf on the western shore of this island, where the boats were kept, and a sentry placed over them. It was necessary, after we had escaped out of the bombproof, to procure a boat, in order to transport ourselves off the island; and as there were none, except what were immediately under the eye of the sentry, the only alternative which remained, was to make the sentry a prisoner, and carry him off with us. As this was a business in which some nicety of conduct was necessary, I chose to trust no one to execute it but myself; and therefore, ordered the seven prisoners round the island, a different way from what I went myself, and directed them to advance to within fifteen rods of the sentinel, and make a noise sufficient to attract his attention towards them. This would bring the sentry between me and the other seven prisoners; and when he was turned towards them, I should be at his back.

Having made these arrangements, all the prisoners silently

crawled out of the hole, following them myself as soon as I saw they all had passed without any accident. We all met at the spot appointed. I told the men to be cautious, not to be in a hurry; not to be in any perturbation; but to proceed leisurely and considerately to the spot appointed. I told them to be five minutes in getting to the spot. I then left them. I hastened around, and arrived as near to the sentry as I thought prudent, about one minute and a half before I heard the noise from the other men. At the noise, the sentry turned and hailed, "Who comes there?" No answer was made. Immediately on seeing the attention of the sentry turned from me, I arose from my position flat on the ground, and advanced as near as twenty feet, and lay down again. Immediately the noise from the seven men was again renewed; and the sentry's attention was fixed to the object of the noise. He again hailed in a very peremptory manner, cocked his gun, and made ready to fire. By this time I had arisen from the ground, and advanced to within about eight feet of the sentry, when I heard the piece cock, and saw him present it! I immediately darted at him, seized him in an instant, and clapped my hand over his mouth, to prevent him from making a noise, which should alarm the other soldiers on guard. When I first laid hold of him, he started, and attempted to get from me, making a noise through his nose as though very much terrified: crying "eh! eh! eh!" I told him that the least noise from him should produce instant death; that I would rip his guts out the first moment he proved refractory. After I had sufficiently terrified him, I took my hand from his mouth, and told him that no harm should befall him, so long as he behaved in a peaceable manner. I took his gun and cartridge-box from him. The other prisoners now coming up, we all went into the barge, carrying ten oars, and put off.

It was now about half an hour past twelve at night, it being extremely dark and rainy, and nothing to steer by, except mere conjecture. We were ignorant of the time of tide, whether it was ebbing or flowing, and consequently could not tell which way we drifted: however, we determined to row until we came to some land. I set myself in the stern sheets, steering the boat; Richards, the sentry, set in the bottom of the boat, between my legs. The gun with the fixed bayonet lay by me, and the cartridge-box hanging by my side. The other men were at their oars, rowing the boat. We had proceeded about far enough, as we judged, to be in the middle of the channel, between the island and Dorchester, whither we meant to direct our course.

It was now demanded of me, by one of the men who sat forward rowing the boat, what I meant to do with Richards? As I did not know where we should in fact land, I was undetermined in my own mind what I should do with him when I came to land, and gave an answer to that amount. The person asking the question, looking upon his escape as certain, began to put on airs of consequence, and answered me in a sarcastic manner, "Well, Captain Burroughs, as you have had the command until you do not know what to do, it is best for some other person to take it, who does know what to do;" and then turning himself to Richards, continued his discourse, "and as for you, Mr. Richards, you'll please to walk overboard, that we may not, after this, hear any of your tales told to your brother swads. If you walk over without fuss, it is well, if not, you shall be thrown over, tied neck and heels."

When I heard this insolent treatment and dastardly language, I could hardly conceive what it meant. Unprovokedly to throw Richards into the water, was a manifestation of a language of the heart, which appeared to me so unnatural, that I could not believe the person using it, to be serious. Yet I could not conceive any propriety in using it in any other light. Richards himself was terrified. He began to supplicate me in the most moving terms, to save him from the destruction which was ready to fall upon him. His entreaties made such an impression upon my mind, that I should have given him my assistance, if I had been opposed by every man in the boat; however I did not yet believe he was in that degree of danger which he appeared to apprehend; but was soon undeceived by the three forward hands shipping their oars and coming aft.

I endeavored to expostulate, but to no effect. I saw they were resolutely bent on their diabolical purpose! I saw the disposition of the infernals pictured in their operations. I let go the helm, started up, and swore by the Almighty, that I'd send the first to hell who dared lay a hand on Richards. The poor fellow, at this time, lay in the bottom of the boat trembling with agony, and crying in the most piteous manner. The blood flew quick through my veins. The plaintive cries of Richards vibrated upon my heart, and braced every nerve. At this moment the first villain who had proposed this infernal plan, laid hold of me by the shoulder to prevent my interposing between Richards and the others, who were about throwing him overboard.

When I found his hand gripping my shoulder, I immediately reached my arm over his back, caught him by the waistband of his breeches and dashed him to the bottom of the boat. The moment of my laying hold of him, I determined to throw him into the sea, and why I did not, I have never since been able to tell. After I had thrown him into the bottom of the boat, I caught the gun on which was a bayonet fixed; this I brought to a charge and made a push at the man nearest me, who drew back, took his seat at the oar, when all again was quiet.

We continued rowing until we struck fast on the ground, but could see no land. We left the boat and waded about until we discovered the shore. When we came to land, we could not determine on what place we had fallen. We were soon satisfied, however, by the drum on the Castle beating the long-roll, and immediately after, beating to arms. We heard the alarm in that direction which plainly pointed out, that we were somewhere near Dorchester Point. We saw the Castle in an uproar, and all the signals of alarm which are usually made on such occasions.

After we had found where we were, the three men who engaged in throwing Richards overboard, left us, and went away together. I then told Richards that he might go where he pleased; that he must be sensible I had saved his life, even at the risk of my own; therefore, the dictates of gratitude would teach him a line of conduct which would not militate against my escape. This he promised in the most solemn manner. He was warm in his expressions of gratitude towards me. I believed him sincere. He departed.

We travelled on with rapidity about one mile further, and then came into a little thicket of houses, and a barn standing immediately on the road among them; this barn we all entered and found two mows of hay. I ascended one mow, and having taken up the hay by flakes, near the side of the barn, to the depth of six feet, three of us went down, and the hay fell back into its former situation, covering us entirely over at the same time. I had ordered the other two to go on to the other mow, and do as they had seen me. They accordingly went, and I supposed all secure.

Not long after this, there came a number of women into the barn to milk the cows. Soon after, I heard children round the barn, as though they were in pursuit of something with a dog. I soon found that a skunk was their object under the barn. However, when the women had finished milking their cows, the children were all ordered into the house, this day being Sunday.

To my astonishment and surprise, the two men who had gone to the other mow, now came over where I was, and told me, they could not find a place to hide; "and indeed," said they, " we do not like to be so far off, for it appears to us, that we shall be taken if we are !" How I felt under the situation you will readily conceive, by supposing yourself in my place, and people expected into the barn every minute to fodder their cattle ! I jumped out of my place, told them to lie down in a moment, covered them over with hay, and returned into my place, just as the young men came into the barn to take care of their cattle. They came on to the mow where we were lying, and took the hay from it for their cows; but made no discovery: and yet, notwithstanding all this, one of our men, by the name of Burrel, whom I had covered over with hay, was asleep before the young men went out of the barn, and snored so loud, as to be heard; but the men did not know what noise it was, nor where it came from.

We heard the various bells ringing at Dorchester meetinghouses for the exercises of the day. The forenoon meeting was finished, and the first bell for the exercises of the afternoon was ringing, when a number of men came into the barn to put a horse into the chaise, standing on the barn-floor. The streets were full of people going to the meetinghouse. A number of children came likewise into the barn with the men, and climbed on to the mow where we lay secreted, looking for hens' nests. At this moment Burrel began to snore, which brought the children immediately to the spot where he lay, and his head being uncovered, they saw it, and cried out, "Daddy, daddy, here's the skunk ! here's the skunk !" It hardly appeared credible to the old gentleman that a skunk should be on the haymow; he therefore manifested some doubt as to his children's report, but they were determined he should believe them, and affirmed it again with warmth, "it certainly is a skunk, daddy, for it has got ears."

The peculiar manner in which this was uttered, made the people, on the barn-floor, think something uncommon was there. They accordingly ascended the mow to the number of eight or nine, in order to satisfy themselves concerning this matter. By this time Burrel awakening, saw he was discovered, and began to pull the hay over his head. Those who were on the mow saw it, and were now convinced, that the children in fact had seen something that had ears. They took the pitchfork and moved the hay, which lay over these two men, and immediately saw that they were convicts, escaped the preceding night from the Castle.

About this time the shops were fitted up sufficient to receive all the prisoners, with conveniences for making nails. Therefore, I was put to work in the shops, and taught to manufacture nails; but the lessons which I received here had but little effect upon my progress in acquiring this noble art. That unaccountable stupidity which I ever possessed, had an unusual influence upon me at this time. It is true, I could make a nail equal to anything you ever saw, of the kind, in beauty and elegance; but the slowness with which I executed this, was a circumstance of great complaint by the overseer, not being able to finish more than five in a day; which cost more than ten times the value of the nails in coal and iron; therefore, it was determined, that I should be more expeditious in my work. I obeyed the commands of those who were over me. I made the next day five hundred nails; but they had as many heads and horns as the beast we read of in scripture. This did not answer the purpose intended. I was reprimanded in severe terms, but all did not signify. When I made good nails, I could not overgo five in a day, and when I made more, they were as varied, in form and magnitude, as the ragged rocks upon the mountains.

The plain truth of the business was here: I viewed the transactions of the government towards me, to be inimical and cruel. I felt none of that confidence in her treatment which a child ought to feel towards the government of a kind parent. I considered that she had declared open war against me; and would take every opportunity to oppress me. Under this view of matters, I meant to make those arrangements in my conduct, which we see one nation making in their conduct towards another, with whom they are at open war.

I was determined to defeat the business of making nails entirely; and accordingly entered into a plan for that purpose.

There was a large well about six rods from the shop, to which we used to repair for water. The well was 20 feet deep, and the water generally near the top. We took our nail-rods, broke them in pieces, put them into the water pail, carried them to the well, and flung them into the water. This we continued for the space of three weeks, until the well was nearly filled with iron. The return of nails did not half pay for the first cost of the rods, so that the commissary was determined to send no more rods to the island, supposing it a waste of the public property. However, the overseer urged another trial, and the commissary with reluctance, consented to send down a small quantity of nail-rods for the last trial. This circumstance I was informed of, by the boat-men, who went after the rods. I therefore exhorted the prisoners to stand this last trial with courage and perseverance. They universally promised to remain inviolate to their trust, and I pleased myself with the speedy accomplishment of my plan.

The universal excuse of the prisoners, for not returning more nails for the iron which they had received, was their inability. They constantly insisted upon it, that they could not make more nails out of the iron; all agreeing in one excuse, and all returning much the same quantity of nails, in proportion to the iron they received; it was thought that the business would not answer its design; and therefore was about being dropped. Yet the overseer was minded to try one more experiment, to see whether the business would bare a profit, or whether it would not. The law, regulating the treatment towards convicts on the Castle, had strictly prohibited the allowance of spirituous liquors, under any consideration; therefore, many, who had been formerly great drunkards, were now wholly debarred their favorite enjoyment; and moreover, being so long habituated to immoderate drinking, and being now wholly deprived of the use of it, they had experienced in reality, great temporary inconveniences, with regard to their health, as well as to the cravings of appetite unsatisfied. Hence, the prospect of spirituous liquor to these, would have a very powerful effect. This the overseer was sensible of; accordingly, offered a gill of rum to every one who should return so many nails, out of such a weight of iron.

This bait I saw. I expostulated with the men to beware of the treachery. I used every argument in my power to convince them of the necessity of this self-denial. I endeavored to show them, that far from kindness, this rum was offered them as the most fatal poison they could drink. They were all convinced, and all seemed resolute to put in practice my advice. But when the rum was brought into the shop, and they saw the precious morsel before them, they fainted under the trial! They could not resist the temptation! They weighed the iron, and returned the full tale of nails; they drank the delicious liquid. They returned into the prison with exultation; they were rich; they felt far exalted above my situation; being able to gain a gill of rum a day; whereas, I was unable to perform one tenth part of the task required.

"Now," said they, "we shall be able to earn a gill of rum every day !" This appeared so great a state of happiness, when compared with what their case had been, that they were almost contented with their situation. They began to despise my wisdom; to think that my head did not contain so much as they were before inclined to believe it did. They exultingly said, "This never would have been the case, if we had followed your advice. We must have a little sense now and then, as well as you all the time." I had no disposition to contradict these haughty Patricians. "Perhaps," said I, "before tomorrow morning you may find yourselves sunken to your former Plebeian state of servile misery." I had rather see the operation of such profound penetration, than undertake to contradict one of these Knights of the Pot, with all his greatness, armed capapee.

After the prisoners had performed their task the next day, and returned their nails in full tale, to their astonishment and sore mortification, they found no rum was to be dealt out to them. They made application for it, but received in return the bitterest reproaches and heavy curses. They were given to understand that they should now do their tasks, and that too without a reward. I found, when they were shut into the prison at night, that they had fallen greatly from their state of exaltation, which they felt the night preceding. They were now not so rich, so great, nor so wise. They could now see the propriety of my expostulations: but alas! they saw it too late.

Seeing the success of this experiment had such a salutary effect in discovering the real cause why the prisoners had not been more profitable in their labors, the overseer thought to make me change my plan of conduct as much as the others had changed theirs: but in this attempt, he found me possessing what the West India Planter would call sullenness, or incorrigible obstinacy, in one of his slaves. Those who felt friendly towards me would call it manly resolution; others, who were inimical, would call it deviltry, wickedness, etc., so that it would have as many names as there are different feelings towards one in those who relate it. You, sir, may call it by what name you find propriety will dictate. The fact was, that by length of time, I did not become any more profitable in my employment.

◇◇◇◇◇◇◇◇◇◇◇◇◇

[*William Stuart, Bridgeport, Conn.*]

Time passed until I was seventeen years of age (1805).

During these four years I employed my leisure hours hammering sixpences into shillings, and twelve and half cent pieces into quarters of dollars.

I was a high boy, rude, bold, fearless, reckless, but shrewd, cunning, artful, and full of mischief. I was ever getting the boys into trouble, and if a girl played me a trick, it was not forgotten until full payment was given. I was a great rambler, engaged in every frolic and in every row.

But I had property now, my father having recently died, leaving me three thousand dollars. I had the frolic, and felt satisfied. I kept hammering out the silver pieces. There is some skill in it. I took two pieces of sole leather and enclosed the silver between them, and with a shoe hammer upon a lap stone, beat over the centre of the coin, and in three minutes, sixpences became shillings, and shillings became quarters. But this sort was not enough. I melted pewter, and run it in moulds, and thus I could coin one hundred quarters in an evening.

There was a man in the neighborhood by the name of Michael Abbot, who kept a grog shop. He reduced his liquors largely, and sold them as genuine. We found out the secret how the old man served his Rum, and as every one then drank Rum, I treated all the boys and girls, and paid him in pewter coin until he got (with some good money,) two quarts of it. He then went to Norwalk village to pay the wholesale dealer and he found out the trick, and then abandoned the business. But my pay was as genuine as his miserable Rum. I was always glad of it.

My intercourse with the young men of our vicinity was of the most perfect frankness. One afternoon Joseph Mills and myself went down to the village to see what "we could scare up" in that quarter. After inquiring for the news, the gossip of the neighborhood, the stories afloat about things in general, and chattering with the inmates of the tavern, we repaired to the bar and took brandy. Soon after, as old acquaintance gathered in, we turned a cent to see who should treat the company. The stake fell upon one of us, and we drank another glass. Conversation now became general, of fast horses, of scrapes, of balls, and of carousals. We became loud and noisy, yet good natured and full of fun.

During this time, a gentleman came in and took his seat. There seemed to be a defect in one of his eyes, for he wore a green shade lying close over one eye ball. After some of our company passed out, this man went to the door and beckoned to me. He probably had heard something fall from my lips which led him to think I was a good deal of a boy. I passed out upon the piazza with him, and in a whisper he asked me, "Can you keep a secret?" I replied, I can if I say I will.

We went out in the rear of a building on a little knoll, where now stands the barn of Stevens' Hotel. The stranger again enquired of me, "Who is that man with you?" I said, Jo. Mills. "Can he keep a secret?" I said yes; and he directed me to call him. I did so. He then asked, "Is there a private place near here, where we can talk over a secret, for I have something to tell you?"

We crossed the Bridge together, and turned into an open piece of woods, out of sight of any of the people, and sat down upon the grass and herbage. I now saw that the patch of silk over his eye was used to blind others — not himself. He appealed to our honor again to keep our transactions hidden from the view of the people, and swore to keep his revelations secret.

[307]

He now took from his person a roll of Bank Bills; told us they were counterfeit, and offered to sell us some of them. Neither of us understood what counterfeit bank money was. He explained it to our satisfaction, and we now saw how suddenly we could become rich — have our pockets lined with gold, and live in affluence and ease.

It was [Stephen] Burroughs' money, and to our eyes at least, as good as genuine. A great fact astounded us both. He engaged to furnish us for ten dollars a hundred, any quantity that we wished; but he said, "Keep the matter dark; say nothing; be prudent and cautious, and in six months you will each be worth $50,000." Was not here a golden bait? What greater inducements could be laid before the senses of an ambitious and unscrupulous youth?

I always had a love of money, intense and ardent, even though I frequently spent it prodigally. I valued it while it was in my possession, and as soon as it was gone I cast about to see what means would avail me to get more. Here I found out the secret, fitted perfectly to this passion of mine. He offered me 300 dollars for my horse, saddle and bridle, and I accepted the offer.

We went back to the tavern and took another drink; then he mounted the horse I sold him and left us. This horse and saddle was worth 35 dollars, good money.

AND NOW, FELLOW CITIZENS

◇◇◇◇◇◇◇◇◇◇◇◇◇

[Timothy Dwight]

Fʀᴏᴍ half to two thirds of the inhabitants sleep round the year without bolting, or locking their doors. This, you will observe, is not done by the tenants of cottages merely; for of these we have very few; but much more numerously by the owners of good houses, well stored with the property which naturally invites plunderers.

I have lived in New-Haven during the last sixteen years. [1795–1811]

This town contains 750 houses, and about 6,000 people. It employs, also, a trading capital, amounting to $2,500,000. No house, within my knowledge, has been broken open here, during this period.

New-Haven is the shire town of the County of New-Haven, in a State distinguished for the rigid execution of its laws. Of course all the capital punishments in the County have been inflicted here. The whole number of these in one hundred and seventy-five years, has been thirteen. Of these, five were whites; five were Indians; and three were blacks. Of the whites, one was a stranger taken up as a spy, as he was passing through this town, and executed, pursuant to a sentence of a court martial. Three of the remaining four were natives of England. It does not appear, that any inhabitant of this town, or County, ever suffered death by the hand of law. There is no reason to conclude, that the people of this County are more distinguished for their morals than most of the other settlements, which have been established for any length of time.

The people of New-England have always had, and have by the law always been required to have, arms in their hands. Every man is, or ought to be, in the possession of a musket. The great body of our citizens, also, are trained with a good degree of skill, and success, to military discipline. Yet I know not a single instance, in which arms have been the instruments of carrying on a private quarrel. Nor do I believe, that such a subject is even thought of by one person in fifty thousand, so often as once in twelve months; I believe I might say with truth, so much as once during life. On a country, more peaceful and quiet, it is presumed, the sun never shone. I must, however, acknowledge that there have been, since the settlement of this country, several mobs, and two or three more serious commotions. In Connecticut, the government, whether of the Colony or the State, has never met with a single serious attempt at resistance to the execution of its laws. That of Massachusetts was for some time opposed during the latter part of the Revolutionary War, and the three years which followed the peace. Several mobs assembled at different times, composed of people from various parts of the County of Hampshire. The first of them were employed in resisting the British government; the rest rose in opposition to that of the State. Their last effort [Shays' Rebellion] was in the proper sense an insurrection; and that which immediately preceded it, deserved substantially the same name. In the last, the insurgents, amounting to several hundreds, attempted to take possession of the public arsenal at Springfield; but were dispersed by Gen. Shepard, with the loss of two or three of their number. Some of the ringleaders were afterwards taken, tried, and sentenced to suffer death; but were pardoned. The cause of these disturbances was the hard pressure of poverty, produced by the ruin of the Continental currency, the want of a circulating medium, and a general train of difficulties, following from these, and enhanced by a taxation, severe in the amount, and distressing in the mode. The period was also that, in which the former government was annihilated, and the new one imperfectly established. In all these inroads upon good order, detestable as mobs are, not a person lost his life, except those just mentioned.

◇◇◇◇◇◇◇◇◇◇◇◇◇

[*Joseph Story, Marblehead*]

During my professional studies in Mr. Sewall's office, I was left very much alone, and with no literary associate in my native town. I was driven, therefore, back upon my own resources, and I not unfrequently devoted for months more than fourteen hours a day to study. Mr. Sewall's absence in congress for about half the year was also a serious disadvantage to me, for I had no opportunity to ask for any explanation of difficulties, and no cheering encouragement to light up the dark and intricate paths of the law.

Beginning my studies in this recluse and solitary manner, I confess that I deeply felt the truth of Spelman's remarks, when he was sent to the Inns of Court for a similar purpose, my heart like his sunk within me; and I was tempted several times to give up the science from a firm belief that I could never master it. The case was very different then from what it is now, in respect both to the plan of studies and the facilities to acquire the elements. Then there were few elementary books; now the profession is inundated with them. Then the student, after reading the most elegant of all commentaries, Mr. Justice Blackstone's work, was hurried at once into the intricate, crabbed, and obsolete learning of Coke on Littleton. Now there are many elementary works which smooth the path towards the study of this great master of the common law. Then, there were scarcely any American Reports, (for the whole number did not exceed five or six volumes,) to enable the student to apply the learning of the common law to his own country, or to distinguish what was in force here, from what was not. Now, our shelves are crowded with hundreds.

Hitherto my pursuits had been wholly of a literary and classical character. I loved literature, and indulged freely in almost every variety of it to which I had access, from the profound writings of the great historians, metaphysicians, scholars, and divines, down to the lightest fiction, the enticing novel, the still more enticing romance, and the endless pageantries and imaginings of poetry. You may judge, then, how I was surprised and startled on opening

[311]

works, where nothing was presented but dry and technical principles, the dark and mysterious elements of the feudal system, the
subtle refinements and intricacies of the middle ages of the common law, and the repulsive and almost unintelligible forms of
processes and pleadings, for the most part wrapped up in black-
letter, or in dusty folios. To me the task seemed Herculean. I
should have quitted it in despair, if I had known whither to turn
my footsteps, and to earn a support. My father had often told me,
in the sincerity of his affection, that he should leave little property;
that the most I could expect would be my education; and that I
must earn my livelihood by my own labors. I felt the truth of the
admonition; and it was perpetually whispered into my secret soul
whenever I felt the overpowering influence of any discouragement.
My destiny was to earn my bread by the sweat of my brow; and I
must meet it or perish.

I shall never forget the time, when having read through Blackstone's Commentaries, Mr. Sewall, on his departure for Washington, directed me next to read Coke on Littleton, as the appropriate
succeeding study. It was a very large folio, with Hargrave and Butler's notes, which I was required to read also. Soon after his departure, I took it up, and after trying it day after day with very little
success, I sat myself down and wept bitterly. My tears dropped
upon the book, and stained its pages. It was but a momentary ir-
resolution. I went on and on, and began at last to see daylight, ay,
and to feel that I could comprehend and reason upon the text and
the comments. When I had completed the reading of this most
formidable work, I felt that I breathed a purer air, and that I had
acquired a new power. The critical period was passed; I no longer
hesitated. I pressed on to the severe study of special pleading, and
by repeated perusals of Saunders's Reports, acquired such a decided
relish for this branch of my profession, that it became for several
years afterwards my favorite pursuit. Even at this day I look back
upon it with a lingering fondness, although many years have
elapsed since I ceased to give it an exclusive attention. It is in my
judgment the best school for the discipline of an acute and solid
lawyer. While in Mr. Sewall's office, I also read through that deep
and admirable work upon one of the most intricate titles of the law,
Fearne on Contingent Remainders and Executory Devises, and I
made a manuscript abstract of all its principles. I am not quite sure
that it may not yet be found among my manuscripts.

At the time of my admission to the bar, I was the only lawyer
within its pale, who was either openly or secretly a *democrat*. Essex

was at that time almost exclusively federal, and party politics were inexpressibly violent. I felt many discouragements from this source. But after a while my industry and exclusive devotion to my profession (and they were very great) brought me clients, so that, in the course of three or four years, I was in very good business and with an increasing reputation.

To young men with my political opinions the times were very discouraging. My father was a republican, as contra-distinguished from a federalist, and I had naturally imbibed the same opinions. In Massachusetts, at that period [1801], an immense majority of the people were federalists. All the offices, (with scarcely an exception, I believe,) were held by federalists. The governor, the judges, the legislature were ardent in the same cause. It cannot be disguised, too, that a great preponderance of the wealth, the rank, the talent, and the civil and literary character of the state, was in the same scale. Almost all the profession of the law were of the party. I scarcely remember more than four or five lawyers in the whole state, who *dared* avow themselves republicans. The very name was odious, and even more offensive epithets (such as Jacobins) were familiarly applied to them. The great struggle was just over between Mr. Jefferson and Mr. Adams, and the former had been chosen to the Presidency. The contest had been carried on with great heat and bitterness; and the defeated party, strong at home, though not in the nation, was stimulated by resentment, and by the hope of a future triumph. Under such circumstances there was a dreadful spirit of persecution abroad. The intercourse of families was broken up, and the most painful feuds were generated. Salem was a marked battleground for political controversies, and for violent struggles of the parties. The republican party was at first very small there; and its gradual growth and increasing strength so far from mitigating added fuel to the flame.

Such was the state of things at the time when I came to the bar. All the lawyers and all the judges in the county of Essex were federalists, and I was the first who was obtruded upon it as a political heretic. I was not a little discouraged by this circumstance, and contemplated a removal as soon as I could find a better position or prospect elsewhere. For some time I felt the coldness and estrangement resulting from this known diversity of opinion; and taking as I did, a firm and decided part in politics, it was not at all wonderful that I should be left somewhat solitary at the bar. Gradually, however, to my surprise, business flowed in upon me; and as I was most diligent and laborious in the discharge of my professional duties, I began in a year or two to reap the reward of my fidelity to my clients. From that time to the close of my career at the bar, my business was constantly on the increase, and at the time when I left it, my practice was probably as extensive and as lucrative as that of any gentleman in the county. Indeed, I contemplated a removal to Boston, as a wider sphere, in which I might act with more success; and I was encouraged to this by retainers from that city in very important causes.

◇◇◇◇◇◇◇◇◇◇◇◇◇

[Henry Adams]

Down to 1850, and even later, New England society was still directed by the professions. Lawyers, physicians, professors, merchants were classes, and acted not as individuals, but as though they were clergymen and each profession were a church. In politics the system required competent expression; it was the old Ciceronian idea of government by *the best* that produced the long line of New England statesmen. They chose men to represent them because they wanted to be well represented, and they chose the best they had. Thus Boston chose Daniel Webster, and Webster took, not as pay, but as *honorarium*, the cheques raised for him by Peter Harvey from the Appletons, Perkinses, Amorys, Searses, Brookses, Lawrences, and so on, who begged him to represent them. Edward Everett held the rank in regular succession to Webster. Robert C. Winthrop claimed succession to Everett. Charles Sumner aspired to break the succession, but not the system. The Adamses had never been, for any length of time, a part of this State succession; they had preferred the national service, and had won all their distinction outside the State, but they too had required State support and had commonly received it.

◇◇◇◇◇◇◇◇◇◇◇◇◇

[John Neal, Portland, Maine]

I was now beginning to breathe freely once more, and, of course, felt obliged to keep the community astir, lest we should all go to sleep together, settle on our lees, or stagnate in our marriage-beds. The "Yankee" was doing wonders; but wonders did not satisfy me. We wanted a city-government. Our old-fashioned municipal government was frightfully expensive and wasteful, if the time of a laboring population was worth any thing, and withal, exceedingly changeable, inefficient, and uncertain. Two attempts, followed by two wretched failures, had been made; one, I believe, by no less a personage than

Mr. F. O. J. Smith, supported by the whole strength of the democratic party, before the first of his many changes. After weighing the matter well, I undertook it, anew. We had town-meetings called: at one of which, my good uncle, James Neal, denounced me, in conversation, as an aristocrat, and insisted upon it, that I had been too long abroad; while others appeared to think I had not been abroad long enough. Meanwhile, I issued a sort of manifesto, on a single page, headed, substantially, in this way: "Thirty-one unanswerable reasons — *answered.*" This finished the business; for I had answered, fully and completely, every objection that had ever been raised, to my knowledge. This I followed up with a pamphlet of about fifty octavo pages, and tables, petitions, on both sides, and statistics, giving undeniable statistics, where necessary. The result of which was, notwithstanding the bitter and exasperated opposition among our wealthiest property-holders, an immediate and overwhelming triumph. An act of incorporation was had, and our present city government organized without losing a day. What next ? We were without side-walks: our streets were impassable at certain seasons of the year; foot-passengers could not wade through portions of Middle-Street; and if you saw an aged man poking about in the mud, with a cane, you were tempted to ask if anybody was missing. Here, too, common sense and foresight prevailed over long-established prejudices; and we soon had, not only brick side-walks, instead of rotten plank; and mica-slate, or talco-slate crossings, instead of cobble-stones, and bottomless pits. And then, we wanted something more: A Park, if it was to be had, or, at any rate, breathing-places, at both ends of the peninsula, where the population could get a mouthful of fresh air, and look out upon panoramas of unequalled beauty and vastness, with the White Hills on one side, and the broad Atlantic on the other, and such skies — you'll excuse me, I hope — as are to be seen nowhere else upon earth; owing to the distribution and arrangement of sea and river, cove and lakelet; and so, after a brief, but exasperating struggle, we had a five-mile drive with the two beautiful promenades, which render Portland so attractive to strangers, poets, and landscape-painters. And, by the way, this reminds me of asking where on earth a population is to be found, varying from about seven or eight thousand, up to thirty-five thousand, or thereabouts, which have turned out so many poets and landscape-painters ? Compare Portland with Baltimore, Philadelphia, New York, Cincinnati, or Chicago, and then tell me, if you can, why Portland has been so fruitful, and they so barren ? We have Neal — that's myself, in order of time, the first — Grenville Mellen, Frederick Mellen, Longfellow, Willis, Cutter, Florence Percy, so called, though born elsewhere, and

PORTLAND, MAINE

at least a dozen other capital newspaper poets, with Codman, Tilton, Brown, Beckett, Hudson, all distinguished, and some celebrated, both abroad and at home, for landscape, with half a score at present undistinguished, but who threaten to be heard of hereafter; and some, I know, will keep their promise. Here, too, we have had Paul Akers, and his brother Charles, and Simmons, now abroad, for sculptors; all the inevitable growth of our large, wholesome, and beautiful scenery, and well-marked individualities.

◇◇◇◇◇◇◇◇◇◇◇◇◇

[*Charles T. Congdon, New Bedford, Mass.*]

We had but a melancholy evening of it when the news came that General Jackson had been elected to the presidency, and that John Quincy Adams was defeated. My impression is that I cried, having arrived at the mature age of eight years, and understanding such things much better than I have since, or, for that matter, do now. I had a strong belief not only that the republic would go to ruin, but that general ignorance would prevail, that no new books would be printed, that public schools would be abolished, that universal poverty would ensue, and that the whaling business especially would come to an end. Why should I not have been thus melancholy when my elders and betters made perfect hypochondriacs of themselves ? I doubt if any public man was ever more thoroughly hated than General Jackson was then in Massachusetts. We even named a cutaneous complaint contracted in barbers' shops after that much admired and much abused hero. Then there was a particularly disagreeable square-toed boot which we called the Jackson. Mr. Adams paid us a visit not long after, and, being always in search of sights, I went down to the pier to see him land. I thought him fearfully old and shaky, but he lived long enough after for me to write his obituary notice in my own newspaper. I was one of a great tail of boys who followed the good man to his hotel. He had some infirmity of the eyes, and my impression was that he was shedding tears at the enthusiastic character of our attentions. I was introduced to him ten years afterward, and it did not appear to me that he was overwarm in his demeanor. His style of handshaking was of the pump-handle sort, and, to say the least of it, he was not hotly affectionate in his greetings; but perhaps he had never heard how I fought his battles when a boy. He was fortunate neither in making friends nor in keeping them: had he been of a more genial manner, he might have been re-elected to the presidency. But what could be expected of a man who used to cut a hole in the ice that he might take his morning bath in the gelid waters of the Potomac? Of course he had a strong constitution, and he had need of it. His life was one of continual disappointments and ceaseless battles.

The general fact that up to 1843 the State of Rhode Island was without a Constitution will strike those who have the usual faith in such paper safeguards with an astonishment bordering upon incredulity. But for two features of the Charter which were hardly democratic, the little State might have gone on pleasantly and prosperously for another century, under that rag of royalty. In the nineteenth century, given as it is to much voting, in the United States, which are trying on a large scale the experiment of a nearly absolute democracy, restrictions of the suffrage will always be sure to make many spirits uneasy; and in Rhode Island the suffrage was restricted to land-owners and to their eldest sons. It was an odd bit of feudalism, — a singular conservation of one of the rights of primogeniture. Again, the legislative representation, which had been fixed by the Charter in 1663, had become singularly unequal and arbitrary. It was, indeed, one of rotten boroughs. Providence, with over 20,000 inhabitants in 1840, had only four representatives, while Newport, with less than 10,000 inhabitants, had six representatives. Towns having altogether only 29,000 inhabitants and about 3,000 voters elected thirty-eight representatives, while but thirty-four were chosen by towns having nearly 80,000 inhabitants and nearly 6,000 voters.

The disfranchised petitioned, — it was all they could do; and their petitions were not always treated as judiciously as they should have been. Once they were referred to a committee, which reported against them in what I still consider one of the most remarkable pieces of the kind which has ever fallen under my notice. It was written by Benjamin Hazard, a hard-headed old lawyer, with a bottomless contempt for political innovations, and was such an essay as an English Tory of the Eldon stamp might have fulminated against the Reform Bill. It demonstrated by the best of legal logic that popular suffrage would be undesirable, and it offered to the popular notions of democracy a perfect *chevaux-de-frise* of special pleading, of replication, rejoinder, and rebutter. It was one of those arguments which one may feel to be all wrong and yet find it difficult to refute; and when, long after, I was asked to write an answer to it, I found the task anything but an easy one, and did the job badly. There were many stories told at bar dinners and suppers of Mr. Hazard's dogmatic and pertinacious ways. One of the drollest was of his rencontre with an antagonist for once too much for him. He had left a convivial party on a dark night, and was found soon after arguing with the town pump. "Get out of my way !" said he. "Move on !" he reit-erated. "What do you mean by this disreputable conduct ?" Still the pump held its position, when the irate lawyer roared, "Get out of my way, in the name of the State of Rhode Island and Providence Plantations !" The pump was proof against even this, and his com-panions coming up, it was found necessary to lead him gently to his domicile.

The year 1840 was one of great political activity everywhere, and the contest in Rhode Island was a particularly lively one. People who could not vote, more than ever envied those who could. In a desperate minority, the Democrats were anxious for a good cry. But the movement which was to grow to such considerable proportions had a personal and somewhat insignificant beginning. There was a Dr. John A. Brown, a botanical physician, who supplied the people of Providence with root-beer of a pleasant and salutiferous quality. Brown's beer was in demand, and, being of a foamy and effervescent sort, it may have had something to do with the ebullitions which fol-lowed. At any rate, when not engaged in building up the constitu-tions of his patients, the doctor was painfully sensible that the an-cient State had no Constitution of its own, — a deficiency which, both as a patriot and a practitioner, he ceased not to lament. He determined to start a free-suffrage agitation: secondly, he resolved to emit a free-suffrage newspaper; and, thirdly, he employed me to edit it. He might have done much better if he had been able to offer a little higher wages; for I engaged to convulse Rhode Island (with the Plantations thrown in) for the modest remuneration of five dol-lars per week. . . .

A name was wanted for the journal, and I suggested "The New Age" as expressive and appropriate, particularly as we proposed to abolish the work of an age which might be considered an old one. So the first number of the newspaper was issued from a little office which had just about type enough to set up a single edition. For some time the public paid but limited attention to our denuncia-tions of Charles II. and his musty old charter; but Dr. Brown was not in the least discouraged, and I am sure that I was not.

Concession came. As early as January, 1841, the General Assembly had called a convention to frame a Constitution. This was not the way, however, in which the Rhode Island Suffrage Association pro-posed to reform the State, and when the legal Constitution was sent to the people for sanction, the suffrage men helped to vote it down. Going back to first principles, and actually assuming that the State was without a government, they held a convention of their own, and got through with their work and had their Constitution ready for the people while the authorized body was still in session. There was no pretence of legality, in the ordinary sense of the word, in their doings. It was simply revolution. In April, 1842, the governor of Rhode Island had appealed to President Tyler for Federal assistance against insurrection; and I think about the best public document which Mr. Tyler ever sent forth, whoever may have written it, was the reply in which he assured the governor of support and protection. The suffrage men assumed that their Constitution had been adopted, and began to organize military companies to defend it. The days of trouble were close at hand.

The leading spirit of the suffrage movement from this time forward was Thomas Wilson Dorr, a Providence lawyer of good family, of fair ability, a man of boundless obstinacy, which his admirers called firmness. He had the reputation in Providence of an excellent hater, and of being influenced in the course which he pursued by what he considered to be personal injuries. In strict historical justice it must be said that the plan upon which the suffrage men proceeded was not his own. It was devised and determined upon in the office of "The New Age" some time before Mr. Dorr had anything whatever to do with the project. At first he was disinclined to lend his name to the enterprise, and he underwent a good deal of importunity before he could be induced to reverse his decision. I was once deputed to ask him to make a public address, or to write a letter, or in some other way to commit himself. He was a slow man, apparently though not really phlegmatic; but he answered me promptly. He said that upon several occasions he had labored for an extension of the suffrage, that he had never been properly supported by those who should have been swiftest in doing so, and that he must respectfully decline all invitations to participate in the proposed agitation. As he said this, he calmly smoked his cigar, looking, I must say, as little like an incendiary and revolutionist as any man whom I have ever encountered. He yielded afterwards, and, curiously enough, he had bitter reason to repeat the same complaint of inadequate support. He organized his government in Providence on the 3d of May, 1842, issued proclamations, sent a regular message to his Legislature, which met in a foundry, and from that time forth was called the Foundry Legislature. The members voted divers sums of money, especially for their own per diem and mileage, but they did not run the risk of levying taxes, — a measure which might have been regarded with disfavor by their constituents. "Governor" Dorr — "Rightful Governor" as his followers styled him — then went away to show himself to his sympathizers in New York, where for a while he was a great favorite with the men of the Pewter Mug. He came back upon the 16th of May, girt with a sword and breathing most belligerently. I saw him draw the weapon and wave it in defiance of the general and State governments, then and there swearing to die rather than yield. I also saw him, still wearing the sword and surrounded by armed men, drawn through the streets of Providence in a barouche. The last time I saw him was at his headquarters, the house of Burrington Anthony, and I can bear testimony to the fact that he was then as dauntless as ever. He was, however, in a desperate situation, — his State officers resigning, his family imploring him to abandon his schemes, all his most respectable followers turning against him. He marched that night upon the arsenal, but his own men had spiked his guns, of which he had six. These he himself tried to discharge. Had he succeeded, he, with a good many of those about him, might have been dead immediately after. A murderous discharge of grape would have saved the government all the trouble which afterward occurred. There would have been no subsequent invasion of the State, nor would its military annals have contained the short but decisive campaign of Chepatchet. Governor Dorr came back again in the last days of June with a motley following, but before the first day of July he had fled again, with his Spartan band, after issuing a general order dismissing his troops upon the ground that the Suffrage party no longer adhered to "the People's Constitution." So ended the Dorr war.

◇◆◇◆◇◆◇◆◇◆◇◆◇◆◇

[*Phineas Taylor Barnum, Danbury, Conn.*]

My store had much to do in giving shape to my future character as well as career, in that it became a favorite resort; the theatre of village talk, and the scene of many practical jokes. For any excess of the jocose element in my character, part of the blame must attach to my early surroundings as a village clerk and merchant. In that true resort of village wits and wags, the country store, fun, pure and simple, will be sure to find the surface. My Bethel store was the scene of many most amusing incidents, in some of which I was an immediate participant, though in many, of course, I was only a listener or spectator.

The following scene makes a chapter in the history of Connecticut, as the State was when "blue-laws" were something more than a dead letter. To swear in those days was according to custom, but contrary to law. A person from New York State, whom I will call Crofut, who was a frequent visitor at my store, was a man of property, and equally noted for his self-will and his really terrible profanity. One day he was in my little establishment engaged in conversation, when Nathan Seelye, Esq., one of our village justices of the peace, and a man of strict religious principles, came in, and hearing Crofut's profane language he told him he considered it his duty to fine him one dollar for swearing.

Crofut responded immediately with an oath, that he did not care a d — n for the Connecticut blue-laws.

"That will make two dollars," said Mr. Seelye.

This brought forth another oath.

"Three dollars," said the sturdy justice.

Nothing but oaths were given in reply, until Esquire Seelye declared the damage to the Connecticut laws to amount to fifteen dollars.

Crofut took out a twenty-dollar bill, and handed it to the justice of the peace, with an oath.

"Sixteen dollars," said Mr. Seelye, counting out four dollars to hand to Mr. Crofut, as his change.

"Oh, keep it, keep it," said Crofut, "I don't want any change, I'll d — d soon swear out the balance." He did so, after which he was more circumspect in his conversation, remarking that twenty dollars a day for swearing was about as much as he could stand.

On another occasion, a man arrested for assault and battery was to be tried before my grandfather, who was a justice of the peace. A young medical student named Newton, volunteered to defend the prisoner, and Mr. Couch, the grand-juryman came to me and said that as the prisoner had engaged a pettifogger, the State ought to have some one to represent its interests and he would give me a dollar to present the case. I accepted the fee and proposition. The fame of the "eminent counsel" on both sides drew quite a crowd to hear the case. As for the case itself, it was useless to argue it, for the guilt of the prisoner was established by evidence of half a dozen witnesses. However, Newton was bound to display himself, and so, rising with much dignity, he addressed my grandfather with, "May it please the honorable court," etc., proceeding with a mixture of poetry and invective against Couch, the grand-juryman whom he assumed to be the vindictive plaintiff in this case. After alluding to him as such for the twentieth time, my grandfather stopped Newton in the midst of his splendid peroration and informed him that Mr. Couch was not the plaintiff in the case.

"Not the plaintiff! Then may it please your honor I should like to know who *is* the plaintiff?" inquired Newton.

He was quietly informed that the State of Connecticut was the plaintiff, whereupon Newton dropped into his seat as if he had been shot. Thereupon, I rose with great confidence, and speaking from my notes, proceeded to show the guilt of the prisoner from the evidence; that there was no discrepancy in the testimony; that none of the witnesses had been impeached; that no defence had been offered; that I was astonished at the audacity of both counsel and prisoner in not pleading guilty at once; and then, soaring aloft on general principles, I began to look about for a safe place to alight, when my grandfather interrupted me with —

"Young man, will you have the kindness to inform the court which side you are pleading for — the plaintiff or the defendant ?"

It was my turn to drop, which I did amid a shout of laughter from every corner of the court-room. Newton, who had been very downcast, looked up with a broad grin and the two "eminent counsel" sneaked out of the room in company, while the prisoner was bound over to the next County Court for trial.

◇◇◇◇◇◇◇◇◇◇◇◇◇

[Harriot K. Hunt]

To Frederick U. Tracy, Treasurer, and the Assessors, and other authorities of the City of Boston, and the citizens generally.

Harriot K. Hunt, physician, a native and permanent resident of the City of Boston, and for many years a tax payer therein, in making payment of her city taxes for the coming year, begs leave to protest against the injustice and inequality of levying taxes upon women, and at the same time refusing them any voice or vote in the imposition and expenditure of the same. The only classes of male persons, required to pay taxes, and not at the same time allowed the privilege of voting, are aliens and minors. The objection in the case of aliens, is, their supposed want of interest in our institutions and knowledge of them. The objection in case of minors is, the want of sufficient understanding. These objections certainly cannot apply to women, natives of the city, all whose property and interests are here, and who have accumulated by their own sagacity and industry, the very property on which they are taxed. But this is not all; the aliens by going through the forms of naturalization, the minor on coming of age, obtain the right of voting, and so long as they continue to exercise it, though so ignorant as not to be able to *sign* their names, or *read* the very votes they put into the ballot boxes. Even drunkards, felons, idiots, or lunatics of *men,* may still enjoy that right of voting, to which no woman, however large the amount of taxes she pays, however respectable her character, or useful her life, can ever attain. Wherein, your remonstrant would inquire, is the justice, equality, or wisdom of this ? That the rights and interests of the female part of the community are sometimes forgotten or disregarded in consequence of their deprivation of political rights, is strikingly evinced, as appears to your remonstrant, in the organization and administration of the city public schools. Though there are open in this State and neighborhood, a great multitude of colleges and professional schools, for the education of boys and young men, yet the city has very properly provided two high schools of its own, one Latin, the other English, at which the *male graduates* of the grammar schools may pursue their education still further at the public expense, and why is not a like provision made for the girls ? Why is the public provision for *their* education stopped short, just as they have attained the age best fitted for progress, and the preliminary knowledge necessary to facilitate it, thus giving the advantage of superior culture to *sex*, not to mind ? The fact that our colleges and professional schools are closed against females, of which your remonstrant has had personal and painful experience, having been in the year 1847, after twelve years of medical practice in Boston, refused permission to attend the lectures of Harvard Medical College, that fact would seem to furnish an additional reason, why the city should provide at its own expense, those means of superior education, which, by supplying our girls with occupation and objects of interest, would not only save them from lives of frivolity and emptiness, but which might open the way to many useful and lucrative pursuits, and so raise them above that *degrading dependence,* so fruitful a source of female misery.

Reserving a more full exposition of the subject to future occasions, your remonstrant in paying her tax for the current year, begs leave to *protest* against the injustice and inequalities above pointed out.

This is respectfully submitted,

HARRIOT K. HUNT, 32 Green street.

Boston, Oct. 18, 1852.

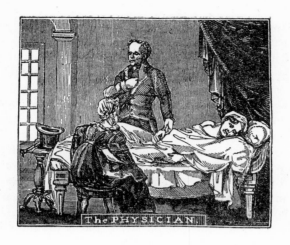

The PHYSICIAN

THE PRACTICE OF PHYSIC

❖❖❖❖❖❖❖❖❖❖❖

[*Samuel Thomson, Alstead, N. H.*]

WHEN I was between three and four years old (1772), my father took me out with him to work. The first business I was set to do was to drive the cows to pasture, and watch the geese, with other small chores, which occupation kept me all day in the fields. I was very curious to know the names of all the herbs which I saw growing, and what they were good for; and, to satisfy my curiosity was constantly making inquiries of the persons I happened to be with, for that purpose. All the information I thus obtained, or by my own observation, I carefully laid up in my memory, and never forgot. There was an old lady by the name of Benton lived near us, who used to attend our family when there was any sickness. At that time there was no such thing as a Doctor known among us, there not being any within ten miles. The whole of her practice was with roots and herbs, applied to the patient, or given in hot drinks, to produce sweating; which always answered the purpose. When one thing did not produce the desired effect, she would try something else, till they were relieved. By her attention to the family, and the benefits they received from her skill, we became very much attached to her; and

[325]

when she used to go out to collect roots and herbs, she would take me with her, and learn me their names, with what they were good for; and I used to be very curious in my inquiries, and in tasting every thing that I found. The information I thus obtained at this early age, was afterwards of great use to me.

Sometime in the summer, after I was four years old, being out in the fields in search of the cows, I discovered a plant which had a singular branch and pods, that I had never before seen, and I had the curiosity to pick some of the pods and chew them; the taste and operation produced was so remarkable, that I never forgot it. I afterwards used to induce other boys to chew it, merely by way of sport, to see them vomit. I tried this herb in this way for nearly twenty years, without knowing any thing of its medical virtues. This plant is what I have called the Emetic Herb, and is the most important article I make use of in my practice. It is very common in most parts of this country, and may be prepared and used in almost any manner. It is a certain counter poison, having never been known to fail to counteract the effects of the most deadly poison, even when taken in large quantities for self-destruction. There is no danger to be apprehended from its use, as it is perfectly harmless in its operation, even when a large quantity is taken; it operates as an emetic, cleanses the stomach from all improper aliment, promotes an internal heat, which is immediately felt at the extremities, and produces perspiration. The exclusive right of using this plant for medical purposes is secured to me by patent, and my right to the discovery has never been disputed; though the Doctors have done every thing they could to destroy the credit of it, by false statements, representing it to be a deadly poison, and at the same time they knew to the contrary, for they have made use of it themselves for several years, and have tried to defraud me of the discovery. I feel perfectly convinced from near forty years' experience of its medical properties, that the discovery is of incalculable importance, and if properly understood by the people will be more useful in curing the diseases incident to this climate, than the drugs and medicines sold by all the apothecaries in the country.

On arriving in Walpole, my father proceeded immediately to the house of the famous Dr. Kittredge, to have him dress my wound, and get his opinion of my situation. The doctor soon came home, and on entering the room where I was, cried out in a very rough manner, Who have you here? His wife answered, a sick man. The devil, replied he, I want no sick man here. I was much terrified by his coarse

[326]

manner of speaking, and thought if he was so rough in his conversa, tion, what will he be when he comes to dress my wound; but I was happily disappointed, for he took off the dressing with great care, and handled me very tenderly. On seeing the strings that were in the wound, he exclaimed, what the devil are these halters here for ? My father told him they were put in to keep the sore open. He said he thought the sore open enough now, for it is all rotten. Being anxious to know his opinion of me, my father asked him what he thought of my situation. What do I think ? said he, why I think he will die; and then looking very pleasantly at me, said, though I think young man, you will get well first. In the morning he dressed my ancle again, and gave me some salve to use in future; and my father asked him for his bill, which was, I think, for our keeping and his attending me, about fifty cents.

Soon after my family had got well of the measles, I was sent for to see a woman by the name of Redding, in the neighborhood. She had been for many years afflicted with the cholic, and could get no relief from the doctors. I attended her and found the disorder was caused by canker, and pursued the plan that my former experience had taught me, which relieved her from the pain, and so far removed the cause that she never had another attack of the disease. In this case the cure was so simply and easily performed, that it became a sub- ject of ridicule, for when she was asked about it, she was ashamed to say that I cured her. The popular practice of the physicians had so much influence on the minds of the people, that they thought noth- ing could be right but what was done by them. I attended in this family for several years, and always answered the desired purpose; but my practice was so simple, that it was not worthy of notice, and being dissatisfied with the treatment I received, I refused to do any thing more for them. After this they employed the more fashionable practitioners, who were ready enough to make the most of a job, and they had sickness and expense enough to satisfy them, for one of the sons was soon after taken sick and was given over by the doctor, who left him to die; but after he left off giving him medicine he got well of himself, and the doctor not only had the credit of it, but for this job and one other similar, his charges amounted to over one hundred dollars. This satisfied me of the foolishness of the people, whose prej- udices are always in favor of any thing that is fashionable, or that is done by those who profess great learning; and prefer long sickness and great expense, if done in this way, to a simple and natural relief, with a trifling expense.

I was called on to attend a woman in the town where I lived. She was an old maid, and had lately been married to a widower, who was very fond of her. She had been much disordered for many years, and was very spleeny; she had been under the care of several doctors without receiving any benefit. I visited her several times and gave general satisfaction; so much so that she allowed that I had done her more good than all the others that had attended her. A short time after I had done visiting her, the old man came out one morning to my house at sunrise, and I being about six miles from home, he came with all speed where I was, and said he wished me to come to his house as soon as possible, for his wife was very sick. I told him to return, and I would be there as soon as he could. I soon after set out, and we both arrived there about the same time; and I was very much astonished to find his wife about her work. I was asked into another room by the old man and his wife, and he said she had something to say to me. She then said that, "if I could not attend her without giving her love powder, she did not wish me to attend her at all." I was very much astonished at her speech, and asked what she meant. She said that ever since she had taken my medicine she had felt so curiously, that she did not know what to make of it. The old man affirmed to the same, and he thought that I had given her love powder, and did not know what the event might be.

This foolish whim of the old man and his wife, caused a great bluster, and was food for those idle minds, who seem to take delight in slandering their neighbors; and was made a great handle of by the doctors, who spread all kinds of ridiculous stories about me during my absence in the summer of 1806. In the autumn, when I had returned home, I found that a certain doctor of Alstead, had circulated some very foolish and slanderous reports about me and the old woman, and had given to them so much importance, that many people believed them. I found that I could prove his assertions, and sued him for defamation; supposing that by appealing to the laws of my country I could get redress; but I was disappointed in my expectations, for I was persuaded to leave the case to a reference, and he had raised such a strong prejudice in the minds of the people against me, that they were more ready to favor a man whom they considered great and learned, because he had been to college, than to do justice to me; so they gave the case against me, and I had to pay the cost. After this, I refused to attend those people who had assisted in injuring me, and gave them up to their fashionable doctor. A curse seemed to follow them and his practice; for the spotted fever prevailed in this place soon after, and the doctor took charge of those who had sided with him against me, and if he had been a butcher and used the knife, there would not have been more destruction among them. Two men who swore falsely in his favor, and by whose means he got his cause, were among his first victims; and of the whole that he attended, about nine tenths died. He lost upwards of sixty patients in the town of Alstead in a short time.

◇◇◇◇◇◇◇◇◇◇◇◇◇◇

[Harriot K. Hunt, Boston]

In October, 1835, we removed to the corner of Spring and Leverett streets, where we lived some time, advertised, and began, as it were, our profession. Our mother was then nearly sixty-five years of age — clear and bright, and, as ever, watchful over her children. Our previous removal being but temporary, this new dwelling-place seemed more like home. There we commenced a life, fraught with absorbing interest; — grasping the past to apply it to the present, and prospectively looking to the future. My medical brother can recur to his first professional year, and remember the varied states of mind it induced in him, and all the shades of his anxiety. But he had "regularly" studied — had passed through an approved college, and been accepted; and with a recognition from the medical faculty, and an M. D. placed at the end of his name, he had a capital to start upon. He had older heads to sustain him — a code of laws to obey — a mistake would not be fatal to him, though it might be to the patient ! — and if he reverently looked to the centre, the centre would kindly regard him. I said he had studied before he practised: — we studied and practised at the same time; for our knowledge seemed very trifling when we commenced, and had we not been constantly brought in contact with the errors, blunders, and lack of applicability among the doctors, we might have shrunk from the overwhelming responsibility attached to the name of physician. But the standard they have placed before the public, will induce many a commonplace woman to enter the profession. Would this were not so !

I remember vividly the earnestness — the enthusiasm — with which we received our first patients. To be sure, they came along very slowly; but every case that did come, was a new revelation — a new wonder — a new study in itself, and by itself. The need of freedom of action — diversity of treatment — was constantly felt by us. Very early in medical life we found ourselves differing from our teachers, and escaping from formal rules. We very soon learned not to trust too much to medication: — not but that we often saw it fully successful; but it did not meet our perception of the dignity of the human body. Anatomy had partially opened its treasures to me; and the wonderful deposits from the blood to develop, perfect, and sustain the system, even the bony structure, filled my soul with reverent awe: — for I never entered the medical life through physics, but through metaphysics. An anecdote on bones comes in place here. A medical journal noticed that we had advertised ourselves as physicians, and, by way of a fling at our presumed ignorance, queried if we knew the difference between the sternum and the spinal column ! This was a thin jest, to be sure, the skeleton of a joke; but, as it involved in its delicate humor the question of our knowledge of the very trunk of the anatomical tree, without which, we could not keep the branches in health, as also anterior, posterior, heart, lungs, and nervous system, — as it included all this, it was quite a palpable hit ! It is but just to say that the editor of that journal became our friend, and I have to thank him for the subsequent use of his library, and many kindnesses.

Reverence for the human organization had much to do with my medical life; and I found myself questioning cases of dyspepsia, constipation, liver complaints, and many others — begging them to tell me why they had imposed their drawbacks on health and life; and they did tell me of fearful abuses through ignorance, passion, luxury, and vice. Were not my cases guides and mentors ?

We studied with unwearying zeal. When our mother was sweetly asleep, we were reciting our lessons to each other — investigating every case that had been presented to us through the day — often thankful that we had declined cases (and numerous were those we did decline) till we were prepared to meet them. My sister, being gifted in the use of her pencil, copied plates. Our leisure hours slipped away like moments, with use stamped on every one of them. There was an abiding faith about us, an enthusiasm which surprised many of our tame friends. They could not understand that barren technicalities, freshened by the atmosphere of love, blossomed with beauty for us; or that the diseases of others, with a fervent wish for their removal, gave us mental life.

Our business gradually increased. One cure opened the way for other cases; and an enforcement of dietetic rules, bathing, and so forth, soon placed on a permanently healthy platform those who consulted us. Our diagnosis was not copied from that of any eminent M. D. Indeed it required a strong and determined effort never to speak disparagingly of the profession, or of physicians, but to be quiet and candid. Very carefully did we venture out into the broad ocean — preferring, at the outset, to keep along shore, till experience could trim the sails, and confidence pilot a larger craft. Soon, opportunities were offered us to visit country towns; I accepted them cheerfully; my sister remained at home. From these journeys I gathered rich knowledge: so many "given up cases" were presented to my notice ! — also chronic diseases of an aggravated character. These last were opportunities for friendly relations and examinations; but not cases to be accepted professionally. My field of observation broadened wonderfully; — if hospitals closed their doors to woman, except as patient and nurse, the public were beginning to perceive the inconsistency — nay, injustice — of the act ! We had, before long, patients from the highly cultivated, the delicate, and the sensible portions of the community.

My mother always objected to our practising midwifery; her reasons were satisfactory. In this early stage of woman in the profession, there was no physician to speak one encouraging word to us, or to whom we could apply. So alone, unaided by any, we established our own code of laws, and wisely concluded not to visit patients at their homes; for we knew if we did, doctors would say, as we were women, that we were insinuating ourselves into families, and weakening confidence in the faculty. To remain in our house, and receive calls, was the best opening for the life in this city. The arrangement was productive of much good to physician as well as to patient. Many homebound, chamber-ridden, used for years to medical calls, would make a desperate effort, saying "live or die." We will go and hear what those strange women have to say to us; that very resolution was the dawn of light, the beginning of new life to them, and a fit preparation for obedience to those physical laws which we insisted upon as absolutely necessary to a cure.

"In from the country so soon ?" said I to another who lived still further off, and brought me a beautiful bouquet. "Yes, I am suffering from *ennui;* any thing for a change; my headaches are relieved, yet I am not grateful; my neuralgia does not trouble me, yet I am discontented and unhappy." "Oh, the fact is, you *miss those pains* and *aches,* and have nothing to talk about. Do you know I once refused to prescribe for a girl who was suffering from tic douloureux, because her life was so aimless, that I thought her only chance for reflection was through pain, and I did not dare to interfere ? Perhaps I should have treated your case in the same way." This rather startled her. "One has no society in a country town." "Invite your city friends to come and see you." "They are so fashionable, they talk about nothing but dress, parties, and servants." "Does that trouble you ?" "Yes." "Very well, then catch that glimmer of light, use it, and it will increase. Offer yourself as a gift to God, and then you can magnetize your friends, and other topics of conversation will be enjoyed."

THE MEETING-HOUSE

◇◇◇◇◇◇◇◇◇◇◇◇◇◇

[*Cotton Mather, Boston*]

H*æc ipse miserrima vidi.** — Four children of John Goodwin, in Boston, which had enjoy'd a religious education, and answer'd it with a towardly ingenuity — children, indeed, of an exemplary temper and carriage, and an example to all about them for piety, honesty, and industry — these were, in the year 1688, arrested by a very stupendous witchcraft. The eldest of the children, a daughter of about thirteen years old, saw cause to examine their laundress, the daughter of a scandalous Irish woman in the neighbourhood, about some linen that was missing; and the woman bestowing very bad language on the child, in her daughter's defence, the child was immediately taken with odd fits, that carried in them something *diabolical*. It was not long before one of her sisters, with two of her brothers, were horribly taken with the like fits, which the most *experienc'd* physicians pronounced extraordinary and preternatural: and one thing that the more confirmed them in this opinion was, that all the children were tormented still just the same part of their bodies, at the *same time,* tho' their pains flew like swift lightning from one part unto another, and they were kept so far asunder, that they neither saw nor heard one another's complaints. At 9 or 10

* These things these wretched eyes beheld.

a-clock at night, they still had a release from their miseries, and slept all night pretty comfortably. But when the day came, they were most miserably handled. Sometimes they were *deaf*, sometimes *dumb*, sometimes *blind,* and often all this at once. Their tongues would be drawn down their throats, and then pull'd out upon their chins, to a prodigious length. Their mouths were forc'd open to such a wideness, that their jaws went out of joint; and anon clap together again, with a force like that of a spring lock; and the like would happen to their shoulder-blades and their elbows, and hand wrists, and several of their joints. They would lie in a benumb'd condition, and be drawn together like those that are ty'd neck and heels; and presently be stretch'd out — yea, *drawn back* enormously. They made piteous out-cries, that they were cut with *knives,* and struck with *blows;* and the plain prints of the *wounds* were seen upon them. Their necks would be broken, so that their neck-bone would seem dissolv'd unto them that felt after it; and yet on the sudden it would become again so stiff, that there was no stirring of their heads; yea, their heads would be twisted almost round; and if the main force of their friends at any time obstructed a dangerous motion which they seem'd upon, they would roar exceedingly: and when devotions were performed with them, their *hearing* was utterly taken from them. The ministers of Boston and Charlestown, keeping a day of prayer with fasting, on this occasion, at the troubled house, the youngest of the four children was immediately, happily, finally delivered from all its trouble. But the magistrates being awakened by the noise of these grievous and horrid occurrences, examined the person who was under the suspicion of having employ'd these troublesome dæmons; and she gave such a wretched account of herself, that she was committed unto the gaoler's custody.

It was not long before this woman (whose name was Glover) was brought upon her trial; but then the court could have no answers from her but in the Irish, which was her native language, although she understood English very well, and had accustom'd her whole family to none but English in her former conversation. When she pleaded to her indictment, it was with *owning*, and *bragging*, rather than *denial* of her guilt. And the interpreters, by whom the communication between the bench and the barr was managed, were made sensible that a *spell* had been laid by another witch on *this,* to prevent her telling tales, by confining her to a language which 'twas hoped nobody would understand. The woman's house being searched, several *images*, or *poppets*, or babies, made of raggs, and stuffed with goats' hair, were thence produced; and the vile woman confessed that her way to torment the objects of her malice, was by wetting of her finger with her spittle, and stroaking of those little images. The abus'd children were then present in the court; the woman kept still stooping and shrinking, as one that was almost prest unto death with a mighty weight upon her. But one of the images being brought unto her, she oddly and swiftly started up, and snatch'd it into her hand: but she had no sooner snatch'd it, than one of the children fell into sad fits before the whole assembly. The judges had their just apprehension at this, and carefully causing a repetition of the experiment, they still found the same event of it, tho' the children saw not when the hand of the witch was laid upon the images. They ask'd her "whether she had any to stand by her ?" She reply'd, "she had:" and looking very pertly into the air, she added, "No he's gone !" and she then acknowledg'd that she had *one*, who was her prince; with whom she mention'd I know not what communion. For which cause, the night after, she was heard expostulating with a devil for his thus deserting her, telling him that "because he had served her so basely and falsely, she had con-fessed all."

However, to make all clear, the court appointed five or six physi-cians to examine her very strictly, whether she was no way craz'd in her intellectuals. Divers hours did they spend with her; and in all that while no discourse came from her but what was *agreeable;* par-ticularly when they ask'd her what she thought would became of her soul, she reply'd, "You ask me a very solemn question, and I cannot tell what to say to it." She profest herself a Roman Catholick, and could recite her *Pater-noster* in Latin very readily, but there was one clause or two always too hard for her, whereof, she said, " she could not repeat it, if she might have all the world."

In the upshot, the doctors return'd her *compos mentis,* and sen-tence of death was past upon her. Divers days past between her be-ing arraign'd and condemn'd; and in this time one Hughes testify'd that her neighbour, (call'd Howen) who was cruelly bewitch'd unto death about six years before, laid her death to the charge of this woman, and bid her (the said Hughes) to remember this; for within six years there would be occasion to mention it. One of Hughes' chil-dren was presently taken ill in the same woful manner that Good-win's was; and particularly the boy, in the night cry'd that a *black person* with *a blue cap* in the room tortur'd him, and that they try'd with their hand in the bed for to pull out his bowels. The mother of the boy went unto Glover the day following, and asked her, "Why she tortured her poor lad at such a rate ?" Glover answered, "Be-cause of the wrong she had receiv'd from her;" and boasted, "that she had come at him as a black person with a blue cap; and with her hand in the bed, would have pulled his bowels out, but could not." Hughes denied that she had wronged her; and Glover, then desiring to see the boy, wished him well; upon which he had no more of his indispositions. After the condemnation of the woman, I did myself give divers visits unto her; wherein she told me that she did use to be at meetings, where her prince with four more were present. She told me who the four were, and plainly said, "that her prince was the devil." When I told her *that* and *how* her prince had cheated her, she reply'd, "If it be so, I am sorry for that !" And when she declin'd answering some things that I ask'd her, she told me, "she would fain give me a full answer, but her spirits would not give her leave;" nor could she consent, she said, without their leave, "that I should pray for her." At her execution, she said the afflicted children should not be reliev'd by her death, for others besides she had a hand in their affliction. Accordingly the three children continu'd in their furnace as before; and it grew rather "seven times hotter" than it was. In their fits they cry'd out [they] and [them] as the authors of all their miseries; but who that [they] and [them] were, they were unable to declare: yet, at last, one of the children was able to discern their shapes, and utter their names. A blow at the place where they saw the spectre, was always felt by the boy himself, in that part of his body that answer'd what might be stricken at: and this, tho' his back were turn'd, and the thing so done, that there could be no collusion in it. But as a *blow* at the spectre always hurt him, so it always help'd him too: for after the agonies to which a push or stab at that had put him, were over (as in a minute or two they would be) he would have a respite from his ails a considerable while, and the spectre would be gone: yea, 'twas very credibly affirmed that a dangerous woman or two in the town receiv'd wounds by the blows thus given to their spectres. The calamities of the children went on till they barked at one another like dogs, and then purred like so many cats. They would complain that they were in a *red-hot oven,* and sweat and pant as much as if they had been really so. Anon they would say that cold water was thrown on them, at which they would shiver very much.

They would complain of blows with great cudgels laid upon them, and we that stood by, though we could see no cudgels, yet could see the marks of the blows in red streaks upon their flesh.

They would complain of being roasted on an *invisible spit;* and lie and roll and groan as if it had been most sensibly so; and by and by shriek that knives were cutting of them. They would complain that their heads were *nail'd* unto the floor, and it was beyond an ordinary strength to pull them from thence. They would be so limber sometimes, that it was judg'd every bone they had might be bent; and anon so stiff, that not a joint of them could be stirr'd.

One of them dreamt that something was growing within his skin, cross one of his ribs. An expert chirurgeon searcht the place, and found there a brass pin, which could not possibly come to lie there as it did without a prestigious and mysterious conveyance. Sometimes they would be very mad; and then they would climb over high fences; yea, they would fly like geese, and be carried with an incredible swiftness through the air, having but just their toes now and then upon the ground, (sometimes not once in *twenty foot*) and their arms *wav'd* like the wings of a bird. They were often very near drowning or burning of themselves; and they often strangled themselves with their neckclothes; but the providence of God still order'd the seasonable succours of them that look'd after them. If there happened any mischief to be done where they were, as the dirtying of a garment, or spilling of a cup, or breaking of a glass, they would laugh *excessively*.

But upon the least reproof of their parents, they were thrown into inexpressible anguish, and roar as excessively. It usually took up abundance of time to dress them or undress them, through the strange postures into which they would be *twisted*, on purpose to hinder it; and yet the dæmons did not know our thoughts: for if we us'd a jargon, and said, "Untie his neckcloth," but the party bidden understood our meaning to be "untie his shooe;" the *neckcloth*, and not the *shooe*, has been by *written postures* rendered strangely *inaccessible*. In their beds they would be sometimes treated so, that no cloaths could for an hour or two be laid upon them. If they were bidden to do a *needless* thing (as to rub a *clean* table) they were able to do it unmolested; but if to do any *useful* thing (as to rub a *dirty* table) they would presently, with many torments, be made uncapable.

They were sometimes hindred from eating their meals, by having their teeth set, when any thing was carrying unto their mouths. If there were any discourse of God, or Christ, or any of the "things which are not seen, and are eternal," they would be cast into *intolerable anguishes*. All praying to God, and reading of his word, would occasion 'em a very *terrible vexation*. Their *own* ears would then be stopt with their *own* hands, and they would roar, and howl, and shriek, and hollow, to drown the voice of the devotions; yea, if any one in the room took up a Bible, to look into it, though the children could see nothing of it, as being in a crowd of spectators, or having their faces another way, yet would they be in *wonderful torments* till the Bible was laid aside. Briefly, *No good thing* might then be

[337]

endur'd near those children, which, while they were *themselves,* lov'd every good thing, in a measure that proclaim'd in them the fear of God. If I said unto them, "Child, cry to the Lord Jesus Christ !" their teeth were instantly set. If I said, "Yet, child, look unto him !" their eyes were instantly pull'd so far into their heads, that we fear'd they could never have us'd them any more.

It was the eldest of these children that fell chiefly under my own observation: for I took her home to my own family, partly out of compassion to her parents, but chiefly that I might be a critical eye-witness of things that would enable me to confute the *sadducism* of this debauch'd age. Here she continu'd well for some days; applying herself to actions of industry and piety: But November 20, 1688, she cry'd out, "Ah, they have found me out !" and immediately she fell into her fits; wherein we often observ'd that she would cough up a ball as big as a small egg into the side of her wind-pipe, that would near choak her, till by stroaking and by drinking it was again carry'd down.

When I pray'd in the room, first her hands were with a *strong,* tho' not *even* force, clapt upon her ears: and when her hands were by our force pull'd away, she cry'd out, "They make such a noise, I cannot hear a word !" She complained that Glover's chain was upon her leg; and, assaying to go, her gait was exactly such as the *chain'd witch* had before she dy'd. When her tortures pass'd over, still frolicks would succeed, wherein she would continue hours — yea, days together — talking perhaps never *wickedly,* but always *wittily* beyond herself: and at certain provocations her torments would *renew* upon her, till we had left off to give them; yet she frequently told us in these frolicks, "That if she might but steal or be drunk, she should be well immediately." She told us, "that she must go down to the bottom of our well," (and we had much ado to hinder it,) "for they said there was plate there, and they would bring her up safely again."

We wonder'd at this; for she had never heard of any plate there; and we our selves, who had newly bought the house were ignorant of it but the former owner of the house just then coming in, told us "There had been plate for many years lost at the bottom of the well." Moreover, one singular passion that frequently attended her, was this:

An *invisible chain* would be clapt about her, and she, in much pain and fear, cry out when [they] began to put it on. Sometimes we could with our hands knock it off, as it began to be fasten'd: But ordinarily, when it was on, she would be pull'd out of her seat with such violence *towards* the fire, that it was as much as one or two of us could do to keep her out. Her eyes were not brought to be perpendicular to her feet, when she rose out of her seat, as the *mechanism* of an humane body requires in them that rise; but she was dragg'd *wholly* by other hands. And if we stamp'd on the hearth, just between her and the fire, she scream'd out, "That by jarring the chain, we hurt her."

I may add, that [they] put an unseen rope, with a cruel noose, about her neck, whereby she was choak'd until she was black in the face: and tho' it was got off before it had kill'd her, yet there were the red marks of it, and of a finger and a thumb near it, remaining to be seen for some while afterwards. Furthermore, not only upon her own looking into the Bible, but if any one else in the room did it, *wholly unknown* to her, she would fall into unsufferable torments.

A Quaker's book being brought her, she could quietly read whole pages of it; only the name of GOD and CHRIST, she still skipp'd over, being unable to pronounce it, except sometimes, stammering a minute or two or more upon it: and when we urg'd her to tell what the word was that she miss'd she would say, "I must not speak it: they say I must not. You know what it is: 'Tis G, and O, and D." But a book against Quakerism [they] would not allow her to meddle with. Such books as it might have been profitable and edifying for her to read, and especially her catechisms, if she did but offer to read a line in them, she would be cast into hideous convulsions, and be tost about the house like a foot ball: But books of jest being shown her, she could read them well enough, and having cunning descants upon them. Popish books [they] would not hinder her from reading; but [they] would from reading books against Popery. A book which pretends to prove "that there are no witches," was easily read by her; only the name devils and witches might not be utter'd. A book which proves "that there are witches," being exhibited unto her, she might not read it; and that experssion in the story of Ann Cole, about running to the rock, always threw her into sore convulsions.

Divers of these trials were made by many witnesses: but I, considering that there might be a snare in it, put a seasonable stop to this fanciful business. Only I could not but be amaz'd at one thing: A certain Prayer-book being brought her, she not only could read it very well, but also did read a large part of it over, calling it her Bible, and putting a more than ordinary respect upon it. If she were going into her tortures, at the tender of this book, she would recover her self to read it: Only when she came to the Lord's Prayer, now and then occurring in that book, she would have her eyes put out; so that she must turn over a new leaf, and then she could read again. Whereas also there are scriptures in that book, she could read them there: but if any shew'd her the very same scriptures in the Bible it self, she should sooner die than read them: and she was likewise made unable to read the Psalms in an ancient metre, which this Prayer-book had in the same volume with it.

Besides these, there was another inexplicable thing in her condition. Ever now and then, an invisible horse would be brought unto her by those whom she only call'd [*them*] and [*her company,*]upon the approach of which her eyes would be still clos'd up: For (said she) " they say I am a tell-tale, and therefore they will not let me see them." Here-upon she would give a spring as one mounting an horse, and settling her self in a riding posture, she would in her chair be agitated, as one sometimes ambling, sometimes trotting, and sometimes galloping very furiously. In these motions we could not *perceive* that she was mov'd by the stress of her feet upon the ground, for often she touch'd it not. When she had rode a minute or two, she would seem to be at a rendezvous with [them] that were [her company,] and there she would maintain a discourse with them, asking them many questions concerning her self, [we gave her none of ours] and have answers from them, which indeed none but her self perceiv'd. Then would she return, and inform us "How [they] did intend to handle her for a day or two afterwards," and some other things that she inquir'd. Her horse would sometimes throw her with much violence; especially if any one stabb'd or cut the air under her. But she would briskly mount again, and perform her fantastick journies, mostly in her chair; but sometimes also she would be carry'd from her chair, out of the room in another, very oddly, in the posture of a riding woman. At length, she pretended that her horse could ride up the stairs; and unto admiration she rode (that is, was toss'd as one that rode) up the stairs. There then stood open the study of one belonging to the family; into which entring, she stood immediately on her feet, and cry'd out, "They are gone ! they are gone ! They say that they cannot — God won't let 'em come here !" Adding a reason for it, which the owner of the study thought more *kind* than *true*. And she presently and perfectly came to her self, so that her whole discourse and carriage was alter'd unto the greatest "measure of sobriety;" and she sate reading of the Bible and other good books for a good part of the afternoon. Her affairs calling her anon to go down again, the dæmons were in a quarter of a minute as bad upon her as before; and her *horse* was *waiting* for her. Some then, to see whether there had not been a fallacy in what had *newly* hapned, resolv'd for to have her up unto the study, where she had been at ease before; but she was then so strangely distorted, that it was an *extream difficulty* to drag her up stairs. The dæmons would pull her out of the people's hands, and make her *heavier* than perhaps *three* of her self. With incredible toil, (tho' she kept screaming, "They say I must not go in,") she was pull'd in; where she was no sooner got, but she could stand on her feet, and, with an alter'd note, say, "Now I am well."

She would be faint at first, and say, "She felt something to go out of her!" (the noises whereof *we* sometimes heard, like those of a mouse) but in a minute or two she could apply her self to devotion, and express her self with *discretion, as well as ever* in her life.

To satisfie some strangers, the *experiment* was divers times, with the same success, repeated; until my lothness to have any thing done like making a charm of a room, caus'd me to forbid the repetition of it. But enough of this. The ministers of Boston and Charlestown kept another day of prayer with fasting, for Goodwin's afflicted family: after which, the children had a sensible, but a gradual abatement of their sorrows, until *perfect ease* was at length restor'd unto them. The young woman dwelt at my house the rest of the winter; having by a vertuous conversation made her self enough welcome to the family. But ere long, I thought it convenient for me to entertain my congregation with a sermon on the "memorable providences" wherein these children had been concern'd, [afterwards publish'd.] When I had begun to study my sermon, her *tormentors* again seiz'd upon her, and manag'd her with a special design, as was plain, to disturb me in what I was then about.

In the worst of her extravagancies formerly, she was more dutiful to myself than I had reason to expect. But now her whole carriage to me was with a *sawciness,* which, I was not used any where to be treated withal. She would knock at my study door, affirming "that some below would be glad to see me," though there was none that ask'd for me. And when I chid her for telling what was false, her answer was, "Mrs. Mather is always glad to see you!" She would call to me with numberless impertinences: And when I came down, she would throw things at me, though none of them could ever hurt me: and she would hecter me at a strange rate for something I was doing above, and threatened me with *mischief* and *reproach,* that should revenge it. Few tortures now attended her, but such as were provok'd. Her frolicks were numberless, if we may call them hers. I was in Latin telling some young gentleman, that if I should bid her look to God, her eyes would be put out: upon which her eyes were presently serv'd so. Perceiving that her troubles understood Latin, some trials were thereupon made whether they understood Greek and Hebrew, which it seemed they also did; but the Indian languages they did seem not so *well* to understand.

When we went unto prayer, the dæmons would throw her on the floor at the feet of him that pray'd, where she would whistle, and sing, and yell, to drown the voice of prayer, and she would fetch blows with her fist, and kicks with her foot, at the man that pray'd: But still her fist and foot would always recoyl, when they came within an inch or two of him, as if rebounding against a wall: and then she would beg hard of other people to strike him, which (you must be sure) not being done, she cry'd out, "He has wounded me in the head." But before the prayer was over, she would be laid for dead, wholly senseless, and (unto appearance) breathless, with her belly swell'd like a drum; and sometimes with croaking noises in her. Thus would she lie, most exactly with the stiffness and posture of one that had been two days laid out for dead. Once lying thus, as he that was praying, was alluding to the words of the Canaanites, and saying "Lord, have mercy on a daughter vex't with a devil," there came a big, but low voice from her, in which the spectators did not see her mouth to move, "There's two or three of us." When prayer was ended, she would revive in a minute or two, and continue as frolicksome as before.

She thus continu'd until Saturday towards the evening; when she assay'd with as nimble, and various, and pleasant an application, as could easily be us'd, for to divert the young folks in the family from such exercises as it was proper to meet the Sabbath withal: But they refused to be diverted, she fell fast asleep, and in two or three hours waked perfectly herself, weeping bitterly to remember what had befallen her. When Christmas arrived, both she at my house, and her sister at home, were by the dæmons made very drunk, though we are fully satisfied they had no *strong drink* to make them so; nor would they willingly have been so to have gained the world. When she began to feel her self drunk, she complained, "Oh! they say they will have me to keep Christmas with them. They will disgrace me when they can do nothing else." And immediately the ridiculous behaviours of one drunk were, with a wondrous exactness, represented in her *speaking,* and *reeling,* and *spewing,* and anon *sleeping,* till she was well again. At last the dæmons put her upon saying that she was dying, and the matter proved such that we fear'd she really *was;* for she lay, she toss'd, she pull'd, just like one dying, and urg'd hard for some one to die with her, seeming loth to *die alone.* She argu'd concerning death, with a paraphrase on the thirty-first Psalm, in strains that quite amaz'd us: And concluded that tho' she was "loth to die," yet, if God said she must, *she must !* Adding, that the Indians would quickly shed much blood in the country, and horrible tragedies would be acted in the land. Thus the vexations of the children ended.

But after a while, they began again; and then one particular minister, taking a particular compassion on the family, set himself to serve them in the methods prescribed by our Lord Jesus Christ. Accordingly, the Lord being *besought thrice* in *three* days of prayer,

with fasting on this occasion, the family then saw their *deliverance* perfected; and the children afterwards, all of them, not only approved themselves devout Christians, but unto the praise of God reckon'd these their afflictions among the special *incentives* of their Christianity.

The ministers of Boston and Charlestown, afterwards accompany'd the printed narrative of these things with their attestations to the truth of it. And when it was reprinted at London, the famous Mr. Baxter* prefixed a preface unto it, wherein he says: "This great instance comes with such convincing evidence, that he must be a very obdurate Sadducee, that will not believe it."

[*Samuel Sewall*]

Decʳ 21, 1696. A very great Snow is on the Ground. I go in the morn to Mr. Willard, to entreat him to chuse his own time to come and pray with little Sarah: He comes a little before night, and prays

* Richard Baxter, author of *Saints' Everlasting Rest.* B. M.

very fully and well. Mr. Mather, the President, had pray^d with her in the time of the Courts sitting. Decr. 22. being Catechising day, I give Mr. Willard a note to pray for my daughter publickly, which he did. Note, this morn Madam Elisa Bellingham came to our house and upbraided me with setting my hand to pass Mr. Wharton's acc^o to the Court, where he obtain'd a Judgm^t for Eustace's farm. I was wheadled and hector'd into that business, and have all along been uneasy in the remembrance of it: and now there is one come who will not spare to lay load. The Lord take away my filthy garments, and give me change of Rayment. This day I remove poor little Sarah into my Bed-chamber, where about Break of Day Decr. 23. she gives up the Ghost in Nurse Cowell's Arms. Born, Nov. 21. 1694. Neither I nor my wife were by: Nurse not expecting so sudden a change, and having promis'd to call us. I thought of Christ's Words, could you not watch with me one hour ! and would fain have sat up with her: but fear of my wives illness, who is very valetudinarious, made me to lodge with her in the new Hall, where was call'd by Jane's Cry, to take notice of my dead daughter. Nurse did long and pathetically ask our pardon that she had not call'd us, and said she was surpriz^d. Thus this very day is rendered fowl to us by reason of the general Sorrow and Tears in the family. Master Chiever was here, the evening before, I desir'd him to pray for my daughter. The Chapt^r read in course on Decr 23. m. was Deut. 22. which made me sadly reflect that I had not been so thorowly tender of my daughter; nor so effectually carefull of her Defence and preservation as I should have been. The good Lord pity and pardon and help for the future as to those God has still left me.

Decr 24. Sam. recites to me in Latin, Mat. 12. from the 6th to the end of the 12th v. The 7th verse did awfully bring to mind the Salem [witchcraft] Tragedie.*

6th day, Decr 25, 1696. We bury our little daughter. In the chamber, Joseph in course reads Ecclesiastes 3^d a time to be born and a time to die — Elisabeth, Rev. 22. Hanah, the 38th Psalm. I speak to each, as God helped, to our mutual comfort I hope. I order'd Sam. to read the 102. Psalm. Elisha Cooke, Edw. Hutchinson, John Bailey, and Josia Willard bear my little daughter to the Tomb.

Note. Twas wholly dry, and I went at noon to see in what order things were set; and there I was entertain'd with a view of, and converse with, the Coffins of my dear Father Hull, Mother Hull, Cousin Quinsey, and my Six Children: for the little posthumous was now took up and set in upon that that stands on John's: so are three, one

* "If ye had known what this meaneth, I will have mercy and not sacrifice, ye would not have condemned the guiltless."

upon another twice, on the bench at the end. My Mother ly's on a lower bench, at the end, with head to her Husband's head: and I order'd little Sarah to be set on her Grandmother's feet. 'Twas an awfull yet pleasing Treat; Having said, The Lord knows who shall be brought hether next, I came away.

Mr. Willard pray'd with us the night before; I gave him a Ring worth about 20ˢ. Sent the President one, who is sick of the Gout. He prayᵈ with my little daughter. Mr. Oakes, the Physician, Major Townsend, Speaker, of whoes wife I was a Bearer, and was join'd with me in going to Albany and has been Civil and treated me several times. Left a Ring at Madam Cooper's for the Governour. Gave not one pair of Gloves save to the Bearers.

Octʳ 2, 1701. [In Margin — Opprobrium. Mr. Cotton Mather speaks hard words of me.] Mr. Cotton Mather came to Mr. Richard Wilkins's book shop, and there talked very sharply against me as if I had used his father worse than a Neger; spake so loud that people in the street might hear him. Then went and told Sam, That one pleaded much for Negros, and he had used his father worse than a Negro, and told him that was his Father. I had read in the morn Mr. Dod's saying; Sanctified Afflictions are good Promotions I found it now a cordial. And this caus'd me the rather to set under my Father and Mother's Epitaph, — Psal. 27. 10.*

It may be it would be arrogance for me to think that I, as one of Christ's Witnesses, am slain, or ly dead in the street.

Octʳ 9. I sent Mr. Increase Mather a Hanch of very good Venison; I hope in that I did not treat him as a Negro.

Octobʳ 22, 1701. I, with Major Walley and Capt. Samˡ Checkly, speak with Mr. Cotton Mather at Mr. Wilkins's. I expostulated with him from 1 Tim. 5.1. Rebuke not an elder. He said he had consider'd that: I told him of his book of the Law of Kindness for the Tongue, whether this were correspondent with that. Whether correspondent with Christ's Rule: He said, having spoken to me before there was no need to speak to me again; and so justified his reviling me behind my back. Charg'd the Council with Lying, Hyprocrisy, Tricks, and I know not what all [in Margin — Surreptitious]. I ask'd him if it were done with that Meekness as it should; answer'd, yes. Charg'd the Council in general, and then shew'd my share, which was my speech in Council; viz. If Mr. Mather should go to Cambridge again to reside there with a Resolution not to read the Scriptures, and expound in the Hall: I fear the example of it will do more hurt than

* "When my father and my mother forsake me, then the Lord will take me up."

his going thither will doe good. This speech I owned. Said Mr. Corwin at Reading, upbraided him, saying, This is the man you dedicat your books to ! I ask'd him if I should suppose he had done some thing amiss in his Church as an Officer; whether it would be well for me to explain against him in the street for it. (Mr. Wilkins would fain have had him gon into the inner room, but he would not.) I told him I conceiv'd he had done much unbecoming a Minister of the Gospel, and being call'd by Maxwell to the Council, Major Wally and I went thither, leaving Capt. Checkly there. 2 Tim. 2. 24. 25. Went to the Council, Sign'd Mr. Mather's order for £25. Hammer'd out an Order for a Day of Thanksgiving.

Thorsday, Octr 23. Mr. Increase Mather said at Mr. Wilkins's, If I am a Servant of Jesus Christ, some great Judgment will fall on Capt. Sewall, or his family.

Octr 24. Rainy Day, yet Judge Atwood comes from Rehoboth to Boston. 25. Visits several, and me among the rest. This day in the morn. I got Mr. Moody to copy out my Speech, and gave it to Mr. Wilkins that all might see what was the ground of Mr. Mather's Anger.

Writ out another and gave it to Joshua Gee. I perceive Mr. Wilkins carried his to Mr. Mathers; They seem to grow calm. (On Friday received Mr. Fitch's Letter and Blessing.) Receive the News of Sister Sewall's being brought to Bed of a Son, which is the Sixth; and the fifteenth Child. Messenger came in when Judge Atwood here. Son Hirst comes to Town. Was in danger to be cast away coming over the Ferry, the wind was so very high.

◇◆◇◆◇◆◇◆◇◆◇◆◇

[*Jonathan Edwards, Northampton, Mass.*]

The people of Hampshire county in general, I suppose, are as sober, and orderly, and good sort of people, as in any part of New England; and I believe they have been preserved the freest by far, of any part of the country from error and variety of sects and opinions. Our being so far within the land, at a distance from sea-ports, and in a corner of the country, has doubtless been one reason why we have not been so much corrupted with vice, as most other parts. But without question, the religion and good order of the country, and their purity in doctrine, has, under God, been very much owing to the great abilities, and eminent piety, of my venerable and honored grandfather Stoddard. I suppose we have been the freest of any part of the land, from unhappy divisions and quarrels, in our

NORTHAMPTON, MASSACHUSETTS

ecclesiastical and religious affairs, till the late lamentable Spring-field contention.

We being much separated from other parts of the province, and having comparatively but little intercourse with them, have from the beginning, till now, always managed our ecclesiastical affairs with ourselves; it is the way in which the country, from its infancy, has gone on by the practical agreement of all, and the way in which our peace and good order has hitherto been maintained.

The town of Northampton is of about eighty-two years standing, and has now about two hundred families; which mostly dwell more compactly together than any town of such a bigness in these parts of the country; which probably has been an occasion that both our corruptions and reformations have been, from time to time, the more swiftly propagated, from one to another, through the town. Take the town in general, and so far as I can judge, they are as rational and understanding a people as most I have been acquainted with: Many of them have been noted for religion, and particularly, have been remarkable for their distinct knowledge in things that relate to heart religion, and Christian experience, and their great regards thereto.

I am the third minister that has been settled in the town: The Reverend Mr. Eleazer Mather, who was the first, was ordained in July 1669. He was one whose heart was much in his work, abundant in labors for the good of precious souls; he had the high esteem and great love of his people, and was blessed with no small success. The Rev. Mr. [Solomon] Stoddard who succeded him, came first to the town the November after his death, but was not ordained till September 11, 1672, and died February 11, 1728–9. So that he continued in the work of the ministry here from his first coming to town, near sixty years. And as he was eminent and renowned for his gifts and grace, so he was blessed, from the beginning, with extraordinary success in his ministry, in the conversion of many souls. He had five harvests as he called them: The first was about fifty-seven years ago; the second about fifty-three years; the third about forty; the fourth about twenty-four; the fifth and last about eighteen years ago. Some of these times were much more remarkable than others, and the ingathering of souls more plentiful. Those that were about fifty-three, and forty, and twenty-four years ago, were much greater than either the first or the last; but in each of them, I have heard my grandfather say, the greater part of the young people in the town seemed to be mainly concerned for their eternal salvation.

After the last of these, came a far more degenerate time, (at least among young people) I suppose, than ever before. Mr. Stoddard, indeed, had the comfort before he died, of seeing a time when there was no small appearance of a divine work amongst some, and a considerable ingathering of souls, even after I was settled with him in the ministry, which was about two years before his death; and I have reason to bless God for the great advantage I had by it. In these two years, there were near twenty that Mr. Stoddard hoped to be savingly converted; but there was nothing of any general awakening. The greater part seemed to be at that time very insensible of the things of religion, and engaged in other cares and pursuits. Just after my grandfather's death, it seemed to be a time of extraordinary dullness in religion: Licentiousness for some years greatly prevailed among the youth of the town; they were many of them very much addicted to night walking, and frequenting the tavern, and lewd practices, wherein some by their example exceedingly corrupted others. It was their manner very frequently to get together in conventions of both sexes, for mirth and jollity, which they called frolicks; and they would often spend the greater part of the night in them, without any regard to order in the families they belonged to: And indeed family government did too much fail in the town. It had become very customary with many of our young people to be indecent in their carriage at meeting, which doubtless would not have prevailed to such a degree, had it not been that my grandfather, through his great age, (though he retained his powers surprisingly to the last) was not so able to observe them. There had also long prevailed in the town, a spirit of contention between two parties, into which they had for many years been divided, by which was maintained a jealousy one of the other, and they were prepared to oppose one another in all public affairs.

But in two or three years after Mr. Stoddard's death, there began to be a sensible amendment of these evils; the young people shewed more of a disposition to hearken to counsel, and by degrees left off their frolicking, and grew observably more decent in their attendance on the public worship, and there were more that manifested a religious concern than there used to be.

At the latter end of the year 1733, there appeared a very unusual flexibleness, and yielding to advice, in our young people. It had been too long their manner to make the evening after the sabbath, and after our public lecture, to be especially the times of their mirth, and company keeping. But a sermon was now preached on the sabbath before the lecture, to shew the evil tendency of the practice, and to persuade them to reform it; and it was urged on heads of families, that it should be a thing agreed upon among

them, to govern their families, and keep their children at home, at
these times; — and withal it was more privately moved, that they
should meet together the next day, in their several neighborhoods,
to know each other's minds; which was accordingly done, and the
motion complied with throughout the town. But parents found
little or no occasion for the exercise of government in the case; the
young people declared themselves convinced by what they had
heard from the pulpit, and were willing of themselves to comply
with the counsel that had been given. And it was immediately, and,
I suppose, almost universally complied with; and there was a thorough reformation of these disorders thence-forward, which has continued ever since.

Presently after this, there began to appear a remarkable religious
concern at a little village belonging to the congregation, called Pas-
commuck, where a few families were settled, at about three miles
distance from the main body of the town. At this place a number of
persons seemed to be savingly wrought upon. In the April following, Anno 1734, there happened a very sudden and awful death of a
young man in the bloom of his youth; who being violently seized
with a pleurisy, and taken immediately very delirious, died in
about two days; which (together with what was preached publicly
on that occasion,) much affected many young people. This was followed with another death of a young married woman, who had
been considerably exercised in mind, about the salvation of her
soul, before she was ill, and was in great distress in the beginnings
of her illness, but seemed to have satisfying evidences of God's saving mercy to her, before her death; so that she died very full of
comfort, in a most earnest and moving manner, warning and coun-
selling others. This seemed much to contribute to the solemnizing
of the spirits of many young persons; and there began evidently to
appear more of a religious concern on people's minds.

In the fall of the year, I proposed it to the young people, that
they should agree among themselves to spend the evenings after lectures, in social religion, and to that end to divide themselves into
several companies to meet in various parts of the town; which was
accordingly done, and those meetings have been since continued,
and the example imitated by elder people. This was followed with
the death of an elderly person, which was attended with many unusual circumstances, by which many were much moved and affected.

About this time began the great noise that was in this part of the
country, about Arminianism, which seemed to appear with a very
threatening aspect upon the interest of religion here. The friends of
vital piety trembled for fear of the issue; but it seemed, contrary to

their fear, strongly to be overruled for the promoting of religion. Many who looked on themselves as in a Christless condition, seemed to be awakened by it, with fear that God was about to withdraw from the land, and that we should be given up to heterodoxy, and corrupt principles; and then their opportunity for obtaining salvation would be past; and many who were brought a little to doubt about the truth of the doctrines they had hitherto been taught, seemed to have a kind of a trembling fear with their doubts, lest they should be led into by-paths, to their eternal undoing: And they seemed with much concern and engagedness of mind to inquire what was indeed the way in which they must come to be accepted with God. There were then some things said publicly on that occasion, concerning justification by faith alone.

It was in the latter part of December that the spirit of God began extraordinarily to set in, and wonderfully to work amongst us; and there were, very suddenly, one after another, five or six persons who were, to all appearance, savingly converted, and some of them wrought upon in a very remarkable manner.

Though the work was glorious, yet I was filled with concern about the effect it might have upon others. I was ready to conclude (though too rashly) that some would be hardened by it, in carelessness and looseness of life, and would take occasion from it to open their mouths, in reproaches of religion. But the event was the reverse, to a wonderful degree. God made it, I suppose, the greatest occasion of awakening to others, of any thing that ever came to pass in the town. I have had abundant opportunity to know the effect it had, by my private conversation with many. The news of it seemed to be almost like a flash of lightning upon the hearts of young people, all over the town, and upon many others. Those persons amongst us, who used to be farthest from seriousness, and that I most feared would make an ill improvement of it, seemed greatly to be awakened with it; many went to talk with her concerning what she had met with; and what appeared in her seemed to be to the satisfaction of all that did so.

Presently upon this, a great and earnest concern about the great things of religion, and the eternal world became universal in all parts of the town, and among persons of all degrees, and all ages; the noise amongst the dry bones waxed louder and louder. All other talk but about spiritual and eternal things was soon thrown by; all the conversation in all companies, and upon all occasions, was upon these things only, unless so much as was necessary for people carrying on their ordinary secular business. Other discourse than of the things of religion, would scarcely be tolerated in any company. The minds of people were wonderfully taken off from the world; it was treated amongst us as a thing of very little consequence. They seemed to follow their worldly business, more as a part of their duty, than from any disposition they had to it; the temptation now seemed to lie on that hand, to neglect worldly affairs too much, and to spend too much time in the immediate exercise of religion; which thing was exceedingly misrepresented by reports that were spread in distant parts of the land, as though the people here had wholly thrown by all worldly business, and betook themselves entirely to reading and praying, and such like religious exercises.

It then was a dreadful thing amongst us to lie out of Christ, in danger every day of dropping into hell; and what persons' minds were intent upon was to escape for their lives, and to *fly from the wrath to come.* All would eagerly lay hold of opportunities for their souls, and were wont very often to meet together in private houses for religious purposes; and such meetings, when appointed, were wont greatly to be thronged.

This work of God, as it was carried on, and the number of true saints multiplied, soon made a glorious alteration in the town; so that in the spring and summer following, Anno 1735, the town seemed to be full of the presence of God. It never was so full of love, nor so full of joy; and yet so full of distress as it was then. There were remarkable tokens of God's presence in almost every house. It was a time of joy in families on the account of salvation's being brought unto them; parents rejoicing over their children as new born, and husbands over their wives, and wives over their husbands. *The doings of God were then seen in his sanctuary, God's day was a delight, and his tabernacles were amiable.* Our public assemblies were then beautiful; the congregation was alive in God's service, every one earnestly intent on the public worship, every hearer eager to drink in the words of the minister as they came from his mouth; the assembly in general were, from time to time in tears, while the word was preached; some weeping with sorrow and distress, others with joy and love, others with pity and concern for the souls of their neighbors.

Our congregation excelled all that ever I knew in the external part of the duty before, the men generally carrying regularly and well, three parts of music, and the women a part by themselves: But now they were evidently wont to sing with unusual elevation of heart and voice, which made the duty pleasant indeed.

When this work of God first appeared, and was so extraordinarily carried on amongst us in the winter, others round about us seemed not to know what to make of it; and there were many that scoffed at, and ridiculed it; and some compared what we called conversion to certain distempers. Strangers were generally surprised to find things so much beyond what they had heard, and were wont to tell others that the state of the town could not be conceived of by those that had not seen it. And those that came from the neighborhood to our public lectures, were for the most part remarkably affected. Many that came to town on one occasion or other, had their consciences smitten, and awakened, and went home with wounded hearts, and with those impressions that never wore off till they had hopefully a saving issue; and those that before had serious thoughts, had their awakenings, and convictions greatly increased.

In the month of March, the people in South Hadley began to be seized with deep concern about the things of religion; which very soon became universal; and the work of God has been very wonderful there; not much, if anything, short of what it has been here, in proportion to the size of the place. About the same time it began to break forth in the west part of Suffield, (where it has also been very great) and it soon spread into all parts of the town. It next appeared at Sunderland, and soon over-spread the town; and I believe was for a season, not less remarkable than it was here. About the same time it began to appear in a part of Deerfield, called Green River, and afterwards filled the town, and there has been a glorious work there. It began also to be manifest in the south part of Hatfield, in a place called the Hill; and after that the whole town, in the second week in April, seemed to be seized, as it were at once, with concern about the things of religion; and the work of God has been great there. There has been also a very general awakening at West Springfield, and Long Meadow; and in Enfield there was, for a time, a pretty general concern amongst some that before had been very loose persons. About the same time that this appeared at Enfield, the Rev. Mr. Bull of Westfield, informed me that there had been a great alteration there, and that more had been done in one week there than in seven years before. — Something of this work likewise appeared in the first precinct in Springfield, principally in the north and south extremes of the parish. And in Hadley old town, there gradually appeared so much of a work of God on souls, as at another time would have been thought worthy of much notice. For a short time there was also a very great and general concern, of the like nature, at Northfield. And wherever this concern appeared, it seemed not to be in vain; but in every place God brought saving blessings with him, and his word attended with his spirit (as we have all reason to think) returned not void. It might well be said at that time in all parts of the country, *Who are these that fly as a cloud, and as doves to their windows?*

This remarkable pouring out of the spirit of God, which thus extended from one end to the other of this country, was not confined to it, but many places in Connecticut have partook in the same mercy. As for instance the first parish in Windsor, under the pastoral care of the Rev. Mr. Marsh, was thus blest about the same time, as we in Northampton, while we had no knowledge of each other's circumstances. There has been a very great ingathering of souls to Christ in that place, and something considerable of the same work began afterwards in East Windsor, my honored father's parish, which has in times past, been a place favored with mercies of this nature, above any on this western side of New England, excepting Northampton; there having been four or five seasons of the pouring out of the spirit to the general awakening of the people there, since my father's settlement amongst them.

There was also the last spring and summer a wonderful work of God carried on at Coventry, under the ministry of the Rev. Mr. Meacham. I had opportunity to converse with some of the Coventry people, who gave me a very remarkable account of the surprising change that appeared in the most rude and vicious persons there. The like was also very great at the same time in a part of Lebanon, called the Crank, where the Rev. Mr. Wheelock,* a young gentleman, is lately settled. And there has been much of the same at Durham, under the ministry of the Rev. Mr. Chauncey; and to appearance, no small ingathering of souls there. And likewise amongst many of the young people in the first precinct in Stratford, under the ministry of the Rev. Mr. Gould, where the work was much promoted by the remarkable conversion of a young woman that had been a great company keeper, as it was here.

Something of this work appeared in several other towns in those parts, as I was informed when I was there the last fall. And we have since been acquainted with something very remarkable of this nature at another parish in Stratford, called Ripton, under the pastoral care of the Rev. Mr. Mills. And there was a considerable revival of religion last summer at New Haven old town, as I was once and again informed by the Rev. Mr. Noyes, the minister there, and by others; and by a letter which I very lately received from Mr. Noyes, and also by information we have had otherwise. This flourishing of religion still continues, and has lately much increased: Mr. Noyes writes, that many this summer have been added to the

* Eleazar Wheelock, who transplanted Dartmouth College to Hanover, N. H. B. M.

church, and particularly mentions several young persons that belong to the principal families of that town.

There has been a degree of the same work at a part of Guilford; and very considerable at Mansfield, under the ministry of the Rev. Mr. Eleazar Williams; and an unusual religious concern at Tolland; and something of it at Hebron, and Bolton. There was also

CONGREGATIONAL CHURCH, LEBANON, CONNECTICUT

no small effusion of the spirit of God in the north parish in Preston in the eastern part of Connecticut, which I was informed of, and saw something of it when I was the last autumn at the house, and in the congregation of the Rev. Mr. Lord, the minister there, who, with the Rev. Mr. Owen of Groton, came up hither in May, the last year, on purpose to see the work of God here. Mr. Lord told me, that when he got home, he informed his congregation of what he had seen, and that they were greatly affected with it, and that it proved the beginning of the same work amongst them, which prevailed till there was a general awakening, and many instances of persons, who seemed to be remarkably converted. I also have lately heard that there has been something of the same work at Woodbury.

This dispensation has also appeared extraordinary in the numbers of those on whom we have reason to hope it has had a saving effect. We have about six hundred and twenty communicants which include almost all our adult persons. The church was very large before; but persons never thronged into it as they did in the late extraordinary time. Our sacraments were eight weeks asunder; and

I received into our communion about an hundred before one sacrament, and four-score of them at one time, whose appearance, when they presented themselves together to make an open explicit profession of Christianity, was very affecting to the congregation. I took in near sixty before the next sacrament day; and I had very sufficient evidence of the conversion of their souls, through divine grace, though it is not the custom here, as it is in many other churches in this country, to make a credible relation of their inward experiences the ground of admission to the Lord's Supper.

I am far from pretending to be able to determine how many have lately been the subjects of such mercy; but if I may be allowed to declare any thing that appears to me probable in a thing of this nature, I hope that more than three hundred souls were savingly brought home to Christ in this town, in the space of half a year, (how many more I don't guess) and about the same number of males as females; which, by what I have heard Mr. Stoddard say, was far from what has been usual in years past, for he observed that in his time, many more women were converted than men. And I hope that by far the greater part of persons in this town, above sixteen years of age, are such as have the saving knowledge of Jesus Christ; and so by what I have heard, I suppose it is in some other places, particularly at Sunderland and South Hadley.

This has also appeared to be a very extraordinary dispensation, in that the spirit of God has so much extended not only his awakening, but regenerating influences, both to elderly persons, and also those that are very young. It has been a thing heretofore rarely heard of, that any were converted past middle age; but now we have the same ground to think that many such have in this time been savingly changed, as that others have been so in more early years. I suppose there were upwards of fifty persons in this town above forty years of age; and more than twenty of them above fifty, and about ten of them above sixty, and two of them above seventy years of age.

It has heretofore been looked on as a strange thing, when any have seemed to be savingly wrought upon, and remarkably changed in their childhood; but now, I suppose, near thirty were to appearance so wrought upon between ten and fourteen years of age, and two between nine and ten, and one of them about four years of age. The influences of God's spirit have also been very remarkable on children in some other places, particularly at Sunderland and South Hadley, and the west part of Suffield. There are several families in this town that are all hopefully pious; yea, there are several numerous families, in which, I think, we have reason to hope that all the children are truly godly, and most of them lately become so. And there are very few houses in the whole town into which salvation has not lately come, in one or more instances. There are several negroes, that from what was seen in them then, and what is discernible in them since, appear to have been truly born again in the late remarkable season.

The work of God's spirit seemed to be at its greatest height in this town, in the former part of the spring, in March and April; so far as I, by looking back, can judge from the particular acquaintance I have had with souls in this work, it appears to me probable, to have been at the rate, at least, of four persons in a day, or near thirty in a week, take one with another, for five or six weeks together. When God in so remarkable a manner took the work into his own hands, there was as much done in a day or two, as at ordinary times is done in a year.

❖❖❖❖❖❖❖❖❖❖❖❖❖

[*Lorenzo Dow, Coventry, Conn.* *]

I thought I heard the voice of God's justice saying, "take the unprofitable servant, and cast him into utter darkness." I put my hands together, and cried in my heart, the time has been, that I might have had religion; but now it is too late; mercy's gate is shut against me, and my condemnation for ever sealed: — Lord, I give up; I submit; I yield; I yield; if there be mercy in heaven for me, let me know it; and if not, let me go down to hell and know the worst of my case. As these words flowed from my heart, I saw the Mediator step in, as it were, between the Father's justice and my soul, and those words were applied to my mind with great power; "Son! thy sins which are many, are forgiven thee; thy faith hath saved thee; go in peace."

The burden of sin and guilt and the fear of hell vanished from my mind, as perceptibly as an hundred pounds weight falling from a man's shoulder; my soul flowed out in love to God, to his ways and to his people; yea, and to ALL mankind.

October 20th, 1796. Satan pursues me from place to place: oh! how can people dispute there being a devil! If they underwent as much as I do with his buffetings, they would dispute it no more. He throwing in his fiery darts, my mind is harrassed like punching the body with forks and clubs. Oh! that my Savior would appear and

* Described on a later page by S. G. Goodrich.

sanctify my soul, and deliver me from all within that is contrary to purity.

23d. I spoke in Hardwick to about four hundred people, thence to Petersham and Wenchendon, to Fitchburgh, and likewise to No-town, where God gave me one spiritual child. — Thence to Ashburnham, where we had some powerful times.

November 1st. I preached in Ringe, and a powerful work of God broke out shortly after, though some opposition attended it; but it was very solemn.

Some here I trust will bless God in the day of eternity, that ever they saw my face in this vale of tears.

In my happiest moments I feel something that wants to be done away: oh! the buffetings of satan! if I never had any other hell, it would be enough.

December 15th, I rode fifteen miles to Brattleborough. About this time, on my way, I took a severe cold on my lungs, and almost lost my voice. The next day my friends advised me not to go to any other appointments, as they thought it presumption; but I feeling impressed on my mind, could not feel content to disappoint the people. Accordingly, in the name of God, I set out in the hard snow storm, and over the mountains, about ten miles, and a solemn time we had. The storm still continuing to increase, the snow had now fallen about knee high, so that the mountains were almost impassable by reason of snow, steepness, mud and logs; the people here thought my life would be endangered by the falling of trees, or the extreme cold in the woods, as there was no house for several miles, and the wind blew exceeding hard: however, out I set, relying upon the strong for strength. The snow being driven in banks more than belly deep, I frequently was obliged to alight and stamp a path for my horse; and though I was much wearied and chilled, yet by the goodness of God, I arrived at my appointment, fourteen miles.

◇◇◇◇◇◇◇◇◇◇◇◇◇

[*Josiah Quincy, Quincy, Mass.*]

The meeting-house in Quincy, so associated with John Adams, may be worth a brief description. I have no distinct remembrance of the building previous to its enlargement, in 1806, but have heard its appearance previous to that date often described by Mr. Adams and by members of my own family. It was built in 1731, and, according to our present ideas, was queer and comfortless. The body of the house was occupied by long seats, the men being placed on one side of the broad aisle and the women on the other. The oldest inhabitants were always seated in front. "I never shall forget," Mr. Adams once said to me, "the rows of venerable heads ranged along those front benches which as a young fellow, I used to gaze upon. They were as old and gray as mine is now."

The deacons were accommodated just under the pulpit, while the sexton had a bench in the rear, perhaps to keep a watch over the young people on the back seats. One of the oddest things about the church was a little hole high up in the wall, through which the bell ringer might be seen in the exercise of his vocation. It was the duty of this functionary to keep his eye upon the congregation, and to mark by the customary tolling the arrival of the minister. As time wore on, some wall pews began to appear in the old meeting-house. These were built by individuals, at their own expense, permission having been first gained by a vote of the town. And there are curious votes upon this subject in the early records. On one occasion it was voted that a prominent personage might "build him a pew over the pulpit, provided he so builds as not to darken the pulpit." And a friend of mine here suggests that, as a figure of speech, pews may now be said to be built over the pulpit with some frequency, and regrets that the good divines of the town, whose lifelong sway was arbitrary and unquestioned, did not have the wit to prevent that perilous permission. For, notwithstanding the wholesome caution of the old record, it has been found impossible "not to darken the pulpit" when the pews are placed above it.

An ancestor of mine was permitted to fence off the first pew, and his example was quickly followed by others. This was a recognition of caste in the one place where men should meet on terms of perfect equality. I cannot but think that this innovation upon the good custom of our fore-fathers has had its effect in alienating from religious services a large portion of our population. A notable addition to the Sunday exercises in the Quincy meeting-house followed the introduction of the pews; for the seats in these aristocratic pens were upon hinges, and were always raised during the long prayer, for the purpose of allowing those who stood to rest themselves by leaning against the railing. At the conclusion of the devotion, the sudden descent of all the seats sounded like a volley of musketry, and was a source of considerable terror to those who heard it for the first time. When the increase of population rendered desirable an enlargement of the meeting-house, it was sawed through the middle; and, the two halves being separated, an addition was built to reunite them. The President's pew was conspicuous in the reconstructed edifice, and there the old man was to be seen at every service. An air of respectful deference to John Adams seemed to pervade the building. The ministers brought their best sermons when they came to exchange and had a certain consciousness in their manner as if officiating before royalty. The medley of stringed and wind instruments in the gallery — a survival of the sacred trumpets and shawns mentioned by King David — seemed to the imagination of a child to be making discord together in honor of the venerable chief who was the center of interest.

PLYMOUTH, CONNECTICUT

[*Lyman Beecher, Litchfield, Conn.*]

Soon after my arrival at Litchfield I was called to attend the ordination at Plymouth [Conn.] of Mr. Heart, ever after that my very special friend. I loved him as he did me. He said to me one day, "Beecher, if you had made the least effort to govern us young men, you would have had a swarm of bees about you; but, as you have come and mixed among us, you can do with us what you will."

Well, at the ordination at Plymouth, the preparation for our creature comforts, in the sitting-room of Mr. Heart's house, besides food, was a broad sideboard covered with decanters and bottles, and sugar, and pitchers of water. There we found all the various kinds of liquors then in vogue. The drinking was apparently universal. This preparation was made by the society as a matter of course. When the Consocation arrived, they always took something to drink round; also before public services, and always on their return.

As they could not all drink at once, they were obliged to stand and wait as people do when they go to mill.

There was a decanter of spirits also on the dinner-table, to help digestion, and gentlemen partook of it through the afternoon and evening as they felt the need, some more and some less; and the sideboard, with the spillings of water, and sugar, and liquor, looked and smelled like the bar of a very active grog-shop. None of the

GOSHEN, CONNECTICUT

Consociation were drunk; but that there was not, at times, a considerable amount of exhilaration, I can not affirm.

When they had all done drinking, and had taken pipes and tobacco, in less than fifteen minutes there was such a smoke you couldn't see. And the noise I can not describe; it was a maximum of hilarity. They told their stories, and were at the height of jocose talk. They were not old-fashioned Puritans. They had been run down. Great deal of spirituality on Sabbath, and not much when they got where there was something good to drink.

I think I recollect some animadversions were made at that time by the people on the amount of liquor drank, for the tide was swelling in the drinking habits of society.

The next ordination was of Mr. Harvey, in Goshen, and there was the same preparation, and the same scenes acted over, and then afterward still louder murmurs from the society at the quantity and expense of liquor consumed.

These two meetings were near together, and in both my alarm, and shame, and indignation were intense. 'Twas that that woke me up for the war. And silently I took an oath before God that I would never attend another ordination of that kind. I was full. My heart kindles up at the thought of it now.

There had been already so much alarm on the subject, that at the General Association at Fairfield in 1811, a committee of three had been appointed to make inquiries and report measures to remedy the evil. A committee was also appointed by the General Association of Massachusetts for the same purpose that same month, and to confer with other bodies.

I was a member of General Association which met in the year following at Sharon, June 1812, when said committee reported. They said they had attended to the subject committed to their care; that intemperance had been for some time increasing in a most alarming manner; but that, after the most faithful and prayerful inquiry, they were obliged to confess they did not perceive that any thing could be done.

The blood started through my heart when I heard this, and I rose instanter, and moved that a committee of three be appointed immediately, to report at this meeting the ways and means of arresting the tide of intemperance.

The committee was named and appointed. I was chairman, and on the following day brought in a report, the most important paper that ever I wrote.

This report was thoroughly discussed and adopted, and a thousand copies ordered to be printed; and that, too, was before people had learned to do much. It was done with zeal and earnestness, such as I had never seen in a deliberative body before.

Dr. [Timothy] Dwight did indeed say — our father and our friend — that while he approved of our zeal, and appreciated the exigency that called it forth, he was not without some apprehension that in their great and laudable earnestness his young friends might transcend the sanction of public sentiment; but, with a smile peculiarly his own, and heavenly, he added, "If my young friends think it best to proceed, God forbid that I should oppose or hinder them, or withhold my suffrage."

I was not headstrong then, but I was *heartstrong* — oh very, very! I had read and studied everything on the subject I could lay hands on. We did not say a word then about wine, because we thought it was best, in this sudden onset to attack that which was most prevalent and deadly, and that it was as much as would be safe to take hold of one such dragon by the horns without tackling another; but in ourselves we resolved to inhibit wine, and in our families we generally did.

[362]

All my expectations were more than verified. The next year we reported to the Association that the effect had been most salutary. Ardent spirits were banished from ecclesiastical meetings; ministers had preached on the subject; the churches generally had approved the design; the use of spirits in families and private circles had diminished; the attention of the community had been awakened; the tide of public opinion had turned; farmers and mechanics had begun to disuse spirits; the Legislature had taken action in favor of the enterprise; a society for Reformation of Morals had been established, and ecclesiastical bodies in other states had commenced efforts against the common enemy. "The experience of one year had furnished lucid evidence that nothing was impossible to faith."

From that time the movement went on by correspondence, lectures, preaching, organization, and other means, not only in Connecticut, but marching through New England, and marching through the world.

I remember that while at New Haven we had a meeting to consult about organizing a society for the promotion of reform. We met in Judge Baldwin's office; and a number of the leading lawyers were invited to meet us, some seven or eight perhaps. We took up the subject, and discussed it thoroughly, Dr. Dwight being the chairman of the meeting, and such men as David Daggett, Judge Baldwin, Roger Minot Sherman participating.

That was a new thing in that day for the clergy and laymen to meet on the same level and co-operate. It was the first time there had ever been such a consultation between them in Connecticut in our day. The ministers had always managed things themselves, for in those days the ministers were all politicians. They had always been used to it from the beginning.

On election day they had a festival. All the clergy used to go, walk in procession, smoke pipes, and drink. And, fact is, when they got together, they would talk over who should be governor, and who lieutenant governor, and who in the Upper House, and their counsels would prevail.

Now it was part of the old "steady habits" of the state, which ought never to have been touched, that the lieutenant governor should succeed to the governorship. And it was the breaking up this custom by the civilians, against the influence of the clergy, that first shook the stability of the standing order and the Federal party in the state. Treadwell was a stiff man, and the time had come when many men did not like that sort of thing. He had been active in the enforcement of the Sabbath laws, and had brought on himself the odium of the opposing party.

[363]

Hence some of the civilians of our own party, David Daggett and others, wireworked to have him superseded, and Roger Griswold, the ablest man in Congress put in his stead. That was rank rebellion against the ministerial candidate. But Daggett controlled the whole Fairfield County bar, and Griswold was a favorite of the lawyers, and the Democrats helped them because they saw how it would work; so there was no election by the people, and Treadwell was acting Governor till 1811, when Griswold was chosen. The lawyers in talking about it, said, "We have served the clergy long enough; we must take another man, and let them take care of themselves."

I foresaw the result as it afterward came to pass. I wrote to Theodore Dwight, President Dwight's brother, a lawyer of Hartford, and told him what the effect would be; that there was a regular course, and the people were attached to it; and that if you throw over the men they revere, and whose turn it is, they will be disgusted; there will be a reaction, and by-and-by you yourselves will be set aside. It is laughable, the fulfillment a few years after just as I predicted. The Democrats came and took them house and lot, slung them out as from a sling. They turned out not only the deacon justices, but the lawyer justices too, and they never got it again; whereas the ministers and churches, by the voluntary system, recovered, and stood better than before.

It was the anticipation of the impending revolution and downfall of the standing order that impelled me to the efforts I made at that time to avert it, and to prepare for it in all possible ways. And one was this association of the leading minds of the laity with us in counsel, and discussing matters with them. They easily fell in with our views, saw the things as we did, and threw in their influence heartily. I remember Roger Minot Sherman especially was highly pleased. "You have never before," he said, "done any thing so wisely and so well as this."

It was not very long after my return from Salem when the tide began to turn. For years we of the standing order had been the scoff and by-word of politicians, sectarians, and infidels, and had held our tongues; but now the Lord began to pour out his Spirit.

Brother Hawkes, then recently settled at Hartford, sent two of his deacons to ask me to come and help him in a revival. I remember, when I saw them and heard their errand, I turned round and said, "Now, wife, it is my turn. Now I will speak." I went to Hartford, and the Spirit of God was there. I spent about three weeks in the work. Preached all the while; it was a powerful revival. I was gone two Sabbaths, getting home on Saturday.

Revivals now began to pervade the state. The ministers were united, and had been consulting and praying. Political revolution had cut them off from former sources of support, and caused them to look to God. Then there came such a time of revival as never before in the state.

I remember how we all used to feel before the revolution happened. Our people thought they should be destroyed if the law should be taken away from under them. They did not think any thing about God — did not seem to. And the fact is, we all felt our children would scatter like partridges if the tax law was lost. We saw it coming. In Goshen they raised a fund. In Litchfield the people bid off the pews, and so it has been ever since.

But the effect, when it did come, was just the reverse of the expectation. When the storm burst upon us, indeed, we thought we were dead for a while. But we found we were not dead. Our fears had magnified the danger. We were thrown on God and on ourselves, and this created that moral coercion which makes men work. Before we had been standing on what our fathers had done, but now we were obliged to develop all our energy.

On the other hand, the other denominations lost all the advantage they had had before, so that the very thing in which the enemy said, "Raze it — raze it to the foundations," laid the corner-stone of our prosperity to all generations. The law compelling every man to pay somewhere was repealed. The consequence unexpectedly was, first, that the occasion of animosity between us and the minor sects was removed, and infidels could no more make capital with them against us, and they then began themselves to feel the dangers of infidelity, and to react against it, and this laid the basis of co-operation and union of spirit.

And, besides, the tax law had for more than twenty years really worked to weaken us and strengthen them. All the stones that shelled off and rolled down from our eminence lodged in their swamp. Whenever a man grew disaffected, he went off and paid his rates with the minor sects; but on the repeal of the law there was no such temptation.

Take this revolution through, it was one of the most desperate battles ever fought in the United States. It was the last struggle of the separation of Church and State.

[*Stephen Burroughs, Hanover, N. H.*]

Weary with life, I returned to my father's, made some small arrangements, and left the country. One pistareen was all the ready cash I had on hand, and the suddenness with which I departed, deprived me of a chance to raise more. Travelling on leisurely, I had time for reflection. Well, said I, again an outcast among mankind ? Where am I going ? What can I do with myself in this world, where I meet with nothing but disappointment and chagrin ? True it is, I am an outcast, but who cares for that ? If I will not use the means for my own preservation and prosperity, what am I to expect ?

Business of some kind I must enter into, and that immediately, in order to answer the present calls of nature. And what can that be ? said I; have not I enumerated all the callings, which are profitable for me to attend to ? I might possibly write in an office, or tend in a store, on wages, had I any person to recommend or introduce me into that business. But what can now be done ? A stranger — moneyless — and friendless. There is one thing, said contrivance, which you may do; and it will answer your purpose; preach ! Preach ? What a pretty fellow am I for a preacher ! A pretty character mine, to tickle the ears of a grave audience ! Run away from my own home for being connected in robbing a bee house, and for my attention to a married woman; having been through scenes of tumult, during my whole career, since I have exhibited on the active stage of life. Besides all this, what an appearance should I make in my present dress ? which consisted of a light grey coat, with silver-plated buttons, green vest, and red breeches. This, said I, is a curious dress for me to offer myself in, as a preacher; and I am by no means able to obtain a different suit.

At any rate, it is best to see what can be done; therefore, in order to obviate the first difficulty, viz. of disagreeable reports following you, it will be necessary to prevent, as much as possible, your being known, where you offer yourself to preach; and in order to prevent that you must change your name. This being done, you must go some distance, where you are not personally known; and the probability is, that you can continue in such business, till some opportunity may offer for your entering into other employment. As for your dress you cannot alter that at present, and therefore, you must make the best of it you can.

I exchanged my horse for another, much worse, and received three dollars for the difference. This furnished me with money for my immediate expenses in travelling. I pursued my course down Connecticut river about one hundred and fifty miles, judging that by this time, I was far enough from home to remain unknown. I concluded to begin my operations. Hearing of a place called Ludlow, not far distant, where they were destitute of a clergyman, I bent my course that way, it being Saturday, and intended to preach the next day, if I proved successful. I arrived about noon, and put up at the house of one Fuller, whom I found to be a leading man in their religious society. I introduced myself to him as a clergyman, and he gave me an invitation to spend the sabbath with them and preach. You will readily conclude that I did not refuse this invitation. The greatest obstacle was now surmounted, as I conceived, viewing myself as fairly introduced into the ministerial function. I had engaged to preach on the morrow. I had almost forgotten to tell you that my name here was Davis. People had been notified that a sermon would be delivered. This business I never had attempted. It is true, the study of divinity had come under my attention, together with every other subject of common concern, in a cursory manner. I concluded that sermonizing would not be so difficult as the other exercises of public worship. Many disagreeable possibilities arose into view. What, said I, would be my feelings, should I make some egregious blunder in travelling this unbeaten road? I once concluded to get up, take my horse privately out of the stable and depart, rather than run the risk of the dangers which were before me. But upon more mature reflection, I found the hard hand of necessity compelled me to stay. When I awoke the next morning, my heart beat with anxious palpitation for the issue of the day. I considered this as the most important scene of my life — that in a great measure, my future happiness or wretchedness depended on my conduct through this day. The time for assembling approached! I saw people began to come together. My feelings were all in arms against me, my heart would almost leap into my mouth.

Why, said I, am I thus perturbed with these whimsical feelings? I know my dress is against me, and will cause some speculation; but I cannot help it, and why need I afflict myself with disagreeables before they arrive? I fortified my countenance with all my resolution, and set out with my bible and psalm book under my arm, those being the only insignia of a clergyman about me. When I made my appearance, I found a stare of universal surprise at my gay dress, which suited better the character of a beau than a clergyman. My eyes I could not persuade myself to raise from the ground till I had ascended the pulpit. I was doubtful whether I had the command of my voice, or even whether I had any voice. I sat a few minutes, collecting my resolution for the effort of beginning; I made the attempt — I found my voice at command — my anxiety was

[367]

hushed in a moment, my perturbation subsided, and I felt all the serenity of a calm summer's morning. I went through the exercises of the forenoon without any difficulty. No monarch, when seated on the throne, had more sensible feelings of prosperity, than what I experienced at this time.

I attended on the afternoon's exercises without any singular occurrence. The meeting being dismissed, and the people retired, I was informed by my landlord, that they did not agree to hire me any longer; accordingly, I found my business here at an end.

I was advised by Mr. Fuller, to make application to Mr. Baldwin, minister of Palmer, about twenty miles distant from Ludlow, for information where were vacancies, and for an introduction into those vacancies. I accordingly set out for Palmer on Monday morning, and arrived at Mr. Baldwin's about four o'clock in the afternoon. I introduced myself to him as a clergyman wanting employment. I saw he noticed my dress, but asked no questions. He examined into my education, knowledge of divinity, tenets, etc., and finding all agreeing with his ideas of orthodoxy, he concluded to recommend me to a town called Pelham, eighteen miles distant from Palmer. The next morning I set off for Pelham, with a letter to one Deacon Gray. I arrived, and delivered my letter, and was hired, in consequence of the recommendation of Mr. Baldwin, without any hesitation, for four sabbaths, five dollars a sabbath; boarding, horse-keeping, etc. etc. — I now found myself, in some measure, settled in business. The want of an immediate relief to my temporary inconveniences was now supplied. I found the family into which I had fallen, to be an agreeable, social circle, and I was much respected in the family, not only on account of my sacerdotal character, but likewise on account of the ease with which I mixed with them, in all their little social enjoyments.

Before I preceed to the relation of succeeding events, it will be necessary to give a description of the people inhabiting this town,* as much will depend on knowing their character, to rightly understand the relation of incidents which will follow.

The town of Pelham was settled with people chiefly from the north of Ireland. They were of course, strict Presbyterians. They valued themselves much on being acquainted with the nice distinctions between orthodox and heterodox principles and practice. They likewise wished to be thought shrewd in their observations on

* Pelham was also the home of Daniel Shays, leader of Shays' Rebellion. It now lays claim to the oldest meeting-house in continuous use in New England. Tiny and impoverished, the town has twice vainly tried to go out of existence by annexing itself to some neighbor. B. M.

ministers and preaching. A people generally possessing violent passions, which once disturbed, raged, uncontrolled by the dictates of reason; unpolished in their manners, possessing a jealous disposition; and either very friendly or very inimical, not knowing a medium between those two extremes. The first settled minister they had among them was one Abicrombie, from Scotland, a man of handsome abilities, but violent passions, resolute and persevering. Not many years after he was settled among them, a difficulty took place between him and the people, which was carried to considerable length, and ended in his dismission. After Mr. Abicrombie left his people, they made application to one Grayham, who at length settled among them, to their universal satisfaction; being a very handsome speaker, and otherwise possessed with popular talents as a preacher. Mr. Grayham was a man of very delicate feelings, of superior refinement, and inheriting a great desire for that peace which establishes the enjoyment of society.

After preaching a number of years to this people, he found an uneasiness prevailing among them, the chief cause of which was, his practicing upon a system of manners more refined than what was prevalent in the place; consequently, they accused him of pride, of attention to the vanities of the world; of leaving the plain path of scripture, and following after the vices of Rome. Mr. Grayham labored to convince them of their mistakes; of his wish to live with them upon the most intimate terms of equality; of his ever having it in view to pursue such measures as would, in their operation, conduce to their good and prosperity; and in that pursuit, he had expected his examples and precepts would answer a valuable purpose. His expostulations, remonstrances and entreaties were all given to the wind. The difficulties increased, and the clamor grew louder. The mind of Mr. Grayham was too delicately strung to bear those strokes of misfortune; they insensibly wore upon his constitution, till at last he fell a sacrifice to the tumult, and sought his rest in the grave.

The town of Pelham remained destitute of a minister for a considerable time. They tried a number of candidates, but not finding any with whom they could agree, no one was yet settled. At length, a Mr. Merrill came among them. He was a man possessing the gift of utterance and flow of expression, perhaps equal to any. He was an eccentric genius, and imprudent to the last degree; possessing violent passions — headstrong and impetuous. The plausible part of his character was so captivating, that the town agreed to settle him. He accordingly was installed. His imprudences soon made their appearance. Complaint was made, but they found one now who paid but little attention to their complaining. Both parties began to give way to passion. Their contention increased, and a flame was kindled which set the whole town in an uproar. Mr. Merrill refused to start from that foundation to which his legal contract entitled him; therefore, the other party determined to use extraordinary and violent measures. This attack Mr. Merrill dared not meet; therefore, he suddenly left the town. Matters were in this situation when I came to Pelham. From the information of Mr. Baldwin, and from the communications of my landlord and family, I soon gained a pretty thorough knowledge of the people whom I was amongst; and I endeavored to adapt my conduct to their genius as far as I was capable. I found myself soon able to dress in a habit fitting my calling. I soon found, likewise, that any endeavors to suit the people had not altogether failed. At the expiration of the four Sabbaths, they engaged me to preach sixteen more. I began to form an acquaintance in the neighboring towns, and with the neighboring ministers.

This happened to be a time of great mortality among women in child-bed; consequently, I was called to preach many funeral sermons in this and the neighboring towns, many of which were destitute of a clergyman of their own. I always attended this business when I had a call. This circumstance began to raise a wonder in the minds of some, how I could be prepared for preaching so constantly, and on so short notice, being as yet only nineteen years of age. I had, in reality, ten sermons with me, written by my father.

At a certain time, being suddenly called to preach a funeral sermon, I had none of my own written, proper for the occasion. I took one of my father's, and delivered it to a crowded audience. As this sermon was delivered in a private house, it was in the power of any to look into my notes. One, who had wondered at my always being prepared to preach, took this opportunity of looking over my notes, and thought they appeared too old to be lately written. The circumstance was mentioned to a number, who began to grow uneasy with apprehension of my preaching sermons not my own. Mr. Baldwin coming to Pelham about this time, they mentioned the matter to him, that he might make some enquiry into the business, and inform them. He accordingly mentioned the matter to me, in a confidential manner, and desired to see the sermon alluded to. I was sensible the handwriting of my father was so different from my own, that the first view must clearly convince any observer, that this sermon was not written by myself; I therefore told Mr. Baldwin, that the sermon was a manuscript which I had in my possession, together with some others, written by another person, and that the want of time to prepare a discourse had induced me to take this, rather than refuse to preach. Mr. Baldwin made some observations with regard to my situation; of the necessity of a great degree of prudence; and of the impropriety of using other sermons as a general thing. He returned to Palmer, without giving the men any account respecting the matter of their suspicion. Not gaining that intelligence by Mr. Baldwin which was expected, those who were uneasy, spread their suspicions among others, until there became uneasiness pretty generally through the town. They, at length, agreed to this method, viz. to send one of their number to me, on Sunday morning, previous to my going into the meetinghouse, and desire me to preach from a passage of scripture, which he should give me. I was informed of all these circumstances previous to the time of trial.

The Sunday following, I was waited on by Mr. Clark, who desired me to oblige him, by delivering a discourse from the first clause of the 5th verse of the 9th chapter of Joshua; the words were, "old shoes and clouted on their feet." I informed him I would deliver a discourse from that text, and accordingly he left me. I truly felt somewhat blanked, at the nature of the passage I had to discourse upon. However, I was determined to do the best on the subject I was capable. I endeavored to make some arrangements in my mind on the subject. I had not thought long on it, before the matter opened to my mind, in such a manner, as to give me much satisfaction. As your patience would hardly endure the repetition of a tedious sermon, I will not trouble you with it.

◇◇◇◇◇◇◇◇◇◇◇◇◇

[David L. Dodge, Connecticut]

In July, 1798, myself and wife took a journey to Hampton to visit my parents, and attended the revival in progress there. As we spent about two weeks, I will enter a little into detail, and the more readily as it was probably a fair sample of the revivals generally of that day. We passed out of Norwich in a pleasant summer day, into a part of Lisbon, and from thence into Scotland, and entered Hampton, descending into the valley of the little river, as it was called, which was thickly settled for a farming community, at about four o'clock P.M., when we discovered on our right, in an orchard of the wide spreading trees, a vast assembly for a country town. We rode abreast of the orchard, got out of our chaise, fastened our horse to the fence, and went over into the orchard. They had selected a hollow, erected a stage covered with boards, on which were a number

[371]

of chairs, (occupied by ministers), and they had also set up shingle bolts in form of a semicircle round it, one row rising, as the ground descended, above another, and stretched on boards sufficient to seat, I suppose, more than a thousand persons. We entered the outer circle in front of four ministers on the platform, one of whom was preaching. What first attracted our notice was the fixed and solemn attention of the audience to the preaching, which was searching,

addressed chiefly to the understandings and consciences of the hearers. When the speaker closed, another rose and gave a pungent exhortation and made a concluding prayer, closing with the benediction, but no one moved from his place. Another minister rose and gave a short exhortation and again dismissed the congregation, still no one retired. Then the pastor, the Rev. Ludovicus Weld, rose and said in substance, "My Christian friends, duty requires that we should all retire to our homes, as the day is far spent, and many have several miles to go," and then repeated the benediction. The congregation then began to move slowly in different ways with down cast look, and we did not notice one speaking to another. Probably, from two to three hundred lingered and began to gather round the staging. Mr. Weld exhorted them to go home and to their closets. The ministers descended from the platform, and quickly broke through the crowd, on their way to the house, the anxious following them like a flock of sheep after their shepherd. We then entered our chaise, solemnly impressed with the scene we had witnessed, and proceeded immediately to visit my parents. After the introduction of my wife, and the salutations had passed, my parents and sister related to us many interesting particulars relative to the revival; and we were gratified to see that my parents appeared to take as deep an interest in the work as those who had made a public profession of religion. One peculiar feature of the revival was, it created a universal solemnity over all the inhabitants of the town, and bore down all open opposition to the work, and engrossed the general conversation.

The sabbath following, a large congregation assembled, many from the neighboring town. The meeting house though large was filled to overflowing, two or three ministers were in the pulpit, the exercises were appropriate, and deep solemnity appeared to pervade every one. We received, after the services were closed, kind salutations from many of my old companions, who understood that we were now professors of religion, several of whom were in an interesting state of mind, and we were affectionately invited to visit them.

◇◆◇◆◇◆◇◆◇◆◇◆◇

[*Timothy Dwight*]

Marriages were formerly festivals of considerable significance in this country. It was customary to invite even the remote relations of the parties, all their particular friends, and a great number of their neighbours. A dinner was made, in form, by the parents of the bride for the bridegroom and a numerous suite. The marriage was celebrated in the evening. Cake and wine were plentifully distributed among the guests; and the festivity was concluded with dancing. At the present time the guests are usually, very few.

Justices of the Peace are throughout New England authorized to marry, but are rarely, if ever, employed to perform this service, when a clergyman can be obtained. As it is every where believed to be a Divine institution; it is considered as involved, of course, within the duties of the sacred office. An absolute decency is observed during the celebration.

At the Funerals in New-England, the friends and neighbours attend, of course. When the assembly is gathered by the ringing of the parish bell, a prayer is made at the house, in which the deceased lived, by the clergyman, and is always adapted to the occasion. The corpse is then conveyed to the grave either upon a hearse, or upon men's shoulders. In the latter case, the young men of the town always voluntarily offer their services in sufficient numbers. A solemn procession accompanies it, and to a great extent it is attended by pall-bearers. After the corpse is committed to the grave, in many places a solemn address is made by the Clergyman to the assembly, and the thanks of the surviving family are returned to those, who are present, for their attendance; and in cases, where the disease had been of long continuance, to such as have exhibited kindnesses to the sick, and mourning family. Sometimes the procession is formed anew, and accompanies the mourners to their habitation; but more frequently the company disperses. In either case an entire decorum is preserved.

At this period [French Revolution] Europe, which annually ships for our shores a vast quantity of useful merchandize, and together with it a proportional assortment of toys and mischief, consigned to these States a plentiful supply of the means of corruption. From France, Germany, and Great-Britain, the dregs of Infidelity were vomited upon us at once. From the Système de la Nature, and the Philosophical Dictionary, down to the Political Justice of Godwin, and the Age of Reason, the whole mass of pollution was emptied on this country. The two last publications, particularly, flowed in upon us as a deluge. An enormous edition of the Age of Reason was published in France, and sent over to America, to be sold for a few pence the copy; and where it could not be sold, to be given away. You may perhaps be astonished, that such men as these, the mere outcasts of creation, could do harm at all. In my apprehension they were exactly fitted for a sphere of mischief, of vast import in the empire of destruction, which perhaps no other men could have filled. Satan needs his scullions, and scavengers, as well as his nobles, and heroes. They were industrious, bold, and enterprising. They were impudent beyond example; were not destitute of imagination, and possessed a popular manner of writing. It is true, they were incapable of understanding the force of an argument, or the nature of evidence; but they were no less delighted with falsehood than better men are with truth; were equally triumphant in a victory and a defeat; and like the Lernoean snake, had a spare head for every new combatant. At the same time they were conveniently lost to principle, and to shame; and uttered villainy, obscenity, and blasphemy, not merely with a brazen front, but with the sober, intrepid serenity of apparent conviction. Such men are incomparably better fitted to persuade ignorance, and embolden vulgar iniquity, than superiour villains. The writings of such villains are beyond the reach of mankind at large. These men are fitted to invade the cottage, and ravage the fireside. On the people of New-England their influence, though sensibly felt, was not extensive: on other parts of the Union it is declared, as I believe with truth, to have been great.

◇◇◇◇◇◇◇◇◇◇◇◇◇◇

[*Samuel Griswold Goodrich*]

In a certain country town within my knowledge, the introduction of stoves into the meeting-house, about the year 1830, threatened to overturn society. The metropolis, which we will call H . . ., had adopted stoves in the churches, and naturally enough some people of the neighboring town of E . . . set about introducing this custom into the meeting-house in their own village. Now, the two master-spirits of society — the Demon of Progress and the Angel of Conservatism — somehow or other had got into the place, and as soon as this reform was suggested, they began to wrestle with the people, until at last the church and society were divided into two violent factions — the Stove Party and the Anti-stove Party. At the head of the first was Mr. Deacon K . . . and at the head of the latter was Mrs. Deacon P . . . The battle raged portentously, very much like the renowned tempest in a teapot. Society was indeed lashed into a foam. The minister, between the contending factions, scarcely dared to say his soul was his own. He could scarcely find a text from "Genesis to Jude," that might not commit him on one side or the other. The strife — of course — ran into politics, and the representative to the assembly got in by a happy knack at dodging the question in such wise as to be claimed by both parties.

Finally, the progressionists prevailed — the stove party triumphed, and the stoves were accordingly installed. Great was the humiliation of the antistoveites; nevertheless, they concluded to be submissive to the dispensations of Providence. On the Sabbath succeeding the installation of the stoves, Mrs. Deacon P . . ., instead of staying away, did as she ought, and went to church. As she moved up the broad aisle, it was remarked that she looked pale but calm, as a martyr should, conscious of injury, yet struggling to forgive. Nevertheless, when the minister named his text — Romans xii. 20 — and spoke about heaping coals of fire on the head — she slid from her seat, and subsided gently upon the floor. The train of ideas suggested was, in fact, too much for her heated brain and shattered nerves. Suddenly there was a rush to the pew, and the fainting lady was taken out. When she came to the air, she slightly revived.

"Pray what is the matter?" said Mrs. Deacon K . . ., who bent over her, holding a smelling-bottle to her nose.

"Oh, it is the heat of those awful stoves," said Mrs. Deacon P. . . .

"No, no, my dear," said Mrs. Deacon K . . . ; "that can't be: it's a warm day, you know, and there's no fire in them."

"No fire in the stoves ?" said Mrs. Deacon P. . . .

"Not a particle," said Mrs. Deacon K. . . .

"Well, I feel better now," said the poor lady; and so bidding her friends good-by, she went home, in a manner suited to the occasion.

In the olden time a country minister's home was a minister's tavern, and therefore I saw, at different periods, most of the orthodox

DURHAM, CONNECTICUT

or Congregational clergymen belonging to that part of the State, at our house. My father frequently exchanged with those of the neighboring towns, and sometimes consociations and associations were held at Ridgefield. Thus, men of the clerical profession constituted a large portion of the strangers who visited us. I may add that my lineage was highly ministerial from an early period down to my own time. The pulpit of Durham, filled by my paternal grandfather, continued in the same family one hundred and twenty-six consecutive years. A short time since, we reckoned among our relations, not going beyond the degree of second cousin, more than a dozen ministers of the Gospel, and all of the same creed.

As to the clergy of Fairfield country, my boyish impressions of them were, that they were of the salt of the earth — rock-salt, the very crystals of Christianity; nor has a larger experience altered my opinion. If I sometimes indulge a smile at the recollection of particular traits of character, or more general points of manners significant of the age, I still regard them with affection and reverence. Some of them were grave and portly, especially those who bore the awe-inspiring title of Doctors of Divinity. I cannot now recollect among them all a single little or emaciated D.D. At the very head of the list, in my imagination, was Dr. Ripley, of Green's-farms, now Southport, I believe. He was a large and learned man — two hundred pounds avoirdupois of solid divinity. He read the Bible in the original tongues for diversion, and digested Hebrew roots as if they had been buttered parsnips. He was withal a hale, hearty old gentleman, with a rich, ruddy smile over his face, bespeaking peace within and without.

Dr. Lewis, of Horseneck, weighed less according to the steelyards: he had perhaps less Greek and Latin in him, but I have an impression that he was a man even more full of godliness. He was in fact the patron saint of my young fancy, and his image still seems before me. He was of the middle size, neither fat nor lean, stooped a little, and had a thin face with a long nose. Yet his countenance was the very seat of kindliness, charity, and sanctity. His thin, white locks floated down his cheeks and over his shoulders in apostolic folds. His voice was soft, yet penetrating. He had not, I think, any prodigious power of intellect, but during his preaching every ear was intent, every heart open. The congregation sometimes nodded, especially of a hot summer Sunday, even beneath the thunders of Dr. Ripley; nay, Deacon Olmstead himself, enthroned in the deacon's seat, was obliged now and then to take out his sprig of fennel, in the very midst of the doctor's twelfthlies and fifteenthlies; but nobody ever slept under the touching and sympathetic tones of Dr. Lewis. The good man has long since been translated to another world, but the perfume of his goodness still lingers amid the churches which were once impressed with his footsteps.

These gentlemen whom I have described, traveled on horseback, and were always well mounted; some of them were amateurs in horseflesh: I have already had occasion to notice the points of Dr. Ripley's beast. In manners they were polite, and somewhat assiduous in their stately courtesies. They spoke with authority, and not as the scribes. Their preaching was grave in manner, and in matter elaborately dovetailed with scripture. The people drank hard cider, and relished sound doctrine: it was not till nearly half a century afterward that — imbibing soda-water, champagne, and other gaseous beverages — they required pyrotechnics in the pulpit. A soul to reach heaven must then have the passport of Saybrook; and in point of fact, orthodoxy was so tempered with charity, that nearly all who died, received it.

I may add that despite their divinity, they were sociable in their manners and intercourse. The state of the Church was no doubt first in their minds; but ample room was left for the good things of life. Those who came to our house examined my brother in his Greek and Latin, and I went out behind the barn to gather tansey for their morning bitters. They dearly loved a joke, and relished anecdotes, especially if they bore a little hard upon the cloth. I remember some of them at which I have heard Dr. Ripley almost crack his sides, and seen even the saintly Dr. Lewis ran over at the eyes with laughing. Shall I give you a specimen ?

Once upon a time there was a clergyman — the Rev. Dr. T . . . of H . . . — a man of high character, and distinguished for his dignity of manner. But it was remarked that frequently as he was ascending the pulpit stairs he would smile, and sometimes almost titter, as if beset by an uncontrollable desire to laugh. This excited remark, and at last scandal. Finally, it was thought necessary for some of his clerical friends, at a meeting of the association, to bring up the matter for consideration.

The case was stated — the Rev. Dr. T . . . being present. "Well, gentlemen," said he, "the fact charged against me is true, but I beg you to permit me to offer an explanation. A few months after I was licensed to preach, I was in a country town, and on a Sabbath morning was about to enter upon the services of the church. Back of the pulpit was a window, which looked out upon a field of clover, then in full bloom, for it was summer. As I rose to commence the reading of the Scriptures, I cast a glance into the field, and there I saw a man performing the most extraordinary evolutions — jumping, whirling, slapping in all directions, and with a ferocious agony of exertion. At first I thought he was mad; but suddenly the truth burst upon me — he had buttoned up a bumble-bee in his pantaloons ! I am constitutionally nervous, gentlemen, and the shock of this scene upon my risible sensibilities was so great, that I could hardly get through the services. Several times I was upon the point of bursting into a laugh. Even to this day, the remembrance of this scene — through the temptation of the devil — often comes upon me as I am ascending the pulpit. This, I admit, is a weakness, but I trust it will rather excite your sympathy and your prayers than your reproaches."

The most conspicuous of the Methodists was the noted Lorenzo Dow. He was a native of Connecticut, and at the period of my boyhood had begun to be talked about chiefly on account of his eccentricities — though he was also a man of some talent. About the time that Methodism began to spread itself in Connecticut, Dow appeared in Ridgefield, and taking a stand on 'Squire Nathan Smith's wood-pile, held forth to a few boys and other people that chanced to be in that quarter. I was returning from school, and stopped to hear his discourse. He was then about thirty years of age, but looked much older. He was thin and weather-beaten, and appeared haggard and ill-favored, partly on account of his reddish, dusty beard, some six inches long — then a singularity if not an enormity, as nobody among us but old Jagger the beggar cultivated such an appendage. I did not comprehend what he said, and only remember his general appearance. He was merely passing through Ridgefield, and soon departed, having produced the impression that he was an odd sort of person, and rather light-headed. I afterward heard him preach twice at camp-meetings.

Lorenzo was not only uncouth in his person and appearance, but his voice was harsh, his action hard and rectangular. It is scarcely possible to conceive of a person more entirely destitute of all natural eloquence. But he understood common life, and especially vulgar life — its tastes, prejudices, and weaknesses; and he possessed a cunning knack of adapting his discourses to such audiences. He told stories with considerable art, and his memory being stored with them, he could always point a moral or clinch a proposition by an anecdote. He knew that with simple people an illustration is better than logic, and when he ran short of Scripture, or argument failed, he usually resorted to some pertinent story or adapted allegory. He affected oddity in all things — in his mode of preaching as well as in dress. He took pains to appear suddenly and by surprise among the people where he proposed to hold forth: he frequently made his appointments a year beforehand, and at the very minute set, he would come like an apparition.

◇◇◇◇◇◇◇◇◇◇◇◇◇

[Catharine E. Beecher, Litchfield, Conn.]

The most remarkable and unique of the demonstrations of sympathy for our mother's death was what in New England is called the *minister's wood-spell*, when, by previous notice, on some bright winter day, every person in the parish who chooses to do so sends a sled load of wood as a present to the pastor. On this occasion we were previously notified that the accustomed treat of dough-nuts and loaf-cake, cider and flip, must be on a much larger scale than common.

With father's rejoicing approval, I was allowed to take both the responsibility and the labor of this whole occasion, with Aunt Esther as my guide, and the younger children as my helpers, and for nearly a week our kitchen was busy as an ant-hill. For preliminaries, the fat was to be prepared to boil the dough-nuts, the spices to be pounded, the sugar to be rolled, the flour to be sifted, and the materials for beer for the flip to be collected. Next came the brewing, on a scale of grandeur befitting the occasion. Then the cake was duly made, and placed in large stone pots or earthen jars set around the kitchen fire, and duly turned and tended till the proper lightness was detected. Lastly came the baking of the loaves and the boiling of the dough-nuts; and were I to tell the number of loaves I put into and took out of the oven, and the bushels of dough-nuts I boiled over the kitchen fire, I fear my credit for veracity would be endangered. Certainly our kitchen, store-room, and pantry were a sight to behold, calling in admiring visitors, while my success was the matter of universal gratulation.

When the auspicious day arrived, the snow was thick, smooth, and well packed for the occasion; the sun shone through a sharp, dry, and frosty air; and the whole town was astir. Toward the middle of the afternoon, runners arrived with news of the gathering squadrons — Mount Tom was coming with all its farmers; Bradleyville also; Chestnut Hill, and the North and the South settlements; while the "town hill" gentry were on the *qui vive* to hunt up every sled and yoke of oxen not employed by their owners. Before sundown the yard, street, and the lower rooms of our house were swarming with cheerful faces. Father was ready with his cordial greetings, adroit in detecting and admiring the special merits of every load as it arrived. The kind farmers wanted to see all the children, and we were busy as bees in waiting on them. The boys heated the flip-irons, and passed around the cider and flip, while Aunt Esther and the daughters were as busy in serving the dough-nuts, cake, and cheese. And such a mountainous wood-pile as arose in our yard never before was seen in ministerial domains !

<><><><><><><><><><>

[*Henry Adams, Boston*]

Nothing quieted doubt so completely as the mental calm of the Unitarian clergy. In uniform excellence of life and character, moral and intellectual, the score of Unitarian clergymen about Boston, who controlled society and Harvard College, were never excelled. They proclaimed as their merit that they insisted on no doctrine, but taught, or tried to teach, the means of leading a virtuous, useful, unselfish life, which they held to be sufficient for salvation. For them, difficulties might be ignored; doubts were waste of thought; nothing exacted solution. Boston had solved the universe; or had offered and realized the best solution yet tried. The problem was worked out.

Of all the conditions of his youth which afterwards puzzled the grown-up man, this disappearance of religion puzzled him most. The boy went to church twice every Sunday; he was taught to read his Bible, and he learned religious poetry by heart; he believed in a mild deism; he prayed; he went through all the forms; but neither to him nor to his brothers or sisters was religion real. Even the mild discipline of the Unitarian Church was so irksome that they all threw it off at the first possible moment, and never afterwards entered a church. The religious instinct had vanished, and could not be revived, although one made in later life many efforts to recover it. That the most powerful emotion of man, next to the sexual, should disappear, might be a personal defect of his own; but that the most intelligent society, led by the most intelligent clergy, in the most moral conditions he ever knew, should have solved all the problems of the universe so thoroughly as to have quite ceased making itself anxious about past or future, and should have persuaded itself that all the problems which had convulsed human thought from earliest recorded time, were not worth discussing, seemed to him the most curious social phenomenon he had to account for in a long life. The faculty of turning away one's eyes as one approaches a chasm is not unusual, and Boston showed, under the lead of Mr. Webster, how successfully it could be done in politics; but in politics a certain number of men did at least protest. In religion and philosophy no one protested.

❖❖❖❖❖❖❖❖❖❖❖❖❖

[*Thomas Low Nichols, Orford, N. H.*]

There is a Yankee anecdote which runs something in this way: "John !" calls the shop-keeper to his assistant; "have you watered the rum ?" "Yes, sir." "Have you sanded the sugar ?" "Yes, sir." "Have you wet the codfish and tobacco ?" "Yes, sir." "Then come to prayers !"

Most of the New England people whom I knew were religious but they made hard bargains. To cheat in swapping horses, or in trade generally, was considered a kind of game, not prohibited, at which the winner was merely a cute fellow. Barnum's autobiography was no severe shock to the conscience of New England; and Barnum himself is only a rather strong specimen of a speculating Yankee. It has never, perhaps, occurred to the average American, that getting the best end of a bargain had any relation to the Commandment, "Thou shalt not steal," or the golden rule of the gospel.

[381]

But it is also true that theft was so rare that I can scarcely remember an instance in my early knowledge. The axe was left in the log, and other tools, where they were used. Granaries were not locked, and not a house for miles was ever fastened at night. Orchards of fruit were safe; and if melon patches in the neighbourhood of some college or academy were liable to robbery, it was because the boys had established a custom of indulging in this kind of plunder, and considered it a sort of practical joke. The rule about orchards was that every one had a right to all the fruit he could eat or carry away in his pockets.

There was, in fact, no temptation to steal, for every one had, or might easily have, plenty. The price of potatoes was six pence a bushel; Indian corn, two shillings; wheat, four shillings. Other articles were in proportion. It was very difficult to find an object of charity, or to give away provisions. I remember a family debate on the subject when we had more turkeys than we needed for one Thanksgiving day. The question was whether there was any one to whom we could send a turkey, who would not feel offended. The result was, that in a district of two or three miles around not a family could be thought of to whom it would probably be a welcome gift.

The greatest vice I knew was drunkenness. The hospitality of the people induced them to offer every neighbour who called something to drink. The rum-bottle stood upon the sideboard, and a cider-barrel was always on tap in the cellar. Whoever called, if only the next neighbour to borrow a hoe or a shovel, was offered a bowl of apples and a mug of cider, if not something stronger.

❖❖❖❖❖❖❖❖❖❖❖❖

[*John Neal, Portland, Maine*]

On the 27th of September, 1851, Mr. [Neal] Dow, the mayor of Portland, published to the world, without qualification or misgivings, these words: *"The watch-house is now used to keep seized liquors in, instead of drunkards."* This went the rounds of all our papers, East, West, North, and South.

And yet, at this very time, September, 1851, there were no less than *forty-eight* persons confined in the watch-house — three for larceny, and *forty-five for drunkenness !*

Yet more. At the time when he was bragging of the reformation he had brought about among our people, by the help of what was called "The Maine-Law," a law, by the way, which was never the same for twelve months together, as if we had been a community of drunkards, a city of groggeries and tippling-shops, I obtained the certificate of Mr. Baker, the jailer, that, from July, 1851, to September, 1853, two years and two months, there had been only eighty-one different *persons* committed, though the number of committals amounted to one hundred and three; a small part of the number having been committed from one to seven times. And this, in twenty-six months; less than three a month, in a city of drunkards, under the vigorous administration of Mayor Dow !

At another time, he declared that no liquor could be found *within five miles of the city;* and at another, that not a drop could be had nearer than Moosehead-Lake ! And yet, he knew, for everybody here knew the fact, that there were hundreds of places within the city of Portland, where liquor, and the worst, might always be had for the asking, and that grog-shops and Irish boarding-houses and negro-shanties, where liquors were kept in oil-cans and pickle jars, under beds and in out-houses, were multiplied to a frightful extent; and just what I had foreseen and foretold, from the first, the most ingenious evasions were resorted to. Liquors were sold in the shape of books, made of tin, painted, and lettered with some attractive title; such as "Drops of Comfort;" "Consolation for the Afflicted;" "Hints for the Ungodly." Drams, too, were sold in the form of eggs, made of porcelain. Walking-sticks and heavy canes were contrived to hold from a half-pint to a quart of brandy. Clubs and associations were formed, for the purpose of drinking and gambling, not only in public, but in private houses. Young men would travel with portmanteaus containing bottles, or take a room, anywhere, and invite their companions to a treat; of course, drinking more and oftener, than if they went openly to a bar. And all this, not so much, perhaps, from a love of liquor, as for a love of what they called *spirit, or fun.* Having been forbidden by law to control themselves, to touch, taste, or handle, under the severest penalties, they determined to have their own way, like so many school-boys, in defiance of the master; in other words, by over-reaching or outwitting the authorities.

The result of all his engineering and manoeuvring was, that, instead of being re-elected the following year, the pleasant gentleman was tumbled, neck-and-heels, out of his chair, and then *shelved* for the rest of his natural life. We elected him first, because we did not know him; and we refused a re-election, because we *did.* Having *tried* him, and he us, we had no choice left, if we would not become a laughing-stock for all generations.

[383]

STIRRING TIMES

FURIOUS TAWNIES

◆◇◆◇◆◇◆◇◆◇◆◇◆

[*A Narrative of the Captivity and Removes of Mrs. Mary Rowlandson*]

ON the 10th of February, 1675, came the Indians with great numbers upon Lancaster [Mass.]: their first coming was about sun-rising; hearing the noise of some guns, we looked out; several houses were burning, and the smoke ascending to heaven. There were five persons taken in one house, the father and mother, and a suckling child they knocked on the head, the other two they took and carried away alive. There were two others, who being out of their garrison upon occasion, were set upon; one was knocked on the head, the other escaped: Another there was who running along was shot and wounded, and fell down; he begged of them his life, promising them money (as they told me) but they would not hearken to him, but knocked him on the head, stript him naked, and split open his bowels. Another seeing many of the Indians about his barn, ventured and went out, but was quickly shot down. There were three others belonging to the same garrison who were killed; the Indians getting up upon the roof of the barn, had advantage to shoot down upon them over their fortification. Thus these murtherous wretches went on burning and destroying all before them.

At length they came and beset our house, and quickly it was the dolefulest day that ever mine eyes saw. The house stood upon the edge of a hill; some of the Indians got behind the hill, others into the barn, and others behind any thing that would shelter them; from all which places they shot against the house, so that the bullets seemed to fly like hail, and quickly they wounded one man among us, then another, and then a third. About two hours (according to my observation in that amazing time) they had been about the house before they prevailed to fire it, (which they did with flax and hemp, which they brought out of the barn, and there being no defence about the house, only two flankers at two opposite corners, and one of them not finished) they fired it once, and one ventured out and quenched it, but they quickly fired it again, and that took. Now is the dreadful hour come, that I have often heard of (in time of the war, as it was the case of others) but now mine eyes see it. Some in our house were fighting for their lives, others wallowing in blood, the house on fire over our heads, and the bloody heathen ready to knock us on the head if we stirred out. Now might we hear mothers and children crying out for themselves and one another, "Lord, what shall we do !" Then I took my children (and one of my sisters her's) to go forth and leave the house: but as soon as we came to the door, and appeared, the Indians shot so thick, that the bullets rattled against the house, as if one had taken a handful of stones and threw them, so that we were forced to give back. We had six stout dogs belonging to our garrison, but none of them would stir, though at another time, if an Indian had come to the door, they were ready to fly upon him and tear him down. The Lord hereby would make us the more to acknowledge his hand, and to see that our help is always in him. But out we must go, the fire increasing, and coming along behind us roaring, and the Indians gaping before us with their guns, spears, and hatchets to devour us. No sooner were we out of the house but my brother-in-law (being before wounded in defending the house, in or near the throat) fell down dead, whereat the Indians scornfully shouted and hallooed, and were presently upon him, stripped off his cloaths. The bullets flying thick, one went through my side, and the same (as would seem), through the bowels and hand of my poor child in my arms. One of my elder sister's children (named William) had then his leg broke, which the Indians perceiving, they knocked him on the head. Thus were we butchered by those merciless heathens, standing amazed, with the blood running down to our heels. My eldest sister being yet in the house, and seeing those woeful sights, the infidels halling mothers one way and children another, and some wallowing in their blood; and her eldest son telling her that her son William was dead, and myself was wounded, she said, and "Lord let me die with them:" which was no sooner said but she was struck with a bullet, and fell down dead over the threshold. I hope she is reaping the fruit of her good labours, being faithful to the service of God in her place. In her younger years she lay under much trouble upon spiritual accounts, till it pleased God to make that precious scripture take hold of her heart, 2 *Cor.* 12. 9. *And he said unto me, My grace is sufficient for thee.* More than twenty years after, I have heard her tell how sweet and comfortable that place was to her. But to return: The Indians laid hold of us, pulling me one way, and the children another, and said, "Come, go along with us:" I told them they would kill me: they answered, "If I were willing to go along with them, they would not hurt me."

Oh ! the doleful sight that now was to behold at this house ! Come behold the works of the Lord, what desolations he has made in the earth. Of thirty-seven persons who were in this one house, none escaped either present death, or a bitter captivity, save only one, who might say as in *Job* 1, 15. *And I only am escaped alone to tell the news.* There were twelve killed, some shot, some stabbed with their spears, some knocked down with their hatchets. When we are in prosperity, Oh the little that we think of such dreadful sights, to see our dear friends and relations lie bleeding out their hearts' blood upon the ground. There was one who was chopt in the head with a hatchet, and stript naked, and yet was crawling up and down. It was a solemn sight to see so many christians lying in their blood, some here and some there, like a company of sheep torn by wolves. All of them stript naked by a company of hell-hounds, roaring, singing, ranting and insulting, as if they would have torn our hearts out: yet the Lord by his almighty power, preserved a number of us from death; for there were twenty-four of us taken alive and carried captive.

I had often before this said that if the Indians should come, I should chuse rather to be killed by them, than taken alive: but when it came to the trial, my mind changed; their glittering weapons so daunted my spirit, that I chose rather to go along with those (as I may say) ravenous bears, than that moment to end my days. And that I may the better declare what happened to me during that grievous captivity, I shall particularly speak of the several Removes we had up and down the wilderness.

The first Remove

Now away we must go with those barbarous creatures, with our bodies wounded and bleeding and our hearts no less than our bodies. About a mile we went that night, up upon a hill within sight of the town, where we intended to lodge. There was hard by a vacant house, (deserted by the English before, for fear of the Indians.) I asked them whether I might not lodge in the house that night ? to which they answered, What, will you love Englishmen still ? This was the dolefulest night that ever my eyes saw. Oh the roaring, and singing, and dancing, and yelling of those black creatures in the night, which made the place a lively resemblance of hell: And miserable was the waste that was there made, of horses, cattle, sheep, swine, calves, lambs, roasting pigs and fowls (which they had plundered in the town) some roasting, some lying and burning, and some boiling, to feed our merciless enemies: who were joyful enough, though we were disconsolate. To add to the dolefulness of the former day, and the dismalness of the present night, my thoughts ran upon my losses and sad bereaved condition. All was gone, my husband gone, (at least separated from me, he being in the Bay: and to add to my grief, the Indians told me they would kill him as he came homeward,) my children gone, my relations and friends gone, our house and home, and all our comforts within door and without, all was gone (except my life) and I knew not but the next moment that might go too.

There remained nothing to me but one poor wounded babe, and it seemed at present worse than death, that it was in such a pitiful condition, bespeaking compassion, and I had no refreshing for it, nor suitable things to revive it. Little do many think, what is the savageness and brutishness of this barbarous enemy, those even that seem to profess more than others among them, when the English have fallen into their hands.

Those seven that were killed at Lancaster the summer before upon a sabbath day, and the one that was afterward killed upon a week day, were slain and mangled in a barbarous manner, by one-eyed John, and Marlborough's praying Indians, which Capt. Mosely brought to Boston, as the Indians told me.

The third Remove

The morning being come, they prepared to go on their way, one of the Indians got upon a horse, and they sat me up behind him, with my poor sick babe in my lap. A very wearisome tedious day I had of it; what with my own wound, and my child being so exceeding sick, and in a lamentable condition with her wound, it may easily be judged what a poor feeble condition we were in, there being not the least crumb of refreshing that came within either of our mouths from Wednesday night to Saturday night, except only a little cold water. This day in the afternoon, about an hour by sun, we came to the place where they intended, viz: an Indian town called Wenimesset, northward of Quabaug. When we were come, Oh the number of Pagans (now merciless enemies) that there came about me, that I may say as *David*, Psal. 27. 13, *I had fainted unless I had believed,* &c. The next day was the sabbath: I then remembered how careless I had been of God's holy time: how many sabbaths I had lost and misspent, and how evilly I had walked in God's sight; which lay so close upon my spirit, that it was easy for me to see how righteous it was with God to cut off the thread of my life, and cast me out of his presence forever. Yet the Lord still shewed mercy to me, and helped me; and as he wounded me with one hand, so he healed me with the other. This day there came to me one Robert Pepper, (a man belonging to Roxbury,) who was taken at Capt. Beer's fight; and had been now a considerable time with the Indians, and up with them almost as far as Albany to see King Philip, as he told me, and was now very lately come with them into these parts. Hearing, I say, that I was in this Indian town, he obtained leave to come and see me. He told me he himself was wounded in the leg at Capt. Beers's fight; and was not able some time to go, but as they carried him, and that he took oak leaves and laid to his wound, and by the blessing of God, he was able to travel again. Then took I oak leaves and laid to my side, and with the blessing of God, it cured me also; yet before the cure was wrought, I may say as it is in Psalms 38. 5, 6. *My wounds stink and are corrupt, I am troubled, I am bowed down greatly, I go mourning all the day long*. I sat much alone with my poor wounded child in my lap, which moaned night and day, having nothing to revive the body, or cheer the spirits of her; but instead of that one Indian would come and tell me one hour, your master will knock your child on the head, and then a second and then a third, your master will quickly knock your child on the head.

This was the comfort I had from them; miserable comforters were they all. Thus nine days I sat upon my knees, with my babe in my lap, till my flesh was raw again. My child being even ready to depart this sorrowful world, they bid me carry it out to another wigwam; (I suppose because they would not be troubled with such spectacles;) whither I went with a very heavy heart, and down I sat with the picture of death in my lap. About two hours in the night, my sweet babe like a lamb departed this life, on Feb. 18, 1675, it being about six years and five months old. It was nine days from the first wounding in this miserable condition, without any refreshing of one nature or another, except a little cold water. I cannot but take notice, how at another time I could not bear to be in a room where a dead person was, but now the case is changed; I must and could lie down with my dead babe all the night after. I have thought since, of the wonderful goodness of God to me, in preserving me so in the use of my reason and senses, in that distressed time, that I did not use wicked and violent means to end my own miserable life. In the morning, when they understood that my child was dead, they sent me home to my master's wigwam. (By my master in this writing must be understood Quannopin, who was a Saggamore, and married King Philip's wife's sister; not that he first took me, but I was sold to him by a Narraganset Indian, who took me when I first came out of the garrison.) I went to take up my dead child in my arms to carry it with me, but they bid me let it alone. There was no resisting, but go I must, and leave it. When I had been a while at my master's wigwam, I took the first opportunity I could get, to go look after my dead child. When I came I asked them what they had done with it? they told me it was on the hill; then they went and showed me where it was, where I saw the ground was newly digged, and where they told me they had buried it; there I left that child in the wilderness, and must commit it and myself also in this wilderness condition, to him who is above all. God having taken away this dear child, I went to see my daughter Mary, who was at the same Indian town, at a wigwam not very far off, though we had little liberty or opportunity to see one another; she was about ten years old, and taken from the door at first by a praying Indian, and afterwards sold for a gun. When I came in sight she would fall a weeping, at which they were provoked, and would not let me come near her, but bid me be gone; which was a heart-cutting word to me. I had one child dead, another in the wilderness, I knew not where, the third they would not let me come near to: *Me* (as he said) *have ye bereaved of my children; Joseph is not, and Simeon is not, and ye will take Benjamin also, all these things are against me.* I could not sit still in this condition, but kept walking from one place to another. And as I was going along, my heart was even overwhelmed with the thoughts of my condition, and that I should have children, and a nation that I knew not ruled over them. Whereupon I earnestly entreated the Lord that he would consider my low estate, and shew me a token for good, and if it were his blessed will, some sign and hope of some relief. And indeed quickly the Lord answered in some measure, my poor prayer: For as

I was going up and down mourning and lamenting my condition, my son came to me and asked me how I did ? I had not seen him before, since the destruction of the town; and I knew not where he was, till I was informed by himself that he was amongst a smaller parcel of Indians, whose place was about six miles off. With tears in his eyes he asked me whether his sister Sarah was dead ? and told me he had seen his sister Mary; and prayed me, that I would not be troubled in reference to himself. The occasion of his coming to see me at this time was this: There was, as I said, about six miles from us a small plantation of Indians, where it seems he had been during his captivity; and at this time, there were some forces of the Indians gathered out of our company, and some also from them (amongst whom was my son's master) to go to assault and burn Medfield: In this time of his master's absence, his dame brought him to see me. I took this to be some gracious answer to my earnest and unfeigned desire. The next day the Indians returned from Medfield. (All the company, for those that belonged to the other smaller company came through the town that now we were at.) But before they came to us, Oh, the outrageous roaring and hooping that there was ! They began their din about a mile before they came to us. By their noise and hooping they signified how many they had destroyed; which was at that time twenty-three. Those that were with us at home, were gathered together as soon as they heard the hooping, and every time that the other went over their number, these at home gave a shout, that the very earth rang again. And thus they continued till those that had been upon the expedition were come up to the Saggamore's wigwam; and then, Oh, the hideous insulting and triumphing that there was over some English men's scalps that they had taken (as their manner is) and brought with them. I cannot but take notice of the wonderful mercy of God to me in those afflictions, in sending me a Bible. One of the Indians that came from Medfield fight, and had brought some plunder, came to me, and asked me if I would have a Bible, he had got in his basket ? I was glad of it, and asked him if he thought the Indians would let me read ? He answered yes; so I took the Bible, and in that melancholy time, it came into my mind to read first the 28 chap. of Deuteronomy, which I did, and when I had read it, my dark heart wrought on this manner, that there was no mercy for me, that the blessings were gone, and the curses came in their room, and that I had lost my opportunity. But the Lord helped me still to go on reading till I came to ch. 30, the seven first verses; where I found there was mercy promised again, if we would return to him, by repentance: and though we were scattered from one end

[393]

of the earth to the other, yet the Lord would gather us together, and turn all those curses upon our enemies. I do not desire to live to forget this scripture, and what comfort it was to me.

Now the Indians began to talk of removing from this place, some one way and some another. There were now besides myself nine English captives in this place, (all of them children except one woman.) I got an opportunity to go and take my leave of them, they being to go one way and I another. I asked them whether they were earnest with God for deliverance ? They told me they did as they were able, and it was some comfort to me, that the Lord stirred up children to look to him. The woman, viz: good-wife Toslin told me she should never see me again, and that she could find in her heart to run away by any means, for we were near thirty miles from any English town, and she very big with child, having but one week to reckon, and another child in her arms two years old, and bad rivers there were to go over, and we were feeble with our poor and coarse entertainments. I had my Bible with me, I pulled it out, and asked her whether she would read; we opened the Bible, and lighted on Psal. 27, in which Psalm we especially took notice of that verse, *Wait on the Lord, be of good courage, and he shall strengthen thine heart, wait I say on the Lord.*

The fourth Remove

And now must I part with the little company I had. Here I parted with my daughter Mary (whom I never saw again till I saw her in Dorchester, returned from captivity) and from four little cousins and neighbours, some of which I never saw afterward, the Lord only knows the end of them. Among them also was that poor woman before mentioned, who came to a sad end, as some of the company told me in my travel: She having much grief upon her spirits about her miserable condition, being so near her time, she would be often asking the Indians to let her go home; they not being willing to that and yet vexed with her importunity, gathered a great company together about her, and stripped her naked, and set her in the midst of them; and when they had sung and danced about her (in their hellish manner) as long as they pleased, they knocked her on the head, and the child in her arms with her. When they had done that, they made a fire and put them both into it, and told the other children that were with them, that if they attemped to go home they would serve them in like manner. The children said she did not shed one tear, but prayed all the while. But to return to my own journey: We travelled about half a day or a little more and came to a desolate place in the wilderness where there were no wigwams or inhabitants before; we came about the middle of the afternoon to this place; cold, wet and snowy, and hungry, and weary, and no refreshing for man, but the cold ground to sit on, and our poor Indian cheer.

Heart-aching thoughts here I had about my poor children, who were scattered up and down among the wild beasts of the forests. My head was light and dizzy, (either through hunger or bad lodging, or trouble, or all together,) my knees feeble, my body raw by setting double night and day, that I cannot express to man the affliction that lay upon my spirit, but the Lord helped me at that time to express it to himself. I opened my Bible to read, and the Lord brought that precious scripture to me. *Jer.* 31. 16. *Thus saith the Lord, refrain thy voice from weeping, and thine eyes from tears, for thy work shall be rewarded, and they shall come again from the land of the enemy*. This was a sweet cordial to me; when I was ready to faint, many and many a time have I sat down and wept sweetly over this scripture. At this place we continued about four days.

The fifth Remove

The occasion (as I thought) of their removing at this time, was the English army's being near and following them: For they went as if they had gone for their lives, for some considerable way; and then they made a stop, and chose out some of their stoutest men, and sent them back to hold the English army in play whilst the rest escaped; and then like Jehu they marched on furiously with their old and young; some carried their old decriped mothers, some carried one, and some another. Four of them carried a great Indian upon a bier; but going through a thick wood with him they were hindered, and could make no haste; whereupon they took him upon their backs, and carried him one at a time, till we came to Bacquag River. Upon Friday, a little after noon, we came to this river. When all the company was come up and were gathered together, I thought to count the number of them, but they were so many and being somewhat in motion, it was beyond my skill. In this travel, because of my wound, I was somewhat favoured in my load: I carried only my knitting-work, and two quarts of parched meal. Being very faint, I asked my mistress to give me one spoonful of the meal, but she would not give me a taste. They quickly fell to cutting dry trees, to make rafts to carry them over the river, and soon my turn came to go over. By the advantage of some brush which they had laid upon the raft to sit on, I did not wet my foot, (while many of themselves at the other end were mid-leg deep,) which cannot but be acknowledged as a favour of God to my weakened body, it being a very cold time. I was not before acquainted with such kind of doings or dangers. *When thou passest through the waters I will be with thee, and through the rivers they shall not overflow thee. Isai.* 43. 2. A certain number of us got over the river that night, but it was the night after the Sabbath before all the company was got over. On the Saturday they boiled an old horse's leg (which they had got) and so we drank of the broth as soon as they thought it was ready, and when it was almost all gone they filled it up again.

The first week of my being among them, I hardly eat any thing: the second week I found my stomach grow very faint for want of something, and yet it was very hard to get down their filthy trash; but the third week (though I could think how formerly my stomach would turn against this or that, and I could starve and die before I could eat such things, yet) they were pleasant and savory to my taste. I was at this time knitting a pair of white cotton stockings for my mistress, and I had not yet wrought upon the Sabbath day. When the Sabbath came they bid me to go to work; I told them it was Sabbath day, and desired them to let me rest, and told them I would do as much more work to-morrow; to which they answered me they would break my face. And here I cannot take but notice of the strange Providence of God in preserving the heathen: They were many hundreds, old and young, some sick and some lame; many had Papooses at their backs; the greatest number at this time with us were Squaws, and they travelled with all they had, bag and baggage, and yet they got over this river aforesaid; and on Monday they sat their wigwams on fire, and away they went; on that very day came the English army after them to this river, and saw the smoke of their wigwams and yet this river put a stop to them. God did not give them courage or activity to go over after us. We were not ready for so great a mercy as victory and deliverance; if we had been, God would have found out a way for the English to have passed this river, as well as for the Indians with their Squaws and children, and all their luggage. *O that my people had hearkened unto me, and Israel had walked in my ways, I should soon have subdued their enemies, and turned my hand against their adversaries. Psal.* 81. 13, 14.

That day, a little after noon, we came to Sqaubeag, where the Indians quickly spread themselves over the deserted English fields, gleaning what they could find; some picked up ears of wheat that were crickled down, some found ears of Indian corn, some found ground-nuts, and others sheaves of wheat that were frozen together in the shock, and went to threshing of them out. Myself got two ears of Indian corn, and whilst I did but turn my back, one of them was stole from me, which much troubled me. There came an Indian to them at that time, with a basket of horse-liver. I asked him to give me a piece: What (says he) can you eat horse liver. I told him I would try, if he would give me a piece, which he did; and I laid it on the coals to roast, but before it was half ready, they got half of it away from me; so that I was forced to take the rest and eat it as it was, with the blood about my mouth, and yet a savory bit it was to me; for to the hungry soul every bitter thing was sweet. A solemn sight methought it was, to see whole fields of wheat and Indian corn forsaken and spoiled, and the remainder of them to be food for our merciless enemies. That night we had a mess of wheat for our supper.

The eighth Remove

On the morrow morning we must go over Connecticut River to meet with King Philip; two canoes full they had carried over, the next turn myself was to go; but as my foot was upon the canoe to step in, there was a sudden outcry among them, and I must step back; and instead of going over the river, I must go four or five miles up the river farther northward. Some of the Indians ran one way, and some another. The cause of this rout was, as I thought, their espying some English scouts, who were thereabouts. In this travel up the river about noon the company made a stop, and sat down, some to eat and others to rest them. As I sat amongst them musing on things past, my son Joseph unexpectedly came to me. We asked of each others welfare, bemoaning our doleful condition, and the change that had come upon us: We had husband and father, and children, and sisters, and friends, and relations, and house, and home, and many comforts of this life; but now we might say as *Job. Naked came I out of my mother's womb, and naked shall I return: The Lord gave, and the Lord hath taken away, blessed be the name of the Lord.* I asked him whether he would read? he told me he earnestly desired it. I gave him my Bible, and he lighted upon that comfortable scripture, *Psalm* 118. 17, 18. *I shall not die but live, and declare the works of the Lord: The Lord hath chastened me sore, yet he hath not given me over to death.* Look here mother (says he) did you read this? And here I may take occasion to mention one principal ground of my setting forth these lines, even as the Psalmist says, to declare the works of the Lord, and his wonderful power in carrying us along, preserving us in the wilderness, while under the enemy's hand, and returning of us in safety again; and his goodness in bringing to my hand so many comfortable and suitable scriptures in my distress.

But to return: We travelled on till night, and in the morning we must go over the river to Philip's crew. When I was in the canoe, I could not but be amazed at the numerous crew of Pagans that were on the bank on the other side. When I came ashore, they gathered all about me, I sitting alone in the midst: I observed they asked one another questions, and laughed, and rejoiced over their gains and victories. Then my heart began to fail and I fell a weeping; which was the first time to my remembrance that I wept before them; although I had met with so much affliction, and my heart was many times ready to break, yet could I not shed one tear in their sight, but rather had been all this while in a maze, and like one astonished; but now I may say as *Psal.* 137. 1. *By the river of Babylon, there we sat down, yea, we wept, when we remembered Zion.* There one of them asked me why I wept? I could hardly tell what to say; yet I answered, they would kill me: No said he, none will hurt you. Then came one of them, and gave me two spoonfuls of meal (to comfort me) and another gave me half a pint of peas, which was worth more than many bushels at another time. Then I went to see King Philip; he bid me come in, and sit down; and asked me whether I would smoke it? (a usual compliment now a days, among the saints and sinners;) but this no ways suited me. For though I had formerly used tobacco, yet I had left it ever since I was first taken. It seems to be a bait the devil lays to make men lose their precious time. I remember with shame, how formerly, when I had taken two or three pipes, I was presently ready for another; such a bewitching thing it is. But I thank God he has now given me power over it; surely there are many who may be better employed, than to sit sucking a stinking tobacco-pipe.

Now the Indians gathered their forces to go against Northampton. Over night one went about yelling and hooting to give notice of the design. Whereupon they went to boiling of ground-nuts, and parching corn (as many as had it) for their provision; and in the morning away they went. During my abode in this place, Philip spake to me to make a shirt for his boy, which I did; for which he gave me a shilling. I offered the money to my mistress, but she bid me keep it, and with it I bought a piece of horse-flesh. Afterward he asked me to make a cap for his boy, for which he invited me to dinner; I went, and he gave me a pan-cake, about as big as two fingers; it was made of parched wheat, beaten and fried in bear's grease, but I thought I never tasted pleasanter meat in my life. There was a Squaw who spake to me to make a shirt for her Sannup: for which she gave me a piece of beef. Another asked me to knit a pair of stockings for which she gave me a quart of peas. I boiled my peas and beef together, and invited my master and mistress to dinner; but the proud gossip, because I served them both in one dish, would eat nothing, except one bit that he gave her upon the point of his knife. Hearing that my son was come to this place, I went to see him, and found him

[398]

lying flat on the ground; I asked him how he could sleep so ? he answered me, that he was not asleep, but at prayer; and that he lay so, that they might not observe what he was doing. I pray God he may remember these things now he is returned in safety. At this place (the sun now getting higher) what with the beams and heat of the sun, and the smoke of the wigwams, I thought I should have been blinded. I could scarce discern one wigwam from another. There was one Mary Thurston of Medfield, who seeing how it was with me, lent me a hat to wear; but as soon as I was gone, the Squaw that owned that Mary Thurston came running after me, and got it away again. Here was a Squaw who gave me a spoonful of meal, I put it in my pocket to keep it safe, yet notwithstanding somebody stole it, but put five Indian corns in the room of it; which corns were the greatest provision I had in my travel for one day.

The Indians returning from North Hampton, brought with them some horses, and sheep, and other things which they had taken: I desired them that they would carry me to Albany upon one of those horses, and sell me for powder; for so they had sometimes discoursed. I was utterly helpless of getting home on foot, the way that I came. I could hardly bear to think of the many weary steps I had taken to this place.

The ninth Remove

But instead of either going to Albany or home-ward, we must go five miles up the river then go over it. Here we abode a while. Here lived a sorry Indian, who spake to me to make him a shirt; when I had done it, he would pay me nothing for it. But he living by the river side, where I often went to fetch water, I would often be putting him in mind, and calling for my pay; at last he told me if I would make another shirt for a Papoos of his, he would give me a knife, which he did when I had done it. I carried the knife in, and my master asked me to give it him, and I was not a little glad that I had anything that they would accept of and be pleased with. When we were at this place, my master's maid came home; she had been gone three weeks into the Narragansett country to fetch corn, where they had stored up some in the ground: She brought home about a peck and a half of corn. This was about the time that their great Captain (Naonanto) was killed in the Narragansett country.

My son being now about a mile from me, I asked liberty to go and see him, they bid me go, and away I went; but quickly lost myself, travelling over hills and through swamps, and could not find the way to him. And I cannot but admire at the wonderful power and goodness of God to me, in that though I was gone from home and met

[399]

with all sorts of Indians, and those I had no knowledge of, and there being no christian soul near me, yet not one of them offered the least imaginable miscarriage to me. I turned homeward again, and met with my master, and he showed me the way to my son. When I came to him, I found him not well; and withal he had a boil on his side, which much troubled him. We bemoaned one another a while, as the Lord helped us, and then I returned again. When I was returned, I found myself as unsatisfied as I was before. I went up and down mourning and lamenting, and my spirit was ready to sink, with the thoughts of my poor children. My son was ill, and I could not but think of his mournful looks, having no christian friend near him, to do any office of love to him, either for soul or body. And my poor girl, I knew not where she was, nor whether she was sick or well, alive or dead. I repaired under these thoughts of my Bible, (my great comforter in that time,) and that scripture came to my hand, *Cast thy burthen upon the Lord, and he shall sustain thee. Psalm 55. 22.*

But I was fain to go look after something to satisfy my hunger; and going among the wigwams, I went into one, and there found a Squaw who shewed herself very kind to me, and gave me a piece of bear. I put it into my pocket, and came home; but could not find an opportunity to broil it, for fear they should get it from me; and there it lay all the day and night in my stinking pocket. In the morning I went again to the same Squaw, who had a kettle of ground-nuts boiling: I asked her to let me boil my piece of bear in the kettle, which she did, and gave me some ground-nuts to eat with it, and I cannot but think how pleasant it was to me. I have sometimes seen bear baked handsomely amongst the English, and some liked it, but the thoughts that it was bear, made me tremble: But now that was savory to me that one would think was enough to turn the stomach of a brute creature.

One bitter cold day, I could find no room to sit down before the fire: I went out, and could not tell what to do, but I went to another wigwam, where they were also sitting round the fire; but the Squaw laid a skin for me, and bid me sit down, and gave me some ground-nuts, and bid me come again; and told me they would buy me if they were able; and yet these were strangers to me that I never knew before.

The tenth Remove

That day a small part of the company removed about three quarters of a mile, intending farther the next day. When they came to the place where they intended to lodge, and had pitched their wigwams, being hungry, I went again back to the place we were before at, to get something to eat; being encouraged by the Squaw's kindness, who bid me come again. When I was there, there came an Indian to look after me; who when he had found me, kickt me all-along. I went home and found venison roasting that night, but they would not give me one bit of it. Sometimes I met with favour, and sometimes with nothing but frowns.

A Squaw was boiling horses feet, she cut me off a piece, and gave one of the English children a piece also. Being very hungry, I had quickly eat up mine; but the child could not bite it, it was so tough and sinewy, but lay sucking, gnawing and slobbering of it in the mouth and hand, then I took it of the child, and eat it myself, and savory it was to my taste. That I may say as *Job, Chap. 6. 7. The things that my soul refuseth to touch, are as my sorrowful meat.* Thus the Lord made that pleasant and refreshing, which another time would have been an abomination. Then I went home to my mistress's wigwam, and they told me I disgraced my master with begging, and if I did so any more, they would knock me on the head: I told them they had as good do that, as starve me to death.

The nineteenth Remove

They said when we went out, that we must travel to Wachuset this day. But a bitter weary day I had of it, travelling now three days together, without resting any day between. At last, after many weary steps, I saw Wachuset hills, but many miles off. Then we came to a great swamp, through which we travelled up to our knees in mud and water, which was heavy going to one tired before. Being almost spent, I thought I should have sunk down at last, and never got out; but I may say as in *Psalm 94. 18. When my foot slipped, thy mercy, O Lord, held me up.* Going along, having indeed my life, but little spirit, Philip (who was in the company) came up, and took me by the hand, and said, "Two weeks more and you shall be mistress again." I asked him if he spake true? he answered, "Yes, and quickly you shall come to your master again," who had been gone from us three weeks. After many weary steps, we came to Wachuset, where he was, and glad was I to see him. He asked me when I washed me? I told him not this month; then he fetched me some water himself, and bid me wash, and gave me a glass to see how I look'd, and bid his Squaw give me something to eat. So she gave me a mess of beans and meat, and a little ground-nut cake. I was wonderfully revived with this favour shewed me. *Psalm 106. 46. He made them also to be pitied of all those that carried them away captive.*

[401]

My master had three Squaws, living sometimes with one, and sometimes with another. Onux, this old Squaw at whose wigwam I was, and with whom my master had been these three weeks: Another was Wettimore, with whom I had lived and served all this while. A severe and proud dame she was; bestowing every day in dressing herself near as much time as any of the gentry of the land; powdering her hair, and painting her face, going with her necklaces, with jewels in her ears, and bracelets upon her hands. When she had dressed herself, her work was to make girdles of wampom and beads. The third Squaw was a younger one, by whom he had two Papooses. By that time I was refreshed by the old Squaw, Wettimore's maid came to call me home, at which I fell a weeping. Then the old Squaw told me to encourage me, that when I wanted victuals, I should came to her and that I should lie in her wigwam. Then I went with the maid, and quickly I came back and lodged there. The Squaw laid a mat under me, and a good rug over me; the first time that I had any such kindness shewed me. I understood that Wettimore thought, that if she should let me go and serve with the old Squaw, she should be in danger to lose (not only my Service) but the redemption-pay also. And I was not a little glad to hear this; being by it raised in my hopes, that in God's due time there would be an end of this sorrowful hour. Then came an Indian and asked me to knit him three pair of stockings, for which I had a hat and a silk handkerchief. Then another asked me to make her a shift, for which she gave me an apron.

Then came Tom and Peter with the second letter from the council, about the captives. Though they were Indians, I took them by the hand, and burst out into tears; my heart was so full that I could not speak to them; but recovering myself, I asked them how my husband did? and all my friends and acquaintance? they said they were well, but very melancholy. They brought me two biskets, and a pound of tobacco, the tobacco I soon gave away. When it was all gone, one asked me to give him a pipe of tobacco, I told him it was all gone; then he began to rant and threaten; I told him when my husband came, I would give him some: "Hang him," rogue, says he, "I will knock out his brains, if he comes here." And then again at the same breath, they would say, that if there should came an hundred without guns they would do them no hurt. So unstable and like madmen they were. So that fearing the worst, I durst not send to my husband, though there were some thoughts of his coming to redeem and fetch me, not knowing what might follow; for there was but little more trust to them, than to the master they served. When the letter was come, the Saggamores met to consult about the captives, and called me to them, to enquire how much my husband would give to redeem me. When I came I sat down among them, as I was wont to do, as their manner is. Then they bid me stand up, and said, they were the general court. They bid me speak what I thought he would give. Now knowing that all that we had was destroyed by the Indians, I was in great strait. I thought if I should speak of but little, it would be slighted, and hinder the matter; if of a great sum, I knew not where it would be procured; yet at a venture, I said twenty pounds, yet desired them to take less; but they would not hear of that, but sent that message to Boston, that for twenty pounds I should be redeemed. It was a praying Indian that wrote their letters for them. There was another praying Indian, who told me that he had a brother, that would not eat horse, his conscience was so tender and scrupulous, though as large as hell for the destruction of poor christians; then he said he read that scripture to him, 2 *Kings* 6. 25. *There was a famine in Samaria, and behold they besieged it, until an ass's head was sold for fourscore pieces of silver, and the fourth part of a cab of dove's dung, for five pieces of silver.* He expounded this place to his brother, and shewed him that it was lawful to eat that in a famine, which it is not at another time. And now, says he, he will eat horse with any Indian of them all. There was another praying Indian, who when he had done all the mischief that he could, betrayed his own father into the English's hands, thereby to purchase his own life. Another praying Indian was at Sudbury fight, though as he deserved, he was afterwards hanged for it. There was another praying Indian, so wicked and cruel, as to wear a string about his neck, strung with christian fingers. Another praying Indian, when they went to Sudbury fight, went with them, and his Squaw also with him, with her papoos at her back. Before they went to that fight, they got a company together to powow. The manner was as followeth:

There was one that kneeled upon a deer-skin with the company round him in a ring, who kneeled, striking upon the ground with their hands, and with sticks, and muttering or humming with their mouths. Besides him who kneeled in the ring, there also stood one with a gun in his hand. Then he on the deer-skin made a speech, and all manifested assent to it, and so they did many times together. Then they bid him with a gun go out of the ring, which he did; but when he was out, they called him in again; but he seemed to make a stand. Then they called the more earnestly, till he turned again. Then they all sang. Then they gave him two guns, in each hand one. And so he on the deer-skin began again; and at the end of every sentence in his speaking, they all assented, and humming or muttering, with their mouths, and striking upon the ground with their hands. Then they bid him with the two guns, go out of the ring again: which he did a little way. Then they called him again, but he made a stand, so they called him with greater earnestness; but he stood reeling and wavering, as if he knew not whether he should stand or fall, or which way to go. Then they called him with exceeding great vehemency, all of them, one and another. After a little while he turned in staggering as he went, with his arms stretched out, in each hand a gun. as soon as he came in, they all sang and rejoiced exceedingly a while, and then he upon the deer-skin made another speech, unto which they all assented in a rejoicing manner; and so they ended their business, and forthwith went to Sudbury fight.

To my thinking, they went without any scruple but that they should prosper, and gain the victory. And they went out not so rejoicing, but they came home with as great a victory. For they said they killed two captains, and almost an hundred men. One Englishman they brought alive with them, and he said it was too true, for they had made sad work at Sudbury; as indeed it proved. Yet they came home without that rejoicing and trumphing over their victory, which they were wont to shew at other times; but rather like dogs (as they say) which have lost their ears. Yet I could not perceive that it was for their own loss of men; they said they lost not above five or six; and I missed none, except in one wigwam. When they went, they acted as if the devil had told them that they should gain the victory, and now they acted as if the devil had told them they should have a fall. Whether it were so or no, I cannot tell, but so it proved: For they quickly began to fall, and so held on that summer, till they came to utter ruin. They came home on a sabbath day, and the pawaw that kneeled upon the deer-skin, came home, I may say without any abuse, as black as the devil. When my master came home, he came to me and bid me make a shirt for his Papoos, of a holland laced pillow-beer. About that time there came an Indian to me, and bid me come to his wigwam at night, and he would give me some pork and ground-nuts. Which I did, and as I was eating, another Indian said to me, he seems to be your good friend, but he killed two Englishmen at Sudbury, and there lie the cloathes behind you; I looked behind me, and there I saw bloody cloathes, with bullet-holes in them; yet the Lord suffered not this wretch to do me any hurt, yea instead of that, he many times refresh'd me. Five or six times did he and his Squaw refresh my feeble carcase. If I went to their wigwam at any time, they would always give me something, and yet they were strangers that I never saw before. Another Squaw gave me a piece of fresh pork, and a little salt with it, and lent me her frying-pan to fry it; and I cannot but remember what a sweet, pleasant and delightful relish that bit had to me, to this day. So little do we prize common mercies, when we have them to the full.

The twentieth Remove

It was their usual manner to remove, when they had done any mischief, lest they should be found out; and so they did at this time. We went about three or four miles, and there they built a great wigwam, big enough to hold an hundred Indians, which they did in preparation to a great day of dancing. They would now say among themselves, that the governor would be so angry for his loss at Sudbury, that he would send no more about the captives, which made me grieve and tremble. My sister being not far from this place, and hearing that I was here, desired her master to let her come and see me, and he was willing to it, and would come with her; but she being ready first, told him she would go before, and was come within a mile or two of the place. Then he overtook her, and began to rant as if he had been mad, and made her go back again in the rain: So that I never saw her till I saw her in Charlestown, but the Lord requited many of their ill-doings, for this Indian her master, was hanged afterwards at Boston.

Another thing that I would observe is, the strange providence of God in turning things about when the Indians were at the highest, and the English at the lowest. I was with the enemy eleven weeks and five days, and not one week passed without their fury and some desolation by fire or sword upon one place or another. They mourned for their own losses, yet triumphed and rejoiced in their inhuman and devilish cruelty to the English. They would boast much of their victories; saying, that in two hours' time they had destroyed such a captain and his company; in such a place; and such a captain and his company in such a place; and boast how many towns they had destroyed, and then scoff, and say, they had done them a good turn, to send them to heaven so soon. Again they would say, this summer they would knock all the rogues on the head, or drive them into the sea, or make them fly the country, thinking surely, Agag-like, *The bitterness of death is past.* Now the heathen begin to think all is their own; and the poor Christians' hopes fail (as to man) and now their eyes are more to God, and their hearts sigh heaven-ward, and they say in good earnest, *Help, Lord, or we perish.* When the Lord had brought his people to this, that they saw no help in any thing but himself, then he takes the quarrel into his own hand; and tho' they had made a pit, as deep as hell for the Christians that summer, yet the Lord hurled themselves into it. And the

Lord had not so many ways before to preserve them, but now he hath as many to destroy them.

But to return again to my going home; where we may see a remarkable change of province. At first they were all against it, except my husband would come for me; but afterward they assented to it, and seemed to rejoice in it: Some asking me to send them some bread, others some tobacco, others shaking me by the hand, offering me a hood and scarf to ride in: not one moving hand or tongue against it. Thus hath the Lord answered my poor desires, and the many earnest requests of others put up unto God for me. In my travels, an Indian came to me, and told me, if I were willing he and his Squaw would run away, and go home along with me. I told them no, I was not willing to run away, but desired to wait God's time that I might go home quietly, and without fear. And now God hath granted me my desire. O the wonderful power of God that I have seen, and the experiences that I have had. I have been in the midst of those roaring lions, and savage bears, that feared neither God, nor man, nor the devil, by night and day, alone and in company; sleeping all sorts together, and yet not one of them ever offered the least abuse of unchastity to me, in word or action. Though some are ready to say, I speak it for my own credit; but I speak it in the presence of God, and to his glory. God's power is as great now, as it was to save Daniel in the lion's den, or the three children in the fiery furnace. Especially that I should come away in the midst of so many hundreds of enemies, and not a dog move his tongue. So I took my leave of them, and in coming along, my heart melted into tears, more than all the while I was with them, and I was almost swallowed up with the thoughts that ever I should go home again. About the sun's going down, Mr. Hoar, myself, and the two Indians, came to Lancaster, and a solemn sight it was to me. There I had lived many comfortable years among my relations and neighbours: and now not one Christian to be seen, or one house left standing. We went on to a farm house that was yet standing, where we lay all night; and a comfortable lodging we had, though nothing but straw to lie on. The Lord preserved us in safety that night, and raised us up again in the morning, and carried us along, that before noon we came to Concord. Now was I full of joy, and yet not without sorrow: joy, to see such a lovely sight, so many Christians together, and some of them my neighbours: There I met with my brother, and my brother-in-law, who asked me if I knew where his wife was? poor heart! he had helped to bury her, and knew it not; she being shot down by the house, was partly burnt, so that those who were at Boston at the desolation of the town, came back afterward and buried the dead, did not know her. Yet I was not without sorrow, to think how many were looking and longing, and my own children among the rest, to enjoy that deliverance that I had now received; and I did not know whether ever I should see them again. Being recruited with food and raiment, we went to Boston that day, where I met with my dear husband; but the thoughts of our dear children, one being dead, and the other we could not tell where, abated our comfort in each other.

◈◈◈◈◈◈◈◈◈◈◈◈

[Cotton Mather]

On March 15, 1697, the salvages made a descent upon the skirts of Haverhill, murdering and captivating about thirty-nine persons, and burning about half a dozen houses. In this broil, one Hannah Dustan, having lain in about a week, attended with her nurse, Mary Neff, a body of terrible Indians drew near unto the house where she lay, with designs to carry on their bloody devastations. Her husband hastened from his employments abroad unto the relief of his distressed family; and first bidding *seven* of his *eight* children (which were from *two* to *seventeen* years of age) to get away as fast as they could unto some garrison in the town, he went in to inform his wife of the horrible distress come upon them. Ere she could get up, the fierce Indians were got so near, that, utterly desparing to do her any service, he ran out after his children; resolving that on the horse which he had with him, he would ride away with *that* which he should in this extremity find his affections to pitch most upon, and leave the rest unto the care of the Divine Providence. He overtook his children, about forty rod from his door; but then such was the *agony* of his parental affections, that he found it impossible for him to distinguish any one of them from the rest; wherefore he took up a courageous resolution to live and die with them all. A party of Indians came up with him; and now, though they fired at him, and he fired at them, yet he manfully kept at the reer of his *little army* of unarmed children, while they marched off with the pace of a child of five years old; until, by the singular providence of God, he arrived safe with them all unto a place of safety about a mile or two from his house. But his house must in the mean time have more dismal *tragedies* acted at it. The nurse, trying to escape with the new-born infant, fell into the hands of the formidable salvages; and those furious tawnies coming into the house, bid poor Dustan to rise immediately. Full of astonishment, she did so; and sitting down in the chimney with an heart full of most fearful *expectation,* she saw the raging dragons rifle all that they could carry away, and set the house on fire. About nineteen or twenty Indians now led these away, with about half a score other English captives; but ere they had gone many steps, they dash'd out the brains of the infant against a tree; and several of the other captives, as they began to tire in the sad journey, were soon sent unto their long home; the salvages would presently bury their hatchets in their brains, and leave their carcases on the ground for birds and beasts to feed upon. However, Dustan (with her nurse) notwithstanding her present condition, travelled that night about a dozen miles, and then kept up with their new masters in a long travel of an hundred and fifty miles, more or less, within a few days ensuing, without any sensible damage in their health, from the hardships of their *travel,* their *lodging,* their *diet,* and their many other difficulties.

These two poor women were now in the hands of those whose "tender mercies are cruelties;" but the good God, who hath all "hearts in his own hands," heard the sighs of those prisoners, and gave them to find unexpected favour from the master who hath laid claim unto them. That Indian family consisted of twelve persons; two stout men, three women, and seven children; and for the shame of many an English family, that has the character of *prayer-less* upon it, I must now publish what these poor women assure me. 'Tis this: in obedience to the instructions which the French have given them, they would have *prayers* in their family no less than thrice every day; in the morning, at noon, and in the evening; nor would they ordinarily let their children *eat* or *sleep,* without first saying their prayers. Indeed, these *idolaters* were, like the rest of their whiter brethren, *persecuters,* and would not endure that these poor women should retire to their English prayers, if they could hinder them. Nevertheless, the poor women had nothing but fervent prayers to make their lives comfortable or tolerable; and by being daily sent out upon business, they had opportunities, together and asunder, to do like another Hannah, in "pouring out their souls before the Lord." Nor did their praying friends among our selves forbear to "pour out" supplications for them. Now, they could not observe it without some wonder, that their Indian master sometimes when he saw them dejected, would say unto them, "What need you trouble your self? If your God will have you delivered, you shall be so!" And it seems our God would have it so to be. This Indian family was now travelling with these two captive women, (and an English youth taken from Worcester, a year and a half before,) unto a rendezvous of salvages, which they call a *town*, somewhere beyond Penacook; and they still told these poor women that when they came to this town, they must be stript, and scourg'd, and run the *ganlet* through the whole army of Indians. They said this was the *fashion* when the captives first came to a town; and they derided some of the faint-hearted English, which, they said, fainted and swoon'd away under the *torments* of this discipline. But on April 30, while they were yet, it may be, about an hundred and fifty miles from the Indian town, a little before break of day, when the whole crew was in a *dead sleep*, (reader, see if it prove not so!) one of these women took up a resolution to imitate the action of Jael upon Siseria; and being where she had not her own *life* secured by any *law* unto her, she thought she was not forbidden by any *law* to take away the *life* of the *murderers* by whom her child had been butchered. She heartened the nurse and the youth to assist her in this enterprize; and all furnishing themselves with hatchets for the purpose, they struck such home blows upon the heads of their sleeping oppressors, that ere they could any of them struggle into any effectual resistance, "at the feet of these poor prisoners, they bow'd they fell, they lay down; at their feet they bow'd, they fell; where they bow'd, there they fell down dead." Only one squaw escaped, sorely wounded, from them in the dark; and one boy, whom they reserved asleep, intending to bring him away with them, suddenly waked, and scuttled away from this desolation. But cutting off the scalps of the ten wretches, they came off, and received *fifty pounds* from the General Assembly of the province, as a recompence of their action; besides which, they received many "presents of congratulation" from their more private friends: but none gave 'em a greater taste of bounty than Colonel Nicholson, the Governour of Maryland, who, hearing of their action, sent 'em a very generous token of his favour.

◇◈◇◈◇◈◇◈◇◈◇◈◇◈◇

[*Samuel Sewall*]

April 29. 5th day is signalised by the Atchievment of Hannah Dustin, Mary Neff, and Samuel Lennerson; who kill'd Two men [Indians], their Masters, and two women and 6 others, and have brought in Ten Scalps.

May 12, 1697. Hañah Dustan came to see us; I gave her part of Coñecticut Flax. She saith her Master, whom she kill'd, did formerly live with Mr. Roulandson at Lancaster: He told her, that when he pray'd the English way, he thought that was good: but now he found the French way was better. The single man shewed the night before, to Sam[1]. Leñarson, how he used to knock English men on the head and take off their Scalps; little thinking that the Captives would make some of their first experiment upon himself. Sam. Leñarson kill'd him.

SPIRIT OF 'SEVENTY-SIX

❖❖❖❖❖❖❖❖❖❖❖❖❖

[George R. T. Hewes, Boston]

Some time after the massacre of our citizens, and before the destruction of the tea, Hewes relates an ancedote of a hair's breath escape. One day, said he, as I was returning from dinner, I met a man by the name of John Malcom, who was a custom-house officer, and a small boy, pushing his sled along, before him; and just as I was passing the boy, he said to Malcom, what, sir, did you throw my chips into the snow for, yesterday? Upon which Malcolm angrily replied, do you speak to me, you rascal; and, as he raised a cane he had in his hand aiming it at the head of the boy, I spoke to Malcolm, and said to him, you are not about to strike that boy with your cudgel, you may kill him; upon my saying that, he was suddenly diverted from the boy, and turning upon me, says you d——d rascal, do you presume too, to speak to me? I replied to him, I am no rascal, sir, be it known to you; whereupon he struck me across the head with his cane, and knocked me down, and by the blow cut a hole in my hat two inches in length. At this moment, one Captain Godfry came up, and raising me up, asked who had struck me; Malcom, replied the by standers, while he, for fear of the displeasure of the populace, ran to his house, and shut himself up. The people, many of whom were soon collected around me, advised me to go immediately to Doctor Warren,* and get him to dress my wound, which I did without delay; and the doctor, after he dressed it, observed to me, it can be considered no misfortune that I had a thick skull, for had not yours been very strong, said he, it would have been broke; you have come within a hair's breath of loosing your life. He then advised me to go to Mr. Quincy, a magistrate, and get a warrant, for the purpose of arresting Malcom, which I did, and carried it immediately to a constable, by the name of Justine Hale, and delivered it to him, to serve, but when he came to the house where Malcom was locked up, it was surrounded by such a multitude he could not serve it. The people, however, soon broke open the door, and took Malcom into their custody. They then took him to the place where the massacre was committed, and their flogged him with thirty-nine stripes. After which, they besmeared him thoroughly with tar and feathers; they then whipped him through the town, till they arrived at the gallows, on the neck, where they gave him thirty-nine stripes more, and then, after putting one end of a rope about his neck, and throwing the other end over the gallows, told him to remember that he had come within one of being hanged. They then took him back to the house from whence they had taken him, and discharged him from their custody.

The severity of the flogging they had given him, together with the cold coat of tar with which they had invested him, had such a benumbing effect upon his health, that it required considerable effort to restore his usual circulation. During the process of his chastisement, the deleterious effect of the frost, it being a cold season, generated a morbid affection upon the prominent parts of his face, especially upon his chin, which caused a separation and peeling off of some fragments of loose skin and flesh, which, with a portion of the tar and feathers, which adhered to him, he preserved in a box, and soon after carried with him to England, as the testimonials of his sufferings in the cause of his country. On his arrival in England soon after this catastrophe Malcom obtained an annual pension of fifty pounds, but lived only two years after to enjoy it.

On my inquiring of Hewes if he knew who first proposed the project of destroying the tea, to prevent its being landed, he replied

* Joseph Warren, the fallen hero of Bunker Hill. B. M.

that he did not; neither did he know who or what number were to volunteer their services for that purpose. But from the significant allusion of some persons in whom I had confidence, together with the knowledge I had of the spirit of those times, I had no doubt but that a sufficient number of associates would accompany me in that enterprise.

The tea destroyed was contained in three ships, laying near each other, at what was called at that time Griffin's wharf, and were surrounded by armed ships of war; the commanders of which had publicly declared, that if the rebels, as they were pleased to style the Bostonians, should not withdraw their opposition to the landing of the tea before a certain day, the 17th day of December, 1773, they should on that day force it on shore, under the cover of their cannon's mouth. On the day preceding the seventeenth, there was a meeting of the citizens of the county of Suffolk, convened at one of the churches in Boston, for the purpose of consulting on what measures might be considered expedient to prevent the landing of the tea, or secure the people from the collection of the duty. At that meeting a committee was appointed to wait on Governor Hutchinson, and request him to inform them whether he would take any measures to satisfy the people on the object of the meeting. To the first application of this committee, the governor told them he would give them a definite answer by five o'clock in the afternoon. At the hour appointed, the committee again repaired to the governor's house, and on inquiry found he had gone to his country seat at Milton, a distance of about six miles. When the committee returned and informed the meeting of the absence of the governor, there was a confused murmur among the members, and the meeting was immediately dissolved, many of them crying out, Let every man do his duty, and be true to his country; and there was a general huzza for Griffin's wharf. It was now evening, and I immediately dressed myself in the costume of an Indian, equipped with a small hatchet, which I and my associates denominated the tomahawk, with which, and a club, after having painted my face and hands with coal dust in the shop of a blacksmith, I repaired to Griffin's wharf, where the ships lay that contained the tea. When I first appeared in the street, after being thus disguised, I fell in with many who were dressed, equipped and painted as I was, and who fell in with me, and marched in order to the place of our destination. When we arrived at the wharf, there were three of our number who assumed an authority to direct our operations, to which we readily submitted. They divided us into three parties, for the purpose of boarding the three ships which contained the tea at the same time.

The name of him who commanded the division to which I was assigned, was Leonard Pitt. The names of the other commanders I never knew. We were immediately ordered by the respective commanders to board all the ships at the same time, which we promptly obeyed. The commander of the division to which I belonged, as soon as we were on board the ship, appointed me boatswain, and ordered me to go to the captain and demand of him the keys to the hatches and a dozen candles. I made the demand accordingly, and the captain promptly replied, and delivered the articles; but requested me at the same time to do no damage to the ship or rigging. We then were ordered by our commander to open the hatches, and take out all the chests of tea and throw them overboard, and we immediately proceeded to execute his orders; first cutting and splitting the chests with our tomahawks, so as thoroughly to expose them to the effects of the water. In about three hours from the time we went on board, we had thus broken and thrown overboard every tea chest to be found in the ship; while those in the other ships were disposing of the tea in the same way, at the same time. We were surrounded by British armed ships, but no attempt was made to resist us. We then quietly retired to our several places of residence, without having any conversation with each other, or taking any measures to discover who were our associates; nor do I recollect of our having had the knowledge of the name of a single individual concerned in that affair, except that of Leonard Pitt, the commander of my division, who I have mentioned. There appeared to be an understanding that each individual should volunteer his services, keep his own secret, and risk the consequences for himself. No disorder took place during that transaction, and it was observed at that time, that the stillest night ensued that Boson had enjoyed for many months.

During the time we were throwing the tea overboard, there were several attempts made by some of the citizens of Boston and its vicinity, to carry off small quantities of it for their family use. To effect that object, they would watch their opportunity to snatch up a handful from the deck, where it became plentifully scattered, and put it into their pockets. One Captain O'Conner, whom I well knew, came on board for that purpose, and when he supposed he was not noticed, filled his pockets, and also the lining of his coat. But I had detected him, and gave information to the captain of what he was doing. We were ordered to take him into custody, and just as he was stepping from the vessel, I seized him by the skirt of his coat, and in attempting to pull him back, I tore it off; but springing forward, by a rapid effort, he made his escape. He had however to run a gaunlet through the crowd upon the wharf; each one, as he passed, giving him a kick or a stroke.

The next day we nailed the skirt of his coat, which I had pulled off, to the whipping post in Charlestown, the place of his residence, with a label upon it, commemorative of the occasion which had thus subjected the proprietor to the popular indignation.

Another attempt was made to save a little tea from the ruins of the cargo, by a tall aged man, who wore a large cocked hat and white wig, which was fashionable at that time. He had slightly slipped a little into his pocket, but being detected, they seized him, and taking his hat and wig from his head, threw them, together with the tea, of which they had emptied his pockets, into the water. In consideration of his advanced age, he was permitted to escape, with now and then a slight kick.

The next morning, after we had cleared the ships of the tea, it was discovered that very considerable quantities of it was floating upon the surface of the water; and to prevent the possibility of any of its being saved for use, a number of small boats were manned by sailors and citizens, who rowed them into those parts of the harbour wherever the tea was visible, and by beating it with oars and paddles, so thoroughly drenched it, as to render its entire destruction inevitable.

The few months that I remained at Wrentham, I was continually reflecting upon the unwarrantable sufferings inflicted on the citizens of Boston, by the usurpation and tyranny of Great Britain, and my mind was excited with an unextinguishable desire to aid in chastising them.

I had fully resolved to take a privateering cruise, and when I informed my wife of my fixed resolution, and requested her to have my clothes in readiness in a short time, by a day appointed, although she was greatly afflicted at the prospect of our separation, and my absence from a numerous family of children, who needed a father's parental care, she without a murmur reluctantly complied with my request. On the day which I had appointed to take my departure, I came into the room where my wife was, and inquired if all was ready? She pointed in silence to my knapsack. I observed, that I would put it on and walk with it a few rods, to see if it was rightly fitted to carry with ease. I went out, to return no more until the end of my cruise.

I then pursued my route to Providence, in Rhode Island, and on my arrival there, immediately stipulated with Captain Thomas Stacy to go with him on a cruise of seven weeks. When that term had expired, and we had seen no enemy during the time, we were discouraged, and threatened to mutiny, unless he would return, as we had served out the time for which we had stipulated. The captain then promised us, that if we would continue with him one week longer, provided we did not see any thing during that time, he would return; to which we assented. The next Sunday after, we espied a large ship, which we took to be a British frigate. We were ordered to down sails and go to fishing, thereby to deceive them; and when she came by us, she took us to be only a fisherman

After she had passed us, our captain said to us, my boys, if you will stand by me, we will take that ship. We immediately gave chase, and overtook her about an hour after dark. The captain hailed us, and asked us where we were from: our captain answered, from St. Johns, Newfoundland. I am a King's tender, and belong to his majesty, King George. Our captain then hailed him, and he said he was from Quebec, bound to London. Our captain then said to him, come aboard and bring your papers, that we may see whether you are a d — d Yankee or not. He came aboard accordingly, and brought his papers. Our captain then took him by the hand, and said to him, you are welcome aboard the sloop Diamond, belonging to the United States. You are my prisoner. Finding his mistake, and that resistance would be useless, he surrendered without a struggle.

Soon after, I went to Boston, and requested of Captain Smedley my discharge from the ship. But he seemed to think he could not with propriety give it. I then requested him to pay me my wages. He told me he was about fitting out an expedition to the West Indies, and could not, without great inconvenience, spare the money then; but said he would call on his way to Providence, where he was going in a short time, and would then pay me; but I never saw him afterwards. Neither have I, at any time since, received a farthing, either of my share of prize money or wages.

◇◇◇◇◇◇◇◇◇◇◇◇◇◇

[Paul Revere, Boston]

In the fall of 1774 and winter of 1775, I was one of upwards of thirty, chiefly mechanics, who formed ourselves into a committee for the purpose of watching the movements of the British soldiers, and gaining every intelligence of the movements of the tories. We held our meetings at the Green Dragon tavern. We were so careful that our meetings should be kept secret, that every time we met, every person swore upon the bible, that they would not discover any of our transactions, but to Messrs. HANCOCK, ADAMS, Doctors WARREN, CHURCH, and one or two more.

About November, when things began to grow serious, a gentleman who had connexions with the tory party, but was a whig at heart, acquainted me, that our meetings were discovered, and mentioned the identical words that were spoken among us the night before. We did not then distrust Dr. Church, but supposed it must be some one among us. We removed to another place, which we thought was more secure; but here we found that all our transactions were communicated to Governor Gage. (This came to me through the then Secretary Flucker; he told it to the gentleman mentioned above.) It was then a common opinion, that there was a traitor in the Provincial Congress, and that Gage was possessed of all their secrets. (Church was a member of that Congress for Boston.) In the winter, towards the spring, we frequently took turns, two and two, to watch the soldiers, by patrolling the streets all night. The Saturday night preceding the 19th of April, about 12 o'clock at night, the boats belonging to the transports were all launched, and carried under the sterns of the men of war. (They had been previously hauled up and repaired.) We likewise found that the grenadiers and light infantry were all taken off duty.

From these movements, we expected something serious was to be transacted. On Tuesday evening, the 18th, it was observed, that a number of soldiers were marching towards the bottom of the Common. About 10 o'clock, Dr. Warren sent in great haste for me, and begged that I would immediately set off for Lexington, where Messrs. Hancock and Adams were, and acquaint them of the movement, and that it was thought they were the objects. When I got to Dr. Warren's house, I found he had sent an express by land to Lexington — a Mr. William Dawes. The Sunday before, by desire of Dr. Warren, I had been to Lexington, to Messrs. Hancock and Adams, who were at the Rev. Mr. Clark's. I returned at night through Charlestown; there I agreed with a Colonel Conant and some other gentlemen, that if the British went out by water, we would shew two lanthorns in the north church steeple; and if by land, one, as a signal; for we were apprehensive it would be difficult to cross the Charles River, or get over Boston neck. I left Dr. Warren, called upon a friend, and desired him to make the signals. I then went home, took my boots and surtout, went to the north part of the town, where I had kept a boat; two friends rowed me across Charles River, a little to the eastward where the Somerset man of war lay. It was then young flood, the ship was winding, and the moon was rising. They landed me on the Charlestown side. When

I got into town, I met Colonel Conant, and several others; they said they had seen our signals. I told them what was acting, and went to get me a horse; I got a horse of Deacon Larkin. While the horse was preparing, Richard Devens, Esq. who was one of the Committee of Safety, came to me, and told me, that he came down the road from Lexington, after sundown, that evening; that he met ten British officers, all well mounted, and armed, going up the road.

I set off upon a very good horse; it was then about eleven o'clock, and very pleasant. After I had passed Charlestown neck, and got nearly opposite where Mark was hung in chains, I saw two men on horseback, under a tree. When I got near them, I discovered they were British officers. One tried to get ahead of me, and the other to take me. I turned my horse very quick, and galloped towards Charlestown neck, and then pushed for the Medford road. The one who chased me, endeavouring to cut me off, got into a clay pond, near where the new tavern is now built. I got clear of him, and went through Medford, over the bridge, and up to Menotomy. In Medford, I awaked the Captain of the minute men; and after that, I alarmed almost every house, till I got to Lexington. I found Messrs. Hancock and Adams at the Rev. Mr. Clark's; I told them my errand, and inquired for Mr. Dawes; they said he had not been there; I related the story of the two officers, and supposed that he must have been stopped, as he ought to have been there before me. After I had been there about half an hour, Mr. Dawes came; we refreshed ourselves, and set off for Concord, to secure the stores, &c. there. We were overtaken by a young Dr. Prescot, whom we found to be a high son of liberty. I told them of the ten officers that Mr. Devens met, and that it was probable we might be stopped before we got to Concord; for I suppose that after night, they divided themselves, and that two of them had fixed themselves in such passages as were most likely to stop any intelligence going to Concord. I likewise mentioned, that we had better alarm all the inhabitants till we got to Concord; the young Doctor much approved of it, and said, he would stop with either of us, for the people between that and Concord knew him, and would give the more credit to what we said. We had got nearly half way: Mr. Dawes and the Doctor stopped to alarm the people of a house: I was about one hundred rods a head, when I saw two men, in nearly the same situation as those officers were, near Charlestown. I called for the Doctor and Mr. Dawes to come up; in an instant I was surrounded by four; — they had placed themselves in a straight road, that inclined each way; they had taken down a pair of bars on the north side of the road, and two of them were under a tree in the pasture. The Doctor being foremost, he came up; and we tried to get past them; but they being armed with pistols and swords, they forced us into the pasture; — the Doctor jumped his horse over a low stone wall, and got to Concord. I observed a wood at a small distance, and made for that. When I got there, out started six officers, on horseback, and ordered me to dismount; — one of them, who appeared to have the command, examined me, where I came from, and what my name was? I told him. He asked me if I was an express? I answered in the affirmative. He demanded what time I had left Boston? I told him; and added, that their troops had catched aground in passing the river, and that there would be five hundred Americans there in a short time, for I had alarmed the country all the way up. He immediately rode towards those who stopped us, when all five of them came down upon a full gallop; one of them, whom I afterwards found to be a Major Mitchel, of the 5th Regiment, clapped his pistol to my head, called me by name, and told me he was going to ask me some questions, and if I did not give him true answers, he would blow my brains out. He then asked me similar questions to those above. He then ordered me to mount my horse, after searching me for arms. He then ordered them to advance, and to lead me in front. When we got to the road, they turned down towards Lexington. When we had got about one mile, the Major rode up to the officer that was leading me, and told him to give me to the Sergeant. As soon as he took me, the Major ordered him, if I attempted to run, or any body insulted them, to blow my brains out. We rode till we got near Lexington meeting-house, when the militia fired a volley of guns, which appeared to alarm them very much. The Major inquired of me how far it was to Cambridge, and if there were any other road? After some consultation, the Major rode up to the Sergeant, and asked if his horse was tired? He answered him, he was — (He was a Sergeant of Grenadiers, and had a small horse) — then, said he, take that man's horse. I dismounted, and the Sergeant mounted my horse, when they all rode towards Lexington meeting-house. I went across the burying-ground, and some pastures, and came to the Rev. Mr. Clark's house, where I found Messrs. Hancock and Adams. I told them of my treatment, and they concluded to go from that house towards Woburn. I went with them, and a Mr. Lowell, who was a clerk to Mr. Hancock. When we got to the house where they intended to stop, Mr. Lowell and myself returned to Mr. Clark's, to find what was going on. When we got there, an elderly man came in; he said he had just come from the tavern, that a man had come from Boston, who said there were no British troops coming. Mr. Lowell and myself went towards the tavern, when we met a man on a full gallop, who told us the troops were coming up the rocks. We afterwards met another, who said they were close by. Mr. Lowell asked me to go to the tavern with him, to get a trunk of papers belonging to Mr. Hancock. We went up chamber; and while we were getting the trunk,

LEXINGTON, MASSACHUSETTS

we saw the British very near, upon a full march. We hurried towards Mr. Clark's house. In our way, we passed through the militia. There were about fifty. When we had got about one hundred yards from the meeting-house, the British troops appeared on both sides of the meeting-house. In their front was an officer on horseback. They made a short halt; *when I saw, and heard, a gun fired,* which appeared to be a pistol. Then I could distinguish two guns, and then a continual roar of musquetry; when we made off with the trunk.

◆◇◆◇◆◇◆◇◆◇◆◇◆·

[*Henry Tufts, New Hampshire*]

In 1775 I left home, and meeting with Captain Clarke, enlisted into his company for two months. We marched directly to Portsmouth, and employed in the building and repairing of forts, in the vicinity of that town. I served as cook to part of the company, as I tarried the whole time of enlistment, without desertion.

One night, however, as I was traveling in the streets of Portsmouth, it was my ill luck to meet with two riflemen, one of whom

accosted me with; *"You are the devil, that served us so today."* Not
knowing to what he alluded, I inadvertently replied, *"Yes."* At
which without more ceremony, he knocked me down with a club;
striking out two of my fore-teeth, and leaving me for dead in the
street. Soon, however, recovering some use of my senses, I made
shift, with very great difficulty, to reach a neighboring house, where
I tarried till morning. Being determined upon revenge, I loaded
my gun at the moment I awaked, and issued forth in quest of the
assassin. I found him at Tilton's tavern, and resolved to shoot him
instantly. In the broad entry, I met General [John] Sullivan and
Colonel [Joseph] Cilley, who having heard of the abusive treatment
I had received, suspected my real motives, and demanded the sur-
render of my arms. Instead of immediate compliance, I showed my
wounds, related the whole adventure, and protested my determina-
tion to have recompense. The general said the villain deserved
chastisement, and should receive it; still peremptorily ordering me
to deliver up my weapons. Not daring to disobey the general, who
was our commander in chief, I complied with his injunctions
though with reluctance. At that moment Col. Cilley approached
the rascal who had thus maltreated me, belabored him soundly
with his sword, and ordered him under guard, to the jail in Portsmouth. There he was confined I know not how long, but my term
of enlistment having expired, I returned home to Lee, and spent
several weeks to little or no advantage. After this, being solicited by
Capt. Denbo, I enlisted into his corps for two months more, and
was directed to repair to Winter Hill, near Boston. Here our troops
fared, at times, so slenderly, that we had to atone for the dearth of
allowance, by stealing pigs, poultry, and such like articles.

One night I went to Mystic, with two others, and stole a number
of dunghill fowls. Just as we had caught and killed them, the
owner happened to hear a disturbance among his poultry, and ran
out to discover what the fracas might be. I happened to espy him,
just as he was stepping out of doors; so to give my comrades a better chance to secrete the plunder, I marched up to the farmer and
made some inquiry for some cider. He said he believed somebody
had been stealing his poultry. *"Nothing more likely,* (quoth I) *for
just now I saw several fellows running down street."* *"Damn them,*
said he, *I believe they have carried off some of my fowls."*

Uttering this, he invited us into the kitchen, and treated us plentifully with cider; we then bid him adieu, and marched off jovially
with our feathered booty. On the way back to quarters we picked
up a couple of geese more, and made a delicate feast on the whole
the same evening; but, the next morning the proprietor of the

geese, paid our commissary a visit, and complained to Capt. Denbo of his loss. The captain told him to search where he pleased, so the farmer made inquiry, till weary of the pursuit, but not being able to track his property, or fasten either upon any one, we had permission to drive him out of the camp; this we exultingly put in execution, pelting him unmercifully with snow balls, and using him, in other respects, I must confess, extremely ill. At the expiration of the two months I was dismissed with the recommendation of having behaved as a good soldier, and returned to Lee.

I stayed at home but a short space, ere I once more enlisted, for other two months, under Capt. Folsom, and marched back to Winter Hill. In a few days our company was stationed at Cambridge College, and assisted in building the forts at Lechmore's point; but while engaged in this business, we were forced to submit to much hardship, and were extremely exposed to the fire of the enemy the whole time. Provisions being also scarce, we were reduced to half allowance, and obliged to spend part of our wages to prevent absolute starvation. — Not relishing such short commons, I resolved to trick, if possible, something out of the commissary, whose name was Smith. Accordingly, with the connivance of several of the subaltern officers, I went and drew our company's quota of pork for the day, and conveyed it to the place of destination. In a few minutes I returned back to the commissary's quarters, who was yet dealing out provision, when spying on the head of the barrel, a large portion of the side of a hog, weighing about forty pounds, I called out in Mr. Smith's hearing, to James Hall, one of our company, saying, "You lazy devil, why don't you take away our meat ? You expect me to do the whole drudgery, but I'll see you hang'd first." The commissary, who heard this rough greeting, turned about in a pet, exclaiming, "What's your meat here for ? If you don't take it out of my way in a twinkling, I'll lay an embargo on the transport." As I was to the full as anxious for the speedy removal of the nuisance, as the gentleman himself could be, I thrust the pork through with a stick, in which manner, Hall and I lugged it off very triumphantly, thus easing the unsuspecting commissary of the incumbrance in a trice.

As our wants had been pressing, the officers of the company were by no means offended at my successful stratagem, justly concluding we should need a moderate quantity of rum, while devouring this acquisition; I told them I would undertake to provide that desideratum likewise. So running out of doors with much alacrity, in order to find a suitable tool to dispatch upon the embassy; whom should I meet with but old Hall, the father of him above named. Without preface, I requested him to go to the sutler's, and get us a gallon of rum, but he declined, unless I would furnish him with the money. As it happened I was destitute of the necessary evil, but knowing Hall to be an illiterate man and very ignorant, I drew from my pocket an old summons, which had been served on me for debt some time before. Presenting this, I told him it was a four dollar bill, and desired him to procure me the rum with all speed, and return the change. His scruples being now removed, he set off to execute his commission, while I, knowing the imposition must be detected by the Sutler, and wishing to make both ends of my project meet, dispatched after Hall another man (whom I let into the secret) with directions to bring away the rum at the moment of its delivery, and before Hall should present his old summons to the tapster. My envoy arrived in the nick of time, and fulfilled articles to a punctilio; but scarce was his back turned, when Hall pulled out the supposed bill to make payment. The sutler, not being familiarized to such odd kind of money, demanded its value. Hall replied it was a four dollar bill, and requested his change. At this the sutler, who was an arch blade, had much ado to repress risibility, but willing to carry on the joke, and knowing Hall to be a responsible man, told him he was unable to break the bill just then, but would charge the rum and take pay another time. With this answer, Hall went away entirely satisfied, and very honestly returned me the old summons, together with a history of proceedings; and here the affair rested, for he never discovered the cheat, till called upon by the sutler to make remittances.

We regaled ourselves like lords upon these goodly things, which we devoured with as keen avidity, as though they had been acquired ever so honestly, while I received the applause of every guest, as well for my zeal, as ingenious contrivance.

◇◇◇◇◇◇◇◇◇◇◇◇◇

[Lyman Beecher]

I remember near the close of the war, when New Haven was attacked by the British, Aaron Burr happened to be there, and took command of a party of militia. Father took his old firelock and went out with them. But the British were too strong for them, and the word came each one to look out for himself. Father was down in the "second quarter," so called, and happened to see a scout; he raised his gun, and stood deliberating whether he could kill a fellow-being. The click of a trigger near by turned his head toward a British marksman, who had no such scruples, but was aiming straight at his head. He popped down into a ravine, losing his gun and hat, and wandered about all that hot July day bareheaded, and got a sunstroke, from which he never wholly recovered.

I remember that day we were plowing, when we heard the sound of cannon toward New Haven. "Whoa !" said Uncle Benton; stopped team, off harness, mounted old Sorrel, bareback, shouldered the old musket, and rode off to New Haven. Deacon Bartlett went too; and Sam Bartlett said he never saw his father more keen after deer than he was to get a shot at the regulars. He had a large-bored, long old shot-gun, that I bought afterwards for ducks.

I remember the firing at the close of the war. They sent us a cannon from New Haven, and we fired it thirteen times, one for every state. The last time they filled it full of stones, and let drive into the top of a great oak-tree.

Then came hard times, taxes, whiskey insurrection, Shays' rebellion, and the new Constitution. Uncle Benton objected to the eight dollars per day for members of Congress; but General Collins smoothed him down, and he voted for it. I remember one day they were discussing who should be president, a knot of them, and I spoke up, "Why, General Washington !" and they looked at each other and smiled.

❖❖❖❖❖❖❖❖❖❖❖❖❖

[Ebenezer Fox, Roxbury, Mass.]

I sought a friend, and found one in a companion with whom I had long associated, John Kelley, who was a little older than myself. To him I imparted my views and wishes in regard to future operations.

Our plan was soon formed, which was nothing less than to furnish ourselves with whatever we thought indispensable for our undertaking, to leave home privately, and take the most direct route to Providence, R. I., where we expected to find employment as sailors on board of some vessel.

Our greatest trouble was to raise the means for the expedition. Having collected what few articles we possessed and securing them in two small bundles, we secreted them in a barn at some distance from our habitation.

The place for our meeting was the steps of the church, which stood where the Rev. Mr. Putnam's now stands. According to appointment, I found my friend Kelley on the spot at eight o'clock in the evening on the eighteenth of April, the night before the memorable battle of Lexington.

Kelley's first question to me was, "How much money have you

got ?" I replied, "A half a dollar." "That is just what I have got," said Kelley, "thought I might have taken as much as I wanted from the old tory; but I thought I would not take any more than what belonged to me." Kelley had lived with a gentleman named Winslow, who was highly esteemed for his benevolence and other virtues; but, being a friend to the royal government, he was stigmatized with the epithet of "Tory."

We started about nine o'clock at night, and travelled till we arrived at Jamaica Plain and stopped on the door-steps of the Rev. Dr. Gordon's church to rest ourselves and hold a consultation.

We concluded to continue on our route, and directed our course to Dedham, where we arrived shortly after ten the same night.

As I have observed, this was on the night previous to the battle of Lexington. At that time, much excitement prevailed in the public mind. Great anxiety was manifested in the country in the vicinity of Boston to know what was going on there. People were out in all directions to hear the "news from town." As we were too young to be very well informed in regard to coming events, and were ignorant of the great plans in agitation, our fears induced us to think that the uncommon commotion that appeared to prevail must have some connexion with our escape, and that the moving multitudes we saw were in pursuit of us.

Before we entered the village, we stopped at a tavern and called for a bowl of bread and milk, the price of which was three pence; but the kindhearted landlord refused to take any compensation. We now were constantly meeting with people, who, anxious to hear the news from Boston, frequently interrogated us respecting whence we came and whither we were going, &c.; in answering which we adhered as nearly to the truth as our fears of discovery would permit.

We stopped at Mann's tavern in Walpole, and here a multitude of people collected, having apparently some great object in agitation. Being seen coming in the direction from Boston, we were again assailed with more questions than we knew how to answer consistently with our safety. The tavernkeeper excited our apprehensions by abruptly asking us whither we were going?

"To seek our fortunes," we replied.

"You have taken hard times for it," and he advised us to return home.

During the conversation, the stage coach from Boston arrived at the tavern, where the passengers were to dine. They brought the news of the Lexington battle, with an exaggerated account of a loss on the side of the British of two hundred men, and on that of the American of only thirty. This was received with loud shouts of exultation, while the militia marched off full of ardor and zeal.

By this time, my companion and myself felt the need of some refreshment; but our funds would not permit us to indulge our appetites with the luxury of a dinner; we therefore contented ourselves with a simple luncheon.

Tired of walking, our next object was to drive a bargain with the coachman for a ride to Providence. The price demanded was one and sixpence for each of us, and that upon condition that one should ride with the coachman and the other on the baggage.

The coachman's seat to stage-coaches in those days was not the comfortable place which it now is; and the baggage used to be fastened directly upon the hind axle-tree. Racks and such-like conveniences are the improvements of modern times. To sit upon the baggage, then, could not be considered a great privilege, and it required not a little exertion to keep one's position. For such accommodations one and sixpence each we considered an exorbitant price; and, after a great deal of haggling, a bargain was made to carry us both for two and eight-pence. We left Walpole about one o'clock and arrived in Providence about sunset.

Our design in coming to Providence naturally led us to the part of the town where the shipping lay. We found a vessel at a wharf, which appeared to have no person on board. We went on to her deck, and, finding the cabin doors open, entered, took possession of two vacant berths, in which we slept soundly till morning, when we left the vessel without meeting with any person belonging to her.

I and my companion then thought it best to separate, for the purpose of seeking employment, in different directions; and we parted without thinking to fix upon any time or place for a subsequent meeting. I have since ascertained, that Kelley found employment on board of a vessel, and went to sea. What was his fate I know not; for after that day I never saw him, nor to the present time have I ever heard any more respecting him than what I have related. Should he meet with these pages, he is informed that I reside in the town from which we absconded sixty-three years ago.

After seeking for a situation on board of some vessel for several days, I at length found one in the service of Capt. Joseph Manchester, who was in the employ of Nathaniel Angier. I shipped in the capacity of cabin boy, for a compensation of twenty-one shillings per month, to go to Cape François in the island of St. Domingo. The wages of the sailors were forty-two shillings a month.

By the assistance of my good aunt, in a few days I was tolerably well equipped for the voyage. The vessel was hauled off into the stream, and shortly after we sailed for our destined port. This being the first time I ever was at sea, I experienced a considerable amount of that mental and bodily prostration called "sea-sickness;" but in a few days I became accustomed to the motion of the vessel, and recovered my usual health and spirits.

Being what is termed a "green hand," I had everything to learn that belonged to my duties; and of course made some blunders, for which I received more curses than thanks.

Among other misfortunes, I unluckily placed a large pot of butter in the larboard locker, without the precaution to fasten it in its place. It rolled out in the course of the night, and the fragments of the pot together with the contents were scattered about near the foot of the cabin steps. At the time of the accident the captain was upon deck, and having occasion to go below, he stepped into the midst of the greasy particles and measured his length upon the floor. The butter received a stamp of considerable magnitude in the form of a head, which, although it served to protect the captain's from any lamentable damage, did not shield mine from a volley of oaths and threats.

After a pleasant voyage of about fourteen days, we arrived in sight of our destined port. That part of St. Domingo in which Cape François is situated was then in possession of the French; and, in regard to certain articles, trade was prohibited between the inhabitants and the American colonies. Some management was therefore necessary to obtain the cargo we wanted. A boat was sent ashore to inform certain merchants who were expecting us, of our arrival. In the morning a pilot came to our assistance, and we were soon anchored in the harbor of Cape François.

We carried our staves and hoops in a state of preparation to be converted into hogsheads; and I worked at coopering till we were ready to receive our cargo. Having filled the hogsheads with molasses, which was apparently all our cargo, we set sail, and afterwards took on board a quantity of coffee, a prohibited article, which was conveyed to us by vessels employed for that purpose.

Our loading being thus completed, we directed our course for Providence, and after a passage of about fifteen days we arrived at Stonington, Connecticut.

During our absence from home, the Revolutionary war had

commenced, and we found that the British had begun their depredations upon our commerce and maritime towns.

We left Stonington in the night, entertaining the hope, that, with a favorable wind, we might get into Providence without being discovered by the British cruisers, which we knew were cruising somewhere between Newport and Providence.

If the breeze had continued favorable, we should have effected our object; but, unfortunately, the wind subsided a little before daylight, and in the morning we found ourselves close by the enemy, consisting of two ships of war, and a small vessel called a tender between them and the land. The American commander, Commodore Whipple, with a naval force greatly inferior to the British, was seen by us, higher up the bay, out of reach of the enemy, making signals for us to press all sail and approach. But unluckily we were ignorant of the meaning of the signals, and did not know whether they came from a friend or an enemy. As the cruisers were to the windward of us, we tacked one way and the other, hoping that we should be able to beat up the bay; but, finding that the tender was about to intercept our progress in one direction, while the cruisers approached us in the other, and no chance of escape appearing, we bore away and ran our vessel ashore.

Preparations were hastily made for leaving the vessel, our captain having given permission to all, who were disposed to run the risk, to make their escape. The mate and crew jumped overboard and swam for shore where they arrived safe, although fired upon by the British tender.

Captain Manchester, supposing that I should be unable to reach the shore by swimming, kindly advised me to remain on board with him and be taken prisoner. I hesitated a short time about taking his advice, but finally concluded to run the risk of being drowned; and with nothing on but a shirt and a pair of trowsers, I plunged into the sea and swam for the shore, where I arrived without injury, but nearly exhausted from fatigue and fear, not a little augmented by the sound of the bullets that whistled around my head while in the water. In dread of pursuit, I ran into a corn-field, and finding my wet clothes an incumbrance, I stripped them off and ran with all speed through the field.

At a little distance in advance of me I could discover a number of men, whom I soon found to be our ship's crew, who had landed before me. My appearance among them in a state of entire nakedness excited not a little mirth. "Holloa! my boy," ex-

claimed one of them, "you cut a pretty figure; not from the garden of Eden, I can swear for it, for you have not even an apron
of fig-leaves to cover you with; you were not born to be drowned,
I see, though you may live to be hanged." But after a few jests at
my expense, the mate took off one of the two shirts, with which
he had taken the precaution to provide himself before he left the
vessel, and gave it to me. This garment answered all the purposes of a covering, as it effectually covered my person from my
shoulders to my feet. After travelling about half of a mile, we
came to a house, where the good woman, taking pity on my grotesque and unique condition, gave me a decent suit of clothes.

Uninterrupted intercourse being now established between Dorchester and Boston, my brother and myself were sent into Boston
to choose our trades and seek our employers. I found employment
in the shop of Mr. John Bosson, a barber and manufacturer of wigs,
as an apprentice upon probation.

After I had been in this situation long enough for all parties to
be satisfied, I was bound by my father in regular form as an apprentice.

The trade of a barber in those days was very different from what
it now is. My principal employment was in the preparation of hair
for the purposes of wigs, crape-cushions, &c.; being occasionally
allowed to scrape the face of some transient customer, who might
be reasonably expected never to call again for a repetition of the
operation.

In Mr. Bosson's service I continued until I was sixteen years old,
and made laudable progress in the mysteries of his art.

The war at this time was fiercely maintained between the United
States and Great Britain; and as soldiers were wanted, a draught
was made upon the militia of Massachusetts for a quota of men to
march to New York, to reinforce the American army then in the
vicinity of that city. My master was unfortunately among the number draughted for that service.

One day, while my fellow-apprentice and myself were at work,
Mr. Bosson entered the shop laboring under great agitation of
mind. He walked rapidly about, occasionally stopping, and honing
several razors that he had put in perfect order previous to his going
out; and attempting to sharpen a pair of shears that at the time
bore the keenest edge. At length, from various ejaculations, and
now and then a half-smothered curse upon his ill luck, we gathered the fact, that he was enrolled among the soldiers who were
soon to take up the line of march for New York. This was an un-

fortunate business for him; a reality he had not anticipated. The idea of shouldering a musket, buckling on a knapsack, leaving his quiet family, and marching several hundred miles for the good of his country, never took a place in his mind.

The reality of his position operated as a safety-valve to let off the steam of his partiotism, and to leave him in a state of languor well calculated to produce in him a degree of resignation for remaining at home. But what was to be done ? A substitute could not be obtained for the glory that might be acquired in the service; and as for money, no hopes could be entertained of raising sufficient for the purpose. Mr. Bosson continued to fidget about, uttering such expressions as his excited feelings prompted, allowing us to catch a disconnected sentence, such as: "Hard times — don't need two apprentices any more than a toad needs a tail;" — "if either of you had the spunk of a louse, you would offer to go for me." With this last remark he quit the shop apparently in high dudgeon.

The truth was now evident, that he wanted somebody to take his place.

To provide ways and means of payment was the principal obstacle in the way of hiring a substitute. Gold and silver had scarcely a physical existence in the country, and the want of a circulating medium was attempted to be supplied by the legislative acts of government in issuing an excessive quantity of paper money, which, as it never had any intrinsic value, soon degenerated from its nominal worth with progressive rapidity. From 1777 to 1781 the state of the money was so fluctuating that no certain calculation could be made of its value; for it was not two days at a time of the same value. The depreciation continued, till prudent people declined taking it at any rate; and they, who did, received it at a depreciation of several hundreds for one. Patriotism, more than a love of gain, prompted men to join the army. More were willing to enlist voluntarily than to serve in the capacity of substitutes for an uncertain compensation. My master, therefore, had but little hope of finding any one willing to serve in his stead.

The spirit of adventure had been suppressed, but not destroyed, within me. The opportunity seemed favorable to my desires; and, as my elder fellow-apprentice was fearful that he might be called upon, he encouraged me in the project, and I resolved upon offering my services.

Mr. Bosson accepted my proposition to act as his substitute with a great degree of satisfaction and gratitude, which he evinced by a liberal supply of clothing and equipments for the service. He did not suffer my zeal to cool, but immediately gave directions to have me enrolled and enlisted for three months, in a company commanded by Capt. William Bird of Boston, in a regiment under Colonel Proctor.

Early in the month of September, 1779, being not quite sixteen, the age required at that time for militia service, our company was paraded on Boston common, and with a heavy knapsack on my back, and a gun on my shoulder, superior in weight to those carried by soldiers at the present time, we took up the line of march.

When we left Boston, each of us received three thousand dollars in Continental money; of the value of which the reader may have already formed some idea, and it had not risen since our departure, for we found on our return that from one hundred to one hundred and fifty dollars of it were required for a simple repast. In addition to this compensation, our monthly pay was forty shillings, in the same valuable currency. My clothes were much worn and damaged in the service, and upon our return were found in a very shabby condition, especially my shoes. Of these I had two pairs, but the good judgment of a thief was shown by stealing the better pair one night while I was asleep, leaving me no other alternative but to go barefoot, or secure the remaining ones to my feet by winding rope-yarn around them in the form of bandages.

My feet were covered with blisters while I marched over the frozen ground and snow; and thus, almost crippled, and worn down with fatigue, I arrived at my father's in Roxbury, whither he had returned, after an absence of about two months.

Our coast was lined with British cruisers, which had almost annihilated our commerce; and the state of Massachusetts judged it expedient to build a government vessel, rated as a twenty-gun ship, named the "Protector," commanded by Captain John Foster Williams. She was to be fitted out for service as soon as possible, to protect our commerce, and to annoy the enemy. A rendezvous was established for recruits at the head of Hancock's wharf, where the national flag, then bearing thirteen stripes and stars, was hoisted. All means were resorted to, which ingenuity could devise, to induce men to enlist. A recruiting officer, bearing a flag and attended by a band of martial music, paraded the streets, to excite a thirst for glory and a spirit of military ambition.

The recruiting officer possessed the qualifications requisite to make the service appear alluring, especially to the young. He was a jovial good-natured fellow, of ready wit and much broad humor. Crowds followed in his wake when he marched the streets; and he occasionally stopped at the corners to harangue the multitude, in order to excite their patriotism and zeal for the cause of liberty.

When he espied any large boys among the idle crowd around him, he would attract their attention by singing in a comical manner the following doggerel:

> All you that have bad masters,
> And cannot get your due;
> Come, come, my brave boys,
> And join with our ship's crew.

A shout and a huzza would follow, and some would join in the ranks. My excitable feelings were roused; I repaired to the rendezvous, signed the ship's papers, mounted a cockade, and was in my own estimation already more than half of a sailor. The ship was as yet far from being supplied with her complement of men; and the recruiting business went on slowly. Appeals continued to be made to the patriotism of every young man to lend his aid, by his exertion on sea or land, to free his country from the common enemy. Promises of gain were held out, which set truth at defiance, and offers the most tempting that the impoverished state of the finances of government could promise. About the last of February the ship was ready to receive her crew, and was hauled off into channel, that the sailors might have no opportunity to run away after they were got on board.

Upwards of three hundred and thirty men were carried, dragged, and driven on board, of all kinds, ages, and descriptions, in all the various stages of intoxication; from that of "sober tipsiness" to beastly drunkenness, with the uproar and clamor that may be more easily imagined than described.

The wind being fair, we weighed anchor and dropped down to Nantasket roads, where we lay till about the first of April; and then set sail for a cruise of six months.

On the morning of June 9th, 1780, the fog began to clear away; and the man at the mast-head gave notice that he saw a ship to the westward of us. As the fog cleared up, we perceived her to be a large ship under English colors to the windward, standing athwart our starboard board. Our relative position gave us an opportunity to escape, but our valiant captain did not see fit to avail himself of it.

As she came down upon us, she appeared as large as a seventy-four; and we were not deceived respecting her size, for it afterwards proved that she was an old East-Indiaman, of eleven-hundred tons burden, fitted out as a letter-of-marque for the West-India trade, mounted with thirty-two guns, and furnished with a complement of one hundred and fifty men. She was called the Admiral Duff, commanded by Richard Strang, from St. Christopher and St. Eustatia, laden with sugar and tobacco, and bound to London. I was standing near our first lieutenant, Mr. Little, who was calmly examining the enemy, as she approached, with his spy-glass, when Captain Williams stepped up and asked his opinion of her. The lieutenant applied the glass to his eye again and took a deliberate look in silence, and replied, "I think she is a heavy ship, and that we shall have some hard fighting; but one thing I am certain, she is not a frigate; if she were, she would not keep yawing, and showing her broadsides as she does; she would show nothing but head and stern; we shall have the advantage of her, and the quicker we get alongside the better." Our captain ordered English colors to be hoisted, and the ship to be cleared for action. The shrill pipe of the boatswain summoned all hands to their duty. The bedding and hammocks of the sailors were brought up from between decks; the bedding placed in the hammocks, and lashed up in the nettings; our courses hauled up; the top-gallant sails clewed down; and every preparation was made, which a skilful officer could suggest, or active sailors perform.

The enemy approached till within musket shot of us. The two ships were so near to each other that we could distinguish the officers from the men; and I particularly noticed the captain on the gang-way, a noble-looking man, having a large gold-laced cocked hat on his head, and a speaking-trumpet in his hand. Lieutenant Little possessed a powerful voice, and he was directed to hail the enemy; at the same time the quartermaster was ordered to stand ready to haul down the English flag and to hoist up the American. Our lieutenant took his station on the after part of the starboard gangway, and, elevating the trumpet, exclaimed "Hallo ! whence come you ?" — "From Jamaica, bound to London," was the answer. "What is the ship's name ?" inquired the lieutenant. "The Admiral Duff," was the reply.

The English captain then thought it his turn to interrogate, and asked the name of our ship. Lieutenant Little, in order to gain time, put the trumpet to his ear, pretending not to hear the question. During the short interval, thus gained, Captain Williams called upon the gunner to ascertain how many guns could be brought to bear upon the enemy. "Five," was the answer. "Then fire, and shift the colors," were the orders. The cannons poured forth their deadly contents, and, with the first flash, the American flag took the place of the British ensign at our mast-head.

[433]

The compliment was returned in the form of a full broadside, and the action commenced. I was stationed on the edge of the quarter-deck, to sponge and load a six-pounder; this position gave me a fine opportunity to see the whole action. Broadsides were exchanged with great rapidity for nearly an hour; our fire, as we afterwards ascertained, produced a terrible slaughter among the enemy, while our loss was as yet trifling.

I happened to be looking for a moment towards the main deck, when a large shot came through our ship's side and killed Mr. Benjamin Scollay, a very promising young man, who was, I think, a midshipman. At this moment a shot from one of our marines killed the man at the wheel of the enemy's ship, and, his place not being immediately supplied, she was brought alongside of us in such a manner as to bring her bowsprit directly across our forecastle. Not knowing the cause of this movement, we supposed it to be the intention of the enemy to board us. Our boarders were ordered to be ready with their pikes to resist any such attempt, while our guns on the main deck were sending death and destruction among the crew of the enemy. Their principal object now seemed to be to get liberated from us, and by cutting away some of their rigging, they were soon clear, and at the distance of a pistol shot.

The action was then renewed, with additional fury; broadside for broadside continued with unabated vigor; at times so near to each other that the muzzles of our guns came almost in contact, then again at such a distance as to allow of taking deliberate aim. The contest was obstinately continued by the enemy, although we could perceive that great havoc was made among them, and that it was with much difficulty that their men were compelled to remain at their quarters.

A charge of grape-shot came in at one of our port-holes, which dangerously wounded four or five of our men, among whom was our third lieutenant, Mr. Little, brother to the first. His life was despaired of, but by the kind attention he received from his brother, and the surgeon, he finally recovered, though he bore evidence of the severity of his wounds through life.

While Captain Williams was walking the quarter deck, which he did during the whole action, a shot from the enemy struck the speaking trumpet from his hand and sent it to a considerable distance from him. He picked it up with great calmness of manner, and resumed his walk, without appearing to have been at all disturbed by the circumstance.

The battle still continued with unabated vigor on both sides, till our marksmen had killed and wounded all the men in the fore, main, and mizen tops of the enemy. The action had now lasted about an hour and a half, and the fire from the enemy began to slacken, when we suddenly discovered that all the sails on her main-mast were enveloped in a blaze. The fire spread with amazing rapidity, and, running down the after-rigging, it soon communi-cated with her magazine, when her whole stern was blown off, and her valuable cargo emptied into the sea. All feelings of hostility now ceased, and those of pity were excited in our breasts for the miserable crew that survived the catastrophe.

Our enemy ship was now a complete wreck, though she still floated, and the survivors were endeavoring to save themselves in the only boat that had escaped the general destruction. The hu-manity of our captain urged him to make all possible exertion to save the miserable, wounded, and burnt wretches, who were strug-gling for their lives in the water. The ship of the enemy was greatly our superior in size, and lay much higher out of the water.

Our boats had been much exposed to his fire, as they were placed on spars between the fore and main masts during the action, and had suffered considerable damage. The carpenters were ordered to repair them with the utmost expedition, and we got them out in season to take up fifty-five men, the greater part of whom had been wounded by our shot or burned when the powder magazine ex-ploded.

After the action was over, I found that I was so deaf, as to cause me to fear that I had totally lost the sense of hearing. I attributed this to the noise of the cannon, which I had been employed in load-ing and sponging for such a period of time. It was nearly a week before my hearing was restored, and then but partially; and, ever since, I have experienced great inconvenience from this deafness.

About the twentieth of the month we sailed from the banks of Newfoundland, and arrived at Broad bay in seven or eight days. Having found a good harbor, we dropped anchor, and made imme-diate preparations to get our sick and wounded men on shore. Cap-tain Williams made a contract with a farmer, who was friendly to the American cause, in comfortable circumstances, having good buildings, to provide for the sick and wounded, and to furnish ac-commodations for our surgeon's mate who was left on shore with medicines and things proper for a hospital.

There was now a constant communication kept up between the ship and the shore, and it was necessary for our officers to exercise great vigilance to protect the property of our friendly farmer from depredation.

[*Andrew Sherburne, Portsmouth, N. H.*]

The continental ship of war Ranger, of eighteen guns, commanded by Thomas Simpson, Esq. was at this time (1778) shipping a crew in Portsmouth. This ship had been ordered to join the Boston and Providence frigates and the Queen of France twenty guns, upon an expedition directed by Congress. My father having consented that I should go to sea, preferred the service of Congress to privateering. He was acquainted with Capt. Simpson. — On board this ship were my two half uncles, Timothy and James Weymouth. Accompanied by my father, I visited the rendezvous of the Ranger and shipped as one of her crew. There were probably thirty boys on board this ship. As most of our principal officers belonged to the town, parents preferred this ship as a station for their sons who were about to enter the naval service. Hence most of these boys were from Portsmouth. As privateering was the order of the day, vessels of every description were employed in the business. Men were not wanting who would hazard themselves in vessels of twenty tons or less, manned by ten or fifteen hands. Placing much dependence on the protection of my uncles, I was much elated with my supposed good fortune, which had at last made me a sailor.

I was not yet fourteen years of age. I had received some little moral and religious instruction, and was far from being accustomed to the habits of town boys, or the maxims or dialect of sailors. The town boys thought themselves vastly superior to country lads; and indeed in those days the distinction was much greater than at present. My diffidence and aversion to swearing, rendered me an object of ridicule to those little profane chaps. I was insulted, and frequently obliged to fight. In this I was sometimes victorious. My uncles, and others, prompted me to defend my rights. I soon began to improve in boxing, and to indulge in swearing. At first this practice occasioned some remorse of conscience. — I however endeavored to persuade myself that there was a necessity for it. I at length became a proficient in this abominable practice. To counterbalance my guilt in this, I at the same time became more constant in praying; heretofore I had only prayed occasionally; now I prayed continually when I turned in at night, and vainly imagined that I prayed enough by night to atone for the sins of the day. Believing that no other person on board prayed, I was filled with pride, concluding I had as much or more religion than the whole crew besides. The boys were employed in waiting on the officers, but in time of action a boy was quartered to each gun to carry cartridges.

I was waiter to Mr. Charles Roberts, the boatswain, and was quartered at the third gun from the bow. Being ready for sea, we sailed to Boston, joined the Providence frigate, commanded by Commodore Whipple, the Boston frigate and the Queen of France. I believe that this small squadron composed nearly the entire navy of the United States. We proceeded to sea some time in June, 1779. We cruised several weeks, made the Western Islands, and at length fell in with the homeward bound Jamaica fleet, on the banks of Newfoundland. The Jamaica fleet, which consisted of about one hundred and fifty sail, some of which were armed, was convoyed by one or two line of battle ships, and several frigates and sloops of war. Our little squadron was in the rear of the fleet, and we had reason to fear that some of their heaviest armed ships were there also. If I am not mistaken, the Boston frigate was not in company with us at this time. My reader may easily imagine that our minds were agitated with alternate hopes and fears. No time was to be lost. Our Commodore soon brought to one of their ships, manned and sent her off. Being to windward, he edged away and spoke to our Captain. We were at this time in pursuit of a large ship. The Commodore hauled his wind again, and in the course of an hour we came up with the ship, which proved to be the Holderness, a three decker, mounting 22 guns. She struck after giving her several broadsides. Although she had more guns, and those of heavier metal than ourselves, her crew was not sufficiently large to manage her guns, and at the same time work the ship. She was loaded with cotton, coffee, sugar, rum, and alspice. While we were employed in manning her, our Commodore captured another and gave her up to us to man also. When this was accomplished, it was nearly night; we were, however, unwilling to abandon the opportunity of enriching ourselves, therefore kept along under easy sail. Some time in the night we found ourselves surrounded with ships, and supposed we were discovered. We could distinctly hear their bells, on which they frequently struck a few strokes, that their ships might not approach too near each other during the night. We were close on board one of their largest armed ships; and from the multitude of lights which had appeared, supposed that they had called to quarters. It being necessary to avoid their convoy, we fell to leeward, and in an hour lost sight of them all.

Having manned our prizes and secured our prisoners, we all shaped our course for Boston, where we arrived some time in the last of July or beginning of August, 1779.

In all we had taken ten prizes, two of which were retaken. The

Ranger made but a short stop at Boston, for as most of our officers and crew belonged to Portsmouth and its vicinity, our vessel could be most conveniently refitted there.

The cargoes of our prizes being divided among our crews, my share was about one ton of sugar, from thirty to forty gallons of fourth proof Jamaica rum, about twenty pounds of cotton, and about the same quantity of ginger, logwood and alspice, and about seven hundred dollars in paper money, probably worth fifty dollars in specie.

Those merchants who were concerned in navigation, rarely made suitable provision for their vessels. The two last voyages I had been, we suffered extremely for provisions. The vessels and our lives were much in danger, in consequence of those vessels not being well found. But it is well known that the yankees will run great risks, and that common seamen are generally too inconsiderate, and there were more of this class at that day than the merchants could employ.

◇◇◇◇◇◇◇◇◇◇◇◇◇

[David L. Dodge, Hampton, Conn.]

My earliest recollection extends to the time when I was but little over two years of age, and the place where my parents resided about that time, in the year 1776.

I recollect our removal to our hired farm in 1779, and the cannonading when New London was burnt.* At that time my father had employed a soldier at home on furlough for a few days, to cut bushes in the pasture, and I was with him to heap up the brush. As we listened, he said, there is fighting somewhere today. He then went and sat down under a large walnut tree, and I followed him. He occasionally uttered in substance such expressions as, "There is hot work somewhere today;" "Blood is flowing to-day;" "Souls are passing into eternity," &c. Such exclamations, together with the expression of his countenance, fastened the day upon my memory. News came the next morning that the forts were stormed, the garrisons put to the sword, New London burnt, and the British were marching upon Norwich, and would proceed up into the country. My mother wrung her hands, and asked my father if we had not better pack up some things to secrete them. He replied, there would be ample time for this work after hearing again, before they could reach us. I particularly recollect the terrible snow-storm

* By Benedict Arnold. B. M.

in the winter of 1780, the intercourse of neighbors being kept up, mainly, on snow-shoes, and many females using them; the snow averaging from five to eight feet deep.

I will here notice an event, as it illustrates the spirit of the times. There was a respectable farmer who resided in Brooklyn, by the name of John Baker, who was called an odd and singular man, be-

cause he openly denounced all kinds of carnal warfare as contrary to the gospel; and, of course, refused to take any part in the revolutionary war. By some he was called a *Tory*, by others a *coward*, while he constantly declared it a matter of conscience. Yet he was drafted for the army, and his neighbors determined he should serve by compulsion. He declared he would die before he would serve as a warrior, and consequently fled to the woods in the fall of 1779. The clergy and the laity urged his compulsion, and the populace turned out and pursued him, as hounds would a fox, and finally they caught and bound him, like Sampson, "with strong cords," placed him in a wagon, and sent two trusty patriots to convey him to Providence, to the troops stationed there. In the course of the night, however he got hold of a knife, cut himself loose, and escaped to the woods. Subsequently he returned and secreted himself in a large dense cedar swamp, about half a mile from our house. He made himself as comfortable a shelter as the thick boughs of the double spruce and cedar would permit. There he remained, without fire, during the severe winter of 1780, without the knowledge of any one, except his brother and my parents, to whom he made himself known to save himself from perishing. His brother furnished him, in the night, with some articles of food and clothing from his own house; and my father, by an understanding with him, was absent at certain times, while my mother would supply him with food, blankets, and other conveniences. There was a wall from the woods connected with the swamp, to our garden, forming the back fence. One day, as I was on a snow-bank in the rear of the garden, I looked over the fence and saw a man creeping along the side of the wall; as soon as he saw me he started and ran for the woods. I, with equal speed, made for the house, supposing he was a "wild Indian," of which class of men I had heard many frightful stories, and screamed to my mother that the Indians had come, and fled into the back room and crept under the bed. The term "wild," was applied to Indians on the frontiers at war with Americans, in distinction from a pretty numerous remnant of several tribes who lived quietly in the State. So frightened was I at a glimpse of poor Baker, that for several nights afterwards I dreamed frightful dreams about "wild Indians."

The facts relative to Mr. Baker, I received from my parents, but do not recollect how he was released. Probably the compassion of the community was aroused, as there was reason to suppose that he might have perished by the severity of the winter. In after years, when a young man, I have visited Mr. Baker. He had one of the best cultivated farms in the vicinity, and I never heard a lisp against his character, except his opposition to war.

◇◇◇◇◇◇◇◇◇◇◇◇◇

[*Thomas Low Nichols, Orford, N. H.*]

We had drills, trainings, officers' drills, and once a year that glorious military spectacle of the muster of a whole regiment, and every few years the general muster of an entire brigade.

Even the company trainings on the green before the meeting house were great days. The spectators gathered in crowds, drank sweet cider and New England rum, and ate molasses-gingerbread. Emulous pedlars sold tin-ware and Yankee notions at auction with stentorian lungs. Our citizen soldiers were dressed in every kind of homespun fashion, and as variously armed, with old Queen's arms which had come down from the colony days of Queen Anne, or been captured with the army of Burgoyne; with fowling-pieces, ducking guns, or rifles. When they were tired of manoeuvring, firing by platoons, and burning powder in a shamfight, full of shouts of command, rattle, and smoke, the captain, if oratorically gifted, made a speech, and the company was dismissed, satisfied that there was glory enough for one day, and that they had served their country.

At the muster of a regiment there was, of course, a large gathering. People came ten or fifteen miles, in waggons and on horseback. The collection of pretty girls was larger; there were more sellers of cider and gingerbread; and the pedlar auctioneers were more vociferous. Besides the "drift-wood" militia, there were companies in uniform. There was a company of cavalry, and one of artillery, with a four or six-pounder, iron or brass, which had to burn a great many blank cartridges, and was used not only on training-days, but also to fire the salutes on the Fourth of July, and for political victories, and on other joyful occasions.

After the morning evolutions came the grand review, and the most interesting ceremony of the day. The regiment formed a hollow square; the chaplain made a prayer, sitting on horseback. I do not exactly see why, but the military prayer on horseback, under the blue sky, with cavalry, infantry, and artillery standing motionless in regular lines, and the crowd of spectators devoutly uncovered, seemed more solemn to me than one made in a pulpit. Then the colonel, if gifted in that line — and there are few Americans who are not more or less so — made a speech to the soldiers, in which he recited the glories won by a citizen soldiery in the past two wars, alluded touchingly to the grey-headed revolutionary heroes there present, and told them they were the pride and strength of their country, the pillars of the State, and defenders of their homes and firesides. Then he wound up with a magnificent spread-eagle flourish about the greatness and glory of the country, which reached from ocean to ocean, and from the great lakes to the Gulf of Mexico; with an intimation, perhaps, that they might be called upon to extend its boundaries in either of these practicable directions.

The first celebration of the anniversary of the Declaration of American Independence I can recollect, was on the brow of the plateau which overlooked the beautiful valley where I was born. I remember the shining river winding off into the distance, the cliffs of grey rock more than perpendicular, the blue mountain-peaks far away on the horizon, the meadows with broad elms, butter-nuts, sugar-maples, the village with its white houses embowered in trees, the sky intensely blue, and the glorious July sunshine.

The music was a fife and drum. The militia company of our district was posted on the field, and later in the day fired off a rattling *feu-de-joie*. I cannot say much for the appearance of the company, as each man wore his ordinary costume, and not much time had ever been given to drill.

There was a salute, to open the ceremonies of the celebration. The hills and mountains were filled with the echoes and reverberations. I have heard the report of a cannon distinctly repeated seven times, besides the roaring thunders of continuous echoes. But we

had no cannon. Our company was infantry, not artillery, and not a four-pounder could be procured. All were noisily engaged elsewhere on the great occasion, when gunpowder enough is wasted every year to fight a hundred battles. We had a grand salute, notwithstanding, fired from a fifty-six; not a fifty-six pounder cannon — there was scarcely so large a piece of field-artillery in those days — but a fifty-six pound weight. These weights of cast iron have a hole about an inch in diameter through the centre, into which melted lead is poured until they are of the standard weight. Into this hole a charge of gunpowder was poured, and upon it driven a wooden plug, with a crease cut in its side for priming. It made all the noise that was necessary, and each discharge was accompanied by the screams of the fife, the roll of the drum, and the shouts of all the boys in the neighborhood.

The prayer was followed by the inevitable reading of the Declaration of Independence, in which Jefferson proclaimed the rights of man, and indicted George the Third for numerous violations of those rights, and declared that the thirteen colonies "are, and of right ought to be, free, sovereign, and independent States;" to which declaration the signers nobly pledged "our lives, our fortunes, and our sacred honour."

After reading came the oration. It was given by an intelligent farmer, militia colonel, and deputy sheriff. It recounted the labours, sacrifices, and perils of the past, the freedom and prosperity of the present, and the glories of the coming future.

After the oration came another national salute — thirteen guns, one for each of the original States, from the fifty-six, a *feu-de-joie* from the old flint-lock muskets of the militia, and then an attack upon the bread and cheese and rum-punch provided by the committee. I sat on the breezy brow of the hill, in the shade of the singing pine-trees, looking down the beautiful valley of my world, thinking of all I had heard of our glorious country and its great destiny, and wondering what share I — a boy then eight or nine years old — was to have in its future — that future which I have lived to see drenched in blood and tears.

CONSTITUTION AND *GUERRIERE*

SECOND WAR WITH GREAT BRITAIN

❖❖❖❖❖❖❖❖❖❖❖❖❖

[*Isaiah Thomas, Worcester, Mass.*]

JUNE, 1812, 16. Mr. E. T. Andrews, his wife, my son's wife and Miss H. Weld came up to see us. Attended at the Bank. No discounts.

18. War declared against Gᵗ. Britain by Congress.

19. Went to Framingham with Judge Nathˡ. Paine in a Chaise to attend Meeting of Worcester Turnpike directors and returned. Lost my Cane, silver headed, which I had owned 40 years.

20. President's Proclamation of War against England. My cane was found in Shrewsbury, and I sent for it, and got it. Mrs. Soper and her husband, came from Boston. Mr. E. T. Andrews, his wife, and her Sisters, went from this place yesterday on their way to the Springs at Stafford. Mrs. Mary Andrews (widow of William Andrews who died about three months ago) died yesterday in Boston of Apoplexy.

❖❖❖❖❖❖❖❖❖❖❖❖❖

[*William Stuart, Bridgeport, Conn.*]

In process of time War was declared, and recruiting officers were found in every large village, and their rendezvous were always in the immediate vicinity of grog shops. There is nothing like Rum to wake up dormant patriotism, inspire cowards with daring, and make fools and madmen. Thus are men constituted, and so long as war is tolerated by nations, the material for manufacturing soldiers is essential. I have often thought that no Maine Law system can be introduced successfully in any nation, until the quarreling and warring propensities of men of influence are subdued.

I and my comrades made frequent visits to these dens of iniquity, and our success was in proportion to our diligence. I occasionally served as enlisting agent, under Col. Morris Ketchum and Capt. Peter Bradley, and added to their stock of soldiers very materially. When a man becomes half drunk, his patriotism rises, and he is ready to shed the blood of his enemies and send his fellow mortals to their last account, without a tear of sympathy. Our gang was a hardened set, and as we had only one object in view, every other consideration was made to bow to it as supreme. We cared not where domestic peace was broken up, neither did we regard the widow's appeal for her only son. We urged onward our suit amid carousals and revelry, and found that every barrier would flee before our skill.

The war was engaged in with spirit. Gen'l Hull was the commander in chief, and promised to do honor to our country's arms The British army, with the Indians, their allies, under the command of General Brock, drew near the American encampment, and demanded a surrendry of the army, and Gen. Hull submitted without firing a gun. The affair was unlooked for by Mr. Madison and his Cabinet, and produced a momentary panic through the country. The loss for a time of the services of so many men, rendered it necessary for the government to raise a large force with the utmost speed, and as an inducement to enrolment a greatly increased bounty was offered. I encouraged Isaac Arnold, a miserably intemperate man, to enlist. The officer paid him the bounty, and the first business he engaged in for the honor of his country, was to get drunk. I saw that his bounty would soon be spent, and I offered to take care of it for him, and he delivered it to me. Arnold was dull and nearly torpid, and I stepped out in the dark, took his money and substituted counterfeit in its place, enwrapped it in a piece of brown paper, and stowed it away in his pocket. During the night he slept away all knowledge of our interview the previous evening.

For several days he spent his money freely, and paid Mr. Marvin a considerable amount for a rum debt. In the course of a few days Arnold's money was all spent, and it was found to be all counterfeit. Here arose the first troubles in the camp. It was currently reported that Col. Ketchum had paid the bounty of the recruits in counterfeit money, as every soldier had more or less of it. This coming to the Colonel's ears, he was placed in a disagreeable attitude.

Many traced their bad money to Arnold, and as he was intemperate and poor before his enlistment, it necessarily followed that he received it from the recruiting officer. It became in the minds of the people a fixed fact that this bad money came from government. As additional evidence, not a man of the whole military company was free from the charge of having counterfeit money. The public became excited, and the more the subject was agitated the more certain it was to the minds of many, that the government had, for the want of sufficient funds, supplied the deficiency with counterfeit money. The community charged the fraud fearlessly upon these recruiting officers. Major Ketchum became indignant, and solemnly swore that if any man thereafter should assert that he had paid the bounties in counterfeit money, he would hold him responsible to the law, and if need be, to the loaded pistol. His resolution stilled the uproar, for he was well known to be courageous and inflexible, and woe be to him who dared to confront him with insult.

◇◇◇◇◇◇◇◇◇◇◇◇◇◇

[Samuel Griswold Goodrich]

I pass over a variety of things, still in my memory: the gradual deepening of the gloom that spread over society as the events of the war drew on; the bankruptcies of merchants; the suspension of specie payments by the banks; the difficulty of getting money; the gradual withering of the resources of the people; the scarcity of a multitude of articles, alike of luxury, convenience, and necessity; the stagnation of trade; the impoverishment and depression of the laboring classes; the crushing of the hopes and prospects of the young, about entering upon the theater of active and independent life: in short, that general sense of anxiety, poverty, and disappointment — which clouded nearly every brow and nearly every heart. I pass over those hells of drinking, deception, and degradation, called recruiting rendezvous. I pass over the scream of fife and tuck of drum — daily exhibited in the streets by a miserable set of young men, for the most part seduced into the army, either by artifice or liquor. I pass over the patriotic pulsations of the democracy, and the lowering disgust of federalism, as the glorious army of patriots — sometimes ten or a dozen men — led by a puffy sergeant, choking with martial ardor or a close-fitting stock, passed through our city on their way to the Conquest of Canada.

I must not omit an episode of the war, in which I was concerned. On the first of June, 1813, Commodore Decatur, in the United States, attended by the Macedonian and the sloop-of-war Hornet, having passed from New York through the Sound, attempted to get out to sea by way of Montauk Point. Here they were met by the British fleet, under Commodore Hardy, and driven into the Thames at New London. The enemy's force was soon increased by the arrival of other ships of war, and these, anchoring off Gull Island so as to block up the port, seemed to threaten a speedy attack. Great panic immediately ensued, as well at New London as along the borders of the Sound. The specie of the banks in that city was removed to Norwich, and the women and children dispersed themselves among the interior towns and villages. No adequate means of defense existed along the line of the New England coast — seven hundred miles in extent. The regular troops had nearly all been marched off to invade Canada.

But now a new state of things had arisen in Connecticut: our own territory was threatened. For this, the State government had made wise preparation, and on their part there was no hesitation. It was midsummer — a period when the husbandmen could ill afford to leave their farms: so orders were sent by Governor Smith to dispatch at once the companies of militia from the larger towns to the defense of New London, and the neighboring country. At that time I belonged to an artillery company, and this was among those ordered to the coast. I received a summons at four o'clock in the afternoon, to be ready to march the next day at sunrise. I went at once to consult my uncle — who, by the way, was at that time not only mayor of the city, but Lieutenant-governor of the State. He had a short time before promised to make me one of his aids, and perhaps thought I should expect him now to fulfill his engagement. He soon set that matter at rest.

"You must of course go," said he. "We old federalists can not shelter our nephews, when there is a question of defending our own territory."

"Ought I not to consult my parents ?" said I.

"I will go down and see them to-morrow," he replied.

"Certainly then I shall go: I wish to go: my only feeling is that my mother may have some anxiety."

"I will see her to-morrow: you may be at ease on that subject. Be ready to march at sunrise, according to your orders. I will come and see you before you start."

The next morning, while it was yet dark, he came, gave me letters of introduction to Judge Brainard, father of the poet, Judge Perkins, and General Williams. He also supplied me with ten dollars, a welcome addition to my light purse. Then he said — "I have only one thing to add — if you come to a fight, *don't run away till the rest do.* Good-by !"

The next morning — June 7, 1813 — about sunrise, the whole company, nearly sixty in number, mounted in wagons, departed. At sunset, we were on the heights, two miles back of New London. No provision had been made for us, and so we went supperless to bed, in a large empty barn. I scarcely closed my eyes, partly because it was my first experiment in sleeping on the floor, and partly because of the terrific snoring of a fellow-soldier, by the name of C . . ., who chanced to be at my side. Never have I heard such a succession of choking, suffocating, strangling sounds as issued from his throat. I expected that he would die, and indeed once or twice I thought he was dead. Strange to say, he got up the next morning in excellent condition, and seemed, indeed, to feel better for the exercise. This man became quite a character before the campaign was over: he got the title of Aeolus, and as he could not be tolerated in the barracks, he was provided with a tent, at a good distance, where he blew his blast without restraint. I need only add, that, at the close of the campaign, he was the fattest man in the company.

I was glad to see the daylight. The weather was fine, and as the sun came up, we saw the British fleet — some half dozen large ships of war — lying off the mouth of the Thames. They seemed very near at hand, and for the first time I realized my situation — that of a soldier, who was likely soon to be engaged in battle. We were, however, not all sentimentalists. There were among us, as doubtless in all such companies, a supply of witty, reckless Gallios, who gave a cheerful turn to our thoughts. We soon dispersed among the inhabitants, scattered over the neighboring hills and valleys, for breakfast. Like hungry wolves, we fell upon the lean larders, and left famine behind. Of course every one offered to pay, but not one person would accept a farthing: we were, indeed, received as protectors and deliverers. It was something, after all, to be soldiers ! With our stomachs fortified, and our consciousness flattered, we came cheerfully together.

At ten o'clock, we were mustered, and began our march, all in our best trim: cocked hats, long-tailed blue coats, with red facings, white pantaloons, and shining cutlasses at our sides. Our glittering cannon moved along with the solemnity of elephants. It was, in fact, a fine company — all young men, and many from the best families in Hartford. Our captain, Johnson, was an eminent lawyer, of martial appearance, and great taste for military affairs. He afterward rose to the rank of General. Mosely, the first-lieutenant, was six feet four inches high — a young lawyer, nephew of Oliver Wolcott — and of high social and professional standing. Screamed the fife, rolled the drum — as we entered New London! The streets presented some confusion, for still the people were removing back into the country, as an attack was daily expected. A few military companies were also gathering into the town. We were, however, not wholly overlooked: Women put their heads out of the windows, and smiled their gratitude as we passed along. Men stopped, and surveyed us with evident signs of approbation. It was a glorious thing to belong to such a company! At last we came to a halt in one of the public squares. Then there was racing and chasing of aid-de-camps, in buff and feathers, for four mortal hours, during which our martial pride wilted a little in the broiling sun. At four o'clock in the afternoon, we were transported across the Thames, to the village of Groton, and took up our quarters in a large house, on the bank of the river, vacated for our use. Two immense kettles — the one filled with junks of salt beef and the other with unwashed potatoes — were swung upon the kitchen trammels, and at six o'clock in the evening we were permitted each to fish out his dinner from the seething mass. That was my first soldier's supper; and after all, it was a welcome and relishing meal.

Opposite to New London is the village of Groton, the main street running along the river bank; on an eminence some hundred rods from the river, and commanding a view of the surrounding country, including the harbor and the islands which lie scattered near it in the Sound, is the site of Fort Griswold — the scene of one of the saddest tragedies in our revolutionary annals.

In my time, Fort Griswold was in tolerable repair. Our company, as well as other portions of the militia, labored upon it, and strengthened it, as well by completing its works as by erecting a small redoubt upon the southeastern side. To the defense of the latter, in case of attack, the Hartford company was assigned.

About a week after our arrival, over a thousand militia, gathered from various parts of the State, were stationed along the river, chiefly on the eastern bank. Decatur had drawn his three ships up the stream as far as possible, some twelve miles from its mouth, and near the city of Norwich. Here the river is reduced to three hundred feet in width, and flows between high rocky banks. On one of these, called Allyn's Mountain — commanding a wide view even as far south as the harbor — light entrenchments were thrown up, being deemed an effectual defense against any attack likely to be made by the enemy.

The British commander, Hardy, conducted with the utmost courtesy and humanity, but still there was a feeling of uneasiness along the shore. This was deepened into anxiety and alarm, on the arrival of Decatur and his ships, and the consequent gathering of the British forces around the harbor, as if for attack. When we arrived, the squadron consisted, I think, of two ships-of-the-line, two frigates, and a number of smaller vessels. There was, however, a constant movement among them — the force being frequently diminished, and as frequently augmented. These changes were the occasion of constant alarm along the shore, and scarcely a day passed that we had not some rumor of a meditated attack.

Such was the state of public affairs on the surface. As to myself, I was soon drilled into the habits of a soldier. I had been permitted to go to New London and deliver my letters of introduction. I received letters from home, and in one of these, from my father, which I have preserved, I find the following passages:

> We hope you will pay very exact attention to your conduct and behavior, while you are a soldier. You have our prayers for your welfare and that of your comrades. Study to ingratiate yourself with them, by your kindness, and especially with your officers, by your cheerful obedience to their orders. We hear that there is an additional British force arrived within a few days. How long they will think it worth while to keep up the blockade at New London, is uncertain: they will not, at any rate, consult our convenience. We are in hopes the British will make no attack upon New London, and that you will not be called into a conflict with them. But we must leave this to the overruling of a merciful God, as also the issue, should he permit such an event. Should you be called to engage with them, I hope and trust that you will do your duty, and defend your country, which is just and right, though it may not be so to engage in offensive war.
>
> I wish to remind you, my dear son, of the necessity of being prepared for death, at all times and by all persons. This is specially important to a soldier. This will arm you with courage to meet whatever God shall call you to experience. It is no evidence of courage for persons to rush into danger in a thoughtless or wicked manner; it is a better and surer courage which rests upon a deep sense of duty, and which always keeps the soldier ready to die at any moment — even at the beat of the drum.

There is a specimen of old Presbyterian, Blue Light,* Hartford Convention Federalism, during the "late war!"

The officers of our company were rigid disciplinarians, and accordingly we were drilled for about four hours each day. We soon gained much reputation for our martial exercises and our tidy appearance. Many people came over from New London to witness our performances. Among these were often persons of distinction. On two occasions, Decatur, Biddle, and Jones came to see us, and complimented us very heartily. On Sundays, we marched two miles to church. Being in our best guise, we caused quite a sensation. Men and women, boys and girls, streamed along at our flanks, often in a broiling sun, yet always with admiring looks.

After the morning drill, we were generally at leisure for the rest of the day, taking our turn, however, on guard, and in other occasional duties. Most of the soldiers gave up their rations of mess beef and potatoes, and lived on their own resources. We formed ourselves into a general club for a supply of fresh fish. Every day three of us went out fishing, and generally returned with a half-bushel basketful of various kinds, among which the blackfish or tataug — now so greatly esteemed — was always abundant. I was employed by the captain to keep his journal of our proceedings, and sometimes I was dispatched to New London, or to some one of the officers along the line, with a letter or a parcel. I established a friendly acquaintance with old Mrs. Avery, who kept a supply of excellent bread and butter, milk and eggs. I visited Fort Trumbull, and the blockaded fleet up the river. Frequently I strolled into the country, and now and then went to see "Mrs. Bailey," who even at that early period was a celebrity of Groton. I have never seen such fierce democracy as in this village, fed, as it doubtless is, upon the remembrance of the British massacre at the fort; and Mrs. Bailey was filled with its most peppery essence. The story of the flannel petticoat† was then

* A term of abuse for the Federalists, derived from blue lights that were alleged to have been shown at night along the coast as a signal to the British fleet. B. M.

† When Decatur took refuge in New London harbor, the inhabitants of Groton were thrown into great alarm. At this moment a messenger was sent to Fort Griswold for flannel, to be used for the cannon. Most of the portable goods had been sent away, and the messenger was unsuccessful, until he met Mrs. Anna Bailey, who instantly took off her flannel petticoat and heartily devoted it to the patriotic cause of defense. It was carried to the fortress, and displayed on a pike. The story being told, the garrison cheered, and the "martial petticoat" became almost as celebrated as Mahomet's breeches. The story went over the whole country, and when General Jackson (then President) came to New London, he visited this lady. She is said to have given him a very demonstrative reception. She died January 10, 1851, aged 92 years.

recent, but it had marked her for immortality. All the soldiers went to see her, and she sang Jefferson and Liberty [this tune was later adopted for *The Star-Spangled Banner*] to them with great spirit. Once a soldier talked "old federalism" to her, by way of jest: whereupon she got up, and holding out her petticoat, danced and sang Jefferson and Liberty at him, as if that were sufficient to strike him dead.

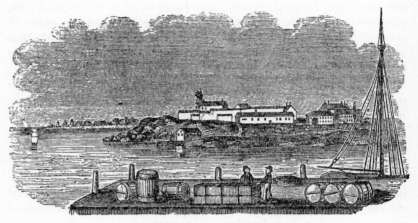

FORT TRUMBULL

I remember that on one occasion H . . . A . . ., my special companion, and myself, were sent with a letter to a lieutenant, who commanded a small picket on the eastern shore, near the mouth of the river — that is, at Point Groton. It was a distance of some three miles. The weather was pleasant, and our route lay along the shore of the stream, which opens into a wide bay, as it meets the Sound. As we approached the southern point of the shore, we found ourselves quite near to the British squadron. One of the vessels, which we knew as the Acasta — for we had learned all their names — was under full sail in a light wind, and coming up toward the shore. She was already so near that we could see the men, and note every movement on the deck. While we were admiring the beautiful appearance of the ship, we suddenly saw several white puffs issue from her sides, and uncoil themselves into volumes of smoke. Then came a deafening roar; a moment after, and in the very midst of it, there were wild howls in the air, above our heads. At a little distance beyond, the ground was plowed up, scattering the soil around, and the top of one of the forest trees, of which a few were scattered here and there, was cut asunder, and fell almost at our feet.

We understood the joke in an instant, and so did the lieutenant who commanded the picket. He was the object of the attack, and the broadside of the Acasta, sending its shot over our heads, had hurled one or two balls crashing through the roof of the little fish-hut, which he and his men occupied. In less than five minutes, they were seen trotting off at a round pace, with their cannon, jerking right and left, over the rough ground behind them. Several other shots were given, but the party escaped in safety. My companion and myself ensconced ourselves behind the rocks, and though it was grave sport, we enjoyed it exceedingly. We could trace the cannon-balls as they flew by looking like globes of mist, twinkling through the air. Several of them passed close over our heads, and grooved the earth, in long trenches, at our sides. The noise they made, as they rose high in the air, was a strange mixture between a howl and a scream. After having thus showed her teeth, and made a great noise, the frigate returned to her anchorage, and all was quiet. I hope I shall not degrade myself, as a soldier, in your eyes, by confessing that this was the only battle in which I was engaged during this glorious war !

I must, however, mention one circumstance, which tried the souls of our company. Let me premise that, on a certain Saturday, a large accession to the British force arrived in the bay, the whole number of vessels, of all kinds, amounting to fourteen. This looked very much like an attack, and accordingly there was a feverish anxiety among the inhabitants of New London and the vicinity, and a general bustle in the army, from Groton Point to Allyn's Mountain. A large body of militia was set to work upon Fort Griswold. Our company was drilled in the little redoubt which we were to defend, and every preparation was made to give the enemy a warm reception. The general idea was, that a landing of British troops would be made on the eastern side, and that we should take the brunt of the first attack.

The sun set in clouds, and as the evening advanced, bursts of thunder, attended by flashes of lightning, muttered along the distant horizon. Our company were admonished to sleep on their arms. Every thing wore a rather ominous appearance. There were no signs of cowardice in the men, but they looked thoughtful; and when Bill W . . ., the laureate wit of the company, let off some of his best jokes — which would ordinarily have set the whole corps in a roar — he was answered by a dead silence. It chanced that I was that night on guard. My turn came at ten o'clock. Taking my gun, I paced the bank of the river, back and forth, in front of our barracks. I had received orders to let nothing pass, by land or water. It was intensely dark, but at frequent intervals, thin flashes of lightning sprang up against the distant sky, behind dark rolling masses of clouds.

Gradually the lights in the streets and windows of New London, stretching in a long line on the opposite side of the river, were extinguished one by one, a few remaining, however, as sentinels, indicating anxiety and watchfulness. The sounds on all sides were at last hushed, and left the world to darkness and to me. More than half of my two-hours' watch had passed, when I heard the dip of oars and the flapping of waves against the prow of a boat. I looked in the direction of the sounds, and at last descried the dusky outline of a small craft, stealing down the river. I cried out — "Boat ahoy! who goes there?" My voice echoed portentously in the silence, but no answer was given, and the low, black, raking apparition glided on its way. Again I challenged, but there was still no reply. On went the ghost! I cocked my gun. The click sounded ominously on the still night air. I began to consider the horror of shooting some fellow-being in the dark. I called a third time, and not without avail. The rudder was turned, the boat whirled on her heel, and a man came ashore. According to my orders, I marshaled him to the guard room, and gave notice of what had happened, to the captain. The man was only a fisherman, going home, but he was detained till morning. So, you see, I can boast that I made one prisoner. My watch was soon over, and returning to my station, I laid down to sleep.

All was soon quiet, and I was buried in profound repose, when suddenly there was a cry in the main barrack-room, overhead — "Alarm! alarm!"

"Alarm! alarm!" was echoed by twenty voices, attended by quick, shuffling sounds, and followed by a hurried rush of men down the staircase. A moment after, the guard in front discharged his musket, and was answered by a long line of reports, up and down the river, from the various sentinels extending for half a dozen miles. Then came the roll of drums, and the mustering of the men. Several of our company had been out to see what was going on: they came back, saying that the enemy was approaching! J. M. . . . distinctly heard the roar of cannon, and positively saw the flashes of muskets. B. W. . . . found out that the attack had already begun upon our southern pickets. Nobody doubted that our time had come!

In a very few minutes our company was drawn up in line, and the roll was called. It was still dark, but the faint flashes gave us now and then a glimpse of each other's faces. I think we were a ghostly looking set, but it was perhaps owing to the bluish complexion of the light. J. S. . . ., of West Hartford, who marched at my left shoulder — usually the lightest-hearted fellow in the company — whispered to me, "Goodrich, I'd give fifty dollars to be at West Division !" For myself, I felt rather serious, and asked a certain anxious feeling in my stomach — "What's to be done ?" I thought of my father's letter, and my uncle's injunctions, and having settled it in my mind that I must fight, I closed my thoughts against all consequences, and felt that I was ready for the conflict. I was indeed almost anxious to have it come, as the suspense was painful. I afterward found, on conversing with several members of the company, that very similar trains of thought had occurred to them. Johnson, our captain, was a man of nerve and ready speech. When the roll was finished, he said in a clear, hearty tone, "All right, my good fellows ! Every man at his post !" These few words — which were, however, more politic than true, for one fellow was taken with sudden colic, and could not be got out — were electrical. We were ready to take our places in the redoubt.

Messengers were now sent to the two neighboring posts to inquire into the state of facts. Word was brought that the first alarm came from our barracks ! The matter was inquired into, and it turned out that the whole affair was originated by our Corporal T . . ., who, in a fit of nightmare, jumped up and cried, "Alarm ! alarm !"

Our martial ardor soon reconciled itself to this rather ludicrous denouement, though several persons who had been somewhat chapfallen, became suddenly inflated with courage, which signalized itself with outbursts of — "D — the British !" "They're a pack of sneaking cowards, after all !" and the like. The next morning was fresh and fair. The skirmishing thunder-gusts of the night had cleared the air, and even distant objects seemed near at hand. Before us lay the whole British fleet, still and harmless, in the glassy bay. My left-hand chum, J. S. . . ., who, in the dark hour, would have given fifty dollars to be at West Division, was now himself again. "Come on here, you black old Ramiles !" said he — dashing the doubled fist of his right hand into the palm of his left: "Come on here, you black-hearted British bull-dogs, and we'll do your business for you !" &c.

Notwithstanding our military duties, you will readily comprehend that we had a good deal of leisure. For the most part, this idle time was wasted, or worse than wasted.

The military spirit is opposed to reflection: it is reckless, banishes thought, and teaches a kind of self-abandonment. Our officers set an excellent example, and there was less of degradation in our

company than in others. Still, among us, there was a general reading
of bad books, a great deal of petty gambling, and not a little tippling. It was easy to see, week by week, the gradual wearing away of
the sense of propriety, of gentlemanly tastes, and general conservatism, in at least one-half the young men of our company. A similar
declension was visible throughout the whole body or militia along
the line.

Fortunately our period of service was brief. In about six weeks
from the time of our departure, we were dismissed, and returned
to our homes. Thus closed my military career, so far as relates to
active service.

My country has not been unmindful of my services; for I have
received two land-warrants — giving me a title to some hundred and
sixty acres — with the fresh virgin soil of the Far West upon them.
Say not that republics are ungrateful !

I remember perfectly well, the universal state of anxiety and depression which prevailed in New England at this time. Such a thing
as silver or gold money was almost unknown. The chief circulation
consisted of bills of suspended banks or what were called "facilities"; that is, bank-notes, authorized by the legislature of Connecticut, redeemable in three years after the war. These were at fifteen
to twenty-five per cent. discount compared with specie. Banks issued
notes of fifty, twenty-five, and twelve-and-a-half cents. Barbers put
out bills, payable in shaving, and various institutions adopted a
similar course. This mass acquired the title of "rag money," "shin-
plasters," &c.: a large portion of it was notoriously worthless, either
as being counterfeit, or issued by irresponsible parties, yet it generally passed without scrutiny. I recollect a person at a turnpike-
gate offered a five-dollar bank-note, and received in change a large,
greasy wad of bills, of various names, hues, and designs. He glanced
at it, and said to the keeper — "Why, half of this is counterfeit !"

"I know it," was the reply; "but it passes just as well as any
other."

At this period, all kinds of British merchandise had become very
scarce, and many had entirely vanished from the market. There was
a small supply of certain articles, from time to time, furnished by
the vessels captured by our ships and privateers, and some convenient and necessary goods were smuggled in from Canada. There was,
in fact, a large amount of money — and this was all specie — sent to
the British Provinces for pins, needles, jewelry, laces, muslins, cam-
brics, chintzes, silks, sewing-silk, buttons, &c., &c. These merchan-
dises were so costly that a man would frequently carry the value of
a thousand dollars in a pair of saddlebags, sometimes on his shoul-

ders, and sometimes on horseback. The life of the smuggler along the line, at this period, was one of danger and adventure. In some instances, persons laid the foundations of future fortune in this illicit traffic. I recollect very well the prices at which we sold some of these articles: calico, now worth twelve and a half cents, readily brought seventy-five cents the yard; cotton-cambric, now twenty cents, then a dollar; linen handkerchiefs, now fifty cents, then two dollars; fine broadcloth, now five dollars, then twelve, or even fifteen dollars. The average prices of British goods, at retail, were about four times what they are now.

In a point of fact, however, our dry-goods trade was almost destroyed. Domestic products were enormously dear — flour at one time eighteen dollars a barrel — at Boston !

◇◆◇◆◇◆◇◆◇◆◇◆◇

[Asa G. Sheldon, Wilmington, Mass.]

In April, 1814, I made a contract with Amos Binney, navy agent, to draw a load of grape shot from Charlestown to Commodore McDonald [Macdonough], in Vergennes, Vt. I brought the load to Wilmington with four oxen and a horse. It weighed 6,700 lbs., at $3\frac{1}{2}$ cents per lb.

Hearing that oxen were much wanted at Vergennes, I bought two other yoke. So I started with four yoke of oxen and a horse. They walked up the hills and through the mud smart and easy. Thinking that I might have some weak bridges to pass, I took with me a chain fifteen feet long to hitch on to the end of the wagon-tongue to save my team should the load break through. My route lay through Tewksbury, Lowell, North Chelmsford. Tyngsborough, Dunstable, Nashua, South Merrimac, Amherst, Mt. Vernon, corner of Lyndborough. New Boston, Francistown, Deering, Antrim, Hillsborough, Washington, Lempster, Unity, Claremont, Weathersfield, Cavendish, Mt. Holly, Ludlow, Trenton, Middlebury, &c., to Vergennes. I crossed the beautiful Connecticut River between Claremont and Weathersfield, where so straight was its course you might discern the bridge five miles distant, the river not varying its width.

On May 5th, I arrived at Vergennes, having undressed but twice on the journey. The shot were counted, found "all right," and I received my pay.

I sold my oxen, horse and harness, yokes and chains. The fifteen feet of chain sold for $5, double what it cost new. These things were wanted by the farmers, who had sold theirs to the government. The two yoke last purchased, brought $25 per yoke more than cost.

I started on the homeward tack the same night, with a market-man, and proceeded fourteen miles, and then, on foot and with occasional rides, I wormed my way home, a distance of one hundred and seventy-five miles.

In Francistown, as the company were seating themselves at the breakfast table, there seemed a lack of room for me, my appearance being rather dirty and repulsive. The inn-keeper seeing this, said, "Gen. Chandler, here, move about and let this man have a seat."

When loading into the stage, it was called out, before I could squeeze in, "No room for you, — no room for you." "Make room for him," said the inn-keeper, "or I'll get in and make room for him; his money is as good as yours." Room was made, and I took my seat by old Gen. Chandler. He inquired, I thought, too minutely into my business and whereabouts, and said, "Wasn't you afraid to carry so much money?" "No, not so much afraid of that as of not being allowed to sit down at the table." A general smile pervaded all faces, and from that time we were chatting companions, he expressing regret that I was not going on to Boston.

◇◇◇◇◇◇◇◇◇◇◇◇◇◇

[*Isaiah Thomas, Worcester, Mass.*]

February, 1815. 10. Bells rung and Cannon discharged in Worcester for the Success of our Arms at New Orleans on the 8th of Jan.y. last.

11. Attended at the Tanyard.

13. About one °Clock last Night, an Express went thro' town from Newyork for Boston with the News of Peace being concluded at Ghent between our Government & that of Great Britain; this intelligence was confirmed this day on the arrival of the Mail from Newyork. The Bells were immediately rung and Cannon fired. Articles of Peace was agreed on on the 24th December last.

YANKEES

◇◇◇◇◇◇◇◇◇◇◇◇◇◇

[*Of Thomas Mortons entertainment at Plimmouth*
and castinge away upon an Island.]

THIS man arrived in those parts, and hearing newes of a Towne
that was much praised, he was desirous to goe thither, and see how
thinges stood, where his entertainement was there best, I dare be
bould to say: for although they had but 3. Cowes in all, yet had
they fresh butter and a sallet of egges in dainty wise, a dish not
common in a wilderness, there hee bestowed some time in the survey of this plantation. His new come servants in the meane time,
were tane to taske, to have their zeale appeare, and questioned what
preacher was among their company; and finding none, did seeme to
condole their estate as if undone, because no man among them had
the guift, to be in Ionas steade, nor they the meanes, to keepe them
in that path so hard to keepe.

Our Master say they reads the Bible and the word of God, and
useth the booke of common prayer, but this is not the meanes; the
answere is: the meanes, they crie; alas poore Soules where is the
meanes, you seeme as if betrayed to be without the meanes; how
can you be stayed from fallinge headlonge to perdition ? *Facilis
descensus averni:* the booke of common prayer sayd they what poore
thinge is that, for a man to reade in a booke ? No, no, good sirs, I
would you were neere us, you might receave comfort by instruction:

give me a man hath the guiftes of the spirit, not a booke in hand. I doe professe sayes one, to live without the meanes, is dangerous, the Lord doth know.

By these insinuations, like the Serpent they did creepe and winde into the good opinion of the illiterate multitude, that were desir· ous to be freed and gone (to them no doubt, which some of them after confessed) and little good was to be done one them after this charme was used, now plotts and factions, how they might get loose, and here was some 35. stout knaves, & some plotted how to steale Master Westons barque, others exasperated knavishly to worke, would practise how to gett theire Master to an Island; and there leave him, which hee had notice of, and fitted him to try what would be done, and steps aborde his shalop bound for Cape Anne to the Massachusetts, with an Hogshead of Wine, Sugar hee tooke along, the Sailes hoist up and one of the Conspirators aboard to steere, who in the mid way pretended foule weather at the harboure mouth, and therefore for a time, hee would put in to an Island neere, and make some stay where hee thought to tempt his Master to walke the woods, and so be gone but their Master to prevent them, caused the sales and oares to be brought a shore, to make a tilt if neede should be, and kindled fire, broched that Hogshead, and caused them fill the can with lusty liquor, Claret sparklinge neate which was not suffered to grow pale and flatt, but tipled of with quick dexterity, the Master makes a shew of keepinge round, but with close lipps did seeme to make longe draughts, knowinge the wine would make them Protestants, and so the plot was then at large disclosed and discovered, & they made drowsie, and the inconstant windes shiftinge at night did force the kellecke home, and billedge the boat, that they were forced to leave her so, and cut downe trees that grew by the shore, to make Caffes: two of them went over by helpe of a fore saile almost a mile to the maine the other two stayed five dayes after, till the windes would serve to fill the sailes. The first two went to cape Ann by land, and had fowle enough, and fowle wether by the way, the Islanders had fish enough, shel-fish and fire to roast, & they could not perish for lacke of foode, and wine they had to be sure; and by this you see they were not then in any want; the wine and goodes brought thence, the boat left there so billedgd that it was not worth the labor to be mended.

Of the Revells of New Canaan.

The Inhabitants of Pasonagessit (having translated the name of their habitation from that ancient Salvage name to Ma-re Mount; and being resolved to have the new name confirmed for a memorial to after ages) did devise amongst themselves to have it performed in a solemne manner with Revels, & merriment after the old English custome: prepared to sett up a Maypole upon the festivall day of Philip and Iacob; & therefore brewed a barrell of excellent beare, & provided a case of bottles to be spent, with other good cheare, for all commers of that day. And because they would have it in a compleat forme, they had prepared a song fitting to the time and present occation. And upon Mayday they brought the Maypole to the place appointed, with drumes, gunnes, pistols, and other fitting instruments, for that purpose; and there erected it with the help of Salvages, that came thether of purpose to see the manner of our Revels. A goodly pine tree of 80. foote longe, was reared up, with a peare of buckshorns nayled one, somewhat neare unto the top of it: where it stood as a faire sea marke for directions; how to finde out the way to mine Host of Ma-re Mount.

The setting up of his Maypole was a lamentable spectacle to the precise separatists: that lived at new Plimmouth. They termed it an Idoll; yea they called it the Calfe of Horeb: and stood at defiance with the place naming it Mount Dagon; threatning to make it a woefull mount and not a merry mount.

There was a merry song made, which (to make their Revells more fashionable) was sung with a Corus, every man bearing his part; which they performed in a daunce, hand in hand about the Maypole, whiles one of the Company sung, and filled out the good liquour like gammedes and Iupiter.

THE SONGE

> Drinke and be merry, merry, merry boyes,
> Let all your delight be in the Hymens joyes,
> Jô to Hymen now the day is come,
> About the merry Maypole take a Roome.
> Make greene garlons, bring bottles out;
> And fill sweet Nectar, freely about,
> Uncover thy head, and feare no harme,
> For hers good liquor to keepe it warme.
> Then drinke and be merry, &c.
> Iô to Hymen, &c.
> Nectar is a thing assign'd,
> By the Deities owne minde,
> To cure the hart opprest with greife,
> And of good liquors is the cheife,
> Then drinke, &c.
> Iô to Hymen, &c.
> Give to the Mellancolly man,
> A cup or two of't now and than;

This physick' will soone revive his bloud,
And make him be of a merrier moode.
Then drinke, &c.
Iô to Hymen, &c.
Give to the Nymphe thats free from scorne,
No Irish; stuff nor Scotch over worne,
Lasses in beaver coats come away,
Yee shall be welcome to us night and day.
To drinke and be merry, &c.
Jô to Hymen, &c.

This harmeles mirth made by younge men (that lived in hope to have wifes brought over to them, that would save them a laboure to make a voyage to fetch any over) was much distasted, of the precise Seperatists: that keepe much a doe, about the tyth of Muit and Cummin; troubling their braines more then reason would require about things that are indifferent: and from that time sought occasion against my honest Host of Ma-re Mount to overthrow his ondertakings, and to destroy his plantation quite and cleane.

Of a great Monster supposed to be at Ma-re-Mount; and the preparation made to destroy it.

The Separatists envying the prosperity, and hope of the Plantation at Ma-re Mount (which they perceaved beganne to come forward, and to be in a good way for gaine in the Beaver trade) conspired together against mine Host especially, (who was the owner of that Plantation) and made up a party against him; and mustred up what aide they could; accounting of him, as of a great Monster.

Many threatening speeches were given out both against his person, and his Habitation, which they divulged should be consumed with fire: And taking advantage of the time when his company (which seemed little to regarde, theire threats) were gone up into the Inlands, to trade with the Salvages for Beaver.

They set upon my honest host at a place, called Wessaguscus, where (by accident) they found him. The inhabitants there were in good hope, of the subvertion of the plantation at Mare Mount, (which they principally aymed at;) and the rather, because mine host was a man that indeavoured to advance the dignity of the Church of England; which they (on the contrary part) would laboure to vilifie; with uncivile termes: enveying against the sacred booke of common prayer, and mine host that used it in a laudable manner amongst his family, as a practise of piety.

There hee would be a meanes to bringe sacks to their mill (such is the thirst after Beaver) and helped the conspiratores to. Suprised mine host, (who was there all alone) and they chardged him, (because they would seeme to have some reasonable cause against him (to sett a glosse upon their malice) with criminall things which indeede had beene done by such a person but was of their conspiracy; mine host demaunded of the conspirators who it was, that was author of that information, that seemed to be their ground for what they now intended. And because they answered, they would not tell him, hee as peremptorily replyed, that hee would not stay, whether he had, or he had not done as they had bin informed.

The answere made no matter (as it seemed) whether it had bin negatively, or affirmatively made for they had resolved what hee should suffer, because (as they boasted,) they were now become the greater number: they had shaked of their shackles of servitude, and were become Masters, and masterles people.

It appeares, they were like beares whelpes in former time, when mine hosts plantation was of as much strength as theirs, but now (theirs being stronger,) they (like overgrowne beares) seemed monsterous. In briefe, mine host must indure to be their prisoner, untill they could contrive it so, that they might send him for England, (as they said,) there to suffer according to the merit of the fact, which they intended to father upon him; supposing (belike) it would proove a hainous crime.

Much rejoycing was made that they had gotten their cappitall enemy (as they concluded him) whome they purposed to hamper in such sort, that hee should not be able to uphold his plantation at Ma-re Mount.

The Conspirators sported themselves at my honest host, that meant them no hurt; & were so joccund that they feasted their bodies, and fell to tippeling, as if they had obtained a great prize; like the Trojans when they had the custody of Hippenus pinetree horse.

Mine host fained greefe: and could not be perswaded either to eate, or drinke, because hee knew emptiness would be a meanes to make him as watchfull, as the Geese kept in the Roman Cappitall: whereon the contrary part, the conspirators would be so drowsy, that hee might have an opportunity to give them a slip, instead of a tester. Six persons of the conspiracy were set to watch him at Wessaguscus: But hee kept waking; and in the dead of night (one lying on the bed, for further suerty,) up gets mine Host and got to the second dore that hee was to passe which (notwithstanding the lock) hee got open: and shut it after him with such violence, that it affrighted some of the conspirators.

The word which was given with an alarme, was, ô he's gon, he's gon, what shall wee doe he's gon? the rest (halfe a sleepe) start up in a maze, and like rames, ran theire heads one at another full butt in the darke.

Their grand leader Captaine Shrimp tooke on most furiously, and tore his clothes for anger, to see the empty nest, and their bird gone.

The rest were eager to have torne theire haire from theire heads, but it was so short, that it would give them no hold; Now Captaine Shrimp thought in the losse of this prize (which hee accoumpted his Master peece,) all his honor would be lost for ever.

In the meane time mine Host was got home to Ma-re Mount through the woods, eight miles round about the head of the river Monatoquit, that parted the two Plantations: finding his way by the helpe of the lightening (for it thundered as hee went terribly) and there hee prepared powther three pounds dried, for his present imployment, and foure good gunnes for him, and the two assistants left at his howse, with bullets of several sizes three hounderd, or thereabouts; to be used if the conspirators should pursue him thether: and these two persons promised theire aides in the quarrell, and confirmed that promise with a health in good rosa solis.

Now Captaine Shrimp, the first Captain in the Land (as hee supposed,) must doe some new act to repaire this losse, and to vinidicate his reputation, who had sustained blemish, by this oversight. Begins now to study, how to repaire or survive his honor in this manner; callinge of Councell: they conclude.

Hee takes eight persons more to him, and (like the nine Worthies of New Canaan) they imbarque with preparation against Ma-re Mount, where this Monster of a man (as theire phrase was) had his denne; the whole number, (had the rest not bin from home, being but seaven,) would have given Captaine Shrimpe (a quondam Drummer,) such a wellcome, as would have made him wish for a Drumme as bigg as Diogenes tubb, that hee might have crept into it out of sight.

Now the nine Worthies are approached; and mine Host prepared: having intelligence by a Salvage, that hastened in love from Wessaguscus, to give him notice of their intent.

One of mine Hosts men prooved a craven: the other had prooved his wits to purchase a little valoure, before mine Host had observed his posture.

The nine worthies comming before the Denne of this supposed Monster, (this seaven headed hydra, as they termed him) and began like Don Quixote against the Windmill to beate a party, and to offer quarter (if mine Host would yeald) for they resolved to send him for England, and bad him lay by his armes.

But hee (who was the Soone of a Souldier) having taken up armes in his just defence, replyed, that hee would not lay by those armes, because they were so needful at Sea, if hee should be sent over. Yet (to save the effusion of so much worthy bloud, as would haue issued, out of the vaynes of these 9. worthies of New Canaan, if mine Host should have played upon them out at his port holes (for they came within danger like a flocke of wild geese, as if they had bin tayled one to another, as coults to be sold at a faier) mine Host was content to yeelde upon quarter; and did capitulate with them: in what manner it should be for more certainety, because hee knew what Captaine Shrimpe was.

Hee expressed, that no violence should be offered to his person, none to his goods, nor any of his Howsehold: but that hee should have his armes, and what els was requisit for the voyage, (which their Herald retornes,) it was agreed upon, and should be performed.

But mine Host no sooner had set open the dore and issued out; but instantly Captaine Shrimpe, and the rest of the worties stepped to him, layd hold of his armes; and had him downe, and so eagerly was every man bent against him (not regarding any agreement made with such a carnall man,) that they fell upon him, as if they would have eaten him: some of them were so violent, that they would have a slice with scabbert and all for haste, untill an old Souldier (of the Queenes as the Proverbe is) that was there by accident, clapt his gunne under the weapons, and sharply rebuked these worthies for their unworthy practises. So the matter was taken into more deliberate consideration.

Captaine Shrimpe and the rest of the nine worthies, made themselves (by this outragious riot) Masters of mine Hoste of Ma-re Mount, and disposed of what hee had at his plantation.

This they knew (in the eye of the Salvages) would add to their glory; and diminish the reputation of mine honest Host, whome they practised to be ridd of, upon any termes, as willingly as if hee had bin the very Hidra of the time.

How the 9. worthies put mine Host of Ma-re-Mount into the inchaunted, Castle at Plimmouth, and terrified him with the Monster Briareus.

The nine Worthies of New Canaan having now the Law in their owne hands (there being no generall Governour in the Land: nor none of the Separation that regarded, the duety they owe their

[465]

Soveraigne, whose naturall borne Subjects they were: though translated out of Holland: from whence they had learned to worke all to their own ends, and make a great shew of Religion, but no humanity, for they were now to sit in Counsell on the cause.

And much it stood mine honest Host upon, to be very circumspect, and to take Eacus to taske: for that his voyce was more allowed of, then both the other: and had not mine Host confounded all the arguments that Eacus could make in their defence: and confuted him that swaied the rest, they would have made him unable to drinke in such maner of merriment any more. So that following this private counsell, given him by one that knew who ruled the rost, the Hiracano ceased that els would split his pinace.

A conclusion was made, and sentence given, that mine Host should be sent to England a prisoner. But when hee was brought to the shipps for that purpose, no man durst be so foole hardy as to undertake carry him. So these Worthies set mine Host upon an Island, without gunne, powther, or shot, or dogge, or so much as a knife, to get any thinge to feede upon or any other cloathes to shelter him with at winter then a thinne suite which hee had one at that time. Home hee could not get to Ma-re-Mount upon this Island. Hee stayed a moneth at least, and was releeved by the Salvages that tooke notice that mine Host was a Sachem of Passonagessit, and would bring bottles of strong liquor to him, and unite themselves into a league of brother hood with mine Host; so full of humanity are these infidels before these Christians.

From this place for England, sailed mine Host in a Plimmouth shipp, (that came into the Land to fish upon the Coast,) that landed him safe in England at Plimmouth, and hee stayed in England untill the ordinary time for shipping to set forth for these parts; and then retorned: Noe man being able to taxe him of any thinge.

But the Worthies (in the meane time) hoped they had bin ridd of him.

❖❖❖❖❖❖❖❖❖❖❖❖

[Edward Johnson, Woburn, Mass.]

And now to the third and great distresse, which lay behind them by reason of their back friends, the Lording Bishops, and other Malignant adversaries, being daily exasperated against them, and in especiall at this time by one Morton, who named himselfe the Host of Merrimount, who wanted not malice, could he possible have attained meanes to effect it; But the Lord Christ prevented both him and his Masters, whom with flattery he sought to please with scurrillous deriding the servants of Christ, to bring them into contempt, yet the Lord prevented all, and delivered this wretched fellow into his peoples hands againe after all this, who dealt as favourably with him as David did with Shimmei.

◇◇◇◇◇◇◇◇◇◇◇◇

[*Timothy Dwight*]

The object of our journey to Shutesbury was to see a man, named Ephraim Pratt, very far advanced in age. The distance is ten miles. We arrived late in the afternoon, and found the object of our curiosity.

He was born at Sudbury (Massachusetts) in 1687; and in one month from the date of our arrival (Wednesday November 13th) would complete his one hundred and sixteen year. He was of middle stature; firmly built; plump, but not encumbered with flesh; less withered than multitudes at seventy; possessed of considerable strength, as was evident from the grasp of his hand, and the sound of his voice; and without any marks of extreme age. About two months before, his sight became so impaired, that he was unable to distinguish persons. His hearing, also, for a short time had been so imperfect, that he could not distinctly hear common conversation. His memory was still vigorous; his understanding sound; and his mind sprightly in its conceptions.

The principal part of the time, which I was in the house, he held me by the hand; cheerfully answered all my questions, readily gave me an account of himself in such particulars, as I wished to know; observed to me, that my voice indicated, that I was not less than forty-five years of age; and that he must appear very old to me: adding however, that some men, who had not passed their seventieth year; probably looked almost, or quite, as old as himself. The remark was certainly just; but it was the first time, that I had heard persons, who had reached the age of seventy, considered as being young. We were informed partly by himself, and partly by his host, that he had been a laborious man all his life; and particularly, that he had mown grass one hundred and one years successively. The preceding summer he had been unable to perform this labour. During this season his utmost effort was a walk of half a mile. In this walk he stumbled over a log, and fell. Immediately afterwards he began evidently to decline; and lost in a considerable degree both his sight and hearing. In the summer of 1802, he walked without inconvenience two miles; and mowed a small quantity of grass.

Throughout his life he had been uniformly temperate. Ardent spirits he rarely tasted: cider he drank at times, but sparingly. In the vigorous periods of life he had accustomed himself to eat flesh, but much more abstemiously than most other persons in this country. Milk, which had always been a great part, was now the whole of his diet. He is naturally cheerful, and humorous; apparently unsusceptible of tender emotions; and not much inclined to serious thinking. According to an account, which he gave his host, he made a public profession of religion near seventy years before our visit to him; but was not supposed by him, nor by others acquainted with him, to be a religious man. He conversed easily; and was plainly gratified with the visits, and conversation, of strangers. When he was ninety-three years old, he made a bargain with his host, (who told us the story,) that he should support him during the remainder of his life for £20.

He was never sick but once; and then with the fever and ague. It is scarcely necessary to observe, that a man one hundred and sixteen years old, without Religion, was a melancholy sight to me.

Three or four years before this time I saw in a newspaper an advertisement, written by a person, who professed, and appeared, to be acquainted with him, and his concerns, in which it was said, that his descendants, some of whom were of the fifth generation, amounted probably to more than 1,500.

The natives of New England are generally straight, and well-formed. I have seen great numbers of Europeans from Great-Britain, Ireland, France, and Germany; and from these specimens have no reason to believe that we are inferior to either of these nations in personal appearance. Deformed persons are found here; but, I have good reason to believe, as rarely as in any country under heaven. There is however one particular, in which we are said to fall behind most, and probably all of these nations. It is supposed that our teeth more generally decay, at an untimely period than theirs.

In energy and activity of mind we are behind no people. There is nothing, which promises a benefit at all adequate to the expense of the effort, which a New-Englander will not cheerfully undertake. Nor are the inhabitants of any country possessed of more numerous, or more efficacious resources, in their own minds to insure success to the undertaking. Whether we are brave, or cowardly, I will leave to be decided by the battles of Breed's Hill, Hoosac, Stillwater, and Saratoga; and by the attack on Stony Point. Their energy is evinced by the spirit, with which they have subdued an immeasurable wilderness, and with which they visited every part of the ocean for fishing, and every town on its shore for commerce. And let me add, that their ingenuity is scarcely less conspicuous in the unceasing succession of inventions, with which they have improved, and are still improving the methods of performing operations in agriculture, manufactures, and the mechanic arts, and increasing the various conveniences of life.

With this active spirit, they unite a general disposition to a quiet, orderly, and obliging deportment, to treat strangers and each other with civility, to submit readily to lawful authority, and to obey even the recommendations of their rulers. They are also social; attached to conversation; accustomed, from early life, to take an interest in the concerns of others; and habitually to feel from childhood that they have, and ought to have, a real interest in these concerns.

The women of New-England are generally well, and often elegantly, formed. Their features have usually a good degree of regularity, are comely, and frequently handsome. Their complexion, like that of the men, is not so generally fair as that of the Irish, British, and other European women in the North, but very sensibly fairer than that of the French women; and a vast number of them have complexions inferiour to none in the world. In great numbers they have fine eyes: both blue and black; and generally possess that bloom, which health inimitably suffuses over a beautiful countenance. But regular features, united with the most delicate complexion, cannot form beauty. This charming attribute, so coveted by one sex, and so fascinating to the other, is, as an eminent poet of your country has said,

> an air divine,
> Through which the mind's all gentle graces shine;
> They, like the sun, irradiate all between;
> And the face charms, because the soul is seen.

In this respect the women of New-England, to a great extent, triumph. Their minds, often possessing a fine share of intelligence, are remarkably distinguished by amiable dispositions. A gentle and affectionate temper, ornamented with sprightliness, and gilded with serenity, may be fairly considered as being extensively their proper character. They are said, by some of your countrymen, to be too feminine; and are certainly less masculine than most of their sex, who have visited these States from England or the European continent. To us, this is a delightful part of their character.

Their manners are in entire symmetry with their minds and faces. An universal sweetness and gentleness, blended with sprightly

[469]

energy, is their most predominant characteristic. There is nothing languid in their deportment, and rarely any thing affected. They are affable, obliging, and cheerful; while they are at the same time grave, discreet, and very rarely betrayed into any impropriety.

Very many of them are distinguished for moral excellence; are unaffectedly pious, humble, benevolent, patient, and self-denying. In this illustrious sphere of distinction, they put our own sex to shame. Were the church of Christ stripped of her female communicants, she would lose many of her brightest ornaments, and, I fear, two thirds of her whole family.

◇◇◇◇◇◇◇◇◇◇◇◇◇

[Samuel Griswold Goodrich]

It may be amusing, to give here a few sketches of the remarkable characters of Ridgefield, at the opening of the present [nineteenth] century.

I begin with the deacons of my father's parish. First was Deacon Olmstead, full threescore years and ten at the opening of the present century. His infancy touched upon the verge of Puritanism — the days of Increase and Cotton Mather. The spirit of the Puritans lived in his heart, while the semblance of the patriarchs lingered in his form. He was fully six feet high, with broad shoulders, powerful limbs, and the august step of a giant. His hair was white, and rolled in thin curls upon his shoulders: he was still erect, though he carried a long cane, like that of father Abraham in the old pictures, representing him at the head of his kindred and his camels, going from the land of Haran to the land of Canaan. Indeed, he was my personification of the great progenitor of the Hebrews; and when my father read from the twelfth chapter of Genesis, how he and Lot and their kindred journeyed forth, I half fancied it must be Deacon Olmstead under another name.

There was something stately, no doubt, in the costume of the olden time: there was also a corresponding air of starchness in the carriage. A cocked hat and powdered wig made it necessary for a man to demean himself warily, like an Italian porter who carries a tub of water upon his head. Thus guised, even little Dr. Marsh,*

* Rev. John Marsh, D.D., of Wethersfield, was the last of the Connecticut clergy to give up the wig. I have often seen him in it, though he left it off a short time before his death. Once, when he was on a journey, he stopped overnight at a tavern. On going to bed, he took off his wig and hung it up. A servant maid happened to see it, and ran down in great terror to her mistress, saying, "Ma'am, that minister has took off his head and hung it up on a nail !"

For many years he was accustomed to mount his old chaise and set off with of Wethersfield, whom I remember in his antique costume, was quite a portly gentleman. The long powdered queues, the small-clothes and knee-buckles, the white-top-boots and silk stockings, with the majestic tread of a Humphries, a Daggett, or a Dana — who flourished forty or fifty years ago in the high places of Connecticut — no doubt made these leaders of society look like the born lords of creation.

But be this as it may, there is no doubt that Deacon Olmstead was in all things a noble specimen of humanity — an honor to human nature — a shining light in the Church. I have spoken of him as having something grand about him, yet I remember how kindly he condescended to take me, a child, on his knee, and how gently his great brawny fingers encircled my infant hand. I have said he was wise; yet his book learning was small, though it might have been as great as that of Abraham, or Isaac, or Jacob. He knew indeed the Bible by heart, and that is a great teacher. He had also lived long, and profited by observation and experience. Above all, he was calm, just, sincere, and it is wonderful how these lamps light up the path of life. I have said he was proud, yet it was only toward the seductions of the world: to these he was hard and stern: to his God, he was simple, obedient, and docile as a child: toward his kindred and his neighbor, toward the poor, toward the suffering — though not so soft — he was sympathetic as a sister of charity.

Deacon Hawley was unlike his associate whom I have described. He was younger, and of a peculiarly mild and amiable temper. His countenance wore a tranquil and smooth expression. His hair was fine and silky, and lay, as if oiled, close to his head. He had a soft voice, and an ear for music. He was a cabinet-maker by trade, a chorister by choice, a deacon by the vote of the church, a Christian by the grace of God. In each of these things he found his place, as if designed for it by nature and Providence.

In wordly affairs as well as spiritual, Deacon Hawley's path was straight and even: he was successful in business, beloved in society, honored in the church. Exceedingly frugal by habit and disposition, he still loved to give in charity, though he told not the world of it. When he was old, his family being well provided for, he spent much of his time in casting about to find opportunities of doing

---

Mrs. Marsh to attend the annual commencement at Cambridge College. Everybody knew him along the road, and bowing, as he passed, said, "How d'ye do, Dr. Marsh?" At last he dismissed his wig; but now, as he went along, nobody recognized him. It was evident that his wig was necessary to insure the accustomed and grateful salute; so, on his journeys to commencement ever after, he put it on, though he discarded it at other times. He died A.D. 1820, aged 79.

good. Once he learned that a widow, who had been in good circumstances, was struggling with poverty. He was afraid to offer money as charity, for fear of wounding her pride — the more sensitive, perhaps, because of her change of condition. He therefore intimated that he owed a debt of fifty dollars to her late husband, and wished to pay it to her.

"And how was that?" said the lady, somewhat startled.

"I will tell you," said the Deacon. "About five and twenty years ago, soon after you were married, I made some furniture for your husband — to the amount of two hundred dollars. I have been looking over the account, and find that I rather overcharged him, in the price of some chairs; that is, could have afforded them at somewhat less. I have added up the interest, and here, madam, is the money."

I know not how it is, but the term *deacon* is associated in many minds with a certain littleness, and especially a sort of affectation, a cant in conversation, an I-am-holier-than-thou air and manner. I remember Deacon C . . . of H . . ., who deemed it proper to become scriptural, and to talk as much as possible like Isaiah. He was in partnership with his son Laertes, and they sold crockery and furniture. One day a female customer came, and the old gentleman being engaged, went to call his son, who was in the loft above. Placing himself at the foot of the stairs, he said, attuning his voice to the occasion, "La-ar-tes, descend — a lady waits!" Deacon C . . . sought to signalize himself by a special respect to the ways of Providence: so he refused to get insurance against fire, declaring that if the Lord wished to burn down his house or his barn, he should submit without a murmur.

From the ecclesiastic notabilities of Ridgefield I turn for a moment to the secular. And first, Colonel Bradley claims my notice, for he was the leading citizen of the place, in station, wealth, education, and power of intellect. He was a tall, gaunt, sallow man, a little bent at the period of my recollection, for he was then well stricken in years. He lived in a two-story white house, at the upper end of the main street, and on the western side. This was of ample dimensions, and had a grave, antique air, the effect of which was enhanced by a row of wide-arching elms, lining the street. It stood on a slight elevation, and somewhat withdrawn from the road; the fence in front was high and close; the doors and windows were always shut, even in summer. I know not why, but this place had a sort of awfulness about it: it seemed to have a spirit and a voice, which whispered to the passer-by, "Go thy way: this is the abode of one above and beyond thee!"

In order to comprehend the impression likely to be made by

such a sombre tenement, you must remember the general aspect of our country villages at that time, and indeed at the present time. Each house was built near the street, with a yard in front and a garden beside it. The fences were low, and of light, open pickets or slats, made to exclude cattle, pigs, and geese, which then had the freedom of the place. There was a cheerful, confiding, wide, open look all around. Everybody peeped from the windows into everybody's grounds. The proprietor was evidently content to be under your eye; nay, as you passed along, his beets and carrots in long beds, his roses and peonies bordering the central walk; the pears and peaches and plums swinging from the trees, all seemed to invite your observation. The barn, having its vast double doors in front, and generally thrown open, presented its interior to your view, with all its gathered treasures of hay, oats, rye, and flax. Near by, but yet apart, stood the crib for the Indian corn, showing its laughing, yellow ears between the slats, designed to give circulation to the air.

There was in all this a liberty and equality which belonged to the age. These had their foundation, partly at least, in two sources — a love of an open, unobstructed view, and a sort of communal familiarity in the intercourse of society. The first settlers of the country found it covered with forests, which, while they sheltered the lurking Indian, the poaching wolf, and the prowling bear, also obstructed civilization. Trees were then the great enemy, and to exterminate them was the first great battle of life. In those days men became tree-haters. The shadow of the wood was associated with dearth and danger — the open space with plenty of peace. It was not till long after, when the burning sun of our summers had taught the luxury of shade, that the people of New England discovered their mistake, and began to decorate their streets and pleasure-grounds with trees.

Col. Bradley was an exclusive. His cold, distant manner bespoke it. He was, I believe, an honorable man. He was a member of the church; he was steady in his worship, and never missed the sacrament. He was a man of education, and held high offices. His commission as colonel was signed by John Jay, president of the Continental Congress, and his office of Marshal of the District of Connecticut was signed by Washington. His commission as judge of the County Court was signed by the governor of the State. He was, as I have said, the most distinguished citizen of the place, and naturally enough imagined that such a position carried with it, not the shadow, but the substance of power. He seldom took an open part in the affairs of the town, but when he did, he felt that his word should be law. He deemed even a nod of his head to be imperative;

people were bound to consult his very looks, and scenting his trail, should follow in his foot-steps. Like most proud men of despotic temper, he sometimes condescended to bring about his ends by puppets and wire pullers. Affecting to disdain all meddling, he really contrived openly or covertly to govern the church and the town. When parties in politics arose, he was of course a federalist; though ostentatiously standing aloof from the tarnish of caucuses, he still managed to fill most of the offices by his seen or unseen dictation.

Such a man could little appreciate the real spirit of democracy, now rising, like a spring-tide, over Connecticut. Believing in the "Good old way," he sincerely felt that innovation was synonymous with ruin. Thinking all virtue and all wisdom to be centered in the few, he believed all folly and mischief to be in the many. The passage of power from the former to the latter, he regarded with unaffected horror. The sanctity of the church, the stability of the law, the sacredness of home, life, and property, all seemed to him put at hazard if committed to the rabble, or what to him was equivalent, that dreaded thing — democracy.

He was certainly a man of ability, well read in history, and of superior mental gifts. He saw the coming storm, which soon lowered and thundered in the sky; but he neither comprehended its force, nor the best manner of combating it. He had not those sensitive feelers — the gift of such born democrats as Jefferson and Van Buren — which wind their invisible and subtle threads among the masses, and bring home to the shrewd sensorium an account of every trembling emotion in the breast of the million. In fact so far as the mass, the people were concerned, he was a profound owl, seeing deeply into the nothingness of night, but stark blind in the open day of real and pressing action. In wielding power, put into his hands by authority, he was a strong man: in acquiring it at the hands of democracy, he was a child.

Col. Bradley, whom I have described as the head of the federal party in Ridgefield, was pretty nearly a type of his kind in those days. There was perhaps a shade of Jesuitism about him, a love of unseen influences, the exercise of invisible power, which was personal and not a necessary part of his principle. I perfectly recollect his appearance at church, and the impression he made upon me. He was bald, and wore a black silk cap, drawn down close over his eyes. These were like jet, not twinkling, but steady and intense, appearing very awful from the dark caverns in which they were set. I hardly dared to look at him, and if perchance his slow but searching gaze fell upon me, I started as if something had wounded me. At long intervals he came to our house, and though he was of course a supporter of my father, being a member of the church, I had the impression that everybody breathed thick and anxiously while he was there, and felt relieved when he went away.

It is not possible to conceive of two persons more unlike than the one I have just sketched and General King. The former was tall, thin, dark; the latter was of middle height, stout, erect, and florid. The first was highly educated, meditative, secret, deep, cold, circumspect; the latter was unschooled, yet intelligent; frank, though perhaps superficial; imperious, yet fearless and confiding. Col. Bradley was a federalist; Gen. King a democrat. These two, indeed, were the leaders of the two great political parties in Ridgefield.

If I were to be asked what made Gen. King a democrat, I should be at a loss to answer. He was fond of authority: his whole presence and manner bespoke it. His carriage was erect, his head set back, his chest protruded. His hair was stiff and bristling, and being long on the top, was combed back in the manner of Gen. Jackson's. Like him he had a decidedly military air and character. He was, no doubt, a very good man on the whole, but I imagine he was not imbued with any special sympathy for the masses, or the rights of man. I have pretty good reasons to believe that his natural disposition was dictatorial — despotic. It is related that one day he came into the field where his men were haying. A thunderstorm was approaching, and he commanded the laborers in a tone of authority to do this and that, thus requiring in fact what was impossible. Jaklin, an old negro, noted for his dry wit, being present, said in an undertone —

"I'm thankful the Lord reigns."

"Why so ?" said a bystander.

"Because," was the reply, "if the Lord didn't reign, the Gineral would !"

Why, then, was he a democrat ? Was it because Col. Bradley and himself were rivals in trade, rivals in wealth, rivals in position ? Was it that by a natural proclivity, derived from this relation, he became an opponent of one who stood in his way, and thus became a democrat ? Who will venture to solve such questions as these ?

General King's house stood on the northern slope of a small swell of ground, midway between the two extremities of the main street, and on the western side. It was a rather large two-story edifice, always neatly kept, and glowing in fresh white paint. Wealth and respectability in the full tide of successful experiment, were as readable in its appearance as if it had been so written in front, like the designation of a railway station.

Contiguous to this fresh and flourishing mansion, on the southern side, was a brown, gable-roofed house, with two venerable, but still green and flourishing button-wood trees in front. The building was marked with age, the surface of its clapboards, unprotected by paint, being softened and spongy through the influence of the seasons. The roof was of a yellowish-green tint, imparted by a gathering film of moss. The windows were contracted, and the casing, thin and plain, bespoke the architecture of our day of small things. All around was rather bare, and the little recess in front, open and uninclosed, was at once shaven close and desecrated by a flock of geese that every night made it their camp-ground. Nevertheless, there was a certain dignity about the button-wood trees in front, and the old brown house in the rear, that excited respect and curiosity in the beholder. There was indeed some reason, for this was the home of the Ingersolls.

The Rev. Jonathan Ingersoll was my father's immediate predecessor, as minister of the First Congregational Church in Ridgefield. Though he has been dead three fourths of a century, tradition still cherishes his memory as an able preacher, a devoted pastor, and a most amiable man. In my boyhood he had long since passed away, but his widow still lingered in the old brown house I have described. She was every way a superior woman — wise, good, loving, and beloved. Her husband's mantle descended upon her shoulders, and she wore it worthily before the world and the Church. By the latter she was cherished as a guardian saint. She was always my father's friend, and in the critical and difficult passages which are sure to arise between a pastor and his people, she was the ready and efficient peacemaker. I remember her, though faintly and as a dream, yet one in which I saw a pale, gray, saintly old lady, almost too good for this wicked world.

Matthew Olmstead, or Mat Olmstead, as he was usually called, was a day laborer, and though his speciality was the laying of stone fences, he was equally adroit at hoeing corn, mowing, and farmwork in general. He was rather short and thick-set, with a long nose, a litle bulbous in his latter days — with a ruddy complexion, and a mouth shutting like a pair of nippers — the lips having an oblique dip to the left, giving a keen and mischievous expression to his face, qualified, however, by more of mirth than malice. The feature was indicative of his mind and character, for he was sharp in speech, and affected a crisp, biting brevity, called dry wit. He had also a turn for practical jokes, and a great many of these were told of him, to which, perhaps, he had no historical claim.

I remember that when the great solar eclipse of 1806 was approaching, he with two other men were at work in one of our fields, not far from the house. The eclipse was to begin at ten or eleven o'clock, and my father sent an invitation to the workmen to come up and observe it through some pieces of smoked glass. They came, though Mat ridiculed the idea of an eclipse — not but the thing might happen — but it was idle to suppose it could be foretold. While they were waiting and watching for the great event, my father explained that the light of the sun upon the earth was to be interrupted by the intrusion of the moon, and that this was to produce a transient night upon the scene around us.

Mat laughed with that low scoffing chuckle, with which a woodchuck, safe in his rocky den, replies to the bark of a besieging dog.

"So you don't believe this?" said my father.

"No," said Mat, shaking his head, and bringing his lips obliquely together, like the blades of a pair of shears. "I don't believe a word of it. You say, Parson Goodrich, that the sun is fixed, and don't move?"

"Yes, I say so."

"Well: didn't you preach last Sunday out of the 10th chapter of Joshua?"

"Yes."

"And didn't you tell us that Joshua commanded the sun and moon to stand still?" "Yes."

"Well: what was the use of telling the sun to stand still if it never moved?"

This was a dead shot, especially at a parson, and in the presence of an audience inclined, from the fellowship of ignorance, to receive the argument. Being thus successful, Mat went on.

"Now, Parson Goodrich, let's try it agin. If you turn a thing that's got water in it bottom up, the water'll run out, won't it?"

"No doubt."

"If the world turns round, then your well will be turned bottom up, and the water'll run out!"

At this point my father applied his eye to the sun through a piece of smoked glass. The eclipse had begun; a small piece was evidently cut off the rim. My father stated the fact, and the company around looked through the glass and saw that it was so. Mat Olmstead, however, sturdily refused to try it, and bore on his face an air of supreme contempt, as much as to say, "You don't humbug me!"

But ignorance and denial of the works of God do not interrupt their march. By slow and invisible degrees, a shade crept over the landscape. There was no cloud in the sky, but a chill stole through the atmosphere, and a strange dimness fell over the world. It was midday, yet it seemed like the approach of night. There was something fearful in this, as if the sun was about to be blotted out in the midst of his glory — the light of the world to be extinguished at the moment of its noon ! All nature seemed chilled and awed by the strange phenomenon.

Mat Olmstead said not a word; the other workmen were overwhelmed with emotions of awe.

At length the eclipse began to pass away, and nature slowly returned to her equanimity. The birds came forth, and sang a jubilee, as if relieved from some impending calamity. The hum of life again filled the air; the old hen with her brood gayly resumed her rambles, and made the leaves and gravel fly with her invigorated scratchings. The workmen, too, having taken a glass of grog, returned thoughtfully to their labors.

"After all," said one of the men, as they passed along to the field, "I guess the parson was right about the sun and the moon."

"Well, perhaps he was," said Mat; "but then Joshua was wrong."

I turn to the town miser. Granther Baldwin, as I remember him, was threescore years and ten — perhaps a little more. He was a man of middle size, but thin, wiry, and bloodless, and having his body bent forward at a sharp angle with his hips, while his head was thrown back over his shoulders — giving his person the general form of a reversed letter Z. His complexion was brown and stony; his eye gray and twinkling, with a nose and chin almost meeting like a pair of forceps. His hair — standing out with an irritable frizz — was of a rusty gray. He was always restless, and walked and rode with a sort of haggish rapidity. At church, he wiggled in his seat, tasted fennel, and bobbed his head up and down and around. He could not afford tobacco, so he chewed, with a constant activity, either an oak chip or the roots of elecampane, which was indigenous in the lane near his house. On Sundays he was decent in his attire, but on week-days he was a beggarly curiosity. It was said that he once exchanged hats with a scarecrow, and cheated scandalously in the bargain. His boots — a withered wreck of an old pair of whitetops — dangled over his shrunken calves, and a coat in tatters fluttered from his body. He rode a switch-tailed, ambling mare, which always went like the wind, shaking the old gentleman merrily from right to left, and making his bones, boots, and rags rustle like his own bush-harrow. Familiar as he was, the school-boys were never tired of him, and when he passed, "There goes Granther Baldwin !" was the invariable ejaculation.

I must add — in order to complete the picture — that in contrast to his elvish leanness and wizard activity, his wife was bloated with fat, and either from indolence or lethargy, dozed away half her life in the chimney corner. It was said, and no doubt truly, that she often went to sleep at the table, sometimes allowing a rind of bacon to stick out of her mouth till her nap was over. I have a faint notion of having seen this myself. She spent a large part of her life in cheating her husband out of *four-pence-ha'pennies,** of which more than a peck were found secreted in an old chest, at her death.

It was the boast of this man that he had risen from poverty to wealth, and he loved to describe the process of his advancement. He always worked in the corn-field till it was so dark that he could see his hoe strike fire. When in the heat of summer he was obliged occasionally to let his cattle breathe, he sat on a sharp stone, lest he should rest too long. He paid half a dollar to the parson for marrying him, which he always regretted, as one of his neighbors got the job done for a pint of mustard-seed. On fast-days, he made his cattle go without food as well as himself. He systematically stooped to save a crooked pin or a rusty nail, as it would cost more to make it than to pick it up. Such were his boasts — or at least, such were the things traditionally imputed to him.

He was withal a man of keen faculties; sagacious in the purchase of land, as well as in the rotation of crops. He was literally honest, and never cheated any one out of a farthing, according to his arithmetic —though he had sometimes an odd way of reckoning.

I need not enlarge upon the adventures between Granther Baldwin and the school-boys, who took delight in pocketing his apples, pears, and nuts. These things were so abundant in those days, that everybody picked and ate, without the idea of trespass. But Granther's heart was sorely afflicted at these dispensations. He could not bear the idea of losing a pocketful of apples, or a handful of butternuts, chestnuts, or walnuts, even if they lay decaying in heaps upon his ground. His house and farm were close by West Lane school, and it was quite a matter of course that this hard, unrelenting conservatism should clash with the ideas of the natural rights of school-boys, entertained by such free-born youths as those at this seminary. They loved the fruit, and considered liberal pickings to be their birthright. Had the old gentleman let them alone, or had he smiled on them in their small pilferings, they had, no doubt, been moderate in their plunder. But when he made war on them — even unto sticks, stones, and pitch-forks — the love of fun and the glory of mischief added an indescribable relish to their forays upon his woods

* According to the old New England currency, the Spanish sixteenth of a dollar — the sixpence of New York and the picayune of Louisiana — was four-pence-halfpenny. This word was formerly the shibboleth of the Yankees — every one being set down as a New Englander who said *fourpence-ha'penny.*

and orchards. I confess to have been drawn in more than once to these misdoings. Perhaps, too, I was sometimes a leader in them. I confess, with all due contrition, that when the old miser, hearing the walnuts rattle down by the bushel in the forest back of his house — knowing that mischief was in the wind — came forth in a fury, pitchfork in hand; when I have heard his hoarse yet impotent threats; I have rather enjoyed than sympathized with his agonies. Poor old gentleman — let me now expiate my sins by doing justice to his memory!

It is true he was a miser — selfish and mean by nature. Born in poverty, and only rising from this condition by threescore years and ten of toil and parsimony, was it possible for him to be otherwise? And yet Granther Baldwin was not wholly lost.

He was a firm believer in the Bible, and set the example of implicit submission to its doctrines, as he discovered them. He made an open profession of his faith, and in sickness and in health, in rain and shine, in summer and winter, he sustained the established institutions of religion. No weather ever prevented him from attending church, though he lived nearly two miles from the place of worship. Often have I seen him on a Sunday morning, facing the keen blast, plodding his way thither, when it seemed as if his heart must be reduced to an icicle. He attended all funerals within the precincts of the place. He was present at every town meeting: he paid his taxes, civil and ecclesiastical, at the appointed day. He kept thanksgivings and fasts — the first gingerly, and the last with all his heart. He had a clock and a noon-mark, and when they varied, he insisted that the sun was wrong. He believed profoundly in arithmetic, and submitted, without repining, to its decrees. Here was the skeleton of a man and a Christian; all that it wanted was a soul!

◆◇◆◇◆◇◆◇◆◇◆◇◆◇

[*Charles T. Congdon, New Bedford, Mass.*]

There was a good deal left in our town, in my boyhood, of old-fashioned manners and of old-timed courtesy, and many a relic of the old colonial days, when the distinction of classes was much wider than it now is. There were still many who pronounced the English language according to Walker, and said, "I am much *obleeged* to you"; many who were not afraid of being considered proud, and thought more of their blood than of their property; who hung their arms upon the wall, — gules, fesse, crest and all; and who left in their wills curious little gold rings, fashioned in the form of a death's head, to be given to their bearers at the last. Years

NEW BEDFORD

and years after, I saw one of these upon the finger of a pretty girl, who told me it had come to her from her great-grandfather, who received it at Squire W —'s funeral. There were fine old ladies then, who showed you with great pride the portraits of their ancestors painted by Copley, and in such lace and velvet and brocades as only Copley has ever painted. One of these ancient dames I well remember, who, when I was taken into her presence by my mother, filled my childish soul with awe, — so stiff, so stately, so grandly mannered was she, as she sat bolt upright in her great chair with no apparent pressure of her eighty years upon her. She fanned herself with the air of an empress. She presided at the tea-table, and poured out the beverage with her old hands into cups which would set a collector of the present day wild. She made every guest her particular care, and asked everyone scrupulously if the tea was agreeable. She had the old way of pressing her visitors to take a little more of this or that, — a custom which had come down from the time when Lady Mary Wortley Montagu carved for her father's guests, and recommended tid-bits to the Whig lords and squires. She was the embodiment of scrupulous decorum and civility, and I doubt if anything could have betrayed her into the discourteous or rude.

❖❖❖❖❖❖❖❖❖❖❖❖

[Henry Adams, Quincy, Mass.]

During these three or four summers the old President's [John Quincy Adams'] relations with the boy [Henry] were friendly and almost intimate. Whether his older brothers and sisters were still more favored he failed to remember, but he was himself admitted to a sort of familiarity which, when in his turn he had reached old age, rather shocked him, for it must have sometimes tried the President's patience. He hung about the library; handled the books; deranged the papers; ransacked the drawers; searched the old purses and pocket-books for foreign coins; drew the sword-cane; snapped the travelling-pistols; upset everything in the corners, and penetrated the President's dressing-closet where a row of tumblers, inverted on the shelf, covered caterpillars which were supposed to become moths or butterflies, but never did. The Madam bore with fortitude the loss of the tumblers which her husband purloined for these hatcheries; but she made protest when he carried off her best cut-glass bowls to plant with acorns or peachstones that he might see the roots grow, but which, she said, he commonly forgot like the caterpillars.

❖❖❖❖❖❖❖❖❖❖❖❖

[*Thomas Low Nichols, Orford, N. H.*]

When I was a small boy in New Hampshire, one very cold winter's day I went into the bar-room of a country tavern to warm myself by the stove, around which a dozen or more men were sitting. The jingle of sleigh-bells came up to the door and stopped. A rough looking up country farmer came in, thawed himself a moment by the fire, looked about him with a grave friendliness, and said: "My name is so and so. I live on a little farm up on Onion river in Vermont. I have got a son in Boston learning the carpenter's trade. Well, it is winter, you see; I had got up my wood, and done all the little chores about, and so I thought I would tackle up my team and take a jag of dried apples, dried pumpkins, and apple sauce, and some socks and mittens that the old woman and gals had been knitting and go down to Boston, see how my boy is getting on, sell my truck, buy a few notions, and get home again. Think there's goin' to be a thaw ?"

All this was as quiet, easy and natural as possible. The good man was at home among his equals; and if the squire, or the governor of the State, had been there, it would have been all the same. A Vermont farmer was holding the plough in his own field one day when a neighbour came across the furrows to tell him that he had been nominated for governor — but, then, the duties of governor of Vermont were not very onerous, and, in those days the salary was five hundred dollars a year.

◇◇◇◇◇◇◇◇◇◇◇◇◇

[*Henry D. Thoreau*]

No people can long continue provincial in character who have the propensity for politics and whittling, and rapid traveling, which the Yankees have, and who are leaving the mother country behind in the variety of their notions and inventions. The possession and exercise of practical talent merely are a sure and rapid means of intellectual culture and independence.

◇◇◇◇◇◇◇◇◇◇◇◇◇

[*John M. Todd, barber, Portland, Me.*]

In 1845, John Neal became a customer of mine, and for thirty-five years I had the benefit of his wisdom, learning and generosity. His library was ever open to me, and much indebted was I to him. And now to that dual nature of Mr. Neal's, that strong, ungovernable temper that brooked no insult, for woe to him who dared to offend him or incur his wrath. Henry Ward Beecher said: "Our virtues consist not in what we do or what we do not do, but in what we have resisted." No one knows what Mr. Neal resisted. He said to me: "I tremble when I think of my ungovernable temper. I know not why I have not killed some one ere this." I will give you an instance of that double nature of his.

I was in his office when a hard looking and very poorly clad Irishman came in, walked up to Mr. Neal, took from his hat a dirty paper, threw it down upon the table in front of Mr. Neal, saying, "There's that bill for digging the house drain." Mr. Neal looked at the footing of the bill, $63. Like a tiger he sprang from his chair, both feet striking the floor together, with eyes flashing and glaring like a wild lion, and screeched, "Out of my office, you villain, or I'll thrash the floor with you !" The poor Irishman shot out of the room like lightning and Mr. Neal commenced pacing the floor back and forth like a wild tiger, and repeating, "Sixty-three dollars, the villain; six dollars would have been a fair price for the job." At that moment poor Michael opened the door about half an inch and, in a low voice, said, "Mr. Neal, the big house drain is there too."

"O dear, dear, will you forgive me, Michael," said Mr. Neal, changing instantly, "have I wounded your feelings ? Will you forgive me ? I had forgotten all about the large house drain. The bill is none too large. The fact is I glanced at the sixty-three dollars, when I thought six dollars was enough, and I see that is just what you have charged for the small house drain." Mr. Neal sat down, took out his check book, wrote a check for the sixty-three dollars, and said again, "Michael, please forgive me, won't you ?" Michael said, "To be sure I will, Mr. Neal, for that is nothing; you are a good man, you are. I know you well and am sure you could not help it at all, for you get mad easy." I stood motionless through it all, perfectly astonished to witness such an outburst of rage and apparently without a sufficient cause. I had not ventured to speak, waiting in silence. Mr. Neal turned to me smiling, and his smile was as fascinating as his frown was terrifying when enraged, and said: "John, you saw the fool John Neal, and you also saw John Neal who professes to be a follower of his beloved Master, and I could not help it. I do try hard to live up to His teaching. Oh, how humiliating it was for me to get upon my knees, figuratively speaking, and humbly ask that man's forgiveness, but justice, honor and the blessed gospel called so loudly upon me, I was obliged to do it."

◇◇◇◇◇◇◇◇◇◇◇◇◇

[*Edward Everett Hale, Boston*]

I wish particularly to describe Fullum, who outlived the class to which he belonged, and had, when he died, in 1886, long been its last representative.

The few New England children who still read the Rollo books will have pleasant remembrances of *Jonas* and *Beechnut,* in whom Mr. Jacob Abbott has presented for posterity the hired boy of New England country life. In life in a little town like Boston this hired boy might grow to be the hired man, and, as in Fullum's exceptional case, might grow to be a hundred years old, or nearly that, without changing that condition. If that happened his presence in a family became a factor of importance to the growing children. In the case of Fullum, if, as he supposed, he was born in 1790, he was thirty-two years old when, in 1822, he took me in his arms before I was an hour old.

Fullum, then, had been a country lad, who came down from Worcester County, to make his fortune. I do not know when, but it was before the time of the short war with England. He expected to be, and was, the hired boy and hired man in one and another Boston family. Early in the business he was in Mr. William Sullivan's service. He was driving Mr. Sullivan out of town, one day, when they found Roxbury Street blocked up by the roof of the old meeting-house, which had been blown into the street by the gale of September, 1815. Afterward he was in Daniel Webster's service, and here also he took care of horses and carriages. He was a born tyrant, and it was always intimated that Mr. Webster did not fancy his rule. Anyway he came from the Websters to us, I suppose when Mr. Webster went to Congress, in the autumn of 1820. And, in one fashion or another, he lived with our family, as a most faithful vassal or tyrant, for sixty-six years from that time.

Here was a faithful man Friday, who would have died for any of us, so strong was his love for us, yet who insisted on rendering his service very much in his own way. If my father designed a wooden horse for me, to be run on four wheels, after the fashion of what were called velocipedes in those days, he would make the drawings, but it would be Fullum's business to take them to the carpenter's and see the horse made. If we were to have heavy hoops from water-casks, Fullum was the person who conducted the negotiation for them. There was no harm in the tutorship to which we were thus intrusted. He never used a profane or impure word while he was with us children; and as he was to us an authority in all matters of gardening, of carpentry, of driving and the care of horses, we came to regard him as, in certain lines, omniscient and omnipotent. Yet this omniscient and omnipotent person, at once the Hercules and the Apollo of our boyhood, could not read, write, or spell so well as any child four years old who had been twelve months at Miss Whitney's school.

TRAVELS IN NEW ENGLAND

◆◇◆◇◆◇◆◇◆◇◆◇◆

[*Thomas Morton, of Merrymount*]

In the Moneth of June, Anno Salutis: 1622. It was my chaunce to
arrive in the parts of New England with 30. Servants, and provision
of all sorts fit for a plantation: And whiles our howses were building, I did endeavour to take a survey of the Country: The more I
looked, the more I liked it.

And when I had more seriously considered of the bewty of the
place, with all her faire indowments, I did not think that in all the
knowne world it could be paralel'd. For so many goodly groues of
trees; dainty fine round rising hillucks: delicate faire large plaines,
sweete cristall fountaines, and cleare running streames, that twine
in fine meanders through the meads, making so sweete a murmur-
ing noise to heare, as would even lull the sences with delight a
sleepe, so pleasantly doe, they glide upon the pebble stones, jetting
most jocundly where they doe meete; and hand in hand runne
downe to Neptunes Court, to pay the yearely tribute, which they
owe to him as soveraigne Lord of all the springs. Contained within
the volume of the Land, Fowles in abundance, Fish in multitude,
and discovered besides; Millions of Turtledoves one the greene
boughes: which sate pecking, of the full ripe pleasant grapes, that
were supported by the lusty trees, whose fruitfull loade did cause
the armes to bend, which here and there dispersed (you might see)
Lillies and of the Daphnean-tree, which made the Land to mee
seeme paradice, for in mine eie, t'was Natures Master-peece: Her

[487]

cheifest Magazine of, all where lives her store: if this Land be not rich, then is the whole world poore.

What I had resolved on, I have really performed, and I have endeavoured, to use this abstract as an instrument, to bee the meanes, to communicate the knowledge which I have gathered, by my many yeares residence in those parts, unto my Countrymen, to the end, that they may the better perceive their error, who cannot imagine, that there is any Country in the universall world, which may be compared unto our native soyle, I will now discover unto them a Country whose indowments are by learned men allowed to stand in a paralell with the Israelites Canaan, which none will deny, to be a land farre more excellent than Old England in her proper nature.

◇◇◇◇◇◇◇◇◇◇◇◇◇

[*Edward Johnson, Woburn, Mass.*]

But to begin, this Town, as all others, had its bounds fixed by the General Court, to the contenese (contents) of four miles square, (beginning at the end of Charles Town bounds). The grant is to seven men of good and honest report, upon condition, that within two year they erect houses for habitation thereon, and so go on to make a Town thereof, upon the Act of Court; these seven men have power to give and grant out lands unto any persons who are willing to take up their dwellings within the said precinct, and to be admitted to al common priviledges of the said Town, giving them such an ample portion, both of Medow and Upland, as their present and future stock of cattel and hands were like to improve, with eye had to others that might after come to populate the said Town; this they did without any respect of persons, yet such as were exorbitant, and of a turbulent spirit, unfit for a civil society, they would reject, till they come to mend their manners; such came not to enjoy any freehold. These seven men ordered and disposed of the streets of the Town, as might be best for improvement of the Land, and yet civil and religious society maintained; to which end those that had land neerest the place for Sabbath Assembly, had a lesser quantity at home, and more farther off to improve for corn, of all kinds; they refused not men for their poverty, but according to their ability were helpful to the poorest sort, in building their houses, and distributed to them land accordingly; the poorest had six or seven acres of Medow, and twenty five of Upland, or thereabouts. Thus was this Town populated, to the number of sixty families, or thereabout, and after this manner are the Towns of New England peopled. The scituation of this Town is in the highest part of the yet peopled land, neere upon the head-springs of many considerable rivers, or their branches, as the first rise of Ipswitch river, and the rise of Shashin * river, one of the most consid-erable branches of Merrimeck, as also the first rise of Mistick river and ponds, it is very full of pleasant springs, and great variety of very good water, which the Summers heat causeth to be more cooler, and the Winters cold maketh more warmer; their Medows are not large, but lye in divers places to particular dwellings, the like doth their Springs; their Land is very fruitful in many places, although they have no great quantity of plain land in any one place, yet doth their Rocks and Swamps yeeld very good food for cattel; as also they have Mast and Tar for shipping, but the distance of place by land causeth them as yet to be unprofitable; they have great store of iron ore; their meeting-house stands in a small Plain, where four streets meet; the people are very laborious, if not exceeding some of them.

Now to declare how this people proceeded in religious matters, and so consequently all the Churches of Christ planted in New-England, when they came once to hopes of being such a competent number of people, as might be able to maintain a Minister, they then surely seated themselves, and not before, it being as unnat-ural for a right N. E. man to live without an able Ministery, as for a Smith to work his iron without a fire; therefore this people that went about placing down a Town, began the foundation-stone, with earnest seeking of the Lords assistance, by humbling of their souls before him in daies of prayer, and imploring his aid in so weighty a work, then they address themselves to attend counsel of the most Orthodox and ablest Christians, and more especially of such as the Lord had already placed in the Ministery, not rashly running together themselves into a Church, before they had hopes of attaining an Officer to preach the Word, and administer the Seals unto them, chosing rather to continue in fellowship with some other Church for their Christian watch over them, till the Lord would be pleased to provide: They after some search meet with a young man named Mr. Thomas Carter, then belonging to the Church of Christ at Water-Town, reverend godly man, apt to teach the sound and wholesome truths of Christ; having attained their desires, in hopes of his coming unto them, were they once joyned in Church-estate, he exercising his gifts of preaching and prayer among them in the mean time, and more especially in a day of fasting and prayer.† Thus these godly people interest their affec-tions one with the other, both Minister and people: After this they

* Shawshin or Shawsheen.   † In April, 1642.

make ready for the work, and the 24. of the 6. moneth * 1642. they assembled together in the morning about eight of the clock; After the reverend Mr. Syms had continued in preaching and prayer about the space of four or five houres, the persons that were to joyn in Covenant, openly and professedly before the Congregation, and messengers of divers Neighbour Churches — among whom the reverend Elder of Boston, Mr. Cotton,† Mr. Wilson, Mr. Allen of Charles-Town, Mr. Shepheard of Cambridg, Mr. Dunster ‡ of Water-Town, Mr. Knowles of Deadham, Mr. Allen of Roxbury, Mr. Eliot § of Dorchester, Mr. [Richard] Mather: As also it is the duty of the Magistrates (in regard of the good and peace of the civil Government) to be present, at least some one of them (not only to prevent the disturbance might follow in the Commonwealth by any, who under pretence of Church-Covenant, might bring in again those cursed opinions that caused such commotion in this and the other Colony, to the great dammage of the people) but also to countenance the people of God in so pious a work, that under them they may live a quiet and peaceable life, in all godliness and honesty; for this cause was present the honored Mr. Increase Nowel — the persons stood forth and first confessed what the Lord had done for their poor souls, by the work of his Spirit in the preaching of his Word, and Providences, one by one; and that all might know their faith in Christ was bottomed upon him, as he is revealed in his Word, and that from their own knowledg, they also declare the same, according to that measure of understanding the Lord had given them; the Elders, or any other messengers there present question with them, for the better understanding of them in any points they doubt of, which being done, and all satisfied, they in the name of the Churches to which they do belong, hold out the right hand of fellowship unto them, they declaring their Covenant, in words expressed in writing to this purpose.

◇◇◇◇◇◇◇◇◇◇◇◇◇◇

[*The Journal of Madam Knight in 1704*]

My Guide's shade on his Hors resembled a Globe on a Gate post. His habitt, Hors and furniture, its looks and going Incombarably answered the rest.

* *I.E.*, Aug. 24. But Woburn town records give the date as Aug. 14.

† John Cotton, in whose honor Boston was named after Boston in Lincolnshire.

‡ Henry Dunster, the first president of Harvard.

§ John Eliot, the apostle to the Indians.

Thus Jogging on with an easy pace, my Guide telling mee it was dangero's to Ride hard in the Night, (wh^{ch} his hors had the sence to avoid,) Hee entertained me with the Adventurs he had passed by late Rideing, and eminent Dangers he had escaped, so that, Remembring the Hero's in Parismus and the Knight of the Oracle, I didn't know but I had met wth a Prince disguis'd.

When we had Ridd about an how'r, wee came into a thick swamp, wch. by Reason of a great fogg, very much startled mee, it being now very Dark. But nothing dismay'd John: Hee had encountered a thousand such Swamps, having a Universall Knowledge in the woods; and readily Answered all my inquiries wch. were not a few.

In about an how'r or something more, after we left the Swamp, we came to Billinges, where I was to Lodg. My Guide dismounted and very Complasantly help't me down and shewd the door, signing to me wth his hand to Go in; wch I Gladly did — But had not gone many steps into the Room, ere I was Interogated by a young Lady I understood afterwards was the Eldest daughter of the family, with these, or words to this purpose, (viz.) Law for mee — what in the world brings You here at this time a night ? — I never see a woman on the Rode so Dreadfull late, in all the days of my versall life. Who are You ? Where are You going ? I'me scar'd out of my witts — with much now of the same Kind. I stood aghast, Prepareing to reply, when in come my Guide — to him Madam turn'd, Roreing out: Lawfull heart, John, is it You ? — how de do ! Where in the world are you going with this woman ? Who is she ? John made no Ansr. but sat down in the corner, fumbled out his black Junk, and saluted that instead of Debb; she then turned agen to mee and fell anew into her silly questions, without asking mee to sitt down.

I told her shee treated me very Rudely, and I did not think it my duty to answer her unmannerly Questions. But to get ridd of them, I told her I come there to have the post's company with me tomorrow on my Journey, &c. Miss star's awhile, drew a chair, bid me sitt, And then run upstairs and putts on two or three Rings, (or else I had not seen them before) and returning, sett herself just before me, showing the way to Reding, that I might see her Ornaments, perhaps to gain the more respect. But her Granam's new Rung sow, had it appeared, would affected me as much. I paid honest John wth money and dram according to contract, and Dismist him, and pray'd Miss to shew me where I must Lodg. Shee conducted me to a parlour in a little back Lento, wch was almost fill'd wth the bedsted, wch was so high that I was forced to climb on a chair to gitt up to yᵉ wretched bed that lay on it; on wᶜʰ having Stretcht my tired Limbs, and lay'd my head on a Sad-colourd pillow, I began to think on the transactions of yᵉ past day.

Tuesday, October yᵉ third, about 8 in the morning, I with the Post proceeded forward without observing anything remarkable; And about two, afternoon, Arrived at the Post's second stage, where the western Post mett him and exchanged Letters. Here, having called for something to eat, yᵉ woman bro't a Twisted thing like a cable, but something whiter; and laying it on the bord, tugg'd for life to bring it into a capacity to spread; wᶜʰ having wᵗʰ great pains accomplished, she serv'd in a dish of Pork and Cabage, I suppose the remains of Dinner. The sause was of a deep Purple, wᶜʰ I tho't was boil'd in her dye Kettle; the bread was Indian, and every thing on the Table service Agreable to these. I, being hungry, gott a little down; but my stomach was soon cloy'd, and what cabbage I swallowed serv'd me for a Cudd the whole day after.

Having here discharged the Ordnary for self and Guide, (as I understood was the custom,) About Three, afternoon, went on with my Third Guide, who Rode very hard; and having crossed Providence Ferry, we come to a River wᶜʰ they Generally Ride thro'. But I dare not venture; so the Post got a Ladd and Cannoo to carry me to tother side, and hee rid thro' and Led my hors. The Cannoo was very small and shallow, so that when we were in she seem'd redy to take in water, which greatly terrified mee, and caused me to be very circumspect, sitting with my hands fast on each side, my eyes stedy, not daring so much as to lodg my tongue a hair's breadth more on one side of my mouth than tother, nor so much as think on Lott's wife, for a wry thought would have oversett our wherey: But was soon put out of this pain, by feeling the Cannoo on shore, wᶜʰ I as soon almost saluted with my feet; and Rewarding my sculler, again mounted and made the best of our way forwards.

Being come to mr. Havens', I was very civilly Received, and courteously entertained, in a clean comfortable House; and the Good woman was very active in helping off my Riding clothes, and then ask't what I would eat. I told her I had some Chocolett, if shee would prepare it; which with the help of some Milk, and a little clean brass Kettle, she soon effected to my satisfaction. I then betook me to my Apartment, wᶜʰ was a little Room parted from the Kitchen by a single bord partition; where, after I had noted the Occurrances of the past day, I went to bed, which, tho' pretty hard, Yet neet and handsome. But I could get no sleep, because of the Clamor of some of the Town tope-ers in next Room. Who were entred into a strong debate concerning yᵉ Signifycation of the name of their Country, [viz.] Narraganset. One said it was named so by ye Indians, because there grew a Brier there, of a prodigious Highth and bigness, the like hardly ever known, called by the Indians Narragansett; And quotes an Indian of so Barberous a name for his Author, that I could not write it. His Antagonist Replyed no — It was from a Spring it had its name, wch hee well knew where it was, which was extreem cold in summer, and as Hott as could be imagined in the winter, which was much resorted too by the natives, and by them called Narragansett, (Hott and Cold,) and that was the originall of their places name — with a thousand Impertinances not worth notice, wch He utter'd with such a Roreing voice and Thundering blows with the fist of wickedness on the Table, that it peirced my very head. I heartily fretted, and wish't 'um tongue tyed; but wth as little succes as a friend of mine once, who was (as shee said) kept a whole night awake, on a Jorny, by a country Left. and a Sergent, Insigne and a Deacon, contriving how to bring a triangle into a Square. They kept calling for tother Gill, wch while they were swallowing, was some Intermission; But presently, like Oyle to fire, encreased the flame. I set my Candle on a Chest by the bed side, and setting up, fell to my old way of composing my Resentments, in the following manner:

> I ask thy Aid, O Potent Rum!
> To Charm these wrangling Topers Dum.
> Thou hast their Giddy Brains possest —
> The man confounded wth the Beast —
> And I, poor I, can get no rest.
> Intoxicate them with thy fumes:
> O still their Tongues till morning comes!

And I know not but my wishes took effect; for the dispute soon ended wth 'tother Dram; and so Good night!

Wednesday, Octobr 4th. About four in the morning, we set out for Kingston (for so was the Town called) with a french Docter in our company. Hee and ye Post put on very furiously, so that I could not keep up with them, only as now and then they'd stop till they see mee. This Rode was poorly furnished wth accommodations for Travellers, so that we were forced to ride 22 miles by the post's account, but neerer thirty by mine, before wee could bait so much as our Horses, wch I exceedingly complained of. But the post encourag'd mee, by saying wee should be well accommodated anon at mr. Devills, a few miles further. But I questioned whether we ought to go to the Devil to be helpt out of affliction. However, like the rest of Deluded souls that post to ye Infernal denn, Wee made all posible speed to this Devil's Habitation; where alliting, in full assurance of good accommodation, wee were going in. But meeting his two daughters, as I suposed twins, they so nearly resembled each other, both in features and habit, and look't as old as the Divel himselfe, and quite as Ugly, We desired entertainm't, but could hardly get a word out of 'um, till with our Importunity, telling them our necesity, &c. they call'd the old Sophister, who was as sparing of his words as his daughters had bin, and no, or none, was the reply's hee made us to our demands. Hee differed only in this from the old fellow in to'ther Country: hee let us depart.

From hence we proceeded (about ten forenoon) through the Narragansett country, pretty Leisurely; and about one afternoon came to Paukataug River, wch was about two hundred paces over, and now very high, and no way over to to'ther side but this. I darid not venture to Ride thro, my courage at best in such cases but small, And now at the Lowest Ebb, by reason of my weary, very weary, hungry and uneasy Circumstances. So takeing leave of my company, tho' with no little Reluctance, that I could not proceed wth them on my Jorny, Stop at a little cottage Just by the River, to wait the Waters falling, wh^{ch} the old man that lived there said would be in a little time, and he would conduct me safe over. This little Hutt was one of the wretchedest I ever saw a habitation for human creatures. It was supported with shores enclosed with Clapbords, laid on Lengthways, and so much asunder, that the Light come throu' every where; the doore tyed on wth a cord in ye place of hinges; The floor the bear earth; no windows but such as the thin covering afforded nor any furniture but a Bedd wth a glass Bottle hanging at ye head on't; an earthan cupp, a small pewter Bason. A Bord wth sticks to stand on, instead of a table, and a block or two in ye corner instead of chairs. The family were the old man, his wife and two Children; all and every part being the picture of poverty. Notwithstanding both the Hutt and its Inhabitance were very clean and tydee: to the crossing the Old Proverb, that bare walls make giddy hows-wifes.

I had scarce done thinking, when an Indian-like Animal come to the door, on a creature very much like himselfe, in mien and feature, as well as Ragged cloathing; and having 'litt, makes an Awkerd Scratch wth his Indian shoo, and a Nodd, sitts on ye block, fumbles out his black Junk, dipps it in ye Ashes, and presents it piping hott to his muscheeto's, and fell to sucking like a calf, without speaking, for near a quarter of an hower. At length the old man said how do's Sarah do? who I understood was the wretches wife, and Daughter to ye old man: he Replyed — as well as can be expected, &c. So I remembered the old say, and suposed I knew Sarah's case. Butt hee being, as I understood going over the River, as ugly as hee was, I was glad to ask him to show me ye way to Saxtons, at Stoningtown; wch he promising, I ventur'd over wth the old mans assistance; who having rewarded to content, with my Tattertailed guide, I Ridd on very slowly thro' Stoningtown, where the Rode was very Stony and uneven. I asked the fellow, as we went, divers questions of the place and way, &c. I being arrived at my country Saxtons, at Stonington, was very well accommodated both as to victuals and Lodging, the only Good of both I had found since my setting out.

Thirsday, Octob^r ye 5th, about 3 in the afternoon, I sat forward with neighbor Polly and Jemima, a Girl about 18 Years old, who hee said he had been to fetch out of the Narragansetts, and said they had Rode thirty miles that day, on a sory lean Jade, wth only a Bagg under her for a pillion, which the poor Girl often complain'd was very uneasy.

Wee made Good speed along, wch made poor Jemima make many a sow'r face, the mare being a very hard trotter; and after many a hearty and bitter Oh, she at length Low'd out: Lawful Heart father ! this bare mare hurts mee Dingely, I'me direfull sore I vow; with many words to that purpose: poor Child sais Gaffer — she us't to serve your mother so. I don't care how mother us't to do, quoth Jemima, in a pasionate tone. At which the old man Laught, and kik't his Jade o' the side, which made her Jolt ten times harder.

About seven that Evening, we come to New London Ferry: here, by reason of a very high wind, we mett with great difficulty in getting over — the Boat tos't exceedingly, and our Horses caper'd at a very surprizing Rate, and set us all in a fright; especially poor Jemima, who desired her father to say so jack to the Jade, to make her stand. But the careless parent, taking no notice of her repeated desires, She Rored out in a Passionate manner: Pray suth father, Are you deaf ? Say so Jack to the Jade, I tell you. The Dutiful Parent obey's; saying so Jack, so Jack, as gravely as if hee'd bin to saying Catechise after Young Miss, who with her fright look't of all coullors in ye Rainbow.

Being safely arrived at the house of Mrs. Prentices in N. London, I treated neighbour Polly and daughter for their divirting company, and bid them farewell; and between nine and ten at night waited on the Rev^d Mr. Gurdon Saltonstall, minister of the town, who kindly Invited me to Stay that night at his house, where I was very handsomely and plentifully treated and Lodg'd; and make good the Great Character I had before heard concerning him: viz. that hee was the most affable, courteous, Genero's and best of men.

From hence wee went pretty briskly forward, and arriv'd at Saybrook ferry about two of the Clock afternoon; and crossing it, wee call'd at an Inn to Bait, (foreseeing we should not have such another Opportunity till we come to Killingsworth.) Landlady come in, with her hair about her ears, and hands at full pay scratching. Shee told us shee had some mutton wch shee would broil, wch I was glad to hear; But I suppose forgot to wash her scratchers; in a little time shee brot it in; but it being pickled, and my Guide said it smelt strong of head sause, we left it, and p^d sixpence a piece for our Dinners, wch was only smell.

So wee putt forward with all speed, and about seven at night come to Killingsworth, and were tolerably well with Travillers fare, and Lodged there that night.

Saturday, Oct. 7th, we sett out early in the Morning, and being something unacquainted wth the way, having ask't it of some wee mett, they told us wee must Ride a mile or two and turne down a Lane on the Right hand; and by their Direction wee Rode on but not Yet comeing to ye turning, we mett a Young fellow and ask'd him how farr it was to the Lane which turn'd down towards Guilford. Hee said wee must Ride a little further, and turn down by the Corner of uncle Sams Lott. My Guide vented his Spleen at the Lubber; and we soon after came into the Rhode, and keeping still on, without any thing further Remarkabell, about two a clock afternoon we arrived at New Haven, where I was received with all Posible Respects and civility. Here I discharged Mr. Wheeler with a reward to his satisfaction, and took some time to rest after so long and toilsome a Journey; and Inform'd myselfe of the manners and customs of the place, and at the same time employed myselfe in the afair I went there upon.

Their Diversions in this part of the Country are on Lecture days and Training days mostly: on the former there is Riding from town to town. And on training dayes The Youth divert themselves by Shooting at the Target, as they call, (but it very much resembles a pillory,) where hee that hitts nearest the white has some yards of Red Ribbin presented him wch being tied to his hattband, the two ends streaming down his back, he is Led away in Triumph, wth great applause, as the winners of the Olympiack Games. They generally marry very young: the males oftener as I am told under twentie than above; they generally make public weddings, and have a way something singular (as they say) in some of them, viz. Just before Joyning hands the Bridegroom quitts the place, who is soon followed by the Bridesmen, and as it were, dragg'd back to duty — being the reverse to ye former practice among us, to steal m^s Pride.

There are great plenty of Oysters all along by the sea side, as farr as I Rode in the Collony, and those very good. And they Generally

[496]

lived very well and comfortably in their famelies. But too indulgent (especially ye farmers) to their slaves; sufering too great familiarity from them, permitting y^m to sit at Table and eat with them, (as they say to same time,) and into the dish goes the black hoof as freely as the white hand. They told me that there was a farmer lived nere the Town where I lodged who had some differences wi^th his slave, concerning something the master had promised him and did not punctually perform; wch caused some hard words between them; Butt at length they put the matter to Arbitration and Bound themselves to stand to the award of such as they named — wch done, the Arbitrators Having heard the Allegations of both parties, Order the master to pay 40^s to black face, and acknowledge his fault. And so the matter ended: The poor master very honestly standing to the award.

There are every where in the Towns as I passed, a Number of Indians the Natives of the Country, and are the most salvage of all the salvages of that kind that I had ever Seen: little or no care taken (as I heard upon enquiry) to make them otherwise. They have in some places Landes of their owne, and Govern'd by Law's of their own making; — they marry many wives and at pleasure put them away, and on the least dislike or fickle humour, on either side, saying *stand away* to one another is a sufficient Divorce.

If the natives commit any crime on their own precincts among themselves, ye English take no Cognezens of, But if on the English ground, they are punishable by our Laws. They mourn for their Dead by blacking their faces, and cutting their hair, after an Awkerd and frightfull manner; But can't bear You should mention the names of their dead Relations to them: they trade most for Rum, for wch they^d hazzard their very lives; and the English fit them Generally as well, by seasoning it plentifully with water.

They give the title of merchant to every trader; who Rate their Goods according to the time and spetia they pay in: viz. Pay, mony, Pay as mony, and trusting. Pay is Grain, Pork, Beef, &c. at the prices sett by the General Court that Year; *mony* is pieces of Eight, Ryalls, or Boston or Bay shillings (as they call them,) or Good hard money, as sometimes silver coin is termed by them; also Wampom, vizt· Indian beads wch serves for change. Pay *as mony* is provisions, as afores^d one Third cheaper then as the Assembly or Gene^l Court sets it; and *Trust* as they and the merch^t agree for time.

Now, when the buyer comes to ask for a comodity, sometimes before the merchant answers that he has it, he sais, *is Your pay redy?* Perhaps the Chap Reply's Yes: what do You pay in? say's the merchant. The buyer having answered, then the price is set; as suppose he wants a six-penny knife, in pay it is 12ᵈ — in pay as money eight pence, and hard money its own price, viz. 6d. It seems a very Intricate way of trade and what *Lex Mercatoria* had not thought of.

Being at a merchants house, in comes a tall country fellow, wᵗʰ his alfogeos full of Tobacco; for they seldom Loose their Cudd, but keep Chewing and Spitting as long as they'r eyes are open, — he advanc't to the midle of the Room, makes an Awkward Nodd, and spitting a Large deal of Aromatick Tincture, he gave a scrape with his shovel like shoo, leaving a small shovel full of dirt on the floor, made a full stop, Hugging his own pretty Body with his hands under his arms, Stood staring rown'd him, like a Catt let out of a Baskett. At last, like the creature Balaam Rode on, he opened his mouth and said: have You any Ribinen for Hatbands to sell I pray ? The Questions and Answers about the pay being past, the Ribin is bro't and opened. Bumpkin Simpers, cryes its confounded Gay I vow; and beckning to the door, in comes Jone Tawdry, dropping about 50 curtsees, and stands by him: hee shows her the Ribin. *Law You,* sais shee, *its right* Gent, do You, take it, *tis dreadfull pretty.* Then she enquires, *have You any hood silk I pray ?* wch being brought and bought, Have You any *thred silk to sew it* wᵗʰ says shee, wᶜʰ being accomodated with they Departed. They Generaly stand after they come in a great while speachless, and sometimes dont say a word till they are askt what they want, which I Impute to the Awe they stand in of the merchants, who they are constantly almost Indebted too; and must take what they bring without Liberty to choose for themselves; but they serve them as well, making the merchants stay long enough for their pay.

We may Observe here the great necessity and bennifitt both of Education and Conversation; for these people have as Large a portion of mother witt, and sometimes a Larger, than those who have bin brought up in Citties; But for want of emprovements, Render themselves almost Ridiculos, as above. I should be glad if they would leave such follies and am sure all that Love Clean Houses (at least) would be glad on't too.

They are generaly very plain in their dress, throuout all yᵉ Colony, as I saw, and follow one another in their modes; that You may know where they belong, especially the women, meet them where you will.

Their Cheif Red Letter day is St. Election, wᶜʰ is annualy Observed according to Charter, to choose their Govenʳ: a blessing they can never be thankful enough for, as they will find, if ever it be their hard fortune to loose it. The present Governor in Conecticott is the Honᵇˡᵉ John Winthrop Esq. A Gentleman of an Ancient and Honourable Family, whose Father was Governor here some-time before, and his Grand father had bin Govr of the Massachusetts.

Dec. 6th we set out from New Haven, and about 11 same morning came to Stratford ferry; wch crossing, about two miles on the other wise Baited our horses and would have eat a morsell ourselves, But the Pumpkin and Indian mixt Bred had such an Aspect, and the Bare-legg'd Punch so awkerd or rather Awfull a sound, that we left both, and proceeded forward, and about seven at night come to Fairfield, where we met with good entertainment and Lodg'd; and early next morning set forward to Norowalk, from its halfe Indian name *North-walk,* when about 12 at noon we arrived, and Had a Dinner of Fryed Venison, very savoury. Landlady wanting some pepper in the seasoning, bid the Girl hand her the spice in the little Gay cupp on ye shelfe.

Saturday, Dec. 23, Having Ridd thro a difficult River we come to Fairfield where wee Baited and were much refreshed as well with th Good things wch gratified our appetites as the time took to rest our wearied Limbs, wch Latter I employed in enquiring concerning the Town and manners of the people, &c. This is a considerable town, and filld as they say with wealthy people — have a spacious meeting house and good Buildings. But the Inhabitants are Litigious, nor do they well agree with their minister, who (they say) is a very worthy Gentleman.

They have abundance of sheep whose very Dung brings them great gain, with part of which they pay their Parsons sallary. And they Grudg that, prefering their Dung before their minister. They Lett out their sheep at so much as they agree upon for a night; the highest Bidder always carries them, And they will sufficiently Dung a Large quantity of Land before morning. But were once Bitt by a sharper who had them a night and sheered them all before morning.

Being got to Milford, it being late in the night, I could go no further; my fellow travailer going forward, I was invited to Lodg at Mrs. ——, a very kind and civil Gentlewoman, by whom I was handsomely and kindly entertained till the next night. The people here go very plain in their apparel (more plain then I had observed in the towns I had passed) and seem to be very grave and serious. They told me there was a singing Quaker lived there, or at least had a strong inclination to be so, His Spouse not at all affected that way. Some of the singing Crew come there one day to visit him, who being then abroad, they sat down (to the woman's no small vexation) Humming and singing and groneing after their

[499]

conjuring way — Says the woman are you singing quakers? Yea say they — Then take my squalling Brat of a child here and sing to it says she for I have almost split my throat wth singing to him and cant get the Rogue to sleep. They took this as a great Indignity, and mediately departed. Shaking the dust from their Heels left the good woman and her Child among the number of the wicked.

[*Joseph Story, Marblehead*]

My native town, like other fishing towns, as I believe, was full of all sorts of superstitions. Ghosts, hobgoblins, will-o'-wisps, apparitions, and premonitions, were the common, I might almost say, the universal subject of belief, and numberless were the stories of haunted houses and wandering spirits, and murdered ghosts, that were told at the fireside, and filled my imagination with every kind of preternatural fear. It is to this circumstance that I principally owe my strong love of the marvellous in novels, and that I yet read with delight the romances of Mrs. Ratcliffe, which always appear to me to be realities, with which I have been long familiar.

Marblehead is, as you know, a secluded fishing town, and having no general connection with other towns, it has not as a thoroughfare much of that intercourse which brings strangers to visit it, or to form an acquaintance with its inhabitants. When I was young there were many discouragements under which it was laboring. Its whole business was annihilated during the revolutionary war. Many of its inhabitants entered the army and navy, or served on board of privateers; and from the various calamities incident to such situations, the close of that war found the town with upwards of nine hundred widows whose husbands had perished in the contest. It was greatly impoverished, and indeed in my earliest recollection seemed struck with a premature and apparently irretrievable decline. The general poverty, combined with other circumstances, made the resources of education narrow; and few books were to be found, and few scholars were nurtured on its rocky shores.

The inhabitants of a town so situated, and especially of a town almost wholly engaged in the fisheries, whose voyages began and ended in the same port, and whose occupation when abroad is in sounding the depth of the ocean, and drawing their lines upon the stormy waves of the Banks of Newfoundland, have little variety in their thoughts or conversation. Their lives have few incidents but those perilous adventures which everywhere belong to a seafaring life. Their habits are necessarily plain, their morals pure, and their manners, if not rough, at least generally unpolished and unpretending. Their very equality of condition as well as uniformity of pursuit bring them all into the same circle, and there is little room for the pride of scholarship, or the triumph of superior knowledge.

The people of Marblehead are a peculiar race; and as utterly unlike their neighbors as though they belonged to another age or country. The lines of their character are perhaps a little less marked than formerly, from their wider intercourse in later years with other places, but still they are deep and permanent, strong and full of meaning. They are a generous, brave, humane, honest, straightforward people; sagacious in their own affairs, but not wise beyond them; confiding and unsuspecting; hospitable by nature, though stinted in means; with a love of home scarcely paralleled, and an indifference to the show and splendor of wealth, which cannot easily be imagined; frugal and laborious; content with their ordinary means, neither rejecting learning nor over anxious for its attainment. The very rocks of their shores, the very barrenness of the strand on which their buildings rest, the very scantiness of the mother soil on which they were born, and in which they expect to lie buried when they are dead, have to them an indescribable charm. They love it with an intensity of interest which neither time nor distance can control. They seem perpetually to exclaim, "This is my own, my native land."

◇◇◇◇◇◇◇◇◇◇◇◇◇◇

[*Samuel Griswold Goodrich*]

In Ridgefield, in the year 1800, there was but a single chaise, and that belonged to Colonel Bradley, one of the principal citizens of the place. It was without a top, and had a pair of wide-spreading, asinine ears. That multitudinous generation of traveling vehicles, so universal and so convenient now — such as top-wagons, four-wheeled chaises, tilburies, dearborns, &c., was totally unknown. Even if these things had been invented, the roads would scarcely have permitted the use of them. Physicians who had occasion to go from town to town, went on horseback; all clergymen, except perhaps Bishop Seabury, who rode in a coach, traveled in the same way. My father's people, who lived at a distance, came to church on horseback — their wives and daughters being seated on pillions behind them. In a few cases — as in spring-time, when the mud had no soundings — the farm wagon was used for transporting the family.

In winter it was otherwise, for we had three or four months of sleighing. Then the whole country was a railroad, and gay times we had. Oh ! those beautiful winters, which would drive me shivering to the fireside now: what vivid delight have I had in your slidings and skatings, your sleddings and sleighings ! One thing strikes me now with wonder, and that is, the general indifference, in those days, to the intensity of winter. No doubt, as I have said before, the climate was then more severe; but be that as it may, people seemed to suffer less from it than at the present day. Nobody thought of staying at home from church because of the extremity of the weather. We had no thermometers, it is true, to frighten us with the revelation that it was twenty-five degrees below zero. The habits of the people were simple and hardy, and there were few defences against the assaults of the seasons. The houses were not tight; we had no stoves, no Lehigh or Lackawanna coal; yet we lived, and comfortably too; nay we even changed burly winter into a season of enjoyment.

◇◇◇◇◇◇◇◇◇◇◇◇◇◇

[Uriel Crocker, Boston]

Travelling in those days was pretty hard work. It took a day and a half, travelling night and day, to get from Boston to New York. I remember that once in 1830 I started from New York for New Haven in a steamboat which was full of Yale students. When we were within about a quarter of a mile of the wharf in New Haven, the boat got frozen up in the ice and could go no farther. The captain said that when the tide came in, it would break up the ice so that he could get his boat through and up to the wharf, which was in plain sight. I concluded to go below and turn in, and went to sleep and slept till about four or five o'clock in the morning, when some one came and woke me up and said he had been up all night, and he thought I ought to let him have a turn at my berth for a while. I thought I had had my share of it, and so I got up and let him take my place. After a while some coaches were sent round to the other side of the bay, and I took my bag and lugged it across the ice and rode round to New Haven, and went to a coffee-house, where after a while I succeeded in getting a fire. This was on Sunday. I stayed there all day and went to church. I intended to take the stage for Boston in the evening; but when the stage came along, Green, the driver, said there were nine inside, and so there was no room for me. So I had to grin and bear it, and stay all night. In the morning I took an extra and started; and when we had gone some six or seven miles we found the stage that had started the night before, stuck in the mud. We reached Hartford late that evening and got up at two or three o'clock the next morning and came on to Boston. That Sunday night was the night on which old Dr. Lyman Beecher's Church was burned.

◇◇◇◇◇◇◇◇◇◇◇◇◇

[Henry D. Thoreau]

He who rides and keeps the beaten track studies the fences chiefly. Near Bangor, the fence-posts, on account of the frost's heaving them in the clayey soil, were not planted in the ground, but were mortised into a transverse horizontal beam lying on the surface. Afterwards, the prevailing fences were log ones, with sometimes a Virginia fence, or else rails slanted over crossed stakes, — and these zigzagged or played leap-frog all the way to the lake, keeping just ahead of us.

I noticed occasionally very long troughs which supplied the road with water, and my companion said that three dollars annually were granted by the State to one man in each school-district, who provided and maintained a suitable water-trough by the roadside, for the use of travelers, — a piece of intelligence as refreshing to me as the water itself. That legislature did not sit in vain. It was an Oriental act, which made me wish that I was still farther down East, — another Maine law, which I hope we may get in Massachusetts. That State is banishing bar-rooms from its highways, and conducting the mountain springs thither.

I think that there was not more than one house on the road to Molunkus, or for seven miles. At that place we got over the fence into a new field, planted with potatoes, where the logs were still

[503]

burning between the hills; and, pulling up the vines, found good-sized potatoes, nearly ripe, growing like weeds, and turnips mixed with them. The mode of clearing and planting is to fell the trees, and burn once what will burn, then cut them up into suitable lengths, roll into heaps, and burn again; then, with a hoe, plant potatoes where you can come at the ground between the stumps and charred logs; for a first crop the ashes sufficing for manure, and no hoeing being necessary the first year. In the fall, cut, roll, and burn again, and so on, till the land is cleared; and soon it is ready for grain, and to be laid down. Let those talk of poverty and hard times who will in the towns and cities; cannot the emigrant who can pay his fare to New York or Boston pay five dollars more to get here, — I paid three, all told, for my passage from Boston to Bangor, two hundred and fifty miles, — and be as rich as he pleases, where land virtually costs nothing, and houses only the labor of building, and he may begin life as Adam did ? If he will still remember the distinction of poor and rich, let him bespeak him a narrower house forthwith.

◇◇◇◇◇◇◇◇◇◇◇◇◇

[*Thomas Low Nichols, Orford, N. H.*]

We traversed our rough New England roads with mailcoaches, drawn by four or six horses, at the rate of six or eight miles an hour. But when I mounted to the driver's seat on a fine autumnal morning, and drove off twenty miles up the romantic valley, to the academy where I was expected to acquire the rudiments of a classical education, there was more joy and triumph in that high seat, and the progress of those well-matched steeds, than I have ever found in the express train at sixty miles an hour.

The roads, never very good, were very bad in the spring, when the melting snows and the upheaving of the frost made mud a foot or more in depth. In swampy places logs and poles were laid across to form a roadway called corduroy, over which vehicles bumped and jolted at the slowest pace. These roads were mended every year, but only by hauling the loam from the gutters at the side towards the centre, and it is a proverb that "no road is so rough as one that has just been mended." There were a few turnpike roads, made and kept in repair by companies, who gathered tolls for their use; but these were never properly made.

These prudent New England farmers, who took their own produce to the best market, and bought their supply of goods at wholesale prices, were of very little profit to the tavern-keepers on the way, or to those in town. They carried their provisions ready cooked, in the shape of bean-porridge frozen into large cakes, ready to be warmed by the tavern fire, doughnuts and cheese, cooked sausages, &c. They also carried oats for their horses, and as much hay as they could stow. The tavern-keeper could only charge for a baiting of hay and a lodging, and their traveling expenses could be scarcely more than a shilling a day.

The snow-road had its difficulties. It was liable to be blown into drifts ten or fifteen feet deep, and the teamsters carried shovels to dig through them. On the other hand, a sudden thaw might carry off all the snow and leave them in the mud. Still, the old fashion of going to the winter market was a jolly one; and a train of twenty teams driving along, with all their bells cheerily jingling, and their drivers at night gathering round the tavern fire, telling stories, cracking homely jokes, and drinking hot cider, or something stronger, when stronger liquors were in fashion, had more life and variety than the railway trains of the present day.

◇◇◇◇◇◇◇◇◇◇◇◇

[*Edward Everett Hale, Boston*]

As late as May, 1845, when I was twenty-three years old, I had an engagement to go from Boston to Worcester Saturday afternoon. I was to preach there the next day. When, at three o'clock, I came to the station of the Worcester road, there was an announcement that, from some accident on the line above, no train would leave until Monday. The three o'clock train, observe, was the latest train on Saturday. I crossed Boston to the Fitchburg station and took the

WORCESTER RAILROAD STATION, BOSTON

[505]

train for Groton or Littleton. There I took a stage for Lancaster, where I slept. In the morning, with a Worcester man who had been caught in Boston as I was, I took a wagon early, and we two drove across to Worcester. That is to say, as late as 1845 there were but two men in Boston to whom it was necessary that they should go to Worcester that afternoon. This was ten years after railroad communication had been established.

A group of children in the country, if they saw a carriage approaching, would arrange themselves hastily in a line on one side of the road and "make their manners." That is, they would all bow as the carriage passed. The last time that I remember seeing this was in 1842, in Hampshire County, as the stage passed by. It was done good-naturedly, with no sign of deference, but rather, I should say, as a pleasant recognition of human brotherhood in a lonely region.

There was a charm in such half-vagrant journeying about which the Raymond tourist knows nothing. There was no sending in advance for rooms, and you took your chances at the tavern, where you arrived, perhaps, at nine o'clock at night. It may be imagined that the sudden appearance at the country tavern of a party of ten, of all ages from three months upwards, was an event of interest. In those times the selectmen knew what they meant, when they said that no person should dispense liquor who did not provide for travellers. Practically it was a convenience to any village to have a place where travellers could stay; and practically the people of that village said to the man whom they licensed to sell liquor, "If you have this privilege, you must provide a decent place of entertainment for strangers." One man kept the tavern, perhaps, for his life long. It had its reputation as good or poor, and you avoided certain towns because So-and-So did not keep a good house.

The New England tavern of the old fashion held its own to the most advantage in later times in the State of Maine, on the roads back into the lumber region, and I dare say such comfortable houses for travellers may be found there now.

These country taverns always had signs, generally swinging from a post with a cross-bar, in front of the house. The sign might be merely the name of the keeper; this was a sad disappointment to young travellers. More probably it was the picture of the American eagle or of a rising sun. Neptune rising from the sea was a favorite device. I remember at Worcester the Elephant. The portrait of General Wolfe still hangs at the Newburyport tavern, and there remain some General Washingtons. After I was a man I had occasion to travel a good deal one summer in Northern Vermont, where the tavern signs still existed. Almost without exception their devices were of the American eagle with his wings spread, or of the American eagle holding the English lion in chains, or of the lion chained without any American eagle. These were in memory of Macomb's and McDonough's victories at Plattsburg and on the lake. They also, perhaps, referred to the fact that most of these taverns were supported by the wagons of smugglers, who, in their good, large peddlers' carts, provided themselves with English goods in Canada, which they sold on our side of the line.

A story tells how Mr. Isaac P. Davis, who was, I think one of the proprietors of the locks and canals which made Lowell, went to the old tavern on the Merrimac, at Lowell, with a party, and inquired what they were to have for dinner. The keeper said that a good salmon had come up the river the night before, and he proposed to serve him — with which answer Mr. Davis was well pleased. Later in the morning he said he should like to see the salmon. But the man only expressed his amazement at such folly on the part of a Boston man. "You don't suppose I would take him out of the water, do you ? He is in the water at the foot of the falls, and has been there since last night. When it is time to cook him, I shall go out and catch him."

◇◇◇◇◇◇◇◇◇◇◇◇◇

[*Timothy Dwight, S.T.D., President of Yale College*]

The area, occupied by New Haven, is probably as large, as that which usually contains a City of six times the number of inhabitants, in Europe. A considerable proportion of the houses have court-yards in front, and gardens in the rear. The former are ornamented with trees, and shrubs; the latter are luxuriantly filled with fruit-trees, flowers, and culinary vegetables. The beauty, and healthfulness, of this arrangement need no explanation.

The houses in the City are generally decent; and many of the modern ones handsome. The style of building is neat and tidy. Fences, and outhouses are also in the same style: and being almost universally painted white, make a delightful appearance to the eye; an appearance, not a little enhanced, by the great multitude of shade-trees: a species of ornament, in which this town is unrivalled. Most of the buildings are of wood; and may be considered as destined to become the fuel of a future conflagration. Building with brick and stone, is, however, becoming more and more frequent. The mode of building with stone, which seems not unlikely to become general, is to raise walls of whin-stone, broken into fragments of every irregular form, laid in strong mortar; and then to overcast them with a peculiar species of cement.

The corners, frames of the doors, arches and sills of the windows, cornices, and other ornamental parts, are of a sprightly coloured free-stone. The cement is sometimes divided by lines at right angles

in such a manner, as to make the whole resemble a building of marble; and, being smooth, and white, is of course very handsome. Several valuable houses have been lately built in this manner: and the cement, contrary to the general expectation, has hitherto perfectly sustained the severity of our seasons. This mode of building is very little more expensive, than building with wood; and will, I suspect, ultimately take the place of every other. I know of no other equally handsome, where marble itself is not the material. Both these kinds of stone are found, inexhaustibly, at a moderate distance.

A general view of the state of Society in the City is given in the following list, taken in the year 1811. At this period there were in New-Haven:

29 houses concerned in foreign commerce,	5 hat stores,
41 stores of dry goods,	4 book stores,
42 grocery stores,	3 rope walks,
4 ship chandlery do.	2 sail lofts,
2 wholesale hardware do.	1 ship-yard,
3 wholesale dry goods do.	17 butchers,
1 wholesale glass and china do.	16 schools,
1 furrier's do.	12 inns,
10 appothecaries do.	5 tallow-chandlers,
6 traders in lumber,	2 brass-founders,
1 in paper hangings,	3 brasiers,
6 shoe stores,	29 blacksmiths,
7 manufactories of hats,	1 bell-founder,
	9 tanners,

30 shoe and boot makers,
9 carriage makers,
7 goldsmiths,
4 watch-makers,
4 harness-makers,
5 cabinet-makers,
50 carpenters and joiners,
3 comb-makers,
4 Windsor-chair-makers,
15 masons,
26 tailors,
14 coopers,
3 stone cutters,

7 curriers,
2 block-makers,
5 barbers,
3 tinners,
1 wheelwright,
1 leather-dresser,
1 nailer,
2 paper-makers,
5 printing offices,
2 book-binders,
5 bakers, and
2 newspapers published.

THERE WERE ALSO,

6 clergmen,
16 lawyers,

9 practising physicians, and
1 surgeon.

The trade of this town is conducted with skill, as well as spirit. Of this the fact, that during the last fifteen years, the number of failures has been proportionally smaller than in almost any town in the Union, is unequivocal proof. At the same time, it is conducted in a manner fair and honourable. A trick in trade is rarely heard of; and when mentioned, awakens, alike, surprise and indignation.

It deserves to be mentioned here, that the vessels built for the merchants of this town, and intended for foreign commerce, are built with more strength, and furnished in a better manner, than in most places on this continent. Those, who command them, are generally distinguished by their enterprise, skill, and probity; and are intrusted with the sale, and purchase, of their cargoes, as well as with the conduct of their vessels; and thus frequently become possessed of handsome property. Several of them, also, are distinguished by their good manners, good sense, and extensive information. From these facts, united, it has arisen, that very few vessels from this port meet with those accidents, which are fatal to others.

The state of Society in this Town is, I think, remarkably happy. The inhabitants, taken together, are not inferiour to those of any town, with which I am acquainted, in intelligence, refinement, morals, or religion. Both sexes are, to a great extent, well informed; much less ceremonious, and perhaps somewhat less polished, but not less refined, than those of the larger cities in this country. Their morals, at the same time, are of a superiour cast; and their religion much more predominant. A general spirit of good neighbourhood prevails among all classes, which nothing, hitherto, has seriously interrupted.

[509]

An extensive revival of religion, within a few years past, has added not a little to the pleasures, furnished by society in New-Haven.

The township of Worcester is, throughout, divided into farms; which wear a cheerful and prosperous aspect. The town is principally built on a single street, extending, from East to West, about a mile and a half on the road. It is situated in a valley; and contains, as I judge, about one hundred and twenty houses; generally well-built; surrounded by neat fences, outhouses, and gardens; frequently handsome; and very rarely small, old, or unrepaired. Few towns in New-England exhibit so uniform an appearance of neatness, and taste; or contain so great a proportion of good buildings, and so small a proportion of those which are indifferent, as Worcester. There is probably more wealth, in it, also, than in any other, which does not exceed it in dimensions, and number of inhabitants. Its trade, considering its inland situation, is believed to be extensive, and profitable. The number of public officers, professional men, merchants, and mechanics, is, proportionally, great; and produces a very lively appearance of activity and business.

There is scarcely a township in New-England, which has not a complete set of grist-mills, and saw-mills. Heylin, who wrote his Geography at the close of the seventeenth century, mentions the town of Reading as being advantageously built near a pond, and as being by this situation peculiarly fortunate in having "one mill for corn, and another for timber." A New-Englander cannot refrain from smiling at this account. There is, probably, no country in the world, where mill-streams are so numerously, and universally dispersed, or grist-mills and saw-mills so universally erected, as in New-England.

The bread, generally used in Worcester County, is made of rye. Rye bread is used in considerable quantities in many places on Connecticut River; but, being made usually of what is called white rye, and managed with great care in every part of the process, often approximates in its colour to wheat and still more in its agreeableness to the palate. But the rye, in this region, is itself of a dark hue; and is ground without being bolted: the flour being afterwards separated from the bran, very imperfectly, by sifting. It is then mixed with a large portion of the meal of maize; and, when baked, is dark, glutinous, and heavy. When a traveller from the Western country sees this bread brought upon the table at an inn; he looks at it with curiosity and wonder; asks what kind of food it is; and is not a little surprised, when he is told that it is bread.

A stranger can hardly be persuaded, that this bread is preferred by the inhabitants, who have been used to it, to the best wheaten loaf; and that not by plain people only, but by gentlemen, accustomed through life to all that is meant by good living. I have seen, in Boston and elsewhere, at tables loaded with the richest dainties, this bread preferred, both by the host and the guests, to the finest white bread.

The white bread, served up at tables in this County, and in the country further East; particularly in the inns; is made in the form of large biscuits; dry and hard, but agreeable to the taste; yet inferiour to the crackers, made in the country farther West.

The trade of Exeter, N. H., is much smaller than it was formerly: five or six vessels, only, being employed by the inhabitants in foreign commerce. A manufactory of sail-cloth, and twine, was established here in 1790, or 1791, by Thomas Odiorne, Esq. and has met with some success. Ship-building was heretofore a considerable, and profitable, business in this town. Since the revolution, it has declined. A few vessels, however are built annually; and a great quantity of saddlery is manufactured: more, probably, than in any other town in New-England.

The morals of the inhabitants have been much improved during the last half century. Formerly, they were employed, to a great extent, in the business of getting lumber. The effects of this dissolute business I shall consider hereafter. Suffice it now, to say, that such of the people of Exeter, as were engaged in it, were poor, idle, haunters of taverns, and devoted to all the baser pursuits of vulgar vice. In consequence of the termination of this business, industry has succeeded to sloth, regularity to dissoluteness, thrift to poverty, and comfort and reputation to suffering and shame.

A cause of the slow progress of settlement has been found in the character of the inhabitants. These, heretofore, have been chiefly lumbermen, and fishermen. Both these classes are usually employed, during the mild season, in severe toil; and not a small proportion of those, belonging to both, spend the winter in idleness and dissipation. At the same time, very many of them are in a great measure destitute of property through life. This is, indeed, less extensively

applicable to fishermen; some of whom almost every where, and most in towns distinguished for sobriety, acquire at least a comfortable living.

But those who are mere lumbermen are almost necessarily poor. Their course of life seduces them to prodigality, thoughtlessness of future wants, profaneness, irreligion, immoderate drinking, and other ruinous habits. The farmers of New-England have never willingly resided among people of such a character.

In their industry, economy, sobriety, and perseverance, the inhabitants of Salem have found a remedy for all the evils of their local situation; and in spite of them all, have arrived at a state of prosperity, unequalled by any other town in the American Union. Happily for the inhabitants, these characteristics seem to remain, (most heartily do I wish they may long remain,) in their full force.

A specimen of this character, particularly of that apprehensiveness of danger, to which the persons, possessing it, will always be awake, was not long since exhibited by the proprietors of the new market. The manager of the Theatre in Boston applied to these gentlemen for leave to occupy the upper story of this building as a theatre. After consulting each other on the proposal, they informed him, that they would sooner set it on fire. Another specimen of the same nature is found in the fact, that there is not (in 1796) a single four wheeled pleasure carriage in this town.

We began to ascend the mountains of Littleton, New Hampshire, in the dusk of the evening. The moment we entered the forests on its side, it became dark. Here all the dangers, mentioned above, assailed us at once. The mire was often so stiff, and so deep, that our horses scarcely struggled through it. The roots also, the stumps, rocks, stones, and causeys, multiplied upon us in almost every part of our progress: while the darkness was such, as to prevent us from

SALEM, MASSACHUSETTS

discerning the extent of our danger, and to keep us in a continual state of anxiety and alarm. At times indeed, the moon glimmered doubtfully on our path; but the forest was so thick, throughout most of the way, as effectually to intercept its light. In this manner we laboured on five miles, before we reached our destined inn.

I consoled myself with a cup of coffee, and a partridge: an entertainment, which I had hardly expected in a house, just built in an almost impenetrable forest, on a high mountain, and in a spot, where the first stroke of the axe was struck scarcely five years before. At that period, as the inn-keeper afterwards informed me, he set out from Andover in the winter, on an ox sled, with his wife and one child, to seek his fortune: i.e. to find a settlement for himself and his family. Providence led him to this place. He was already beginning to live comfortably. When I visited Littleton in 1803, I found him in possession of a good house; a good farm, well cleared, and cultivated; and in prosperous circumstance.

What motives could induce a man, even as enterprising, and determined, as our host appeared to be, to plant himself in a spot, so desolate and forlorn, with the expectation of living at all, it is not easy to imagine. I found, however, by conversing with him, that those, which appeared to me insuperable difficulties, he laughed at

[513]

as mere trifles. Happy resolution. Were all men as easily deterred from difficult enterprises, as votaries of pleasure, or even of study; a great part of the earth would now be a desert.

A considerable number of those, who first claimed, and acquired influence in the State of Vermont during its early periods, were men of loose principles, and loose morals. They were either professed Infidels, Universalists, or persons, who exhibited the morals of these two classes of mankind. We cannot expect, therefore, to find the public measures of Vermont distinguished, at that time, by any peculiar proofs of integrity, or justice.

The Connecticut may perhaps with as much propriety, as any in the world, be named the beautiful river. From Stuart to the Sound, it uniformly sustains this character. The purity, salubrity, and sweetness, of its waters; the frequency, and elegance, of its meanders; its absolute freedom from all aquatic vegetables; the uncommon and universal beauty of its banks; here a smooth and winding beach; there covered with rich verdure; now fringed with bushes; now crowned with lofty trees; and now formed by the intruding hill, the rude bluff, and the shaggy mountain; are objects, which no traveller can thoroughly describe, and no reader adequately imagine. When to these are added the numerous towns, villages, and hamlets, almost every where exhibiting marks of prosperity and improvement; the rare appearance of decline; the numerous churches, lifting their spires in frequent succession; the neat school-houses, every where occupied; and the mills, busied on such a multitude of streams; it may be safely asserted, that a pleasanter journey will rarely be found than that, which is made in the Connecticut Valley.

In the Quinipiac, near its mouth, is a very large and most prolific bed of oysters. These shell fish are annually caught, between the months of September and May, in vast quantities. Many of them are opened, and put into casks; and sent, during the cold season, over large tracts in Connecticut, New-York, Massachusetts, Vermont, and New-Hampshire. As women and children are extensively employed in opening them, the expense of this fishery, which is quite profitable to the inhabitants, is inconsiderable. With these advantages, united with a little commerce, the inhabitants are in prosperous circumstances.

A considerable number of Indians reside in Stonington township; and possess a tract of land, on and about Lantern Hill, in the Northern part of the township, and the most elevated spot in this region. Here some of them live in weekwams; and others, in houses, resembling poor cottages; at the best small, ragged, and unhealthy. Others, still, live on the farms of the white inhabitants in houses, built purposely for them; and pay their rent by daily labour. Two thirds of them are supposed to be contained in the Indian families; the remaining third are employed in the service of the farmers. One half of the former division live on the lands, reserved for them. These are held in fee simple; and cannot be disposed of without the consent of the Legislature, or of the Overseer.

The whole body of these Indians are a poor, degraded, miserable race of beings. The former, proud, heroic spirit of the Pequod, terrible even to other proud heroic spirits around him, is shrunk into the tameness and torpor of reasoning brutism. All the vice of the original is left. All its energy has vanished. They are lazy in the extreme; and never labour, unless compelled by necessity. Nor are they less prodigal than lazy. The earnings of a year, hardly as they are acquired, they will spend in a day, without a thought of the morrow. Wherever they can obtain credit, they involve themselves in debt; and never dream of paying their debts, unless under the iron hand of law. Thieves they are of course; but have too little enterprise to steal any thing of importance. It is hardly necessary to observe, that they are liars. They have no such thing among them as marriage; but cohabit without ceremony, or covenant; and desert each other at pleasure. Their children, when young, they place in English families, as servants. In the earlier parts of life these children frequently behave well; but, when grown up, throw off all that is respectable in their character, and sink to the level of their relatives. Some of them, when hired as labourers, and servants, are tolerably industrious; from a conviction, that they cannot safely be indolent. The rest, and even these when not employed, doze away life in uniform sloth and stupidity. To strong drink their devotion is complete; and for ardent spirits, or cider, they will part with every thing, which they possess. Generally, they are healthy; but, when sick, seem in a great measure to be beyond the reach of medicine. Those, who live by themselves, are half-naked, and often half-starved.

The Indian of the latter character lounges; saunters; gets drunk; eats, when he can find food; and lies down to sleep under the nearest fence. Without any present or future object in view, without proposing any advantage to himself, or feeling any interest in what is proposed by others, he leads the life, not of a man, but of a snail; and is rather a moving vegetable, than a rational being.

To these remarks there are some exceptions. The women, who live in English families, retain, at times, a degree of that fondness for dress so remarkable, and universal, among such as still continue in a savage state. Those who are educated in these families, are often seen at church. A small number also, of both men and women, are reputed to be honest; and are, therefore, safely believed to merit this character.

The houses in Yarmouth are inferiour to those in Barnstable, and much more generally of the class, which may be called, with propri-

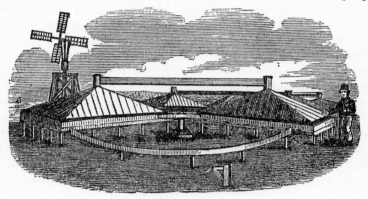

SALT VATS

ety, Cape Cod houses. These have one story, and four rooms on the lower floor; and are covered on the sides, as well as the roofs, with pine shingles, eighteen inches in length. The chimney is in the middle, immediately behind the front door; and on each side of the door are two windows. The roof is straight. Under it are two chambers; and there are two larger, and two smaller, windows in the gable end. This is the general structure, and appearance, of the great body of houses from Yarmouth to Race Point. There are, however, several varieties, but of too little importance to be described. A great proportion of them are in good repair. Generally, they exhibit a tidy, neat aspect in themselves, and in their appendages; and furnish proofs of comfortable living, by which I was at once disappointed, and gratified. The barns are usually neat, but always small.

At Yarmouth, also, may be said to commence the general addiction of the people on this peninsula to fishing. From this source is derived their wealth, and much of their subsistence.

In Yarmouth we first found the salt-works, which are now beginning to engross the attention of the people on this peninsula.

On Sunday we found a large and very decent congregation in the old church at Plymouth. A singular custom was here exhibited to us. More than fifty bills were read by the Clergyman, desiring the prayers of the congregation for families in affliction. They were principally occasioned by the death of nine inhabitants, almost all of them at sea, which had either happened, or been first heard of, during the preceding week. In such a case, it seems a bill is presented for every branch of the family, which is particularly interested in the melancholy event.

❖❖❖❖❖❖❖❖❖❖❖❖❖

[Samuel Griswold Goodrich, Ridgefield, Conn.]

I have somewhere heard of a traveler on horseback, who, just at eventide, being uncertain of his road, inquired of a person he chanced to meet, the way to Barkhamstead.

"You are in Barkhamstead now," was the reply.

"Yes, but where is the center of the place ?"

"It hasn't got any center."

"Well — but direct me to the tavern."

"There ain't any tavern."

"Yes, but the meeting-house ?"

"Why didn't you ask that afore ? There it is, over the hill !"

So, in those days, in Connecticut — as doubtless in other parts of New England — the meeting-house was the great geographical monument, the acknowledged meridian of every town and village. Even a place without a center or a tavern, had its house of worship, and this was its initial point of reckoning. It was, indeed, something more. It was the town-hall, where all public meetings were held, for civil purposes; it was the temple of religion, the ark of the covenant, the pillar of society — religious, social, and moral — to the people around. It will not be considered strange then, if I look back to the meeting-house of Ridgefield, as not only a revered edifice — covered with clapboards and shingles, though it was — but as in some sense the starting point of my existence. Here at least, linger many of my most cherished remembrances.

A few rods to the south of this, there was, and still is, a tavern, kept in my day, by Squire Keeler. This institution ranked second only to the meeting-house; for the tavern of those days was generally the center of news, and the gathering place for balls, musical entertainments, public shows, &c.; and this particular tavern had special claims to notice. It was, in the first place, on the great thoroughfare of that day, between Boston and New York, and had become a general and favorite stopping-place for travelers. It was, moreover, kept by a hearty old gentleman, who united in his single

[517]

person the varied functions of publican, postmaster, representative, justice of the peace, and I know not what else. He besides had a thrifty wife, whose praise was in all the land. She loved her customers, especially members of Congress, governors, and others in authority, who wore powder and white-top boots, and who migrated to and fro, in the lofty leisure of their own coaches. She was indeed a woman of mark, and her life has its moral. She scoured and scrubbed and kept things going, until she was seventy years old, at which time, during an epidemic, she was threatened with an attack. She, however, declared that she had not time to be sick, and kept on working, so that the disease passed her by, though it made sad havoc all around her — especially with more dainty dames, who had leisure to follow the fashion.

Besides all this, there was an historical interest attached to Keeler's tavern, for deeply imbedded in the northeastern corner-post, there was a cannon-ball, planted there during the famous fight with the British in 1777. It was one of the chief historical monuments of the town, and was visited by all curious travelers who came that way. Little can the present generation imagine with what glowing interest, what ecstatic wonder, what big round eyes, the rising generation of Ridgefield, half a century ago, listened to the account of the fight as given by Lieutenant Smith, himself a witness of the event and a participator of the conflict, sword in hand.

This personage was, in my time, a justice of the peace, town librarian, and general oracle in such loose matters as geography, history, and law — then about as uncertain and unsettled in Ridgefield, as is now the fate of Sir John Franklin, or the longitude of Lilliput. He had a long, lean face; long, lank, silvery hair, and an unctuous, whining voice. With these advantages, he spoke with the authority of a seer, and especially in all things relating to the revolutionary war.

The agitating scenes of that event, so really great in itself, so unspeakably important to the country, had transpired some five and twenty years before. The existing generation of middle age, had all witnessed it; nearly all had shared in its vicissitudes. On every hand there were corporals, sergeants, lieutenants, captains, and colonels — no strutting fops in militia buckram, raw blue and buff, all fuss and feathers — but soldiers, men who had seen service and won laurels in the tented field. Every old man, every old woman had stories to tell, radiant with the vivid realities of personal observation or experience. Some had seen Washington, and some Old Put; one was at the capture of Ticonderoga under Ethan Allen; another was at Bennington, and actually heard old Stark say, "Victory this day, or my wife Molly is a widow !" Some were at the taking of Stony Point, and others in the sanguinary struggle of Monmouth. One had witnessed the execution of André, and another had been present at the capture of Burgoyne. The time which had elapsed since these events, had served only to magnify and glorify these scenes, as well as the actors, especially in the imagination of the rising generation. If perchance we could now dig up, and galvanize into life, a contemporary of Julius Caesar, who was present and saw him cross the Rubicon, and could tell us how he looked and what he said — we should listen with somewhat of the greedy wonder with which the boys of Ridgefield listened to Lieutenant Smith, when of a Saturday afternoon, seated on the stoop of Keeler's tavern, he discoursed upon the discovery of America by Columbus, Braddock's defeat, and the old French war — the latter a real epic, embellished with romantic episodes of Indian massacres and captivities. When he came to the Revolution, and spoke of the fight at Ridgefield, and punctuated his discourse with a present cannonball, sunk six inches deep in a corner-post of the very house in which we sat, you may well believe it was something more than words — it was, indeed, "action, action, glorious action !" How little can people nowadays — with curiosity trampled down by the march of mind and the schoolmaster abroad — comprehend or appreciate these things !

◇◇◇◇◇◇◇◇◇◇◇◇◇

[*Samuel Maverick, 1660*]

Concord — Above Twelve miles above Watter Towne is an In-land Towne called Concord. It lyeth on the River Meromack I conceive about 20 miles above the first ffalls but good passing on it there in small Boats from place to place. They subsist in Husbandry and breeding of Catle.

Sudbury. — About 4 or 5 Miles more Southerly on the same River is a Towne called Sudbury a very pleasant place, the River runing to & againe in it, In which I have seen Excellent ffishing both with hooks & Lynes and Netts, They plant and breed Catle, and gett something by Tradeing w^t the Indians.

Nashoway. — About ten or twelfe miles aboue these Two Townes is a Countrey Towne called Nashoway first begun for Love of the Indians Trade, but since the ffertility of ye Soyle and pleasantness of the River hath invited many more. There is Excellent Salmon and Trout.

Now we must returne to the mouth of Charles River againe or rather the entrance of the Bay of Massachusits, It hath three entrances, two of them difficult and dangerous without a good wind and Pylot. The Southernmost called Nasascot in the usuall Channell; w'in this Bay are 12 or 13 pretty Islands between some of which yow must saile about 2 leagues before yow come up to Boston Rode yow must passe within halfe a Cable length of Castle Island,

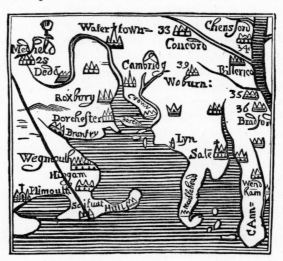

on which is a ffort above and a strong Battery below, closs by Highwater marke. on this Island I conceive there be thirtie good Gunns.

Boston. — Two miles aboue this Island is the Towne of Boston, the Metropolis of New England lying pleasantly on a plaine and the ascending of a High Mount which lyes about the midle of ye plaine, The wholl Towne is an Island except two Hundred paces of land at one place on the Southside it is large and very populous. It hath two handsome Churches in it, a handsome market place, and in the midest of it a Statehouse. In the Towne are fouer full companys of ffoote and a Troope of horse On the Southeast side of the Towne on a little Hill there is a Fort, and under it a Batterie both having a dozen of Gunns or more in them, and on the Northeast side of the Towne there is a Battery of 6 Gunns commanding the Rode and the entrance of Charles River. and on the tope of the Hill aboue the Towne and in the strats are severall good Gunns, The Towne is full of good shopps well furnished with all kind of Merchandize and many Artificers, and Trad's men of all sorts. In this Towne are kept the Courts of Election ye Generall quarter Court besids the Country Courts.

Roxberry. — About two miles to the Southward of Boston is the

Towne of Roxberry. The sea which surrounds Boston comes on both sides of it. It is well seatted, for the Body of the Towne lyeth on both sides a small Rivolet of water. There are many considerable ffarmes belonging to it, and by Farmeing is there most subsistance.

Dorchester. — Two miles near east from this Town lyeth Dorchester, which claimes the third dignity as being ye third Towne setled by the English in the year 1630. They are a very industrious people, and have large bounds on wch are many gallant Farmes, by these bounds runes the Massachusets River.

Dedham. — And on Charles River stands the Towne of Dedham about 8 Miles either from Boston or Roxberry, a very pleasant place and the River affoords plenty of good ffish In this Towne leiveth many Bisquett makers and Butchers and have Vent enough for their Commodities in Boston.

Medfeild. — Five or six Miles from Dedham is a small in-land Towne called Medifield handsomely seatted for Farming and breeding of Cattle.

Braintree. — Three or fouer miles Southward is a Towne once called Mount Wolaston, now Braintree. There was a Patent granted for a considerable tract of land in this place in the yeare 1632 or thereabouts to Capt Wollaston and Mr Thomas Morton. Wollaston returned for England and Morton was banished, his house fired before his face, and he sent prisoner to England but for what offence I know not who some yeares after (nothing being laid to his Charge) returned for New England, where he was soon after apprehended and keept in the Common Goale a whole winter, nothing laid to his Charge but the writeing of a Booke entituled New Canaan, which indeed was the truest discription of New England as then it was that euer I saw, The offence was he had touched them too neare they not proveing the charge he was sett loose, but soone after dyed, haveing as he said and most believed received his bane by hard lodging and fare in prison. This was done by ye Massachusetts Magistrats and the land by them disposed of. It subsists by raiseing provisions, and furnishing Boston with wood.

Weymouth. — Two or three miles from hence Sowthward is ye Towne of Weymouth, wherein are some quantity of Inhabitants, & leive as their neibo^rs who have commerce with Boston.

Higham. — Three Miles from hence Easterly on the South shoare of Massachusits Bay is the Towne of Higham a handsome Towne supplying Boston also with wood, timber, leather and board, Some Masts are had there and store of provisions.

Hull. — Three Miles further tending more to the East, at the very entrance into the Massachusetts Bay is the Towne of Hull, the Inhabitants of which leives well being by Water not above 7 Miles from Boston tho neare 20 by land.

Three miles South from this place is the utmost south bounds of the Massachusits Government and Territories, beyond which they have not gone although they have gone soe farr beyond them to the Northward.

◇◇◇◇◇◇◇◇◇◇◇◇◇

[*Timothy Dwight*]

The Bostonians, almost without an exception, are derived from one country and a single stock. They are all descendants of Englishmen; and of course are united by all the great bonds of society; language, religion, government, manners, and interests. You will easily believe therefore, that they exhibit as much unity of character, as can accord with the nature of free and civilized society. With a very small number of exceptions, they speak the English language in the English manner; are protestants; and hold the great principles of English liberty.

Boston is distinguished for its habits of business. A man, who is not believed to follow some useful business, can scarcely acquire, or retain, even a decent reputation. A traveller passing through it is struck with the peculiar appearance of activity, everywhere visible. Almost all, whom he meets, move with a sprightliness, differing very sensibly from what he observes in New-York and Philadelphia.

Not less distinguished are the inhabitants, particularly the middle and inferiour classes, for their intelligence and information. In a singular degree are they acquainted with the affairs of the town itself; and with the residence, and character, of almost every inhabitant. I have rarely met a child, who could not tell me both the street and the house for which I enquired.

Nor are they less distinguished for civility. A Bostonian, if not pressed by business of his own, will readily accompany a stranger to the house, which he wishes to find; and will scarcely appear to feel as if he had conferred the least obligation. In the superiour classes this disposition appears often, with peculiar advantage.

Better tables are nowhere spread than in Boston: and nowhere does a guest find himself more at ease, more secure from solicitations, or entertained with more graceful or cordial hospitality. The best bred women here are charming examples of grace and amenity.

The people of Boston are characteristically distinguished by a lively imagination; and ardour easily kindled; a sensibility soon felt, and strongly expressed; a character, more resembling that of the

[522]

Greeks than that of the Romans. They admire, where graver people would only approve; detest where cooler minds would only dislike; applaud a performance, where others would listen in silence; and hiss, where a less susceptible audience would only frown. This character renders them sometimes more, sometimes less, amiable; usually less cautious; and often more exposed to future regret. From this source their language is frequently hyperbolical; and their pictures of objects, highly coloured.

Hence, also, their enterprises are sudden, bold, and sometimes rash. A general spirit of adventure prevails here, which in numerous instances has become the means of attempts, made with honour and success, in cases, where many of their commercial neighbours would have refused to adventure at all. The manner, in which they commenced the trade of Nootka Sound, and circumnavigated the globe, advantageously illustrates this observation. A ship, belonging to Joseph Barrell, Esq. and others, sailed round the earth three times; and a sloop, of moderate size, once. Few merchants in America would, I believe, have resolved on these enterprises; and few seamen executed them. On the other hand, the dealers in Georgia lands found many more customers in Boston, than in New-York. The tea, shipped to Boston by the East-India company, was destroyed. In New-York, and Philadelphia, it was stored.

The *Boston Style* is a phrase, proverbially used throughout a considerable part of this country to denote a florid, pompous manner of writing; and has been thought by persons at a distance to be the predominant style of this region. It cannot be denied, that several publications, written in this manner, have issued from the press here, and for a time been much celebrated. Most of the orations delivered on the 5th of March, may be produced as examples. Still it has never been true, that this mode of writing was either general in this town, or adopted by men of superiour talents. The most respectable writers, here, have been distinguished for the chasteness, and simplicity, of their compositions.

◇◇◇◇◇◇◇◇◇◇◇◇◇

[*Thomas Low Nichols*]

The people of Boston, so far as I could see, were as honest in the eighteen-twenties as the residents of the rural districts. When I wandered out in the early morning, losing no time to see as much as possible of the town before our brief visit was over, I saw on almost every door-sill loaves of bread, vessels of milk, and the morning papers. Bakers, milkmen, and newsmen left their treasures on the door-step. There was smoking brown bread of rye and Indian corn, hot rolls, and loaves of wheaten bread waiting for the dilatory housemaids.

How long, I wonder, would piles of bread and newspapers lie upon London street-door steps in the early morning, over all its quiet streets ? There were no policemen then in Boston that I ever heard of. A few constables kept order in a town of sixty thousand people. There were watchmen, for I heard them in the night crying the hours: "Twelve o'clock, and a cloudy night; all's well !" And they shouted "Fire !" and sprung their terrible rattles sometimes; and the volunteer fire-engine companies, with torches, speaking-trumpet bellowings, and shoutings of "Fire !" thundered over the cobble-stone pavements. I went up through the skylight upon the flat roof of the house, and saw the smoke and flame, and heard the roar, with the clamour of fifty bells all ringing their alarum, and torch-lit engines dashing in from distant suburbs.

I remember a story told me by a Boston merchant in my boyhood. His son and I were schoolmates in an academy in the country, and I went to pay him a visit when I went to town. The merchant was a very handsome man; he had elegant manners, a charming family, a delightful residence, and a prosperous business had made him rich.

"I was born in the country," he said, "and my father, who was a poor farmer with a large family, used to come to Boston to market. One day, when I was twelve years old, I came with him, hoping to find some work to do, to earn my living. We got in early in the morning, by driving nearly all night; and while we were in the street, waiting for somebody to buy our load, I took a newspaper off a door-step and began to read it. Almost the first thing I saw was an advertisement of 'Boy wanted.' When father had sold his load we went to look for the place. It was a large house, on a handsome street, belonging to a merchant; and the boy was wanted to work in the kitchen, help the cook, clean knives, black boots, and wait at table. The work seemed easy enough, and the pay good, so I stayed. The merchant was pleased with me, and after a while took me into the store to do errands and such light work. Then I became a clerk, then a partner. The merchant's daughter was as partial to me as her father always had been, and I got married; and here I am — and all from looking into a newspaper one frosty morning in the streets of Boston !"

[*Edward Everett Hale, Boston*]

As late as 1817, in a description of Boston which accompanied a show which a Frenchman had made by carving and painting the separate houses, it was said, with some triumph, that there were nine blocks of buildings in the town. This means that all the other buildings stood with windows or doors on each of the four sides, and in most instances with trees, or perhaps little lanes, between; as all people will live when the Kingdom of Heaven comes.

The reader must imagine, therefore, a large, pretty country town, where stage-coaches still clattered in from the country, and brought all the strangers who did not ride in their own chaises. Large stables, always of wood, I think, provided for the horses thus needed.

When I was nine or ten years old my father, who was thought to be a fanatic as a railroad prophet, offered in Faneuil Hall the suggestion that if people could come from Springfield to Boston in five hours an average of nine people would come every day. This prophecy was then considered extravagant.

Furniture was stately, solid, and expensive. I use chairs, tables, and a sideboard in my house to-day, which are exactly as good now as they were then. Carpets, then of English make, covered the whole floor, and were of what we should now call perfect quality. In summer, by the way, in all houses of which I knew any thing, these carpets were always taken up, and India mattings substituted in the "living-rooms." Observe that very few houses were closed in summer. Dress was certainly as elegant and costly as it is now; so were porcelain, glass, table linen, and all table furniture. Every house, by the way, was warmed by open fires; and in every kitchen cooking was done by an open fire. I doubt if I ever saw a stove in my boyhood except in a school or an office.

What we call buggies were unknown, and a gentleman and lady would certainly ride in a chaise, which was not the English chaise, but a two-wheeled covered vehicle, hung on C-springs. In such a town the supplies of food, unless brought from the immediate neighborhood, came from the seaboard or the Western rivers in sloops or schooners. We drew our flour from points as far south as Richmond. I remember that, in more than one winter, when my grandmother, in Westhampton, had sent us a keg or two of home apple-sauce, the sloop which brought the treasure was frozen up in Connecticut River below Hartford, so that it was four or five months before we hungry children enjoyed her present.

The boys were in touch with the large public in their unauthor-
ized and unrecognized connection with the fire department. Boston
was still a wooden town, and the danger of fire was, as it is in all
American cities, constantly present. There hung in our front entry
two leather buckets; in each of them was certain apparatus which
a person might need if he were in a burning house. Strange to say,

there was a bed-key, that he might take down a bedstead if it were
necessary. These were relics of a time when my father had been a
member of one of the private fire companies. In those associations
each man was bound to attend at any fire where the property of
other members of the association was in danger; and there were
traditions of father's having been present at the great Court Street
fire, for instance. But these fire clubs either died out or became
social institutions, as the Fire Club in Worcester exists to this day;
and nothing was left but the bucket as a sort of memorial of a former existence.

Before our day the volunteer fire department system of Boston
had been created, and there were similar systems in all large cities.
Of course we boys supposed that ours was the best in the world;
each boy in Boston supposed that the engine nearest his house was
the best engine in the world, and that, on occasion, it could throw
water higher than any other engine. It could likewise, on occasion,
pump dry any engine that was in line with it. I need not say that

these notions of the boys were simply superstitions, wholly un-founded in fact. Our engine was the *New York*. The engine-house was one of a curious mass of public buildings that occupied the place where Franklin's statue now stands, in front of what was the court-house of that day. There was no electric fire alarm in those early days. The moment fire broke out everybody who had any lungs ran up the street or down the street, or both ways, crying "Fire!" and as soon as the churches could be opened, all the bells in Boston began to ring. Then the company which was to drag the *New York* to the fire began to assemble at its house, and naturally there was great pride in seeing that your engine was first in place. You learned where the fire was, not by any signal, but by the rumor of the street. It was at the North End, or at the South End, or on the wharves, or on "Nigger Hill." As soon as boys and men, of whatever connection, arrived, sufficient in combined strength to drag the engine, it started, under the direction of such officer of the company as might be present. The members of the company had no uniforms, so far as I remember; they joined the lines as quickly as they could, but there were always enough people to pull. As I have intimated, it was everybody's business to attend at the fire.

When you arrived at the spot there would be a general caucus as to the method of attack, yet I think there were people in command. Afterwards a gentleman named Amory, highly respected by all of us, was chief engineer. Whatever the caucus directed was done, with as much efficiency as was possible under such democratic insti-tutions. But, in the first place, the probability was that there was no water near. The Jamaica Pond aqueduct carried water in log pipes to the lower levels of the city; but, for fully half the city, there was no such supply, and wells had to be relied upon. Every engine, therefore, which was good for anything, was a "suction engine," as it was called; that is, it was able to pump from a well, as well as able to throw water to an indefinite height. The engine that ar-rived first repaired to the well best known in that neighborhood, or, if the occasion were fortunate, to the sea, and began to pump. The engine that arrived next took station next to this, and pumped from it through a long line of hose; and so successive engines car-ried the water to the place where some foreman directed it upon the flames. It was thus that the different engines attained their celebrity, as one pumped the tub of another dry, while the unfor-tunate members were "working the brakes" to their best to keep it full.

The buckets of which I have spoken were the remains of a yet earlier period, when people formed themselves in line to the well or to the sea, and passed buckets backward and forward — full if they were going toward the fire, empty if they were going away; and the water was thus thrown upon such flames as chose to wait for it.

❖❖❖❖❖❖❖❖❖❖❖❖

[*Josiah Quincy*]

The War of 1812 put a stop to navigation and compelled all transfers of property to be made by wagons. It was said to cost six thousand dollars to transport a piece of ordnance from New York to Buffalo. A great number of teams bearing produce from Vermont and New Hampshire, and smuggled goods from Canada, passed through Andover. In the absence of mercantile news, the arrival of these wagons was announced under the head of "Horse-marine news." One of the humors of the war was an amusing parody upon the "Mariners of England" entitled the "Wagoners of Freedom," a ditty of which I can still repeat several verses. These teamsters had, however, adopted one article of the sailors' faith that was by no means acceptable to the people of Andover. They held that "there was no Sunday off soundings," and continued their progress on that day greatly to the scandal of the righteous town. It was plain that the law must be enforced, and accordingly tithing-men lay in wait on Sunday at the tavern, and at the corners of the public roads. They succeeded in stopping the heavy teams, but horsemen and light carriages slipped through their fingers. But a way was soon devised to meet this difficulty. A deacon was joined to the tithing-men the very next Sunday, and the party were put in command of the tollgate, about a mile out of the town on the road leading to Boston. It was known about the school that a trap had been set which no Sunday traveler could hope to escape, and great was the interest in waiting for a victim. At length a gentleman driving a fine horse passed along the street, and, all unconscious of his fate, proceeded towards the tollgate. The excitement was now intense, for we expected to see him brought back by the deacon in ignominious captivity. But the spectators were disappointed, for this part of the programme was not carried out. In what wonderful way the traveler had managed to elude the deacon and his guard we could not divine. The return of the party at sunset brought the explanation, and a doleful tale of depravity passed from mouth to mouth. It appeared that the gentleman had been duly stopped at the tollgate and informed that he could go no farther. But instead of showing the indignation which his captors had expected, he expressed himself as delighted to find Andover was bent on enforcing the admirable Sunday laws, and had selected agents so prompt and capable as to preclude all chance of their evasion. "But the law, gentlemen," he went on to say, "as you well know, excepts those who travel upon errands of necessity or mercy; and I assure you that my mother is lying dead in Boston." Upon this statement the gate was reluctantly opened, and the traveler allowed to proceed. But no sooner was he fairly out of danger than he reined in his horse and delivered himself of these heartless word: "Good-by, Deacon; tell the busybodies of Andover that my mother is lying dead in Boston, — and you may add, if you like, that she has been lying dead there *for the last twenty years !*"

It need not be said that this occurrence was improved, as the text of a lecture to the boys on the sin of prevarication, which is, perhaps, the reason why I remember it so vividly. A short time after this, another attempt to enforce the Sunday law was much talked of in the town. One Sabbath morning, a hack containing four gentlemen drove through the place and took the road to Salem. The deacon and a tithing-man, who were again on the alert, stopped the carriage, and ordered the passengers to return to the tavern. As there was no tollgate in the way this time, the travelers irreverently consigned the ecclesiastical functionaries to hot quarters, and commanded their driver to whip up and go on. This greatly exasperated the deacon and his companion, who, considering that the arrest of such hardened offenders was undoubtedly a work of necessity and mercy, hired a light carriage and gave pursuit. But a stern chase, as the sailors say, is apt to be a long chase, and the hack kept on till it reached Salem, where the pursuers felt certain of making a capture. And this might have been effected had the parties stopped at any tavern or house, as it was reasonable to suppose that they would. But, unhappily, on went the hack till it reached the end of the wharf. Here the passengers jumped out, sprang into a boat that was in waiting, and were instantly rowed to a frigate which was lying in the harbor, — their would-be captors gazing after them in mute consternation. As it did not seem quite prudent for an Andover deacon to attempt the arrest of officers on board a man-of-war, there was nothing to be done but to retrace a tedious journey, and to submit to such chaff as a heartless world bestows upon unsuccessful attempts to make it better.

ADAMS HOUSE, QUINCY, MASSACHUSETTS

[*Henry Adams*]

Though Quincy was but two hours' walk from Beacon Hill, it belonged in a different world. For two hundred years, every Adams, from father to son, had lived within sight of State Street, and sometimes had lived in it, yet none had ever taken kindly to the town, or been taken kindly by it. The boy inherited his double nature. He knew as yet nothing about his great-grandfather, who had died a dozen years before his own birth: he took for granted that any great-grandfather of his must have always been good, and his enemies wicked; but he divined his great-grandfather's character from his own. Never for a moment did he connect the two ideas of Boston and John Adams; they were separate and antagonistic; the idea of John Adams went with Quincy. He knew his grandfather John Quincy Adams only as an old man of seventy-five or eighty who was friendly and gentle with him, but except that he heard his grandfather always called "the President," and his grandmother "the Madam," he had no reason to suppose that his Adams grandfather differed in character from his Brooks grandfather who was equally kind and benevolent. He liked the Adams side best, but for no other reason than that it reminded him of the country, the summer, and the absence of restraint. Yet he felt also that Quincy was in a way inferior to Boston, and that socially Boston looked down on Quincy. The reason was clear enough even to a five-year-old child. Quincy had no Boston style. Little enough style had either; a simpler manner of life and thought could hardly exist, short of cave-dwelling. The flint-and-steel with which his grandfather Adams used to light his own fires in the early morning was still on the mantelpiece of his study. The idea of a livery or even a dress for servants, or of an evening toilette, was next to blasphemy. Bathrooms, water-supplies, lighting, heating, and the whole array of domestic comforts, were unknown at Quincy. Boston had already a bathroom, a water-supply, a furnace, and gas. The superiority of Boston was evident, but a child liked it no better for that.

YANKEE LIVES

YANKEE LIVES

❖❖❖❖❖❖❖❖❖❖❖❖❖

HENRY ADAMS (Boston, 1838–1918) was the most brilliant writer and the most penetrating analyst in all the great dynasty of Adamses. He and Edward Everett Hale (*q.v.*) shared an uncle in Edward Everett. The quotations are taken by permission of the publishers, Houghton Mifflin Company, from
The Education of Henry Adams. Boston, 1918.

JAMES MONTGOMERY BAILEY (Albany, N. Y., 1841–Danbury, 1894) , "The Danbury-News Man," was in his day a celebrated humorist, and the first modern "colyumist." The quotations are from
Life in Danbury. Boston, Lee & Shepard, 1873.

PHINEAS TAYLOR BARNUM was born at Bethel, Connecticut in 1810, and died in 1891. The quotations are from
Struggles and triumphs; or, forty years' recollections of P. T. Barnum. Buffalo, N. Y., The Courier Company, 1875. (First edition, Hartford, 1869.)

LYMAN BEECHER (New Haven, 1775–Brooklyn, N. Y., 1863) was the first celebrated member of the Beecher family, father of Harriet Beecher Stowe and Henry Ward Beecher. His sermons were a great influence in the temperance movement that swept America and then the world in the first half of the nineteenth century. The quotations are from
Autobiography, Correspondence, Etc., of Lyman Beecher, D.D., edited by Charles Beecher. New York, Harper & Bros., 1864.

JOSEPH TINKER BUCKINGHAM (Windham, Connecticut, 1779–Cambridge, Mass., 1861) was a leading Boston journalist, the editor of *The New England Galaxy* and *The Boston Courier.* He was an apprentice at the Walpole (New Hampshire) branch of Isaiah Thomas' (*q.v.*) far-flung enterprise. The quotations are from
Personal memoirs and recollections of editorial life. Boston, Ticknor, Reed & Fields, 1852.

STEPHEN BURROUGHS (Hanover, N. H., 1765–Three Rivers, Canada, 1840) recited most of what is known about his rough-hewn career in his book (the source of the quotations) :

Memoirs of the Notorious Stephen Burroughs. New York, Lincoln McVeagh The Dial Press, 1924. (First edition, 1798.)

CHARLES TABER CONGDON (New Bedford, Mass., 1821–New York, 1891) was a prominent journalist, author, and poet, known in his time as the right-hand man of another Yankee, Horace Greeley of the New York Tribune. The quotations are from *Reminiscences of a Journalist.* Boston, James R. Osgood and Company, 1880.

JULIA COWLES (Farmington, Conn., 1785–1803) was engaged to John Treadwell, ("T-ll"), son of former Governor John Treadwell of Connecticut. Her death of consumption prevented their marriage. The quotations are taken by permission of the Yale University Press from *The Diaries of Julia Cowles,* edited from the Original Manuscripts in the possession of Anna Roosevelt Cowles by Laura Hadley Moseley. New Haven, Yale, 1931.

URIEL CROCKER (Marblehead, Mass., 1796–1887) was a member of the Boston publishing house of Crocker & Brewster, whose respected and prosperous career extended from 1818 to 1876. Crocker and Osmyn Brewster were the successors to Samuel Turell Armstrong, a former workman at Isaiah Thomas' (*q.v.*) Boston branch. The quotations are from *Memorial of Uriel Crocker.* [Boston, privately printed for Uriel Haskell Crocker, 1891.]

RICHARD HENRY DANA, Jr., (Cambridge, Mass., 1815–Rome, 1882) needs no remarks from me. Though he lived to be an eminent lawyer and leading citizen of Boston, he is always remembered for his first book. (Incidentally, after being away for two years, he graduated at the head of the Harvard class of 1837.) The book, of course, is *Two Years Before the Mast.* Boston, Houghton Mifflin Company. (First edition, 1840.)

REUBEN DELANO is known to me only as the ostensible author of a pamphlet, the source of the quotation: *Wanderings and adventures of Reuben Delano, being a narrative of twelve years life in a whale ship.* Worcester, Thomas Drew, Jr., 1846.

"LORD" TIMOTHY DEXTER (Malden, Mass., 1743–Newburyport, 1806) was probably the most famous and surely the most eccentric Yankee eccentric ever to stay out of a madhouse. In commerce he had a golden touch; he was crazy only in the way he used his riches. The mansion that he bought and fantastically adorned with wooden statues still stands at Newburyport. Although he maintained a poet laureate (who gave up reading the great poets because it put him out of conceit with his own efforts), he obviously disdained to use a ghost in writing his only book, the source of our quotations

A Pickle for the Knowing Ones, or Plain Truths in a Homespun Dress. Newburyport, John G. Tilton, 1848. (First edition 1802.)

DAVID L. DODGE (Brooklyn, Conn., 1774–New York, 1852) was a pious merchant and manufacturer who reveals himself pretty completely in the book that served as our source:

Memorial of Mr. David L. Dodge. Boston, S. K. Whipple & Co., 1854.

LORENZO DOW (Coventry, Conn., 1777–Georgetown, Md., 1834) was a famous itinerant evangelist, the founder of camp-meetings, whose wanderings covered not only the whole eastern United States but England and Ireland as well. The quotations are from

The Dealings of God, Man, and the Devil, as exemplified in the Life, Experience, and Travels of Lorenzo Dow. . . . Fourth edition, Norwich, Conn., William Faulkner, 1833.

TIMOTHY DWIGHT, S.T.D. (Northampton, Mass., 1752–1817), a grandson of Jonathan Edwards (*q.v.*), became President of Yale College in 1795, and held that office until his death. He was popularly known as "Old Pope Dwight," and was so fierce in his attacks on the infidel Whigs that one of his parishioners, a woman of New Haven, is said to have hung her Bible down the well lest the infidels should get it. The book whence the quotations come is a mine of information on thirty years of New England:

Travels; in New-England and New-York. New Haven, Timothy Dwight [Jr.], 1821–2 (4 volumes).

JONATHAN EDWARDS (East Windsor, Conn., 1703–Princeton, N. J., 1758), one of the first American philosophers and theologians, was for years pastor of his grandfather Solomon Stoddard's parish at Northampton. He was later made President of Princeton, but died before he could assume office. The quotations are from

A narrative of many surprising conversions in Northampton & vicinity written in 1736. Worcester, Moses W. Grout, 1832. (First edition, Boston and London, 1737.)

EBENEZER FOX (Roxbury, Mass., 1763–1843) is remarkable only as the author of a book describing his part in the Revolution, from which the quotations are taken. It is
The adventures of Ebenezer Fox in the Revolutionary War. Boston, Charles Fox, 1848. (First edition, 1838.)

SAMUEL GRISWOLD GOODRICH (Ridgefield, Conn., 1793–1860) was a literary figure of some prominence even before he began in 1827 writing children's books under the name of "Peter Parley." The success of Peter Parley almost passes belief — even in England the mere name would sell a book. Goodrich listed 28 spurious English Parley books, and said there were more. His autobiography is the source of the quotations:
Recollections of a lifetime. Auburn, N. Y., Miller, Orton & Mulligan, 1856.

EDWARD EVERETT HALE (Boston, 1822–1909), a nephew of the orator, Edward Everett, always lived in Boston except for 1846–56, when he was minister in Worcester. He was in his time the most popular preacher in Boston, though now of course better remembered for *The Man Without a Country.* The quotations are taken by permission of the publisher, Little, Brown & Co., from
A New England Boyhood. Boston, 1927. (First edition, 1893.)

CHESTER HARDING (Conway, Mass., 1792–Boston, 1866) was a prominent portrait-painter whose fame extended to England, and whose career was practically an epitome of American history. The source of the quotations is one of the most attractive of autobiographies:
My Egotistography. Cambridge, John Wilson & Son, 1866. (Two later editions under the title *A Sketch of Chester Harding, Artist.*)

GEORGE ROBERT TWELVES HEWES was remarkable only as one of the last survivors of the Boston Tea Party. Nearly sixty years after, two biographies based on interviews appeared. The quotations are from one of these:
A retrospect of the Boston tea-party, with a memoir of George R. T. Hewes [by James Hawkes]. New York, S. S. Bliss, printer, 1834.

Of SETH HUBBELL I know only that his descendants were prominent at Wolcott within living memory, and what is told in his scarce pamphlet, the source of the quotations:
A narrative of the sufferings of Seth Hubbell & family, in his beginning a settlement in the town of Wolcott, in the state of Vermont.

[538]

(Third edition) Danville, Vt., E. & W. Eaton, Printers, **1826.** (First edition, 1824.)

HARRIOT KEZIA HUNT, M.D., (Boston, 1805–1875) was a reformer, feminist, and woman doctor — one of the first to practise in Boston. Her book, whence the quotations are taken, describes her struggles against prejudice and obstruction. It is
Glances & Glimpses; or fifty years social, including twenty years professional life. Boston, John P. Jewett & Co., 1856.

CAPTAIN EDWARD JOHNSON (Canterbury, England, 1598–Woburn, Mass., 1672) was among the most substantial early settlers of eastern Massachusetts, whither he went from England in 1630. His book, a prime source of early New England history, first appeared anonymously, under another title, in 1653. Our quotations were drawn from
The Wonder-Working Providence of Sions Saviour in New England, edited by J. Franklin Jameson. New York, Charles Scribner's Sons, 1910.

SARAH KEMBLE KNIGHT (Boston, 1666–1727) was a former schoolmistress, a widow, who kept, during a business trip to New York, the journal from which the quotations are taken:
The Journal of Madam Knight. New York, Peter Smith, 1935. (First edition, 1825.)

LUCY LARCOM (Beverly, Mass., 1824–1893) was a poetess and teacher of some celebrity. Her early life is charmingly described in the book whence the quotations are taken (by permission of Houghton Mifflin Co., authorized publisher) :
A New England Girlhood. Boston, 1890.

AMOS LAWRENCE (Groton, Mass., 1786–Boston, 1852) was one of the family of merchants and industrialists for whom the mill town of Lawrence was named. The quotations are from
Extracts from the diary and correspondence of the late Amos Lawrence, edited by his son, William R. Lawrence, M.D. Boston, Gould & Lincoln, 1856.

COTTON MATHER (Dorchester 1662/3–1727/8) was a leading member of the theocracy which ruled early Massachusetts. The quotations are taken from his celebrated historical work
Magnalia Christi Americana. Hartford, Silas Andrus & Son, 1853. (First edition, 1702.)

SAMUEL MAVERICK (England 1602 ?–1676 ?) was an early Massachusetts colonist, a leading figure in the colony, a Maine landowner; he was noted for his kindness to the Indians, but got involved in religious controversy which darkened his later years. The quotations are from

A briefe discription of New England. Boston, Massachusetts Historical Society, 1885.

THOMAS MORTON (1575–1646–7) was celebrated for his plantation, Merry Mount, which as a center of Episcopalian revelry was a thorn in the side of the Plymouth Puritans. In dealing with Morton, the Pilgrim Fathers showed their worst side (although he probably deserved little better), as Morton demonstrates in the quotations from

New English Canaan. Washington, D. C., P. Force, 1838. (First edition, London?, 1693.)

JOHN NEAL (Portland, Me., 1793–1876) was a brilliant and quarrelsome Quaker who in his time tended store, studied law, wrote novels, acted as secretary to Jeremy Bentham, mixed in politics, and wrote for an incredible variety of journals. He put much of the flavor of this fiery career into the book from which the quotations are taken:

Wandering recollections of a somewhat busy life. Boston, Roberts Bros., 1869.

THOMAS LOW NICHOLS (Orford, N. H., 1815–France 1901) was once a celebrated journalist and reformer. Much of his fascinating career was lived outside New England; the most material on him is to be found in the book which furnished our quotations:

Forty Years of American Life: 1821–1861. New York, Stackpole Sons, 1937. (First edition, London, 1864.)

JOSIAH QUINCY (1802–1882), the fourth of that name, was the son of Josiah Quincy (1772–1864), mayor of Boston 1823–28, President of Harvard 1829–45; the father of Josiah Phillips Quincy (1829–1910); and grandfather of Josiah Quincy (1859–1919), mayor of Boston 1895–99. He himself, a member of the Harvard class of 1821, was mayor of Boston 1845–49. The quotations are taken by permission of the publishers, Little, Brown & Co., from

Figures of the Past from the Leaves of old Journals. Boston, 1926. (First edition, 1883.)

PAUL REVERE (Boston, 1735–1818) has been treated ably and at length by Esther Forbes. Our quotation comes from a letter to

Jeremy Belknap, corresponding secretary of the Massachusetts Historical Society, in

Massachusetts Historical Society Collections, Vol. V., 1798.

MARY WHITE ROWLANDSON was born about 1635, probably in England; she was the daughter of John White, the wealthiest of the original proprietors of Lancaster, Massachusetts. About 1656 she married Joseph Rowlandson, the first minister of Lancaster. They had four children. Her and their fate during captivity by the Indians is described in our extract. She was ransomed on May 2d, 1676, for £20, and the two children still in captivity were released soon after. Her book, from which the extracts come, was enormously popular; first printed at Cambridge by Samuel Green in 1682, it has been reprinted more than thirty times since. The edition here used is

A Narrative of the Captivity, Sufferings, and removes of Mrs. Mary Rowlandson. Boston, Massachusetts Sabbath School Society, 1856.

SAMUEL SEWALL (England, 1652–1730) was a prominent figure in the life of his time. He was a judge, and the only one concerned in the Salem witchcraft trials who afterward acknowledged himself in error. The quotations are from his diary, one of the chief sources for early New England life:

Diary of Samuel Sewall, 1674–1729. Boston, Massachusetts Historical Society, 1878–82 (3 volumes).

ASA G. SHELDON (born 1788, in Lynnfield, Mass.) was a versatile and highly articulate farmer and contractor. He tells nearly all about himself, and certainly all I know, in the source of the quotations:

The Life of Asa G. Sheldon, Wilmington Farmer. Woburn, Mass., E. T. Moody, Printer, 1862.

ANDREW SHERBURNE (born in 1765 at Rye, New Hampshire) became a minister, and wound up in the west — New York State. To help make ends meet, he issued his autobiography, the source of the quotations:

Memoirs of Andrew Sherburne: A Pensioner of the Navy of the Revolution. Second edition, Providence, H. H. Brown, 1831. (First edition, 1828.)

JOHN S. SPRINGER was the author of a book that tells practically all there is to know about its subject, and that even the keen-eyed Thoreau (*q.v.*) drew heavily on in writing about the Maine woods. The quotations came from it.

Forest Life and Forest Trees. New York, Harper and Brothers, 1851.

JOSEPH STORY (Marblehead, 1779–1845) was among the most eminent legal authorities of his day, and an associate justice of the United States Supreme Court for thirty-four years. The quotations are drawn from

Life and Letters of Joseph Story, edited by his son, William W. Story. Boston, Little and Brown, 1851.

WILLIAM STUART (born about 1788, apparently not far from the present Bridgeport, Conn.) was another turbulent autobiographical rogue in the style of Henry Tufts and Stephen Burroughs (*qq. v.*), and indeed tells of distributing Burroughs' counterfeit output. The quotations are from

Sketches of the Life of William Stuart, the First and Most Celebrated Counterfeiter of Connecticut. Bridgeport, printed and published for the author, 1854.

ISAIAH THOMAS (Boston, 1749–Worcester, 1831) was the greatest printer, publisher, and bookseller of New England. His *Massachusetts Spy* was a leading Revolutionary organ. His chain of branches blanketed northern New England. He founded the American Antiquarian Society, by whose permission the quotations are taken from:

The diary of Isaiah Thomas, 1805–1828. Worcester, Mass., American Antiquarian Society, 1909.

SAMUEL THOMSON (Alstead, N. H., 1769 — Boston, 1843) was a self-taught herb doctor who gained a very wide following throughout New England and the west, despite the embittered and often bigoted opposition of the regular medical faculty, against whose habits of bleeding and drugging he made a firm stand. Both his career and his system are detailed in the source of our quotations:

New Guide to Health; or Botanic Family Physician. . . . To Which is Prefixed, a Narrative of the Life and Medical Discoveries of the Author. Boston, printed for the author at the office of the Boston Investigator, J. Q. Adams, printer, 1835. (First edition, 1822.)

HENRY DAVID THOREAU (Concord, Mass., 1817–1862) as a subject for comment here would be an impertinence. He made two trips to the forests of Maine, the second in 1853, but his book on the subject was not published until after his death:

The Maine Woods. Boston, 1864.

JOHN M. TODD (born in 1821 at Durham, Me.) was a talkative Portland barber who (perhaps influenced by his numerous literary customers) put some of his monologues into print, whence they are taken for this book.

A Sketch of the Life of John M. Todd (*Sixty-two Years in a Barbershop*) . Portland, Me., William W. Roberts Company, 1906.

JOHN TRUMBULL (Lebanon, Conn., 1756–1843) came of a distinguished Connecticut family, and fought through the revolution, quarreling the while with his superiors over tardy promotion. He did diplomatic service abroad, studied under Benjamin West, and was in his later years the grand panjandrum of American painting. Both his art and his life are displayed in the source of the quotations:

Autobiography, Reminiscences and Letters of John Trumbull, from 1756 to 1841. New York, Wiley and Putnam, 1841.

HENRY TUFTS (1748–1831) was perhaps as thorough a bad egg as New England ever produced. He was practically illiterate, and his autobiography, the source of the quotations, was evidently ghost-written; but its facts bear the stamp of truth.

The autobiography of a criminal, Henry Tufts, edited, with an introduction, by Edmund Pearson. New York, Duffield & Co., 1930. (First edition,

A narrative of the life, adventures, travels and sufferings of Henry Tufts. Dover, N. H., Samuel Bragg, jun., 1807.)

ANNA GREEN WINSLOW (Marshfield, Mass.?, 1760–1779) was sent by her loyalist parents from Nova Scotia to Boston, their birthplace, to live with relatives while being "finished." She is believed to have died of consumption, like our other girl diarist, Julia Cowles. The quotations are taken by permission of the publishers, Houghton Mifflin Co., from

Diary of Anna Green Winslow, a Boston School Girl of 1771, edited by Alice Morse Earle. Boston, 1894.

INDEX

[INCLUDING ILLUSTRATIONS]

◇◇◇◇◇◇◇◇◇◇◇

academies, 64

Adams, Henry, 75, 234, 314, 380–1, 482, 530–1, 535

Adams, John Quincy, 317, 482

Adams houses, Quincy, Mass. (illus.), 530

agriculture, 136

Alstead, N. H., 325–8

amusements, 4, 29–34, 139–40

Andover (Phillips Andover Academy), 67–70, (illus.), 67

Andover, Mass., 528–9

applesauce, 27, 525

auctioneering, 204, (illus.), 204

Bacon Academy (illus.), 64

Bailey, Mrs. Anna, 451–2

Bailey, J. M., 49–50, 166, 276–8, 535

baking, 42

Barnum, P. T., 218–22, 268–70, 275, 321–3, 535

Beecher, Catharine, 379–80

Beecher, Lyman, 4–8, 25–8, 51–4, 90–6, 118, 360–5, 423–4, 535

bees (gatherings), 150–1, 164–5

Bethel, Conn., 219–22, (illus.), 221

Beverly, Mass., 40–5, 70–2, (illus.), 41

books, 10, 46, 140

Boston, 3–4, 23–5, 29–40, 213–18, 257–68, 295–306, 329–32, 343–6, 520, 522–8; Brattle Street Meeting-House, 36; Castle Island, 295–306; Common, 30–4, (illus.), 31; Harbor (illus.), 171; honesty, 523; Latin School, 63; schools, 62–4; State Street (illus.), 234; style, 523, 530; Tea Party, 411, (illus.), 411–15; Worcester Railroad Station (illus.), 505

Bowditch, Nathaniel, 86

Bozrahville, Conn., 227–8

Braintree, Mass., 521

Brattle Street Meeting-House, Boston, 36

Brattleboro, Vt., 358

bread, 510–11

Bridgeport, Conn., 306–8

Brooklyn, Conn., 54

Buckingham, J. T., 8–11, 254–62, 267–8, 535

Burroughs, Stephen, 73–4, 96–103, 167–70, 295–306, 366–71, 535

Cambridge, Vt., 127

Cape Cod, 516

Castle Island, Boston, 295–306

centenarian, 467–8

churches, founding of, 489–90

churning (illus.), 163

cider mill (illus.), 138

Class Day, Harvard, 89–90

clearing land, 504

climate, 135

clockmaking, 224

clothes, 3–4, 18, 154–5

coal, 86

Commencement, Harvard, 87–9

Concord, Mass., 519

Congdon, Charles T., 46–8, 317–21, 480–2, 536

Connecticut, 363–5, 447–57

Connecticut River, 514

conscientious objector, 439–40

Constitution, U.S.S. (illus.), 444

Copley, J. S., 272

costume, 3–4, 18, 154–5

Cotton, John, 490

cotton mills, 229–34, (illus.), 230

counterfeiting, 308, 446, 456

courtship of Sewall, 108–17

Cowles, Julia, 14–17, 536
Craigie House, 81–2, (illus.), 82
Crocker, Uriel, 165–6, 262–5, 502–3, 536

dame school, 56–8, 59, 70–2, (illus.), 59
Dana, Richard Henry, Jr., 170–9, 536
Danbury, Conn., 268–70, 276–8, 321–3
Dartmouth College, 96–104, (illus.), 97
Dartmouth Indian scare, 100–1
Decatur, Stephen, 447
Dedham, Mass., 521
Delano, Reuben, 179–96, 536
depression of 1812–15, 456
Dexter, Timothy, 199–201, 536–7, (illus.), 200
Dexter Mansion (illus.), 201
disestablishment of clergy, 363–5
Dodge, David L., 54, 201–6, 226–8, 371–3, 438–40, 537
Dorchester, Mass., 521
Dorr, T. W., 320
Dorr's Rebellion, 318–21
Dow, Lorenzo, 357–8, 378–9, 537
drinks, 138, 147–8
drunkenness, 382–3
Dunster, Henry, 490
Durham, Conn. (illus.), 376
Dustan, Hannah, 407–10, (illus.), 410
Dwight, Timothy, 55, 64–5, 78, 93–5, 103–4, 119–23, 134–41, 224, 251, 309–11, 373–4, 467–70, 507–17, 522–3, 537
dye-tub, 143–4

Edwards, Jonathan, 346–57, 537
Election Day, 32–4, 45
Eliot, John, 490
elocution, 65–6, 279
Emerson, Ralph Waldo, 87, 88
Exchange Coffee House, Boston, burned, 85
Exeter, N. H., 291–2, 511–12

Fair Haven, Mass. (illus.), 180
Fairfield, Conn., 499
farming, 136

Farmington, Conn., 14–17, (illus.), 14
feminism, 323–4
fences, 503
fire companies, 165–6
fire department, 526–8, (illus.), 526
fire, laying, 145
fireplace, 40
fireside (illus.), 47
fishing, 7, 500–1, 512, (illus.), 512
flax, 5, 148
flax-breaker (illus.), 148
food, 6, 38, 41–2, 137–9, 144–7, 153–4
forest fire (illus.), 247
Fort Griswold, 449–55
Fort Trumbull (illus.), 452
fourpence-halfpenny, 479
Fourth of July, see Independence Day
Fox, Ebenezer, 424–35, 538
Fullum, hired man, 485–6
furniture, 152–3, 525

Goodrich, S. G., 11–13, 55–62, 142–159, 225–6, 375–9, 446–57, 470–80, 501–2, 517–19, 538
Goshen, Conn. (illus.), 361
Great Awakening, 347–57
Greenfield, Mass., 254–6
gristmills, 510–11, (illus.), 511
Groton, Conn., 449–55
Guilford, Conn., 5–8

Hale, Edward Everett, 29–40, 62–4, 89–90, 278–9, 485–6, 505–7, 525–8, 538
Harding, Chester, 273–5, 538
Hartford, Conn., 205–6
Harvard College, 77–90, (illus.), 80; Class Day, 89–90; Commencement, 87–89; Fire Department, 84–5; Washington Corps, 83
help, 154, 162
Hewes, G. R. T., 411–16, 538
Hingham, Mass., 521
hired man, 485–6
house furnishings, 152–3
Hubbell, Seth, 124–34, 538
Hull, Mass., 521
Hunt, Harriot K., 23–5, 323–4, 329–32, 539
hunting, 157–8, 165

husking bee, 164–5, (illus.), 164
Hyde Park, Vt., 124, 130

Independence Day, 441–2, (illus.),
442
Indians, 497, 514–16
inn signs, 506–7

Johnson, Edward, 466, 488–90, 539
Johnson, Vt., 124, 127

King Philip, 398
Kingston, R. I., 493
Kirkland, John T., 79
Knight, Sarah Kemble, 490–500, 539

Lancaster, Mass., 387–9
language, 61
Larcom, Lucy, 40–6, 70–2, 228–32,
539
Lawrence, Amos A., 216–18, 539
Lebanon, Conn., 354, 355, (illus.),
355
lectures, 278
Lenox, Mass., 275
Lexington, Battle of, 418–20
Lexington, Mass. (illus.), 420
Litchfield, Conn., 25–9, 379–80
Littleton, 513
log cabin (illus.), 120
log houses, 134
log jam (illus.), 243
logging, 236–47
logging camp (illus.), 245
Lowell, Mass., 228–34
lumbering, 511–12

magazines, children's, 30
Maine, 123, 583–4
maple sugar, 145–7, (illus.), 146
Marblehead, 500–1, (illus.), 500
Marlborough pie, 38
Massachusetts, 107–17; school sys-
tem, 76
Massachusetts Bay (map), 520
Mather, Cotton, 111, 333–43, 345–6,
407–9, 539
Maverick, Samuel, 107–8, 519–22,
539–40
Medfield, Mass., 521
meeting, 35–6
meeting-house, 517

Merrymount, 460–4
Mattawamkeag River, 240
Milford, Conn., 499
militia, 34
mills, cotton, 229–34, (illus.), 230
mills, grist, 510–11, (illus.), 511
Morton, Thomas, 459–66, 487–8,
521, 540
mourning rings, 480
music, 140
Muster (holiday), 34

Narragansett country, 493
Nashua, N. H., 519
naval life, 436–8
Neal, John, 17–23, 65–6, 207–16,
265–8, 314–17, 382–3, 483–4, 540
New Bedford, 46–8, 480–2, (illus.),
481
New Concord, N. H., 134
New Hampshire, 160
New Haven, Conn., 309–10, 496–7,
502–3, 507–10, (illus.), 508
New London, Conn., 448–9, 495;
Burning of (illus.), 439
Newburyport, Mass., 167
newspapers, 140, 142
Nichols, Thomas Low, 72, 160–5,
225, 232–4, 381–2, 440–3, 483, 504–
5, 523–4, 540
Northampton, Mass., 346, 347, (il-
lus.), 347
Norwalk, Conn., 499
Norwich, Conn. (illus.), 202
nutting, 26

Orford, N. H., 161–3
oysters, 514

painter (illus.), 271
payment, methods of, 497
Pelham, Mass., 368–71
pens, 48
perquisites, 10
pest-houses, 12–13
Phi Beta Kappa, 86
Philip, King, 398
Phillips Andover Academy, 67–70,
528–9, (illus.), 67
physical characteristics of Yankees,
468–9

pioneers, 119–22
Plymouth, Conn. (*illus.*), 360
Plymouth, Mass., 459–60, 466, 516
pork, 138, 144
Portland, Maine, 19–23, 65–6, 315–17, 382–3, (*illus.*), 316
Portsmouth, N. H., 436
Pratt, Ephraim, centenarian, 467–8
privateering, 415–16
professions, influence of, 314

quilting, 164–5
Quincy, Josiah, 67–70, 79–89, 358–60, 528–9, 540
Quincy, Mass., 358–60, 482, 530–1

railroads, 35, 505, (*illus.*), 35
religion, disappearance of, 380–1
Revere, Paul, 416–20, 540–1
revival meeting, 371–3
Rhode Island, 318–21
Ridgefield, Conn., 11–13, 55–62, 142–59, 225–6, 470–80, 501–2, 517–19, (*illus.*), 144
roads, 504; corduroy, 134
Rowlandson, Mrs. Mary, 387–407, 541
Roxbury, Mass., 520

Sabbath, 35, 41–2, 52
Sabbath laws, 528–9
Saco, Maine, 284–6
Salem, Mass., 512, 513, (*illus.*), 513
salt vats (*illus.*), 516
sawmill, 236, 248–50, (*illus.*), 236
Saybrook, Conn., 495–6
schoolmasters, 72
Scott, novels of, 28
seafaring, 43–4
servants, 154, 162
Sewall, Samuel, 77, 108–17, 343–6, 409–10, 541, (*portrait*), 109
shearing (*illus.*), 6
Sheldon, Asa G., 222–3, 457–8, 541
Sherburne, Andrew, 436–8, 541
shipbuilding (*illus.*), 167
shooting, 165
slavery, 6
sleighing, 139, 160–1, (*illus.*), 139
sliding, 19–21, (*illus.*), 20
snowshoeing, 130

snowstorms, 135
spinning, 7, 148–9, (*illus.*), 7
Springer, John S., 236–7, 238–40, 241–4, 246–50, 541
stagecoaches, 504
State Street, Boston (*illus.*), 234
Stiles, Ezra, 92
Stoddard, Solomon, 348
stone bees, 150–1
Stonington, Conn., 495, 514–16
storekeeping, 201–22
Story, Joseph, 311–14, 500–1, 542
Stowe, Harriet Beecher, 25–9
Stuart, Gilbert, 273
Stuart, William, 306–8, 445–6, 542
Sudbury, Mass., 519
superstition, 500

taverns, 504, 506, 517–19
temperance, 360–3
Thanksgiving, 36–40, (*illus.*), 37
Thomas, Isaiah, 251–3, 444, 458, 542
Thomson, Samuel, 325–9, 542
Thoreau, Henry David, 123, 237–8, 240–1, 244–6, 250, 483, 503–4, 542
tin peddlers, 197–9
Todd, John M., 483–4, 542–3
trade in New Haven, 508–9
training day, 440–1, 496
Trumbull, John, 271–2, 543
Trumbull house (*illus.*), 272
Tufts, Henry, 280–95, 420–3, 543
turkeys, 144

vehicles, 225–6, 501–2, 525
Vergennes, Vt., 457
Vermont, 119–21, 124–34; morals of, 514

Walpole, N. H., 254
Warren, Samuel, 412, 417
Waterbury, Conn., 224–5, (*illus.*), 224
watering troughs, 503
weather, 135
Weymouth, Mass., 521
whaling, 179–96, (*illus.*), 185, 187, 188, 189, 195
Whitney, Eli, 226
Whittier, John Greenleaf, 265
whittling, 156–7

Willis, N. P., 266
Wilmington, Mass., 222–3
Windham, Conn., 9–11
Winslow, Anna Green, 3–4, 543
witchcraft, 333–43; execution (*illus.*), 343
Woburn, Mass., 488–90
Wolcott, Vt., 124–34
women, 469–70

"wood-spell," 379–80
Worcester, Mass., 251–3, 510–11
Worcester Railroad Station, Boston, 505
Worthington, Conn., 197–9, (*illus.*), 197

Yale, 76, 90–6, (*illus.*), 76, 91
Yarmouth, Mass., 516

A NOTE ON THE TYPE USED IN THIS BOOK

This book was set on the Linotype in a type-face called "Baskerville." The punches for this face were cut under the supervision of George W. Jones, the eminent English printer and the designer of Granjon and Estienne. Linotype Baskerville is a facsimile cutting from type cast from the original matrices of a face designed by John Baskerville, a writing-master of Birmingham, for his own private press. The original face was the forerunner of the "modern" group of type faces, known today as Scotch, Bodoni, etc. After his death in 1775, Baskerville's punches and matrices were sold in France and were used to produce the sumptuous Kehl edition of Voltaire's works.

This book was composed, printed, and bound by The Plimpton Press, Norwood, Massachusetts. The binding is based on original designs by W. A. Dwiggins. The reproductions of old engravings were made by Eagle Photo-Engraving Company, New York.